ENCYCLOPEDIA OF THE
JAZZ AGE

From the End of World War I to the Great Crash

Volume Two

Edited by James Ciment

SHARPE REFERENCE
an imprint of M.E. Sharpe, Inc.

SHARPE REFERENCE

Sharpe Reference is an imprint of M.E. Sharpe, Inc.

M.E. Sharpe, Inc.
80 Business Park Drive
Armonk, NY 10504

Library of Congress Cataloging-in-Publication Data

Encyclopedia of the Jazz Age: from the end of World War I to the great crash / James Ciment, editor.
   p. cm.
Includes bibliographical references and index.
ISBN 978-0-7656-8078-5 (hardcover: alk. paper)

1. United States—History—1919–1933—Encyclopedias. 2. Nineteen twenties—Encyclopedias.
I. Ciment, James.

E784.E53 2007
973.91'503—dc22
2007023928

Cover Images provided by Getty Images and the following: (top row, left to right) Time & Life Pictures; Hulton Archive/Stringer; Hulton Archive; Stringer/Hulton Archive; (middle row) American Stock/Hulton Archive; Transcendental Graphics; Edward Gooch/Stringer/Hulton Archive; Kirby/Stringer/Hulton Archive; (bottom row) Harold Lloyd Trust/Hulton Archive; Getty UK/Hulton Archive; Frank Driggs Collection/Hulton Archive; Stringer/Hulton Archive.

Printed and bound in the United States of America

The paper used in this publication meets the minimum requirements of
American National Standard for Information Sciences
Permanence of Paper for Printed Library Materials,
ANSI Z 39.48.1984.

MV (c) 10 9 8 7 6 5 4 3 2 1

Publisher: Myron E. Sharpe
Vice President and Editorial Director: Patricia Kolb
Vice President and Production Director: Carmen Chetti
Executive Editor and Manager of Reference: Todd Hallman
Executive Development Editor: Jeff Hacker
Project Editor: Jeanne Marie Healy
Program Coordinator: Cathleen Prisco
Editorial Assistant: Alison Morretta
Text Design: Carmen Chetti and Jesse Sanchez
Cover Design: Jesse Sanchez

Contents

Sidebars

Topic Finder

Business, Economics, and Labor

Consumer and Popular Culture

ENCYCLOPEDIA OF THE JAZZ AGE

Volume Two

Immigration

In the 1920s, as prejudice increased toward the foreign born, Americans turned away from providing a haven for "huddled masses yearning to breathe free," as Emma Lazarus's poem on the Statue of Liberty read. Instead, new policies reflected a general opposition to large-scale immigration, especially from certain parts of the globe. Immigration restrictions in the 1920s reduced the percentage of foreign-born Americans to its lowest level since before the Civil War. America's foreign-born population as a percentage of all residents never again reached pre-1920 levels.

Points of Origin

Immigrants entered America from all parts of the globe. But in the wake of World War I, more than a million Poles, Russians, and other Eastern Europeans displaced by the war migrated to the United States. The first two years of the decade brought more than 1.2 million refugees and migrants seeking a better life for their families to U.S. shores. Many of them were Catholic, Greek or Russian Orthodox, or Jewish. American consuls in Europe warned that millions more were preparing to escape the desperate circumstances in their homelands. Before they could arrive, however, the U.S. government established limits on immigration.

Legislation in 1882, the Chinese Exclusion Act, had restricted the immigration of Chinese laborers, but the immigration laws of the 1920s constituted the first effort to limit incoming European populations as well as those from other areas. The immigration laws of 1921 and 1924 restricted immigration to a percentage of the nationalities already in the United States. The 1921 legislation, the Emergency Quota Act, set the limit at 3 percent of the foreign-born populations as reflected in the 1910 U.S. Census; the 1924 National Origins Act reduced this to 2 percent of the 1890 census figures. Such quotas dramatically reduced the overall number of immigrants, but they significantly affected the new waves of immigrants that had been coming from Austria, Hungary, Czechoslovakia, Yugoslavia, Italy, Poland, Russia, and the Baltic states. Meanwhile, the quotas favored the Northern and Western European nations from which most immigrants had come in the past.

Prior to the 1920s, as many as 30 percent of immigrants eventually returned to their country of birth. In 1920, less than 50 percent of America's foreign-born residents applied for citizenship, suggesting that their stays in America might prove temporary. But the depressed economic conditions in Europe and elsewhere following World War I discouraged out-migration after arrival in the United States. The percentage of those applying for citizenship increased by an estimated 8 percent during the course of the decade, suggesting that more immigrants regarded the move as permanent; for males over the age of twenty-one, the increase exceeded 11 percent.

Quotas prompted a change in the socioeconomic background of immigrants. Because the limitations created competition for open slots, the better connected, more educated, and more affluent held an advantage over others. The number of general laborers fell from 162,859 (20 percent of the total migration) in 1921 to 18,080 (7 percent) in 1930. Commissioner General of Immigration W.W. Husband declared, "We are now receiving a better class of immigrants as a whole than we have done in thirty-five years." Husband's comment referred only to legal immigrants, however; estimates of undocumented immigration ranged from 100 to 1,000 per day.

Because of the new prejudicial legislation, the percentage of European-born Americans decreased by almost 3 percent during the decade. Canadians and Latin Americans made up the difference. Canadians represented the largest documented migration to the United States, numbering more than 1 million new arrivals from 1920 to 1930. "Visitors" and those migrating from the Western Hemisphere were neither counted nor restricted. Efforts to include these countries in the quota system were defeated by the U.S.

Government workers attend to newly arrived immigrants at Ellis Island, belying America's increasingly hostile attitude toward foreigners and newcomers. In 1921 and 1924, Congress passed laws dramatically restricting immigration from Eastern and Southern Europe. *(Topical Press Agency/ Hulton Archive/Getty Images)*

State Department, congressmen from the West, and business interests in the Southwest, especially mining, agribusiness, and construction. But because immigration officials counted only people who arrived by boat, people who landed in Canadian or Mexican ports could then travel overland to the United States. Some were able to purchase false credentials in Latin America. This traffic created a flourishing illegal alien industry with which the American Border Patrol could not keep pace, despite great increases in budget and staffing. Congress did not make illegal entry a criminal offense until 1929.

From 1910 to 1930, because of political and economic instability in Mexico, several hundred thousand Mexicans sought new opportunities north of the border. A growing economy in need of low-wage labor in Texas, New Mexico, Arizona, and California attracted potential migrants, while the integration of northern Mexican railroad lines with those in the southwestern United States made such a journey more feasible. America's mid-decade immigration laws and revolution in Mexico during the latter half of the 1920s spurred even greater numbers to the United States from that country. More than 450,000 Mexicans received permanent visas to enter the United States during this period—more than double the number in the 1910s. But visa-holding Mexican immigrants counted for only a portion of the Mexicans who migrated during this period. The Mexican-born population of the United States reached

about 2 million by 1930. The border between the two countries remained fluid, with some migrants moving back and forth regularly. It is estimated that as many as 1 million Mexican migrants returned to Mexico during the decade.

Points of Settlement

Approximately 30 percent of U.S. immigrants during the 1920s moved to the Midwest, usually as part of a chain migration—that is, one family or community member settled in a given location, prompting relatives and friends to follow. The majority of immigrants, however, lived near their ports of entry. As a result, the Northeast and West Coast contained the highest percentage of immigrants. Immigrants composed about a quarter of the population in New York, Rhode Island, Massachusetts, and Connecticut. On the West Coast, immigrants made up about 15 percent of the population, and only about 2 percent in the South.

Almost 80 percent of the immigrants lived in urban areas (23 percent higher than the national average). More than half of all immigrants resided in cities with more than 100,000 people (twice the rate of native-born Americans). Immigrants represented more than a quarter of the population in America's fifteen largest cities. By contrast, only one-fifth of immigrants lived in rural areas in 1930. This trend toward greater urbanization among immigrants continued uninterrupted into the twenty-first century. The vast majority of voluntary immigrants to the United States prior to the twentieth century came to work on farms. But by the end of the 1920s, fewer than one in eleven immigrants owned or worked on farms. These immigrants comprised just 4 percent of the total farming population.

Social Changes

In previous decades, immigrants relied heavily on the assistance of previous arrivals belonging to the same ethnic group. In the 1920s, however, ethnic aid societies and fraternal organizations lost momentum due to the lack of immigrants. In fact, many social organizations, such as the League of United Latin American Citizens, forbade foreign-born membership, failed to assist in the acculturation process, and refused to petition on behalf of the recent arrivals. Foreign-language newspapers lost readership and continued the rapid decline first realized during Word War I.

The Soviet Ark

Fear ran rampant in the United States during the early twentieth century as immigrants from Italy, Russia, and the Austro-Hungarian Empire poured into the country. These people were different, it was believed, from previous immigrants. They came from lands where democracy had not taken root, or where ideologies such as anarchism, socialism, and communism were supported.

In late 1917, Communist revolutionaries known as Bolsheviks seized control of the Russian government and pulled Russia's armies off the battlefields of World War I. The Bolsheviks talked of overthrowing capitalism and abolishing Christianity. With the end of the war in 1918, America's own working classes proved restive, launching a general strike in Seattle in February 1919 and a national steel strike from September 1919 through January 1920. U.S. Attorney General A. Mitchell Palmer was determined to nip trouble in the bud, and he knew exactly whom to go after—anarchists like Emma Goldman and Alexander Berkman, who preached a message of revolutionary action at home while supporting worker uprisings across Central and Eastern Europe.

On November 7, 1919, on the second anniversary of the Russian Revolution, America's top law enforcement official made his move, sending police to raid the headquarters of radical organizations across the United States. The Palmer Raids netted thousands of alleged anarchists and Communists. A month later, 249 foreign-born radicals—some resident aliens, others whose citizenship had been revoked under the wartime Sedition Act—boarded the SS *Buford* and, accompanied by one guard for every two deportees, were shipped off to the Soviet Union.

The former U.S. Army transport ship, dubbed the "Soviet Ark" by the press, departed at dawn on December 21 from the very place many of the immigrant passengers had first arrived in America—Ellis Island in New York Harbor. On January 17, the ship landed at Hangö, Finland, and two days later, the deportees were turned over to Soviet authorities at the Russian border town of Belo Ostrov. "The revolutionary hymn, played by the military Red Band, greeted us as we crossed the frontier," Berkman recalled. "The hurrahs of the red-capped soldiers, mixed with the cheers of the deportees, echoed through the woods, rolling into the distance like a challenge of joy and defiance. With bared head I stood in the presence of the visible symbols of the Revolution Triumphant."

It did not take long for disappointment to set in. Both Berkman and Goldman, his ideological comrade and lover, were horrified by the forced labor camps and dissident prisons they witnessed in revolutionary Russia. They left the country for Germany in 1921. Two years later, Goldman published a memoir titled *My Disillusionment in Russia*. Four years after that came Berkman's *The Bolshevik Myth*.

With the fear of radical subversion dissipating by the early 1920s, American authorities eased up on their repression of radicals. A few of the passengers of the Soviet Ark were eventually allowed to return to the United States. Goldman and Berkman were not among them, at least not in life. In May 1940, Goldman died of a stroke in Toronto, Canada. Immigration authorities granted the request of her friends and family to allow her body to enter the country for interment in a cemetery near Chicago.

James Ciment

Immigrant children learned English in school, and ethnic church parishes started adding services in English.

Anti-immigrant sentiment reached a plateau during the 1920s, as fears promoted by fringe elements became part of the cultural mainstream. The attitudes of the 1920s resulted in policies that promoted a more ethnically homogeneous nation and a general antipathy toward immigrants, if not immigration itself.

Michael Jacobs

See also: Americanization; Asian Americans; Eugenics; German Americans; Immigration Laws of 1921 and 1924; Irish Americans; Italian Americans; Jewish Americans; Ku Klux Klan; Latinos and Latinas; Migration, Great; Population and Demographics.

Further Reading

Carter, Susan. B. *Historical Statistics of the United States: Earliest Times to the Present.* New York: Cambridge University Press, 2006.

Dinnerstein, Leonard, and David M. Reimers. *Ethnic Americans: A History of Immigration.* 4th ed. New York: Columbia University Press, 1999.

Dumenil, Lynn. *The Modern Temper: American Culture and Society in the 1920s.* New York: Hill and Wang, 1995.

Gibson, Campbell J., and Emily Lennon. *Historical Census Statistics on the Foreign-Born Population of the United States: 1850–1990.* Washington, DC: U.S. Bureau of the Census, 1999.

Higham, John. *Strangers in the Land: Patterns of American Nativism, 1860–1925.* New York: Atheneum, 1963.

Immigration Laws of 1921 and 1924

U.S. immigration legislation passed during the Jazz Age is notable for establishing quotas for immigrants based on nationality, or excluding some groups outright. A host of factors created an environment that was conducive to such restrictions.

Before the late nineteenth century, the majority of immigrants to America had come from Northern and Western Europe and were generally of white Anglo-Saxon Protestant (WASP) stock. After the Civil War, immigrants from other areas began arriving in larger numbers. Typically from Southern and Eastern Europe, these immigrants were generally non-Protestant—many were Catholic, Greek Orthodox, or Jewish—and they came from cultures that many Americans considered socially backward. The idea of America as a "melting pot," a place where immigrants of varied backgrounds could become assimilated into the mainstream culture, began to erode as anxieties grew about urban deterioration and economic competition from desperately poor immigrants.

Intolerance was increasing, reflected in the legal segregation of African Americans in the South, the aggressive assimilation policies toward Native Americans, and the growing discrimination aimed at immigrants, who were stereotyped as lazy, dishonest, crude, and prone to radical politics and criminality. While the Chinese Exclusion Act of 1882 had restricted immigration from a specific country, calls for widespread immigration restriction were being voiced in the early twentieth century and had become common by World War I. However, the economic demand for labor had slowed the translation of resentment into immigration control. As the labor market became saturated, the calls became more urgent. The Ku Klux Klan became a potent antiforeign, anti-Catholic organization numbering about 4 million members in the early 1920s.

The Russian Revolution of 1917 and the subsequent Red Scare further exacerbated anxieties by raising the specter of foreign radicals destabilizing America. The idea that Southern and Eastern Europeans were somehow inferior became common currency, fueled by widespread anti-Catholicism and anti-Semitism. And in the increased nativism and xenophobia that followed World War I, many Americans sought not only to restrict immigration but to protect American society from undesirables. Even big business interests, which had the most to gain from immigrant labor driving costs down, began to add their voice to the chorus.

Major immigration legislation followed in 1921 and 1924. By the end of 1920, immigration numbers were averaging 52,000 per month. The 1921 Emergency Quota Act set quotas equal to 3 percent of the nationalities already in the United States, based on the figures in the 1910 U.S. Census. This immediately restricted total annual immigration to about 350,000, and the majority of immigrants would be from Northern and Western Europe. In addition, no more than one-fifth of a nation's annual quota could be filled in any single month.

Under the 1924 National Origins Act, or Johnson-Reed Act, nationalities were restricted to 2 percent of their numbers in the 1890 census. This more drastic cutback ensured that total immigration would never reach prewar peaks, and it favored the nationalities that had immigrated in large numbers before 1890. Initially, total annual immigration was limited to about 165,000, less than 20 percent of the prewar average. The legislation also imposed stricter bars on Asians, except for Filipinos (the Philippines being an American-controlled country). Consequently, approximately 86 percent of immigrants were from Britain, Ireland, Germany, and other Northern and Western European countries. Germany had the largest quota, 51,227, while Poland, with only 5,982, had the largest among Southern or Eastern European countries. Immigrants from Italy had averaged 200,000 in the years immediately before World War I but numbered just 3,845 per year after the legislation went into effect.

With modifications made in 1929 and again in 1952, the 1924 quota act remained largely in effect until passage of the 1965 Immigration and Nationality Act, which replaced tight national quotas with broader and more liberal hemispheric ones.

Sam Hitchmough

See also: Americanization; Immigration; Ku Klux Klan; Migration, Great; Population and Demographics.

Further Reading

Barkan, Elliott Robert. *And Still They Come: Immigrants and American Society, 1920 to the 1990s.* Wheeling, IL: Harlan Davidson, 1996.

Higham, John. *Strangers in the Land: Patterns of American Nativism, 1860–1925.* New Brunswick, NJ: Rutgers University Press, 2002.

Industrial Workers of the World

The Industrial Workers of the World (IWW)—popularly known as the Wobblies—was a radical industrial union of the early twentieth century. While the rival American Federation of Labor (AFL) primarily organized skilled workers and focused on winning higher wages and better working conditions for its members, the IWW sought to organize all workers regardless of skill level and advocated overthrowing the capitalist system and putting workers in control of the government. In the decade or so after its founding in 1905, the IWW reached its peak of influence by organizing highly publicized strikes in industries as diverse as mining and textiles.

When IWW leaders spoke out and organized against U.S. participation in World War I—they saw the war as an exercise in defense of capitalism and empire—the federal government responded with raids on IWW meeting halls across the country and the arrest of 165 IWW officials. Members were accused of conspiring to resist the military draft, encouraging desertion among members of the armed forces, and using intimidation tactics against strikebreakers. Under the Espionage Act of 1917, federal officials successfully prosecuted more than 100 IWW leaders, including many who were no longer members of the union; some received prison sentences as long as twenty years.

Despite government repression, the IWW survived the war relatively intact and was especially strong in western states. Union officials were instrumental in organizing the Seattle general strike of February 1919, a coordinated walkout by more than 60,000 workers in various industries, including 3,500 IWW members. The strike effectively shut down the city for five days. The action was largely unsuccessful, however. The key constituency—35,000 of the city's shipyard workers—failed to win the higher wages for which they had originally walked out.

The Seattle general strike was one in a series of domestic and foreign events—including a nationwide steel strike, a series of anarchist bombings, and the Russian Revolution—that led government officials and the American public to conclude that the nation was under grave threat of radical subversion. Along with anarchist groups and the Socialist and Communist parties, the IWW was viewed as one of the most dangerous institutions in America. The Red Scare of 1919–1920 resulted in raids conducted by U.S. Attorney General A. Mitchell Palmer and the newly formed Bureau of Investigation (later the Federal Bureau of Investigation) against the IWW and other radical organizations. In these raids, dozens of IWW officials, especially those of foreign birth, were arrested. In December 1919 a few of those arrested were deported to the Soviet Union. Nine union leaders, including IWW co-founder William "Big Bill" Haywood, jumped bail in 1921 while on trial for violating the Espionage Act and fled to the Soviet Union; Haywood died there in 1928.

Public opinion, never very supportive of the Wobblies, turned outright hostile during and immediately after World War I. In some locales, citizens took the law into their own hands, attacking IWW members and organizers and driving them out of town. The most notorious postwar incident occurred in Centralia, Washington, a town that had long been a site of IWW organizing in the timber industry. On November 11, 1919, the first anniversary of the armistice that ended World War I, townspeople seized army veteran and IWW activist Wesley Everett from the local jail. The mob beat and then shot Everett, dumping his body in an unmarked grave. The coroner's report listed the death as a suicide.

Still, the IWW continued to organize successfully, particularly in the mining and timber camps of the West and industrial towns in the Northeast. In 1923, the union counted roughly 100,000 members on its rolls, the highest in its history, and IWW leaders claimed that it had strong support from another 300,000 workers. During the first few years of the 1920s, the union organized strikes from San Pedro, California, to Philadelphia, but these were largely minor affairs, usually aimed at winning the release of IWW activists jailed for civil disobedience. None of these strikes approached the scale of the great timber and mining industry actions of the early 1900s or the Lawrence, Massachusetts, textile worker strike of 1912.

Increasing prosperity, as well as ongoing repression, soon took their toll on the IWW, as did internal divisions. In 1924, the organization split between its western and eastern halves, largely over whether the union should be run centrally or with different locals operating autonomously. There was also growing resentment in the ranks over the influence of Communist Party members on union leadership. While the IWW conducted one last important strike in 1927–1928, in the Colorado mining industry, its power and numbers had already shrunk considerably. By 1930, the IWW had fewer than 10,000 members, and it played only a minor role in the labor-organizing wave that spread across America in the middle and late 1930s.

James Ciment and Leigh Kimmel

See also: Anarchism; Communist Party; Flynn, Elizabeth Gurley; Labor Movement; Socialism and the Socialist Party of America.

Further Reading

Dubofsky, Melvin. *We Shall Be All: A History of the Industrial Workers of the World.* Chicago: Quadrangle, 1969.

Laslett, John. *Labor and the Left: A Study of Socialist and Radical Influences in the American Labor Movement, 1881–1924.* New York: Basic Books, 1974.

Noggle, Burl. *Into the Twenties: The United States from Armistice to Normalcy.* Urbana: University of Illinois Press, 1974.

Irish Americans

Like other Americans of the Jazz Age, the 4.5 million people who identified themselves as ethnically Irish faced rapid social and economic change. They also faced unique issues of their own. There was strife in Ireland, continuing anti-Irish prejudice among some Americans, and a changing balance in the Irish American population between recent immigrants and third- and fourth-generation Americans. The decade that began with harsh civil wars in Ireland ended with an Irish American running for president of the United States for the first time, albeit unsuccessfully.

Ireland was in turmoil during the early years of the Jazz Age, with supporters of Irish independence engaged in guerrilla warfare against British forces. Then, after the signing of the Anglo-Irish Treaty in 1921, civil war raged in the new state for another two years. Moreover, U.S. President Woodrow Wilson did not deliver on the promise he made at the 1919 Paris Peace Conference to support Irish independence. The Irish rebel leader Eamon de Valera, who had been born in New York but raised in Limerick, had toured the United States in 1919–1920, seeking political recognition of the Irish Free State and money to support the cause. The Friends of Irish Freedom, an organization formed in New York City in 1917, played a great part in raising funds, but diplomatic support from Washington was not forthcoming.

The Irish American population was not a solid bloc. By 1920, almost three-quarters of those who identified themselves as Irish American also identified themselves as at least third-generation American. For them, the wars and political divisions in the home country may have been of less intense interest than they were for more recent generations or immigrants. Religion also diversified the Irish American population. Many of the Irish immigrants who had arrived since the Great Hunger in the mid-nineteenth century were Catholic, while many of those who came during the colonial and early republic periods were Protestant.

By the 1920s, some Irish American families had begun climbing the economic and social ladder. It was common to find Irish Americans working, for example, as teachers, in business, and in law enforcement. The majority of Irish Americans were city dwellers, with concentrations in New York, Boston,

Detroit, Baltimore, and Philadelphia. Even small towns in New England had concentrations of Irish living in sections known as "Little Dublin" or "Little Ireland." In part this cohesion was for familiarity, but it was for protection as well. The revived Ku Klux Klan in the 1920s had among its targets both Irish and Catholic people, and the decade brought marches and other displays of ethnic hatred in a number of cities in the North.

One of the ways in which Irish Americans protected themselves was by becoming involved in political machines and alliances. In earlier decades, these machines had often been hotbeds of graft and corruption, but by the 1920s, even the most notorious of such groups, including Tammany Hall in New York City, were shaking off that reputation to reinvent themselves as organizations concerned with social welfare and antidiscrimination. This was nowhere more apparent than in the career of Tammany Hall member, New York Governor Al Smith, who championed laws for the rights of workers and child welfare. In his 1928 bid for president, however, the Democratic candidate ran into strong anti-Catholic prejudice outside of the Northeast, and he lost the election to Republican Herbert Hoover in a landslide.

Other Irish Americans of note during the Jazz Age included playwright Eugene O'Neill, the son of immigrants from Kilkenny and Tipperary. During the 1920s, three of his plays won the Pulitzer Prize: *Beyond the Horizon* in 1920, *Anna Christie* in 1922, and *Strange Interlude* in 1928. Among novelists, F. Scott Fitzgerald stood out for his American masterpiece *The Great Gatsby* (1925). George M. Cohan staged shows that helped create the modern Broadway theater, and John Barrymore acted on stage and in film. Notre Dame University's successful football team officially took on the name "Fighting Irish," and Jack Dempsey reigned as the heavyweight boxing champion during the first half of the decade. Just beginning their careers were singer Bing Crosby and actress Helen Hayes, both of whom would go on to world renown. Buster Keaton acted in his first films, and Walt Disney created his first two short animated series.

Kerry Dexter

See also: Catholics and Catholicism; Immigration; Immigration Laws of 1921 and 1924.

Further Reading

Gedutis, Susan. *See You at the Hall: Boston's Golden Era of Irish Music and Dance.* Boston: Northeastern University Press, 2004.

Meagher, Timothy J. *Inventing Irish America: Generation, Class, and Ethnic Identity in a New England City, 1880–1928.* South Bend, IN: Notre Dame University Press, 2000.

Miller, Kerby. *Emigrants and Exiles: Ireland and the Story of Irish Emigration to America.* New York: Oxford University Press, 1985.

Italian Americans

Until the 1920s, Italian Americans were among the least assimilative of the nation's ethnic groups. Italian immigrants were among the least likely to bring their families or to apply for citizenship, and they were the most likely to return to their native land. The restrictive federal immigration laws of 1921 and 1924 changed that. Cut off from the possibility of returning to the United States if they left, few Italian Americans made the trip to their homeland and more applied for U.S. citizenship.

The roughly 1.6 million native Italians who lived in the United States in 1920 did not constitute a uniform ethnic group. Those who came from northern Italy were markedly different in culture, dialect, and lifestyle from those who came from southern Italy—so much so that the U.S. government kept separate immigration statistics for the two regions of the country. Those originating from northern Italy represented about 15 percent of the 5.5 million Italian immigrants who arrived between 1870 and passage of the restrictive National Origins Act of 1924. By the 1920s, most northern Italians were fully integrated into American society and were indistinguishable from the larger culture. Unlike other ethnic groups, they did not tend to help subsequent immigrants, and they tended to distance themselves from southern Italians, who made up the bulk of foreign-born Italians in the United States in 1920.

Prior to the National Origins Act of 1924, as many as 60 percent of the Italian immigrants returned to Italy within five years of their arrival in America. Because of the transitory nature of their migration, Italians had the lowest rate of application for citizenship and brought the fewest number of children of any major European migrant group. The prospect of returning to Italy slowed acculturation, and learning English was a lower priority for Italians than for many other immigrants. Limitations imposed by the National Origins Act of 1924 served to homogenize America's ethnic communities by decreasing the number of new migrants and marginalizing cultural links with the country of origin. This affected Italian migration and culture less severely. Instead, the immigration restrictions prompted a decline in return migration (the *ritornati*) and an unanticipated increase in Italian-speaking, foreign-born people. Italian was the second most popular non-English language spoken among the foreign born in American homes throughout the 1920s, after German. While most non-English languages experienced a dip in home use, Italian actually increased by more than 10 percent during the decade.

Large Italian colonies were located in New York, Philadelphia, Chicago, Boston, Baltimore, San Francisco, and Detroit. Fewer than two-thirds of Italian immigrants settled more than fifty miles beyond New York City, and regional residence had a significant effect on community development. Outside these few major cities, there were not Italian neighborhoods so much as there were Italian streets or concentrations, requiring that Italians intermingle with other ethnic groups and native-born Americans.

Most Italian American mutual aid societies reflected the provincialism of Italy—an Italian location name or patron saint indicated the origin of its constituents, such as San Gennaro for those from the Naples region. The spirit of localized cohesion was known as *campanilismo,* loyalty to those who live within the sound of the church bells. Most Italian Americans married other Italian Americans, usually from the same area of Italy; unions between Italians from the south and north of the country were relatively rare.

Italian Americans of the first and second generation often were forced by economic circumstances to make work a higher priority than education. Italian American children often worked in family or neighborhood businesses rather than attend school. At the end of the 1920s, 42 percent of New York City's high school students graduated, but only 11 percent of the Italian American students earned their diplomas. Over 30 percent of Italian Americans in the city worked as laborers. Italians made up the largest group of workers in the largely unskilled garment industry during the decade. Meanwhile, employers often held a strong prejudice against Italians. This pushed a few Italians into the informal or underground economy.

Many Italian Americans came to the United States as part of the *padroni* system, in which immigrants had their passage to America paid by accepting the employment offered to them by *padroni,* or labor contractors. In the 1920s, as the padroni system started to wane, an increasing number of Italian Americans joined labor unions. Although once drawn to radical unions like the International Workers of the World, many shifted to the more mainstream unions of the American Federation of Labor to win concessions from employers.

Italian Americans also set up service organizations. The Sons of Italy, established in New York City's Little Italy neighborhood in 1905, emerged as an umbrella organization for Italian mutual aid societies. By 1922, the order numbered 1,300 lodges across the country.

At the same time, Italian Americans faced strong pressure to assimilate from patriotic groups like the Daughters of the American Revolution and the American Legion. And no immigrant group faced more nativist violence than Italian Americans, especially in the Midwest. Italian Americans, especially Sicilians, were unfairly stigmatized as criminals because a small number of them participated in organized crime. In the public mind they were associated with anarchism and other radical political doctrines. When Italian American anarchists Nicola Sacco and Bartolomeo Vanzetti were executed in 1927, convicted of a double murder and robbery in 1920, many claimed they were convicted and executed partly because they were Italian.

Italian Americans were nevertheless making their mark on America in a positive way in the 1920s. Some of Jazz Age America's most celebrated public figures were Italian Americans. These included the legendary film star Rudolph Valentino, whose funeral in 1926 drew more than 100,000 people. In 1922, Gene Sarazen won golf's U.S. Open at age twenty, the youngest player to do so. And Fiorello La Guardia served in Congress as a representative of New York City throughout the decade and later was one of the city's most famous mayors.

Michael Jacobs

See also: Catholics and Catholicism; Immigration; Immigration Laws of 1921 and 1924; Sacco and Vanzetti Case (1920–1921).

Further Reading

Mangione, Jerre, and Ben Morreale. *La Storia: Five Centuries of the Italian American Experience.* New York: HarperCollins, 1992.

Nelli, Humbert S. *From Immigrants to Ethnics: The Italian Americans.* New York: Oxford University Press, 1983.

Rolle, Andrew. *The Italian Americans: Troubled Roots.* New York: Free Press, 1980.

Schiavo, Giovanni. *Four Centuries of Italian American History.* New York: Vigo, 1955.

Japan, Relations with

Relations between the United States and Japan during the 1920s were affected by several issues and misunderstandings that would result in tragic consequences in the following decade. Japan emerged from World War I believing that it had achieved equality with the major Western powers, but it could not gain the acceptance it believed it had earned. For example, Japan failed to secure the equality-of-nations clause it wanted in the Treaty of Versailles; the white rulers of South Africa, Australia, and New Zealand strenuously opposed the clause.

In late 1921, the U.S. government invited Japan and the world's other naval powers to Washington, D.C., for discussions on naval disarmament and the situation in China and the Pacific. The resulting Four-, Five-, and Nine-Power treaties limited the construction of warships, promised respect for China's territorial integrity, permitted Great Britain to abrogate the Anglo-Japanese Alliance of 1902 (which was up for renewal), and compensated Japan with a joint Anglo-American promise not to fortify Pacific holdings west of Hawaii and north of Singapore.

Also at issue were American immigration policies that insulted many Japanese. Cresting in the decade before World War I, the third great wave of immigration to the United States brought millions of people from the crumbling Russian and Austro-Hungarian empires as well as from Japan. Many Americans resisted the increased ethnic and cultural differentiation, and one result was increasingly strict immigration laws in the 1920s. The Emergency Quota Act of 1921 limited immigration based on each ethnicity's population in the 1910 U.S. Census. The National Origins Act of 1924 went further, using the 1890 census, before the onset of the third great wave, to determine quotas. In both cases, immigration was limited to 2 percent of the total of a particular nationality in the baseline year. The legislation thus clearly favored emigration from northwest Europe and included no quota for Japan. (The Chinese Exclusion Act of 1882 had already ended legal Chinese immigration.) Despite the protests of the Japanese government, President Calvin Coolidge signed the bill into law.

The hard feelings arising from the Washington Naval Conference and the immigration laws affected U.S.-Japanese relations for the remainder of the 1920s. There were other important issues, to be sure, including differing views on the situation in China, the status of Korea and the Philippines, and the willingness of the United States to recognize Japan as a great, if not entirely equal, power.

China presented a significant challenge. In 1921, the leader of the nationalist movement, Sun Yat-sen, allied with the Soviet Comintern. In 1926, his successor, Jiang Jieshi (Chiang Kai-shek), organized a military campaign, the Northern Expedition, to unify China. Japan had long viewed parts of China as attractive for its own expansion, while the United States believed itself to be a friend of China and remained committed to the Open Door trade policy to provide opportunities for American business. These conflicting views of East Asia, and the respective roles of China, Japan, and the United States, would come to the fore as Japan's increasing aggression led finally to its invasion of China.

The respective situations of Korea and the Philippines also posed a challenge. Japan had gained paramountcy in Korea in 1905, incorporating the former Hermit Kingdom into the Japanese Empire after 1910. By contrast, the U.S. government had announced its intention to quit the Philippines by 1946. These islands, strategically located about a day's steaming time from major sites in Southeast Asia and the western Pacific, were a likely target if Japan sought control of the great natural resources in the region.

Perhaps the key to U.S.-Japanese relations was the view each government held of the other. Japan had great respect for the United States and sought to be regarded as an equal. To Americans, by contrast, Japan was a land of cheap products ("gimcracks" and "gewgaws") and exotic customs, not nearly equal to the European nations that had sent the majority of immigrants to America. The volatile situation of the 1920s worsened throughout the 1930s and finally exploded on December 7, 1941.

Charles M. Dobbs

See also: China, Relations with; Four-Power Treaty (1921); Siberian Intervention; Versailles, Treaty of (1919); Washington Naval Conference (1921–1922).

Further Reading

Bamba, Nobuya. *Japanese Diplomacy in a Dilemma: New Light on Japan's China Policy, 1924–1929.* Vancouver, Canada: University of British Columbia Press, 1972.

Cohen, Warren I. *Empire Without Tears: American Foreign Relations, 1921–1933.* Philadelphia: Temple University Press, 1987.

Ellis, L. Ethan. *Republican Foreign Policy, 1921–1933.* New Brunswick, NJ: Rutgers University Press, 1995.

Iriye, Akira. *After Imperialism: The Search for a New Order in the Far East, 1921–1931.* Cambridge, MA: Harvard University Press, 1965.

Jazz

F. Scott Fitzgerald, the great chronicler of 1920s American culture, coined the lasting nickname for the era—the Jazz Age. (The title of his second collection of short stories, published in 1922, was *Tales of the Jazz Age.*) For Fitzgerald, and for his contemporaries, jazz music—with its fast-paced, syncopated rhythms, improvisation, and hedonistic associations—symbolized all that was modern, carefree, and sometimes illicit in the years following the reform-minded Progressive Era and the sacrifices of World War I. Jazz spoke to the carefree, modern spirit of the times.

Jazz was not invented in the 1920s, but that decade saw its popularity grow exponentially, spreading beyond the confines of New Orleans and other black urban centers in the South and North to a wider white audience. The Great Migration, during which waves of African Americans moved northward, brought many musicians and their audiences from the Deep South to the urban centers of the Northeast, Midwest, and West. In addition, radio and the spread of phonographs made jazz available to a much larger audience.

Origins and Migration

Jazz originated at the turn of the twentieth century in New Orleans, a melting pot of French, Spanish, Anglo, and, most important, African cultures (the word *jazz* may have derived from an African American slang term for sex). There, two musical influences—minstrel show bands and Creole (mixed-race) marching bands—came together to create ragtime, the direct precursor of jazz. Until about 1920, the terms *jazz* and *ragtime* were often used interchangeably to describe the infectious and danceable music played in New Orleans nightclubs and brothels. But jazz and ragtime are quite different musical forms. Whereas ragtime is meant to be played as written, jazz is improvised.

As large numbers of rural blacks began to move to urban New Orleans in the first two decades of the twentieth century, they brought a new musical influence to the emerging jazz style: the blues, a rural African American folk music that was itself a musical hybrid of African rhythms, old slave work songs, and black spirituals. The blues was a highly soulful form of music, and its incorporation provided emotional depth and resonance to balance the more carefree rhythms of ragtime.

By the end of World War I, jazz had established itself as a major musical influence in cities up and down the Mississippi Valley, into the Northeast, and across to the West Coast. The primary force behind its spread was the Great Migration, the stream of predominantly African American migrants out of the rural South that began in the early 1900s and continued well after World War II. Driven out of the South by the grinding poverty of tenant farming and the daily indignities of racial oppression, Southern blacks were drawn north and west by relatively high-paying factory jobs—especially plentiful during World War I and the prosperity of the 1920s—and a life away from Jim Crow segregation.

The migration produced new or enlarged African American neighborhoods in urban centers such as New York, Chicago, and Detroit, and created new audiences for New Orleans musicians. These included the two most important purveyors of jazz music in the first two decades of the twentieth century: cornet player Joe "King" Oliver and his Creole Jazz Band, and pianist and composer Ferdinand "Jelly Roll" Morton and his Red Hot Peppers. From 1904, Morton had worked as an itinerant musician, playing with bands in cities from St. Louis to New York, settling in Chicago from 1911 to 1915. Oliver, along with his influential saxophonist Sidney Bechet, moved to Chicago in 1918. Other important jazz musicians moving northward and westward included trombonist Edward "Kid" Ory (to California in 1919 and Chicago in 1925) and trumpet player and Oliver protégé Louis Armstrong (to Chicago in 1922 and New York in 1924).

Jazz Culture

Jazz was more than just a popular musical form of the 1920s. It was the centerpiece of a whole new black—and sometimes racially integrated—urban nightlife. The outlawing of alcohol by the Eighteenth Amendment in 1920 created a new underground culture in America's large cities, focused on the illegal bar, or speakeasy. There were hundreds of speakeasies in most cities during Prohibition; New York had as many as 30,000. Some were just back-alley dives where a patron could obtain cheaply made liquor at a makeshift bar. Others were more elegant affairs, with fancy interiors, strict dress codes, and customers from the upper echelons of business, culture, and politics.

Many of these upscale—and some downscale—establishments featured jazz, which helped to draw customers and provided work for musicians. Jazz was the ideal musical form for the speakeasy; its syncopated rhythms called out for dancing, and its improvisational style spoke to a clientele eager to let their inhibitions be washed away with illegal drinking. Of course, jazz flourished in legitimate clubs, too. Perhaps the most important jazz venue of the 1920s was Harlem's Cotton Club in New York City. Although briefly closed down for selling alcohol in 1925, its owner, bootlegger Owney Madden, usually paid off enough police and politicians to keep it open.

The big Northern cities offered more than an income for jazz and blues musicians from the South. They also infused jazz with the rhythms of modern urban life and provided meeting places where different jazz styles could cross-pollinate, for it was not just New Orleans that produced the African American jazz greats of the 1920s. Pianist, composer, and bandleader Edward "Duke" Ellington came out of Washington, D.C. Singer and bandleader Cab Calloway came from Baltimore. Singer Bessie Smith, who perhaps did more than any other musician to infuse mournful blues riffs into early jazz, was from Chattanooga, Tennessee.

In addition, Northern cities, with their large and well-patronized nightclubs, required larger bands. The improvisational nature of jazz encouraged musicians to learn from and modify each other's playing styles, and large bands meant that more musicians were exposed to a variety of styles, leading to further innovation. Fletcher Henderson recruited Louis Arm-

Jazz pianist, composer, and bandleader Duke Ellington rose to prominence in the clubs of New York City during the 1920s. He wrote more than a thousand pieces in a career that spanned more than half a century. (*Frank Driggs Collection/Hulton Archive/Getty Images*)

strong for his New York ensemble in 1924, while Duke Ellington hired pioneering alto saxophonist Johnny Hodges to play in his band at the Cotton Club in 1928. The hiring of such virtuoso talent led to perhaps the most important innovation in jazz of the 1920s: the solo. Unlike ragtime and early jazz, which consisted primarily of ensemble playing, the jazz form pioneered by emerging bands such as Ellington's and virtuoso players such as Armstrong featured lengthy, improvisational solos alternating with stretches of ensemble playing. Armstrong and Bessie Smith were also critical in the development of jazz singing, which began to be featured in band music of the 1920s, though Armstrong's and Calloway's signature scat style—the rhythmic vocalization of nonsensical syllables—would not emerge until the 1930s.

Jazz crossed racial lines in the 1920s, and not just because white audiences flocked to the jazz-featuring speakeasies and clubs in black parts of town. Whites increasingly began to play the music as well. Paul Whiteman, the self-proclaimed "king of jazz," was a popular bandleader of the 1920s; among his musicians was Bix Beiderbecke, an innovative cornet player from Iowa. Jazz music also influenced American classical music. It was Whiteman who commissioned composer George Gershwin's *Rhapsody in Blue,* a classical composition heavily inflected with jazz rhythms that Whiteman debuted in 1924.

Given the intense racial prejudice of the era, however, most jazz bands—white and black—remained segregated, as did most clubs, despite being located in supposedly integrated cities in the North. The Cotton Club, in the predominantly black Harlem neighborhood of Manhattan, featured black musicians such as Ellington and his band but served white customers only. Moreover, the Cotton Club featured jungle-themed, sexually provocative jazz dance routines that would seem offensive stereotyping to modern audiences, but they played to white audiences' fascination with the exoticism of black culture.

Musicians, however, were perhaps less prejudiced. Recognizing the talent of black musicians—as well as black audiences' greater acceptance of rawer and more innovative musical styles—many white musicians flocked to black clubs and speakeasies after their own gigs at white venues were finished for the night.

Recordings and Radio

By the mid-1920s, the center of American jazz had shifted northward to Chicago and, by the late 1920s, eastward to New York City, the country's recording capital during the Jazz Age. Because of segregation in most recording studios, the first jazz recordings were made by all-white bands in the late 1910s. Most music historians cite a February 28, 1917, recording by the all-white Original Dixieland Jass Band as the first jazz record ever made. It was not until around 1921 that Kid Ory's group performed for the first black jazz recording. The first integrated record, from 1923, featured Jelly Roll Morton playing with the all-white New Orleans Rhythm Kings.

Recordings tempered the improvisational quality of jazz but helped popularize it beyond the major urban centers where audiences might hear it performed live. Records also brought new jazz sounds to musicians in far-flung places, allowing for further cross-pollination of styles. Equally important for jazz's diffusion was the new medium of radio. Following the opening of the first commercial station in

Pittsburgh in 1920, radio stations sprang up across the country, and the sale of sets skyrocketed, with seven in ten households owning a radio by 1930. By the mid-1920s, radio stations in major cities across the country were featuring live jazz music for audiences in the millions.

By the end of the 1920s and the onset of the Great Depression, jazz was the most popular musical form of urban America, at a time when the nation was being transformed from a predominantly rural to a predominantly urban society. Jazz, in effect, provided the sound track for that transition, and it would go on to even greater heights of popularity in the era of Big Band and swing in the late 1930s and 1940s. But no period is more closely associated with this American musical form—perhaps America's greatest contribution to world music—than the uninhibited era it gave its name to: the Jazz Age.

James Ciment

See also: Armstrong, Louis; Baker, Josephine; Beiderbecke, Bix; Blues; Dance, Popular; Gershwin, George; Harlem Renaissance; Migration, Great; Oliver, Joe "King"; Smith, Bessie.

For Further Reading

Burns, Ken. *Jazz.* Documentary film. Alexandria, VA: PBS Films, 2001.
Ogden, Kathy J. *The Jazz Revolution: Twenties America and the Meaning of Jazz.* New York: Oxford University Press, 1989.
Shaw, Arnold. *The Jazz Age: Popular Music in the 1920s.* New York: Oxford University Press, 1987.
Williams, Martin. *Jazz in Its Time.* New York: Oxford University Press, 1989.

Jewish Americans

At the beginning of the 1920s, the Jewish population of the United States was estimated at 3.6 million. In the peak year of 1921, 119,000 Jewish immigrants arrived on American shores, mainly from Poland, representing almost 15 percent of total U.S. immigration. But with more restrictive immigration laws, such as the National Origins Act of 1924, the number of newcomers dipped sharply, averaging 10,000 to 11,000 annually from 1925 to 1929. By the end of the Jazz Age, American Jews numbered over 4 million. In all, over a third of Eastern European Jews left their countries of origin (mainly Poland, Russia, and Romania), and 90 percent of them went to the United States.

Jewish immigrants from Eastern Europe were fleeing pogroms, economic privation, political oppression, and restrictive government policies. They came intending to stay. On average, only 4.6 percent of them ended up leaving the United States. Many came with their families; often men made the crossing first, then sent for their wives and other family members as soon as possible.

Jewish immigrants tended to settle in poorer neighborhoods of big cities, typically in the commercial, industrial, and cultural centers of the Northeast (New York, Philadelphia, Boston, and Baltimore) and the Midwest (Chicago in particular). At the end of the 1920s, 70 percent of Jewish Americans lived in the Northeast; another 20 percent lived in the upper Midwest. Although the numbers were small, there was a Jewish presence in every state.

Eastern European and Russian immigrants found an already ensconced Jewish community in America: the 250,000 German Jews who had arrived in the period 1820–1880. The Jewish groups were different from each other, leading to tensions. Many of the newcomers were more orthodox in their religious beliefs and worship than the earlier immigrants. The established German Jews' reform ideology was more modern and the services more sedate. German Jewish "uptowners," respectable, progressive, and well-to-do, were disdainful of the impoverished and uncouth "downtowners," while many of the poor Eastern Europeans regarded wealthier and more prestigious Jews with envy.

The 1920s, and earlier years as well, were filled with conflicts between the Jewish elite and the Jewish masses, between political conservatives and liberals, democrats and Socialists. The Eastern Europeans wanted an all-embracing American Jewish community, which, due to their greater numbers, they could hope to control. The Germans wanted decentralization and the right to go their own way, by which they hoped to undermine challenges to their traditional leadership.

But the various Jewish groups were joined by a consensus: the consciousness of a common past and a common tradition. Kinship ties remained very strong and obliged Jews to help one another, whatever their differences. The quota laws of the 1920s reduced the number of new arrivals from Eastern Europe, hastening the Americanization of Jews in the United States. Antagonisms notwithstanding, the Jewish community was in the process of becoming integrated and united. Instead of seeing themselves as Russian Jews or German Jews, for example, more and more considered themselves American Jews.

Studies in the 1920s of more than 50,000 Jews in various cities found that about 60 percent of males were salesmen, 27 percent carpenters, 8 percent foremen in manufacturing establishments, and 4 percent physicians and surgeons. Among women, 67 percent worked in clothing factories and 22 percent were stenographers or typists. Overall, the economic structure of American Jewish society changed dramatically between World War I and the end of the 1920s: the number of Jews in trades, clerical occupations, and the professions increased, while the percentage of industrial and other workers decreased.

Jews had a strong impact on America's film industry. By 1926, movies were America's fifth-largest industry, making $1.5 billion a year and accounting for 90 percent of the world's motion pictures. Many of the major studios were run by émigré Jews, such as Samuel Goldwyn, Louis B. Mayer, Harry Cohn, and Jack Warner. At the other end of the spectrum, Jewish gangsters were powerful forces in the ghettos of New York, Chicago, and Detroit. Arnold Rothstein, a gambler and racketeer, allegedly fixed the 1919 World Series. "Greasy Thumb" Guzik was the business manager of Al Capone's mob. The notorious Purple Gang were bootleggers, hired murderers, and kidnappers.

During the Jazz Age, American Jews experienced upward economic mobility. Neither the foreignness of the Eastern European immigrants nor anti-Semitism kept them from improving their lot amid the general prosperity of the period. Many Jews were able to quit the Lower East Side of New York City and its counterparts in other cities, moving to better neighborhoods. They left proletarian occupations and peddling to become shopkeepers, entrepreneurs, and white-collar workers. The number of Jewish teachers, accountants, lawyers, and physicians increased, and many Jews had high hopes for the economic and social advancement of their children.

Leslie Rabkin

See also: Anti-Semitism; Immigration.

Further Reading

Diner, Hasia. *The Jews of the United States, 1654 to 2000.* Berkeley: University of California Press, 2004.

Hertzberg, Arthur. *The Jews in America.* New York: Columbia University Press, 1988.

Sachar, Howard M. *A History of Jews in America.* New York: Vintage Books, 1993.

Jones, Bobby (1902–1971)

Considered by many the greatest golfer of all time, Bobby Jones dominated the game in the 1920s, becoming an iconic athletic figure alongside baseball's Babe Ruth, boxing's Jack Dempsey, football's Red Grange, and tennis's Bill Tilden. Remaining an amateur throughout his playing career and known for his gentlemanly ways and good sportsmanship, Jones won thirteen major championships over an eight-year span (1923–1930), including a sweep of all four majors in 1930—at the time, the Grand Slam consisted of the U.S. Open, British Open, U.S. Amateur, and British Amateur. He remains the only player in golf history to win the Grand Slam in a single year.

Born Robert Tyre Jones, Jr., on St. Patrick's Day, March 17, 1902, in Atlanta, Georgia, he was an only child, the son of Robert P. Jones, an attorney, and Clara Thomas. When Jones was six, the family moved near Atlanta's East Lake Country Club. He did not have formal golf lessons but learned to play by mimicking the swing of East Lake's Scottish professional, Stewart Maiden. Encouraged by his father, Jones soon took up competitive play. He won his first title in an informal tournament that summer when he defeated three other children at East Lake.

In 1916, at age fourteen, he won the Georgia Amateur championship. In the finals of that match-play event (pitting player against player), he defeated fellow Atlanta native and friend Perry Adair. When Adair's father took Perry to the Merion Cricket Club in Ardmore, Pennsylvania, to attempt to qualify for the U.S. Amateur, Jones went along and qualified for the match-play portion of the event. His first taste of national competition proved to be successful for Jones, as he defeated 1906 U.S. Amateur champion Eben Byers in the first round and Pennsylvania Amateur champion Frank Dyer in the second round. Although Jones lost in the third round to defending U.S. Amateur champion Bob Gardner, his debut in national competition caught the eye of the golfing world.

Jones continued to play in national competitions, with his best finish coming at the 1920 U.S. Amateur, when he advanced to the semifinals. He played in all four major championships the following year, traveling to Great Britain to play in the British Amateur and British Open. He did not fare well in either tournament and actually withdrew from the British Open. His breakthrough came in the 1923 U.S. Open at Inwood Country Club in New York, where he won his first national championship in a playoff. The win cleared the way for Jones's domination of the sport for the next eight years, as he won at least one major championship each year—thirteen of the twenty-one he entered. His two primary rivals—Walter Hagen and Gene Sarazen—never won a U.S. Open or a British Open in which Jones was entered. During that span, Jones competed in eight U.S. Opens and three British Opens, finishing either first or second in all of them (including playoff losses in the 1925 and 1928 U.S. Opens).

The Associated Press would later call Jones's Grand Slam sweep of 1930 the single greatest individual achievement in sports history. He was on top of the golfing world—and chose to retire. He had compiled a remarkable career record: five U.S. Amateur championships, four U.S. Open championships, three British Opens, and one British Amateur title. He was also a member of five Walker Cup teams for the United States, all of which defeated their British adversaries.

Part of Jones's appeal to contemporaries and historians of the sport, aside from his great skill, is that

The greatest golfer of his generation—and perhaps the most popular athlete of the 1920s—Bobby Jones won the British Open three times and the U.S. Open four times between 1923 and 1930. He remained an amateur for his entire playing career. *(Kirby/Stringer/Hulton Archive/ Getty Images)*

he remained a part-time amateur, never playing the sport for money. Even as he perfected his game, Jones earned degrees in mechanical engineering and English literature, the latter from Harvard University in 1924. After attending Emory University in 1926 and 1927, he passed the Georgia bar and went to work in his father's law firm.

Jones's retirement from competitive golf did not mean that he left the game altogether. One of his greatest legacies is the Augusta National Golf Club in Georgia, which he designed and helped establish with financier Clifford Roberts. Jones also supported the game by advising on educational golf films and assisting the A.G. Spalding Company in the development of matching sets of golf clubs.

During World War II, Jones served in the U.S. Army Air Corps. In the 1950s, he was diagnosed with a degenerative spinal-cord disease that left him in a wheelchair. Jones died on December 18, 1971.

Rob Hardin

See also: Celebrity Culture; Golf.

Further Reading

Frost, Mark. *The Grand Slam: Bobby Jones, America, and the Story of Golf.* New York: Hyperion, 2004.
Keeler, O.B. *The Bobby Jones Story: The Authorized Biography.* Chicago: Triumph, 2002.

Journalism

The Jazz Age began with the ascendancy to the White House of a newspaper publisher, Warren G. Harding, whose scandal-ridden administration supplied plenty of inspiration for the nation's increasingly sensationalist press. It was the well-respected *Wall Street Journal* that broke the first news of the infamous Teapot Dome bribery scandal in 1922, but even the country's new crop of tabloids, normally preoccupied with sex and crime, caught Teapot Dome fever.

Rise of the Tabloid

The colorful excesses of the tabloid style suited the Jazz Age perfectly. Although tabloids and penny papers had long been the rage in England, the first major tabloid in America, the New York *Daily News,* was less than two years old when Harding took office in 1921.

Joseph Medill Patterson and Robert McCormick, grandsons of Joseph Medill and co-publishers of the *Chicago Tribune* since 1914, had launched the *Daily News* at the behest of Lord Northcliffe, formerly Alfred C. Harmsworth. As publisher of the *Daily Mirror* in London, Harmsworth saw profit potential in bringing the tabloid format to the United States. The New York *Daily News,* which originally appeared as the *Illustrated Daily News,* floundered at first. But by 1924, its circulation of 750,000 was the largest in the country. Two years later, it reached 1 million. Patterson became sole publisher of the tabloid in 1925.

Then, as today, tabloids differed in appearance from traditional newspapers. Tabloid pages were roughly half the size of broadsheet general-circulation dailies. With their priority on photos and short articles, tabloids took far less time to read. Photographs covered their front pages, usually accompanied by one eye-catching headline. When the *Daily News* launched its first issue, *The New York Times* contained no photographs—something that would change for most dailies during the 1920s, as readers voted with their wallets in favor of pictures.

The success of the *Daily News* drew media giant William Randolph Hearst into the New York tabloid market, where he launched the New York *Daily Mirror* in 1924. Ambitious publisher and fitness promoter Bernarr Macfadden soon started the New York *Evening Graphic,* which often exceeded the *News* and *Mirror* for shock value, melodrama, and lurid detail. But even as the tabloid market expanded, the country's total number of newspapers shrank.

Media Giants

The U.S. population had increased from 92 million in 1910 to 122 million in 1930, yet the number of English-language general-circulation dailies shrank during that same period, from 2,200 to 1,942. Dominant media companies like Hearst and Scripps-Howard aggressively snatched up and shut down newspapers according to market forces and the rising costs of the printing technology that audiences demanded. Between 1918 and 1926, Hearst shut down sixteen newspapers. More and more, smaller cities were left with only one newspaper in town, if they had any at all.

Hearst remained the country's top media mogul through the Jazz Age, followed by the Scripps family. Between 1893 and 1926, E.W. Scripps bought thirty-four newspapers, including the *Indianapolis Times* (1922) and *Pittsburgh Press* (1923). Scripps re-

The Execution Photo of Ruth Snyder

By the late 1920s, New Yorkers had come to expect lurid headlines and shocking cover photos from the popular tabloids. The *Daily News,* for example, begun in 1919, had earned a reputation for its emphasis on crime stories and high-society scandal, all presented in a photo-rich tabloid format designed to appeal to busy working-class commuters eager to be entertained as well as informed by their daily paper. Nevertheless, the photo that appeared on page one on January 13, 1928, shocked even the most jaded denizens of New York. For there, on newsstands throughout the city, was the grainy image of a woman strapped to the state's electric chair, in mid-execution.

Her name was Ruth Snyder, and her story of adultery and murder had captivated the country since it broke the year before. Unhappily married to Albert Snyder, the editor of a boating magazine, she had been having an affair with a corset salesman named Judd Gray since 1925. In an age when divorce was much more difficult to obtain than it is today, the two concocted a plan to murder the husband and then get married. First, Snyder persuaded Albert to take out a $48,000 life insurance policy. Then, on the night of March 20, 1927, Gray slipped into the couple's Queens, New York, home and attempted to bludgeon the husband to death. When he proved unable to complete the job, Ruth finished it for him. Snyder and Gray then ransacked the house to make it appear that a burglary had turned deadly.

The lovers were quickly apprehended. Even before the trial, an outraged press and public called for their execution. In one of the most followed criminal trials of the Jazz Age, the *Daily News* and other papers prejudged the couple in their press coverage of the story. As most people expected, Snyder and Gray were found guilty and sentenced to death.

By the 1920s, public executions had become a thing of the past in the United States. Death sentences were carried out inside prison walls, in this case New York's notorious Sing Sing penitentiary. While journalists were permitted to view executions, cameras were strictly prohibited. But Tom Howard, an intrepid news photographer with the *Chicago Tribune*—the flagship paper of the company that owned the *Daily News*—was determined to cap the Snyder coverage with a last photo. By strapping a small camera to his ankle, Howard was able to snap one of the most infamous and shocking photos in American journalistic history.

Politicians, social commentators, and other newspapers expressed shock and disgust at the photo and at the editors of the *Daily News* for publishing it—but the public was fascinated. The January 13, 1928, issue of the *Daily News* sold an extra half million copies, more than doubling the paper's circulation for the day. State authorities around the country beefed up their security at executions. As for the murder and its grisly denouement, they soon became part of the cultural landscape. Playwright Sophie Treadwell used the story as the basis for her surrealist theater classic *Machinal* (1928), and crime writer James M. Cain was inspired to write his best-selling 1935 novella *Double Indemnity*.

Catherine W. Dolinski and James Ciment

The most powerful media baron of the Jazz Age, William Randolph Hearst owned twenty-eight metropolitan daily newspapers as well as two news services and several major national magazines at the height of his power in the mid-1920s. *(Library of Congress, LC-USZ62–68941)*

tired from the business in 1922, turning over his share of the company, then known as the Scripps-McRae League, to his son. Robert Scripps partnered with Roy Howard, the former president and general manager of the United Press, and Scripps-McRae was renamed Scripps-Howard.

New York publisher Frank Gannett was probably next in terms of influence. Gannett, who built his empire during the 1920s, merged papers in half a dozen New York cities, including Ithaca and Rochester, by 1930. He acquired fifteen dailies in New York State and several in Connecticut, New Jersey, and Illinois.

Top Stories

One of the biggest stories for journalists of the Jazz Age was Charles Lindbergh's solo flight from New York to Paris on May 21, 1927. The *St. Louis Globe-Democrat* poured money into the flight itself, and newspapers gave the event a big buildup. In New York, photos of Lindbergh's takeoff from Roosevelt Field covered the newspapers. When news broke of Lindbergh's successful touchdown in France, newspaper sales exploded. *The New York Times* dedicated fifteen pages to Lindbergh when he returned to America.

Sensational trials grabbed headlines in both mainstream and tabloid papers throughout the 1920s. The *Daily Mirror,* for example, reopened the unsolved 1922 double murder of the Reverend Edward Wheeler Hall and Mrs. Eleanor Mills, a member of the church choir. The bodies had been discovered in a rural area of New Jersey, and evidence uncovered by the *Daily Mirror* led to the arrest of the preacher's wife and several of her relatives. Coverage highlighted a love affair between the two victims and conflicting evidence. In the end, no one was convicted.

Innovations

Readers of the *Daily Graphic* in 1926 witnessed the birth of the composograph. By assembling a composite photo of reporters and jury members, the tabloid fabricated a courtroom scene from which photographers had been barred. A hit with readers, this would be the first of several composographs printed in the *Daily Graphic* and the forerunner of illustration methods used by modern supermarket tabloids.

Innovations in mainstream journalism included the rise of specialized reporting and news services. The nonprofit Science Services, created in 1921 by E.W. Scripps, improved newspaper and magazine coverage of the sciences by offering regular science features and pages. Reporter Louis Stark joined *The New York Times* in 1917 and began specializing in labor reporting, a field he would dominate during the Jazz Age and later decades.

Magazines

Many of the news magazines that had prospered through World War I struggled or disappeared in mergers during the 1920s, among them *The Century, The Forum,* and *World's Work*. In 1925, however, a distinguished and promising newcomer arrived on the scene: *The New Yorker*. Harold Ross, editor of the *Stars and Stripes* armed forces newspaper during World War I, began publishing the magazine with the same blend of humor, cultural musings, and serious analysis of current affairs that characterizes the magazine today. *Reader's Digest*, appearing in 1922, offered condensed versions of articles that had originated in other magazines, to the commercial detriment of many of those publications. *Harper's,* which began as a literary magazine, evolved into a public affairs journal during the latter half of the decade.

American Mercury was founded in 1924 under the editorship of drama critic George Jean Nathan and social critic and curmudgeon H.L. Mencken. In characteristic Mencken style, the publication declared in its first pages that it would "attempt a realistic presentation of the whole gaudy, gorgeous American scene," rather than "offer for sale any sovereign balm, whether political, economic or aesthetic, for all the sorrows of the world." The magazine's rebelliousness and contrariness quickly made it as fashionable and popular as it was controversial.

New Media

In 1920, radio station KDKA in Pittsburgh covered the Harding–Cox presidential race, expanding journalism into new formats. Two years later, WHA of Madison, Wisconsin, and WLB of Minneapolis, Minnesota, were launched as the country's first educational radio stations, broadcasting a mix of sports, news, market forecasts, and school programming.

Radio stations were cropping up throughout the country, and some newspapers saw the potential of radio as an outlet. The 1921 heavyweight boxing championship match between Jack Dempsey and Georges Carpentier in Jersey City, New Jersey, was the first widely broadcast sports event in the United States. The fight aired on both coasts, on stations like WJY in Hoboken, New Jersey, and courtesy of media companies like the Seattle *Post-Intelligencer,* which contracted with a local radio distributor to broadcast the bout.

Though heralded at the start of the decade for its vast potential to inform and educate, radio eventually became a favorite object of scorn by the intelligentsia of print journalism. Among the sources of disillusionment were the increasing consolidation and commercialization that swept the industry in the second half of the Jazz Age. The first of the major mergers came in 1926, when American Telephone and Telegraph (AT&T) sold WEAF in Newark and its network

of affiliates for $1 million to a group of companies: General Electric, the Westinghouse Company, and Radio Corporation of America (RCA). The purchase created the National Broadcasting Company (NBC), which encompassed both the WEAF chain of stations and the radio group's existing network linked to WJZ in New York. Although NBC stated that its mission would be to educate and enlighten, critics disparaged it for pandering to low-culture tastes in an effort to maximize advertising revenue.

The arrival of sound in movie theaters ushered in the era of the newsreel. In July 1926, Fox Film reproduced a sound interview with President Calvin Coolidge. That same year, Fox launched Movietone and showed its first newsreels in January 1927 in New York City. Fox debuted a biweekly newsreel feature in New York City in October, expanding to nationwide distribution in December. Hearst was financing weekly newsreels in 1927, the same year that Paramount launched "The Eyes of the World" silent newsreel.

By 1928, Paramount, Universal, Warner-Pathé, Hearst Metrotone, and Fox Movietone were distributing newsreels covering everything from the Lindbergh flight to the South Pole expeditions of Hubert Wilkins that Hearst sponsored and had filmed. As the Jazz Age came to an end, most U.S. newsreels were talkies and reflected the format and tone of the nation's daily newspapers.

Catherine W. Dolinski

See also: American Mercury; Hearst, William Randolph; Luce, Henry; Mencken, H.L.; New York *Daily News*; *New Yorker, The*; *Reader's Digest*; Ross, Harold; *Time.*

Further Reading

Bessie, Simon M. *Jazz Journalism: The Story of American Newspapers.* New York: E.P. Dutton, 1938.

Doerksen, Clifford J. *American Babel: Rogue Radio Broadcasters of the Jazz Age.* Philadelphia: University of Pennsylvania Press, 2005.

Emery, Edwin. *The Press and America: An Interpretative History of the Mass Media.* Englewood Cliffs, NJ: Prentice Hall, 1972.

Mott, Frank L. *American Journalism—A History: 1690–1960.* New York: Macmillan, 1965.

Sloan, William D., and James D. Startt. *The Significance of the Media in American History.* Northport, AL: Vision, 1994.

Teachout, Terry. *The Skeptic: A Life of H.L. Mencken.* New York: HarperCollins, 2002.

Keaton, Buster (1895–1966)

Affectionately known as the Great Stone Face, referring to his serious demeanor despite all manner of surrounding comedy and chaos, Buster Keaton stands as one of the three greats of the silent era in motion picture comedy, alongside Charlie Chaplin and Harold Lloyd. From his appearance in silent short films, Keaton moved to acting in and directing silent features throughout the 1920s, before losing his independence with a move to MGM Studios in 1928.

Joseph Frank Keaton was born into a vaudeville family in Piqua, Kansas, on October 4, 1895. His father, Joseph Hallie Keaton, and mother, Myra Edith Cutler, integrated him into their repertoire at a young age and called themselves the Three Keatons. The most popular account of the origin of the name "Buster" is that it was bestowed on him by magician Harry Houdini, the Keatons' traveling-show companion and business partner.

Roscoe "Fatty" Arbuckle, the star comedian and director, guided Keaton into film. Keaton's first film appearance was in Arbuckle's *The Butcher Boy* (1917). He went on to make fourteen shorts with his comic mentor and assisted Arbuckle in the direction of several of them. Keaton served in France during World War I. After his release from the army, he undertook his last collaboration with Arbuckle, *The Garage,* a short released in 1920. Keaton codirected and starred in the popular *One Week* (1920). The following year, he cowrote, codirected, and starred in *The High Sign,* but he was so disappointed with the film that he shelved it until the following year, when a broken leg prevented him from working. Indeed, over the course of his career, Keaton would suffer a number of serious injuries as he insisted on doing all of his own stunts, which became increasingly elaborate and often more dangerous as time went on.

At this time, Keaton was developing the screen persona that would make him famous: the poker-faced, porkpie-hat-wearing, physical comedian, sub-tle and realistic, who performed his own stunts. He made a flurry of shorts in the early 1920s—including *Neighbors* (1920), *The Boat* (1921), and *Cops* (1922)—that displayed his creativity, showcasing his mix of parody, satire, surrealism, and social commentary. *The Paleface* (1922) depicted Native Americans as victims of white greed, while the Romeo and Juliet plot of *Neighbors* (1920) dealt with ethnic prejudices of the families of the star-crossed lovers.

Keaton's wife, Natalie, was the sister of film star Norma Talmadge, who was married to producer Joseph Schenck. Under Schenck's tutelage, Keaton began his career as a writer, director, and star of feature-length films. But Keaton made little money from his early feature successes, as Schenck had secured the rights to all his output. His first feature, *Three Ages* (1923), a spoof of D.W. Griffith's *Intolerance* (1916), is seen by most film historians as an uneven work. Not so his next two feature films, *Our Hospitality* (1923) and *Sherlock, Jr.* (1924), which have been praised as comic masterpieces. As the sole director of *Sherlock, Jr.* (he had codirectors for many of his other films), Keaton introduced unprecedented special effects. Keaton's character, a film projectionist, is able to enter into and interact with the film he is showing. The effect was achieved by switching from a previously filmed sequence to an identical off-screen staging.

The Navigator (1924) was followed by *Seven Chances* (1925), *Go West* (1925), and *Battling Butler* (1926). Then came the film that is often regarded as his greatest work, although at the time, it was an expensive flop. *The General* (1926), set during the Civil War, featured the most expensive sequence of the silent era: a train crashing through an actual burning bridge. Keaton had refused to use a scale model. *The General,* like many of Keaton's films, showcased many of his filmmaking preferences, in this case, shooting natural locations. He also avoided speeding up the action, a common technique in the comedies of the 1920s, instead allowing the slow unfolding of the visual comic effects. And he employed numerous long shots to create an effective showcase for his character's extraordinary physical stunts, all of which he performed himself. Two more silent features, *College* (1927) and *Steamboat Bill, Jr.* (1928), while praised by film critics, are seen as lesser works, and his career from this point forward began a downward spiral.

Schenck persuaded Keaton to move to MGM in 1928, but Keaton did not fit into the emerging studio system, where the studio heads had final say over film content. His MGM bosses edited much of the improvisation and idiosyncrasies out of the films Keaton made for them. His films from this time include *The Cameraman* (1928) and *Spite Marriage* (1929); the latter was his last silent feature, released at the dawn of the sound era. Unable to adapt to either sound or the rigidity of the studio system, Keaton was released from his contract in 1933, ostensibly for unreliability. His creative demise appears to have been reflected in his private life, as he was divorced in 1932, losing custody of his children and possession of his house.

Keaton was involved in a variety of small projects thereafter. He was rehired by MGM in 1937 as a gagman, and he had a number of roles and cameos in films of the 1940s–1960s. He made several forays into television, including *The Buster Keaton Show, Playhouse 90,* and various series of the 1950s–1960s, such as *Route 66* and *The Donna Reed Show. The Buster Keaton Story,* a film biography starring Donald O'Connor, was made in 1957, and Keaton was presented an honorary Academy Award in 1959. His last film role was in *A Funny Thing Happened on the Way to the Forum* (1966). Keaton died on February 1, 1966, in Los Angeles.

Sam Hitchmough

See also: Film; Film Industry.

Further Reading

Keaton, Buster. *My Wonderful World of Slapstick.* Reprint ed. New York: Da Capo, 1982.

Knopf, Robert. *The Theater and Cinema of Buster Keaton.* Princeton, NJ: Princeton University Press, 1999.

McPherson, Edward. *Buster Keaton: Tempest in a Flat Hat.* New York: Newmarket, 2005.

Kellogg-Briand Pact (1928)

The Kellogg-Briand Pact (also referred to as the Pact of Paris), signed by fifteen nations on August 27, 1928, was a renunciation of war. The agreement was named for its chief negotiators and authors, U.S. Secretary of State Frank B. Kellogg and French Foreign Minister Aristide Briand. The original impetus for the pact came from France, where policy makers were concerned about Germany's growing economic and potential military power.

Despite its defeat in World War I and the imposition of steep reparations, Germany had become the dominant power in Central Europe, with growing influence in the small nation-states that had emerged out of the collapse of the Austro-Hungarian Empire. In 1925, Germany was admitted to the League of Nations, helping to end its pariah status as the nation responsible for starting World War I. But French leaders worried that Germany's greater population and potentially more powerful economy might lead Germany to attempt a reversal of the losses it had suffered after the war, including the loss of the Alsace-Lorraine region to France.

Briand sought a U.S.-French alliance as a deterrent against possible German aggression. He proposed a pact on April 6, 1927, the tenth anniversary of the U.S. entrance into World War I, taking advantage of a strong American peace movement led by diplomats and educators such as Nicholas Murray Butler and James T. Shotwell. The movement remained disappointed that the U.S. government had not decided to join the League of Nations in 1919. As Briand noted, "in the eyes of the world," this agreement would help "to enlarge and fortify the foundation on which the international policy of peace is being erected." Briand was persistent and by mid-June had presented a "Draft Pact of Perpetual Friendship" between France and the United States. Unlike many diplomatic treaties, the draft pact had only two articles: One committed the two nations to renouncing war "as an instrument of their national policy toward the other," and the other stated that the two signatories would settle conflicts between them by "pacific means."

In the end, however, Kellogg outmaneuvered Briand. He recognized that simply turning down the invitation would cause political difficulties for the Coolidge administration and with the peace movement and its allies in Congress. But he did not want to provide security guarantees for France, holding to America's long-standing tradition of avoiding what George Washington had called "entangling alliances." Kellogg therefore both broadened and weakened Briand's idea by calling for a multilateral pact in which all nations could become signatories. Kellogg understood that each successive signature would weaken its enforcement provisions, since it would be much harder to get many nations to agree on a plan to halt international aggression by a single power. In addition,

Secretary of State Frank Kellogg signs the Kellogg-Briand Pact in Paris on August 27, 1928. The ambitious treaty outlawed war and provided the legal basis for the prosecution of Nazi war criminals, but it failed to stop the outbreak of World War II. *(Topical Press Agency/Stringer/Hulton Archive/Getty Images)*

Kellogg intended to ensure that the pact did not formally commit any signatory to come to the defense of a threatened nation. Such a decision, he insisted, should remain the province of sovereign nations acting in their own best interests.

France, in the weaker geostrategic position, accepted Kellogg's counterproposal. A third article was added, opening the agreement to any and all nations. Negotiations began in January 1928, and on August 27, the treaty was signed in Paris by representatives of the United States, France, Australia, Belgium, Canada, Czechoslovakia, Germany, Great Britain, India, Ireland, Italy, Japan, New Zealand, Poland, and South Africa. The signing nations agreed to "condemn recourse to war for the solution of international controversies, and renounce it as an instrument of national policy in their relations with one another." They further agreed to settle all disputes "by pacific means." In time, the number of adherents increased to sixty-two nations.

People around the world celebrated the signing of the pact and its apparent commitment to end war, and in 1929, Kellogg received the Nobel Peace Prize for his work. However, the Japanese seizure of Manchuria in 1931–1932, and the Italian seizure of Ethiopia several years later, exposed the pact as toothless. Indeed, it did little to prevent the outbreak World War II in 1939, just a dozen years after Briand had put forward the original idea.

Charles M. Dobbs

See also: Europe, Relations with; Geneva Arms Convention of 1925; League of Nations; Military Affairs; Washington Naval Conference (1921–1922).

Further Reading

Cohen, Warren I. *Empire Without Tears: American Foreign Relations, 1921–1933.* Philadelphia: Temple University Press, 1987.

Ellis, L. Ethan. *Republican Foreign Policy, 1921–1933.* New Brunswick, NJ: Rutgers University Press, 1995.

Ferrell, Robert H. *Peace in Their Time: The Origins of the Kellogg-Briand Pact.* Hamden, CT: Archon, 1968.

Johnson, Robert D. *The Peace Progressives and American Foreign Relations.* Cambridge, MA: Harvard University Press, 1995.

Kennedy, Joseph (1888–1969)

Joseph Patrick Kennedy, the father of the most famous political clan in twentieth-century America, was a Wall Street investor, film producer, and adviser to several important Democratic politicians during the

1920s. The son of a successful liquor dealer who was active in local Democratic politics, Kennedy was born in Boston, Massachusetts, on September 6, 1888. Descended from Irish Catholic immigrants, he graduated from Harvard University in 1912 and, fueled by what seemed to be almost limitless ambition, set out on a course that would make him one of the wealthiest and most influential people in the United States.

After serving as a state banking examiner, Kennedy borrowed money and purchased a controlling interest in a small bank, the Columbia Trust Bank of Boston. Kennedy, twenty-five years old, began touting himself as "the country's youngest bank president." In 1914, he enhanced his professional, political, and social status by marrying Rose Fitzgerald, a childhood friend who was the daughter of Boston Mayor John Francis "Honey Fitz" Fitzgerald. Among their nine children were John (a U.S. senator from Massachusetts and president of the United States from 1961 to 1963), Robert (a U.S. senator from New York and presidential candidate in 1968), and Edward (a U.S. senator from Massachusetts and presidential candidate in 1980).

In 1917, Kennedy left the bank to take a management position at the Fore River Shipyard in Quincy, Massachusetts, a subsidiary of Bethlehem Steel. While there, Kennedy met Franklin D. Roosevelt, then serving as assistant secretary of the navy. As he began making money during the 1920s, Kennedy remained active in Democratic politics as a fund-raiser for his father-in-law and other candidates, and he would later give a considerable amount of his time, energy, and money to Roosevelt's presidential campaigns.

The shipyard had prospered as a result of America's involvement in World War I, but when the war ended, business slowed at Fore River. Kennedy, who throughout his business career was known for his keen sense of timing, left the organization for Wall Street and a position managing the brokerage house of Hayden, Stone and Company. He took a cut in salary to join the firm, but he was willing to accept the reduction for the opportunities afforded by an unregulated stock market. In the right place at the right time, he made significant amounts of money through clever and aggressive stock market and real estate deals. As he commented in the 1920s, "It's easy to make money in this market. We'd better get in before they pass a law against it." By the time the stock market crashed in 1929, the astute Kennedy had liquidated most of his holdings and, in the process, amassed his first fortune.

Critics have accused Kennedy of insider trading and stock-price manipulation—two commonly practiced and largely legal activities before the creation of the Securities and Exchange Commission (SEC). When President Roosevelt was criticized for appointing Kennedy as the first head of the SEC in 1934, the president responded that a former speculator was the best person to keep an eye on illegal and unethical marketplace operations. In any case, Kennedy was never indicted for breaking any financial laws.

Rumors alleged that Kennedy had supplemented his income by dealing in illegal alcohol during Prohibition and was involved with mob figures Meyer Lansky and Frank Costello, who later told a journalist that he was "partners" with Kennedy. In the years following the repeal of Prohibition, Kennedy would make millions in the legal liquor trade as the U.S. import agent for Haig & Haig scotch, John Dewar's scotch, and Gordon's gin, but rumors of nefarious past associations would follow him for the rest of his life and surface periodically when his sons began seeking high public office.

Already a well-known figure on Wall Street by the mid-1920s, Kennedy increased his public profile through the motion picture industry. In 1926, he became chief executive officer of Film Booking Office, a distributor of low-budget features, merging it with several other film studios to create Radio-Keith-Orpheum (RKO) Pictures, a major producer of feature films in the 1930s and 1940s. For a time, he managed the career of film star Gloria Swanson, and word went around the film community that the two were having an affair. Although his business acumen remained finely honed during the period, Kennedy produced one of the great debacles in the history of film, *Queen Kelly* (1929), with Swanson in the lead role. That production, which went way over budget and bombed at the box office, was a major reason Kennedy abandoned Hollywood in 1929, though his efforts behind the creation of RKO added millions more to his fortune.

Kennedy emerged from the Jazz Age a wealthy man. With his fortune and his growing influence in the Democratic Party, he began to set his sights on high political office, hoping to become the first Catholic president of the United States. However, his controversial praise of the Nazi regime while serving as U.S. ambassador to Great Britain in the late 1930s undermined any chance he had. Instead, Kennedy would pin his White House hopes on his sons. His oldest son, Joseph Kennedy, Jr., died in World War II, but his second-oldest son, John F. Kennedy, was elected president in 1960. John was assassinated in November 1963, and Robert was assassinated in April 1968 while campaigning for the presidency. Joseph P. Kennedy died on November 18, 1969.

Ben Wynne

See also: Democratic Party; Film Industry; Irish Americans; Prohibition (1920–1933); Stock Market.

Further Reading

Goodwin, Doris Kearns. *The Fitzgeralds and the Kennedys: An American Saga.* New York: Simon & Schuster, 1987.

Kessler, Ronald. *Sins of the Father: Joseph P. Kennedy and the Dynasty He Founded.* New York: Warner, 1996.

Maier, Thomas. *The Kennedys: America's Emerald Kings.* New York: Basic Books, 2003.

Whalen, Richard. *The Founding Father: The Story of Joseph P. Kennedy: A Study in Power, Wealth, and Family Ambition.* Washington, DC: Regnery, 1993.

King Tut's Tomb

Archeologist Howard Carter examines the sarcophagus of ancient Egyptian pharaoh Tutankhamen, whose tomb he discovered in 1922. The event triggered a worldwide craze for anything associated with the art and design of ancient Egypt. *(Mansell/Stringer/Time & Life Pictures/Getty Images)*

Among the most famous archeological finds in history, the 3,000-year-old tomb of the ancient Egyptian pharaoh Tutankhamen (or Tutankhamun), discovered by American archeologist Howard Carter in 1922, triggered a wave of fascination for all things Egyptian. In Europe and America, houses, fashions, and everyday consumer products incorporated motifs and imagery of ancient Egypt.

By the early twentieth century, many thought that all of the buried treasures of ancient Egypt had already been discovered or, worse, plundered by tomb robbers. But a number of archeologists—both amateur and professional—were convinced that at least one major tomb, that of Tutankhamen, a young pharaoh of the Eighteenth dynasty who ruled from 1333 to 1324 B.C.E., remained undiscovered and preserved intact.

Among the amateur archeologists working in Egypt was American businessman and lawyer Theodore Davis, who conducted a series of excavations in the Valley of the Kings in the late nineteenth and early twentieth centuries. Davis's work offered evidence that a hidden tomb might be located there, although Davis remained unconvinced. His 1912 book *The Tombs of Harmhabi and Touatânkhamanou* ends with the notorious line, "I fear that the Valley of Kings is now exhausted." One of Davis's assistants, Howard Carter, a trained archeologist with the Egyptian Antiquities Service, was not so sure.

Carter was a precocious Egyptologist, having worked on Egyptian antiquities since his teens. In 1899, when he was just twenty-five, he became renowned in the field by unearthing the remains of Queen Hatshepsut, the longest-reigning queen of any indigenous Egyptian dynasty. By the early twentieth century, Carter was on the hunt for Tutankhamen's tomb, and in 1907, he convinced a wealthy amateur British archeologist, Lord George Carnavon, to finance his work.

Other than a hiatus during World War I, Carter conducted his search uninterrupted for fifteen years. By 1922, Carnavon was beginning to lose interest and told Carter that he had one more season to find the tomb. On November 4, Carter's expedition discovered the steps that led to Tutankhamen's burial chamber. He quickly wired Carnavon, who was staying nearby, to visit the dig. There, on November 26, Carter dug out a tiny breach in the tomb's doorway. Months of work followed, and on February 16, 1923, Carter and his team opened the sealed doorway, becoming the first people to enter the inner chamber of the tomb in more than three millennia. The archeologist later spoke of a faint smell of perfume and oil filling the air.

With candles in hand, Carter, Carnavon, and other members of the expedition laid eyes on a wealth of objects, including gold furniture, statues, and a sarcophagus containing the mummified body of Tutankhamen. The ancient Egyptians had believed in an afterlife that paralleled life in the living world.

Wealthy citizens and royalty were buried with all of the possessions—and sometimes the slaves—they would need to carry on a pampered life in the netherworld.

Carter's discovery of an intact pharaoh's tomb made headlines around the world, and the "King Tut" phenomenon was born. Within days, *The New York Times* was reporting that someone had bought the rights to film the tomb scenes. The Patent Office in Washington received a flood of applications for Tut-related objects, chiefly items for use on women's vanity tables and in their boudoirs. Fashion designers invaded the galleries of New York's Metropolitan Museum of Art to copy Egyptian imagery for clothing, shoes, jewelry, and other accessories. American couturiers readily adopted the Egyptian style, making a name for themselves in a fashion world dominated by French and other European designers. Magazines and newspapers not only featured articles on archeology and ancient Egypt but incorporated Egyptian motifs into their design and print styles.

The fad also infected industrial design and architecture, with Egyptian motifs featured in all varieties of products and on buildings across America. Most noteworthy was the work of Raymond Hood, among the most celebrated American architects of the Jazz Age, though many of his most notable Egypt-styled projects, including Radio City Music Hall and the New York Daily News Building, would not be completed until the 1930s. Perhaps the most obvious architectural paean to Carter's discovery was the massive Egyptian Theater in Hollywood, a particularly kitschy example of early movie-palace architecture erected by impresario Sid Grauman on Los Angeles's famed Hollywood Boulevard.

The irony of "Egyptomania," as it was called at the time, has not been lost on historians and archeologists. Tutankhamen, who died at the age of eighteen, was only a minor figure in ancient Egyptian royalty, and the treasures of his tomb, now stored in Egypt's Cairo Museum, were modest by pharaonic standards. Still, America's fascination with King Tut proved long enduring. A 1970s national museum tour of the pharaoh's artifacts, called "Treasures of Tutankhamen," was among the best-attended artistic events in U.S. history, and similar exhibits remain popular into the twenty-first century.

James Ciment

See also: Fads and Stunts; Fashion, Women's; Science.

Further Reading

Battersby, Martin. *The Decorative Twenties.* New York: Whitney Library of Design, 1988.

Frayling, Christopher. *The Face of Tutankhamun.* London: Faber and Faber, 1992.

James, T.G.H. *Howard Carter: The Path to Tutankhamun.* New York: Kegan Paul, 1992.

Winstone, H.V.F. *Howard Carter and the Discovery of the Tomb of Tutankhamun.* London: Constable, 1991.

Ku Klux Klan

Renowned Hollywood director D.W. Griffith catalyzed the resurgence of the Ku Klux Klan in the early twentieth century when, after the organization had undergone more than forty years of dormancy, he sympathetically portrayed the group in his 1915 film *The Birth of a Nation*. Griffith's film, which portrayed the nativist and violent Klan as protecting the South from ignorant freed slaves and avaricious Northern carpetbaggers following the Civil War, even caught the attention of the White House. After a screening of the film, President Woodrow Wilson is purported to have said, "It is like writing history with lightning, and my only regret is that it is all so terribly true." The Klan subsequently used the film as a recruitment tool, combining it with a series of events that would make the Klan a formidable cultural and political phenomenon in the Jazz Age.

The Klan's mixed agenda corresponded with the spirit of the times. Aside from being racist, anti-Semitic, and anti-Catholic, the organization promoted Protestant, Anglo-Saxon (or Nordic) superiority along with conservative, village values in a period characterized by nativist "one hundred percent Americanism." During Prohibition, the Klan also stood against speakeasies, bootleggers, flappers, and vice in general. Members saw themselves as a bulwark against the decline in morals and manners into a disorderly modern sensibility. The Klan also reflected America's move away from earlier liberal, cosmopolitan programs of assimilation and toward protectionism.

Simmons and the Early Years

William J. Simmons, a Spanish-American War veteran and itinerant Methodist preacher, founded the new Klan organization after being inspired by the sensationalism of the Leo Frank case in 1915. Frank, a Jewish merchant from the North, was found guilty—on flimsy evidence—of murdering a white employee,

The Ku Klux Klan, a violent and racist organization originating in the post–Civil War South, made a comeback in the 1920s, as evidenced by this march down Pennsylvania Avenue in Washington, D.C. *(Library of Congress, LC-USZ62–59666)*

Mary Phagan, at his Atlanta pencil factory. Frank was sentenced to death, but before the sentence could be carried out, a mob calling themselves the "Knights of Mary Phagan" kidnapped him from prison and lynched him. The act of vigilantism had been stoked by Thomas Watson, a former member of the U.S. House of Representatives and owner of the Atlanta-based magazine *Weekly Jeffersonian.* In its pages, Watson published sensational, hate-filled pieces about the "hideous, ominous" lust of black men for white women, as well as "libidinous priests" and the "ravenous appetite" of Jewish men for the "forbidden fruit" of non-Jewish women. In a September 1915 issue, Watson called for "another Ku Klux Klan" to "restore HOME RULE" (his emphasis). Not coincidentally, that same month, Simmons declared himself Imperial Wizard of the Invisible Empire of the Knights of the Ku Klux Klan.

An organizer and compulsive joiner of fraternal orders such as the Masons, Knights Templar, and the Woodmen of the World, Simmons was described by the historian John Higham as a "mellifluous orator." His father was said to have belonged to the original Ku Klux Klan, founded in Tennessee in 1866. In accordance with his affinity for organizing, Simmons allegedly instituted the practice of designating all Klan offices and functions with names beginning with "kl." This gave rise to such odd terms as "klonversation" (secret talk), "klonvocations" (national conventions), the "Kloran" (the Klan constitution), "klaverns" (Klan units or lodges), and "Klankrest" (the headquarters at 1840 Peachtree Road in Atlanta).

The practice of cross burning, a Scottish tradition, came from Thomas Dixon's 1905 book *The Clansman,* the inspiration for *The Birth of a Nation.* The first cross burning took place on Thanksgiving 1915 on Georgia's Stone Mountain—staged to preempt by one week the Atlanta premiere of *The Birth of a Nation.*

For the next five years, the Klan floundered. In 1920, however, the son-in-law of publicity agent Elizabeth Tyler joined the organization, and Simmons contracted the services of Tyler's Southern Publicity Association, run with business partner Edward Y. Clarke. In June 1920, the firm became the Klan's "Propagation Department," and over the course of the next year, it recruited 1,100 new members.

National Expansion

Tyler and Clarke's recruiters—or kleagles—were wildly successful in expanding the new Klan. Recruiters canvassed showings of the still widely circulating *Birth of a Nation.* Masons were found to be a particularly receptive group. The Klan took advantage of local problems to promote itself, favoring organized labor versus undocumented workers, promising to help enforce Prohibition, promoting Americanism, and holding fast against the "New Negro." Simmons's status as a Methodist preacher was stressed when recruiters approached conservative Evangelical and Fundamentalist Protestant ministers.

With these strategies in place, the Klan gained prominence throughout the South, Midwest, and West, particularly Texas, Oklahoma, Arkansas, Ohio, Indiana, Colorado, Utah, and Oregon. By fall 1921, the New York *World* estimated the Klan at 500,000 members. As of 1924, according to one scholar, membership stood at about 4 million nationally. Although the estimates vary, a reflection by Simmons perhaps best sums up the situation in the early 1920s: "There was so much money in sight that we could lay almost any sort of plans."

Many historians have characterized the Ku Klux Klan as a rural phenomenon. Many farmers populated its ranks, and Simmons and later Klan leaders railed against the "menace" of American cities. At one point, Simmons declared New York City "the most un-American city of the American continent." Nevertheless, the Klan existed—and in sizable numbers—in urban areas. Anywhere that Catholics, Jews, and African Americans lived in concentrated numbers served as a breeding ground for Klan activity. The organization is said to have taken root in Atlanta, Chicago, Dallas, Denver, Detroit, Indianapolis, Knoxville, Memphis, New York, and Portland.

Klan membership in Chicago was especially large. In 1921, an Indianapolis Klansman named C.W. Love began recruiting in Chicago, and Simmons himself oversaw the initiation of approximately 2,400 candidates in an August 1921 ceremony near Lake Zurich. An estimated 10,000 local Klansmen attended the event. The Chicago City Council responded to the gathering by voting unanimously to ban the Klan the next month. However, by 1922, with eight units, Chicago became the U.S. city with the largest membership.

Edward Clarke declared later that Chicago's chapter had 30,000 members and more than twenty Klan units. Several were found on the South Side, near neighborhoods with growing African American populations such as Woodlawn and Hyde Park. Chicago suburbs such as Harvey, Aurora, and Cicero also became part of the growth. Like many urban chapters, these Chicago chapters consistently avoided public violence and vigilantism. To wit, one of the Chicago chapter's biggest successes consisted of a publication, *Dawn: A Journal for True American Patriots*, that ran from October 1922 to early 1924. The Klan's influence in Chicago waned after the formation of the American Unity League in 1922, which sought to expose Klan members in its weekly newspaper *Tolerance*.

Politics and Decline

The years 1922–1923 proved controversial for the Klan. Although it was at its peak in terms of political influence and numerical strength, the organization began to be weakened by internal divisions. The Klan had survived a September 1921 congressional investigation and Governor John C. Walton's declaration of martial law in Oklahoma after the Tulsa race riot. A faction of the Klan's leadership maneuvered Simmons out of power in November 1922. It took Simmons three months to realize that he now held only the symbolic office of Emperor, while Hiram Wesley Evans of Dallas held the more powerful position of

Imperial Wizard. Evans would remain the Imperial Wizard for the next seventeen years.

In 1923, the Klan faced more internal maneuvering and infighting. Simmons failed in his attempt to start a women's Klan, which he would have called "Kamelia," and Evans nullified the contract with Tyler and Clarke. A number of chapters split over the ongoing feud between Simmons and Evans. Finally in January 1924, the organization banished Simmons from the Invisible Empire and paid him a cash settlement.

Despite these problems, the Klan proved influential at all political levels in the early 1920s. It swore in President Warren G. Harding as a member—a symbolic gesture—and helped campaign for federal immigration restrictions, which were enacted by Congress in 1921 and 1924. The Klan aided in the election of eleven governors and sixteen U.S. senators, including future Supreme Court Justice Hugo Black, an Alabama senator in 1926. (Black later renounced the Klan.) At the Democratic Party's 1924 national convention in New York's Madison Square Garden, an anti-Klan plank lost by one vote. The Klan's voting bloc then forced Democrats to pass over two anti-Klan presidential candidates, Oscar Underwood (another Alabama senator) and Al Smith (New York's governor and an anti-Prohibition Catholic), for a compromise candidate, John W. Davis. Imperial Wizard Hiram Evans was featured on the cover of *Time* magazine on June 23, 1924. The Klan was a topic throughout the regular campaign, but Republican candidate Calvin Coolidge kept silent on the issue. Davis eventually came out against the Klan but lost in a Coolidge landslide.

The Klan's voting bloc became increasingly irrelevant after 1925. Earlier that year, the Klan was dealt a major blow from a scandal involving former Grand Dragon David C. "Steve" Stephenson, who had served as the Klan's state leader of Indiana until 1923. The incident occurred in March 1925, more than a year after Evans had left the national organization to form a rival Ku Klux Klan. According to the findings at a trial later that year, Stephenson had abducted a young schoolteacher named Madge Oberholtzer, forced her to consume liquor, and raped and killed her. Although some charged that Stephenson had been framed, his conviction almost single-handedly ruined the Klan's national influence. The sordid details revealed a hypocritical organization far removed from the moral values it professed. In Indiana, Klan membership dropped from 350,000 to 15,000 within a year. By 1929, anti-Klan Democrats held most state offices.

The Klan revived briefly in 1928, when New York Governor Al Smith, a Catholic, received the Democratic Party's presidential nomination. Hiram Evans and a new Klan supporter, James S. Vance, spoke against Smith and published pieces around the country in the months before the vote. The Klan's default choice, Republican Herbert Hoover, won the balloting, but by 1930, the Klan's national membership had dwindled to 45,000.

Tim Lacy

See also: African Americans; Anti-Catholicism; Anti-Semitism; Immigration.

Further Reading

Chalmers, David M. *Hooded Americanism: The History of the Ku Klux Klan.* Durham, NC: Duke University Press, 1987.

Dumenil, Lynn. *The Modern Temper: American Culture and Society in the 1920s.* New York: Hill and Wang, 1995.

Higham, John. *Strangers in the Land: Patterns of Nativism, 1860–1925.* 2nd ed. New York: Atheneum, 1965.

Jackson, Kenneth T. *The Ku Klux Klan in the City, 1915–1930.* Chicago: Ivan R. Dee, 1992. First published 1967 by Oxford University Press.

May, Lary. *Screening Out the Past: The Birth of Mass Culture and the Motion Picture Industry.* Chicago: University of Chicago Press, 1983.

Wade, Wyn Craig. *The Fiery Cross: The Ku Klux Klan in America.* New York: Oxford University Press, 1987.

La Follette, Robert (1855–1925)

Uncompromising in pursuing the progressive causes in which he believed, Robert La Follette of Wisconsin was dubbed "Fighting Bob" by his contemporaries. In the U.S. Congress and as governor of Wisconsin, he took on such controversial issues as minority rights, corporate corruption, and U.S. participation in World War I. A lover of words, he often gave long, statistic-filled yet fiery speeches that rallied crowds. He also used his oratory skills to filibuster Congress on a number of occasions.

The youngest of five children, Robert Marion La Follette was born on June 14, 1855, in a log cabin in Primrose, Wisconsin, to Josiah and Mary La Follette. In 1856, his father, a local businessman and politician, died of complications from pneumonia and diabetes. Thus, as his biographers note, the future progressive never knew his father except as the faultless, righteous man of his mother's memory. She insisted that La Follette strive to emulate his father, encouraging him always to stand strong and "do the right thing."

As a child, La Follette loved to perform, reciting poetry and entertaining guests. He later considered an acting career but decided in favor of law and enrolled at the University of Wisconsin in 1875. While there, he found a father figure in university president John Bascom, who influenced La Follette's views on women's rights and social and economic justice. During his time at the university, La Follette fell in love with fellow student Belle Case, the first woman graduate of the University of Wisconsin law school (1879), a temperance activist, and a suffragist. They married in 1881. Together they founded *La Follette's Weekly Magazine* (1909), in which they propounded their views on various political issues.

La Follette was a member of the U.S. House of Representatives from 1885 to 1891, served as governor of Wisconsin from 1901 to 1905, and returned to the U.S. Congress as a senator in 1906, serving until 1925. A Republican turned Progressive, he was a firm believer in democratic reforms and strove to be "the people's" politician.

During World War I, the press and a number of politicians vilified La Follette because of his outspoken opposition to the war. Concerned with preserving civil liberties, he denounced the Espionage and Sedition acts of 1917 and 1918, respectively, and fought to repeal them. He declared that nations fought wars to make corporate moguls rich while common men paid the price with their blood. After the war, he was highly critical of President Woodrow Wilson's handling of the peace process and accused him of usurping authority by unilaterally making decisions rather than consulting Congress. La Follette condemned the Treaty of Versailles as undemocratic and opposed the League of Nations, concerned that it would lead to further U.S. involvement throughout the world. In later years, opponents tried to use his antiwar stance against him, painting him in an unpatriotic light.

Most of the issues La Follette took up in the years immediately following World War I were contrary to the conservative, probusiness politics of the day. In 1919, he opposed a coal and oil bill that permitted the leasing of public lands to private companies and threatened to undo Progressive Era conservation efforts. He also opposed the Esch-Cummins Transportation Act of 1920, charging collusion between the railroads and government. The legislation, which terminated the federal regulation of railroads imposed during the war, was passed by Congress, but the publicity that arose from the debate led to the electoral defeat of a number of its congressional supporters, including co-author John J. Esch (R-WI). La Follette also opposed the Fordney-McCumber Tariff of 1922, which would have entailed the sale of federally owned ships to private companies for a fraction of their cost. Declaring that sovereignty had gradually been "wrested from the people and usurped by the courts," La Follette called for reforms of the U.S. Supreme Court.

At every turn, it seemed, Fighting Bob fought the congressional majority in the name of the public good. He was finally triumphant in April 1922, when he successfully put forth a resolution calling for an investigation of the Interior Department's leasing of naval oil reserves in Wyoming to Harry F. Sinclair's Mammoth Oil Company. Investigations revealed corruption in connection with the awarding of the leases and resulted in the Teapot Dome scandal, one of several corruption scandals in the administration of President Warren G. Harding, and led to the incarceration of Secretary of the Interior Albert B. Fall.

Despite declining health, La Follette attempted a bid for the presidency on the Progressive Party ticket in the 1924 election. With Senator Burton K. Wheeler (D-MT) as a running mate, La Follette appealed to voters to help him break "the private monopoly system over . . . political and economic life" by supporting his third-party candidacy. He proclaimed there would be no corruption in his administration because he planned to clean house of all "the henchmen of special interests . . . the incompetents and time servers." His supporters included Socialists, labor unions, farmers, railway workers, and newly enfranchised women voters. His forthright opposition to the growing Ku Klux Klan won him the support of African American groups. Unfortunately, deep-seated tensions and contradictory objectives among his diverse groups of supporters weakened the campaign. Still, La Follette took 17 percent of the vote and carried his home state of Wisconsin. It was the third most successful third-party showing by a presidential candidate in the twentieth century, after Theodore Roosevelt's candidacy in 1912 and H. Ross Perot's run in 1992.

After the campaign, La Follette's health declined further and he suffered a heart attack in May 1925. He died in Washington, D.C., on June 18, 1925. Two of his sons would enjoy successful political careers—Robert, Jr., as a U.S. senator from Wisconsin and Philip as the state's governor.

Jennifer Aerts Terry

See also: Election of 1924; Progressivism; Republican Party.

Further Reading

Burgchardt, Carl R. *Robert M. La Follette, Sr.: The Voice of Conscience.* Westport, CT: Greenwood, 1992.

Maxwell, Robert S., ed. *Great Lives Observed: La Follette.* Englewood Cliffs, NJ: Prentice Hall, 1969.

Thelen, David P. *Robert La Follette and the Insurgent Spirit.* Boston: Little, Brown, 1976.

Unger, Nancy C. *Fighting Bob La Follette: The Righteous Reformer.* Chapel Hill: University of North Carolina Press, 2000.

Labor Movement

For the American labor movement, the period from the end of World War I to the onset of the Great Depression began with optimism and ended in despair. Before the war, the unions of the American Federation of Labor (AFL)—with which most unions in the United States were affiliated—were under attack from employers, the courts, and rival unions. Employers in many industries maintained "open shops," free of unions and union contracts. Local and federal courts, including the U.S. Supreme Court, consistently granted injunctions that hindered the effectiveness of strikes and boycotts. The AFL, led by Samuel Gompers, spurned state intervention in labor disputes and avoided partisan politics.

Furthermore, most AFL unions represented skilled workers and were organized on a craft basis. Generally moderate to conservative in their politics, these unions were dominated by white males. Excluded from their ranks were the growing numbers of unskilled workers—often women, African Americans, and immigrants from Southern and Eastern Europe. These workers started to organize industrial unions, like the Western Federation of Miners and the International Ladies' Garment Workers Union, that united all workers in an industry across divisions of skill and nationality. The AFL also faced opposition from the Industrial Workers of the World (IWW, or Wobblies), a radical union whose members sought to organize all workers into revolutionary industrial unions, which would, they hoped, eventually overthrow capitalism.

World War I, Labor Revolt, and Reaction

The AFL reaped political benefits by backing Woodrow Wilson, the successful Democratic presidential candidate in 1912. In his first term, Wilson secured such progressive reforms as the Clayton Anti-Trust Act (1914) and the Seaman's Act (1915), which expanded protections for union activity. He also established the Department of Labor in 1913 to help settle labor disputes. Production of war materials for the Allied nations in Europe boosted the U.S. economy, and unions took advantage of high employment by striking in record numbers. The AFL endorsed Wilson again in 1916, and union leaders hoped to win more labor-friendly reforms by supporting Wilson's intervention in the European war. Even though

Open-Shop Movement

In the early twentieth century, closed-shop agreements enabled many unions to exercise unprecedented power in individual workplaces and industries. A closed-shop agreement between a union and a particular company barred nonunion members from employment with that company. Unions thus gained control over the supply of labor, had the membership numbers necessary to sustain themselves financially, and could effectively engage in strikes and confrontations with employers. In the years leading up to World War I, U.S. businesses waged several intense campaigns to eliminate closed-shop unionism in various industries, especially construction. The clamor for "open shops" subsided during the war, however, when the federal government's progressive interventions in industrial labor policy sanctioned considerable growth in union numbers and strength.

The government's retreat from these wartime regulations, followed by worker unrest in 1919 and 1920, caused many employers to abandon their toleration of unions. Seattle businesses fired the first postwar salvo for the open shop in March 1919, when they responded to a general strike by forming the Associated Industries of Seattle to coordinate anti-union efforts. Seizing on Americans' patriotism and postwar anxieties about labor unrest and radicalism, some employers began referring to the open shop as the "American plan." Across the country, national trade and industrial associations were established to counter unions. By September 1920, some 540 open-shop organizations existed in 247 cities. In 1921, the U.S. Chamber of Commerce, taking its first position on labor matters, officially endorsed the open shop.

Although advocates failed at several attempts to create a nationwide federation of open-shop organizations, the National Association of Manufacturers (NAM) played a central role in supporting the movement by creating an Open Shop Department in 1920. The NAM produced pamphlets and debaters' manuals for open-shop associations and other supporters and also disseminated its message and materials to clergy, college professors, and women. Open-shop advocates attacked the closed shop as a violation of employers' and workers' constitutional right to freely contract for work. NAM literature presented evidence indicating that closed shops endangered economic prosperity, caused inflation, raised rents, depressed wages and personal savings, and increased unemployment. Some employers argued that the open shop, which ostensibly prohibited all forms of discrimination in hiring, was not necessarily anti-union. However, the open shop gave employers another tool, along with blacklists, labor spies, and strikebreakers, with which to decimate the labor movement's recent gains and prevent union organizing.

Aided by the economic recession of 1921–1922, the open-shop crusade produced significant results. Total trade union membership declined by about 28 percent between 1920 and 1923, from just over 5 million to 3.6 million. Thereafter, the decline slowed; in 1929, unions claimed 3.4 million members. By the mid-1920s, movement leaders such as Walter Drew, who for decades had battled unions and closed shops in the construction and steel industries, succeeded in persuading business leaders to temper the open-shop message. Open-shop activity faded as more firms turned to the softer approach of welfare capitalism, adopting insurance programs, pension plans, and other measures to curry workers' favor and deter unions.

Justin F. Jackson

some AFL unions pledged not to strike for the war's duration, emboldened workers defied employers and labor leaders. During the war, workers engaged in a total of 6,025 strikes, most of them unauthorized.

In 1918, unions also benefited enormously from representation on the federal War Industries Board and the National War Labor Board (NWLB). These agencies arbitrated disputes and granted many workers the eight-hour workday, the forty-eight-hour workweek, pay increases, and improved working conditions. During the war, the federal government also raided IWW offices and arrested IWW leaders for their opposition to the war, silencing an important AFL rival. In these circumstances, U.S. union membership grew dramatically: from 1917 to 1920, total membership increased by nearly 70 percent, from 2.9 million workers to just over 5 million.

In 1919, workers exercised their new power by striking in record numbers. More than 4 million, 22 percent of the entire workforce, participated in more than 3,000 strikes across the country. In the context of the recent Communist revolution in Russia and surging revolutionary movements across postwar Europe, these strikes inspired many on the Left while frightening many Americans who feared imminent revolution in their own country. In Seattle, a walkout of shipyard workers ignited a general strike of 35,000 workers (many of whom were in AFL unions). The action paralyzed the city and took on a revolutionary flavor, as workers formed their own police units and public health committees.

Most strikers, however, were not radicals but simply workers who believed that their calls for "industrial democracy" merely applied democratic Wilsonian ideals to their workplaces. Although strikers in the textile and telephone industries won some concessions, intervention (or the threat of it) by local, state, and federal governments contributed to the defeat of many strikes. A 1919 strike by Boston's largely Irish police force was broken by conservative Governor Calvin Coolidge. A massive coal miners' strike withered in the face of federal injunctions and Wilson's threat to send the National Guard to occupy the mines. The radical labor organizer William Z. Foster led the largest strike of the year—360,000 steel workers attempting to organize a notoriously anti-union industry. Unsupported by conservative AFL leaders, the steel strike succumbed to strikebreakers, police and National Guard attacks, and employers who used ethnic, cultural, and racial differences to divide their workforce.

The defeats of 1919 marked the beginning of a period of reaction that eroded the labor movement's recent gains. The Wilson administration retreated from its wartime alliance with labor leaders and dismantled the NWLB and other federal agencies that had checked employers' power during the war. In the 1920 elections, antilabor Republicans were elected to majorities in Congress, and the new president, Republican Warren G. Harding, was decidedly less sympathetic to labor than Wilson had been. Employers seized the recession of 1921–1922 (which created 19.5 percent unemployment) as an opportunity to promote open shops in an effort to drive unions out of industry. In 1920 and 1921, American unions lost 1.5 million members. The rout of the labor movement was complete in 1922, when striking textile workers and coal miners suffered defeat and a sweeping federal injunction doomed 400,000 striking railroad shopmen.

New Economy and Labor Conservatism

Transformations in the American economy and other changes greatly weakened the labor movement in the 1920s. Industries in which unions were weak or nonexistent, such as the service and retail industries, expanded considerably. Industries in which industrial unions had gained a foothold before the war, such as textiles, mining, and brewing, were weakened and employment too unstable for unionism to thrive. Employment increased among workers traditionally ignored by most AFL unions—such as those in steel mills and automobile assembly plants. And although these developed limited ways to resist difficult working conditions and low pay, few were unionized.

African American and Mexican employment increased once new immigration restrictions dried up surplus labor from Europe. Employers intentionally manipulated labor markets and segregated African Americans and Mexicans from mainstream whites to exacerbate racism and stymie union organizing. Many AFL unions continued to bar nonwhite workers from membership. Although the AFL allowed the all-black Brotherhood of Sleeping Car Porters to affiliate with the federation, it did not grant those members full "international union" status.

More women joined the labor force, especially in clerical work, the fastest-growing occupation in 1930. However, that year only 250,000 of 4 million women wage earners belonged to any union.

Many manufacturers adopted mass-production methods pioneered in the factories of automobile magnate Henry Ford to reduce worker control over production and mechanize work formerly done by skilled employees. Although these methods increased manufacturers' productivity by 64 percent, factory workers saw only a 26 percent increase in real wages. Most workers benefited little from higher profits, and many skilled workers lost precious job control.

Unions were also hurt by "company unions" (under company control) and different forms of "welfare capitalism" widely instituted by business in the 1920s. Four hundred firms had company unions—also called "works councils" or "industrial associations"—which enabled employers to create the appearance of worker participation in workplace decision making. While worker representatives sometimes achieved improvements through these groups, management invariably had the final say on vital matters. For the first time, many employers also established different welfare measures and benefits for nonunion employees than had been negotiated for union members. In 1928, company life insurance plans covered 5.8 million workers, 3.7 million workers had old-age pensions, and 800,000 workers in 315 firms owned stocks. Without union contracts, however, these benefits easily disappeared. The Great Depression forced many companies to reduce or cut these benefits entirely, losses that eventually motivated many workers to join unions in the 1930s.

AFL leaders struggled to maintain standards won before the war in union-heavy industries. Yet AFL unions compounded the difficulties imposed on them by business and government by failing to adapt to the changing economy, and by refusing to organize the growing numbers of unskilled workers into industrial unions. Few labor leaders better epitomized labor's conservatism and weakness in the 1920s than William Green. A former miner and United Mine Workers official under John L. Lewis, Green was elected AFL president in 1924 following the death of Samuel Gompers because AFL union leaders knew he would not threaten their power. Green did little to counter labor's decline, and he actually urged unions in certain industries to cooperate with management to improve efficiency even if it degraded union-won standards. Green reassured economic and political leaders when he affirmed that unions' "best interests are promoted through concord rather than by conflict," and defended labor unions because they would "increase production, eliminate waste, and maintain continuity of service."

Despite their moderation, AFL unions consistently found little support from Congress, the courts, or the Republican administrations of Presidents Harding and Coolidge. Labor progressives, Socialists, and other radicals turned to independent politics several times with little success. In the tumult of 1919, workers organized a Farmer-Labor Party, which won some local elections but fared poorly in national elections the next year. In 1922, the railroad unions formed the Conference for Progressive Political Action and elected some labor-friendly candidates to Congress but balked at forming a national third party. The Farmer-Labor Party was briefly revived in 1923 but faded when Communists gained control of it. In 1924, several unions endorsed Wisconsin Senator Robert La Follette in his unsuccessful Progressive Party bid for the presidency.

Labor activists in the Communist Party, led by the formidable William Z. Foster, organized the Trade Union Educational League in the early 1920s to push workers and the AFL unions into a more oppositional stance. AFL leaders responded by expelling Communists from the unions and barring them from membership. In 1928, the Communists abandoned work within the AFL unions and formed independent industrial unions under their own federation, the Trade Union Unity League. Communists also played critical roles in the Passaic, New Jersey, and Gastonia, North Carolina, textile strikes at the end of the decade. These strikes prefigured the labor unrest and organizing that would lead to the labor movement's successes in the 1930s, despite the fact that only 12 percent of all American workers belonged to unions in 1930.

Justin F. Jackson

See also: American Federation of Labor; Automobile Industry; *Bailey v. Drexel Furniture Company* (1922); Boston Police Strike of 1919; Child Labor; Coal Industry; Coal Strike of 1919; Economic Policy; Flynn, Elizabeth Gurley; Gary, Elbert H.; Gastonia Strike of 1929; Industrial Workers of the World; Lawrence Textile Strike of 1919; Lewis, John L.; Passaic Textile Strike of 1926; Railroad Shopmen's Strike of 1922; Railroads and Railroad Industry; Railway Labor Act (1926); Recession of 1921–1922; Seattle General Strike of 1919; Steel Strike of 1919–1920; Welfare Capitalism.

Further Reading

Bernstein, Irving. *The Lean Years: A History of the American Worker, 1920–1933*. Boston: Houghton Mifflin, 1960.
Cohen, Lizabeth. *Making a New Deal: Industrial Workers in Chicago, 1919–1939*. New York: Cambridge University Press, 1990.

Dubofsky, Melvyn. *The State and Labor in Modern America.* Chapel Hill: University of North Carolina Press, 1994.

Green, James. *The World of the Worker: Labor in Twentieth-Century America.* Urbana: University of Illinois Press, 1998.

McCartin, Joseph. *Labor's Great War: The Struggle for Industrial Democracy and the Origins of Modern American Labor Relations, 1912–1921.* Chapel Hill: University of North Carolina Press, 1997.

Montgomery, David. *The Fall of the House of Labor: The Workplace, the State, and Labor Activism, 1865–1925.* Cambridge, UK: Cambridge University Press, 1987.

Landis, Kenesaw Mountain (1866–1944)

A U.S. federal judge who became the first commissioner of major league baseball, Kenesaw Mountain Landis is best known for fining John D. Rockefeller's Standard Oil Company a record sum for antitrust violations and for permanently banning eight Chicago White Sox players from professional baseball after they allegedly conspired with gamblers to lose the 1919 World Series. Born on November 20, 1866, in Millville, Ohio, Landis was the sixth of the seven children of Abraham Hoch Landis and Mary Kumler Landis. He was named for a Civil War battle site (Kennesaw Mountain, Georgia) where his father, a surgeon for the Union army, had been wounded.

Little in Landis's youth suggested that he would find great success in life. His brothers fashioned careers in journalism or politics, two of them winning seats in Congress. Kenesaw, by contrast, dropped out of high school and ran errands for the Vandalia Railroad. He competed in bicycle races in Indiana fairgrounds, operated a roller-skating rink, and worked for a newspaper. While covering court cases for the Logansport *Journal* in Indiana, however, he became interested in the law. He studied at the YMCA Law School in Cincinnati and received his law degree from the Union College of Law (now part of Northwestern University) in Chicago in 1891.

In 1893, Landis traveled to Washington, D.C., to serve as personal secretary to the new secretary of state, Walter Quinton Gresham, an Indiana lawyer and judge. After the death of his patron in 1895, Landis returned to Chicago to marry Winifred Reed. The couple had three children.

Landis began practicing law in Chicago, and in 1905, he was appointed to a judgeship in the U.S. District Court for the Northern District of Illinois. He quickly became known for the manner in which he dispensed judgments, often delivering his decisions with an air of drama and flamboyance.

President Theodore Roosevelt, who appointed Landis to the federal bench in 1905, was known as the "Trust Buster" for his efforts to break up corporate monopolies. The largest monopoly of all, John D. Rockefeller's Standard Oil, controlled 85 percent of the nation's refined oil and posted enormous profits each year; the company employed a railway rebate system that virtually ensured its competitors' failure. Standard Oil's refusal to obey antitrust laws finally brought Rockefeller before Landis's bench. On March 4, 1907, testimony began in *United States v. Standard Oil Company of Indiana.* Five months later, Judge Landis fined Rockefeller and Standard Oil an astounding $29,240,000 for violations of federal antitrust regulations. It was the largest fine ever imposed by a U.S. court to that time and caused widespread celebration. Landis's ruling was later reversed, but in 1911, the U.S. Supreme Court ordered the breakup of Standard Oil.

The slender Landis was physically unimpressive—standing five feet, seven inches tall—but exuded power and authority. His white hair sprouted in a bold and unkempt fashion, and his face was craggy and raw. Contemporaries described his personality as flinty and colorful, and his hard-line approach toward Rockefeller and the Standard Oil monopoly attracted national attention.

In 1915, Landis tried another highly controversial case of national interest. A baseball organization named the Federal League had formed in 1913 and the following year began luring away players from the established National and American leagues, which threatened to sue. Federal League representatives announced their own lawsuit, claiming that the exclusive ownership structure of the existing major league system constituted a monopoly.

Federal League officials were pleased at first that Landis, who had already ruled against the country's largest monopoly, would preside over the case. Landis, however, felt that professional baseball was different and strict application of antimonopoly laws did not be apply to it. Landis delayed making a decision and the longer he delayed, the more deeply in debt the Federal League fell. By December 1915, the renegade league had dissolved.

In 1918, Landis oversaw the trial of more than 100 members of the Industrial Workers of the World (IWW, or Wobblies), a labor union formed in 1905 now accused of violating the Espionage Act by attempting to hinder the draft and encouraging desertion from the military during World War I. (The IWW believed that U.S. participation in the war was for the purpose of protecting the overseas interests of wealthy Americans.) All defendants were found guilty, with punishments ranging from ten days to twenty years in prison and $30,000 fines.

On November 12, 1920, the owners of major league baseball teams, who were grateful for Landis's handling of the Federal League lawsuit and his refusal to undermine the structure of the game, elected him as the first commissioner of professional baseball. He would hold that position from 1921 to 1944. He was to receive the substantial salary of $50,000 per year and, initially at least, would remain a federal judge. His selection to the post came amid rumors that eight members of the Chicago White Sox had, in exchange for payoffs from gamblers, deliberately lost the 1919 World Series against the Cincinnati Reds. The players ultimately were cleared of conspiracy charges in court, but Landis banned them from the game for life; none ever played professional baseball again after the 1920 season.

Although this was Landis's best-known decision as baseball commissioner, it was not his only disciplinary action. In 1922, he suspended George Herman "Babe" Ruth for six weeks for participating in unauthorized barnstorming. In 1926, he oversaw a case in which star players Tris Speaker and Ty Cobb were accused of a gambling scheme; evidence proved scanty, however, and no disciplinary consequences ensued.

Landis is widely credited with restoring trust, order, and integrity to the sport of baseball. However, detractors contend that he prevented players of color from entering the major league system for decades; they also point to the capricious nature of many of his decisions. Shortly after his death on November 26, 1944, Landis was elected to the National Baseball Hall of Fame, and the title of the Most Valuable Player Award was officially renamed the Kenesaw Mountain Landis Award.

Kelly Boyer Sagert

See also: Baseball; Black Sox Scandal.

Further Reading

Lieb, Fred. *Baseball As I Have Known It.* Lincoln: University of Nebraska Press, 1996.

Pietrusza, David. *Judge and Jury: The Life and Times of Judge Kenesaw Mountain Landis.* South Bend, IN: Diamond, 1998.

Sagert, Kelly Boyer. *Baseball's All-Time Greatest Hitters: Joe Jackson.* Westport, CT: Greenwood, 2004.

Lasker, Albert (1880–1952)

Albert Davis Lasker pioneered the idea—so deeply ingrained in modern American culture—that advertising is more than a means of informing the public about a product and its attributes. An advertisement, he believed, is an intentional selling tool, utilizing print, image, and voice.

Lasker was born on May 1, 1880, in Freiburg, Germany, but his family migrated to Galveston, Texas, when he was an infant. Raised in relative wealth, Lasker was nevertheless ambitious. At the age of twelve he started a successful community newspaper and, while in his teens, he became a reporter for a Galveston daily. When he turned eighteen, however, his father insisted that he find a more lucrative profession, and Lasker took a job with the Chicago advertising firm of Lord and Thomas. He later wrote that he intended to return to journalism in a few months, but gambling debts forced him to remain in the better-paying field of advertising.

American advertising at the turn of the twentieth century had changed little since the early days of the republic. Print advertisements were essentially news stories told from the point of view of the manufacturers. Copy was dull and informational, little more than an inventory of the product's components and attributes. Set in the same type as the rest of the newspaper or magazine, advertisements were often visually indistinguishable from the surrounding stories. The chief responsibility of advertising firms like Lord and Thomas was to purchase space and place ads in print media. They did not create original ad copy for their clients' products or services.

With his background as a journalist, Lasker at first adhered to the idea of advertising as purely informational. Talking to salesmen in the late 1890s, however, he began to change his views. Advertising, he realized, should be motivational, using words and images to convey the idea that a product is desirable beyond mere functionality—that people should buy it to fill a personal need or desire.

Lasker first put his ideas to use for the 1900 Washer Company. Lasker's advertising copy was so successful that the company increased its billings with Lord and Thomas from $15,000 a year to $30,000 a month, becoming one of the biggest advertisers in America. Other consumer product manufacturers signed on as well. From 1903 to 1912, when Lasker purchased the firm from his employers, Lord and Thomas's annual billings increased from $3 million to $10 million, making it the largest advertising firm in the world. Over the next twenty years, Lasker would launch successful advertising campaigns for brands that, through his expertise, would become household names: Palmolive dish soap, Schlitz beer, Goodyear tires, and Sunkist oranges.

Ever the gambler, Lasker was willing to risk public reproach by using advertisements to challenge taboos. In the early 1920s, he depicted actresses and female opera stars smoking cigarettes. These images and the slogan he created for Lucky Strike cigarettes— "Reach for a Lucky instead of a sweet"—made the brand one of the most successful of the day. Lasker also introduced new products for his clients, among them Kotex in 1921 and Kleenex in 1924. Through his advertising campaigns, these products not only became sales leaders in their categories, but the brand names entered the English language, replacing the generic terms "feminine napkins" and "facial tissues."

A longtime supporter of the Republican Party, Lasker was hired in 1920 to run the presidential campaign of Ohio Senator Warren G. Harding who was relatively unknown in national politics. Recognizing that Americans were tired of the crusades of progressivism and of World War I, Lasker helped Harding hone a message of a return to earlier values and insisted that he remain vague about the pressing issues of the day. In a sense, Lasker was applying the lessons he had learned in commercial advertising—that a promotional campaign, whether on behalf of a consumer product or a political candidate, should be more about sales than information. Harding won the election in a landslide, capturing more than 60 percent of the popular vote—the highest margin in U.S. history to that time.

Lasker ran Lord and Thomas for thirty years, but the pressure of high-stakes business led to three nervous breakdowns. In 1942, he sold the firm and devoted the rest of his life to medical philanthropy, founding the Lasker Foundation with his wife, Mary, in 1942. He died in New York City on May 30, 1952.

James Ciment and Steven Koczak

See also: Advertising.

Further Reading

Gunther, John. *Taken at the Flood: The Story of Albert D. Lasker.* New York: Harper, 1960.
Lasker, Albert. *The Lasker Story As He Told It.* Chicago: Advertising, 1963.
Morello, John A. *Selling the President, 1920: Albert D. Lasker, Advertising, and the Election of Warren G. Harding.* Westport, CT: Praeger, 2001.

Latin America, Relations with

U.S. interventions in Latin America in the two decades before the 1920s strained relations between the United States and many Latin American nations. A history of antagonism was further complicated by the dispatch of U.S. troops to Cuba, the Dominican Republic, Honduras, and Panama under President Theodore Roosevelt; Nicaragua under President William Howard Taft; and Mexico, Haiti, Nicaragua, and the Dominican Republic under President Woodrow Wilson. As the 1920s began, American troops still occupied the latter three countries. The United States also effectively managed the Cuban government. Even nations not occupied by U.S. troops were anxious about the growing political and economic hegemony, as American investments in many Latin American states grew dramatically during the first two decades of the twentieth century. World War I caused a decrease in trade between Latin America and Europe, and the United States was quick to fill the vacuum, becoming an even stronger economic force in the region.

Although the United States withdrew troops from the Dominican Republic and reduced forces in Haiti and Nicaragua during the decade, U.S. economic dominance continued. By 1929, over 20 percent of U.S. exports went to Latin America, the highest percentage to that time. Direct U.S. investment grew from $1.26 billion in 1914 to $3.52 billion by 1929. In some nations, certain American corporations dominated the economy, as United and Standard Fruit did in Honduras. Even without troops, the United States dominated political affairs in Cuba and Panama during the decade and exercised influence in other nations. Still, the decade ended with new, more cooperative relations that would pave the way for President Franklin D. Roosevelt's Good Neighbor Policy in the mid-1930s.

Harding Administration

President Warren G. Harding, inaugurated in 1921, inherited the troubled relations fostered by previous U.S. presidents. During the election campaign, he had said little about foreign policy, especially as it pertained to Latin America. However, he condemned the practice of torture that some government officials argued was going on in Cuba and Haiti, the latter under American occupation. And when Democratic vice-presidential candidate Franklin D. Roosevelt commented that he had personally written the constitution for Haiti, Harding expressed dismay that any American would dictate a constitution to another nation. But Harding did not question the leadership role that the United States had taken in Latin America, or its right to influence affairs there. He claimed to be a staunch supporter of the Monroe Doctrine and believed the region was destined to be dominated by the United States, to Latin America's benefit. Harding, like most Americans, did not heed the few dissenting voices; Senator William Borah (R-ID), for example, advocated immediate withdrawal of all U.S. troops from Latin America.

During the Harding administration, U.S. foreign policy in Latin America did shift away from the use of troops to enforce American views, in part because Harding's economic advisers—especially Treasury Secretary Andrew Mellon—were looking for ways to cut federal spending, and overseas campaigns were costly. Also, many Latin American states were achieving a stability greater than at any period in the previous two decades. U.S. and global demand for raw materials produced in Latin America, such as oil, sugar, and coffee, grew, bringing increased revenues to the region. The enhanced economic security in turn decreased internal tensions.

In light of these conditions, the Harding administration began to withdraw troops. In 1924, after two years of negotiations, U.S. troops were withdrawn from the Dominican Republic. The United States also sponsored negotiations between Latin American states to settle border disputes. A 1921 meeting aboard the USS *Tacoma* in the Gulf of Fonseca involved Honduras, El Salvador, and Nicaragua, and a similar conference was held to discuss a border dispute between Peru and Chile.

In an attempt to produce a shift in U.S. policy toward Latin America, Secretary of State Charles Evans Hughes began a dialogue about the Monroe Doctrine and its misuse as an excuse for American military intervention in Latin America. Hughes believed that Europe was too battered by World War I to interfere in Latin America and that the Monroe Doctrine did not support U.S. action in Latin America under the current circumstances. While not rejecting outright intervention, he was critical of the Roosevelt Corollary, which called for intervention when U.S. interests were threatened by political subversion—often cited by past presidents as a reason for sending troops.

Coolidge Administration

President Calvin Coolidge wanted to follow the policies of his predecessor with a continued reduction in U.S. forces in Latin America, but circumstances made achieving these goals more difficult. Nicaragua, for example, had made economic progress since U.S. forces took control of the nation in 1912. During the occupation, Nicaragua had paid off two-thirds of its foreign debt and regained control of its railroads and utilities from international receivers.

While occupied by U.S. troops, Nicaragua held a number of elections in which conservative, pro-U.S. candidates won, though there were suspicions of fraud on the part of the victors. With liberals demanding fair elections, the United States advised the newly elected president, Diego Chamorro, that they would not recognize his victory in 1920 unless he supported open, monitored balloting in the 1924 election. The conservative Chamorro agreed, which led to a split within his own party. Hard-liners wanted to continue fighting, while another group sought to create a coalition with liberal opponents so they might maintain some power if they lost the election in 1924.

The 1924 coalition of conservative Carlos Solozarro and liberal Juan Sacasa won a contentious election by a narrow margin. Despite Solozarro's request that U.S. troops stay until he was firmly in power, the troops were withdrawn within months of his victory. Immediately following the withdrawal, civil war broke out. Supporters of conservative Emiliano Chamorro (nephew of Diego Chamorro), who had been president in 1917–1920 and assumed the office again in 1926, forced a collapse of the coalition government, and U.S. troops returned in August 1926. Chamorro was forced from power and replaced by a pro-U.S. former president, Adolfo Díaz. This led liberal former vice president Sacasa to build an opposition force and launch his own rebellion.

U.S. officials charged that Mexico was interfering in the region by backing Sacasa and that U.S. troops were in Nicaragua to help maintain its autonomy and protect American lives. By 1927, U.S. negotiator Henry Lewis Stimson was dispatched to meet with rebel leader José María Moncada and to promise a free election in 1928 in which liberals would have a fair chance. In addition, U.S forces would be withdrawn in return for a cease-fire with the Díaz government until the elections. Moncada, deciding this was the best he could expect, agreed to the plan. He was joined by all other rebel leaders except Augusto César Sandino, who moved his forces into the northwest mountains and continued his fight.

A battle between U.S. Marines and Sandino's forces that led to the death of hundreds of Nicaraguan civilians, made headlines in the United States and prompted criticism of the Coolidge administration. Coolidge responded that Sandino was a bandit, much like Pancho Villa had been in Mexico. But U.S. organizations like the Committee on Cultural Relations with Latin America began organizing opposition to Coolidge's Nicaraguan policy. Anxious to get rid of a political liability, the administration pressured the Nicaraguan legislature to pass electoral reforms. Moncada won the 1928 election, and U.S. troops stayed until a new Nicaraguan military could be built. U.S. forces were finally withdrawn in 1933.

Hoover Administration

President Herbert Hoover was more successful than his predecessor in building relations with Latin America. Under Coolidge, State Department official Ruben Clark had written a lengthy memorandum analyzing the Monroe Doctrine and pointing out it did not support intervention in Latin America. Clark's memorandum helped move the Hoover administration in the direction of rethinking intervention. The 1928 Pan American Conference, held in Havana, led to open criticism of U.S. intervention in Latin America, and the U.S. delegation fought to avoid passage of a statement condemning intervention.

Even as the conference was going on, the U.S. State Department and the public at large began questioning the value of intervention. Hoover worked to improve relations in Latin America, as he hoped to complete the withdrawal of troops from Haiti and Nicaragua. The Great Depression and the need to cut government costs further spurred his interest but also distracted him from concentrating on Latin America and achieving these goals.

Despite these challenges, Hoover made it clear that he valued the friendship of Latin America. He embarked on a goodwill tour shortly after his election and appointed ambassadors who would continue building relationships in the region. He reduced troop levels in Haiti and Nicaragua, and laid the groundwork for Franklin D. Roosevelt's Good Neighbor Policy. U.S. troops did not leave Nicaragua until 1933 and Haiti until 1934. They were replaced by U.S.-trained National Guard units. In Nicaragua, the commander of the guard later became the country's dictator.

Michael Faubion

See also: Dominican Republic, Intervention in; Haiti, Intervention in; Havana Conference of 1928; Mexico, Relations with; Nicaragua, Intervention in.

Further Reading

Curry, Earl. *Hoover's Dominican Diplomacy and the Origins of the Good Neighbor Policy.* New York: Garland, 1970.

DeConde, Alexander. *Herbert Hoover's Latin American Policy.* New York: Octagon, 1951.

Gobat, Michel. *Confronting the American Dream: Nicaragua Under U.S. Imperialism.* Durham, NC: Duke University Press, 2005.

Louria, Margot. *Triumph and Downfall: America's Pursuit of Peace and Prosperity, 1921–1933.* Westport, CT: Greenwood, 2000.

Munro, Dana. *The United States and the Caribbean Republics in the 1920s.* Princeton, NJ: Princeton University Press, 1972.

Shoultz, Lars. *Beneath the United States: A History of U.S. Policy Toward Latin America.* Cambridge, MA: Harvard University Press, 1998.

Tulchin, Joseph. *Aftermath of War: World War I and U.S. Policy Toward Latin America.* New York: New York University Press, 1971.

Wood, Bryce. *The Making of the Good Neighbor Policy.* New York: Columbia University Press, 1961.

Latinos and Latinas

In general, Latinos are individuals with ancestries or personal origins in Mexico, the Caribbean, Central America, or South America. The Latino presence in the United States ranges from recent immigrants to those whose families have lived for many generations inside the United States. In addition, Latinos in America occupy all socioeconomic levels, a factor that further contributes to the complex diversity of this group in America. These differences sometimes make cooperation difficult among Latinos—who often have conflicting interests.

The 1920s saw one of the largest increases in Latino immigration to the United States, with roughly 600,000 arriving during that decade. Latin American states were subjected to the severe restrictions placed on immigration during and immediately after World War I, and Puerto Ricans, who had been granted U.S. citizenship in 1917, were not covered under immigration laws at all. The low wages offered by American landowners and manufacturers were generally better than the pay workers could find in their native countries. Thus, Latinos were a good source of cheap labor for agriculture and industry.

Mexican Americans

Persons of Mexican heritage made up the largest group of Latinos in the United States during the 1920s. Although most lived in Texas, New Mexico, Arizona, and California, a growing number of Latinos of Mexican descent were moving to other Western states and to the Midwest during the 1920s. Some were descendants of the 80,000 Mexicans living in territory taken from Mexico in the mid-nineteenth century. By 1900, Mexican Americans may have numbered 500,000, with roughly 75 percent born in the United States. Revolutions in Mexico from 1910 to 1920 and increasing job opportunities in the United States served to both push and pull immigration, with at least 31,000 Mexicans arriving in the United States during the 1910s and 500,000 during the 1920s. The latter figure accounted for 10 percent of total U.S. immigration for the decade; the percentage was even higher in the years after 1924, when federal legislation began restricting arrivals from Southern and Eastern Europe.

Mexican Americans made up substantial populations in many cities in the Southwest during the decade, among them San Antonio, Houston, El Paso, Albuquerque, Phoenix, San Diego, and Los Angeles. Housing covenants and other forms of racism, combined with poverty, forced Mexican Americans in these cities to move into segregated communities, or barrios. In the 1920s, about 40 percent of the Mexican American population lived in barrios. A small middle class of professional and merchant Mexican Americans, many of them descendents from earlier immigrants, also occupied the barrio. As the overall population swelled, many of the barrios became overcrowded or spilled over into neighboring communities.

The largest number of Latinos in the West and Southwest, especially among the most recent immigrants, were part of the unskilled or semiskilled labor force, often working as domestics or blue-collar workers in local manufacturing. Canneries, packinghouses, and mines provided many of the jobs. The low pay, while better than in their nation of origin, often kept them poor and caused many to band together to help each other or challenge employers. Mexican Americans tried to join unions but often found the doors blocked. Most of the established labor groups in the United States resented Mexican American workers, viewing them as strikebreakers, and thus did not work hard to recruit them.

Mutualistas, or mutual aid societies, such as the Texas-based *La Gran Liga Mexicanista de Beneficencia y Protección* (Grand Mexican Benevolence and Protection League), were formed to help with burials, weddings, or other situations that might cripple a family financially. Some established schools to provide children with cultural education about Mexico or to supplement the meager education received in segregated public schools. In 1926, a number of mutualistas in San Antonio joined together to form *La Alianza de Sociedades Mutualistas* (the Alliance of Mutual Aid Societies), with more than 2,000 members.

As more and more immigrants arrived from Mexico, they spread out across the United States. Industrialists in the Midwest needed new pools of cheap labor now that tougher immigration laws had reduced the numbers from Europe. The Mexican American population in Chicago and Detroit grew particularly fast as Latinos took jobs in the auto and steel industries. Mexican Americans also filled the demands of agriculture in the South and West, moving to Louisiana, Florida, Oregon, Washington, and Colorado in previously unseen numbers. Western railroads also attracted Mexican American labor. These rural occupations, however, often isolated Mexican Americans in *colonias,* segregated communities in the countryside.

No matter where they lived or how long their families had been in the country, Mexican Americans often faced discrimination in the form of segregation and limitations on civil rights. In 1929, the League of Latin American Citizens (LULAC) was founded in Corpus Christi, Texas, to promote the political and social interests of Mexican Americans. Formed through the merger of Mexican American organizations in South Texas, LULAC soon emerged as a national organization. Although largely organized and run by upper- and middle-class Mexican Americans, the league claimed to promote the interests of all Mexican Americans. Its agenda was not dissimilar from that of its African American counterpart, the National Association for the Advancement of Colored People (NAACP). LULAC called on the leaders of the Mexican American community to break down barriers and promote assimilation of Mexican Americans into mainstream American culture.

Other Groups

Immigrants from the West Indies came predominantly from Cuba and the U.S. possession of Puerto Rico. Among these, Puerto Ricans constituted the largest community. Although the island's status as a U.S. protectorate and the rules governing movement into the United States made travel to the mainland much easier than for other Caribbean immigrants, the cost of travel was often beyond the means of the poorest Puerto Ricans in the 1920s. As a result, a significant portion of Puerto Ricans moving stateside in the 1920s were upper and middle class. This represented a change from prior years, when the largest portion of Puerto Rican immigrants were brought to the United States by corporations operating plantations on the West Coast and in the South.

During the 1920s, approximately 30,000 Puerto Ricans arrived in the United States, representing about 40 percent of all newcomers from the Caribbean. Despite their relatively high position in island society, many settled for low-paying menial jobs in major cities such as New York and Philadelphia. Serving as garment workers and service workers, they strove to achieve a better life. Like Mexican Americans, they formed mutual aid societies and worked hard in their communities to establish their own middle class.

Immigrants from Cuba began arriving in the United States in small numbers as early as the 1830s, particularly in Florida and along the eastern seaboard. This pattern continued in the 1920s. Many of these immigrants took unskilled jobs, but because of the reputation of the Cuban tobacco industry, many found work in relatively well-paying and often unionized cigar-rolling factories, particularly in the Tampa Bay region of Florida.

South American nations, especially Venezuela and Colombia, sent more than 40,000 immigrants to U.S. shores during the decade. Central America sent 15,000. These newcomers often located in major urban centers and mixed freely with Latino immigrants from other regions. When possible, they joined in mutual aid societies.

Notables

Latinos made significant contributions in many fields of American life during the 1920s. Luis Alonzo (Gilbert Roland), Lupe Vélez, Ramon Novarro, and Dolores Del Rio all made names for themselves in the movie industry. Adolfo Luque became the first Latino

to pitch in the World Series, in 1923. The following year, boxer José Salas became the first Mexican American to represent the United States in the Olympics. In 1928, New Mexico became the first state to elect a Latino U.S. senator, choosing former governor Octaviano Larrazolo to represent its citizens on Capitol Hill.

While Latinos faced many challenges during the 1920s and were not always united, they made steady progress as a community. Repatriation programs and the Great Depression in the 1930s, however, presented more challenges and reversed some of the gains of the previous decade.

Michael Faubion

See also: Immigration; Immigration Laws of 1921 and 1924; Latin America, Relations with; Mexico, Relations with.

Further Reading

Acuña, Rodolfo. *Occupied America: A History of Chicanos.* 2nd ed. New York: Harper & Row, 1981.

Fernandez-Shaw, Carlos M. *The Hispanic Presence in North America from 1492 to Today.* New York: Facts on File, 1999.

Gutierrez, David. *Walls and Mirrors: Mexican Americans, Mexican Immigrants, and the Politics of Ethnicity.* Berkeley: University of California Press, 1995.

Marquez, Benjamin. *LULAC: The Evolution of a Mexican American Political Organization.* Austin: University of Texas Press, 1993.

Meier, Matt, and Feliciano Rivera. *Mexican Americans/American Mexicans.* New York: Hill and Wang, 1993.

Law and the Courts

U.S. state and federal courts of the 1920s were confronted with a host of novel issues arising from changes in American society. Litigants and their lawyers presented perplexing questions resulting from Prohibition and progressive reforms of the previous decade. Thus, much litigation concerned the interpretation of regulatory acts, such as workers compensation statutes, and the birth of administrative law governing the activities of new government agencies, commissions, and boards. Drawing less attention, but more judicial effort, were disputes created by the advent of the automobile. State court dockets swelled with lawsuits involving accident liability, negligence, and insurance.

The new types of disputes and the urbanization of American society encouraged the development of specialized courts, such as traffic and city courts and administrative agency tribunals. Appellate judges had the opportunity to write decisions affecting the law for generations to come and to establish their judicial reputations. One of the most notable judges of the period was Benjamin Cardozo of the New York Court of Appeals. Cardozo's fame and influence was further established by the publication of *The Nature of the Judicial Process* (1921), a collection of the lectures he delivered at the Yale Law School.

During the 1920s, controversy often arose from injunctions issued by state and federal trial judges against labor strikes. In response to these actions, unions and their allies sought limitations on the law's ability to provide such relief at the request of business. Nevertheless, despite the occasional controversial ruling, recent studies have concluded that state courts were not enemies of progressive reform. Although generally conservative in outlook, state supreme courts usually deferred to legislatures and upheld progressive measures. The deference to legislative authority reflected traditional ideals of judicial restraint at the state level.

State trial courts also drew attention due to press coverage by radio, newspapers, and popular magazines. Perhaps reflecting the problems and fears of the times, sensational criminal trials, such as the 1921 Black Sox trial in Chicago, the 1921 Sacco and Vanzetti trial in Dedham, Massachusetts, the 1924 Leopold and Loeb trial in Chicago, and the 1925 Scopes trial in Dayton, Tennessee, enthralled and entertained the nation, while flamboyant lawyers such as Clarence Darrow won unprecedented acclaim.

Supreme Court Jurisprudence

In the 1920s, a conservative, probusiness U.S. Supreme Court, unlike more restrained state supreme courts, struck down much economic regulation, such as statutes concerning minimum wage and work conditions, and declared unconstitutional a state law that barred judges from issuing injunctions in labor disputes. The Court was also inclined to uphold presidential authority in relation to Congress and the federal judiciary, such as the power to remove federal officials despite congressionally mandated limitations and the power to pardon contempt of court citations.

Leading the conservative cause on the Supreme Court was Chief Justice William Howard Taft of Ohio, who was nominated by President Warren G. Harding in 1921 to replace Chief Justice Edward White, who died the same year. With Harding's three subsequent appointments (George Sutherland

of Utah, Pierce Butler of Minnesota, and Edward Sanford of Tennessee), all urged by Taft, a seemingly invincible conservative bloc (also including the affable Willis Van Devanter of Wyoming and the combative James McReynolds of Tennessee) set about what Taft called ending "socialist raids on property rights."

Often in dissent were the two Bostonians on the Court, the scholarly Louis Brandeis and the eloquent Oliver Wendell Holmes, Jr. By the end of the decade, Harvard Law Professor Felix Frankfurter observed: "Since 1920 the Court has invalidated more legislation than in fifty years preceding." The Court's primary method of overturning economic regulation was an interpretation of the due process clauses of the U.S. Constitution's Fifth and Fourteenth Amendments to encompass property and "liberty of contact" rights. This interpretation was termed "substantive" or "economic due process."

Conservatives saw nothing new in the Supreme Court's decisions. They argued that it was the legislative not the judicial power that had overreached. Yet progressives claimed that the Court was protecting the existing political and economic order, and even making policy choices of its own, under the guise of an impartial methodology. In the ultimate rejection of the Court's conservative philosophy, liberal legal scholars began to espouse "sociological jurisprudence." This reform-minded view would encourage judges to craft case law in response to societal needs. At the core of this new theory was a consideration of expediency rather than the traditional search for objective, timeless law.

Angered by conservative Supreme Court rulings that declared prolabor statutes unconstitutional and by lower-court injunctions against strikers, Senator Robert La Follette, the 1924 Progressive Party presidential nominee, made the federal courts a central issue of his campaign. La Follette advocated the election of federal judges, the barring of lower federal courts from declaring acts of Congress unconstitutional, and the empowering of Congress to overturn decisions by the Supreme Court. Although there was little chance that such measures would be adopted, President Calvin Coolidge forcefully defended the Supreme Court and criticized La Follette's proposed judicial reforms—much to the delight of Chief Justice Taft.

Federal Judicial Reform and Appointments

Chief Justice Taft focused on the quality and efficiency of the federal judiciary. He created the Judicial

Early Wiretapping

The surreptitious interception and deciphering of wire communications began almost as soon as nineteenth-century inventions made it possible for messages to be sent by wire. The public quickly became concerned that wire messages were being intercepted and communicated to unintended recipients. Indeed, state and local law enforcement agencies wasted little time making use of wiretapping in the late 1800s and early 1900s, tapping telegraph and telephone wires primarily to investigate and document suspected criminal activity.

By the beginning of the Jazz Age, many U.S. states enacted laws to allay not only the public's concerns but those of the business community as well. Illinois, for example, passed statutes in 1891 and 1903 that criminalized tapping or connecting into telegraph or telephone lines for the purpose of making unauthorized copies of any social or business message, sporting news, or commercial report. These measures had been designed in part to prohibit the use of tapped news, known to one party but not the other, in sports betting and business transactions. An Illinois statute adopted as early as 1895 criminalized wiretapping for the purpose of taking or making use of news dispatches. Passed to stop newspapers from stealing each other's scoops, the legislation called for fines of up to $2,000 and jail sentences of up to one year for violations.

During World War I, after authorizing President Woodrow Wilson to take over any telephone or telegraph systems he deemed necessary for national security, Congress made it a federal crime to tap into telephone or telegraph lines operated by the federal government. The latter provision, directed against enemy agents, was only briefly useful, as it was enacted less than two weeks before the armistice in 1918.

Wiretapping was widely used by federal officers during the Jazz Age to enforce Prohibition. This usually involved inserting small wires alongside existing phone lines, which then picked up conservations on those lines. Since this often did not require entering a person's house or place of business, justices were presented with a quandary. Was this a violation of the Fourth Amendment's prohibition on unreasonable searches and seizures of "persons, houses, papers, and effects"?

In 1927, convicted bootleggers in the Pacific Northwest challenged the constitutionality of the taps on their telephone lines, but a bare 5–4 majority of the U.S. Supreme Court in *Olmstead v. United States* (1928) held that telephone taps outside of people's homes and offices did not violate their rights under the Fourth Amendment. (The ruling remained in effect until *Katz v. United States* in 1967, which extended Fourth Amendment protections to include phone conversations.) In his majority opinion in *Olmstead,* Chief Justice William Howard Taft added that the illegality of the taps under Washington state law was irrelevant, since federal rather than state law governs what can and cannot be used as evidence in federal trials. Federal laws covering peacetime wiretapping would not be enacted until 1934.

Steven B. Jacobson

Chief Justice and former President William Howard Taft (front row, second from right) accompanies U.S. circuit court judges on a visit to the White House in 1929. As chief justice, Taft focused his energies on reforming the federal judiciary. *(Library of Congress, LC-USZ62–132905)*

Conference of the United States in 1922 to foster cooperation among all federal courts, expanded the role of the chief justice as head of the entire federal judicial system, secured the appropriation of funds to build the Supreme Court Building, secured pay raises for federal judges, and obtained President Coolidge's assistance in killing a bill that would have limited federal judges' latitude in charging juries.

Of greater importance was the landmark Judiciary Act of 1925, better known as the "Judges' Bill." Along with other major procedural and jurisdictional reforms making the federal judicial system more open and fair, the act granted the Supreme Court wide discretion concerning cases it accepts for review. Liberated from the heavy burden of routine appeals, justices could concentrate on important constitutional and federal law questions. Crafted and tirelessly pushed by Taft, this modernization won the chief justice widespread praise as an architect of modern judicial administration. Nevertheless, the Judges' Bill could not have overcome congressional opposition without President Coolidge's skillful intervention. Ironically, the judicial reforms, which made it easier for litigants to gain access to the federal judicial system, also encouraged social reformers to turn to litigation instead of legislation as the most promising avenue for achieving their agendas.

Taft was also persistent in attempting to influence judicial appointments by Presidents Harding, Coolidge, and Herbert Hoover. Although Taft was concerned with judicial competence, his chief goal was political. He viewed his unprecedented lobbying of the White House as part of his mission to reverse "radical" trends. Accordingly, Taft repeatedly blocked the appointment of Benjamin Cardozo to the Supreme Court, fearing that he would align himself with Brandeis and Holmes. Taft furthermore relentlessly promoted the appointment of conservative jurists at all levels. His strongest influence came during the Harding administration, when the chief justice simply conveyed his choices to Attorney General Harry M. Daugherty and had most of them approved without hesitation.

Unlike Harding, President Coolidge was a lawyer and greatly interested in judicial appointments. Coolidge therefore spent an extraordinary amount of time personally investigating and evaluating potential nominees, and on a number of occasions he resisted political pressure from Taft and senators. Sometimes, to circumvent Senate opposition, Coolidge made controversial recess appointments of lower federal judges.

Coolidge's attention resulted in high-quality appointees at the federal trial and intermediate appellate levels. Although he almost always nominated Republicans, legal qualifications overrode ideological purity or political pull. Coolidge's circuit court judges included such legal giants as Thomas Swan, former dean of Yale Law School, John Parker, and Learned and Augustus Hand. When the time came to appoint a replacement for the aging Justice Joseph McKenna of California, Coolidge ignored demands that another Westerner be named to the High Court. Instead, he emphasized the candidate's skill as a lawyer over political considerations when, in 1925, he nominated fellow Amherst graduate and Attorney General Harlan Fiske Stone of New Hampshire, a former dean of Columbia Law School and Wall Street lawyer, to the Supreme Court. Stone would be Coolidge's sole Supreme Court nominee.

Stone's nomination encountered stiff opposition from Senators Burton Wheeler of Montana and George Norris of Nebraska. Burton was angry over a Justice Department prosecution of himself, and Norris feared that Stone would be a puppet of Wall Street. After rejecting suggestions that he withdraw Stone's nomination, the president applied considerable pressure on the Senate. Stone aided the effort when he broke precedent by being the first Supreme Court nominee to appear before the Senate Judiciary Committee. After undergoing grueling questioning with dignity, Stone was recommended by the committee and won confirmation. To Taft's disappointment, within a year of arriving at the Supreme Court, Justice Stone was increasingly found in the Court's liberal camp, particularly in civil rights and liberties cases. Nevertheless, the Supreme Court remained a bastion of judicial conservatism throughout the 1920s.

Russell Fowler

See also: American Civil Liberties Union; *Bailey v. Drexel Furniture Company* (1922); Baldwin, Roger; Criminal Punishment; *Gitlow v. New York* (1925); Holmes, Oliver Wendell, Jr.; Sacco and Vanzetti Case (1920–1921); *Schenck v. United States* (1919); Scopes Trial (1925); Taft, William Howard.

Further Reading

Gilmore, Grant. *The Ages of American Law.* New Haven, CT: Yale University Press, 1977.

Mason, Alpheus T. *Harlan Fiske Stone: Pillar of the Law.* New York: Viking, 1965.

———. *William Howard Taft: Chief Justice.* New York: Simon & Schuster, 1964.

O'Brien, David M. *Storm Center: The Supreme Court in American Politics.* New York: W.W. Norton, 2002.

Rembar, Charles. *The Law of the Land: The Evolution of Our Legal System.* New York: Simon & Schuster, 1980.

Swindler, William F. *Court and Constitution in the Twentieth Century: The Old Legality, 1889–1932.* New York: Bobbs Merrill, 1969.

Lawrence Textile Strike of 1919

One of many labor actions that rocked the United States in 1919, the textile strike in Lawrence, Massachusetts, marked the beginning of efforts by a largely immigrant and female workforce to establish a union that could address new industrial and economic conditions. The Industrial Workers of the World (IWW, or Wobblies), a radical Socialist labor organization, had led the famously successful "Bread and Roses" strike of 1912 in Lawrence but had failed to establish a permanent union presence in the mills that dominated the city. Seven years later, Lawrence's textile workers emerged from another long and bitter strike as victors and as leaders of a new industrial union.

When the strike began on February 3, 1919, few of Lawrence's 30,000 textile workers were unionized. In fact, the United Textile Workers (UTW), the union whose call for an eight-hour workday had sparked the strike movement, had only a few members in the city. Led by the conservative John Golden, the UTW was made up almost entirely of skilled British and Irish members. Differences over unequal pay, religion, and ethnic and national politics separated the majority of Lawrence's mill workers from the UTW. While the unskilled immigrant workers of the city's mills had supported the IWW in the 1912 strike, the UTW had denied them membership.

Most of Lawrence's mill employees were recently arrived immigrants from Southern and Eastern Europe, and they proved more receptive to radical and Socialist politics. Moreover, most of the jobs in the mills were dangerous, entailed long hours for little pay, and required little skill. Workers could be easily trained and easily replaced; thus, many women and immigrant employees viewed their jobs as temporary. These factors, along with the staunchly anti-union mill owners, contributed to the inconsistency of worker organization in Lawrence.

World War I dramatically changed conditions in Lawrence and other centers of textile production in the northeastern United States. The government's demand for clothing and other material generated record profits for America's textile firms, and by the war's end in November 1918, Lawrence textile workers had been granted significant wage increases. However, the rising cost of living negated much of the pay raises, and once the war ended, the mills began to lay off workers. The UTW responded by calling on mill owners to adopt the eight-hour workday on February 3, or employees would refuse to work more than eight hours.

In calling for a shorter workday, UTW leaders did not insist that workers retain their current salary. However, leaders of the textile workers, many of whom were former IWW members or Socialists, refused to accept an eight-hour workday as a pay cut. Instead, they called for "forty-eight hours of work for fifty-four hours' pay." The mill owners accepted the reduction in the workday but not the wage demands, and on February 3, 10,000 picketing workers shut down most of Lawrence's mills. Thousands of textile workers in other New England mill towns, as well as in Passaic and Paterson, New Jersey, also went on strike.

Workers with experience from the 1912 conflict quickly created effective strike organizations. By the end of the first week, 15,000 workers, or about 60 percent of all Lawrence textile employees, had joined the strike and crippled most of the mills. Strike leaders also called for outsiders' help to build support beyond Lawrence. Three Socialist-pacifist Protestant ministers from Boston, including A.J. Muste, who later became a prominent labor and antiwar leader, soon arrived on the scene and proved capable strike leaders. The Amalgamated Clothing Workers of America (ACWA), a recently formed, Socialist-led industrial union in New York, also sent organizers who provided critical aid. Despite the arrests of strike leaders, a ban on parades, and dwindling funds, a critical mass of striking workers stayed out of the mills until late May, when a routine springtime increase in factory orders forced mill owners to capitulate after 107 days of the strike.

The ACWA contributed enormously to the success of the strike, and in April 1919, that union's leaders invited textile workers from throughout the Northeast to New York, where they founded the Amalgamated Textile Workers of America (ATWA), basing it on the parent ACWA. With Muste as its head, the ATWA built vibrant local chapters in Lawrence and other textile cities in the Northeast, until ideological infighting, weak shop-floor organization, the Palmer Raids of 1919–1920, and the devastating 1920–1921 recession destroyed its promise. Nevertheless, the short-lived ATWA proved that a mass of unskilled textile workers could build a powerful alternative to the UTW's conservative, craft-based model of textile unionism, and it prefigured the longer-lasting Textile Workers Union of America that formed in the late 1930s.

Justin F. Jackson

See also: Industrial Workers of the World; Labor Movement.

Further Reading

Goldberg, David J. *A Tale of Three Cities: Labor Organization and Protest in Paterson, Passaic, and Lawrence, 1916–1921.* New Brunswick, NJ: Rutgers University Press, 1989.

Hartford, William F. *Where Is Our Responsibility? Unions and Economic Change in the New England Textile Industry, 1870–1960.* Amherst: University of Massachusetts Press, 1996.

Robinson, Jo Ann O. *Abraham Went Out: A Biography of A.J. Muste.* Philadelphia: Temple University Press, 1981.

League of Nations

The League of Nations was an international organization created in the wake of World War I. Much like the United Nations, which superseded it after World War II, the League had several missions. Above all, it provided a forum for the peaceful resolution of international conflict. It was also designed to be a mutual security pact of sorts, calling on members to thwart any aggression against other member nations. The League also comprised constituent commissions and organizations to address labor, refugee, health, and other issues.

The League was largely the brainchild of U.S. President Woodrow Wilson, who first presented his idea for an international organization in a speech to Congress on January 8, 1918. It was the last of his Fourteen Points for the democratic international order he wanted to create for the post–World War I world. In that speech, he called for "a general association of nations . . . for the purpose of affording mutual guarantees of political independence and territorial integrity to great and small nations alike." The League of

Nations was intended to establish a new order based on adherence to international law rather than brute force. It reflected Wilson's vision of progressivism on a global scale. For the peoples of Europe, weary from four years of catastrophic war, the League represented a utopian vision that would break from centuries of military alliances and war.

While Wilson was the strongest advocate, the plan for the League of Nations was drawn up largely by two legal scholars, Cecil Hurst of Great Britain and David Miller of the United States, each attached to his nation's respective delegation to the Paris Peace Conference of 1919. The Hurst-Miller plan ultimately became the basis for the Covenant of the League of Nations, which established the foundations on which negotiations between the Allies and the Central powers would be conducted and was an integral part of the Treaty of Versailles.

The covenant was made up of twenty-six articles, many of which focused on the organization's structure and operations. But the key articles defined what the organization would actually do, albeit in vague terms so as to get all nations to agree. Article 8, for example, described a process by which nations might reduce their armaments, though it did not go into the specifics of how this was to be accomplished or to what ends. Article 15 laid out the procedures by which nations could refer their international disputes to the League, how the League would take up such disputes, and how they would be resolved. Article 22 established the mandate system, whereby former colonies of the defeated World War I powers would be administered by the Allies and prepared for eventual independence. But it was Article 10 that served as the keystone of the League and proved the most controversial in the United States. This article committed all member states to come to the defense of any other member state facing external aggression.

The Covenant of the League of Nations was part of the Versailles peace treaty that officially ended the state of war between Germany and the Allies. The treaty was signed by Wilson and other leaders in June 1919, but under the terms of the U.S. Constitution, it would not become binding on the United States until it was affirmed by the Senate. There, Wilson faced a major challenge in the form of a Republican majority determined to steer America away from direct involvement in the affairs of Europe and the world outside the Western Hemisphere. Isolationist opponents of the treaty argued that the doctrine of

The League of Nations meets for the first time at the Salle de Reform in Geneva, Switzerland, on November 15, 1920. America's refusal to join the sixty-three-member organization was partly responsible for the failure of the League's peacekeeping efforts. *(Stringer/Hulton Archive/Getty Images)*

collective security would undermine U.S. sovereignty by requiring the United States to assist any other member that was attacked. When Wilson refused to compromise on releasing the United States from the obligations of Article 10, the Senate, in November 1919, rejected ratification of the Treaty of Versailles and the League of Nations covenant.

Despite the nonparticipation of the United States, the League of Nations officially came into being on January 10, 1920, with headquarters in Geneva, Switzerland. British diplomat Eric Drummond served as the League's first secretary-general from its creation until 1933. The organization was divided into three bodies: the Assembly, the Council, and the Secretariat. The Assembly, or legislative branch, included representatives of all member states and decided the general policy of the League. The Secretariat, or executive branch, prepared the agenda for the Assembly and prepared League reports. The Council, consisting of the major powers as permanent members and additional members chosen by the Assembly for three-year terms, was (like the later UN Security Council) the body that oversaw security issues, such as those dealt with under Article 10. Originally, the Council was to have five members, but when the United States refused to join, it became a body of four permanent members—Great Britain, France, Italy, and Japan—and four nonpermanent members. Germany joined as a permanent member in 1925, followed by the Soviet Union in 1934. The number of nonpermanent members grew from four in 1920 to six in 1922 to nine in 1926. The Council, which convened every four months, had the right to apply economic and financial sanctions against members that did not abide by its decisions.

Throughout the 1920s, the League of Nations served as a body of arbitration, resolving several international disputes, such as one between Sweden and Finland over the Åland Islands, a border dispute between Albania and Yugoslavia, and another between Poland and Germany over Upper Silesia, all in 1921. In 1923, the League defused a crisis in the former German territory of Memel, which was handed over to Lithuania, and in 1925, the League mediated a border dispute between Greece and Bulgaria and averted war.

Despite the League's successes, the nonparticipation of the United States robbed the organization of much credibility. Because it did not have its own military force, the League was dependent on the armies of the great powers. By the 1930s, therefore, the League proved unable to deter German, Italian, and Japanese aggression, doing little to prevent another world war. In 1945, President Franklin D. Roosevelt helped establish the United Nations, which addressed the weaknesses of the League of Nations.

Dino E. Buenviaje

See also: Europe, Relations with; Geneva Arms Convention of 1925; Kellogg-Briand Pact (1928); Locarno Treaties (1925); Paris Peace Conference of 1919; Versailles, Treaty of (1919); Washington Naval Conference (1921–1922).

Further Reading

Goldstein, Erik. *The First World War Peace Settlements, 1919–1925.* London: Pearson Education, 2002.

Moore, Sara. *Peace Without Victory for the Allies, 1918–1932.* Oxford, UK: Berg, 1994.

Pratt, Julius W. *Challenge and Rejection: The United States and World Leadership, 1900–1921.* New York: Macmillan, 1967.

Walworth, Arthur. *Wilson and His Peacemakers: American Diplomacy at the Paris Peace Conference, 1919.* New York: W.W. Norton, 1986.

League of Women Voters

With ratification of the Nineteenth Amendment to the U.S. Constitution in 1920, suffragists won a long, hard-fought battle for women's enfranchisement. The National American Woman Suffrage Association (NAWSA) and Alice Paul's more militant Congressional Union and later Woman's Party had campaigned for suffrage on the nationwide level while numerous state and local chapters rallied support at the grass-

roots level. Even before the legislation was passed, women in these various organizations prepared for the next step in women's political involvement, launching the nonpartisan League of Women Voters as a means of continuing interest in women's political work.

NAWSA leaders, including Carrie Chapman Catt, were the driving force behind the creation of the League of Women Voters. The organization's first president, Maude Wood Park, was chosen from delegates to the NAWSA Victory Convention in 1920. During the 1920s and beyond, the majority of members in the League of Women Voters came from the NAWSA, although only one-tenth of the women from that group joined the league. Like its predecessor, the League of Women Voters sought to win support for women's and children's initiatives, social welfare reforms, and overall improvement and expediency in government.

For several years following women's formal entrance into politics, the League of Women Voters found success alongside other women's organizations advocating reforms. By the mid-1920s, major victories included passage of the Sheppard-Towner Act (1921) to protect mothers and children and the formation of the Women's Bureau (1920). Although Congress failed to renew the Sheppard-Towner Act in 1927, this legislation is noteworthy for creating the first federally funded social welfare plan in America.

However, the League of Women Voters opposed one of the most progressive pieces of legislation introduced, but not passed, during the 1920s, an equal rights amendment stating, "Men and women shall have equal rights throughout the United States and every place subject to its jurisdiction." The league argued that this proposed amendment to the U.S. Constitution would eliminate protective legislation for women's working conditions, a key component of reform that had long been a priority of women in the NAWSA and other groups, such as the Women's Trade Union League (WTUL) and the National Consumers League (NCL). Not until 1969 did the League of Women Voters change its stance to offer support to a later equal rights amendment.

While the nearly 200,000 members of the League of Women Voters continued to press for reform initiatives and women's political participation during the decade following the passage of the Nineteenth Amendment, many women believed their active role in the movement had ended with the achievement of suffrage. With dismay, the league watched as the overall number of participating voters dropped during the 1920s. Indeed, only half of registered male and female voters participated in elections during the course of the decade. The lackluster turnout was especially disheartening for women in the league, some of whom had labored for years to gain the basic right of citizenry that many women now chose not to exercise. To educate women voters, the league developed its Voters Service program, which provided women with unbiased information on parties and candidates and alerted them to primary elections and polling places.

When research showed that women voted independently of one another, thus discrediting the myth of the "woman's bloc," it seemed to some that woman suffrage had failed in its aim of bringing women's perceived moral high ground into the political process. Since the women who ran for and won election to political office did not necessarily represent a unified women's platform, the League of Women Voters soon realized that its most effective method for exacting change lay in its ability to encourage legislation beneficial to the health and welfare of women and children.

As more women entered professions in the 1920s, fewer women had time for, or sufficient interest in, volunteer work. Moreover, a surge of antifeminism reduced women's interest in joining the league. The organization thus adopted a less inflammatory tack by championing children's welfare reform as well as continuing its efforts to inform voters about candidates and elections.

Margaret L. Freeman

See also: Women's Movement.

Further Reading

Scott, Anne Firor. *Natural Allies: Women's Associations in American History.* Urbana: University of Illinois Press, 1991.

Woloch, Nancy. *Women and the American Experience.* 3rd ed. New York: McGraw-Hill, 2000.

Young, Louise M. *In the Public Interest: The League of Women Voters, 1920–1970.* Westport, CT: Greenwood, 1989.

Leisure and Recreation

The Jazz Age marked what contemporary social observers and critics often called the "Age of Play." Indeed, several of the era's most dramatic changes occurred in the realm of recreation and leisure. Older, established forms of commercial entertainment such as amusement parks, vaudeville shows, dance halls, and poolrooms continued to attract millions of Americans, but newer forms of recreation, particularly joyriding, listening to the radio, attending motion pictures, and drinking and dancing in speakeasies, became popular pastimes. Meanwhile, technological innovations such as lighted athletic fields, heated swimming pools, and artificial ice rinks extended the hours and seasons of certain sports, thus contributing to the increased popularity and growth of recreational sports. During the 1920s, the nation's expanding commercial entertainment and new technologies offered Americans an unprecedented number and variety of diversions to fill their leisure hours.

Increased Options

Several interrelated trends contributed to the expansion of recreation and leisure during the 1920s. Workweeks shortened, and wages and salaries rose, while the cost of living remained comparatively stable. Paid vacations, a new fringe benefit of white-collar employment, became increasingly common. Modern advertisements glorifying leisure and consumption encouraged Americans to spend money on consumer products and commercial recreation in order to achieve self-fulfillment and happiness. Equally important was America's emergence as an urban, industrial nation, a situation that changed people's attitudes toward recreation and leisure. Once considered unnecessary and even frivolous, recreation and leisure came to form a significant feature of modern life. Educators and social workers argued that exercise was essential for healthy physical and mental development. Recreation also provided cathartic relief from the monotony and stress produced by industrial labor and office work. By 1929, according to one government survey, Americans were spending more than $10 billion a year on recreation and leisure, a figure not surpassed until after World War II.

The most revolutionary changes in Jazz Age recreation and leisure resulted from new technologies, and none transformed American life more than the automobile. The 1920s marked the first decade in which automobile ownership became widespread; automobile registrations in the United States soared from 8 million in 1920 to 23 million in 1930. Driving for sheer pleasure, or joyriding, emerged as a popular pastime, especially for younger Americans. On weekends, urban families motored out to the rural countryside to go picnicking, camping, or sightseeing. Rural families

Miniature Golf

During the Jazz Age, miniature golf became a pervasive and enduring pop culture activity, with anywhere between 25,000 and 50,000 courses across America. In California, a woman sued the local zoning board for the right to build a course in a cemetery on her property, with the headstones to be used as hazards. The owners of the luxury ocean liner *Ile de France* built a course on the deck of the ship.

Miniature golf is believed to have begun as a private amusement rather than a commercial venture. The origin has been traced by pop culture historians to 1916, when James Barber, the former president of Barber Steamship Lines, built the first miniature golf course at his estate, Thistle Dhu, in Pinehurst, North Carolina. Architect Edward H. Wiswell was hired to design and build the course at Barber's summer home, not far from the famous Pinehurst Golf Club. The miniature course, not open to the public, was featured in the popular magazine *Country Life* in 1920.

An important technological breakthrough came two years later with the invention of an artificial putting surface. Thomas McCulloch Fairbairn, who owned a cotton plantation in Mexico, had built a small golf course on his estate but found that the harsh Mexican sun was killing the grass on his putting greens. In seeking a solution, Fairbairn discovered that cottonseed hulls, when compacted and mixed with sand, oil, and green dye, made an excellent substitute for the well-manicured grass normally found on golf courses. In 1925, he joined with Robert McCart and Albert S. Valdespino in patenting this artificial putting surface, which proved critical to the success of public miniature golf courses.

A year later, entrepreneurs Drake Delanoy and John Ledbetter built a miniature course on the rooftop of a building in the financial district of New York City. Their targeted market was the lunch-hour office crowd, and they were successful enough to open 150 other rooftop courses throughout the city.

A major breakthrough in terms of miniature golf course design came atop Lookout Mountain on the Tennessee–Georgia border. There, at the Fairyland Inn, owners Frieda and Garnet Carter designed and built the first of the franchise chain of Tom Thumb golf courses. Frieda Carter is usually credited with the design, which included whimsical statues and hazards in the form of elaborate, Rube Goldberg–type contraptions.

The Tom Thumb franchise helped to spread the miniature golf fad across America. In 1930, the Fairyland Inn held the First National Tom Thumb Open golf tournament, drawing participants from all forty-eight states and awarding a prize of $2,000 to the winner. Like so many other distractions of the Jazz Age, the miniature golf craze dropped off during the Great Depression, but it was revived after World War II.

William Toth

drove to cities and towns where they could shop, attend a dance, or take in a movie. Young couples escaped parental scrutiny by driving to amusement parks, movie theaters, nightclubs, dance halls, and soda parlors.

Day trips to amusement parks, the seashore, or the countryside remained common recreational activities, but vacations of a week or more, spent either at a single location or touring about in an automobile, became common among middle-class Americans.

Travel and tourism became increasingly popular in the prosperous years of the Jazz Age. Automobile access, the Miss American pageant, and a beach setting helped make Atlantic City, New Jersey, a popular leisure destination. *(H. Armstrong Roberts/Stringer/Retrofile/Getty Images)*

Florida, with its miles of beaches, warm weather, and numerous amusements, attracted more than half a million tourists a year by 1925.

During the 1920s, commercial entertainments, especially radio and motion pictures, amused millions of Americans. With the advent of regular commercial broadcasting in 1920, radio soon emerged as an all-consuming national obsession. Radio and radio equipment sales skyrocketed from $1 million in 1920 to $430 million in 1925; by 1929, an estimated one-third of American families owned a radio. Entire families often tuned in to listen to musical programs, news, political speeches, sporting events, westerns, detective shows, soap operas, and serial comedies.

Hollywood films formed a significant component of American entertainment and leisure. After World War I, films attracted audiences in unprecedented numbers, and going to the movies became a common form of weekly or even daily recreation. In 1922, Americans purchased an average of 40 million movie tickets per week; with the advent of synchronized-sound films, or "talkies," in 1926, ticket sales soared to even greater heights. By 1930, average weekly attendance of motion pictures exceeded 100 million—at a time when the nation's population stood at just 123 million people. Motion pictures, in fact, remained one of the few commercial entertainments whose audiences did not decline as a result of the Great Depression.

During the Jazz Age, spectator sports became the pervasive, all-consuming national pastime that we recognize today. College football reigned as the nation's most popular spectator sport of the 1920s, and by the end of the decade, gate receipts at college football games exceeded even those for major league baseball. Baseball, however, captivated millions of sports fans. Despite the Black Sox scandal of 1919, annual major league attendance averaged more than 9 million throughout the 1920s, with millions more attending semiprofessional and sandlot games. Boxing, once considered a corrupt, lowbrow sport, also won a widespread following. In 1927 more than 100,000 spectators watched Gene Tunney retain his heavyweight boxing championship in a much-publicized rematch against Jack Dempsey in Chicago. This heavily touted bout generated some $2 million in gate receipts—a record that stood for half a century.

During the 1920s, American spectator sports mushroomed into an enormous industry, encompassing not just athletes and coaches but also press agents, promoters, sportswriters, and radio announcers. Expanding media coverage of sporting events transformed athletes such as Babe Ruth, Jack Dempsey, Red Grange, and Gertrude Ederle into national heroes.

Tens of millions of Americans not only followed but also played sports. Golf and tennis became particularly popular among middle-class Americans; the number of golf courses in the United States swelled from 743 in 1916 to 5,856 in 1930. Public support for athletics led to a boom in the construction of public playgrounds, baseball diamonds, football fields, basketball courts, swimming pools, and skating rinks. Social dancing was a rather athletic activity during the 1920s. A parade of new dance fads, including the Charleston, black bottom, Lindy Hop, and varsity drag, fueled dancing's tremendous popularity.

Americans also participated in nonathletic forms of recreation during the 1920s. Literacy rates reached new highs, and reading remained a favorite pastime for people of all ages, particularly for the upper and middle classes. Popular reading included romance novels, historical fiction, westerns, crime stories, religious tracts, and children's books. The advent of subscription book clubs, such as the Book-of-the-Month Club, founded in 1926, boosted book sales and brought best-selling titles into tens of thousands of American homes. Americans also read mass-circulation magazines, pulp magazines, newspapers, and tabloids in record numbers during the 1920s;

national-circulation magazines were selling a combined annual total of 202 million copies by 1929. Table games, such as bridge, poker, and mah-jongg as well as the solitary pastimes of gardening and crossword puzzles were also popular.

The Effect on Families and Communities

Americans' recreation and leisure activities varied extensively during the 1920s, but they also revealed sharp class divisions among participants and consumers. Some performances, such as operas, orchestral concerts, ballets, and Broadway shows, attracted affluent urban patrons, while baseball games, boxing matches, vaudeville shows, and amusement parks appealed to the working-class. Generally, most forms of commercial entertainment tended to be inexpensive and within the reach of even many working-class patrons. Jim Crow segregation nonetheless restricted and in many cases prevented African Americans from participating fully in some recreational pursuits. As a result, black customers who could do so patronized black-owned theaters, nightclubs, and speakeasies or attended all-black sporting events such as the games of the National Negro Baseball League, founded in 1920.

In some ways, the growth of recreation and leisure undermined the cohesion of American families. Children and parents increasingly pursued separate forms of recreation. College life in particular offered young people an enormous amount of relatively unsupervised leisure time during which to attend football games, go to dances, and otherwise socialize with friends. During the 1920s, millions of young Americans consciously abandoned their parents' behavioral and moral codes and participated in fast-changing fads in fashion, music, dancing, and speech. This brash, new youth culture often disturbed ministers, educators, and conservative Americans.

Leisure and recreation became increasingly organized during the 1920s as a result of expanding membership in fraternal orders, civic organizations, and social clubs, such as the Shriners, Elks, and Kiwanis. These organizations sponsored meetings, conventions, parties, and dances. So, too, did chambers of commerce, country clubs, athletic clubs, drama clubs, literary societies, bridge groups, and church groups.

Children's recreation reflected similar trends. During the 1920s, millions of children participated in outdoor activities and sports sponsored by the YMCA, Boy Scouts, Cub Scouts, Girl Scouts, Brownies, Camp Fire Girls, and other youth organizations. Hundreds of manufacturing companies, particularly in the South, sponsored baseball teams, brass bands, guitar clubs, and other forms of recreation in an effort to promote employee loyalty and to help recent rural migrants adjust to industrial life.

During the Jazz Age, the emergence of a national mass culture led to increasingly standardized forms of recreation and leisure. Motion pictures, radio, phonograph records, modern advertising, and mass-circulation magazines and tabloids contributed to the homogenization of American popular culture by quickly disseminating the latest songs, dances, fads, and catchphrases across the nation. Thus, Americans from coast to coast saw the same motion pictures, heard the same hit songs, and read the same magazines and tabloids.

The expansion of commercial entertainment, particularly motion pictures, radio, and spectator sports, encouraged a growing trend of passive recreation and resulted in what Silas Bent, writing in *Machine Made Man* (1930), called "spectatoritis." Sociologists Robert and Helen Lynd noted similar patterns of sedentary recreation in their classic 1929 community study of Muncie, Indiana, titled *Middletown: A Study in American Culture*. The chief recreational activities of the city's residents, the Lynds observed, tended to be "largely passive," and "the leisure of virtually all women and most of the men over thirty is mainly spent sitting down." But whether joyriding in an automobile, playing a round of golf, or reading a movie magazine, Americans of the 1920s spent unprecedented hours and dollars on recreational and leisure pursuits.

Patrick Huber

See also: Atlas, Charles; Baseball; Boxing; Fads and Stunts; Film; Football; Golf; Tennis; Travel and Tourism.

Further Reading

Aron, Cindy S. *Working at Play: A History of Vacations in the United States.* New York: Oxford University Press, 1999.

Dumenil, Lynn. *The Modern Temper: American Culture and Society in the 1920s.* New York: Hill and Wang, 1995.

Erenberg, Lewis A. *Steppin' Out: New York Nightlife and the Transformation of American Culture.* Chicago: University of Chicago Press, 1981.

Fass, Paula. *The Damned and the Beautiful: American Youth in the 1920s.* New York: Oxford University Press, 1977.

Jakle, John A. *The Tourist: Travel in Twentieth-Century North America*. Lincoln: University of Nebraska Press, 1985.

Lynd, Robert S., and Helen Merrell Lynd. *Middletown: A Study in American Culture*. New York: Harcourt Brace, 1929.

May, Lary. *Screening Out the Past: The Birth of Mass Culture and the Motion Picture Industry*. New York: Oxford University Press, 1980.

Nasaw, David. *Going Out: The Rise and Fall of Public Amusements*. New York: Basic Books, 1993.

Leopold and Loeb Case (1924)

Among the most celebrated criminal cases of the twentieth century was the 1924 Leopold and Loeb case, which contemporaries referred to as the "trial of the century." The case was named for Nathan Leopold and Richard Loeb, two University of Chicago students who were arrested, tried, and convicted for the kidnapping and murder of fourteen-year-old Robert Franks.

The facts of the case were not in dispute. In May 1924, Leopold (then nineteen) and Loeb (eighteen), driving in a rented car, picked up Franks—an acquaintance of both—as he walked along a Chicago street. In what they conceived as the "perfect crime," the two young men killed Franks with a chisel, drove the car to a marsh in Indiana, poured acid over the body to prevent identification, and stuffed it in a concrete drainage ditch. They then issued a demand to Franks's wealthy parents for $10,000 in ransom. During the exchange with the victim's father, Jacob Franks, Leopold was apprehended, and the body was soon found by a day laborer.

Aside from the grisly details of the murder, several elements of the case horrified and fascinated the media and the public, including the background and characters of the defendants. Both came from privilege and moved in Chicago's high society. Leopold, who spoke eight languages, was a millionaire's son and a nationally renowned ornithologist. Loeb, at the time the youngest graduate of the University of Michigan, was the son of a former vice president of Sears, Roebuck and Company. What had led these two sons of privilege to commit such a crime?

Both young men harbored a fascination with crime and murder, and both were students of the philosophy of Friedrich Nietzsche, a nineteenth-century German thinker who, among other things, argued that there are superior individuals who exist beyond the reach of conventional societal restraints. Leopold and Loeb interpreted this to mean that such individuals are exempt from the morals, laws, and ethics that apply to the rest of society.

The two young men had a stormy relationship, with homosexual overtones. Leopold was obsessed with Loeb and had at one time contemplated murdering him for a breach of trust. Most of those who knew the two insisted that Loeb was the mastermind of the crime and that Leopold had gone along to please him. Prosecutors argued that the crime was committed to raise money for Loeb to pay off gambling debts.

Whatever the motive, the two spent many hours planning what they thought would be a perfect crime—kidnapping a rich man's son, murdering him so he could not identify them, and disposing of the body in a place so remote that it would not be found for years. But a random happenstance sunk them. Leopold had lost his eyeglasses alongside the body. This later allowed prosecutors to identify the suspects.

Finally, the case received so much attention due to the presence of Clarence Darrow as the defense attorney. Darrow, who would go on to defend Tennessee teacher John Scopes in the famous "Monkey" trial the following year, was America's most famous criminal defense lawyer. Recognizing that the evidence against his clients was overwhelming, he put in a plea of guilty to charges of kidnapping and murder. His strategy was to keep the young men from being executed by raising an insanity defense. Homosexuality was widely considered a form of mental illness at the time, and Darrow described Leopold and Loeb's relationship as based on "twisted biological satisfactions."

The celebrated attorney then persuaded Judge John Caverly to allow expert psychiatric testimony, a rarity in criminal trials of the day. Darrow hoped to convince the judge that Leopold and Loeb's relationship was a result of mental illness and thus a mitigating circumstance in their crimes. The defense used a wide variety of testimony to prove this—from associates, who described how the young men laughed in the wrong way, to experts who described their abnormal glands.

The prosecutor condemned the psychiatrists, lashed out at the defendants as "cowardly perverts" and "spoiled smart alecks," and called for a fitting punishment—death. But Darrow closed with a twelve-hour summation arguing that the death penalty was inhumane, that a life sentence might be more fitting than the death penalty, that the desire for vengeance was not enough to justify a death sentence, and that society would benefit more from a study of the defendants over time than from a quick execution. The defense moved the judge, as well as many observers, to tears. The two defendants were found guilty and sentenced to life plus ninety-nine years in jail.

Both were sent to Joliet Penitentiary. Loeb was murdered in a prison shower in 1936 by an inmate who said that he was resisting Loeb's advances. Leopold spent thirty-four years in prison; during this time he continued his studies, becoming fluent in more than twenty-five languages. After his release from prison, he taught classes and obtained a master's degree. He died in 1971.

Scott Merriman and James Ciment

See also: Criminal Punishment; Darrow, Clarence; Law and the Courts.

Further Reading

Gertz, Elmer. *A Handful of Clients.* Chicago: Follett, 1965.
Higdon, Hal. *Leopold and Loeb: The Crime of the Century.* Urbana: University of Illinois Press, 1999.
McKernan, Maureen. *The Amazing Crime and Trial of Leopold and Loeb.* Holmes Beach, FL: Gaunt, 1996.

Lewis, John L. (1880–1969)

One of the most influential union leaders in American labor history, John L. Lewis reached national prominence in the 1920s as president of the United Mine Workers of America (UMWA). Both admired and despised by workers, industrialists, politicians, and the public, Lewis led the union through a tumultuous decade with temerity, skill, and an often autocratic iron fist. However, anti-union offensives, rapid changes in coal production, and unsympathetic federal policy makers during the 1920s helped to undermine the UMWA's status as the largest and most powerful union in the United States at the end of World War I.

Early Career

John Llewellyn Lewis was born on February 12, 1880, in a small Iowa mining community. His parents were Welsh immigrants; his father worked in coal mines in both Britain and the United States. Although his family was no different from that of most poor coal miners, and although the young Lewis worked in the mines and participated in the local UMWA branch alongside his father and brothers, he displayed higher ambitions. As a young man, he performed as an ama-

teur singer in local talent shows and tried his hand at politics and business. Failing in the latter two, he moved to Illinois and started his career as a union official in 1908. In rapid succession, Lewis was elected president of his local UMWA branch, named UMWA state lobbyist, and, in 1911, appointed as an organizer for the American Federation of Labor (AFL). In 1917, he returned to the UMWA as an appointee and quickly worked his way up the union's hierarchy. In replacing an ailing UMWA president on January 1, 1920, Lewis assumed leadership of America's most powerful union.

Union Struggles and Achievements

Aided by wartime federal intervention in the coal industry, the UMWA grew dramatically, to more than half a million members by 1919. Two years earlier, the government had pressured the union and coal companies into a three-year nationwide agreement that ensured increased production and banned strikes but also standardized and increased miners' wages—benefits the UMWA tried to extend to nonunion mines. In 1919, the coal miners, encouraged by major strikes in steel and other core industries and angered by a no-strike policy and wages that did not match rising inflation, pressed Lewis and other UMWA leaders into calling a November 1 walkout.

The government, armed with injunctions and the threat of federal troops, forced Lewis to suspend the strike after only fourteen days. However, he secured a 14 percent raise and a government commission that soon granted more significant pay hikes. Although some UMWA militants criticized Lewis's retreat, many miners welcomed the pay raises, and they elected him union president in January 1921.

Postwar developments placed Lewis and the union in a defensive position for the rest of the 1920s. The coal companies' increasing mechanization of the mines robbed the workers of precious control and slashed jobs. Mine owners also gradually shifted production to nonunion mines that were difficult for the UMWA to organize. The companies not only began to violate existing agreements with the union but also fiercely resisted the union's attempts to organize miners in the Appalachian states and other regions.

To preserve the UMWA's diminishing wartime gains, Lewis adopted a traditional strategy of collective bargaining and strikes. In 1922, nonunion miners joined UMWA members in the largest coal miners' strike in history, more than 600,000 strong. Threats of federal intervention forced Lewis into separate settlements, which fragmented the national agreement and further eroded the union's strength. The settlements also ignored nonunion strikers; UMWA dissidents criticized Lewis for losing another opportunity to help fellow miners.

The fortunes of the coal industry and the union fell as energy technology changed and as competition from nonunion mines increased. In meetings with mine operators in 1924 in Jacksonville, Florida, Lewis managed to wrest three-year contracts that secured the status quo in wages but little else. The coal companies soon disregarded this agreement, and Lewis again called out the miners in 1925. However, the administration of President Calvin Coolidge was unwilling to help the weakened UMWA, and the settlement that followed a disastrous 1927 strike did little to stop the union's heavy losses. The UMWA's ranks and finances declined precipitously: From 1921–1922 to 1928, the union's membership fell from more than 500,000 to 80,000 (two-thirds of these were in Illinois); in 1928, the union paid $3 million in relief to its growing number of unemployed members.

A staunch Republican, Lewis repeatedly asked the Warren G. Harding and Coolidge administrations to refrain from intervening in strikes and to enforce the few extant prolabor laws. They often ignored Lewis and instead allowed coal companies free reign in their dealings with the union. Lewis also appealed to the public. In his book *The Miners Fight for American Standards* (1925), he portrayed unions as patriotic institutions that were both natural and beneficial to modern capitalism. Unions, the conservative labor leader argued, ensure the high wages that enable the mass consumption necessary for economic stability and continued prosperity. While his considerable power and charisma won him public notoriety and enabled him to mingle with the nation's political and economic elite (activities he seemed to relish), his heightened stature could not stop the union's temporary decline.

Decline and Resurgence

Throughout the 1920s, many criticized Lewis's increasingly autocratic control of the union's affairs and his seeming inability to stem its decline. In many ways, Lewis personified the image of the shrewd and tough union boss. A master of procedure, he skillfully outmaneuvered opponents during often raucous union conventions. By controlling appointments and siphoning funds, he supported an expansive patronage system, thereby assuring his continued reelection as union president.

Lewis's leadership practices thus fueled the enmity of various contenders for power in the UMWA. In 1926, conservatives as well as liberals and Communists assembled an anti-Lewis "Save the Union" coalition that supported John Brophy for union president. Lewis Red-baited the opposition and handily defeated Brophy. In 1927, the union banned Communists from membership, and Lewis expelled the Communists and other Brophy supporters, calling them "dual unionists" who wanted to create a competing coal miners union.

During the 1930s, Lewis would grow increasingly critical of the conservatism of the American Federation of Labor, pulling the UMWA out of the AFL and using the union as the base for the Congress of Industrial Organizations (CIO). The 1920s had prepared him for a leading role in the creation of a massive industrial union movement which, when aided by New Deal labor laws, gave organized labor unprecedented power for several decades. Lewis remained head of the UMWA through 1960, when he retired. He died at his home in Alexandria, Virginia, on June 11, 1969.

Justin F. Jackson

See also: American Federation of Labor; Coal Industry; Coal Strike of 1919; Labor Movement.

Further Reading

Dubofsky, Melvyn, and Warren Van Tine. *John L. Lewis: A Biography.* Urbana: University of Illinois Press, 1986.

Singer, Alan. "Communists and Coal Miners: Rank-and-File Organizing in the United Mine Workers of America During the 1920s." *Science & Society* 35:2 (1991): 132–51.

Zieger, Robert H. *John L. Lewis: Labor Leader.* Boston: Twayne, 1988.

Lewis, Sinclair (1885–1951)

Perhaps no other writer of the twentieth century so effectively described, denigrated, and exalted small-town American life as Sinclair Lewis. Although almost completely unknown at the beginning of the 1920s, by the end of the decade he was an important influence in American arts and thought. In 1930, he became the first American to receive the Nobel Prize in Literature.

Harry Sinclair Lewis was born on February 7, 1885, in Sauk Centre, Minnesota, a prairie town with a population of less than 3,000. He was the youngest of three sons of a country doctor. His mother died when he was six, and his father remarried a year later. Despite being bookish and unathletic, Lewis was fairly popular in high school. After a year at Oberlin College, "Red" Lewis (so called for his flaming red hair) enrolled in Yale University in the fall of 1903. He became an editor for the Yale literary magazine but dropped out for a time to work as a janitor in a utopian Socialist colony. After travel to Panama and an attempt at a professional writing career, he returned to Yale, graduating in 1908.

Early Career

Lewis's first serious novel, *Our Mr. Wrenn,* was published in 1914. After his marriage in the same year to Grace Hegger, he worked as an editor while continuing to write in his spare time. His next four novels, all published before the end of 1919, attracted little attention. Lewis's fortunes finally changed with the publication of *Main Street* in October 1920.

Main Street was an instant success and immediately hailed as a classic. A simple fish-out-of-water story, often disparaged for its seeming lack of plot, *Main Street* is the story of Carol Kennicott, a young college graduate from St. Paul who marries a country doctor and moves with him to a fictional small town in Minnesota—a place much like Lewis's birthplace. The novel's impact derives from its satirical description of the dullness of small-town American life and the small-mindedness of the population of "Main Street America." All of the protagonist's attempts to reform the town and revitalize its culture are thwarted by nosy, dull neighbors, who prefer their endless rounds of card games, church suppers, and gossip to her oriental parties, theater group, and book discussion society.

The success of *Main Street* was followed by that of *Babbitt* (1922), *Arrowsmith* (1925), *Elmer Gantry* (1927), and *Dodsworth* (1929). Although he published two other novels and a good deal of nonfiction pieces during the 1920s, Lewis's reputation rests primarily on these five novels. *Babbitt,* the story of George P. Babbitt, a successful businessman, continues the examination of American middle-class morals and values that Lewis began in *Main Street.* Babbitt has everything a successful American could want, but still something is missing. The irony of his situation and the struggle between what an individual wants and what society tells him he must be is vintage Lewis, whose characters typically have a rich inner life that is at odds with what they must do to get along.

Arrowsmith demonstrated another aspect of this struggle. Martin Arrowsmith, an impoverished young medical student, discovers his destiny when he trains as a bacteriological researcher. The struggle to make a living at "real work" of importance is contrasted with his inability to overcome the social pressures that come into play during times of financial ease. Arrowsmith leaves his millionaire wife to start a small lab in the Vermont woods, realizing that a life of poverty is a small price to pay for the chance to do his research his way.

Elmer Gantry, the story of a corrupt evangelist, is probably Lewis's most controversial work; its depiction of the drunken, misogynistic Gantry made Lewis the target of death threats and open vilification. *Dodsworth* tells the story of successful American Sam Dodsworth as he ventures abroad. Possessed of a pioneering, entrepreneurial spirit, Dodsworth reaches a dead end in Paris when he realizes that his marriage is over and there is no longer any place for him in the world.

1930 and Beyond

Lewis won the Pulitzer Prize in 1926 for *Arrowsmith* but refused to accept the award. He did accept the 1930 Nobel Prize in Literature, however, and delivered an acclaimed acceptance speech, "The American Fear of Literature." Ten more novels followed, but only two of them—*It Can't Happen Here* (1935), the story of a fascist takeover of the U.S. government, and *Kingsblood Royal* (1947), regarding race relations in America—are widely read today. The 1940s brought personal tragedy to Lewis: in 1942, he was divorced from his second wife, the journalist Dorothy Thompson; in 1944, his son Wells was killed while serving in World War II.

Lewis died in Rome, Italy, on January 10, 1951, heart disease claiming him at the age of sixty-five. Popular in his time, his compelling work is always polemical in nature, original in execution, and American in spirit. Remembered now as a "writer's writer," Lewis exerted a profound influence on succeeding generations of American authors.

Kevin Wozniak

See also: Fiction.

Further Reading

Lundquist, James. *Sinclair Lewis.* New York: Frederick Ungar, 1973.

Vidal, Gore. "The Romance of Sinclair Lewis." *The New York Review of Books,* October 8, 1992, 14, 16–20.

Lindbergh Flight (1927)

By flying a single-engine airplane nonstop from New York to Paris, Charles A. Lindbergh became the first aviator to cross the Atlantic Ocean solo. In the specially built *Spirit of St. Louis,* he completed the 3,600-mile (5,800-kilometer) journey in thirty-three and a half hours, landing at Le Bourget airfield on May 21, 1927.

Six aviators had died and others were injured attempting to win the $25,000 prize offered in 1919 by French American hotel owner Raymond Orteig to anyone who could make the nonstop flight. Such well-known aviators as Richard E. Byrd, who had made headlines in May 1926 by flying over the North Pole, had assembled and trained crews in large

Perhaps the most celebrated achievement of the 1920s was Charles Lindbergh's nonstop solo flight across the Atlantic Ocean in May 1927. The young pilot was hailed in a ticker tape parade down Fifth Avenue in New York City on June 13. *(General Photographic Agency/Stringer/Hulton Archive/ Getty Images)*

multiengine planes in preparation for the crossing. Byrd, flight endurance record-holder Clarence Chamberlin, the American Legion–supported Noel Davis, and World War I flying ace René Fonck of France all encountered difficulties in their attempts. French pilots Charles Nungesser and Francois Coli departed Le Bourget in France on May 8 and were never seen again.

Lindbergh, a Detroit native who had grown up in Little Falls, Minnesota, was the only contestant to use a single-engine plane, and the only one to forgo the use of radio communications and a copilot to share flying time. He was virtually unknown, not just to the public but even to many in the aviation establishment. Younger than the other aviators, Lindbergh had not flown in the Great War, nor had he established any records or pioneering feats; he was, in fact, a working pilot in service of the air mail. His plane, *The Spirit of St. Louis,* named in honor of the group of businessmen who backed him, was made by Ryan Aircraft, a relatively unknown manufacturer in San Diego, and consisted almost exclusively of a cockpit surrounded by fuel tanks with an engine in front. Because of the need for fuel and aerodynamics, a tank was placed directly in front of the cockpit, obscuring vision out of the front of the plane.

When Lindbergh landed at Le Bourget, he encountered a mob of thousands gathered to witness his historic achievement. He spent two weeks in Europe, with massive crowds attending his every move. He returned to the United States aboard a U.S. Navy ship supplied by President Calvin Coolidge, and for the next several months, he was celebrated in parades and special ceremonies across the country. New York City honored him with a ticker tape parade on Fifth Avenue. For more than a year after the flight, Lindbergh toured North and South America promoting air travel before donating *The Spirit of St. Louis* to the Smithsonian Institution in Washington, D.C.

To the American people, Lindbergh represented traits long treasured as characteristically American: individuality, courage, and self-sufficiency. His achievement created visions of a future that included an expanded national horizon. Air travel, the first major advance in overseas mobility since the steamship, piqued the public's interest and gave a boost to the fledgling airline industry. As a result, a whole new branch of aviation-related occupations emerged calling for the skills and knowledge of engineers, mechanics, aircraft designers, flight instructors, and meteorologists.

News of the flight spread around the world via the medium of the day, the radio. Newspaper accounts and photographs were accessible within hours of Lindbergh's landing, and once in Paris, he was able to telephone across the Atlantic to his mother to let her know all was well. The vast network of individuals and technologies involved in completing and reporting the great event underscored the promise of American industry, organization, and society.

Charles J. Shindo

See also: Aviation; Celebrity Culture; Fads and Stunts.

Further Reading

Berg, A. Scott. *Lindbergh.* New York: G.P. Putnam's Sons, 1998.

Lindbergh, Charles A. *The Spirit of St. Louis.* 1953. St. Paul: Minnesota Historical Society Press, 1993.

Ward, John W. "The Meaning of Lindbergh's Flight." *American Quarterly* 10 (Spring 1958): 15.

Literature

See Fiction; Poetry

Locarno Treaties (1925)

At Locarno, Italy, in October 1925, representatives of Great Britain, France, Italy, Belgium, Germany, Poland, and Czechoslovakia agreed on a series of nonaggression and arbitration pacts designed to ensure mutual security. These agreements, known as the Locarno treaties, grew out of French and German efforts to normalize relations and to resolve problems of security, disarmament, and reparations left undetermined by the 1919 Paris peace settlement that ended World War I. The treaties signaled a period of conciliation, sometimes called the Locarno Era, that seemed to portend lasting peace in Europe. But the newfound harmony proved fleeting. In the 1930s, Nazi dictator Adolf Hitler would violate the agreements, and France and Great Britain would prove unwilling to enforce them.

Europe during the early 1920s was rife with resentment and discontent fostered by the Treaty of Versailles. The settlement had severely punished the defeated Germany, stripping away overseas colonizes, sharply reducing the size of the German military, demanding costly reparations, and forcing Germany to sign a war-guilt clause asserting that Germany alone was responsible for the war. These provisions angered the German people, and the reparation payments plunged Germany's economy into chaos. Beset by these and other problems, the Weimar Republic, Germany's new government, struggled to gain broad political support. In redrawn Eastern Europe, various national groups demanded further border adjustments. The victorious powers, France especially, repeatedly charged that the terms of the peace were being enforced inadequately and fretted that Germany might one day regain its military might and threaten the balance of power in Europe.

German Foreign Minister and former Chancellor Gustav Stresemann, who believed that improved diplomacy would help ameliorate the crisis within his country, sought friendlier terms with Germany's neighbors. French Foreign Minister Aristide Briand, also seeking a more hospitable diplomatic climate, proved receptive to his overtures. Together with Britain's foreign secretary, Austen Chamberlain, they negotiated the Locarno treaties in October 1925. The agreements reaffirmed the Franco-German border as delineated in the Paris peace settlement and upheld the provision of that agreement forbidding Germany from deploying troops in the Rhineland. France agreed to withdraw its occupation force from the Rhineland in 1930, five years earlier than specified at Paris.

In addition, Germany, Belgium, and France pledged not to wage war against each other except in "legitimate defense" or in a support role for the League of Nations. They also agreed that future disputes between them would be settled through diplomatic channels. Germany reached a similar arbitration agreement with Poland and Czechoslovakia. Agreements between France and Poland and France and Czechoslovakia bound those countries to come to the other's aid in case of unprovoked attack. France also supported German membership in the League of Nations.

Wearied by World War I and the subsequent years of bickering, many Europeans hailed the Locarno treaties as an overwhelming success. The accords, formally signed in London in December, seemingly initiated a new, harmonious era in international relations. Enthusiasm greeted Germany's entry into the League of Nations, and Chamberlain, Briand, and Austen shared the Nobel Peace Prize for 1926. Continuing the spirit of Locarno, the leading European states, Japan, and the United States signed the Kellogg-Briand Pact in 1928, renouncing "war as an instrument of national policy."

The enthusiasm proved unwarranted. In Germany and France, politicians who supported conciliation were in the minority. In Germany, especially, many viewed the Locarno treaties as an extension of the despised Paris peace settlement; Stresemann was denounced for his efforts. The conciliation of the Western powers unsettled the Soviet Union, which felt isolated and vulnerable in Eastern Europe; consequently, it moved to strengthen its position with France and Turkey.

Moreover, the Locarno treaties were effective only as long as the signatory powers enforced them, which they proved unwilling to do. In 1936, in clear violation of the Paris peace settlement and the Locarno treaties, Hitler dispatched troops into the demilitarized Rhineland. The signatory powers denounced the move and there was talk of sanctions, but no punitive measures were taken. In taking the Sudetenland in 1938, Germany failed to abide by the arbitration agreement it had reached with Czechoslovakia at Locarno. A year later, Germany broke its arbitration pledge with Poland when it invaded that country, thereby setting in motion World War II.

John Paul Hill

See also: Europe, Relations with; Kellogg-Briand Pact (1928); League of Nations; Military Affairs; Paris Peace Conference of 1919; Versailles, Treaty of (1919).

Further Reading

Jacobson, John. "The Conduct of Locarno Diplomacy." *Review of Politics* 34:1 (1972): 67–81.
Newman, William J. *The Balance of Power in the Interwar Years, 1919–1939.* New York: Random House, 1968.
Sontag, Raymond J. *A Broken World, 1919–1939.* New York: Harper & Row, 1971.

Locke, Alain
(1885–1954)

One of the preeminent African American thinkers of the twentieth century, Alain Locke was a philosopher by training and an educator and cultural critic by profession; his intellectual endeavors spanned the fields of art, music, literature, and anthropology. A self-described "midwife" of the Harlem Renaissance, he helped to promote the black literary and artistic awakening centered in that New York City neighborhood in the 1920s and early 1930s.

Locke was born on September 13, 1885, in Philadelphia, Pennsylvania. A descendant of free blacks and the son of schoolteachers Mary Hawkins and Pliny Ishmael Locke, he was a member of the city's black elite. As a child, he played the violin and piano, demonstrating musical as well as academic talent. Af-

ter attending Central High School and the Philadelphia School of Pedagogy, he enrolled in Harvard University in 1904. Graduating magna cum laude with a degree in philosophy in 1907, he became the first African American to receive a Rhodes Scholarship. After studying at Oxford University and the University of Berlin, Locke returned to Harvard and earned a doctorate in philosophy in 1918.

Locke became a member of the faculty at Howard University in 1912 and went on to become chair of the philosophy department in 1921, although he would not publish his first serious article in the field until 1935. Instead, his early reputation was built on his championship of the careers of the writers and artists who were members of the Harlem Renaissance, also referred to as the New Negro movement.

On March 21, 1924, Charles S. Johnson, editor of *Opportunity* magazine, the periodical of the National Urban League, hosted a gathering of established intellectuals and emerging African American writers at Manhattan's Civic Club. Locke served as master of ceremonies at the event, which highlighted the resurgence in black literary output then under way. In 1925, capitalizing on the rich talent of these young writers, Locke edited a special edition of the sociology magazine *Survey Graphic* devoted to the works of African American writers. The issue reached 42,000 readers, prompting Locke to expand the collection into an anthology, *The New Negro,* which appeared in 1927.

It was a landmark effort, bringing together the work of thirty-eight writers, only four of whom were white. An interdisciplinary undertaking, the anthology included poetry by Countee Cullen, Claude McKay, and Langston Hughes; fiction by Jean Toomer and Zora Neale Hurston; drawings by Aaron Douglas; and essays by W.E.B. Du Bois, E. Franklin Frazier, and Walter White. Locke wrote the introduction to the collection as well as four essays, "The New Negro," "Negro Youth Speaks," "The Negro Spirituals," and "The Legacy of the Ancestral Arts." The essays included in the volume articulated the aesthetic, political, and interpretive issues that defined the era, earning Locke a reputation as the premier chronicler and critic of the movement. Above all, *The New Negro* expanded the audience for African American literature.

Locke was at once an advocate of racial pride and of an integrationist vision of American society. In 1924, on sabbatical from Howard, he traveled to Egypt to witness the reopening of Tutankhamen's tomb. His experiences in Africa made a deep impression on him, convincing him of African Americans' rich cultural heritage. Returning to America, he urged black artists to draw on their African antecedents. "Even with the rude transplanting of slavery," he argued, "the American Negro brought over as an emotional inheritance a deep-seated aesthetic endowment." Locke compiled an extensive collection of African art and studied the various styles and techniques. Seeking to dispel popular notions of African "primitivism," he emphasized the technical virtuosity and refined aesthetic sensibilities of traditional African artists.

Despite advocating a distinctive black aesthetic, Locke believed in interracial cooperation, arguing that African Americans played the role of "collaborator and participant in American civilization." He championed the idea of cultural pluralism, claiming that individual groups should be proud of their heritage and that society should honor diversity. Divergent ethnic identities and racial pride, he maintained, need not diminish patriotism. In his influential 1925 essay "The New Negro," Locke described black cultural outpouring as a "gift" to white America. Like many of the other intellectuals active in the New Negro movement, Locke pointed to African American artists to refute claims of racial inferiority.

As one of the leading black intellectuals in America and chair of Howard University's philosophy department, Locke was instrumental in the school's development of a curriculum that included a strong African studies component. He published several books in the course of the next decade, including *Negro Art: Past and Present* (1936), *The Negro and His Music* (1936), and *The Negro in Art: A Pictorial Record of the Negro Artists and the Negro Theme in Art* (1940).

Although he remained interested in art throughout his life, Locke's thinking in his later years revolved around the issue of race relations and advocacy for cultural pluralism. In 1942, he co-edited *When Peoples Meet: A Study in Race and Culture Contacts*, a pioneering anthology about race relations around the globe. Locke remained a high-profile public intellectual, department chair, and popular lecturer until his death from heart disease on June 9, 1954.

Jennifer Jensen Wallach

See also: African Americans; Art, Fine; Fiction; Harlem Renaissance; Journalism; Poetry.

Further Reading

Baker, Houston. *Modernism and the Harlem Renaissance.* Chicago: University of Chicago Press, 1987.

Huggins, Nathan. *Harlem Renaissance.* New York: Oxford University Press, 1971.

Lewis, David Levering. *When Harlem Was in Vogue.* New York: Alfred A. Knopf, 1981.

Locke, Alain, ed. *The New Negro.* New York: Simon & Schuster, 1927.

Washington, Johnny. *Alain Locke and Philosophy: A Quest for Cultural Pluralism.* Westport, CT: Greenwood, 1986.

Lost Generation

The Lost Generation was the name bestowed on a group of young American writers, many of them living and working in Paris after World War I, who gained notoriety in the 1920s. The name comes from Gertrude Stein's remark to Ernest Hemingway that "you young people who served in the war . . . are a lost generation." Along with Hemingway, Sherwood Anderson, F. Scott Fitzgerald, and John Dos Passos are perhaps the group's most prominent representatives.

The men of Hemingway's generation, born between the early 1880s and the turn of the twentieth century, had been decimated by the Great War. The United States suffered 125,000 combat deaths, and the major European antagonists together buried more than 7 million soldiers. In the wake of the armistice, the generation that had fought in the trenches seemed spiritually adrift. Mechanized mass slaughter on the battlefield had made a mockery of Victorian bywords such as "chivalry" and "honor," and disillusionment with the peace had done a great deal to undermine faith in the liberal democratic world that the victors promoted. Critic Edmund Wilson saw in the rootless, aimless protagonists of F. Scott Fitzgerald's novels the representative figures of this Age of Confusion: men and women who had known only war and chaos, and who had abandoned the values of their forebearers without finding new ones to replace them.

Fitzgerald, like Stein, Dos Passos, and many others, fled an American milieu that seemed at once puritanical, dishonest, and vapidly materialistic. In Europe, they found an environment that, if not necessarily more open to their literary experimentation, was at least indifferent to their eccentricities. Perhaps just as important, it was cheap. The weakness of the French franc in the immediate postwar years meant that an American of no great means could live extravagantly in Paris. In his novel *The Sun Also Rises* (1926), Hemingway drew from life to depict these bored expatriates in their dissipations fueled by alcohol and buoyed by a congenial café culture.

The writers of the Lost Generation would produce some of the finest American literature of the twentieth century. Dos Passos's *Manhattan Transfer* (1925) offered a stinging critique of metropolitan life. In *The Great Gatsby* (1925), Fitzgerald traced the rise and collapse of a brilliant Long Island socialite. *A Farewell to Arms* (1929), which confronted the war and its human aftermath, showed Hemingway at the height of his powers.

Many of the writers who made up the Lost Generation were brought together by Shakespeare and Company, an English-language bookstore in Paris run by Sylvia Beach, made famous by publishing the first edition of James Joyce's *Ulysses* (1922). Throughout the 1920s, the store acted as a meeting place for aspiring American writers, a lending library, and a resource for the many editors who scouted the store for new talent for the numerous transatlantic literary journals.

Author Ernest Hemingway and bookstore owner Sylvia Beach pose in front of Shakespeare and Company, Paris's leading purveyor of English-language books, in 1928. Hemingway and other members of the "Lost Generation" of American writers and artists were drawn to the French capital for its culture and low cost of living. *(RDA/Hulton Archive/Getty Images)*

With the coming of the Great Depression and the drying up of literary opportunity, however, the expatriate writers began to filter home. Yet the productive years of the Lost Generation writers would last well into midcentury, and Fitzgerald, Hemingway, Dos Passos, and Stein would have an influence on American letters that remains profound.

Eric Paras

See also: Fiction; Fitzgerald, F. Scott, and Zelda Fitzgerald; Hemingway, Ernest; Poetry; Stein, Gertrude.

Further Reading

Fitch, Noel Riley. *Sylvia Beach and the Lost Generation.* New York: W.W. Norton, 1983.

Hemingway, Ernest. *A Moveable Feast.* New York: Scribner's, 1964.

Wohl, Robert. *The Generation of 1914.* Cambridge, MA: Harvard University Press, 1979.

Luce, Henry (1898–1967)

Henry Robinson Luce was one of the great American media magnates of the twentieth century. The publications he helped to found—*Time, Life, Fortune,* and dozens of others—aimed to synthesize vast amounts of information for busy readers. Their success made Luce not only very wealthy but also one of the most influential figures in the country.

Boy from China

Born on April 3, 1898, in Tengzhou, China, where his parents Henry and Elizabeth were Protestant missionaries, Luce would not set foot in America until 1913, when a scholarship allowed him to attend the Hotchkiss School in Lakeville, Connecticut. At Hotchkiss, where Luce waited tables to support himself, he quickly became editor of the *Hotchkiss Literary Journal.* He also befriended classmate Briton Hadden, who edited the *Hotchkiss Record.* The two young men carried their friendly rivalry to Yale, which they both entered in 1916. Hadden won the position Luce coveted, the editorship of the *Yale Daily News,* but the pair remained close enough to enlist together for war service in 1918. Both trained at Camp Jackson in South Carolina, and both rose to the rank of second lieutenant. The armistice of November 1918 kept them from seeing combat.

Success after success greeted Luce upon his return to Yale and civilian life. He was admitted to Phi Beta Kappa and tapped for the university's prestigious Skull and Bones society. After graduating from Yale with highest honors, he studied for a year at Oxford University in England, and he returned to a job as a reporter for the *Chicago Daily News*. In late 1921, he accepted a position at the *Baltimore News*, where he was reunited with Hadden.

Making *Time*

Hadden and Luce saw a market opportunity for news synthesis for busy readers. Having worked for years in journalism, both were aware of the shortcomings of the genre: a glut of information and a dearth of analysis. A new kind of publication, they thought, might address these failings by condensing the week's news, placing it in perspective, and doing so in lively prose.

Luce and Hadden left the *Baltimore News* in 1922 and set about raising capital for their projected "news magazine," which they called *Time*. With $86,000 in hand, most of it raised through acquaintances from Yale, they set up shop at 9 East Fortieth Street in Manhattan. Hadden served as the creative engine of the partnership while Luce focused more on business matters, though they took turns editing the magazine; some half-dozen Harvard and Yale graduates of similar age rounded out the magazine's staff. On March 3, 1923, the first issue of *Time* made its appearance.

As business manager, Luce watched in dismay as the magazine proceeded to lose almost $40,000 in its first year, attracting fewer than 20,000 subscribers. Skeptics noted that a flourishing weekly review, the *Literary Digest,* already held the field. Others noted that the educated audience Luce and Hadden sought already had the highbrow *New Yorker* to keep them informed. However, by 1926, *Time* was in the black, and by 1928, it was one of the hottest magazines in America.

A number of innovative features attracted people to *Time*. It was opinionated but not strident. It was dense but concise enough to be consumed in a single sitting. It personalized current events by emphasizing individuals; its "Man of the Year" feature, conceived in 1927 and initiated in 1928, would become an enduring favorite. White-collar readers found the *Time* formula particularly appealing; by the second decade of its existence, three of every five subscribers were businesspeople. This, in turn, fueled advertising revenue, as makers of high-end goods and services strove to reach *Time*'s affluent readership.

Hadden's sudden and unexpected death in 1929 left Luce alone at the helm of the magazine. *Time* was reaching nearly 300,000 subscribers, forcing its competitors to adopt its methods or risk irrelevance. But Luce was not finished.

An American Century

In 1930, Luce founded *Fortune* magazine. With its untimely celebration of big business and its shocking price of one dollar per issue, *Fortune* aimed itself at the wealthiest stratum of *Time*'s audience. Then, in 1936, Luce turned his attention to the mass market and launched the magazine that would transform his publishing venture into a media empire: *Life*. The magazine's simple concept, as Luce wrote in introducing it to the public, was to "see life; to see the world . . . to see and to take pleasure in seeing." *Life* was resolutely visual, offering readers quality photojournalism for ten cents an issue. In its first year, it captured more than 1 million readers.

The enormous audience that *Time-Life* reached ensured that Luce's personal opinions would carry enormous weight. Detractors charged that his publications were biased at best, and outright propaganda at worst. Luce was unapologetic. "If everyone hasn't brains enough to know by now that I am a Presbyterian, a Republican and a capitalist," he told *Time* readers, "I am biased in favor of God, the Republican party and free enterprise."

Luce had spoken approvingly in the 1920s of Italian leader Benito Mussolini, but by 1940, Luce was antifascist and an interventionist. In the wake of World War II, he continued to stress America's global responsibilities and to denounce the Soviet Union and its sympathizers. The twentieth century, Luce declared, was to be the "American Century": It was incumbent upon the world's most powerful nation to "exert upon the world the full import of our influence, for such purposes as we see fit and by such means as we see fit."

Having already suffered one heart attack, Luce stepped down as the head of Time, Inc., in 1964, at the age of sixty-six. He died in Phoenix, Arizona, on February 28, 1967.

Eric Paras

See also: Journalism; *Time.*

Further Reading

Baughman, James L. *Henry R. Luce and the Rise of the American News Media.* Boston: Twayne, 1987.

Herzstein, Robert Edwin. *Henry R. Luce: A Political Portrait of the Man Who Created the American Century.* New York: Scribner's, 1994.

Jessup, John K., ed. *The Ideas of Henry Luce.* New York: Atheneum, 1969.

Kobler, John. *Luce: His Time, Life, and Fortune.* New York: Doubleday, 1968.

Swanberg, W.A. *Luce and His Empire.* New York: Scribner's, 1972.

Lynching

In the American context, lynching has been closely associated with racism; most victims have been African American and the perpetrators almost always have been white. The vast majority of lynchings have occurred in the South, usually because the victim was suspected of challenging the social or political order of the region by talking back to a white man, acting inappropriately toward a white woman, insisting on legal rights, or simply becoming economically successful.

Lynchings peaked in the American South in the late nineteenth and early twentieth centuries, with more than 1,100 occurring in the 1890s alone. Most scholars attribute these high numbers to two causes. First, the period saw the final undoing of the racial progress of the Reconstruction era and the full implementation of racial segregation and black disenfranchisement. Second, populist efforts to create a political coalition of poor whites and blacks was met with extreme violence by the established white elite.

The 1920s marked a critical turning point in the history of lynching. The decade witnessed a major decline in incidence; from a peak of fifty-nine in 1921, the number of known lynchings fell steadily, to only seven in 1929. In all, there were an estimated 270 lynchings during the 1920s, about one-fifth of them occurring after 1925. The decline in number was partly due to the activities of anti-lynching crusaders.

African American civil rights leaders such as Ida B. Wells-Barnett had been fighting to expose the horrors of lynching since the 1890s. Wells-Barnett and other activists had shown that black victims of lynchings were, in the vast majority of cases, innocent of any crime, and that racist white mobs and legal authorities actually undermined law and order in an effort to preserve racial and sexual hierarchies. By the 1920s, African American activists had gained enough social and political power to address the lynching issue at the federal level. The multiracial National Association for the Advancement of Colored People (NAACP) spent most of the early Jazz Age working to gain passage of a federal anti-lynching law.

After World War I, African American leaders began working with U.S. Congressman Leonidas Dyer (R-MO), whose district included many black voters, to create the Dyer Anti-Lynching Bill. If passed, the measure would have enabled the federal government to prosecute both lynchers and the local law enforcement officials that colluded with them, and allowed relatives of victims to file a civil suit in the county where the lynching took place. Removing jurisdiction over lynching cases to the federal government was seen as crucial by anti-lynching activists, who believed that local white prosecutors and juries were unlikely to actively pursue legal cases against those responsible for lynchings.

James Weldon Johnson of the NAACP and other leading African Americans spent most of 1921 attempting to push the Dyer bill through Congress. They were initially hopeful that the federal government would act because the Republican Party, the party of Lincoln and long regarded as responsive to African Americans, controlled the House, Senate, and White House. The bill moved through the House Judiciary Committee with only minor adjustments, after which it was presented to the full House of Representatives for debate. Despite the Fourteenth Amendment, which guaranteed equal protection under the law, Southern members of Congress attempted to argue that the federal government had no jurisdiction over what they considered local criminal acts. They also attempted to defend lynching by arguing that it was necessary to protect white women from black rapists, a claim that had repeatedly been proven unfounded. The Dyer bill passed the House on essentially a party-line vote, with only eight Northern Democrats voting in favor.

Getting the bill through the Senate would prove much more difficult. Few members of that body felt a strong need to win the favor of black voters—in no state was there a black majority. When Southern Democrats filibustered the bill, tying up all other work, Republican senators backed down. Neither President Warren G. Harding nor Vice President Calvin Coolidge, both Republicans, spoke out in favor of the bill. They, like most Northern whites, claimed to be repulsed by lynching, but they were unwilling to alienate Southern supporters or expend political capital on the issue.

Although the Dyer bill failed to gain passage, African American civil rights leaders continued to pressure politicians and the American public to end lynching during the 1920s. The Great Migration was making African Americans an increasingly potent political force in the North, and the rapid expansion of national media and culture made it easier for NAACP field agents and other activists to expose the horrors of lynching to the whole country. Some Southern politicians and business leaders, hoping to attract Northern industry and jobs to their states, became increasingly sensitive about the South's image. Northern politicians hoping to attract the growing black vote in their own districts wanted to appear sympathetic to the plight of Southern blacks.

When a white mob burned three young black men at the stake in the town square in Kirvin, Texas, in 1922, and when the Ku Klux Klan mobilized 1,000 people to witness the murder of three black youths in South Carolina in 1925, the NAACP was able to send its own investigators to the scenes of the lynchings. In the South Carolina case, pressure from the NAACP and the *New York World* forced the governor to convene a grand jury. Although the grand jury did not issue any indictments, South Carolina newspapers condemned the lynching and the cover-up that followed it.

Despite such progress, lynching remained a problem after the Jazz Age. In the economically depressed early 1930s, the numbers rose briefly—twenty in 1930 and twenty-four in 1933—before declining in the late 1930s. Efforts to pass federal anti-lynching legislation continued to fail, blocked by the same political obstacles that had arisen in the 1920s. It would take the civil rights movement of the 1950s and 1960s, as well as federal legislation like the Civil Rights Act of 1964, to put an end to lynching and the segregated racial order that gave rise to it. By the late 1960s, lynching had become an extremely rare phenomenon, and one that was taken seriously by local, state, and federal officials.

Michael A. Rembis

See also: African Americans; Du Bois, W.E.B.; Ku Klux Klan; National Association for the Advancement of Colored People.

Further Reading

Raper, Arthur F. *The Tragedy of Lynching.* New York: Negro Universities Press, 1969.

Schneider, Mark Robert. *African Americans in the Jazz Age: A Decade of Struggle and Promise.* Lanham, MD: Rowman & Littlefield, 2006.

Wells-Barnett, Ida B. *On Lynchings.* Amherst, NY: Humanity Books, 2002.

Marriage, Divorce, and Family

Ideas about marriage and divorce in America changed tremendously during the 1920s, especially among the white middle class, but getting married and raising a family remained the norm for most people. In 1920, approximately 60 percent of men and women over the age of fifteen lived as married couples, and most Americans lived in family households. Whereas only one in eighteen marriages ended in divorce during the 1880s, one in six marriages ended in divorce during the 1920s, but remarriage became quite common. Despite the increase in the rate of divorce, only slightly more than 1 percent of respondents to the 1930 U.S. Census indicated that they were divorced.

New Sexual Mores

"Dating" was a relatively new concept during the 1920s. Before this, courtship rituals, primarily among the middle and upper classes, had taken place in the young woman's home. If a man was interested in a woman, he came "calling," and the two sat in the parlor and talked, shared refreshments, or possibly played the piano and sang. But the rise of cities and commercialized forms of leisure, such as dance halls, amusement parks, restaurants, movie theaters, and perhaps most important, the automobile, changed courtship rituals permanently. Young men and women of the 1920s increasingly went on dates outside the home, which afforded them more opportunity for socialization with peers and increased sexual experimentation.

More than 80 percent of males and nearly 50 percent of females engaged in premarital sexual activity during the Jazz Age. Young men and women of the 1920s were not promiscuous, however. In most cases, they limited their sexual experimentation to a single partner they intended to marry. Despite changing sexual mores, the old taboo against premarital sex remained important to most Americans, especially young women. By channeling their sexual activity toward marriage, young men and women were able to push at the edges of existing social boundaries without completely dismantling the Victorian social-sexual system.

Young men and women who experimented with premarital sex faced intense public pressure to legitimize their actions through marriage, and conflicting views about sex, even within marriage, remained prevalent during the 1920s. In the end, however, new courtship rituals, dating practices, and sexual expressiveness changed how most Americans viewed marriage during the Jazz Age. A new notion of companionate marriage emerged in which an ideal marriage was thought to consist of mutual devotion, sexual attraction, and respect for spousal equality. This view of marriage was popularized by magazines, movies, mental health professionals, social service providers, and educators.

Ideas of romantic love, sexual fulfillment, and finding the ideal partner often became more important than economic concerns or a sense of family loyalty. The few individuals who sought to end their marriages during the 1880s did so because the husband was not an adequate or reliable provider, or because the wife failed to carry out her duties in the home. During the 1920s, these claims appeared in divorce petitions less frequently; more often couples cited a lack of attention, consideration, or romantic appeal in their decision to end their marriage. By that time, fewer Americans, especially those in the middle class, relied upon family members for economic survival, and the social network that once centered on the family had become less important in the wake of commercialized leisure and peer-group socialization outside the home. This resulted in an increasing number of couples looking to end emotionally, romantically, or sexually unfulfilling marriages.

Rising Divorce Rates

Some states, such as New York and South Carolina, maintained restrictive divorce laws or denied their residents any right to divorce. The Roman Catholic

Divorce became increasingly prevalent in Jazz Age America. While looking radiant at her March 1920 wedding to actor Douglas Fairbanks, Hollywood idol Mary Pickford, "America's Sweetheart," had divorced her first husband less than a month before and would divorce Fairbanks in 1936. *(General Photographic Agency/Stringer/Hulton Archive/ Getty Images)*

Church also opposed divorce. But some states made it easier for unhappy couples to end their marriages. During the 1920s Nevada became the easiest place to get a divorce. One had only to live in the state for six months in order to obtain a divorce. Realizing that divorce seekers were an economic opportunity—and that other states, such as Arkansas, Idaho, Oklahoma, and the Dakotas, were competing for the same dollars—Nevada legislators lowered the residency requirement for divorce to three months in 1927, and to six weeks in 1931. Although Nevada was the least populous state, with only 77,000 residents, it had the highest divorce rate during the interwar period.

Despite a 300 percent increase in the rate of divorce during the 1920s, marriage remained the norm for most Americans. Divorces, if they could be obtained at all, were often physically, emotionally, and financially draining, and traveling out of state to end a marriage was an option reserved mostly for the rich. Moreover, individuals who divorced or who remained single, especially women, often faced social stigmatization.

Families

Including those who were remarried, nearly 70 percent of all American adults were married during the 1920s. The age at first marriage declined somewhat during the course of the decade, to just over twenty-four for males and just over twenty-one for females.

Children remained the center of married life during the Jazz Age. However, the relationship between parents and their children changed significantly after World War I. The increase in the number of children being schooled outside the home, a youth-oriented peer culture, wage labor, and the automobile meant that middle-class children were no longer as dependent on their parents as they had been in the past. The strict discipline and harsh punishment that were once the norm for parental authority gave way to a more open, loving, nurturing relationship. Older children who helped their parents navigate through an increasingly modern, urban society could actually gain power and status within the family. New notions of the ideal family during the 1920s did not focus on traditional modes of discipline and gender and generational hierarchies but emphasized more democratic, expressively affectionate relations between parents and children. Popular media and a vast array of experts, educators, and social observers contributed greatly to changing attitudes toward child rearing during the 1920s.

Although it seemed that marriage in the 1920s was intended to promote the happiness and sexual satisfaction of both spouses, both men and women faced intense pressures to fulfill the traditional ideas about gender roles. Husbands and wives felt increasingly empowered to end an unhappy marriage, but divorces could be difficult to get and often carried with them the price of social stigmatization. Children remained the central focus of most married couples, but those couples were caring for their children in new ways. Despite the changing ideas about marriage, divorce, and the family during the 1920s, many long-standing social traditions and realities of daily living continued.

Michael A. Rembis

See also: Birth Control; Children and Child Rearing; Health and Medicine; Housing; Population and Demographics; Sex and Sexuality; Sheppard-Towner Act (1921); Social Gospel; Suburbs; Women and Gender; Youth.

Further Reading

Fass, Paula S. *The Damned and the Beautiful: American Youth in the 1920s.* New York: Oxford University Press, 1977.

Kyvig, David E. *Daily Life in the United States, 1920–1940: How Americans Lived Through the "Roaring Twenties" and the Great Depression.* Chicago: Ivan R. Dee, 2002.

May, Elaine Tyler. *Great Expectations: Marriage and Divorce in Post-Victorian America.* Chicago: University of Chicago Press, 1980.

Mayer, Louis B. (1882–1957)

Louis Burt Mayer, a founder of the Hollywood studio system and head of Metro-Goldwyn-Mayer (MGM), serves as the classic example of the paternalistic, tyrannical, ruthless, and egocentric movie mogul lording over his studio kingdom. Yet he believed that his power should be used for a greater purpose—to produce family-friendly motion pictures with a clear moral center.

He was born Eliezer Mayer in Minsk, Russia, in 1882, but his exact birth date is unknown. He later adopted July 4, America's Independence Day, as his birthday. In 1886, his family emigrated to Saint John, New Brunswick, Canada, where his father started a scrap-metal business. As a teenager, Mayer began working in the business full-time, but he did not get along with his father. In 1904, he went to Boston to strike out on his own.

When it became clear that he would never make it rich in the junk business, Mayer turned his sights to the motion picture industry. In 1907, he opened his first movie theater, in Haverhill, Massachusetts. Within a few years, he owned the largest theater chain in New England. But he had greater ambitions. In 1914, he purchased the New England distribution rights to D.W. Griffith's hit film *Birth of a Nation* and received a substantial return on the investment, as the film generated nearly $5 million in revenues, an extraordinary amount for filmmakers of the day. Then, with various partners, Mayer began producing original films, first through a company called Alco, which later became Metro Pictures Corporation, and later through First National and others. After a series of power struggles with his partners, he went west to start his own Hollywood production company, Louis B. Mayer Pictures, in 1917.

He produced a string of romantic melodramas, or "women's pictures," featuring Jazz Age stars such as Anita Stewart, Anna Q. Nilsson, and Norma Shearer. His first feature film, *Virtuous Wives* (1918), starring Stewart, the first actress he signed to a contract, was a modest success. Mayer, however, was more interested in the financial and power-broking aspects of moviemaking than in the films themselves, so in 1923, he lured Irving Thalberg away from Universal Studios to become his new production chief. It would prove a winning partnership.

In 1924, Marcus Loew bought Louis B. Mayer Pictures and made Mayer the West Coast head of the new company, Metro-Goldwyn-Mayer. The first property Mayer and Thalberg took on, *Ben Hur* (1925), was a big hit. For decades to come, MGM would set the Hollywood standard for glamorous stars appearing in big-budget pictures, resulting in huge box-office returns. In the 1920s and 1930s, Hollywood's golden age, MGM created such stars as Rudolph Valentino, Clark Gable, Greta Garbo, Lon Chaney, Mickey Rooney, Joan Crawford, Katharine Hepburn, Judy Garland, and Jean Harlow. Directors such as King Vidor, George Cukor, and Ernst Lubitsch did some of their best work at MGM. Films such as *The Big Parade* (1925) and *Broadway Melody* (1929) represent some of MGM's consistently high-end, high-quality productions.

While Thalberg was undoubtedly the creative force and received most of the credit for the studio's dominance, Mayer played a key role in MGM's success. In fact, Thalberg never produced a film without first getting Mayer's approval. Although Mayer's taste in movies may have run toward the mawkish and sentimental, he excelled at deal making and was a feared and respected manager of employees. Creating glamorous, escapist movies, Thalberg and Mayer kept MGM, the "Tiffany of studios," consistently profitable, even through the worst years of the Depression.

Mayer, the father of two daughters who married powerful men in the filmmaking community, saw himself as a father figure to his employees. If they pleased him, he could be generous and protective. If they displeased him, he could be spiteful and cruel. When the actor Clark Gable demanded a raise, Mayer threatened to tell Gable's wife about her husband's extramarital affairs. Mayer was jealous of his position at MGM and did not like to share power. When Thalberg survived a heart attack in 1932, he returned to work to find he was no longer head of production, as Mayer, according to some, was growing resentful of Thalberg's power and success. The MGM head offered Thalberg a production deal instead.

After Thalberg died in 1937, Mayer became head of production as well as studio chief, making him the sole titan of MGM's West Coast operations. As the 1930s passed into the 1940s, Mayer became the highest paid man in America. He was also a firm supporter of Republican politics, a breeder of thoroughbred horses, and Hollywood's leading ambassador. As the public face of the industry, he was always working to achieve more prestige and mainstream respectability for the movie business—and himself. Mayer lorded over Hollywood's most prosperous studio during the most prosperous times in the film industry.

After World War II, however, audiences began demanding realism in their movies, and Mayer would not comply. Sticking to the formula of recognizable stars in wholesome films, MGM's output was typified by the Andy Hardy series, and profits began to shrink. In the late 1940s, producer Dore Schary was brought in, and MGM began releasing more realistic "message pictures." Schary was no Thalberg, however, and MGM was unable to retain its market dominance. A long-brewing feud with East Coast headquarters resulted in Mayer's firing in 1951. Refusing to accept defeat, he tried to wrest control of MGM through a corporate coup, but the attempt failed. He retired from public life quietly, and bitterly. Mayer died of leukemia on October 29, 1957, at the age of seventy-two.

Tom Cerasulo

See also: Film; Film Industry.

Further Reading

Altman, Diana. *Hollywood East: Louis B. Mayer and the Origins of the Studio System.* Secaucus, NJ: Carol, 1992.
Crowther, Bosley. *Hollywood Rajah.* New York: Holt, 1960.
Eyman, Scott. *Lion of Hollywood: The Life and Legend of Louis B. Mayer.* New York: Simon & Schuster, 2005.
Gabler, Neal. *An Empire of Their Own: How the Jews Invented Hollywood.* New York: Anchor, 1989.
Higham, Charles. *The Merchant of Dreams: A Biography of Louis B. Mayer.* New York: Macmillan, 1993.

McAdoo, William G. (1863–1941)

As U.S. secretary of the treasury from 1913 to 1918, William Gibbs McAdoo was one of the most visible members of President Woodrow Wilson's cabinet. In the 1920s, he attempted to parlay his experience and reputation into a successful bid for the presidency but ran afoul of his own mistakes and of the deep-seated cultural and ideological divisions within the Democratic Party and the nation as a whole.

McAdoo was born on October 31, 1863, in Marietta, Georgia. His family lived in Milledgeville, Georgia, until 1877, when they moved to Knoxville, Tennessee, where his father accepted a professorship at the University of Tennessee. After attending the university until 1882, McAdoo served as deputy clerk of the U.S. Circuit Court in Chattanooga, during which time he read law and was admitted to the Tennessee bar in 1885. In addition to practicing law, McAdoo invested $25,000 in, and became president of, the Knoxville Street Railway Company in 1889. When this venture failed in 1892, he moved with his wife, Sara Fleming McAdoo, and their children to New York City, where he became involved in the sale of securities and the transit business. Later, as president of the Hudson and Manhattan Railroad Company, he achieved his most notable early success supervising the completion of the Hudson Tunnel that linked New York and New Jersey.

McAdoo was an early and active supporter of Woodrow Wilson's bid for the Democratic presidential nomination in 1912. Having proved himself to be an efficient businessman and a progressive leader, as demonstrated by his equitable treatment of his employees and his advocacy for women's rights, Wilson rewarded McAdoo's efforts on his behalf and appointed him secretary of the treasury. In this position, he was involved in such Wilsonian economic policies as tariff reduction, establishment of the Federal Reserve System, inauguration of the federal income tax, and creation of a system of farm credit. During World War I, McAdoo successfully argued for the establishment of a shipping board to maintain the flow of goods to Europe, coordinated the Liberty Loan campaign, and served as director general of the nation's rail system following its nationalization in 1918. After the armistice, McAdoo resigned from the Wilson cabinet and returned to New York to resume the practice of law, justifying his departure on the grounds of fatigue and the need to address the deteriorating condition of his personal finances.

McAdoo's reputation as a progressive and able treasury secretary, along with his personal ties to Wilson, whose daughter he had married following the death of his first wife, caused many Democrats to view McAdoo as heir apparent to Wilson. Although he aspired to the presidency, McAdoo was somewhat ambivalent about seeking the nomination in 1920, in part because of uncertainty about whether Wilson would seek a third term and in part because the Republicans appeared to have a good chance of winning the White House. By the time of the Democratic National Convention, however, he was clearly willing to become a candidate. In the early roll calls, McAdoo received the largest number of delegate votes but was unable to muster sufficient support to secure the nomination. Finally, on the forty-fourth ballot, after Attorney General A. Mitchell Palmer released his delegates, Ohio Governor James M. Cox won the nomination. (Cox subsequently lost the presidential election to Warren G. Harding.)

McAdoo remained an important party leader throughout the early 1920s. His move from New York to California, where the political climate seemed more hospitable to his brand of progressive politics, was a clear signal that he intended to seek the nomination in 1924. McAdoo campaigned that year as the heir of the William Jennings Bryan and Woodrow Wilson tradition within the Democratic Party, hoping to forge what he regarded as a progressive, Southern, and Western coalition against the conservative, machine-dominated urban North and Northeast. He portrayed himself as the champion of the common people, a foe of special privilege, and a supporter of Prohibition.

Many Democrats believed McAdoo would win his party's nomination, but in early 1924, news was released that McAdoo had accepted an annual retainer of $25,000 from oil executive Edward L. Doheny, who was implicated in the Teapot Dome scandal. Although McAdoo's legal services to Doheny were unrelated to Teapot Dome, his association with Doheny and his legal representation of large corporate interests eroded his image as an antagonist of big business. In addition, his failure to renounce the backing of the Ku Klux Klan and his support for Prohibition undermined his strength with the Northern urban wing of the party, where many conservative machine politicians were already hostile to his brand of progressivism.

The 1924 Democratic National Convention has become legendary as one of the most acrimonious and protracted political gatherings in U.S. history. It mirrored the polarities within American society of Protestant versus Roman Catholic, rural versus urban, dry versus wet, and traditional versus modernizing, as well as the ideological, geographic, and cultural schisms within the Democratic Party. When the delegates convened at Madison Square Garden in New York, McAdoo had a formidable opponent in governor Alfred E. Smith of New York. For more than two weeks, delegates struggled to decide on a nominee. As a result of the deadlock between the two frontrunners, John W. Davis of West Virginia emerged as a compromise candidate and was nominated after 103 ballots.

After his failed bid for the nomination in 1924, McAdoo's influence in national party politics declined. He returned to Washington as a senator from California in 1933, a role in which he served as a valuable ally to President Franklin D. Roosevelt. He resigned in 1938 after California Democrats did not renominate him as a candidate for his Senate seat. McAdoo died on February 1, 1941, in Washington, D.C.

Robert F. Martin

See also: Davis, John W.; Democratic Party; Election of 1920; Election of 1924; Wilson, Woodrow.

Further Reading

Broesamle, John J. *William Gibbs McAdoo: A Passion for Change 1863–1917.* Port Washington, NY: Kennikat, 1973.

Craig, Douglas B. *After Wilson: The Struggle for the Democratic Party, 1920–1934.* Chapel Hill: University of North Carolina Press, 1992.

McKay, Claude (1889–1948)

Claude McKay, along with Langston Hughes, Zora Neale Hurston, and Countee Cullen, helped create the artistic movement known as the Harlem Renaissance during the 1920s. Like these other African American authors, McKay struggled not only against American racism but also against divisions within the African American community. Also like other writers during the Harlem Renaissance, McKay sought to establish a distinctly African American cultural voice that was founded on ethnic pride and individual expression.

He was born Festus Claudius McKay on September 15, 1889, to a farming family in the Jamaican village of Sunny Ville. His father, Thomas Francis McKay, owned enough land to be allowed to vote and encouraged his sons to further their education. McKay showed an early aptitude for literature and published his first book of poems, *Songs of Jamaica,* in 1912 with the assistance of Walter Jekyll, an English landowner and McKay's first patron. Under Jekyll's tutelage the young McKay developed a respect for traditional English poetic forms, in particular the sonnet. But Jekyll also encouraged McKay to explore traditional Jamaican idiom and meter, and *Songs of Jamaica* was written in the Jamaican patois.

McKay's second volume of poetry, *Constab Ballads,* about his experiences as a Jamaican police officer, came out the same year. It was in 1912, as well, that he moved to the United States, to attend the Tuskegee Institute in Alabama. McKay was dismayed by the level of racism he encountered in the American South and transferred the following year to Kansas State University to study agronomy. After two years in Kansas, however, McKay dropped his agricultural studies and relocated to Harlem. He married a friend from Jamaica, Eulalie Lewars, but the couple soon divorced.

In 1917, McKay published his first two poems in the United States: "The Harlem Dancer" and "Invocation." A departure from his earlier work in Jamaican dialect, the poems caught the attention of two men who would become important patrons: Frank Harris, editor of *Pearson's* magazine, and Max Eastman, editor of the Socialist publication *The Liberator.* Among the earliest celebrations of African American life in Harlem, in "The Harlem Dancer," McKay painted the scene of a dancer whose body is "devoured" by the stares of lustful young men and their prostitute escorts, but whose own eyes are far away from the scene. Unlike fellow Harlem Renaissance poet Langston Hughes, who was strongly influenced by the early modernism of poets such as Carl Sandburg, McKay's poetic form was traditional. "The Harlem Dancer" was a sonnet with an unconventional theme. Like his Jamaican works, it mingled different cultures and poetic forms.

In 1919, McKay published "If We Must Die" in *The Liberator.* In this sonnet, McKay attacked the race riots that swept the United States in the aftermath of World War I. Whereas Hughes, in such poems as "The Negro Speaks of Rivers," took on a voice that was distinctly African American, McKay used tone and meter that were more heroic and Victorian: "Like men we'll face the murderous, cowardly pack / Pressed to the wall, dying, but fighting back!" It was this willingness to use traditional form with contemporary subjects that distinguished McKay from his Harlem Renaissance contemporaries.

Meanwhile, McKay was becoming increasingly involved in left-wing politics. Living in London from 1919 to 1921, he read extensively in Communist literature and theory and wrote for *The Workers' Dreadnought,* a London Socialist publication. In 1921, he returned to Harlem to edit *The Liberator* and published another collection of poetry, *Harlem Shadows.* Between 1922 and 1933, he visited the Soviet Union and North Africa, addressed the Comintern in Moscow, and traveled throughout Europe.

His novel *Home to Harlem* (1928), a popular success, won the Harmon Gold Award for Literature, but in some African American circles, it met with severe criticism for its portrayal of the underside of life in Harlem. W.E.B. Du Bois claimed to be nauseated by the book, believing that it helped sustain negative impressions of African Americans and thereby undermined the quest for equality. Nevertheless, McKay's other works of fiction in the 1920s and early 1930s—the novel *Banjo* (1929), the short-story collection *Gingertown* (1932), and the novel *Banana Bottom* (1933)—all followed similar themes: the damage done to an individual when an essential element of personal identity is repressed or misconstrued by society. In *Banana Bottom,* for example, McKay tells the story of a Jamaican expatriate, Bita Plant, who, after studying in London, returns to her home and suffers from an identity divided between her English education and her Jamaican roots.

In 1936, with financial support from the Federal Writers' Project, McKay wrote an autobiography, *A Long Way from Home* (1937). *Harlem: Negro Metropolis* (1940) was also autobiographical. McKay continued to write for Socialist periodicals, including *The Nation* and *The New Leader,* but his prose writing during this period never achieved the popularity of his early poetry or the novel *Home to Harlem.*

In 1940, McKay rejected his agnostic inclinations and converted to Catholicism; four years later, he moved to Chicago and worked for the Catholic Youth Organization. He died of heart failure on May 22, 1948, and was buried in New York City. His *Selected Poems* (1953) was published posthumously, as was *My Green Hills of Jamaica* (1977), another autobiographical work.

Jason Stacy

See also: Harlem Renaissance; Hughes, Langston; Locke, Alain; Poetry.

Further Reading

Egar, Emmanuel. *The Poets of Rage: Wole Soyinka, Jean Toomer, and Claude McKay.* Lanham, MD: University Press of America, 2005.

Gosciak, Josh. *The Shadowed Country: Claude McKay and the Romance of the Victorians.* Piscataway, NJ: Rutgers University Press, 2006.

McKay, Claude. *Complete Poems.* Champaign: University of Illinois Press, 2004.

Rameesh, Kotti Sree. *Claude McKay: The Literary Identity from Jamaica to Harlem and Beyond.* New York: McFarland, 2006.

McPherson, Aimee Semple (1890–1944)

Among the most famous Evangelical preachers of the Jazz Age, Aimee Semple McPherson had one of the largest congregations in the country, the Foursquare Gospel Church in Los Angeles, which she built with the donations of her many parishioners. "Sister Aimee," as she was called, was also one of the first preachers to make use of the new medium of radio to broadcast her sermons to a regional audience.

She was born Aimee Elizabeth Kennedy on October 9, 1890, in the small town of Salford, Ontario. Her first exposure to religion came from her parents; her father, James Morgan Kennedy, was a struggling Methodist farmer, and her mother, Minnie, was a member of the Salvation Army. Through her mother, Aimee was grounded in theological conservatism, Christian service, and self-discipline. It was not until age seventeen, however, that she was "born again," under the influence of the traveling preacher Robert James Semple, whom she married in 1908. Together, the couple led revival meetings throughout North America and in 1910 went to China as Christian missionaries. Both came down with malaria in Hong Kong and Robert died; Aimee gave birth to a daughter later that year.

She returned to North America and settled in New York City, working with her mother at the Salvation Army. While in New York, she met Harold McPherson, an accountant, and the two married in 1912. The following year, after giving birth to a son, she claimed to have had a near-death experience during childbirth, a claim that may have stemmed from postpartum depression.

McPherson later said she tried to restrict herself to the duties of a housewife and mother, but the call to evangelize was too strong to resist. She embarked on a preaching tour of Canada in 1913 and, by 1916, was permanently touring both Canada and the United States in her "Gospel Car," a Packard festooned with religious signs. In 1917, she launched a monthly religious newspaper, *The Bridal Call,* for which she wrote most of the copy. Harold McPherson became increasingly frustrated by his wife's constant touring, and the two separated in 1918. Three years later, he filed for divorce on grounds of abandonment.

Although her education was limited to a few semesters of high school, McPherson proved to be a quick study of the Bible. Physically attractive and charismatic, she preached in the dramatic and emotional Pentecostal style. She also began wearing white gowns while preaching, lending her a virginal air that became part of her performance and appeal.

Despite her growing following, McPherson remained poor, and she looked for new territory in which to spread the gospel and establish herself as a successful preacher. In 1918 she moved with her children and mother to Los Angeles. At that time, Los Angeles was gaining a reputation as a center of Evangelical Christianity, a form of religion popular among the many conservative Midwesterners who flocked to the fast-growing city for its climate and economic opportunities. McPherson's flamboyant and theatrical preaching style also appealed to the citizens of a city in which moviemaking was becoming a major industry.

While preaching in revival tents around Southern California in 1921, McPherson claimed to have experienced a vision. In it, she said, she saw the four-faced figure referred to by the prophet Ezekiel in the Bible, consisting of the four animals associated with the gospels of Matthew (human), Mark (lion), Luke (bull), and John (eagle). She proclaimed her vision the "four square gospel" of Jesus as savior, baptizer, healer, and coming king of mankind. This theology is part of the Pentecostal movement, which also stresses that individuals, through gifts of the Holy Spirit, can experience a direct connection to God. Such gifts, supernaturally bestowed on the believer by God, include, among other things, faith healing, speaking in tongues, and prophecy.

Her vision brought her even more followers, who soon flocked to her revival tents in the thousands. With their donations, she erected the Angelus Temple, or Foursquare Gospel Church, in 1923, which still stands in the Echo Park neighborhood of Los Angeles. The facility seated 5,000 parishioners and was soon equipped with radio-broadcasting equipment, making McPherson the first woman to preach over the airwaves. When she started her own station, KFSG, in 1924, she became the first woman to be granted a

Radio preacher Aimee Semple McPherson strikes a dramatic pose at an Evangelical meeting. Her sermons at the Foursquare Gospel Church in Los Angeles drew thousands of parishioners before a sex scandal in 1926 undermined her credibility and popularity. *(Library of Congress, LC-USZ62-92329)*

broadcasting license by the Federal Radio Commission (later the Federal Communications Commission). McPherson also tried to spread the gospel in more traditional ways. In 1926, she founded a Bible school—the Lighthouse of International Foursquare Evangelism of Los Angeles. And in 1927, she declared her church the base for a new sect of Christianity, the International Church of the Foursquare Gospel.

While McPherson had a national following among Evangelicals, it was her mysterious but temporary disappearance in 1926 that captivated the media and the general public. On the evening of May 18, she went to swim in Ocean Park, a beachside community near Santa Monica, with her secretary. An experienced swimmer, she went beyond the breakers, as was her habit, and then vanished. With the media playing the story to a national audience, an intensive search was conducted—with a widespread following. After several days, however, she was given up as drowned. Then, six weeks later, a ransom note came to the Angelus Temple demanding that church officials pay $500,000 or McPherson would be sold overseas in the "white slave trade." Before the church could react, the preacher's mother received a call from her, saying she was in the border town of Douglas, Arizona. McPherson told police and the press that she had been abducted, taken to Mexico, and tortured before escaping through the desert to Douglas.

Both the media and officials were skeptical, as she showed signs of neither torture nor a desert journey on foot. Then came news of witnesses who claimed to have seen her at the seaside resort of Carmel, on the central California coast, with a man who looked like her former radio engineer. But the fraud could not be proved, and a grand jury failed to indict her or her alleged accomplice.

To restore her image, McPherson went on a grand revival tour of the country in the late 1920s that included high-profile preaching engagements at underground speakeasies, but the scandal had hurt her. While some came to see her out of curiosity, few were willing to donate money or embrace her preaching. She returned to Los Angeles, where her congregation shriveled. In 1931, she married a former choir member, David Hutton, but that marriage also ended in divorce. Although donations dwindled with the Great Depression, she became active in opening and running soup kitchens and free health clinics for the poor. During World War II, she sold war bonds. She died on September 27, 1944, of an overdose of barbiturates, complicated by a kidney ailment. The coroner ruled her death accidental.

James Ciment and Andrew J. Waskey

See also: Evangelicals and Evangelical Christianity; Fundamentalism, Christian; Radio.

Further Reading

Blumhofer, Edith. *Aimee Semple McPherson: Everybody's Sister.* Grand Rapids, MI: W.B. Eerdmans, 1993.

Epstein, Daniel M. *Sister Aimee: The Life of Aimee Semple McPherson.* New York: Harcourt Brace Jovanovich, 1993.

Thomas, Lately. *Storming Heaven: The Lives and Turmoils of Minnie Kennedy and Aimee Semple McPherson.* New York: William Morris, 1970.

———. *The Vanishing Evangelist.* New York: Viking, 1959.

Mead, Margaret (1901–1978)

Anthropologist Margaret Mead was an iconic figure in twentieth-century America. She was the rare social scientist who became a household name, and the rare woman in a field dominated by men. Mead was well-known by the press and public for fifty years, from the time she published her first book, *Coming of Age in Samoa* (1928), a surprise best seller that, through her scientific research, presented yet another challenge to the Victorian sexual and social codes under siege during the Jazz Age.

Mead was born in Philadelphia on December 16, 1901. Her father, Edward, taught economics at the prestigious Wharton School of Business at the

University of Pennsylvania. He once told his precocious young daughter, "It's a pity you aren't a boy; you'd have gone far." Mead later said she took this as a challenge. Mead had a powerful role model in overcoming the sexual constraints of her day in her mother, Emily Fogg Mead, a prominent feminist and sociologist of immigrant family life.

At Barnard College in New York during the early 1920s, Mead found her life's calling under the tutelage of German-born Franz Boaz and his assistant Ruth Benedict. Boaz and Benedict were interested in demonstrating, through cross-cultural fieldwork and analysis of non-Western, premodern tribes and cultures, that "nurture" is more important than "nature" in the construction of social mores and practices. This point of view ran counter to some of the beliefs held by conservative Christian Fundamentalists at a time when events such as the Scopes trial, youth rebellion, and the "New Woman" were challenging their traditional assumptions.

Boaz originally wanted Mead to do her fieldwork among American Indians, but Mead insisted on going to Polynesia. In 1926, she embarked on an arduous, ambitious expedition of several months to the South Pacific, to live and work among the young women of the island culture of Samoa. This endeavor was the basis for the doctoral dissertation she presented to Boaz at Columbia University, in which Mead's most famous claim was that "adolescence is not necessarily a time of stress and strain, but that cultural conditions make it so." Exploring the cultures of traditional peoples and using her discoveries to critique Western cultural practices became a hallmark of Mead's work. In New Guinea and elsewhere, Mead criticized as needless and artificial the neurosis-inducing structures of Western life, with their repressive sexual codes of chastity and monogamy, prolonged sheltering of children from initiation into adult life, and focus on the nuclear family as the necessary building block of society. To this system she contrasted the Samoan girls she interviewed and observed, who exhibited a more casual approach to premarital sex, marriage, and divorce; early involvement in the rituals and responsibilities of the community; and devotion to an extended family with many adult role models.

Coming of Age in Samoa, written in an accessible, descriptive (rather than densely scientific) style, became a sensation upon its publication in 1928. While there is little in the study that would seem particularly daring to twenty-first-century readers, it is easy to understand the firestorm of interest it attracted in

Margaret Mead's research on South Pacific youth, published in the best-selling *Coming of Age in Samoa* (1928), offered readers one of the first positive firsthand portrayals of a non-Western culture and broke new ground in the field of cultural anthropology. *(APA/Hulton Archive/Getty Images)*

the late 1920s, amid the culture wars and generational battles of the Jazz Age. Mead would go on from this debut to decades of prominence as a researcher, social critic, and feminist from her post as curator of the American Museum of Natural History. In the 1960s, another period of rebellion and cultural conflict, Mead was esteemed by many in the younger generation for her tireless energy, independence in both her personal and professional life, her stature as a founding figure of the "sexual revolution," and her activism in human rights, environmental, and other social causes. Her opinion on all manner of issues made news until her death on November 15, 1978.

Controversy about Mead's methods and conclusions continued posthumously. In 1983, New Zealand professor Derek Freeman assailed Mead's landmark Samoa study as "a work of anthropological fiction," misrepresenting and romanticizing the realities of "primitive" peoples due to the unreliability of the subjects she interviewed and, in general, an insufficiently rigorous methodology. The debate about Mead's methods and conclusions will no doubt continue indefinitely, but her impact on the ferment of the Jazz

Age, and on American cultural discussions throughout the twentieth century, is lasting and undeniable.

Gregory D. Sumner

See also: Children and Child Rearing; Science; Sex and Sexuality; Youth.

Further Reading

Bowman-Kruhm, Mary. *Margaret Mead: A Biography*. Westport, CT: Greenwood, 2003.

Howard, Jane. *Margaret Mead, a Life*. New York: Simon & Schuster, 1984.

Mead, Margaret. *Coming of Age in Samoa: A Psychological Study of Primitive Youth for Western Civilisation*. New York: Perennial Classics, 2001.

Medicine

See Health and Medicine

Mellon, Andrew (1855–1937)

As U.S. secretary of the treasury during the administrations of three presidents (Warren G. Harding, Calvin Coolidge, and Herbert Hoover), Andrew Mellon was the dominant figure in setting U.S. economic policy during the boom years of the Jazz Age. Holding the position from the beginning of the Harding administration in March 1921 until being replaced by Ogden Mills late in the Hoover administration in February 1932, he was the longest-serving treasury secretary in U.S. history. During his tenure, the country experienced the "Republican prosperity" of the 1920s, as well as the dramatic economic decline following the stock market crash of 1929. His policies favoring tax cuts for the wealthy and limiting public spending are often cited by historians as contributing to both the economic boom of the Jazz Age and the Great Depression that followed.

Andrew Mellon was born in Pittsburgh, Pennsylvania, on March 24, 1855. His father, Thomas Mellon, was a prominent local banker who taught him about finance. Mellon graduated from Western University of Pennsylvania (now the University of Pittsburgh) in 1873 and started a lumber company with his brother, Richard. Within a few years, he and his brother joined his father's banking firm, and by 1882, at the age of twenty-seven, Mellon took over management of the institution. In 1898, the bank reorganized as the Union Trust Company and in subsequent years became a major investor in Gulf Oil, the Aluminum Company of America (Alcoa), and the Pittsburgh Coal Company. In 1900, he married Nora McMullen, and the couple had two children.

Treasury Secretary

On the advice of Pennsylvania Republican leader Philander Knox, President Harding nominated Andrew Mellon to serve as secretary of the treasury, and he was confirmed by the Senate on March 4, 1921. Mellon's philosophy became central to the Republican administration's fiscal policies. He believed that lowering government expenses would allow a reduction in taxes, while the government would receive an increase in revenues due to the greater earning and purchasing power of the taxpayers. He successfully challenged an early Republican-led effort in Congress to replace the income tax with a federal sales tax, arguing that the former was less regressive, but he was also critical of what he saw as excessively high tax rates and wasteful government spending, made worse during World War I. Mellon believed that the $24 billion federal debt and the $6.5 billion budget for 1921 were undermining the economy. He proposed to lower federal spending by cutting waste while lowering taxes. If this was done with proper planning, he believed, government revenues would exceed spending and allow the government to reduce the federal debt.

Mellon's first steps as treasury secretary indicated his support for big business. In 1921, he proposed and got a reduction in the corporate income tax. He supported the return of railroads to their owners after World War I at no cost to the owners, despite heavy government investment in overhauling the lines. He also pushed for the nomination of businessmen to federal regulatory agencies to decrease red tape. The next year he supported and received from Congress an increase in the tariff rate to help protect American industries.

In 1923, he proposed the "Mellon Plan," his first comprehensive proposal to establish principles for government finance. The plan called for a reduction of income tax rates (dropping the maximum rate from 50 percent to 30 percent) and a reduction or elimination of other taxes, such as the inheritance tax, luxury tax, and capital gains tax. Most of the plan was adopted by Congress as the Revenue Act of 1924. By that year, Mellon had lowered federal spending to $3.5 billion, cutting the federal budget nearly in half. By 1930, he had managed to raise revenue and decrease spending enough to reduce the federal deficit to $16 billion.

Mellon's tenure in the 1920s also saw organizational changes in the Treasury Department. Under his charge, the Bureau of the Budget was created to report on government expenditures and centralize spending. Overseas, he helped establish the World War Foreign Debt Commission in 1922 to negotiate specific payment plans for nations that owed money to the United States. France and Great Britain, the two biggest debtors, together owed more than $7 billion.

After the Crash

With the onset of the Great Depression in 1929, Andrew Mellon's financial policies, once popular, came under increasing criticism. As late as 1930, he counseled President Herbert Hoover not to take any drastic action in the face of the Depression, arguing that the decline was a necessary adjustment that eliminated weak companies in the economy. Although this advice ran counter to Hoover's own inclinations, the president followed Mellon's advice during the first full year of the Depression. As the economic decline continued, even Mellon thought that some revision in strategy should be considered. But the change of heart came too late. Facing declining support within the administration, Mellon left the cabinet on February 12, 1932, to assume the position of ambassador to Great Britain, a post he held for a year, until being replaced early in the Franklin D. Roosevelt administration.

Mellon never served in public office again. In 1935 the government investigated his 1931 income tax return for fraud; he was cleared of all charges, but not until after his death on August, 27, 1937. Shortly before he died, Mellon donated $10 million and his private art collection, worth an estimated $15 million, to establish the National Gallery of Art in Washington, D.C.

Michael Faubion

See also: Coolidge, Calvin; Economic Policy; Harding, Warren G.; Hoover, Herbert.

Further Reading

Barber, James. *From New Era to New Deal: Herbert Hoover, the Economists, and American Economic Policy.* Cambridge, UK: Cambridge University Press, 1985.

Cannadine, David. *Mellon: An American Life.* New York: Alfred A. Knopf, 2006.

Love, Alfred. *Andrew W. Mellon: The Man and His Work.* Whitefish, MT: Kessinger, 2003.

Soule, George. *Prosperity Decade: From War to Depression, 1917–1929.* New York: Rinehart, 1947.

Mencken, H.L. (1880–1956)

Best known for his satirical representations of the American middle class, H.L. Mencken was an influential journalist and social critic in the first half of the twentieth century. Because of his wit, Mencken is often quoted. His book *The American Language* (1919), a comparison of British and American English, still stands as one of the most comprehensive linguistic analyses of American English to date.

Henry Louis Mencken was born on September 12, 1880, in Baltimore, Maryland. His father, August Mencken, was a cigar manufacturer. At nineteen, Mencken began a career in journalism, first at the *Baltimore Morning Herald* and, in 1906, at the

Journalist H.L. Mencken of the *Baltimore Sun* won a national following as the cynical chronicler of American popular culture in the 1920s. Among academics, he is perhaps best remembered for *The American Language,* his 1919 treatise on American English. *(MPI/Stringer/Hulton Archive/Getty Images)*

Baltimore Sun. Though Mencken also wrote fiction and poetry in these years, he first established his reputation as a literary critic. His first nonfiction book was *George Bernard Shaw: His Plays* (1905). In 1908, he began writing literary criticism for *The Smart Set,* a well-known literary magazine of the day, becoming editor in 1914. There, Mencken helped new authors such as Theodore Dreiser and Sinclair Lewis find wide audiences.

An early interest in Nietzschean philosophy led Mencken to a libertarian ideology and a distrust of grand schemes for the improvement of humanity. Mencken's 1907 *The Philosophy of Friedrich Nietzsche* was one of the first analyses of that philosopher published in the United States. Mencken's rejection of Woodrow Wilson's justifications for American entrance into World War I in 1914 and his tacit sympathy for Germany inspired many to label him unpatriotic during the war years. In the next decade, however, Mencken's contrarian nature fueled his popularity.

His iconoclastic personality made Mencken a celebrity on American college campuses during the 1920s. In 1924, with support from Alfred A. Knopf, Mencken and drama critic George Jean Nathan launched *American Mercury* magazine, a favorite among college students and faculty until the onset of the Great Depression. Mencken lent public support to many of the authors whose names would be equated with literature in the 1920s, including F. Scott Fitzgerald, Dorothy Parker, and Eugene O'Neill. In addition to his work on the magazine, Mencken contributed columns to the *Chicago Tribune, The Nation,* and the *New York American.*

Mencken's editorials, which typically dealt with timely topical issues, often served as starting points for broad critiques of society, politics, and culture. Although he is remembered for his respect for individual freedom and the scorn he heaped on American puritanism and the "booboisie"—his term for middle-brow culture—most of his writing was in direct response to contemporary issues. For example, his well-known quips against organized religion were a response to the reemergence of Evangelical Christianity in the 1920s. In regard to the trial of the Tennessee teacher John Scopes for teaching evolution to his students, Mencken declared in an article for the *Baltimore Sun* titled "Homo Neanderthalis" that "great masses of men, even in this inspired republic, are precisely where the mob was at the dawn of history. They are ignorant, they are dishonest, they are

cowardly, they are ignoble. They know little if anything that is worth knowing, and there is not the slightest sign of a natural desire among them to increase their knowledge."

Mencken wrote in hyperbole to raise his voice over what he felt was the din of contemporary opinions. Thus, the state of Arkansas became the "apex of moronia," the Anglo-Saxon people became the most slavish in human history, a good laugh was worth more than the most logical of deductions, every decent man must be ashamed of the government under which he lived, and puritanism was the fear that "someone, somewhere, may be happy."

Mencken's modern critics charge him with racism and sexism. Indeed, Mencken sometimes resorted to ethnic slurs in his writing and expressed what modern readers would interpret as misogynistic statements. But he also argued that white Southerners had debased themselves by implementing segregation and discriminating against African Americans. Mencken expressed similarly flammable sentiments toward Jews, Germans, WASPs, Britons, and Asians. However, as the author and critic Gore Vidal noted about Mencken, "irritability is of no consequence when compared to what really matters, public action." Mencken was one of the first American journalists to denounce the treatment of Jews in Nazi Germany and counted among his best friends the African American author George Schuyler. Mencken's *American Mercury* published more works by African American authors than many other publications of equivalent circulation during the 1920s.

In addition to his many other unpopular positions, Mencken was a notorious "wet," or anti-Prohibition advocate. Although his arguments against Prohibition were generally personal and humorous (he called himself "ombibulous" which, he claimed, meant that he liked to drink just about anything alcoholic), he also claimed that none of the promises of temperance advocates had come to pass. According to Mencken, there was more drunkenness in the country, more crime, and less respect for the law—all the result of the Eighteenth Amendment.

In 1948, Mencken suffered from cerebral thrombosis that damaged his brain. He spent his last years collecting and organizing his published writings and private correspondence. He died on January 29, 1956.

Jason Stacy

See also: American Mercury; Journalism; Scopes Trial (1925).

Further Reading

Mencken, H.L. *The Vintage Mencken.* New York: Vintage Books, 1990.

Rogers, Marion Elizabeth. *Mencken: The American Iconoclast.* New York: Oxford University Press, 2005.

Teachout, Terry. *The Skeptic: A Life of H.L. Mencken.* New York: Harper Perennial, 2003.

Mexico, Relations with

Relations between Mexico and the United States were in a state of transition throughout the Jazz Age, shifting from a period of open hostility in the 1910s to one of warmer but still guarded relations in the 1920s. Under the dictatorship of Porfirio Díaz, Mexico had enjoyed the image of a modern, industrial society that was eager for ties with the United States and Europe. But revolutionaries such as Emiliano Zapata and Pancho Villa sought reform of the elitist system, and Mexico was hit with a period of revolution between 1910 and 1920. Díaz was overthrown in 1911 by Francisco Madero, whose own government came to an end in 1913 when Madero was overthrown and executed.

Military, Political, and Economic Affairs

Over the course of the revolution, the United States generally supported the forces of reformer Venustiano Carranza and recognized him as president of Mexico in 1915. This led to conflict with Pancho Villa, who staged a raid on a U.S. cavalry post near Columbus, New Mexico, in 1916 and looted the town. Villa continued to stage attacks throughout northern Mexico. The United States responded with a military incursion into northern Mexico under the command of General John J. Pershing. He was unable to locate Villa but nearly provoked a war between the nations when U.S. forces skirmished with Carranza's forces in the state of Chihuahua. Although Carranza was at war with Villa, he resented U.S. interference in the country. Mexican outrage over U.S. military interference was one of the key factors leading to a new constitution in 1917 that was decidedly hostile to the rights of foreigners in Mexico.

The constitution of 1917 set the tone for relations between the United States and Mexico throughout the first half of the 1920s. It established a strong central government in Mexico and encouraged the use of power against foreign interests. Of particular concern to U.S. officials were the articles that broke up large estates and placed restrictions on foreign ownership of real estate and mineral resources. Moreover, the government reserved the legal right to seize any private property, a direct statement of support for the principle of nationalization. The constitution also aimed to prevent the exploitation of workers by establishing an eight-hour workday and protecting workers' right to strike. These provisions were especially alarming for U.S. oil companies, as they had invested heavily in Mexico. In 1917, Mexico was the third-largest oil producer in the world, and most of its petroleum went directly to the United States, which re-exported it to other nations, especially its allies in Europe.

American relations with Mexico in the 1920s were also shaped by the legacy of World War I. In January 1917, three months before America entered the war, German Foreign Secretary Arthur Zimmermann had sent a telegram to his country's ambassador in Mexico City, instructing him to make an offer to the Carranza government: If the United States went to war with Germany, Berlin would support a Mexican offensive against the American Southwest and the return of lands taken from Mexico during the Mexican-American War. When the telegram came to light, it produced two strong reactions in the American public: anger at Germany and suspicion of Mexico.

When World War I ended in November 1918, the United States was free to deal with Mexico without fear of German interference. President Woodrow Wilson again sent General Pershing into northern Mexico in 1919 after Villa's forces attacked the Mexican border city of Ciudad Juárez. Wilson feared that fighting from the conflict would spill over onto American territory. Meanwhile, U.S. diplomats demanded that Carranza soften the constitution of 1917, especially the provisions in Article 27 that threatened the land rights of U.S. oil companies. But the issue dragged on through the Mexican political process for years. In 1920, when Alvaro Obregón forced Carranza out and became the president of Mexico, the United States refused to recognize his government until the matter of Article 27 was resolved.

In 1923, the Mexican and U.S. governments finally reached an understanding in the form of the Bucareli Agreement, an accord that protected the property rights of U.S. oil companies in Mexico as long as those companies had been actively drilling for oil prior to 1917. It also helped to stabilize the position of the Mexican government by giving it U.S. diplomatic recognition and providing it with U.S. military aid, including airplanes, machine guns, and rifles, which Obregón promptly used to crush a rebellion led by Adolfo de la Huerta, governor of the northern Mexican state of Sonora.

Religion and Culture

Following the settlement of economic disagreements, the Mexican government's antichurch policies became one of the most significant points of contention with the United States. In 1923, President Plutarco Elías Calles took over from Obregón and attempted to break the hold of the Roman Catholic Church in Mexico by placing a special emphasis on the secularization of education and enforcement of anticlerical laws. In 1925, the issue provoked a violent backlash when defrocked priests launched an uprising against the secular government of Mexico called the Cristero War, and Mexico's bishops shut down the churches in protest over government interference. After almost three years of guerrilla warfare, U.S. Ambassador Dwight Morrow set up a meeting between Calles and the liberal American priest John J. Burke, who brokered a settlement between the government and the bishops.

The Jazz Age was also the era in which social and cultural relations between the United States and Mexico began to blossom. The ideals of the Mexican revolution attracted many American leftists, such as writer John Dos Passos and philosopher John Dewey. Many leftists, as well as other Americans, traveled to Mexico during the 1920s. Ambassador Morrow and his wife, Elizabeth Cutter Morrow, played an active role in encouraging social and cultural relations. Among their many guests were the Mexican painters Diego Rivera and Frida Kahlo, as well as the famous American aviator Charles A. Lindbergh, who introduced the Mexican elite to the emerging culture of air travel. In short, the Jazz Age saw Mexico and the United States come closer together, through economic, political, social, and cultural ties that would continue to strengthen over the decades that followed.

David Stiles

See also: Immigration; Immigration Laws of 1921 and 1924; Latin America, Relations with; Latinos and Latinas.

Further Reading

Delpar, Helen. *The Enormous Vogue of Things Mexican: Cultural Relations Between the United States and Mexico, 1920–1935.* Tuscaloosa: University of Alabama Press, 1992.

Langley, Lester D. *Mexico and the United States: The Fragile Relationship.* Boston: Twayne, 1991.

Raat, W. Dirk. *Mexico and the United States: Ambivalent Vistas.* 3rd ed. Athens: University of Georgia Press, 2004.

Redinger, Matthew A. *American Catholics and the Mexican Revolution, 1924–1936.* Notre Dame, IN: University of Notre Dame Press, 2005.

Migration, Great

The Great Migration was the twentieth-century mass movement of African Americans from the rural South to the cities primarily of the North and West. In the view of some historians, the migration began around the turn of the twentieth century and continued through the 1950s. Others set narrower parameters, arguing that the Great Migration began with World War I and ended with World War II. All agree, however, that the shift fundamentally altered the history of African Americans and of American society as a whole.

The number of persons on the move was substantial. In 1910, roughly 90 percent of America's 10 million African Americans lived in the South, a figure roughly unchanged since the formal ending of slavery in 1865. Of these 9 million, roughly eight in ten lived in rural areas. Between 1915 and 1920, somewhere between 500,000 and 1 million African Americans left the rural South for the urban North and West. A similar number made the move in the 1920s. Like many migrants, a number of these individuals returned to the South. Still, enough stayed that of the roughly 12 million African Americans in 1930, 20 percent were living in the urban North and West.

Cities in the Northeast and Midwest received the bulk of the migrants. New York's black population rose from about 92,000 in 1910 (1.9 percent of the total population) to just over 150,000 in 1920 and to nearly 330,000 by 1930 (4.8 percent). Chicago's rose from about 44,000 (2.0 percent) to nearly 110,000 to more than 230,000 in the same period (6.8 percent). Detroit's black population rose from under 6,000 (1.3 percent) to almost 41,000 to more than 120,000 (7.6 percent). Los Angeles saw its black population rise from about 8,000 in 1910 (2.5 percent) to almost 40,000 in 1930 (3.2 percent).

Southern cities also saw significant growth. Atlanta's black population went from just under 52,000 in 1910 (33.8 percent) to nearly 63,000 in 1920 and more than 90,000 (33.3 percent) in 1930; that of Memphis climbed from around 50,000 (38.2 percent) to about 60,000 to roughly 100,000 (39.5 percent).

The population of heavily African American states in the South, particularly those without large urban areas, declined in relative terms, as black majorities in Louisiana, Mississippi, and South Carolina turned into minorities.

Like most other mass migrations in modern world history, the Great Migration was caused by a host of factors, which scholars divide into two general categories: push and pull. Push factors included environmental, economic, and social conditions. During the Reconstruction period after the Civil War, African Americans in the South had made significant economic and political gains. Later, however, their right to vote was largely taken away from them by the poll tax and other restrictive laws. Their economic gains were whittled away by declines in the prices for the commodities they raised as well as high rents and interest rates charged by landholders and merchants. Also damaging was an infestation by the boll weevil, an insect pest that destroyed much of the cotton crop in the mid-1910s. And the 1896 U.S. Supreme Court decision in *Plessy v. Ferguson* upholding segregation greatly restricted African Americans' place in society.

The pull factors were largely economic but included some political and social elements as well. First and foremost was the lure of relatively high-paying jobs, particularly in heavy industry, made possible by a booming manufacturing economy in both the urban North and a few Southern cities such as Richmond and Birmingham. World War I, with its huge demand for labor, opened new opportunities for blacks in defense plants, as did passage of the Naturalization Acts of 1921 and 1924, which severely restricted the number of unskilled immigrant workers from Southern and Eastern Europe. While blacks were often restricted to the lowest-paying maintenance jobs in many factories, such employment still represented an economic improvement for former sharecroppers who, as late as the early twentieth century, were still barely connected to the cash economy.

Northern cities, though largely segregated, also offered greater social inclusiveness for blacks, who formed impoverished but culturally dynamic neighborhoods in virtually every major city north of the Mason-Dixon line. The Jazz Age was the decade of the "New Negro"—urbanized, literate, and assertive—and the Harlem Renaissance, a black cultural efflorescence centered in the Harlem section of New York City. Also, by moving North, blacks were able to reenter the political process, as most Northern states had no restrictions on black voting. The result was

that blacks became part of the calculation of urban political machines, their needs addressed by their representatives who, though limited in number, served in city and state governments and, after 1928, in the U.S. Congress as well.

Yet African Americans who moved North did not escape racism entirely. While in their own neighborhoods they were largely free of the daily indignities and humiliations of the Jim Crow South, many Northern urban whites resented their growing numbers, seeing in African Americans a threat to their own precarious economic and social position. Many white workers saw blacks as economic competitors, a situation exacerbated by employers who used African Americans as strikebreakers. In addition, many immigrants feared that their tentative rise up the social ladder was jeopardized by intermingling with a caste of people—African Americans—uniformly looked down upon by the native born. Not surprisingly, the major antiblack riots of the late 1910s—in East St. Louis and Chicago—were triggered in part by white perceptions that blacks were trying to move into their neighborhoods.

Despite this backlash, the Great Migration continued, slowed only by the depressed manufacturing economy of the 1930s. With the defense-industry demands of World War II and the great postwar economic boom of the 1950s, the Great Migration—whether called by that name or not—continued. By 1960, roughly 40 percent of all African Americans lived in the North and West, and nearly 75 percent were urban.

James Ciment and Sam Hitchmough

See also: African Americans; Chicago Race Riot of 1919; Harlem Renaissance; Immigration.

Further Reading

Grossman, James. *Land of Hope: Chicago, Black Southerners, and the Great Migration.* Reprint ed. Chicago: University of Chicago Press, 1991.

Harrison, Alferdteen. *Black Exodus: The Great Migration from the American South.* Oxford: University Press of Mississippi, 1992.

Lemann, Nicholas. *The Promised Land: The Great Black Migration and How It Changed America.* New York: Vintage Books, 1992.

Military Affairs

Other than during wartime, throughout the nineteenth and early twentieth centuries the United States maintained a relatively small military, considering its population and economic size in comparison to comparable industrial states in Europe and Japan. And the country had always been quick to demobilize following the cessation of hostilities. That pattern played out again before, during, and after World War I. In early 1917, before America's entry into the conflict in Europe, the U.S. Army numbered approximately 100,000 soldiers. At the height of the war in the autumn of 1918, that number swelled to 3.7 million. Following the armistice in November, the number dropped to 2.7 million by June 1919. The National Defense Act of 1920 authorized an army of 296,000, and legislation in 1922 cut it to 136,000 soldiers—an army nineteenth in the world, just behind that of Portugal.

Demobilization was popular with Congress and the American people. The Paris Peace Conference, which officially ended the conflict and set the terms for the postwar world, seemed to many Americans a contradiction of the very democratic principles for which the war had been fought. The general sentiment in the country was to wash the nation's collective hands of Europe and go back to an isolationist foreign policy.

But the isolationism Americans yearned for was never practiced in reality. Although troops returned home from Europe in 1918–1919, the United States maintained forces in several Latin American countries, including the Dominican Republic, Haiti, Mexico, and Nicaragua—though the numbers of servicemen involved, a few hundred to a few thousand in each, were tiny by World War I standards. These ventures to countries caught up in internal strife were justified as protecting U.S. citizens and commercial interests.

There was also unfinished business from the Great War. In 1917, Russia had undergone a Communist revolution and pulled its troops out of the wider European conflict. The new Bolshevik government then became embroiled in a civil war with counterrevolutionary forces that the United States, several European countries, and Japan supported. To that end, the United States had dispatched several thousand troops to Siberia. When it became clear that the "white Russian" forces were losing, however, the United States pulled out its troops. At the same time, the United States retained a small contingent of soldiers in defeated Germany until January 1923.

New Technologies, New Missions

Even as it demobilized after the war, the American military was developing new technologies—particularly in aviation—increasing both the number and size of the aircraft in its arsenal. Many of the great World War I aces, such as Eddie Rickenbacker and Billy Mitchell, had demonstrated the usefulness of air power. Aerial bombing could achieve not only tactical goals, such as terrorizing a local population, but strategic ones as well.

The U.S. Navy, too, was interested in aircraft as well as more modern warships. Under the limitations of the 1922 Washington Naval Treaty, the navy scrapped twenty-six battleships. To counter the shortfall in big ships, the navy started to look at other means of force projection, especially aircraft carriers. In addition, the navy saw the need for fighter aircraft support. In 1922, the USS *Langley,* the navy's first aircraft carrier, was commissioned, followed shortly thereafter by the *Saratoga* and the *Lexington.* Meanwhile, the U.S. Army moved toward a more mechanized force, replacing horses and wagons with trucks and other motorized vehicles.

The most active military force during the Jazz Age was the U.S. Marine Corps. A number of Marine units were deployed in Central America to stabilize local governments. The skills learned by Marine commanders such as Smedley Butler and Lewis "Chesty" Puller in those conflicts became the stuff of Marine Corps legend. The expeditions honed Marine tactics to the extent that the corps eventually published the *Small Wars Manual* (1940). But U.S. occupation forces often proved unpopular and were met by rebel resistance, leading in turn to brutal antiguerrilla campaigns that resulted in many civilian fatalities.

Career Opportunities

Officers who wanted to stay in the military could find advancement through an appointment to one of the war colleges. The most prominent of these was the General Staff and Application College at Fort Leavenworth, Kansas. There, officers who learned their craft on the battlefields of Europe passed on their lessons and skills to soldiers coming up in the ranks. Another option was the Industrial Military School, established in 1924 to deal with the logistics of manufacturing the instruments of war, how to move those items to the front, and how to apply new technologies (such as radio telephones) to military use. The Naval War College applied knowledge of sea tactics to new technology such as aircraft and the aircraft carrier. Marine officers could be appointed to naval schools or to a "practical school" such as U.S.-occupied Nicaragua,

Haiti, or Cuba, where Marines conducted operational exercises.

In the early 1920s, as a tighter approach to the federal government's finances held sway in Washington, politicians often downplayed the needs and concerns of the military. But the threat of a new world war in the late 1930s and the outbreak of actual hostilities reenergized the U.S. military establishment and popular support for it.

Cord Scott and James Ciment

See also: Demobilization, Industrial; Dominican Republic, Intervention in; Four-Power Treaty (1921); Fourteen Points; Geneva Arms Convention of 1925; Haiti, Intervention in; Havana Conference of 1928; Locarno Treaties (1925); Nicaragua, Intervention in; Siberian Intervention; Versailles, Treaty of (1919); Veterans; War Finance Corporation; Washington Naval Conference (1921–1922).

Further Reading

Kennedy, David M. *Over Here: The First World War and American Society.* New York: Oxford University Press, 1980.

Smith, Daniel. *The Great Departure: The United States and World War I, 1914–1920.* New York: John Wiley and Sons, 1965.

Weigley, Russell Frank. *The American Way of War: A History of United States Military Strategy and Policy.* New York: Macmillan, 1973.

Mississippi Flood of 1927

The most widespread natural disaster in American history at the time, the Great Mississippi Flood of 1927 inundated almost 30,000 square miles (78,000 square kilometers), displaced more than 700,000 people, and left 246 dead in seven states (more than half of them African American). The total damage was estimated at $400 million (roughly $4 billion in 2007 dollars), including the destruction of roughly 5 million acres (more than 2 million hectares) of prime farmland.

Flooding on the Mississippi River was nothing new in 1927. Levees were primitive compared to today's flood-control system, and the river frequently overflowed its banks and flooded the wide, flat valley. But the flooding of 1927 was unusual. The previous year had brought unprecedented rainfall to the watershed, and by September 1926, the river's tributaries in Iowa and Kansas had reached capacity. By January 1927, the Cumberland River at Nashville had overflowed its levees by more than fifty-six feet (seventeen meters).

During the winter, tributaries began flooding in Oklahoma and Kansas, Kentucky and Illinois. That spring, the rains came even harder, in some places ten times more than the normal precipitation. On April 15, 1927, Good Friday, the Memphis *Commercial Appeal* warned that the flood might be the greatest in history because the river was already on the verge of overflowing banks and levees from St. Louis downriver. It rained that day over Missouri, Illinois, Arkansas, Mississippi, Texas, and Louisiana—an area covering several hundred thousand square miles. New Orleans got fifteen inches (thirty-eight centimeters) in eighteen hours. By May, the Mississippi River was sixty miles (ninety six kilometers) wide at Memphis.

The U.S. Army Corps of Engineers—responsible for flood-control projects—tried to reassure a nervous populace that the levees would hold and that the excess would be diverted into the Gulf of Mexico. But critics of the Army Corps had long argued that the system was not as effective as the government claimed. Engineer James Buchanan Eads, who built the first railroad bridge over the Mississippi, had argued for cutoffs to straighten the river and get the water running through faster—a step never taken. As the water rose during the spring of 1927, the Army Corps desperately tried to make up for the shortcomings in the system by raising the levees. The river, however, undercut the levees, and vast quantities of water poured through from Missouri and Illinois southward, flooding more than 27,000 square miles (70,000 square kilometers).

A respite in the precipitation came in June, and the river began to recede by July 1. But then the skies opened up again, the result of an unusual low-pressure system that persisted over the Mississippi Valley for months. The rising river proceeded to break the levees in nearly 150 places, and water up to thirty feet (nine meters) deep covered parts of the valley. Some 13 percent of the state of Arkansas was underwater.

Residents and local officials desperately tried to save land, property, and lives. In Mississippi, planters sent their sharecroppers to the levees to pile sandbags, sometimes at gunpoint. Field kitchens and tents were set up to serve them, and National Guardsmen were dispatched to prevent any of the sharecroppers from using the flood to flee their obligations. Ultimately, the flood helped accelerate the Great Migration of African Americans from the rural South to the urban North.

To protect New Orleans, the levees at Caernarvon, Louisiana, were dynamited as the flood approached. The water diverted through the hole flowed at 250,000 square feet (23,000 square meters) per second. The effort saved New Orleans but left thousands of square miles of farmland underwater. The dynamiting was probably unnecessary, experts later concluded, because the river broke through the levees in other places, diverting floodwaters there.

To cope with the problem of displaced people—some 700,000 altogether, including 330,000 African Americans—the Red Cross set up 154 camps, but these only housed only about 325,000 persons and generally excluded blacks. The organization—which collected more than $17 million in donations for flood relief—provided clothing, furniture, food, seed, livestock, and vocational training after the flood to help the displaced get back on their financial feet. It also immunized thousands against flood-related diseases, including pellagra, typhoid fever, malaria, and smallpox. Working with the Red Cross was the Colored Advisory Commission, a committee of influential African Americans established by Tuskegee Institute President Robert R. Moton. For the most part, the federal government did little to relieve the suffering, as President Calvin Coolidge believed that relief efforts should be local. However, he did dispatch Secretary of Commerce Herbert Hoover, a veteran of relief operations in Europe after World War I, to coordinate those local efforts.

Although the floodwater receded by August 1927, it would not be until May 1928 that the last displaced-persons camps were closed. In the long term, the Great Flood of 1927 spurred the Army Corps to expand its flood-control system on the Mississippi River.

James Ciment and John Barnhill

See also: Agriculture; Coolidge, Calvin.

Further Reading

Barry, John M. *Rising Tide: The Great Mississippi Flood of 1927 and How It Changed America.* New York: Touchstone, 1998.
Saxon, Lyle, and Lyle Sanon. *Father Mississippi: The Story of the Great Flood of 1927.* New York: Century, 1927.

Music, Classical

American classical music in the 1920s can be divided into two general styles: modernist and neoclassical. Modernist composers were the more experimental, incorporating a number of non-Western musical techniques, such as atonality, polytonality, and polyrhythm. The music was notable for its dissonant sound. The modernists included a group of composers that music historians call the American Five: Henry Cowell, Riegger Wallingford, John Becker, Carl Ruggles, and Charles Ives.

Neoclassical composers also incorporated nontraditional elements like polyrhythm, but they avoided the dissonant sound associated with the polytonality and atonality of the modernists. Neoclassicists also incorporated melodic themes from folk music and jazz. The finest exemplars of 1920s neoclassicism were Roy Harris, Aaron Copland, and George Gershwin, who also composed jazz and popular music.

Because they adhered more closely to the established melodic and rhythmic traditions of classical music, the neoclassicists enjoyed more popularity in the 1920s than the modernists. Still, both styles represented a rejection of the lush, emotional compositions of late Romantic music. Modernists offered a break from tonality, while neoclassicists emphasized a return to the pre-Romantic rationalism of late eighteenth-century composers Wolfgang Amadeus Mozart and Franz Joseph Haydn. And while both styles were also being developed by European composers of the period—such as Arnold Schoenberg, a modernist, and Igor Stravinsky, a neoclassicist—American practitioners wanted to create a distinctively American style.

Like modernists in literature and the visual arts, the modernist composers were responding to rapid social, economic, and technological changes of the early twentieth century, from the rise of great urban centers to the increasing dominance of the machine in everyday life and the horrors of mechanized death in World War I. Nineteenth-century European and American certainties about human progress and the superiority of Western civilization gave way to a more questioning attitude about modern society and the ability of humans to make sense of a world where change was occurring at an ever more rapid pace.

Just as modernist American poets like T.S. Eliot were abandoning the assured lyrical voice and lush imagery of the Romantic poets, so composers like Cowell and Ives were moving away from the rhythmic, tonal compositions of the Romantic composers—Ives in such compositions as *Three Places in New England,* a set of orchestral pieces composed between 1903 and 1921, and Cowell in *Quartet Euphometric,* composed between 1916 and 1919, and the piano piece "The Banshee" in 1925. Moving away from the Romantic tradition of taking refuge in nature, the modernists embraced the machine age, most notably in the dissonant sounds of atonal music.

While late twentieth-century critics and audiences gave Ives the more important place in the American musical canon, he was largely ignored in the 1920s. Instead, it was Cowell, among the modernists, who had the widest influence in the 1920s and 1930s. He toured extensively as a pianist, playing his own experimental polytonal pieces for audiences in Europe and North America. Cowell also wrote one of the seminal books on modernist music, *New Musical Resources* (1930).

Even as the modernists were making a nearly complete departure from classical music, neoclassicists like Harris and Copland were attempting to give it an American imprint—one that reflected the expansive geography and democratic impulses of the country. Harris's best-known piece of the decade is the 1929 symphony *American Portrait,* while Copland's most important composition of the decade is the 1925 *Dance Symphony.*

Harris, Copland, and other American neoclassicists were students of the French composer, conductor, and music professor Nadia Boulanger, who taught at the American Conservatory in Fontainebleau, outside Paris. Boulanger emphasized classical harmony while encouraging her American students to apply these harmonies to their own distinctive musical traditions. All of these American neoclassicists would incorporate folk melodies and patriotic tunes in their compositions. Still, it was the syncopated rhythms of jazz that influenced what is arguably the most popular American neoclassical music composition of the Jazz Age—Gershwin's *Rhapsody in Blue* (1924). Notably, the piece was first performed not by a symphonic orchestra but by the leading jazz ensemble of the 1920s, Paul Whiteman and His Orchestra.

James Ciment

See also: Dance, Performance; Gershwin, George.

Further Reading

Gann, Kyle. *American Music in the Twentieth Century.* New York: Schirmer, 1997.

Simms, Brian R. *Music of the Twentieth Century: Style and Structure.* New York: Schirmer, 1996.

National Association for the Advancement of Colored People

Founded in New York City in 1909 in reaction to the Springfield, Illinois, race riot of 1908, the National Association for the Advancement of Colored People (NAACP) was initially a predominantly white organization devoted to promoting civil rights for African Americans. Notable founding members included the journalist Mary White Ovington, labor activist William English Walling, settlement worker Jane Addams, philosopher John Dewey, editor William Dean Howells, journalist Lincoln Steffens, journalist Ray Stanard Baker, journalist Ida B. Wells-Barnett, educator Mary McLeod Bethune, and sociologist W.E.B. Du Bois. Of these, only the last three were African American.

From the beginning, the organization published a newspaper called *The Crisis,* edited by Du Bois, which during World War I advocated black support for the war effort. During its first decade, the NAACP succeeded in convincing President Woodrow Wilson to condemn the rampant practice of lynching, persuaded the U.S. War Department to commission blacks as officers in the armed forces, and won the U.S. Supreme Court case *Buchanan v. Warley* (1917), which outlawed segregation in urban residential neighborhoods. Despite such successes, the organization was little known to the American public and had a negligible effect on politics or race relations during its early years. Only after the war and in the 1920s did the association begin to be a major player in shaping public opinion on racial issues.

By 1919, the Great Migration of African Americans from the fields of the South to the industrial centers of the North had greatly altered the racial composition of some of the nation's largest cities. Many of the migrants joined the fledgling NAACP, and with the recruiting efforts of National Field Secretary James Weldon Johnson and his assistant Walter White, membership in the organization swelled tenfold, to nearly 50,000 nationwide, with some 165 branch offices. Monthly circulation of *The Crisis* was more than 100,000.

In 1919, the NAACP published its first report, *Thirty Years of Lynching in the United States, 1898–1918,* and the organization began a national media crusade against lynching. The crusade raised public awareness of the issue but failed to produce effective legislation. Johnson, better known as a poet of the Harlem Renaissance, moved up in the ranks in 1920 to become the first black executive secretary of the organization. White, meanwhile, continued to rally the anti-lynching crusade. In 1929, he published *Rope and Faggot: A Biography of Judge Lynch,* which again helped raise public awareness of the problem but did little to bring about federal anti-lynching legislation.

From its inception, the NAACP clashed with other notable African American organizations and leaders of the day. Booker T. Washington and his successors at the Tuskegee Institute and the National Negro Business League denounced the NAACP's politically confrontational tactics as antithetical to their accommodationist approach to race relations reform—with its emphasis on economic self-improvement rather than demands for political equality. Du Bois and NAACP leaders fired back equally scathing rebukes of the Bookerites, saying their compromises with racist whites merely reinforced discrimination and put off needed political and legal reforms.

Black nationalist Marcus Garvey and his Universal Negro Improvement Association criticized the NAACP for its lack of black leadership, observing the irony of a black civil rights organization dominated by whites and mixed-race "coloreds." Du Bois, Johnson, and White tried to discourage African Americans from supporting Garvey and black nationalist or back-to-Africa movements, urging them to stay in the United States and fight for their constitutional rights.

The NAACP also suffered internal strife in its early years because of its espousal of woman suffrage

Members of the National Association for the Advancement of Colored People, the leading civil rights organization of the 1920s, march in New York City for passage of federal anti-lynching legislation—the organization's predominant issue of the time. *(MPI/Stringer/Hulton Archive/Getty Images)*

Further Reading

Kellogg, Charles F. *NAACP: A History of the National Association for the Advancement of Colored People.* Baltimore: Johns Hopkins University Press, 1967.

National Association for the Advancement of Colored People. http://www.naacp.org.

Ovington, Mary White. *The Walls Came Tumbling Down.* New York: Harcourt, Brace, 1947.

Ross, Barbara J. *J.E. Spingarn and the Rise of the NAACP: 1911–1939.* New York: Atheneum, 1972.

White, Walter. *Rope and Faggot: A Biography of Judge Lynch.* New York: Alfred A. Knopf, 1929.

National Association of Manufacturers

The National Association of Manufacturers (NAM) was established in Cincinnati, Ohio, in 1895, to represent the interests of small and medium-sized manufacturing businesses, acting primarily as an advocate of policies to increase American exports. It rose to prominence as one of the leading organizations representing the interests of American business during the Jazz Age.

NAM was a small and quiet organization for its first seven years, until the national Anthracite Coal Strike of 1902 resulted in the organization's transformation into the bastion of the open-shop movement, which sought to prevent unions from making union membership a condition of employment. Militantly antilabor and confrontational, NAM opposed unionization and national reforms. The National Civic Federation (NCF), then the leading organization of large-scale enterprises, viewed NAM's position as shortsighted and dangerous. The NCF sought to collaborate with organized labor and other reformers in order to prevent more radical confrontations, and it counted Samuel Gompers, head of the American Federation of Labor (AFL), among its signature members.

Business executives were held in high regard as natural leaders of society during the 1920s, and NAM supported this role. The organization held yearly conferences and developed nonpartisan "Platforms of American Industry" that both the Democratic and Republican parties sought to incorporate. NAM was on the cutting edge of the professional lobbying industry that arose during the 1920s, and it sponsored weekly luncheons for lobbyists to meet and discuss policy. Beginning in 1924, NAM launched an innovative "Get Out the Vote Campaign" to increase voter participation rates, and it participated in the era's

and women's rights. Indeed, women played as vital a role in the leadership of the NAACP as they did in any political organization of the Progressive Era.

By 1930, White had replaced Johnson as executive secretary and won a major victory for the NAACP by defeating President Hoover's nomination of North Carolina Judge John J. Parker, an avowed racist, to the Supreme Court. White also drove out the increasingly left-wing Du Bois as editor of *The Crisis,* replacing him with the more politically moderate Roy Wilkins. To lead a crusade against segregation in the nation's public schools and universities, White added black lawyers Charles Houston and Thurgood Marshall to the staff in the 1930s. In the 1932 presidential election, he led the NAACP's effort to persuade African Americans to switch their allegiance from the Republican Party of Abraham Lincoln to the Democratic Party of Franklin D. Roosevelt.

The NAACP continued its civil rights activism through World War II and into the civil rights era, monitoring Roosevelt's promise to pressure manufacturers to hire and promote blacks within the defense industry and spearheading the legal struggle to end segregation and disenfranchisement in the South in the 1950s and 1960s.

Thomas Adams Upchurch

See also: African Americans; Du Bois, W.E.B.; Lynching; Migration, Great.

Americanization campaigns through a program of free films directed to immigrant workers that emphasized shop safety, good workplace habits, and civic values.

The labor question was the most important issue for NAM during the 1920s. NAM released a number of economic studies purporting to show that American workers enjoyed better wages and benefited from lower prices in regions where unions were weak. The organization argued that workers were fully capable of negotiating salaries and working conditions with their employers on an individual basis and had no need for union representation. NAM opposed a 1924 constitutional amendment that would have empowered Congress to restrict child labor, calling the proposal "socialistic" and not a matter of government concern. Additionally, NAM bitterly resisted efforts to protect unionized workers, such as the unsuccessful Shipstead Anti-Injunction Bill of 1928, which would have prohibited the use of judicial injunctions to break union activity.

Economic issues unrelated to union activity were important to NAM as well. The organization favored a high protective tariff and endorsed the protectionist Fordney-McCumber Tariff of 1922. NAM repeatedly petitioned for the reduction of personal and corporate income tax rates, arguing that producers of value deserved to retain the fruits of their labor. Immigration was an issue with an economic component; NAM feared that strict immigration reform would cause a shortage of unskilled labor in the United States. It fought unsuccessfully for larger immigrant quotas in the National Origins Act of 1924 and opposed the literacy requirement for admission. NAM also endorsed the Federal Reserve System and called for its continuation.

The National Association of Manufacturers thrived in the probusiness 1920s. The organization's relationship with the Republican Party, which dominated this period, was particularly strong. For many Americans, NAM retained its legitimacy as a leading organization in American society as long as prosperity reigned, and it was one of the most influential groups that shaped the character of this period. When prosperity imploded during the Great Depression, many Americans blamed the business community and the strongly probusiness President Herbert Hoover for having gone too far. They elected Franklin D. Roosevelt to the White House in 1932 on the premise that the government had not served the people's interests. The Great Depression temporarily eviscerated the legitimacy of businesspeople as social leaders in America, but NAM continues to be a force in the ebb and flow of American politics.

Charles E. Delgadillo

See also: Chamber of Commerce, U.S.; Commerce Department, U.S.; Economic Policy; Labor Movement.

Further Reading

Weinstein, James. *The Corporate Ideal in the Liberal State.* Boston: Beacon, 1968.

Wiebe, Robert H. *Businessmen and Reform: A Study of the Progressive Movement.* Cambridge, MA: Harvard University Press, 1962.

National City Bank

National City Bank was the largest commercial and investment bank in the United States during the 1920s. Innovative management and services had enabled it to grow dramatically, particularly in overseas operations, so that by 1930, it had more than one hundred branches in twenty-three countries. But many regarded the bank's aggressive sale of bonds of questionable value and other activities as a major contributing cause of the Great Depression.

National City Bank was founded in 1812 as the City Bank of New York. The bank thrived as the city grew to economic preeminence during the nineteenth century, and by 1894, it had become the largest bank in the United States as well as a pioneer in foreign investment. National City Bank became the first contributor to the Federal Reserve Bank of New York, the dominant bank in the twelve-branch national Federal Reserve system, established in 1913.

The same act that established the Federal Reserve also permitted U.S. banks to establish foreign branches, and National City Bank became the first to do so, founding a branch in Argentina in 1914. During World War I, National City maintained its preeminence as the country's leading international bank. It also held the lead in assets, becoming the first U.S. bank to top the $1 billion mark in 1919.

Much of this growth was due to the leadership of Frank Vanderlip, the bank's president from 1909 to 1919, who strove to make investment banking more accessible to middle-class Americans. To achieve this, he hired Western Electric executive Charles E. Mitchell in 1916 to head the National City Company, an affiliate that sold securities. In his five years running the company, Mitchell established branches in more than fifty American cities.

In 1921, when Mitchell became president of National City Bank as a whole, he established a management fund to motivate bank officers to open new accounts and sell more securities. After dividends and salaries were paid, the remaining profits were divided among the stockholders and the managers. Thanks to the bank's success, Mitchell personally received over $1 million in both 1928 and 1929. Making good on his promise to establish National City Bank as the "bank for all," Mitchell introduced services to draw in working- and middle-class customers. National City was the first U.S. bank to offer compound interest on savings accounts and the first to offer unsecured personal loans to depositors. By 1929, National City Bank had 230,000 individual accounts and was the largest commercial bank in the world.

National City Bank did much to fuel the expansion of the U.S. economy during the 1920s. Its large sales staff sold securities and bonds to large and small investors. During the 1920s, the bank originated or participated in almost a quarter of all the bonds issued in the United States. In its aggressiveness, however, National City Bank sometimes skirted the limits of responsible banking; many of the bond issues it offered were of questionable value. Working with the dictator of Cuba, Gerardo Machado, bank managers converted $31 million of Cuban sugar loans into bonds that were sold to American investors. In 1927, $90 million of Peruvian government bonds were sold, even though Mitchell and others believed they were not a good risk. These and other bond sales were technically legal, but most American investors were ignorant of the technical details of the bond issues and relied on National City Bank and other banks as guarantors.

At a time when business leaders were lionized by the press and the public, Mitchell became something of a national celebrity. He was popular with the media, who nicknamed him "Sunshine Charlie" for his optimistic view of the American economy. When the stock market crashed in October 1929, Mitchell, who had just become bank chairman, used his influence and power to try to stabilize the banking industry. He remained optimistic that the economy would soon recover.

In 1933, when Congress held hearings on the causes of the Great Depression, Mitchell was one of the first witnesses. The questionable practices of Mitchell and National City Bank in regard to the selling of risky bonds and the profits enjoyed by the bank officers were made public. People were outraged to find that Mitchell had paid no income tax in 1929, based on losses from the sale of stock to his wife. *Time* magazine coined the term "banksters" to describe Mitchell and other officers of National City Bank.

Mitchell was forced to resign as chairman of National City Bank in 1933. Although prosecuted for income tax evasion, he was never convicted. He later successfully resumed his role in the investment industry. National City Bank managed to survive the Depression and continued to thrive. Known today as Citibank, part of Citigroup, it remains the largest financial institution, by assets, in the United States.

Tim J. Watts

See also: Credit and Debt, Consumer.

Further Reading

Hutchison, Robert A. *Off the Books*. New York: Morrow, 1986.

Mayer, Robert Stanley. *The Influence of Frank A. Vanderlip and the National City Bank on American Commerce and Foreign Policy, 1910–1920*. New York: Garland, 1987.

van Cleveland, Harold B., and Thomas F. Huertas. *Citibank, 1812–1970*. Cambridge, MA: Harvard University Press, 1985.

Winkler, John K. *The First Billion: The Stillmans and the National City Bank*. New York: Vanguard, 1934.

Native Americans

By the beginning of the Jazz Age in 1919, the western frontier of the United States had been closed for more than a generation, and the last major conflict between the government and Native Americans—at Wounded Knee, South Dakota, in 1890—was nearly thirty years in the past. In those intervening years, the situation of American Indians in terms of land, culture, and population had deteriorated significantly. The 1920s witnessed the tentative start of a revival in American Indian life. During the course of that decade, American Indians won full citizenship, and new restrictions were put into place to safeguard Native American land rights.

First, and most important, the Native American population underwent major growth in the 1920s. Between 1890, when the U.S. Census Bureau officially declared the frontier closed, and 1920, the Native American population had stagnated at about a quarter of a million, its lowest point in recorded history. Between 1920 and 1930, the population grew to more than 330,000, a gain of nearly 30 percent. This increase marked only the beginning of an upward climb that would bring the Native American population to more than 2 million by century's end. Improved health care, more plentiful food supplies, and a decline in the loss of land to whites all contributed to the turnaround of the 1920s.

Along with the reversal in population decline came the beginning of a new relationship between Americans Indians and the federal government. Traditionally, Native Americans had not been considered citizens of the United States but rather members of sovereign nations, although it was possible to gain U.S. citizenship by marrying whites, by serving in the U.S. military, or by means of special treaties or private acts of Congress. Moreover, the naturalization procedures for foreigners had not been open to Native Americans. In 1924, facing increasing pressure from Native American leaders, Congress passed the Indian Citizenship Act (also known as the Snyder Act), which declared "That all non citizen Indians born within the territorial limits of the United States be, and they are hereby, declared to be citizens of the United States." The legislation did not come without controversy, however, as some Indian leaders, among the Iroquois, for example, feared that U.S. citizenship would undermine tribal sovereignty.

The U.S. government's approach to Indian lands also changed. Under the Dawes General Allotment Act of 1887, communal or tribal ownership of land had ended, replaced by deeds giving land to individual Native Americans and Native American families. The federal government was supposed to hold title to each allotment for twenty-five years, to make sure that American Indians did not lose their lands to unscrupulous speculators. But throughout the Woodrow Wilson administration, from 1913 to 1921, the government proved willing to turn over title to individual Native Americans prematurely. Impoverished and often unfamiliar with real estate laws and practices, many American Indians sold their individual allotments. Between 1887 and 1920, American Indian landholdings declined from 138 million acres to fewer than 65 million acres.

In 1921, the Bureau of Indian Affairs (BIA), under the incoming administration of Warren G. Harding, instituted policy changes designed to halt the alienation of Native American lands. But the policies were generally ignored in the field, and the losses continued. By 1934, when the Dawes General Allotment Act was superseded by the Indian Reorganization Act, which once again recognized tribal ownership of land, the amount of land under Native American ownership had fallen to just over 50 million acres.

So bad was the situation that Congress ordered an investigation into Native American living conditions. The 1928 Meriam Report noted high levels of poverty and a general lack of educational services and health care. While the report maintained the importance of the long-standing federal policy of assimilating American Indians into the national mainstream, it emphasized for the first time the need to preserve aspects of Native American culture. The Meriam Report resulted in no immediate or dramatic changes in Native American policy, but it did lay the foundation for the 1934 Indian Reorganization Act.

Reformers and Native American groups in the 1920s fought against the privatization of American Indian lands and in favor of traditional communal ownership. Groups such as the Indian Rights Association, the Indian Council Fire, and activist John Collier's Indian Defense Association advocated American Indian self-awareness and an end to governmental abuses of native rights. Collier worked on behalf of the Pueblos to oppose legislation threatening their land, stymied the government's attempt to end American Indian dances, and advocated that American Indians receive royalties for their waterpower sites and mineral land. Collier began his work, however, during the period of tension between assimilationist policies and the emerging idea of cultural pluralism. In this atmosphere, the nation struggled to find the proper place of American Indians in American society.

James Ciment and Maria Reynolds

See also: Agriculture; Snyder Act (1921).

Further Reading

McDonnell, Janet A. *The Dispossession of the American Indian, 1887–1934.* Bloomington: Indiana University Press, 1991.

Olson, James, and Raymond Wilson. *Native Americans in the Twentieth Century.* Provo, UT: Brigham Young University Press, 1984.

Philp, Kenneth R. *John Collier's Crusade for Indian Reform, 1920–1954.* Tucson: University of Arizona Press, 1977.

Ness, Eliot (1903–1957)

U.S. Treasury agent Eliot Ness earned lasting fame for helping to indict one of the most notorious gangland figures of Prohibition-era America, Chicago crime boss Al Capone. Ness was born on April 19, 1903, in Kensington, a Scandinavian neighborhood on Chicago's South Side. His parents, immigrants from Norway, were master bakers, and by the time

Ness was nine, he was helping out in the bakery after school. He later said that this experience imbued him with the strong work ethic that he put to use in his meticulous investigations of criminal activities.

Ness attended the University of Chicago, earning a degree in business and law in 1925. After graduating from college he spent two years investigating the finances of clients of an Atlanta-based retail credit company. He found the work tedious, however, and on the urging of his brother-in-law, an agent for the Bureau of Investigation (later the Federal Bureau of Investigation), Ness moved to law enforcement, accepting a position with the Chicago division of the U.S. Treasury Department's Bureau of Prohibition. As its name implied, the bureau was the main federal agency responsible for enforcing laws against the manufacture and distribution of alcohol.

Ness spent his first two years with the bureau conducting raids on bootleg operations (where illegal alcohol was produced) and distribution centers. In later years, Ness admitted that he had been no strong proponent of Prohibition, noting that it lacked support among large segments of the population and, by criminalizing a very popular vice, created an atmosphere of lawlessness. Indeed, by the time Ness joined the bureau, Chicago was engulfed in a wave of gangland violence. During the Jazz Age, hundreds of people were killed each year, some of them innocent bystanders, as a result of mob infighting. Moreover, gang leaders, including Capone, were using their vast revenues from the illegal alcohol trade to bribe local police and members of the bureau. Because of corruption in the department, the raids were sometimes failures, as police officials tipped off mobsters in advance.

Two events in early 1929 helped turn the tide against gangland violence in Chicago. On February 14, in a shootout dubbed the St. Valentine's Day massacre by the press, Capone's hit men murdered seven members of a rival gang led by George "Bugsy" Malone. The brazenness of the attack outraged the public. It also led incoming President Herbert Hoover to declare that breaking up Capone's criminal operation would be a top priority of the Treasury Department, and the Chicago division set up a task force with the sole purpose of convicting Capone. Ness, who had already gained a reputation for incorruptibility, was put in charge.

To guard against corruption, Ness closely checked the records of all 300 members of the Chicago division of the bureau. Eventually, he settled on eleven men he thought he could trust. Among them was Frank Wilson of the Treasury Department's Bureau of Internal Revenue (later the Internal Revenue Service). Using extensive wiretapping to gain information, the team launched a series of raids on bootlegging and distribution operations that Ness claimed were worth $1 million.

The bureau also recognized that bringing down Capone required more than raids and other traditional law enforcement practices. Because Capone was a master of publicity—using high-profile charitable contributions to win public favor—Ness decided that he, too, would have to appeal to the public, both to keep pressure on corrupt politicians and to gain eyes and ears on Capone's operations around the city. Ness made sure the media was present when he conducted his raids, and when Capone unsuccessfully tried to bribe one of his men, Ness went to the press with the story. Thus his team became known as "the untouchables." Ness also narrowly avoided several assassination attempts, which further contributed to his growing image as a folk hero.

Ultimately, it was not Capone's Prohibition violations that got him indicted. Wilson was able to link Capone to large sources of illegal income for which he had paid no taxes. Thus, the man who was reputed to have ordered the deaths of dozens of people, and was said to have killed several by his own hands, was sent to prison in 1931 for eleven years for not paying his taxes.

Ness's success in putting Capone behind bars led to his promotion to head of the Chicago division of the Bureau of Investigation. When Prohibition ended in 1933, he was hired by the city of Cleveland to clean up corruption in its fire and police departments and to shut down illegal gambling. In 1944, Ness left government service, becoming chair of the Diebold Corporation, a manufacturer of safes. He ran for mayor of Cleveland in 1947, but suffered a humiliating defeat. He went on to hold several other jobs in the private sector. Ness died on May 16, 1957, shortly before publication of his memoir *The Untouchables,* which became a best seller.

James Ciment and Leigh Kimmel

See also: Capone, Al; Crime, Organized; Prohibition (1920–1933); Volstead Act (1919).

Further Reading

Heimel, Paul W. *Eliot Ness: The Real Story.* Coudersport, PA: Knox, 1997.

Kobler, John. *Capone: The Life and World of Al Capone.* New York: Da Capo, 1992.

Ness, Eliot, and Oscar Farley. *The Untouchables.* New York: Messner, 1957.

New York *Daily News*

The New York *Daily News* was the first, largest, and most successful of the photo-laden tabloid newspapers that sprang up in the United States during the 1920s. Unlike most of its competitors, the *Daily News* survived and remains a major daily newspaper to this day.

During World War I, many American soldiers serving in Europe became familiar with the London *Daily Mirror,* which was extremely popular because of its plentiful use of photographs and tabloid format, which made it easy to read on public transportation. Among those soldiers was one Captain Joseph Patterson, a member of the family that published the *Chicago Tribune.* With his cousin, Robert McCormick, Patterson founded the *Illustrated Daily News* in New York in 1919; "Illustrated" was soon dropped from the title. From the beginning, Patterson was determined to publish a newspaper that would appeal to the working class by utilizing a punchy writing style, lots of photographs, and an emphasis on sensationalist stories. Rushing to beat a similar tabloid planned by press mogul William Randolph Hearst, Patterson published the first issue on June 26, 1919.

At first, few advertisers were willing to invest in the new format, but readers quickly took to the sensational content, numerous photos, and convenient size. Within a year of its founding, the *Daily News* had jumped from eighteenth to eighth among New York dailies in terms of circulation. By December 1925, the *Daily News* was selling over a million copies each day and was the most widely read daily in the United States.

From the beginning, Patterson stressed sex and sensationalism. An early ad, published in the rival *New York Times,* told readers they could "see New York's most beautiful girls every morning in the *Illustrated Daily News.*" The first issue featured pictures of the Prince of Wales, the most eligible bachelor of his day, according to the paper. Scandal also filled the pages, including divorces of well-known figures, tales of extramarital sex, and the legal problems of Hollywood stars. Gangster wars and licentious murders were also stock in trade for the *Daily News.*

Patterson had a keen sense of what the ordinary man and woman wanted to read about, so he also covered popular culture. Sports figures such as Babe Ruth, Knute Rockne, and Gertrude Ederle had their

photographs in the *Daily News* on a regular basis. Movie stars such as Rudolph Valentino and Greta Garbo had their celebrity status enhanced by regular coverage.

The paper's format also differed from that of more established newspapers. Instead of dense columns of type, like those featured in *The New York Times,* the *Daily News* emphasized large headlines and many photographs. It could be read quickly by people who wanted to be entertained as well as informed.

Many journalists, editors, and publishers looked down on the *Daily News* as low class and fit only for semi-educated working-class readers. Initially, many established journalists refused to work for the paper. However, when the circulation of the *Daily News* skyrocketed, making it possible for the paper to pay some of the highest wages in the business, attitudes soon changed.

Still, the *Daily News* continued to shock many. After extensively covering the trial of Ruth Snyder, who was ultimately convicted of conspiring with her lover to kill her husband, the paper ran a front-page photo in 1928 of her electrocution, after a reporter sneaked a camera into the death chamber.

The newspaper continued to thrive after the Jazz Age. Until the 1980s, it had the largest circulation of any local newspaper in America and remained among the top ten in the country into the early 2000s.

Tim J. Watts

See also: Journalism.

Further Reading

Chapman, John. *Tell It to Sweeney: The Informal History of the New York Daily News.* Garden City, NY: Doubleday, 1961.

Tebbel, John. *An American Dynasty: The Story of the McCormicks, Medills, and Pattersons.* Garden City, NY: Doubleday, 1947.

Wallace, Aurora. *Newspapers and the Making of Modern America: A History.* Westport, CT: Greenwood, 2005.

New Yorker, The

Founded as a weekly humor magazine by editor Harold Ross and *New York Times* journalist Jane Grant, *The New Yorker,* first published in 1925, soon emerged as the preeminent literary magazine in America. In covering cultural, social, political, and economic topics, it featured the work of some of America's finest writers, poets, and illustrators.

Ross provided the main inspiration for the magazine. A working journalist since his teen years in the West and an editor for the army newspaper *Stars and Stripes* during World War I, Ross had moved to New York City in 1919, where he edited *Home Sector,* a magazine for veterans. When that publication folded in 1920, he became editor of the humor magazine *Judge,* which would remain a competitor of *The New Yorker* during the 1920s. He and Grant were married in March 1920 but would later divorce.

While at *Judge,* Ross fell in with a group of New York literary figures known as the Algonquin Round Table, who frequently met for lunch at the Manhattan hotel of the same name. With the encouragement of Round Table writers and critics such as Dorothy Parker, Alexander Woollcott, and Heywood Broun, Ross decided to found a magazine of his own. He and Grant soon met with Raoul Fleischmann, a wealthy bread manufacturer with an interest in journalism and literature.

In the prospectus to investors, Ross laid out his plan for a publication that would appeal to a more sophisticated audience than *Judge* and would be "more than a jester." Rather, it would become a "necessity for the person who knows his way about, or wants to." Unlike its contemporaries *The Nation* and *The New Republic,* two intellectual, left-leaning magazines, *The New Yorker* would eschew any political agenda, publishing only items that had literary merit and might appeal to the well-read person. Ross also designed the magazine as a source of information on cultural and artistic events, particularly in New York City, offering reviews of the latest movies, theater performances, art shows, and sporting events.

On February 19, 1925, the first issue hit the newsstands. Among its features was a front section consisting of a column titled "Talk of the Town," a series of short essays under the heading "Behind the News," and a light opinion piece called "Of All Things." But perhaps the most memorable thing about the first issue was its cover, which featured an illustration of a monocled and top-hatted dandy. The character, Eustace Tilley, became a mascot for the magazine and is still featured on the cover of every anniversary issue.

The first issue sold well, some 15,000 copies, partly because it was a novelty. Soon, sales began to lag, falling to just 8,000 by April. In the wake of the circulation troubles, Ross reworked the front of the magazine. Though gossip was now banished, the heading "Talk of the Town" endured for the front section of every issue. Each "Talk of the Town" opened with an opinion piece under the subheading "Notes and Comment." Ross brought in noted feature writer Morris Markey, previously of the *New York World,* to write many of these articles. Within a few years, essayist E.B. White and humorist James Thurber would assume much of the responsibility for them. After "Notes and Comment" came a series of short features, in the style of the old "Behind the News" segments. This new "Talk of the Town" became the magazine's signature, attracting readers and distinguishing it from competitors like *Life.*

Ross also brought in literary editors and well-known writers. Perhaps his most important hire came in the summer of 1925, when writer and editor Katharine Sergeant Angell joined the staff. Ross's interests tended away from the literary—he personally enjoyed reference books instead—so he developed a keen trust in Angell regarding matters of literary taste. The genteel Angell, from a prominent New England family and Bryn Mawr educated, was an odd match for the cantankerous Ross, but she quickly became a trusted editorial voice, especially regarding fiction.

Angell mostly eschewed the kind of modernist fiction practiced by European authors like James Joyce, Marcel Proust, and Virginia Woolf, preferring more straightforward writing. She also favored stories written without what she called the "heavy burden of plot." Therefore, *The New Yorker* shunned the popular genre fiction, such as crime, featured in other magazines, preferring more atmospheric work. In time, this approach to short fiction would be dubbed "the *New Yorker* short story."

Other key personnel brought aboard that first year included managing editor Ralph Ingersoll and staff writers E.B. White, James Thurber, Peter Arno, and Helen Hokinson. Dorothy Parker and Alexander Woollcott also contributed important pieces. It was White and Thurber, however, who became the magazine's most prominent writers. Within a few years, much of "Talk of the Town" came from their pens. White later credited Ross with allowing young writers like Thurber and himself to develop their distinctive light touch, saying the editor "allowed humor to infect everything."

In the fall of 1925, Fleischmann initiated a massive national marketing campaign, helped along by Ross's decision to publish an exposé on Jazz Age lifestyle titled "Why We Go to Cabarets: A Post-Debutant Explains." The piece revealed that the daughters of many of New York's most prominent families preferred the "flapper" scene at local nightclubs over traditional high-society balls. Drawing major media attention, and front-page notice in *The New York Times, New York Tribune,* and *New York World,* the story helped make a name for the young journal.

By 1927, *The New Yorker* boasted a newsstand circulation of over 50,000 copies per issue. The magazine's playfulness continued, as E.B. White was allowed to tweak political figures like President Calvin Coolidge in his "Notes and Comment" pieces. Even the 1929 stock market crash could not completely dampen the magazine's spirits. Only nine days after Black Thursday, the magazine published "Is Sex Necessary? Or, Why You Feel the Way You Do," a White–Thurber collaboration that parodied books about sexuality that had been popular that year.

Guy Patrick Cunningham

See also: Fiction; Journalism; Parker, Dorothy; Poetry; Ross, Harold.

Further Reading

Kramer, Dale. *Ross and the New Yorker.* Garden City, NY: Doubleday, 1951.
Yagoda, Ben. *About Town: The New Yorker and the World It Made.* New York: Scribner's, 2000.

Nicaragua, Intervention in

In 1926, the U.S. government under President Calvin Coolidge dispatched a contingent of Marines to Nicaragua on the pretext of protecting American citizens, property, and interests against the political turmoil that was engulfing that Central American nation. Over the next seven years—until their withdrawal in 1933—U.S. troops sought to quell a left-wing insurgency led by nationalist Augusto César Sandino and to build a Nicaraguan National Guard. In subsequent years, Nicaragua's National Guard would be the military force used by the Somoza dynasty of dictators to remain in power until 1979.

Nicaragua had long been seen by U.S. policy makers and business leaders as crucial to American security and commercial interests. This was largely a function of the nation's geography. A relatively narrow strip of land between the Atlantic and Pacific oceans, and possessing the largest lakes in Central America, Nicaragua provided a popular transit route for Americans traveling from the East Coast to California during the Gold Rush of the mid-nineteenth century. Even after the completion of the Panama Canal in 1914, Nicaragua offered an alternate sea route between the Pacific and Atlantic that might be exploited by economic and strategic rivals of the United States, particularly Germany. Nicaragua was also home to several U.S. companies that had invested heavily in the nation's infrastructure or in its land, utilizing the latter to grow bananas, coffee, and other tropical crops. More generally, as part of Central America, Nicaragua was viewed as within America's sphere of influence under the Monroe Doctrine and the Roosevelt Corollary, which held that the United States had a legitimate interest in maintaining pro-U.S. regimes throughout the hemisphere.

Like other Central American republics, however, Nicaragua had been plagued by political instability for most of its history since independence from Spain in 1838. As U.S. business and strategic interests in Nicaragua grew in the late nineteenth and early twentieth centuries, the United States became more involved in those tempestuous politics. Indeed, the 1926 U.S. intervention was not the first time the United States had dispatched troops to the country. In 1912, some 2,700 Marines were sent to Nicaragua as political turmoil between conservative and liberal factions engulfed the country. Four years later, the two countries signed the Chamorro-Bryan Treaty, giving the United States exclusive rights to build an interoceanic canal. While not explicitly allowing for U.S. intervention in the case of threats to American interests, the treaty made Nicaragua a virtual U.S. protectorate. U.S. troops remained in the country through 1925, establishing a National Guard, the country's first truly national military force.

When President Carlos Solórzano was overthrown by conservatives in November 1925, political violence once again gripped the country. In May 1926, a battalion of roughly 2,000 U.S. Marines landed on Nicaragua's Caribbean coast. The following year, the United States brokered a truce between the conservative government of President Adolfo Díaz and liberal forces under General José María Moncada. The troops were supposed to remain through the 1928 elections and help to augment Nicaragua's National Guard.

But a rebel group under Augusto César Sandino refused to go along with the agreement. A strong nationalist and labor activist—radicalized by his years in Mexico during that country's revolution of the early twentieth century—Sandino resented both the U.S. military presence and the stranglehold of the nation's

A company of U.S. Marines musters in Nicaragua, one of several Central American and Caribbean countries occupied by U.S. forces during the 1920s. *(Library of Congress, LC-USZ62-99697)*

elite over Nicaragua's economy, regardless of whether liberals or conservatives held power. Sandino, and his largely worker and peasant army, insisted on land reforms and better wages for workers, particularly in the country's mining sector. In 1926, Sandino launched a rebel movement that consisted of several thousand guerrillas (the Nicaraguan government insisted the group never numbered more than a few hundred). Through the rest of the decade and into the 1930s, U.S. troops, alongside the Nicaraguan National Guard, fought the insurgents in a bloody campaign that left hundreds of civilians dead and created havoc with the nation's economy, particularly as much of the fighting occurred in the country's mining and plantation regions.

By the early 1930s, several factors came into play that would bring America's Marines and navy personnel home. One was the rising U.S. casualty numbers; forty-eight died in the fighting by 1933, and another sixty-eight were wounded. Also, President Franklin D. Roosevelt was determined to build a new and less interventionist relationship between the United States and Latin America, which he dubbed the "Good Neighbor Policy." Perhaps most importantly, the Roosevelt administration came to believe that the Nicaraguan National Guard under the leadership of Anastasio Somoza García—whom Roosevelt famously described as "our son of a bitch"—was capable of handling the insurgency on its own.

U.S. troops left Nicaragua in 1933. A year later, Somoza had Sandino assassinated and launched a brutal campaign that crushed the guerrillas. In 1937, Somoza became dictator of Nicaragua. He was succeeded by his son, Anastasio Somoza Debayle, and the Somoza dynasty ruled the country with a corrupt and iron hand until it was overthrown in 1979 by a new insurgency. That movement, Frente Sandinista de Liberación Nacional (Sandinista National Liberation Front), followed in the footsteps of the rebel leader who had battled the U.S. Marines to a standoff in the late 1920s and early 1930s.

James Ciment

See also: Latin America, Relations with; Military Affairs.

Further Reading

Gobat, Michel. *Confronting the American Dream: Nicaragua Under U.S. Imperial Rule.* Durham, NC: Duke University Press, 2005.

Selser, Gregorio. *Sandino.* Trans. by Cedric Belfrage. New York: Monthly Review, 1981.

Nonpartisan League

For some farmers, the first fifteen years of the twentieth century could rightly be called the golden years of American agriculture. Prices were generally good, the weather cooperated, and the social standing of the nation's farmers remained firm. For North Dakotans, however, little could have been further from the truth. High interest rates, shady practices by grain traders and railroad lines, and comparatively low prices led to unrest and social decline.

Thwarted by the 1915 state legislature in their request for funding to support a state-run grain elevator, the farmers in North Dakota grew frustrated. Told by Tredwell Twitchell, a Bismarck legislator, to "Go home and slop the hogs!" they became angry at the dismissiveness of their elected officials. Coalescing behind Arthur C. Townley, a flax farmer who more than once had declared bankruptcy and in recent years had served as an organizer for the Socialist Party, western North Dakota farmers laid forth a platform. Initially calling themselves the Farmers' Nonpartisan Political League, the small band of McHenry County growers demanded a state government that would build and operate a grain mill and elevator, packing plants, and cold storage plants. Moreover, in their view, the state should use its power to operate a hail insurance corporation, with a state-owned bank offering farmers low-interest loans. The group determined to affiliate with no political party, nor to form their own, but to support individual candidates of either party who supported their agenda. The organization changed its name to the Nonpartisan League (NPL) to broaden its appeal.

The league quickly gained adherents, claiming 40,000 members by June 1916 and spreading to other states, particularly the in the Midwest. In the November election, NPL-supported candidates claimed North Dakota's governorship, the cabinet, and the state House of Representatives. Regardless of the roadblocks imposed by a Republican-controlled Senate, much of the NPL's nonagricultural agenda was accomplished. In 1917, for example, the legislature approved a state highway commission, a significantly improved grain grading system, and increased aid to education.

NPL strength reached its zenith in 1918, and with Townley calling for a "New Day for North Dakota," little seemed outside the realm of possibility, particularly given that the state supreme court had been elected in essence to serve the purposes of the NPL. With control of the state firmly in hand, the NPL within a matter of weeks created the framework for the North Dakota State Mill and Elevator Association, the Home Building Association, the Bank of North Dakota, a state-sponsored hail insurance program, and an Industrial Commission to oversee it all.

Problems arose almost immediately from a lack of administrative experience and a measure of corruption.

Compounding the NPL's failure to turn around the economy of the state was the criticism directed toward the league for its Socialist roots. While such underpinnings had not been a burden in 1916, the Bolshevik takeover in Russia in 1917, the French soldiers' strike during World War I, and the generally negative attitude toward the war held by many members of the NPL, particularly its leadership, began to turn the tide.

The election of 1920 saw Governor Lynn J. Frazier gain his third term in office under the banner of the NPL, but the victory was narrow. Opposition to the league was fermenting throughout the state and the Midwest. The Independent Voters' Association and the Citizens' Economy League organized against the NPL, undermining the league at every juncture and publishing the *Red Flame*, a scurrilous tabloid that called into question the morality, patriotism, and honesty of NPL leaders.

By October 1921, the opponents of the NPL had built enough support to hold a recall election targeting North Dakota's governor, the attorney general, and the commissioner of agriculture. Citizens could also vote to overturn the entirety of the NPL's agriculturally oriented program. When the ballots were counted, the officials had all been removed from office. But the institutions spawned by the NPL remained intact and still function to this day, indicating that the ideals of the organization struck an important chord with North Dakotans. The Nonpartisan League essentially dissolved with the recall of its officials, but its name is resurrected from time to time as a study in populism.

Kimberly K. Porter

See also: Agriculture; American Farm Bureau Federation; Farmer-Labor Party; Progressivism.

Further Reading

Campbell, Patrick K., and Charles R. Lamb, eds. *The Nonpartisan League, 1915–1922: An Annotated Bibliography.* St. Paul: Minnesota Historical Society, 1985.

Morlan, Robert L. *Political Prairie Fire: The Nonpartisan League, 1915–1922.* St. Paul: Minnesota Historical Society, 1985.

Robinson, Elwyn B. *History of North Dakota.* Lincoln: University of Nebraska Press, 1966.

Normalcy

In 1920, while campaigning for the presidency of the United States, Republican nominee Warren G. Harding promised that, if elected, he would return the country to "normalcy" following the upheaval of U.S.

involvement in World War I and the idealistic and embattled administration of President Woodrow Wilson. His promise to restore what many Americans perceived as the "good old days" resonated with voters, who elected Harding the nation's twenty-ninth president.

The presidency of Wilson, whose first term saw the adoption of landmark economic measures such as the creation of the Federal Reserve System and the Federal Trade Commission, was marred in its second term by the outbreak of World War I and global pressure on the United States to join the Allied powers. By 1917, the Wilson administration, in preparation for U.S. military involvement, had taken several dramatic measures, including a military draft, nationalization of some industries, and suppression of antiwar groups and other dissenters. U.S. involvement in the war, although brief, resulted in more than 53,000 American combat deaths and Wilson's commitment to increased U.S. involvement in global affairs.

Social and political upheavals surrounding the war resulted in an influx of European immigrants to the United States, most of whom settled in the already crowded cities of the East and Midwest. By 1919, a postwar economic recession had set in, exacerbating social and racial tensions and fueling labor unrest. Violent strikes and urban riots ensued, accompanied by attacks on major American financial institutions by radical political groups. By this time, unbeknownst to the American public, Wilson had been incapacitated by a stroke and was unable to carry out his duties as president.

In the midst of this tumult, many Americans longed for the perceived simplicity and stability of an earlier age. Fear of widespread immigration and alien political ideologies sparked a growth in anti-immigration sentiment, isolationist ideology, and reactionary politics typified by the revival of the Ku Klux Klan. Harding sought to establish a sharp contrast in the minds of voters between his agenda and that of his Democratic opponent, Ohio Governor James M. Cox, whom he cast as a standard-bearer for the progressive policies of Wilson.

Promising a return to the conservative, business-friendly policies of William McKinley, Harding seized upon the country's growing uneasiness with the outward-looking philosophy of progressivism and its emphasis on government activism in effecting social and economic reform. Yet Harding capitalized on the progressives' success in securing woman suffrage by actively supporting the Nineteenth Amendment, which granted voting rights to women. In 1920, in the first national election in which women were allowed to vote, Harding won with 60 percent of the popular vote.

Despite his promise to restore "normalcy" to American life, Harding's presidency was far from normal, marred by scandal and accusations of incompetence and cut short by his death of cardiovascular disease on August 2, 1923. His brief administration saw the resignation, arrest, and conviction of several of its officials for bribery and fraud. Among those convicted was Secretary of the Interior Albert B. Fall. A key figure in the Teapot Dome scandal, Fall became the first member of a U.S. presidential cabinet to serve time in prison. Upon Harding's death, Calvin Coolidge assumed office, continuing Harding's probusiness policies. Coolidge also instituted modest labor reforms and initiated the Kellogg-Briand Pact (1928), a multinational agreement that set a precedent for post–World War II international relations.

Harding's "normalcy" became a subject of ridicule to some. Contemporary critics such as journalist H.L. Mencken scoffed at Harding's use of the word, citing it as yet another example of the president's tendency to misuse the English language. Most believed that Harding inadvertently coined the word while trying to articulate the more common term "normality." Harding's defenders, however, cite evidence that "normalcy" existed long before its association with Harding and may have been in use as early as the mid-nineteenth century, though not in the political sense Harding gave it. The term is currently part of common usage, and most English-language dictionaries deem "normalcy" grammatically acceptable.

Michael H. Burchett

See also: Election of 1920; Harding, Warren G.

Further Reading

Miller, Nathan. *New World Coming: The 1920s and the Making of Modern America.* New York: Scribner's, 2003.

Morello, John A. *Selling the President, 1920: Albert D. Lasker, Advertising, and the Election of Warren G. Harding.* New York: Praeger, 2001.

Murray, Robert K. *The Politics of Normalcy: Governmental Theory and Practice in the Harding-Coolidge Era.* New York: W.W. Norton, 1973.

Norris, J. Frank (1877–1952)

A pioneering radio preacher and outspoken opponent of communism, evolution, and Catholic immigrants,

J. Frank Norris emerged as a notable figure just as fundamentalism was coalescing into a significant movement. His combative temperament was, in some ways, well suited to the militant fundamentalism of the 1920s, whose followers believed they were embroiled in a desperate struggle with currents of change that were eroding the religious and cultural foundations of American civilization. Yet his harsh rhetoric and uncompromising positions alienated allies and enemies alike and made him one of the most controversial religious figures of his time.

John Franklin Norris was born in Dadeville, Alabama, on September 18, 1877. In the early 1880s, his family moved to the village of Hubbard on the Texas frontier. There, in his early teens, Norris experienced a religious conversion at a revival meeting that led to his career in the ministry. He attended Baylor University, in Waco, Texas, and Southern Baptist Theological Seminary, in Louisville, Kentucky, from which he graduated at the top of his class. In 1905, Norris became pastor of the McKinney Avenue Baptist Church in Dallas. Two years later, he temporarily abandoned the pulpit to become editor and part owner of a Texas religious periodical, the *Baptist Standard*. In 1909, he accepted a position as minister of the First Baptist Church of Fort Worth, his primary base of operations for the next forty-three years.

Norris was hardworking, colorful, combative, and controversial. His pugnacious but folksy style and the anti-elitist message of his preaching gave him considerable appeal among the masses. During the late 1910s and early 1920s, he championed Prohibition, battled vice, and warred with politicians, educators, and the regional Southern Baptist establishment. During the 1920s, he allied himself with conservative Christian leaders outside his region and emerged as the leading Southern spokesman for the developing fundamentalist movement. He was a charter member of the World's Christian Fundamentals Association and helped organize the conservative Baptist Bible Union. In 1924, his militancy led a liberal periodical, the *Christian Century*, to describe him as "probably the most belligerent fundamentalist now abroad in the land."

Using his pulpit, his ministry on radio station KSAT in San Antonio, his newspaper *The Searchlight*, and eventually his seminary, the Southwestern Baptist Theological Seminary, Norris championed religious fundamentalism. He believed in the literal truth of the Bible, God's direct intervention in human affairs, and the idea that history is an unfolding of God's will. Although he lived in the most religiously conservative section of the nation, he repeatedly warned that Christianity in the South was in danger of falling victim to the modernism he believed was sweeping the North. For Norris as for many other fundamentalists, "modernism" was an ill-defined term connoting religious, social, and cultural ills besetting the country. He tended to equate change with decay and believed that orthodox Christianity, as he understood it, was the most effective bulwark against that decay.

Throughout the 1920s, Norris zealously supported the enforcement of Prohibition and resisted the growing movement for its repeal. He was an ardent opponent of evolution and published a stenographic record of the Scopes trial of 1925. He warned of the detrimental effects of the growing immigrant population on the nation and espoused the need for segregation of the races. Norris's premillennialist theology, a belief in the return of Jesus as messiah, seems to have precluded him from embracing the anti-Semitism of many of his contemporaries, but he was virulently anti-Catholic. Believing, as did many conservative Protestants, that the Catholics' first loyalty was to the pope and Rome rather than to the United States, he vigorously campaigned against the Democratic presidential candidate Al Smith, a Catholic, in 1928 and helped Republican Herbert Hoover carry Texas.

In 1927, Norris's anti-Catholicism contributed to the most notorious incident of his career. Previously, in 1912, he had been charged with, tried for, and acquitted of perjury and arson as a result of a fire that destroyed the auditorium of his church in Fort Worth. In 1926, Norris alleged that the Catholic mayor of Fort Worth, H.C. Meacham, was guilty of a number of misdeeds, including the misappropriation of public funds for Catholic causes. When a friend of the mayor, Texas lumberman Dexter Elliot Chipps, confronted Norris in his church office, the clergyman shot him to death. A jury acquitted Norris on the grounds of self-defense, but the incident further tainted his already controversial reputation.

As the 1920s drew to a close, Norris interpreted the stock market crash and onset of the Great Depression as divine judgment on an increasingly godless and immoral nation. But he also had compassion for the suffering masses, which at first led him to support the New Deal of President Franklin D. Roosevelt. By the mid-1930s, however, as he expanded his ministry to include both his church in Fort Worth and the Temple Baptist Church in Detroit, of which he became pastor in late 1934, Norris had become a vocal critic of what he regarded as the liberal, even communistic, tendencies of the Roosevelt administration.

Norris seems to have been relatively unconcerned about communism during much of the 1920s, but in the late 1930s, it surpassed modernism in his thinking as the greatest threat to the religious and moral well-being of the nation. His anti-Catholicism of the 1920s gave way to pragmatic cooperation with the Catholic Church, which he now regarded as an important ally in the struggle against the radical Left. The last years of his career in the 1940s and early 1950s were characterized by an unfaltering conservative commitment to counter what he perceived as the threat of Communist aggression from abroad and subversion from within. He died of a heart attack in Keystone Heights, Florida, on August 20, 1952.

Robert F. Martin

See also: Evangelicals and Evangelical Christianity; Fundamentalism, Christian.

Further Reading

Hankins, Barry. *God's Rascal: J. Frank Norris & the Beginnings of Southern Fundamentalism.* Lexington: University Press of Kentucky, 1996.

Norris, J. Frank. *Inside History of First Baptist Church, Fort Worth, and Temple Baptist Church, Detroit: Life Story of Dr. J. Frank Norris.* New York: Garland, 1988.

Office Work

The period from 1918 to 1930 saw a dramatic increase in the amount of office work available in America, and a corresponding shift in the social composition of office workers. Changes inside the office affected social structures in the world outside and opened new opportunities to women, the working class, and first-generation immigrants, particularly those from Eastern Europe. By 1930, the American office had been transformed; instead of earnest male clerks scattered around various departments in factories and businesses, clerical work was done in large central offices, often by young women of varying social backgrounds under the supervision of a male or older female "middle management" figure.

The massive increase in the amount of office work available during the 1920s occurred as a result of earlier developments in business and industry. One major factor was the evolution of scientific management systems to organize labor processes and make them more efficient. Engineer Frederick Taylor pioneered this technique, and his model was adopted by many of the postwar college-educated executives. Offices that adopted his methods were said to be "rationalized" or "Taylorized," and managers hired efficiency experts who introduced timecards, cost-accounting procedures, and auditing systems into the workplace.

A second factor affecting office work was the growth in industrial production and popular consumption. Americans were making and buying more consumer goods. Banks, insurance companies, and utility companies extended their operations to keep pace with the growth of consumer culture. Profitable growth, however, relied on accurate accounting procedures. Careful record keeping required a sizeable staff of workers to type, take dictation, and record and file the numerous pieces of information generated by a profitable business or scientifically managed workforce.

One of the notable features of the expanded office force in the 1920s was the higher proportion of women. The accompanying table of clerical and office work professions shows the shift in gender composition between 1920 and 1930.

Women's entry into office work was partially due to the impact of World War I, which sent many women into offices to substitute for men who were away at war, but it was also a function of prevailing ideas regarding women and work. In contrast to factory jobs, office work was widely viewed as respectable and clean, and thus appropriate for young middle-class women. Many clerical tasks, such as typing, were thought suitable for women's "nimble fingers." Higher management welcomed younger women, in particular, as an attractive addition to the workplace. Some employment bureaus barred women over thirty, while one executive of the era stipulated that his secretaries must be "attractive and add to the general appearance of the office."

In economic terms, women were a relative bargain for employers; it was generally held that women could be paid less than men because they did not need a "family wage" to survive. Some male clerical workers believed that women were responsible for forcing down wages. Many men, therefore, sought to climb

As corporations and other enterprises grew in size during the 1920s, so did the need for clerical workers—providing new employment opportunities for women. (*Topical Press Agency/Hulton Archive/Getty Images*)

Selected Clerical and Office Work Professions, 1920–1930 (in thousands)

	1910	1920	1930
Bookkeepers/cashiers	446.8	615.5	738.2
	(100%)	(100%)	(100%)
Male	263.3	269.8	272.5
	(59%)	(44%)	(37%)
Female	183.6	345.7	465.7
	(41%)	(56%)	(63%)
Stenographers/typists	387.0	786.0	1,097.0
	(100%)	(100%)	(100%)
Male	76.0	80.0	66.0
	(20%)	(10%)	(6%)
Female	311.0	706.0	1,031.0
	(80%)	(90%)	(94%)
Business-machine operators	—	—	38.1
			(100%)
Male			5.4
			(14%)
Female			32.7
			(86%)
Clerical and related jobs not classified elsewhere	654.3	1,323.3	1,680.5
	(100%)	(100%)	(100%)
Male	578.5	990.9	1,260.7
	(88%)	(75%)	(75%)
Female	75.8	332.3	419.9
	(12%)	(25%)	(25%)
Managers, officials, salespeople, and agents in selected categories	441.4	641.1	1,043.1
	(100%)	(100%)	(100%)
Male	426.1	607.3	971.9
	(97%)	(95%)	(93%)
Female	15.3	33.8	71.2
	(3%)	(5%)	(7%)

Source: David L. Kaplan and M. Claire Casey, "Occupational Trends in the United States, 1900–1950," Bureau of the Census Working Paper no. 5, Washington, DC: Department of Commerce, 1958.

the professional ladder rather than be stuck with "women's wages" in lower-ranked clerical positions.

Women office workers also faced a "marriage bar"—the perception that young female office workers were simply marking time before marriage and would never seek serious advancement in their careers. Older women, single or married, also faced this obstacle. The few women who remained in the workforce for the long term, however, tended to command higher pay and rise to management positions.

Despite prejudices, the preference for hiring female clerical workers initiated a "feminization" of office work by 1930. Two million "girls in the office" made up 20 percent of the female labor force. An American Management Association survey of 1928 listed 152 firms with "bookkeeping and billing machines" and indicated that 90 percent of clerical operatives were women; 95 percent were under twenty-five years of age.

Office work transcended some class barriers during the Jazz Age. Working-class women and men with a minimal education were often employed in entry-level positions. There were far fewer black clerical workers than white, and under 3 percent of all office workers were Hispanic. But the number of Eastern European immigrant women in the white-collar workforce doubled between 1918 and 1930. For these first-generation Americans, and for many working-class women and men, office work opened a door to financial independence and upward social mobility. It guaranteed a wage that gave young people, especially those living at home, a bit of discretionary income. It also widened their social horizons because the office served as a place for social mixing. A song, popular with the men of the Pennsylvania Railroad service in 1918, declared,

The office is really a different place,
For every man works with a smile on his face,
It's certainly evident such is the case,
Because we've got girls in the office.

The ability to consume goods, to mix with Americans from different social backgrounds, and to absorb mainstream American values often brought young immigrant clerical workers into conflict with family traditions. But office work also offered them independence and a chance to become more American. In this respect, as well as many others, the expansion of office work in Jazz Age America had profound social effects, in addition to its impact on labor systems and production practices.

Rachel Gillett

See also: Labor Movement; Women and Gender.

Further Reading

Davidson, Janet F. "Now That We Have Girls in the Office." In *Boys and Their Toys? Masculinity, Technology, and Class in America,* ed. Roger Horowitz. New York: Routledge, 2001.

Kocka, Jurgen. *White-Collar Workers in America, 1890–1940: A Socio-Political History in International Perspective.* London: Sage, 1980.

Kwollek-Folland, Angel. *Engendering Business: Men and Women in the Corporate Office, 1870–1930.* Baltimore: Johns Hopkins University Press, 1998.

Strom, Sharon Hartman. *Beyond the Typewriter: Gender, Class, and the Origins of Modern American Office Work, 1900–1930.* Urbana: University of Illinois Press, 1992.

Oil and Oil Industry

The use of petroleum and its by-products as a lubricant, an illuminant, and particularly a fuel was well established in American life before the Jazz Age. By the 1920s, the oil industry had taken on its modern oligarchic form; a few major corporations controlled most of the nation's refining, distribution, and marketing capacity. Still, the decade witnessed rapid growth in the production and consumption of oil, a commodity that had become critical to the economy and strategic position of the United States.

Early History

Oil and its by-product tar had been used since ancient times for illumination, ship caulking, ammunition, and even medicine. Initially, most oil was simply gathered from spots where it bubbled to the earth's surface. The modern oil industry began in America with the drilling of the first oil well in Pennsylvania in 1859. In the late nineteenth century, America's oil came primarily from Pennsylvania and nearby states, and it was used mostly in the form of kerosene as an illuminant. But the spread of electrical illumination, particularly in the more advanced economies of Europe and North America, decreased the demand for kerosene, and the internal combustion engine created an even bigger market for oil in the form of gasoline. Whereas about 12 percent of U.S. crude oil production was refined into kerosene in 1918, that figure dropped to about 5 percent in 1929. At the same time, gasoline's share rose from 25 percent to 50 percent. The rest went into diesel, fuel oils for heating and electricity generation, and lubricants.

Adding to the demand for oil was the decision of the world's major navies to switch from coal to diesel fuel. Thus, oil became a strategic asset for many nations, including the United States. World War I helped to solidify the importance of the commodity with policy makers in the United States and Europe. The warring powers had become so dependent on gasoline and diesel fuel to run tanks and trucks that, in the opinion of many historians, Germany's decision to sue for peace in November 1918 resulted in part from its inability to seize critical oil fields in Romania before they were destroyed by Allied forces. In the United States, huge new discoveries in Texas, Oklahoma, and California expanded supply dramatically in the 1910s and 1920s, as did new foreign oil fields in the Caucasus region of Russia and in Persia (modern-day Iran).

In the 1860s and 1870s, the early years of the American oil industry, the business was highly competitive, with numerous small firms producing, refining, and distributing the product. By the 1880s, however, a single firm—Standard Oil, headed by John D. Rockefeller—had emerged to control refining and distribution, though production remained under the control of many different firms. While Standard Oil's domination helped stabilize prices, it also invited criticism that one company controlled so much of such a crucial product.

In response to a lengthy investigation by the federal government into Standard Oil's monopolistic pricing practices, in 1911 the U.S. Supreme Court ordered the dissolution of the company into a number of smaller firms, including Standard Oil of New York (later Mobil), Standard Oil of Indiana (later Amoco), Standard Oil of California (later Chevron), and the largest of them all, Standard Oil of New Jersey (later Exxon). These companies, along with such major independents as Union Oil (later Unocal), Atlantic Richfield (later ARCO), and Sinclair Oil, controlled the vast majority of America's refining capacity in the 1920s, as well as its distribution network, from pipelines and tank farms down to retail gas stations. Production, however, remained largely in the hands of independent firms and individuals.

Production and Consumption

Domestic production of crude oil climbed dramatically in the 1920s, from roughly 443 million barrels (a barrel equals 42 gallons) in 1920 to just over 1 billion barrels in 1929, making the United States the largest producer of oil in the world. U.S. production of coal—the dominant fuel of nineteenth-century industry—declined from 658 million tons in 1920 to 609 million in 1929. With the rapid growth in the number of automobiles, as well as the transition from coal power to diesel in railroads and shipping, oil consumption grew dramatically. In 1924, domestic demand stood at roughly 685 million barrels, while another 110 million barrels were exported.

The United States remained the world's largest producer of oil during the 1920s, with major fields in Texas, Oklahoma, Louisiana, and California, including this one in the Venice Beach section of Los Angeles. *(Keystone/Hulton Archive/Getty Images)*

The United States was the largest producer and exporter of petroleum in the world during the 1920s, accounting for roughly two-thirds of world production. It also imported oil, largely from Mexico and Venezuela, as it was sometimes cheaper to bring oil from those countries to various parts of the United States by tanker rather than by pipeline or railroad car from domestic supply points. By 1929, U.S. domestic demand had climbed to about 940 million barrels, with another 160 million barrels exported. At the beginning of the decade, California was the largest producer, followed by Oklahoma and Texas. By 1929, Texas had surpassed California for the top spot.

While production rose dramatically over the decade, it was not a steady climb from year to year. Dramatic new discoveries in Texas in the early 1920s, as well as a sharp recession in 1921–1922, sent oil prices plummeting from about $3 per barrel in 1920 to about $1.30 per barrel in 1923. Rising demand and a lack of new discoveries pushed the price back up to nearly $2 per barrel in 1926. Then, big discoveries in Texas and Oklahoma sent the price down to a decade low of about $1.25 per barrel in 1929, while gasoline fell to just ten cents per gallon in some markets in the late 1920s. Oil prices would drop even more sharply in the early 1930s, to a paltry fifteen cents per barrel, a result of the Great Depression lowering demand and the discovery of huge new fields in East Texas.

Many of the discoveries were made possible by new prospecting techniques. Traditionally, drillers would put down experimental wells based on surface features, usually in the form of distinctive domes in the land. But growing use of geophones, seismographic devices that send sound waves into the earth to detect pockets of oil, dramatically raised the likelihood of finding oil. New refining techniques allowed oil companies to get more gasoline from each barrel of oil, and new pipeline technologies cut down on leakage.

Increased U.S. and worldwide production in the 1920s, and the constant flux in oil supplies, led the major oil companies of the world to negotiate the Achnacarry Agreement in 1928, named after the Scottish castle where it was reached. Also known as the "as-is" agreement, Achnacarry set a quota for each oil company in various markets around the globe. A company could sell more oil in that market if overall demand went up, but its percentage would remain the same. This arrangement was intended to stop the oil companies from trying to gain market share by underselling their competitors and driving down prices to ruinous levels. Ultimately, Achnacarry would be undone through massive violations by various oil companies during the desperate Depression years.

Oil and Power

Oil took on an increasingly high and sometimes controversial profile in Jazz Age America. With the number of automobiles on the road steadily climbing—production rose from 2.2 million units in 1920 to 5.3 million in 1929—oil companies began to market their oil products in a more consumer-friendly fashion. They also started marketing higher-octane gasoline and introduced lead to reduce engine "knocking." In 1920, there were roughly 100,000 establishments selling gasoline, half of them as a sideline to their main grocery or hardware business. By 1929, 300,000 establishments in America were selling gasoline, and nearly all of them were solely devoted to that business, as well as automobile repair. Previously, gasoline had been stored in overhead tanks (often converted hot-water tanks) and siphoned down into car gas tanks by hose. However, the new stations used specially designed pumps with glass bulbs at the top so consumers could see the purity of the gasoline for themselves. In addition to gas and repairs, these stations sold almost every accessory a driver might need, from batteries to tires. As gasoline became increasingly branded in the 1920s, the major oil companies opened chains of stations, each with its distinctive logo.

Yet oil also had a darker image in the 1920s. As part of the plan to convert the U.S. Navy from coal to oil, the federal government had set aside three oil reserves in the 1900s and 1910s, two of them located in California and one at Teapot Dome, Wyoming. When Warren G. Harding took office as president in 1921, he appointed Republican Senator Albert Fall of New Mexico to head the Department of the Interior. A successful rancher and miner, Fall believed that the oil reserves should be turned over to private developers and, to that end, wrested control of the reserves from the Department of the Navy. In 1922, Fall arranged to have the reserve at Teapot Dome leased to Harry Sinclair, the founder of Sinclair Oil, and assured him that the U.S. government would buy the oil Sinclair produced from the reserve. Fall made a similar deal with California oil producer Edward Doheny for the Elk Hills reserve in that state. When a congressional investigating committee discovered that Fall had received kickbacks from Sinclair and Doheny, the resulting scandal tarnished the Harding administration and led to Fall's imprisonment on conspiracy and bribery charges. Fall was the first cabinet member to be jailed for misconduct in office. Doheny was acquitted of all charges. Sinclair, although his case ended in a mistrial, was eventually sentenced to six months in prison on contempt of court charges for attempting to spy on jurors.

The Teapot Dome scandal spelled out to Jazz Age Americans the growing political and economic influence of the oil industry. By the end of the decade, oil had become more than a commodity. It had become the very incarnation of power in every sense of that word—from the power to run the economy to the power that corrupts the political process.

James Ciment

See also: Automobile Industry; Automobiles and Automobile Culture; Coal Industry; Sinclair, Harry; Teapot Dome Scandal.

Further Reading

Williamson, Harold F., Ralph L. Andreano, Arnold R. Daum, and Gilbert C. Klose. *The American Petroleum Industry: 1899–1959, The Age of Energy.* Evanston, IL: Northwestern University Press, 1959.

Yergin, Daniel. *The Prize: The Epic Quest for Oil, Money, and Power.* New York: Free Press, 1991.

O'Keeffe, Georgia (1887–1986)

Georgia O'Keeffe garnered recognition both as an artist and as a muse during a time when visibility in the art world was difficult for women. That she had not trained in Europe was often held against her, and she constantly strove to prove herself to artists and critics.

Born on November 15, 1887, in Sun Prairie, Wisconsin, the second of the seven children of Francis O'Keeffe and Ida Totto, she grew up listening to her mother read from books, especially marveling at stories featuring pioneer days and adventure. She was keenly aware of and inspired by the natural world.

Defying convention, O'Keeffe declared as a child that she would be an artist when she grew up. When she was twelve, she received private art lessons and the next year took painting with a local amateur painter. Her aptitude with paintbrush and pencil soon became evident, and she flourished artistically when the family moved to Williamsburg, Virginia, in 1903. After five years of private art lessons and obtaining her high school diploma in

1905, O'Keeffe studied at the Art Institute of Chicago for one year, before being forced to spend time at home recuperating from typhoid. In 1907, she left for Manhattan, where she joined the Art Students League and studied portraiture and still life with American Impressionist painter William Merritt Chase, whose encouragement of individual style among his students influenced O'Keeffe's artistic development.

During the next few years, she alternately attended school and taught art classes, spending summers in Charlottesville, Virginia, where her family had moved in 1909, and the school year at Teachers College at Columbia University in New York; Columbia College in Columbia, South Carolina; and West Texas State in Canyon, Texas. Singularly devoted to her work, she put all her energies into pursing a career as an artist as opposed to fulfilling traditional gender expectations of marriage and family.

While teaching at Columbia College in the mid-1910s, O'Keeffe sent some of her charcoal drawings to fellow artist and friend Anna Pollitzer, who showed them to Alfred Stieglitz, a pioneer in photography who exhibited avant-garde works of Auguste Rodin, Henri Matisse, and other European artists at his gallery. O'Keeffe secured a studio owned by Stieglitz's sister and moved to New York. Initially serving as her mentor, Stieglitz eventually left his wife and moved in with O'Keeffe. Past his professional peak by the time they met, Stieglitz subsequently produced some of his best work while documenting the passionate period early in their relationship.

O'Keeffe had shown her work publicly as early as 1917, but it was Alfred Stieglitz's photography show at the Anderson Galleries in New York, on February 2, 1921, that established her as a major artist. The forty-five seminudes by O'Keeffe thrust her into the public eye, and the publicity created an audience for her paintings that would prove enduring. It was during this period that her signature style and subject matter took shape. Many of her early charcoal drawings and watercolors were curvilinear abstractions, but by 1919 her experiments with oil frequently featured flowers, a subject with which she would always be associated. Over the course of the Jazz Age, O'Keeffe developed the triad—symbolism, abstraction, and photography—that characterized her mature work.

In 1921, several of her oils were included in an exhibit of modern art that Stieglitz organized at the

Pennsylvania Academy of Fine Arts. Although her work appeared in Stieglitz's gallery along with that of other artists, it was not until January 1923 that her first major solo exhibit, featuring 100 paintings, opened at the Anderson Galleries. This show, which further established her as an artist, was followed by a joint show with Stieglitz at the Anderson Galleries in 1924 that included fifty-one of her paintings, including the first of her large-scale flower paintings, from which she reaped positive reviews and critical attention. In their reports, the media focused on the rarity of an American woman artist. The show attracted crowds of women who became O'Keeffe's most enthusiastic supporters.

In June 1924, Stieglitz's divorce from his wife became final, and O'Keeffe and Stieglitz married in December. During the years they lived in New York, the couple immersed themselves in the city's cultural offerings, and their apartment off Park Avenue attracted a regular flow of artists, writers, and socialites. Summers were spent at Lake George, New York. In 1928, a group of O'Keeffe's small paintings of calla lilies sold for $25,000 (equal to several hundred thousand dollars in 2007 terms) to an American living in France. As the largest amount of money paid to a living American artist to date, the sale made headlines and generated even more interest in O'Keeffe's work.

In the winter of 1928–1929, O'Keeffe painted very little. With the inspiration of Lake George waning, O'Keeffe yearned to return to the West. In April 1929, O'Keeffe accepted the invitation of art patron Mabel Dodge Luhan to spend the summer painting in Taos, New Mexico. She returned to New Mexico every summer until 1949, when, after Stieglitz's death, she moved there permanently. O'Keeffe died on March 6, 1986, in Santa Fe, New Mexico.

Rebecca Tolley-Stokes

See also: Art, Fine.

Further Reading

Hogfre, Jeffery. *O'Keeffe: The Life of an American Legend.* New York: Bantam, 1992.

Lisle, Laurie. *Portrait of an Artist: A Biography of Georgia O'Keeffe.* Albuquerque: University of New Mexico Press, 1986.

Peters, Sarah Whitaker. *Becoming O'Keeffe: The Early Years.* New York: Abbeville, 1991.

Pollitzer, Anna. *A Woman on Paper: Georgia O'Keeffe.* New York: Simon & Schuster, 1988.

Wagner, Anne Middleton. *Three Artists (Three Women): Modernism and the Art of Hesse, Krasner, and O'Keeffe.* Berkeley: University of California Press, 1996.

Oliver, Joe "King" (1885–1938)

Jazz cornet player Joe "King" Oliver came out of New Orleans, traveled North with tens of thousands of other Southern blacks during the Great Migration of the early twentieth century, and established a band that would fundamentally shape and define early jazz. He is notable for the use of the mute and for the emergence of his protégé Louis Armstrong. "I still think that if it had not been for Joe Oliver," Armstrong wrote in his autobiography, "Jazz would not be what it is today."

Oliver was born in Abend, Louisiana, on December 19, 1885. He first took up the trombone before switching to the cornet. He began playing professionally in 1907 with various brass bands, dance bands, street parade bands, and small bar and cabaret groups in the city. He played with Edward "Kid" Ory in one of New Orleans's most in-demand "hot" jazz bands, performing for both black and white audiences. It was Ory who dubbed Oliver "King of the Cornet."

By 1918, Oliver had established himself as one of the finest cornet players in New Orleans. The following year, he moved to Chicago with Ory, in part because of the World War I closure of the "red light" Storyville district in New Orleans and possibly as a result of a fight after one of his concerts. He joined Bill Johnson's band at the Dreamland Ballroom and also toured with the band, traveling to California before returning to the Chicago in 1922.

Oliver became a strong and effective bandleader in his own right in Chicago, carrying the New Orleans jazz tradition onto the national stage. He established what would become the celebrated King Oliver's Creole Jazz Band, particularly famous for the duets that Oliver played with the band's second cornet player, twenty-two-year-old Louis Armstrong. Legend has it that Oliver bought Armstrong his first cornet and, while in New Orleans, showed him how

Joe "King" Oliver's Creole Jazz Band, performing here in Chicago in 1923, was the first black ensemble to make a commercial recording. Oliver (rear, second from left) played the cornet; a young Louis Armstrong (front, center) played the slide trumpet. *(Frank Driggs Collection/Hulton Archive/Getty Images)*

to play before calling for him to join the band in Chicago. Armstrong was so influenced by Oliver that he called him "Papa Joe."

The band's relatively short residency at the city's Lincoln Gardens (it disbanded in 1924) nevertheless proved highly influential in the evolution of jazz, with such tracks as "Dipper Mouth Blues" (1923). The band, including Lil Hardin (piano), Honore Dutrey (trombone), Johnny Dodds (clarinet), and Baby Dodds (drums), was the perfect example of New Orleans collective improvisation. In 1924, Oliver also recorded duets with jazz pianist Jelly Roll Morton. The following February, Oliver took over leadership of a larger group that included saxophones from Dave Peyton. The group played at the Plantation Cafe in Chicago as King Oliver and the Dixie Syncopators until spring 1927. This collective was a blending of his New Orleans traditional jazz background and the fast-emerging craze for Big Band dance music. His new band would become famous for such numbers as "Dead Man Blues" and "Someday Sweetheart" (both recorded in 1926). Like the Creole Jazz Band, the Dixie Syncopators made a series of seminal recordings that would become jazz standards.

Oliver is one of the musicians to bridge the unrecorded prehistory of jazz and its early documented and recorded history. He married early blues, ragtime, and popular song, and he helped to shape and define jazz as it emerged. He is widely recognized as one of the leading proponents of the New Orleans style and became famous for the use of timbre modifiers, or mutes, on the cornet and for the "wah-wah" sound. Interested in tonal texture, he would employ a range of cups, bottles, glasses, kazoos, and derby hats to alter the sound. This was showcased in the three-chorus solo on "Dipper Mouth Blues," much mimicked by musicians throughout the 1920s and 1930s. But Oliver was more a strong bandleader and ensemble player than a soloist.

The rapidly evolving jazz of the 1920s, with the creative dynamo of the Harlem Renaissance as its backdrop, soon meant that other, younger musicians and different styles jarred with Oliver's music. As early as 1924, his impact was waning, in part because he suffered from severe and recurring tooth and gum problems—he enjoyed eating sugary foods, particularly sugar sandwiches—and these ailments somewhat affected his ability to play the cornet. His protégé, Louis Armstrong, eventually inherited Oliver's position as jazz's premier cornetist.

The Dixie Syncopators were engaged at Manhattan's Savoy Ballroom in May 1927, but Oliver never sparked the same level of success that he had experienced in Chicago in the mid-1920s. His managers took advantage of him on several occasions, and he made several ill-advised business decisions, such as turning down a regular slot at Harlem's Cotton Club because he thought the fee too low. The spot was subsequently taken by Duke Ellington, for whom it proved enormously valuable.

Luis Russell took over the Dixie Syncopators in 1929, but Oliver remained in New York, playing and recording frequently with various groups. Most of his teeth were removed because of ongoing dental problems, and his gums bled constantly. He lost money in the stock market crash of 1929 and tried to generate funds by touring in the 1930s with a number of bands. Oliver stopped recording in April 1931, but his early recordings were highly sought after by collectors. Moneyless, he took a job as a janitor at a pool hall in Savannah, Georgia, where he died on April 8, 1938.

Sam Hitchmough

See also: Armstrong, Louis; Jazz.

Further Reading

Armstrong, Louis. *Satchmo: My Life in New Orleans.* New York: Prentice Hall, 1954.

Williams, Martin. *King Oliver.* London: Cassell, 1960.

O'Neill, Eugene (1888–1953)

Eugene O'Neill's career as a playwright spanned three decades. From his fruitful participation in the East Coast theater scene of the mid-1910s through his increasingly hermetic California isolation of the mid-1940s, O'Neill continued to write, to innovate, and to confront timeless themes in a modern American setting. His efforts earned him four Pulitzer Prizes, the Nobel Prize, and a reputation as the most significant American dramatist of the twentieth century.

Waiting in the Wings

O'Neill was born on October 16, 1888, in New York City. From the beginning, the theatrical world was his natural milieu. His father, James O'Neill, was a successful stage actor who toured the country performing alongside his wife, Ella. O'Neill traveled with his parents until the age of seven, when he was enrolled in Catholic boarding school: the Mount Saint Vincent School of New York in 1895, and the Betts Academy in Stamford, Connecticut, in 1900.

In 1902, Ella O'Neill attempted suicide. In this way did the fifteen-year-old O'Neill learn that his mother had suffered from morphine addiction brought on by his own complicated birth. O'Neill, an alcoholic, adopted a wild lifestyle that resulted in his ejection from Princeton University after less than a full year. Not until 1914, when he found inspiration in the playwriting class of Harvard professor George Pierce Baker, did O'Neill have a consistent direction. He began writing and, in 1916, removed himself to Cape Cod to work with one of the nation's most forward-looking theatrical companies, the Provincetown Players.

New Horizons

The period that followed was one of remarkable creativity and productivity—to say nothing of success—for the still-youthful O'Neill. Plays such as *Bound East for Cardiff* (1916) and *The Long Voyage Home* (1918) carried him to the New York stage and made him a nationally known figure. Consecutive Pulitzer Prizes for *Beyond the Horizon* and *Anna Christie* in 1920 and 1921, respectively, set him securely atop the hierarchy of American playwrights. Critics admired him because he departed from convention, exploring the possibilities of serious drama conducted in American vernacular. Broadway liked him because his plays were hits.

In *The Emperor Jones* (1920), O'Neill traces the rise and fall of Brutus Jones, a Pullman porter turned Caribbean despot. *The Hairy Ape* (1922) follows the decline of Yank, a ship's stoker whom society cages and ultimately annihilates. O'Neill's weaknesses are on display in these plays: tiresome forays into faux dialect strain viewers' credulity, while major characters appear as composites of stereotypes rather than fleshed-out human beings. Yet audiences found compensation in the playwright's vivid expressionist style and his willingness to confront the dehumanizing effects of modern society. Moreover, the daring that O'Neill showed in his themes and casting had a catalyzing effect on American theater. The New York productions of *The Emperor Jones* and *All God's Chillun Got Wings* (1923), both of which featured black actors in lead roles, helped to incite the vogue for black musicals that underlay the Harlem Renaissance.

By the mid-1920s, O'Neill was a towering figure, acknowledged by the most skeptical of critics as a genius. Yet these years of critical success also brought harrowing loss; from 1920 to 1923, O'Neill lost in succession his father, mother, and brother. The effects would resonate through his work for the rest of his career.

Mourning and Overcoming

Personal loss, grief, and mourning are themes to which O'Neill constantly returned—but not to offer consolation. As a great reader of the nineteenth-century German philosopher Friedrich Nietzsche (he claimed that he reread *Thus Spoke Zarathustra* every year), O'Neill painted a universe without order or meaning. Nietzsche's rigorous atheism found direct translation in the playwright's tragedies.

Strange Interlude (1928), for which O'Neill received his third Pulitzer Prize, allegorized an America torn between puritan values and modern capitalism and science. The ill-received *Dynamo* (1929) juxtaposed the collapse of the old religious order with the failure of the new technological order to produce any principle worthy of mankind's veneration. *Mourning Becomes Electra* (1931), perhaps the most successful of O'Neill's plays from this period, interwove the *Oresteia* of Aeschylus and the Theban plays of Sophocles against the background of a modern New England setting. The theme of the piece, the tyranny that history exercises over life, was one that drew not only from Nietzsche and Sigmund Freud but also from O'Neill's own family saga.

Long Day's Journey into Night (1940), which would not be performed until 1956, portrayed this family situation in painful detail, and incidentally revealed the directness of the connection between O'Neill's life and work. In the play, the Tyrone family is torn apart by mutual guilt, fear, and mistrust. Mrs. Tyrone's self-destruction by morphine parallels a son's self-laceration through alcohol. The Tyrones are unable to speak healing words to one another without pushing each other closer to a terrifying fate. Here again, the paradigm is Greek tragedy.

O'Neill received the Nobel Prize in Literature in 1936. In his acceptance speech, he avowed the debt he owed to Swedish playwright August Strindberg, and he declared that his receiving the award was "a symbol of the recognition by Europe of the coming-of-age of the American theater." After suffering many years from a physically paralyzing ailment, O'Neill died in Boston on November 27, 1953.

Eric Paras

See also: Theater.

Further Reading

Alexander, Doris. *Eugene O'Neill's Creative Struggle: The Decisive Decade, 1924–1933.* University Park: Pennsylvania State University Press, 1992.

Black, Stephen A. *Eugene O'Neill: Beyond Mourning and Tragedy.* New Haven, CT: Yale University Press, 1999.

Bloom, Harold, ed. *Eugene O'Neill.* New York: Chelsea House, 1987.

Sheaffer, Louis. *O'Neill: Son and Playwright.* Boston: Little, Brown, 1968.

Organized Crime

See Crime, Organized

Osborn, Henry Fairfield (1857–1935)

A paleontologist, eugenicist, and adviser to the defense in the 1925 Scopes "Monkey" trial, Henry Fairfield Osborn was born on August 8, 1857, in Fairfield, Connecticut, to Virginia Reed Sturges and William Henry Osborn. Born into New York's mercantile elite, Osborn never had to worry about earning an income. He spent his life pursuing a deep passion for scientific inquiry that developed while he was an undergraduate at Princeton University (1873–1877).

Osborn received his doctorate from Princeton in 1881 and was immediately hired by the university to teach comparative anatomy and embryology. In 1891, he left for New York City, where he had accepted a joint appointment at Columbia University and the American Museum of Natural History. Although he continued to teach until 1910, Osborn abandoned his administrative duties at Columbia in 1897 to become increasingly involved in developing the museum, as well as other public institutions in New York City dedicated to the study of biology.

In 1908, Osborn became museum president. Although much of his scholarship lacked intellectual rigor and was quickly discredited, he proved himself an apt organizer and motivator. He was also skilled at cultivating relationships with elite donors. Under his leadership, the American Museum of Natural History became the largest, most famous science museum in the United States.

During the 1910s, Osborn's lifelong quest to discover the first humans, record the progress of human evolution, and legitimize his contention that an individual's characteristics are the result of biological and geographical differences led him to become increasingly involved in the eugenics movement, as well as the campaign to restrict immigration. He allied himself closely with leading eugenicists, such as Charles Davenport, Harry Laughlin, Lothrop Stoddard, and Madison Grant, and during the 1920s, he became an outspoken proponent of both eugenics and human evolution.

Osborn's connection with the Scopes trial began in February 1922, when *The New York Times* asked him to write a response to an editorial published by three-time populist presidential candidate and Christian Fundamentalist William Jennings Bryan. Bryan had publicly supported a state bill in Kentucky that would have made it illegal to teach human evolution in any school receiving public funds, including universities. When the bill failed to pass the state legislature, Bryan published an editorial in the *Times* condemning Darwinism as an unproven theory that was antithetical to proper Christian doctrine. Osborn, a devout Presbyterian, rebutted by arguing that evolution did indeed occur and was inspired by a higher divine law that operated methodically over eons. In reply, Bryan dismissed this argument and equated Osborn and the Princeton biologist Edward Grant Conklin with monkeys swinging in trees, chattering nonsense. Osborn pursued the subject of evolution in several books: *Evolution and Religion* (1923), *The Earth Speaks to Bryan* (1925), and *Evolution and Religion in Education: Polemics in the Fundamentalist Controversy of 1922 to 1926* (1926).

In summer 1925, Osborn seemed the ideal scientific witness to testify on behalf of John Thomas Scopes, the young high school teacher accused of violating a Tennessee law that forbade teaching evolution in public schools. In June 1925, Scopes met with Osborn, Charles Davenport, James McKeen Cattell, and representatives from the American Civil Liberties Union in New York to discuss the case, and it appeared that Osborn would support the young defendant in his battle against a prosecution team led by none other than William Jennings Bryan. When the trial began in July, however, in Dayton, Tennessee, Osborn did not participate. Instead, he sent a copy of *The Earth Speaks to Bryan* (1925).

Some scholars believe that Osborn did not appear at the trial because he did not want to be associated publicly with the leader of the defense team, the out-spoken, Socialist, anti-eugenicist, agnostic Clarence Darrow. Osborn was, after all, a politically conservative member of America's social and economic elite, a eugenicist, and a devout Presbyterian. Another explanation for Osborn's absence during the trial involves one of his pet projects: Nebraska Man.

For years, Osborn had a team of researchers traveling the world in search of the fossilized remains of an early human ancestor, and in 1906, he thought he had found his "missing link" when an amateur fossil hunter unearthed the remains of a human skull from the Nebraska soil. Osborn, who had very little hands-on experience with fossils, traveled to the site, examined the skull, and declared it the remains of a prehistoric ancestor of modern humans. Although he was proven wrong, he was not discouraged by these finding, and he continued his search. Coincidentally, a second Nebraska Man—or *Hesperopithecus* ("ape of the Western world")—turned up in 1917, in the form of a tooth discovered by another amateur fossil hunter. In the summer of 1925, the verdict on the origins of the tooth was still out, and some historians argue that Os-born did not want the issue raised during the Scopes trial. If *Hesperopithecus* was introduced during the trial and turned out to be anything other than the remains of an early human ancestor, it could have been damaging to the defense as well as to Osborn's already questionable reputation as a scientist.

Osborn served as president of the American Museum of Natural History until 1935, building one of the world's great fossil collections. He died on November 6 of that year. Although his theories concerning human evolution were either discredited or forgotten shortly after his death, the contemporary press touted him as "Darwin's successor."

Michael A. Rembis

See also: Science; Scopes Trial (1925).

Further Reading

Aldershot, Brian Regal. *Henry Fairfield Osborn: Race, and the Search for the Origins of Man.* Burlington, VT: Ashgate, 2002.

Larson, Edward J. *Summer for the Gods: The Scopes Trial and America's Continuing Debate over Science and Religion.* New York: Basic Books, 1997.

Palmer, A. Mitchell (1872–1936)

Alexander Mitchell Palmer is best known for initiating a series of federal raids on suspected radicals from November 1919 to January 1920. The Palmer Raids helped fuel the anticommunist campaign known as the Red Scare in the years after World War I.

Palmer was born to Quaker parents on May 4, 1872, in Moosehead, Pennsylvania. At the age of nineteen, he graduated with high honors from Swarthmore College. Two years later, in 1893, he was admitted to the Pennsylvania bar. Palmer immediately became active in local political affairs in Stroudsburg, Pennsylvania, and went on to pursue a political career at the state and national levels. He was elected to Congress three times from 1908 through 1912 on the reform ticket of the Democratic Party, and in 1912, he served as vice chairman of the Democratic National Committee. That year he also served as chairman of the Pennsylvania delegation to the Democratic National Convention and was instrumental in securing the presidential nomination for Woodrow Wilson.

After winning the election, President Wilson offered Palmer the War Department portfolio, but Palmer declined as a Quaker and a man of peace. Wilson then appointed Palmer to a judgeship in the U.S. Court of Claims. In 1917, Wilson offered Palmer the job of alien property custodian, a new post created under the 1917 Trading with the Enemy Act, to manage property in the United States seized from America's wartime enemies or enemy aliens. Palmer remained at that position until March 5, 1919, when he became attorney general of the United States.

Attorney General Palmer had firsthand experience in the growing Red Scare as a result of the bombing of his residence in Washington, D.C. Just after Palmer and his family retired for the evening on June 2, 1919, an explosion demolished the front of their home and shattered windows in neighboring houses. The assistant secretary of the navy, Franklin D. Roosevelt, who lived directly across the street,

called the police. Authorities determined that the bomb thrower, who had been killed in the blast, was an Italian immigrant from Philadelphia and an anarchist. Palmer and his family survived the blast unscathed, but he emerged a changed man.

Following the incident, Palmer asked for and received an appropriation of $500,000 from Congress to facilitate the Justice Department's apprehension of suspected radicals and subversives. On August 1, 1919, he established the antiradical General Intelligence Division (GID) in the Department of Justice's Bureau of Investigation. He named twenty-four-year-old J. Edgar Hoover as the head of the new division and set him the task of gathering and coordinating all information concerning potentially subversive activity within the United States. The new unit spearheaded the government's aggressive investigation of radicals and radical organizations at a time when both politicians and the public were gripped by fear of communism and revolution, an episode of American history known as the Red Scare.

Within months of its creation, the GID had established an index system consisting of more than 200,000 cards with detailed information on all known radical organizations and publications in the United States. By late fall, the card system also contained the complete case histories of more than 60,000 suspected subversives. The GID also engaged in the creation and distribution of antiradical propaganda through newspapers and magazines.

On November 7, 1919, Attorney General Palmer began what would later become known as the Palmer Raids. He organized a nationwide attack on the Union of Russian Workers, founded in 1907 and headquartered in the Russian People's House in New York City. The organization had more than 4,000 members alleged to be "atheists, communists, and anarchists." In reality, most members were ordinary workers of Russian descent who spoke little or no English and who had no intention of overthrowing the government or confiscating personal wealth. Palmer initiated simultaneous raids in eleven cities but focused primarily on the organization's New York headquarters. State and local organizations conducted their own raids on other organizations suspected of subversive activity.

Although thousands of suspected radicals were arrested and detained, fewer than 250 were considered deportable under the 1918 Alien Act. Despite opposition from civil libertarians and leftists, the government deported 249 suspected radicals on December 21, 1919. The deportees set sail aboard the *Buford* from New York to Hango, Finland, where they were then escorted into Soviet Russia.

On January 2, 1920, Attorney General Palmer initiated a second wave of raids, this time focusing on the newly created Communist and Communist Labor parties. More than 4,000 suspected subversives were arrested and detained in thirty-three major cities; 591 suspected radicals were deported.

Although there was significant opposition on the Left and among those concerned with violations of civil liberties, most Americans cheered the November and January raids. In the aftermath, Palmer continued to press Congress for tougher sedition laws, but none were passed. In March 1920, Palmer announced his plans to run for president, hoping to ride the wave of public support for the raids straight to the White House. But support for his antisubversive campaign declined almost as rapidly as it had grown.

During the weeks leading up to May 1 (May Day), 1920, Palmer and the GID released warnings to the public to guard against imminent attacks by radicals. As the date drew near, GID warnings included everything from a nationwide plot to kill government officials and blow up government buildings to a massive general strike. Local police forces and state militias were mobilized. Buildings, churches, and homes were heavily guarded. In Boston, trucks with machine guns were placed in strategic locations. May 1 came and went without incident. And this was not the first false alarm. A similar situation had occurred on July 4, 1919. Palmer never recovered politically from what quickly became known as the May Day fiasco.

Palmer died on May 11, 1936, from complications following an operation for appendicitis. He was buried in a Quaker cemetery in Stroudsburg, Pennsylvania.

Michael A. Rembis

See also: Bureau of Investigation; Hoover, J. Edgar; Red Scare of 1917–1920.

Further Reading

Coben, Stanley. *A. Mitchell Palmer: Politician.* New York: Columbia University Press, 1963.

Murray, Robert K. *Red Scare: A Study in National Hysteria, 1919–1920.* Minneapolis: University of Minnesota Press, 1955.

Paris Peace Conference of 1919

The Paris Peace Conference was entrusted with the difficult task of establishing a peace following World War I. From its inception, the conference faced a variety of obstacles. Part of the problem was that disagreements among the participating powers could not be worked out by a simple majority vote. All important represented states, primarily Great Britain, the United States, France, and Italy, had to reach a consensus.

The conference formally began on Saturday, January 18, 1919, in Paris, with seventy representatives from twenty-seven countries in attendance. Germany was excluded from the peace negotiations primarily because of French insistence that the defeated power not attend. Russia, who originally had fought against the Central powers, was not invited to the proceedings because it had dropped out of the war effort after the Russian Revolution in 1917. Although the Allied countries originally agreed to base the terms of peace on U.S. President Woodrow Wilson's Fourteen Points, this became increasingly difficult due to the varying interests of the powers represented at the conference.

Organizational Structure

The Council of Ten, or Supreme Council, was the primary decision-making body at the Paris Peace Conference from its beginning to March 25, 1919. The Council of Ten was made up of the prime ministers and foreign ministers of Great Britain, Italy, and France; the president and secretary of state of the United States; and two representatives from Japan. Among its responsibilities, the Council of Ten was charged with creating other bodies, including the Plenary Conference, which all states attended and whose workings were evaluated and regulated by the Council of Ten, and the Bureau of the Conference, which consisted of the most important Allied countries and possessed the real decision-making power at the conference. In addition to monitoring these

Delegates meet in the Hall of Mirrors at Versailles in January 1919 for the opening of the Paris Peace Conference at the end of World War I. President Woodrow Wilson, head of the American delegation, urged his allies to pursue lenient postwar policies toward a defeated Germany. He was unsuccessful. *(Stringer/Time & Life Pictures/Getty Images)*

organizations, the Council of Ten created commissions to research complex issues and compose expert reports for the conference delegates. These commissions, particularly those considering reparations and other financial matters, played a substantial role in the Paris Peace Conference.

Eventually the Council of Ten broke into two separate bodies. The leaders of the four great powers—President Woodrow Wilson of the United States, Prime Minister David Lloyd George of Great Britain, Premier Georges Clemenceau of France, and Prime Minister Vittorio Emanuele Orlando of Italy—met alone as the Council of Four (Japan's leader abstained). The remaining Council of Ten members (the foreign ministers), renamed the Council of Five, met on approximately forty occasions. This body was responsible for studying the reports of the commissions and passing the reports and their findings on to the Council of Four.

Conflicting Interests

Wilson, Lloyd George, and Clemenceau held the greatest power in the Council of Four, which met more than 200 times and became the dominant body at the conference. Their meetings were often filled with conflict, due to the significantly different interests of the member states.

Unlike most of the European leaders, Wilson did not wish to punish the powers defeated in the Great War. Wilson's Fourteen Points called for democratic self-determination for all peoples and an international conflict resolution body known as the League of Nations.

The British believed that Germany should pay reparations until the death of the generation they blamed for World War I. Like the United States, the British also wanted self-determination, at least within Europe, to play an important role in establishing new boundaries on the continent. The British also held that world markets and resources must be accessible to Germany on a basis equal to that of the other countries. In addition, Lloyd George advocated armaments limitations under the League of Nations. The British also believed that the Germans should administer the terms of the peace treaty themselves.

While France agreed with Britain that Germany be required to pay the costs of the war, France's primary concern was the desire to protect itself from future German aggression. As no natural boundary separated the two countries before the war, the French wanted to disconnect the Rhineland from Germany, to create a boundary along that major riverway. France also sought the use of the coal mines of Germany's Saar region as compensation for the French mines that were deliberately destroyed by the Germans during their 1918 retreat. Wilson and Lloyd George opposed both of these conditions.

The basic conflict among the victors at the Paris Peace Conference was the lenient peace that Wilson wanted to impose on Germany as opposed to the tough approach that Britain and particularly France wanted. Self-determination issues also separated the United States and its former European war partners, as neither the British nor the French were willing to seriously discuss independence for their many colonies around the world. Wilson's uncompromising approach may have hampered American aims. Britain and France held to their harsh terms and saw them ratified in the final treaty. Wilson's unwillingness to bend to political winds would also undo his efforts to sell the League of Nations to the U.S. Senate.

Treaty of Versailles

The Treaty of Versailles was the peace agreement between Germany and the victorious powers. Although it did not encompass many of President Wilson's Fourteen Points, it did allow for the creation of the League of Nations. The treaty forced Germany to make territorial concessions, placed severe limitations on German armaments, and required that all those accused of war crimes and the former German emperor, Kaiser Wilhelm II, stand trial. Article 231 of the Versailles treaty, also known as the war-guilt clause, forced the Germans to accept all responsibility for the war, an admission that justified the European powers' desire for Germany to pay reparations. Germany was required to pay 20 billion marks gold by May 1, 1921. Additionally, by the same day, the Reparations Committee would decide the total sum of reparations to be paid.

Other Treaties

The signing and ratification of the Treaty of Versailles did not end the peace process. Following the signing of the treaty between the Allies and the Germans, a new Supreme Council, known as the Heads of Delegation, became the primary decision-making group for the remainder of the peace conference.

The Heads of Delegation supervised negotiations for the treaty with Austria, the Treaty of Saint-Germain, which was signed by the Allies on September 10, 1919. Saint-Germain confirmed the dissolution of the Hapsburg monarchy. Austria was required to cede territory and accept the independence of Poland, Hungary, Yugoslavia, and Czechoslovakia. The Austrian military was limited, and Austria was required to pay reparations for a period of thirty years. The treaty also forbade an Austro-German union, a stipulation violated in 1938 by the *anschluss*, or political union, of Austria and Nazi Germany.

The Treaty of Neuilly with Bulgaria was signed on November 27, 1919. Bulgaria was required to recognize the independence of Yugoslavia, accept arms limitations, and pay reparations in the amount of $445 million. The treaty also prevented Bulgaria from possessing a seaboard on the Aegean Sea.

On June 4, 1920, the Treaty of Trianon, which ended the war between the Allies and Hungary, was signed. The treaty significantly reduced the size of Hungary, removing approximately three-quarters of the territory and two-thirds of the inhabitants. Like the other defeated powers, Hungary was required to pay reparations, and its military strength was reduced.

The Treaty of Sèvres, the agreement ending the war with the Ottoman Empire, was signed on August 10, 1920. However, this treaty was later renegotiated, and a new treaty was signed with Turkey at Lausanne on July 24, 1923.

Legacy

Much of what was created at the Paris Peace Conference would come undone over the next decade. The reparations imposed on Germany proved too much for its fragile economy, resulting in default, renegotiations, and loans from the United States. The League of Nations, without the United States as a member, was unable to achieve its full effectiveness as a conflict resolution body as evidenced by its inability to stem aggression by Germany, Italy, and Japan in the 1930s. It would take the creation of the United Nations after World War II to establish a more efficient conflict resolution body.

April Smith Coffey

See also: Europe, Relations with; Fourteen Points; League of Nations; Reparations and War Debts; Versailles, Treaty of (1919).

Further Reading

House, Edward Mandell, and Charles Seymour, eds. *What Really Happened at Paris: The Story of the Peace Conference.* New York: Scribner's, 1921.

Sharp, Alan. *The Versailles Settlement: Peacemaking in Paris, 1919.* London: Macmillan Education, 1991.

Tardieu, André. *The Truth About the Treaty.* Indianapolis, IN: Bobbs-Merrill, 1921.

Walworth, Arthur. *Wilson and His Peacemakers: American Diplomacy at the Paris Peace Conference, 1919.* London: W.W. Norton, 1986.

Parker, Dorothy (1893–1967)

A prominent writer, critic, and wit in the early twentieth century, Dorothy Parker attained her greatest notoriety as a member of the Algonquin Round Table, a circle of authors and critics whose celebrated luncheons at New York City's Algonquin Hotel between 1919 and 1929 became famous for their conversational wit and humor. Parker was one of the founding members of the Algonquin Round Table, along with columnist Robert Benchley and playwright Robert E. Sherwood.

Dorothy was born in Long Branch, New Jersey, on August 22, 1893, the fourth and last child of Jacob and Annie Rothschild. Her father was a garment manufacturer, and she was raised on New York City's Upper West Side. Her mother died when she was five years old, and her father remarried soon thereafter. Her stepmother, Eleanore Lewis, was Roman Catholic, which may account for Dorothy's education at the Blessed Sacrament Convent School in New York City—from which she was expelled. She continued her education at a finishing school in New Jersey but withdrew when she was thirteen when her father died. In 1917, she married Edwin Parker, a Wall Street broker, but the two became estranged soon thereafter (they would not divorce until 1928).

Parker's first published work, largely theater criticism, appeared in such popular magazines as *Vanity Fair* and *Vogue.* Her poem "Any Porch" was published in *Vanity Fair* in 1914. After working briefly as an editor at *Vogue* in 1916, she found a steady job the following year as a writer and theater critic at *Vanity Fair.* In 1919, she and her colleagues Sherwood and Benchley began having daily lunches at the Algonquin Hotel on Manhattan's 44th Street. Out of those lunches emerged the fabled Algonquin Round Table, which grew to include Franklin Pierce Adams, columnist (under the pen name F.P.A.); Alexander Woollcott, a theater critic and social commentator who eventually wrote for *The New Yorker;* Harold Ross, journalist and founder of *The New Yorker;* Harpo Marx, comedian and musician; and Douglas Fairbanks, actor.

Parker was fired from *Vanity Fair* in 1920 for her mocking critique of the actress Billie Burke, the wife of one of the magazine's major advertisers, theatrical impresario Florenz Ziegfield. Benchley and Sherwood resigned from the magazine in protest. In 1925 Parker joined the staff of Harold Ross's newly founded *New Yorker,* where she wrote book reviews under the name "Constant Reader." She published her first collection of poetry, *Enough Rope,* in 1926. A best seller, *Enough Rope* contained examples of the wit for which Parker became famous, such as "Men seldom make passes / At girls who wear glasses." *Enough Rope* was followed by two more collections of poetry: *Sunset Girls* (1928) and *Death and Taxes* (1931).

During the 1920s, Parker lived the carefree, hedonistic lifestyle for which Jazz Age Manhattan became renowned. She attended literary salons at the Algonquin Hotel and the homes of her wealthy patrons, traveled to Europe, listened to jazz in speakeasies, and had several love affairs. But her life during these years was also beset by tragedy. She drank heavily and attempted suicide at least three times. An affair with writer Charles MacArthur ended in pregnancy and abortion. Much of the turmoil found its way into sardonic verse: "Razors pain you; / Rivers are damp; / Acids stain you; / And drugs cause cramp. / Guns aren't lawful; / Nooses give; / Gas smells awful; / You might as well live."

In the late 1920s and 1930s, Parker turned away from literary pursuits and became more interested in politics. She was arrested during a 1927 protest for the condemned anarchists Nicola Sacco and Bartolomeo Vanzetti. In the aftermath of the stock market crash of 1929, she and other prominent

New York writers and artists began discussing Socialist solutions to the ills of the Great Depression. Also during this period, she helped raise money for republican forces in the Spanish Civil War (1935–1939) and for the defense of the African American Scottsboro Boys, who she believed were wrongly accused of assault and rape. Also during the 1930s, Parker helped found the Anti-Nazi League, which organized economic boycotts of Nazi Germany.

In the early 1930s Parker relocated to Hollywood and helped establish the Screen Actors Guild. Together with her husband, Alan Campbell, whom she married in 1931, Parker wrote thirty-nine films during the 1930s, including *A Star Is Born* (1937), for which she was nominated for an Academy Award. Despite her film successes, she was blacklisted by the Hollywood movie studios in the 1950s for her previous antifascist activities and investigation by the Federal Bureau of Investigation. In 1947, Parker divorced Campbell, though they remarried in 1950.

Her life became increasingly unstable through the 1950s. Her work was published only sporadically; she drank heavily; and three plays she co-authored, *The Coast of Illyria* (1949), *The Ladies of the Corridor* (1953), and *The Ice Age* (1955), met with little critical or popular success. Parker and Campbell separated from 1952 to 1961, and Campbell died from an overdose of sleeping pills in 1963. Parker died of a heart attack in New York City on June 7, 1967.

Jason Stacy

See also: Algonquin Round Table; *New Yorker, The*; Poetry; Ross, Harold.

Further Reading

Calhoun, Randall. *Dorothy Parker: A Bio-Bibliography.* Westport, CT: Greenwood, 1993.

Kinney, Arthur F. *Dorothy Parker, Revised.* New York: Twayne, 1998.

Parker, Dorothy. *Complete Poems.* New York: Penguin, 1999.

———. *Complete Stories.* New York: Penguin, 1995.

Passaic Textile Strike of 1926

Lasting almost an entire year and involving more than 20,000 participants at its peak, the landmark strike by textile workers in and around Passaic, New Jersey, in 1926 captured the attention of the American public and inspired many in the labor movement and political Left. Even in an industry long known for its low pay and unreliable employment, working and living conditions for mill workers in Passaic were extremely poor and belied celebrations of widespread prosperity during the Calvin Coolidge presidency. The strikers' determination to wrest concessions from Passaic mill owners seemed to reverse the labor movement's decline. For those on the Left, the Passaic strike—the first mass job action led by organizers who openly admitted membership in the Communist Party—seemed to signal a renewed receptivity among American workers to anticapitalist politics.

The strike was precipitated by a 10 percent wage cut by the Botany Company in October 1925. As textile workers, the plant's employees earned much less than workers in most other U.S. industries. They also lacked a permanent union; an organization that had been established during the 1919 textile strikes in Passaic and nearby Paterson quickly dissolved. Most Passaic textile workers were Hungarian, Polish, and Italian immigrants employed as unskilled labor. They were shunned by the mainstream United Textile Workers (UTW), a union affiliated with the American Federation of Labor (AFL). Women worked long night shifts (night work for women, while illegal in most states, was legal in New Jersey); they even worked during pregnancy, sometimes giving birth on the factory floor. Conditions in the mills were crude, and 90 percent of workers' families lived in cramped tenements of the kind that had been outlawed in New York City.

Following the wage cut, workers at the Botany mill began to organize a union. On January 25, 1926, after the company fired a union supporter, forty-five workers confronted the mill owner, demanding that he reverse the wage cut and stop firing union activists. He proceeded to fire all of them, and the activists raced through the mill announcing the strike. The mill's 1,000 union members led Botany's 5,000 other employees out of the plant. Within a week, 3,000 workers at two other Passaic mills joined the strikers, who added to their demands a 10 percent pay increase, a forty-four-hour workweek, humane conditions in the mills, and most important, recognition of their union.

To strengthen the strike, the workers marched to the Forstman-Huffman factory in neighboring Clifton, but police attacks prevented them from reaching the plant. Photos of the police beating strikers garnered the attention of major newspapers and the public. Forstman-Huffman locked out their workers in the fourth week of the strike. By the end of March, the job action had spread to several more mills, increasing the number of strikers to 16,000. The strikers organized mass picket lines to keep strikebreakers out of the factories, but city officials attempted to limit the picketing and harassed strike leaders. Spirited battles with police became so routine that tour buses from New York City began to make trips, promising riders a chance to "See the Police Clubbings in Passaic."

City officials, mill owners, and a few local citizens blamed the strike on Communists seeking to destroy American industry and foment revolution. While the strike was undoubtedly a local response to unbearable working conditions, its leader, Albert Weisbord, was an avowed Communist. Weisbord, the son of a New York clothing manufacturer, had once attempted to unionize his father's employees. The twenty-five-year-old Weisbord was a graduate of City College and Harvard Law School and had worked in textiles in New England and Paterson. He was a capable strike leader who earned the love and respect of the strikers, but his Communist affiliation ultimately proved too great a liability. The strikers hoped to affiliate their union with the AFL's United Textile Workers, but the AFL refused to help a strike led by Communists. When Botany mill owners signaled that they would negotiate if Weisbord was removed, he stepped down from union leadership; the strikers joined the UTW just before Labor Day.

Recalcitrant mill owners now refused to meet with AFL or UTW officials. But the workers stayed united, and mounting pressure from political and religious leaders finally brought settlements with the mill owners, beginning with the Botany mill on December 13. Although the hated pay cuts were rescinded, the workers failed to secure union recognition from most mills. The Passaic workers were eventually expelled from the UTW for supporting the Communist-led New Bedford textile workers' strike in 1928. The Communists abandoned all hopes of working within the mainstream AFL unions and established their own competing unions, including the National Textile Workers Union, with Weisbord as its first national secretary.

Justin F. Jackson

See also: American Federation of Labor; Communist Party; Labor Movement.

Further Reading

Murphy, Paul L., with Kermit Hall and David Klaassen. *The Passaic Textile Strike of 1926.* Belmont, CA: Wadsworth, 1974.

Weisbord, Albert. *Passaic: The Story of a Struggle Against Starvation Wages and for the Right to Organize.* New York: AMS, 1976.

Weisbord, Vera Buch. *A Radical Life.* Bloomington: Indiana University Press, 1977.

Paul, Alice (1885–1977)

Alice Paul was a prominent crusader for women's rights in the twentieth century. She participated in and founded various organizations dedicated to securing the right to vote for women, and her efforts were critical to the passage and ratification of the Nineteenth Amendment to the U.S. Constitution, guaranteeing women's right to vote.

Paul was born on January 11, 1885, in Moorestown, New Jersey, to Quaker parents. She graduated from Swarthmore College in 1905 with a degree in biology, and in 1907, she earned a master's degree in sociology from the University of Pennsylvania. In the fall of that year, she traveled to England to study at the London School of Economics. After returning to America in 1910, she earned a Ph.D. in sociology from the University of Pennsylvania.

In 1912, Paul joined the National American Woman Suffrage Association and went to Washington, D.C., to lobby Congress to pass a constitutional amendment securing women's right to vote. On the eve of Woodrow Wilson's inauguration as president in 1913, she organized a march of approximately 8,000 women in the nation's capital. In April of that year, she founded the Congressional Union for Woman Suffrage (CUWS), which was dedicated to gaining passage of the amendment.

Paul founded the Woman's Party in 1915 to organize women living in the West who had already been granted voting rights by state legislatures. In 1916, CUWS and the Woman's Party merged and became the National Woman's Party (NWP). In January 1917, Paul orchestrated NWP picketing at the White House. She and her fellow suffragists became known as the "Silent Sentinels."

Over the next eighteen months, more than 1,000 women picketed at the White House. After the United States entered World War I, the picketers carried signs that connected their plight to the war. One banner read, "Democracy Should Begin at Home," prompting spectators to verbally and physically assault Paul and the other women. On October 20, 1917, Paul was arrested for obstructing traffic in Washington and sentenced to seven months in prison. When she went on a hunger strike, prison doctors force-fed her. Newspapers across the country reported on her suffering, which generated support for the suffrage cause and criticism of the government. In November, Paul was released from prison.

In January 1918, Congress agreed to debate the suffrage amendment, which President Wilson declared that he supported. The House of Representatives passed it by a vote of 274–136. The Senate debated the amendment over a period of many months, during which time Paul continued to organize mass demonstrations that resulted in hundreds of women being arrested. Because the nation was at war, many Americans accused Paul and her supporters of being unpatriotic. Finally, the Senate held a vote in October, but the amendment failed to pass by two votes. With elections coming in November, Paul urged women voters in the West and male supporters of suffrage to vote against those members of Congress who did not support the amendment.

The new Congress in 1919 consisted primarily of those who supported the suffrage amendment. Paul and the NWP continued to hold public protests and picketing to keep the pressure on Congress to pass the amendment. The House of Representatives again passed the measure, this time by a vote of 304–89. In June 1919, the Senate passed the amendment by a single vote. It then went to the states to be ratified by a three-fourths majority, and Paul and the NWP began lobbying state legislatures. On August 26, 1920, Tennessee, the last state needed to ratify the Nineteenth Amendment, did so, guaranteeing women the right to vote.

In the fall of 1920, Paul began to raise funds for a statue to be placed in the Capitol to honor suffrage activists. On February 15, 1921, a statue sculpted in Italy was unveiled in the rotunda. It depicted Lucretia Mott, Elizabeth Cady Stanton, and Susan B. Anthony, all of whom helped found the women's rights movement in the nineteenth century. The back portion of the statue was left unfinished because Paul wanted this to represent forthcoming female leaders.

Now that women had secured the right to vote, Paul wanted to focus on other legal impediments that prevented women from enjoying the same rights as men. She enrolled in the Washington College of Law, earning a bachelor of law degree in 1922. She then attended American University, earning a master of law degree in 1927 and a doctorate of civil law in 1928.

In 1923, she began to lobby Congress to pass an equal rights amendment to ensure that men and women would have the same legal rights. In the late 1920s, she founded the World Woman's Party for Equal Rights, using this organization to work for the rights of women throughout the world, lobbying the League of Nations and its successor, the United Nations (UN). Paul successfully lobbied the UN to establish the Commission on the Status of Women, which still exists today. From the 1950s through the 1970s, she continued to champion women's rights in the United States.

At the age of seventy-nine, Paul led a lobbying campaign in Congress to include a sex discrimination provision in the Civil Rights Act of 1964. In her eighties, she participated in women's rights rallies and protested against the Vietnam War. Congress finally passed an equal rights amendment in 1972, but not enough states were willing to ratify the measure. Alice Paul died on July 9, 1977; she was ninety-two years old.

Gene C. Gerard

See also: Women's Movement.

Further Reading

Baker, Jean H. *Sisters: The Lives of America's Suffragists.* New York: Hill and Wang, 2005.

Ford, Linda G. *Iron-Jawed Angels: The Suffrage Militancy of the National Woman's Party, 1912–1920.* Lanham, MD: University Press of America, 1991.

Irwin, Inez Hayes. *The Story of Alice Paul and the National Woman's Party.* Fairfax, VA: Delinger's, 1977.

Lunardini, Christine A. *From Equal Suffrage to Equal Rights: Alice Paul and the National Woman's Party, 1910–1928.* New York: New York University Press, 1986.

Pickford, Mary (1893–1979)

During the early years of film, Mary Pickford was "America's Sweetheart," an international star and the most adored figure of her day. But she was also a shrewd businessperson who knew how to market herself and how to obtain top dollar for her work. Pickford was the financial brains behind United Artists, the film distribution corporation she started with Charlie Chaplin, director D.W. Griffith, and her husband, actor Douglas Fairbanks.

America's Sweetheart was actually Canadian. She was born Gladys Louise Smith on April 8, 1893, in Toronto. Her father, an alcoholic, had a hard time keeping a job. When he died of a brain hemorrhage, the family was left destitute. To help support her mother and siblings, the young Gladys began acting on the stage. Audiences responded to the little girl, and she appeared in a number of touring shows during her childhood. At age fifteen, she moved to New York to break into Broadway. Her plan was to wait outside the office of the producer David Belasco until he agreed to see her. After a few weeks, he finally consented—and signed her on the spot. Rechristening her Mary Pickford, he gave her a part in the 1908 Broadway production of *The Warrens of Virginia.* Her next show, which ran for five months, was *A Good Little Devil.*

Now seventeen years old, Pickford was too mature to play juveniles but not yet ready for adult roles. On her mother's advice, she decided to appear in movies—at least until she was old enough to play dramatic leads on the stage. Again, she knocked on the door of the most powerful person in the industry. This time it was director D.W. Griffith of the Biograph film company, who offered her a contract of $5 per day—which she quickly negotiated up to $10 per day. Pickford began with small roles in such films as *The Violin Maker of Cremona* and *Her First Biscuits* (1909).

Recognizing that the new medium required a different kind of acting than did the stage, Pickford adjusted her style for the camera. Her performances began to emphasize subtle facial expressions rather than grand gestures and a loud voice. Audiences responded to the curly-haired, plucky actress, whom they identified as the "Biograph Girl." By jumping from one film company to another, Pickford was able to snowball her growing renown into higher and higher salaries.

In 1911, she married the actor Owen Moore, a marriage she at first hid from her mother and the public, sensing that both might disapprove of her choice. Moore was an alcoholic with a nasty temper; over the next few years, the rise in Pickford's career would be mirrored by a downward spiral in her marriage.

In 1913, Pickford made a deal with Adolph Zuckor's Famous Player Film Company for a salary of $500 a week. The next year she played a poverty-stricken, heroic waif in *Tess of the Storm Country,* a breakthrough film that made her a national celebrity. Subsequent features included *Cinderella* (1914), *Madame Butterfly* (1915), and *The Foundling* (1916). Now making $10,000 a week, she was well on her way toward becoming the richest woman in America. Along with the increase in salary came increased control over scripts, crews, editing, and publicity. Not only did she star in movies such as *The Poor Little Rich Girl* (1917), *Rebecca of Sunnybrook Farm* (1917), *The Little Princess* (1917), *Stella Maris* (1918), *M'Liss* (1918), and *How Could You, Jean?* (1918), but she also produced them.

While on tour promoting Liberty Bonds during World War I, Pickford fell in love with the cheerful, athletic, married actor Douglas Fairbanks. In 1919, along with Charlie Chaplin and D.W. Griffith, Pickford and Fairbanks announced the formation of United Artists, a distribution company they had founded. The following year, risking damage to their images and careers, Pickford and Fairbanks went public with their relationship, divorced their spouses, and married each other. The public not only forgave the couple but also embraced them. Living in a Hollywood mansion known as "Pickfair," they reigned as the king and queen of Hollywood society.

But the viewing public seemed to accept Pickford only in juvenile roles. A woman with total creative and financial control of her films, she inevitably played a young girl in peril. In 1920, at the age of twenty-eight, she starred in *Pollyanna,* about a bright-eyed orphan girl. In 1921, she played both the mother and son in *Little Lord Fauntleroy.* During the course of the 1920s, she attempted more mature roles in films such as *Rosita* (1923) and *Dorothy Vernon of Haddon Hall* (1924), but audiences did not want to see her playing anyone older than a teen. After *Little Annie Rooney* (1925), Pickford was fed up. In preparation for adult roles, she cut off the babyish blonde ringlets that had made her famous—only to don a curly wig for an ingénue role in *Sparrows* (1926).

Pickford's transition to talking pictures, *Coquette* (1929), won her an Oscar for best actress, but the sentiment in Hollywood was that the award was really for her earlier work. The Depression public was losing interest in the sentimental roles they had locked her into. Sexy, quick-witted dames like Mae West and exotic sophisticates like Greta Garbo overshadowed the wholesome, old-fashioned screen persona of America's Sweetheart. When her 1933 film *Secrets* tanked at the box office, she stepped away from the limelight.

Meanwhile, Pickford's marriage to Fairbanks was also in decline, largely because of his infidelity. The couple divorced in 1936, and the next year she married the bandleader Charles "Buddy" Rogers. She kept busy with writing, producing, and philanthropy, but Pickford's last years were marred by drinking. In 1976, at the age of eighty-four, she received a Lifetime Achievement Award from the Academy of Motion Picture Arts and Sciences. Because she was too ill to attend the ceremony, a film crew was sent to her living room at Pickfair. The television audience was shocked to see how elderly and confused America's Sweetheart now appeared. She died three years later, on May 29, 1979.

Tom Cerasulo

See also: Celebrity Culture; Chaplin, Charlie; Fairbanks, Douglas; Film; Film Industry.

Further Reading

Brownlow, Kevin. *Mary Pickford Rediscovered.* New York: Harry H. Abrams, 1999.

Carey, Gary. *Doug and Mary.* New York: E.P. Dutton, 1977.

Pickford, Mary. *Sunshine and Shadow.* New York: Doubleday, 1955.

Whitfield, Eileen. *Pickford: The Woman Who Made Hollywood.* Lexington: University Press of Kentucky, 1997.

Poetry

Jazz Age poetry was marked by the modernist aesthetic that dominated music and the visual arts as well as literature. In poetry, this meant innovation in both content and form. Modernist poetry represented a departure from Victorian and Romantic certainties about the poetic "self." Eschewing the mantle of a well-defined narrator speaking to an idealized reader, modernist poets conveyed uncertainty, challenged established ideas, and rejected Romantic notions of the ideal in nature and humanity. Many wrote about social anomie, cultural banality, and the dehumanization of modern civilization. Modernist poetry also moved away from strict meter and rhyme to explore the possibilities of free verse. Yet modernists also emphasized precision in language and imagery.

European antecedents to modernist poetry included John Donne and the other English metaphysical poets of the seventeenth century, as well as Charles Baudelaire and the French symbolists of the late nineteenth century, the latter exploring the dreams and imagined reality below the surface of daily life. In America, the leading precursors of modernist poetry included Walt Whitman, for his expansive free-verse celebrations of everyday life, and Emily Dickinson, whose linguistic compression and precise imagery stood in stark contrast to the lush verbiage of the late Romantics. While Whitman's poetry would find parallels in the longer poems of the high modernist period of the

Expatriate American poet T.S. Eliot, a leading figure of the modernist movement in literature, was awarded the Nobel Prize in Literature in 1948. His best-known work of the 1920s is the fragmented and allusion-rich epic poem "The Waste Land" (1922). *(Imagno/Hulton Archive/Getty Images)*

1920s and 1930s, Dickinson's influence could be found in the tight, lyrical poetry of the Imagists, whom literary scholars sometimes refer to as protomodernists.

The Imagists of the first two decades of the twentieth century were the first to reject what they considered the poetic artifice of the Romantic and Victorian poets, insisting on the precise connection between the words on the page and the imagery they conveyed, achieving this connection through startling juxtaposition of form and content. In this, American-born Imagists including Ezra Pound, William Carlos Williams, and Hilda Doolittle (writing under the pen name H.D.) were inspired by the lyrical simplicity of the ancient Greeks and the poetic compression of Japanese haiku, as in Pound's "In a Station of the Metro" (1913):

The apparition of these faces in the crowd:
Petals on a wet, black bough.

True modernist poetry, according to literary historians, emerged from roughly 1915 to the early 1920s. The two elements that marked this poetry—the questioning of the poetic self and innovations in structure—were intimately connected. For modernists, the poet's authority to convey ideas was called into question by the poets themselves. At the same time, the standard poetic structure was discarded as modernists explored linguistic collage—a sampling of voices and allusions, often from the press or popular song, but also from other languages and eras in human history.

Perhaps no poet adopted the questioning narrative and the linguistic and imagistic juxtaposition better than American expatriate poet T.S. Eliot, whose lengthy poem "The Waste Land" (1922) marks the transition from the compressed lyrical poetry of the Imagists to the more extended explorations of the high modernists of the 1920s. In that poem and others, Eliot invokes ancient Greek verse, press headlines, children's doggerel, and other collage elements to explore the alienation of modern society. The narrator seems to be personally addressing the reader at one moment, lost in his own consciousness the next, and speaking with a God-like authority after that. In adopting different narrative voices within the same work, Eliot was creating the poetic equivalent of cubist painting, a modernist style that questioned the meaning of perspective in the same way that Eliot undermined the standard narration of traditional poetry.

Other poets of the period are known for the ways in which they explored different aspects of the modernist aesthetic. E.E. Cummings employed unorthodox punctuation and syntax to convey the disjointedness of modern life. Poets of the Harlem Renaissance, including Langston Hughes, Jean Toomer, Claude McKay, Countee Cullen, and others, introduced the language of everyday African American speech and the rhythms of jazz and blues, predominantly black musical forms, into their verse. Wallace Stevens offered the most startling juxtaposition of all, suggesting in his work that imagination coexisted with reality.

Not all poets of the Jazz Age, however, were modernist in their outlook and approach. Carl Sandburg, Robert Frost, and Edwin Arlington Robinson, three of the most popular poets of the period, adopted some of the linguistic precision and compression of the modernists, but they nevertheless maintained links to the nineteenth-century traditions of narrative certainty. Sandburg celebrated the common folk of the American working class, most notably in the 1920 collection *Smoke and Steel,* and Frost wrote dark and earthy explorations of everyday life in New England, perhaps best represented by the 1923 collection *New Hampshire.*

Robinson seemed the least influenced by modernist trends. His Pulitzer Prize–winning volumes about Arthurian England—*Merlin* (1917), *Lancelot* (1920), and *Tristram* (1927)—were lush historical character studies evocative of the poetry of the late Romantics. Critics lambasted the works' sentimentality and purple prose, or overly ornate style. However, Jazz Age readers of the best sellers found Robinson's poetry accessible, a sharp contrast to modernist poetry that was difficult to understand and alien to many readers—in short, a jarring departure from poetic traditions.

James Ciment

See also: Cummings, E.E.; Eliot, T.S.; Harlem Renaissance; Hughes, Langston; Locke, Alain; Lost Generation; McKay, Claude; Parker, Dorothy.

Further Reading

Beasley, Rebecca. *Theorists of Modernist Poetry: T.S. Eliot, T.E. Hulme, and Ezra Pound.* New York: Routledge, 2006.

Watson, Steven. *The Harlem Renaissance: Hub of African-American Culture, 1920–1930.* New York: Pantheon, 1995.

Young, David. *Six Modernist Moments in Poetry.* Iowa City: University of Iowa Press, 2006.

Ponzi Schemes

Ponzi schemes, or pyramid schemes, are illegal investment rackets in which investors are lured in by the promise of huge returns. Those returns are initially paid from money that comes in from new investors, with the organizer skimming off part of the take. Ultimately, the Ponzi scheme collapses when the pool of new investors dries up and the existing investors can no longer be paid. While pyramid schemes have existed for hundreds of years, the most famous one in American history was dreamed up in the 1920s by an Italian immigrant named Charles Ponzi, whose name quickly became synonymous with fraud.

Carlo Ponzi was born in Parma, Italy, in 1882. In November 1903 he immigrated to the United States, changing his first name to Charles. For the next decade and a half, he held various menial jobs and twice got in trouble with the law, once for embezzling money from a restaurant where he waited tables and another time for smuggling illegal aliens into the United States.

In 1919, while working in Boston as a clerk handling foreign mail, he discovered the wonders of international postal reply coupons. Because of differences in international exchange rates from one country to the next, the same coupon that was bought for a low sum in one country could be redeemed for a higher amount in another country. Always alert for a way to get rich quick, Ponzi decided to buy large sums of coupons and take advantage of the exchange rates to make several times the amount of his initial investment. Ponzi created the Security Exchange Company to carry out his plan.

Starting with $150, Ponzi convinced a large number of people that they could obtain fantastic rates of return by investing in his company. But when red tape and delays in transferring currency (in the age before electronic banking) devoured any profits, Ponzi used the money from later investors to repay earlier investors' notes, often in a mere forty-five days instead of the ninety he had originally stipulated. The speed and rate of return created such confidence in Ponzi's ability to make money that enormous numbers of new investors came pouring in. Some of the earliest investors immediately reinvested their returns in additional notes. The operation soon became so busy that Ponzi's staff could not keep up with the money flooding in. By the summer of 1920, Ponzi had become a very wealthy man and was living a life of luxury.

Soon, however, as the number of investors grew, the need for new investors to pay off existing ones increased exponentially. The first sign of trouble came on July 26, when the *Boston Post* published an article questioning the logic of Ponzi's scheme and hinting about its illegality. Within hours, more than a thousand people came to Ponzi's offices demanding to pull their money out of the investments.

Ponzi was able to satisfy their demands by drawing from the cash he was taking in from investors in other cities. As a result, he was regarded by many as a hero. But on August 10, auditors and bank officials announced that Ponzi lacked enough money to pay off all his obligations. His admission two days later of his criminal record further undermined his credibility with investors. On August 13, he was arrested by federal authorities and indicted on eighty-six federal counts of fraud. Three months later, he was sentenced to five years in federal prison for mail fraud. It took almost eight years to settle ac-

counts stemming from the scheme, and most investors were able to recover only 30 percent on their notes.

Ponzi served out three and a half years of his federal sentence. Upon his release in 1924, a Massachusetts prosecutor put him on trial for fraud, and a state court sentenced him to seven to nine years in state prison. He never served the second jail term, jumping bail and absconding to Florida, where he became involved in fraudulent real estate sales. Convicted of fraud there in early 1926, he jumped bail and boarded a freighter headed back to his native Italy. He was later captured in New Orleans, however, and returned to Massachusetts to serve his sentence for the original postal scam. A request to President Calvin Coolidge that he be deported to Italy was refused. In 1935, after he had served his time, he was sent back to Italy. He worked briefly for Italy's national airline during the Mussolini era, but the fall of fascism in 1943 left him stranded in Brazil. He tried various businesses but died a pauper in January 1949.

Leigh Kimmel

See also: Fads and Stunts; Stock Market.

Further Reading

Dunn, Donald H. *Ponzi! The Boston Swindler.* New York: McGraw-Hill, 1975.

Ponzi, Charles. *The Rise of Mr. Ponzi.* Naples, FL: Inkwell, 2001.

Walsh, James. *You Can't Cheat an Honest Man: How Ponzi Schemes and Pyramid Frauds Work and Why They're More Common Than Ever.* Los Angeles: Silver Lake, 1998.

Population and Demographics

The population of the United States in the decade following World War I reflected a continuation of a number of trends that had been established since the 1800s, particularly in the areas of growth, vital statistics, and westward movement. But new trends in internal migration and immigration fundamentally changed the demographic profile of the country for years to come.

The nation's total population grew from roughly 105.7 million in 1920 to 122.7 million in 1930. The 15.7 percent adjusted rate of increase this represents was comparable to the previous decade's increase (15.4 percent, adjusted). Significantly, however, it shows the continuation of a general reduction of the rate of increase compared to the decades before 1910, during which these rates routinely exceeded 20 percent and even 30 percent. The population per square mile showed a steady increase, from 35.5 to 41.3, the largest decennial increase recorded to that time.

Migration

The geographic center of the U.S. population continued its movement westward, accelerating from an uncharacteristically small move during the 1910s. Between 1920 and 1930, the center point moved from Owen County, Indiana, to a location 23.6 miles southwest near Linton in Greene County, Indiana. This reflected a significant regional shift in population, particularly to the West Coast, which increased by 47.2 percent—three times the national rate. California's population increased by 2.25 million people, at 65.7 percent, its largest rate of growth since the days of the Gold Rush. More modest but still significantly high rates of increase also occurred in Florida (51.6 percent, 500,000 people), Michigan (32 percent, 1,174,000), Texas (24.9 percent, 1,161,000), and New York (21.2 percent, 2,203,000). Although

Mr. and Mrs. John Herrin pose in front of their farmhouse in Whitehall, Indiana. The plaque marks the exact population center of the United States as determined in the 1920 U.S. Census. The census showed a continuing migration south and west. *(General Photographic Agency/Stringer/Hulton Archive/Getty Images)*

some of these increases came from foreign immigration, more than 23 percent of Americans moved from their native state to another during this period.

People were not only moving to new regions at this time; they were also moving to towns and cities. Although the trend toward urbanization had started in the early nineteenth century, the 1920 U.S. Census was the first to show that a majority of the population (51.4 percent) now lived in urban areas. By 1930, 56.2 percent of the population was urban, and the number of cities of more than 100,000 had increased to ninety-three, a 37 percent increase from that in 1920 and 86 percent more than the 1910 number. The New England and Mid-Atlantic states continued to be the most urbanized, with Massachusetts topping 90 percent and New York and New Jersey in excess of 80 percent. But the burgeoning state of California was not far behind at 73 percent. The city of Los Angeles leaped from the nation's eleventh largest city to the fifth largest, with a 115 percent increase in population. Rural nonfarm (village) populations largely kept pace with the growth of the country as a whole, but rural farm populations decreased in every major region of the United States except the West Coast (which grew by 11.7 percent) and the central Southwest (Texas, Oklahoma, Louisiana, Arkansas, up 1.9 percent).

Although interregional movement and urbanization were long-standing trends in U.S. history, the 1910s and 1920s marked some significant new demographic realities as well. African Americans, for example, played an important role in these trends through the Great Migration. In record numbers, African Americans began moving away from rural areas in the South and predominantly into the urban areas of the North, often to take up factory work. African American populations in the Middle Atlantic states of New York, New Jersey, and Pennsylvania increased by 453,000 (75.4 percent), and in the Midwest states of Ohio, Indiana, Illinois, Michigan, and Wisconsin by 416,000 (80.8 percent) during the 1920s. Michigan witnessed a 182 percent increase in its African American population, and New York a 108 percent increase.

Some significant movement to other areas was part of this phenomenon, with Florida's African American population rising by 31.1 percent (102,000), Texas's by 15.3 percent (113,000), and California's by 109.1 percent (42,000). In contrast, all Southeastern states (with the exception of Florida) posted losses of native African Americans through interstate migration in the 1920s. In Virginia, South

Carolina, and Georgia, these losses exceeded natural increase levels, and the states actually had fewer African American residents in 1930 than they did in 1920.

As a result of these movements, the percentage of African Americans in the populations of some Northern states reached double digits for the first time. The percentage of African Americans living in urban areas rose from under 30 percent in 1910 to 44 percent in 1930.

The first waves of this migration were disproportionately male. Although African Americans claimed a ratio of 97 males to 100 females nationwide in 1930, recipient states like Ohio and Michigan had ratios of 106 and 110.5 respectively; donor states like Georgia and South Carolina had ratios of 92.1 and 91.5. This generalization does not hold true everywhere, however, as recipients such as New York (93.5) and the District of Columbia (89.1) seem to have drawn disproportionately female migrants.

Perhaps partially as a result of these disruptions, growth of the African American population lagged significantly behind that of whites, increasing only by 6.5 percent from 1910 to 1920 and 13.6 percent from 1920 to 1930 (compared with a steady 15.7 percent for whites). As a result, African Americans' share of the population shrank from 10.7 percent in 1910 to 9.7 percent in 1930.

Immigration

Another new demographic phenomenon during the 1910s and 1920s was a significant change in the flow of immigrants to the United States. Whereas the foreign-born population had grown dramatically in the decades before 1910, these numbers dropped precipitously in the 1910s and 1920s. Two main factors were responsible for this shift. First, disruptions caused by World War I sharply curtailed transatlantic migration until 1918. Second, in 1921 and 1924 Congress passed restrictive immigration laws designed to reduce most immigration from Southern and Eastern Europe. As a result, the United States saw the smallest rate of increase in immigration since the early 1800s. While the foreign-born population in the United States had grown by more than 3 million from 1900 to 1910, it increased by only 405,000 from 1910 to 1920, and by 283,000 from 1920 to 1930. From 14.7 percent of the overall population in 1910, the foreign born dropped to 13.2 percent in

1920 and 11.6 percent in 1930—the lowest level since 1850.

Furthermore, because of quotas in the 1921 and 1924 statutes, the immigrants who arrived during this period were different in origin from those who had immigrated earlier. For example, among the Southern and Eastern Europeans in the United States in 1930, 308,000 of the Italian born and 220,000 of the Russian born had come in the four years 1911–1914. Largely due to restrictive quotas, however, only 82,000 of the Italian born and 24,000 of the Russian born had come in the six years 1925–1930. Conversely, some Western and Northern European countries saw increases in their immigration to the United States at this time. Only 71,000 German born and 48,000 Irish born Americans came in the years 1911–1914, compared to 204,000 and 92,000 respectively in 1925–1930. It should be noted that Congress placed no major restrictions on immigration from North and South America, so although the vast majority of the country's 14.2 million foreign-born population in 1930 were from Europe, nearly 15 percent came from the Americas, including 1.3 million from Canada and 641,000 from Mexico.

Wherever their origin, the foreign-born population of the United States was disproportionately male (115.1 to 100 male/female ratio in 1930) and disproportionately urban (nearly 80 percent). Indeed, the foreign born were the most significant cause of the rapid urbanization in the United States during the late 1800s and early 1900s.

Apart from African Americans and the foreign born, other minorities were relatively rare in the United States during the Jazz Age. Latinos represented less than 2 percent of the population in 1930, but this number had tripled from the estimated level in 1910. Native Americans decreased in population, from 266,000 in 1910 to 244,000 in 1920, but rebounded to 331,000 by 1930. Still, Native Americans made up only 0.3 percent of the population. Japanese, Chinese, and other people of South Asian and East Asian descent represented 0.2 percent and were located mostly on the West Coast.

Demographic Trends

The U.S. population was continuing to get older and to marry earlier. The median age of the population was 26.4 in 1930, up from 25.2 in 1920, 24.1 in 1910, and 22.9 in 1900. At the same time, the median age at first marriage was dropping, especially for men.

Whereas it had been 25.1 for men and 21.9 for women in 1910, by 1930 it had dropped to 24.3 and 21.3, respectively. A higher proportion of people were married, too: 60 percent of men and 60.1 percent of women fifteen years of age and older in 1930 were married, compared with 55.8 and 58.9, respectively, in 1910. The divorce rate, at just over 1 percent among men and women in 1930, represented a 48 percent increase over 1920.

Kevin Kern

See also: Birth Control; Children and Child Rearing; Health and Medicine; Immigration; Immigration Laws of 1921 and 1924; Marriage, Divorce, and Family; Suburbs.

Further Reading

Nugent, Walter. *Crossings: The Great Transatlantic Migrations, 1870–1914.* Bloomington: Indiana University Press, 1992.

U.S. Census Bureau. *Thirteenth Census of the United States Taken in the Year 1910.* Washington, DC: National Archives, 1910.

———. *Fourteenth Census of Population, 1920.* Washington, DC: National Archives, 1920.

———. *Fifteenth Census of Population, 1930.* Washington, DC: National Archives, 1930.

Progressivism

During the 1920s, Americans witnessed the end of a reform movement known as progressivism. The movement began during the 1890s, primarily among well-educated, white, native-born, middle-class men and women who looked to science—especially the new social sciences—and to the state to rid society of the problems brought on by rapid industrialization, urbanization, and immigration. Progressives gained a national voice with the rise of Theodore Roosevelt, who became president of the United States in 1901. In 1912, Roosevelt formed the Progressive—or Bull Moose—Party and ran for an unprecedented third term as president in a hard-fought election with viable candidates from four different parties, all of whom incorporated elements of progressivism into their campaign rhetoric. Under the new president, Woodrow Wilson, progressive reform continued to flourish, but by the mid-1920s, the period known as the Progressive Era was over.

World War I

In many ways, World War I marked the culmination of the Progressive movement, as it enabled reformers to achieve many of their long-standing goals. Once President Wilson declared American entry into World War I on April 2, 1917, and justified the campaign as an effort to "make the world safe for democracy," most progressives became supportive of the war effort. While some continued to oppose U.S. participation on ideological grounds, most reformers saw it as their moment to create a more activist federal state. Mobilizing troops, food, and materiel, and winning the support of the American public, would require an unprecedented expansion of the federal government.

Progressives were not disappointed. A 1918 government handbook listed nearly 3,000 mostly new government agencies engaged in wartime mobilization. At the center of that effort was the War Industries Board, which promoted the conservation of scarce resources, influenced prices through the Price Fixing Committee, and oversaw procurement for the Allies. The Food and Fuel administrations, the U.S. Shipping Board, and the U.S. Railroad Administration served similar functions and were instrumental in the mobilization effort. To pay for the war, the Wilson administration established the Liberty Loan program and signed the Federal Revenue Act (1917), which taxed the wealthiest Americans' incomes and levied an excess profits tax on businesses. The Committee on Public Information (CPI), the government's main publicity arm, together with advertisers, was responsible for mobilizing popular support for the war. The CPI employed 150,000 people on twenty-one separate committees and produced more than 100 million pieces of literature ranging from leaflets and posters to book-length studies.

For a brief time, progressives seemed to be witnessing the managed society that many of them desired. But the federal government dismantled almost all the wartime agencies and regulations after the war ended. President Wilson, who suffered a stroke in the midst of his campaign to promote the League of Nations, had also abandoned his former progressive allies. In the wake of the Great War, it seemed to many progressives that their moment to occupy center stage in the American political arena was fading as quickly as it had come.

Demise of Progressivism

The social and political unrest that followed World War I was largely responsible for the demise of progressivism in the United States. During the immediate postwar period, Americans witnessed a rise in labor militancy and a backlash from employers and the government. In 1919, more than 4 million workers at 3,600 establishments from Seattle to Boston walked off the job. Roughly twenty-five race riots of differing intensity broke out across the country. The worst and most heavily publicized riot occurred in Chicago, where thirty-eight people died and more than 500 people were injured in July 1919. Americans also were embroiled in a nationwide Red Scare, aimed largely at organized labor. Although few progressives were involved directly in the unrest after the war, they were still the targets of ridicule and condemnation. Even Jane Addams, the longtime social reformer, could not escape criticism.

Robert La Follette, the progressive former governor and senator from Wisconsin, never recovered politically after the war. Progressive candidates across the country suffered crushing defeats in the elections of 1920. Following the upheaval of the immediate postwar period, Americans ushered in a new wave of conservatism characterized by Warren G. Harding's campaign promise to return the country to "normalcy." During the campaign, Harding openly rejected the activism of Theodore Roosevelt and the idealism of Woodrow Wilson. Harding won the election in a landslide, gaining 76 percent of the electoral vote and 60 percent of the popular vote.

By 1924, the national Progressive Party had collapsed. La Follette made one final bid for the White House in 1924, but he finished a distant third, gaining more than 4 million votes in an election that saw Calvin Coolidge sweep the country with 72 percent of the electoral vote and more than 15 million popular votes. The only state that La Follette won was his home state, birthplace of the political reform movement known as the Wisconsin Idea and La Follette's own brand of progressivism.

In spite of a significant backlash, progressivism in many ways can be viewed as a victim of its own success. In the wake of World War I, Congress passed key pieces of progressive legislation. On January 16, 1920, the Eighteenth Amendment to the U.S. Constitution, prohibiting the manufacture, sale, and transportation of intoxicating liquor, went into effect, ending a decades-long struggle among progressives to rid the country of the ill effects of alcohol. In August 1920, Congress enacted the Nineteenth Amendment, which guaranteed the franchise for women, ending a struggle that had begun formally in 1848. In 1921, Congress passed the Maternity and Infancy Care Act, better known as the Sheppard-

Towner Act. Although it remained in effect only until 1929, many contemporaries considered it a great victory for women progressives. Passage of the Sheppard-Towner Act resulted in federal grants to states for child and adult health programs and the development of full-time maternal and child health services in state health departments. Having achieved many of its major goals, the highly diverse movement focused on the minutiae of social, political, and economic reform—and it fractured.

Although the national movement was dead by 1926, progressive reformers continued to wage their battles at the local level. Many of the prominent progressive reformers, such as Theodore Roosevelt, Woodrow Wilson, and Robert La Follette, were dead. But the spirit of the Progressive Era lived on, not only in legislation and agencies designed to protect workers, improve the environment, empower voters, and make government more equitable, but also in the liberalism of President Franklin D. Roosevelt's New Deal and President Lyndon B. Johnson's Great Society.

Michael A. Rembis

See also: Borah, William; Democratic Party; Election of 1924; La Follette, Robert; Republican Party; Socialism and the Socialist Party of America.

Further Reading

McGerr, Michael E. *A Fierce Discontent: The Rise and Fall of the Progressive Movement in America, 1870–1920.* New York: Free Press, 2003.

Wiebe, Robert H. *The Search for Order, 1877–1920.* New York: Hill and Wang, 1968.

Prohibition (1920–1933)

The Eighteenth Amendment to the U.S. Constitution, ratified in January 1919 and going into effect one year later, banned the manufacture, transportation, and sale of liquor, including beer and wine, throughout the United States. The nation remained officially "dry" from 1920 until 1933, when the Twenty-first Amendment repealed the Eighteenth. But liquor continued to flow during the Prohibition period. Federal, state, and local officials in some areas enforced the liquor ban, but those elsewhere did not. As many Americans continued to drink, the trade in illegal liquor—called "bootlegging," from the custom of hiding liquor flasks in boots—became robust and contributed to the growth of organized crime in America.

Law enforcement authorities in New York pour illegal liquor down a sewer in 1921. Prohibition, in force for more than a year by then, banned the manufacture, distribution, and sale of alcohol in the United States. *(Library of Congress, LC-USZ62–123257)*

Rise of Prohibition

The nationwide liquor ban was the culmination of an extensive campaign led by the Women's Christian Temperance Union and the Anti-Saloon League of America. The latter gained considerable political influence in the first three decades of the twentieth century. It was primarily responsible for convincing Congress to adopt the Eighteenth Amendment and for mobilizing support for the amendment at the state level.

American entrance into World War I in 1917 aided the Prohibition effort, as the nation saw a greater need for industrial efficiency, which liquor consumption hindered. The war also heightened the desire to conserve grain (as food) by disallowing its fermentation into spirituous liquors. Congressional investigation into the pro-German activities of the German-American Alliance and its ties to the United States Brewers' Association increased patriotic opposition to the brewers and to beer. Amid this anti-liquor mood, Congress passed the War Prohibition Act in November 1918, forbidding the manufacture or sale of beer and wine after May 1, 1919, and banning the manufacture or sale of all liquor after June 30, 1919. Although the war ended long before the liquor ban took effect, supporters argued that a wartime condition continued to exist in America. By this time, Congress had passed the Eighteenth Amend-

ment, and thirty-six states had approved it. The War Prohibition Act banned production of liquor in America during the remainder of 1919, and the Volstead Act—providing for the enforcement of constitutional prohibition—took effect on January 16, 1920.

The Eighteenth Amendment banned the production and sale of all intoxicating liquor. Some Americans had expected beer and wine to be exempt from the new law, as they held that these beverages were not intoxicating, when compared to hard alcohol such as whiskey, gin, or rum. The Volstead Act, however, defined "intoxicating" as any substance containing 0.5 percent alcohol by content. The law allowed for the possession of liquor purchased or manufactured before January 1920, and for the production of fruit juices and cider that might be intoxicating.

Enforcement

Not all Americans supported the Eighteenth Amendment equally. Religious populations split on the topic. Catholics, Episcopalians, Jews, and German Lutherans generally opposed Prohibition, while Methodists, Baptists, Presbyterians, Congregationalists, and smaller Evangelical denominations endorsed the liquor ban. Recent immigrants often voted against Prohibition. Middle-class Americans tended to favor the ban; many working-class Americans opposed it. The urban states of the Northeast produced the most political resistance to the Eighteenth Amendment. New Jersey did not ratify it until 1922. Connecticut and Rhode Island never ratified it. The Maryland legislature failed to pass a state enforcement law. Massachusetts did not pass such a law until 1924, and New York repealed its enforcement law in 1923.

National Prohibition called for joint enforcement by state and federal officials. The lack of enforcement legislation in the Northeast proved problematic. In other regions, state and local enforcement officers often deferred to their federal counterparts. Some did so because local voters disliked strict enforcement of the liquor ban, others because liquor enforcement was extremely expensive and time-consuming. Officials in Kansas and Oklahoma, two states that had banned liquor long before national Prohibition took effect, gladly surrendered responsibility for liquor enforcement to federal officers. Their decision was politically wise, as enforcement efforts drew some criticism when officers, engaged in gun battles with determined bootleggers, fired on automobiles thought to be transporting liquor and killed innocent travelers.

Prohibition enforcement also created a backlog in state and federal courts and overcrowding in prisons. To alleviate pressure on the justice system and to accommodate local sentiment, judges and juries refused to impose harsh sentences or voted to acquit. To reduce the court's caseload, some judges scheduled "bargain days" on which they offered short sentences in return for guilty pleas.

The Internal Revenue Service took control of federal enforcement under the direction of Prohibition Commissioner Roy A. Haynes. Congress allocated $2 million for enforcement during the first six months and $6.35 million in 1921. Mabel Willebrandt, named assistant attorney general in 1921, became a prominent and resolute liquor enforcement official. She had few allies in the Justice Department, however, as federal officers often ignored bootlegging, while some succumbed to the temptation of bribe money offered by bootleggers if the officers looked the other way. The federal government dismissed numerous liquor enforcement agents for corruption. Willebrandt succeeded in reducing the flow of liquor from the Caribbean to Florida but enjoyed much less success against larger liquor interests such as those in New York City and complained that many members of Congress purchased liquor from bootleggers right in Washington, D.C. In protest, Willebrandt resigned her office in 1929. That same year, Congress passed the Jones Act, which increased the maximum penalty for bootlegging from six months and $1,000 to five years and $10,000. It further stipulated that officials could charge with a felony those who had knowledge of a liquor offense but did not report it.

In the early years of Prohibition, Americans generally accepted the liquor ban. Consumption, which had been rising, seems to have declined, though the statistics are sketchy. Prohibition certainly did increase the price of liquor. A shot of whiskey costing five cents before Prohibition cost as much as $2 during the liquor ban. Some of the price hike occurred in the weeks before the ban took effect as customers stockpiled liquor for future consumption.

Despite Prohibition, a significant number of Americans continued to purchase and consume alcohol, and this number grew as the 1920s progressed. Liquor entered the United States illegally from Canada, Mexico, and the Caribbean islands. Much of the original financing of prominent Canadian liquor companies came from the illegal shipments of liquor into the United States. The island of St. Pierre, off the Newfoundland shore, was a central shipping point for liquor bound for the Northeast, as was Puget Sound for the Northwest. Rumrunners became common along all of America's borders. In 1925, Brigadier General Lincoln C. Andrews, the Treasury Department's secretary in charge of the Coast Guard, customs, and Prohibition enforcement, reported to Congress that officers confiscated only 5 percent of the liquor smuggled into the United States.

Some liquor originated within the country's borders, as Americans distilled or fermented intoxicants illegally in their homes. Sales of hoses, copper tubing, and other materials pertinent to home liquor production increased. Bathtub gin, moonshine, and home-brewed beer became common drinks. In 1926, General Andrews told Congress that he believed half a million Americans were involved in the moonshine business, and Chicago Mayor William E. Dever testified that perhaps 60 percent of his police force was involved in bootlegging. As violations grew, so did the public's disregard for the legal system, further reducing officials' will to enforce the law.

Breaking the Law

Prohibition aided the growth of organized crime, as gangsters such as Al Capone and Arnold Rothstein took control of liquor sales in different regions of the country. Organized crime had existed before Prohibition, but the liquor ban provided gangs with an illegal commodity that was in high demand. From 1924 to 1928, Capone battled with rival gangs for control of Chicago and its liquor market at an estimated cost of 800 lives. At the height of his power, he employed 6,000 people and brought in $2 million per week. At the end of the 1920s, Capone dominated Chicago, Max "Booboo" Hoff controlled liquor in Philadelphia, and Lucky Luciano attempted to unify the New York gangs into a cartel. Meyer Lansky, Dutch Schultz, Benjamin "Bugsy" Siegel, Jack "Legs" Diamond, Frankie Yale, George "Bugs" Moran, and Frank Costello also ran thriving illegal liquor operations. Following repeal, these gangs largely abandoned bootlegging to focus on gambling, prostitution, and the illegal drug trade.

Illegal nightclubs, called speakeasies, sprouted up throughout the nation, providing Americans with liquor and helping to perpetuate the Jazz Age emphasis on instant gratification and merriment. Speakeasy patrons, many of whom were middle-class, white Americans who ventured into the nightclubs to experience an exotic, dangerous underworld, witnessed the conjunction of illegal liquor, organized crime, jazz, and the flapper. Club owners addressed the stiff competition for customers by hiring jazz orchestras to entertain patrons; it was during this time that Duke Ellington's group became the house band at New York's Cotton Club.

Social Changes

Prohibition brought a number of changes in American society. According to government statistics, it reduced liquor consumption. In 1910, per capita consumption was 2.60 gallons; in 1940 (seven years after the end of Prohibition), it was 1.56 gallons. These numbers do not measure consumption of illegal liquor, however, which might have been higher in 1940 as a lasting effect of Prohibition. Before the ban, most people drank in saloons; during the 1920s many Americans drank at home. This was particularly true of working-class Americans who could not afford to patronize the speakeasies.

Although saloons had been a primarily male institution, middle-class women began to frequent speakeasies during Prohibition. The presence of women in these establishments softened some of the coarse aspects of the earlier saloons. Among young people, drinking became associated with recreation and courtship. Prohibition led to the glamorization of drinking by popular culture, particularly in motion pictures, but also in the popular novels of Ernest Hemingway, F. Scott Fitzgerald, and others that portrayed drinkers as individualists displaying moral courage.

Some criticism of Prohibition grew from the inordinate political power that the Anti-Saloon League held during the 1920s. Wayne Wheeler became league superintendent in 1924 and proceeded to adopt a number of heavy-handed tactics, including bribery of politicians, an activity that Wheeler and other Prohibition supporters earlier had attributed to a corrupt liquor industry. Because Wheeler had written the Volstead Act, he became the authority on this law. Judges and officials asked him to explain or interpret passages for the courts, and he gained significant influence in Washington.

Wheeler died unexpectedly in 1927, and Bishop James Cannon of the Methodist Church assumed leadership of the Anti-Saloon League. Cannon became virulently anti-Catholic, particularly during the 1928 presidential campaign of Al Smith, a Catholic who argued that Prohibition had accomplished its mission to destroy the old-time saloon and should be relaxed. Smith, who proposed the legalization of beer and wine, failed in his presidential bid, but Prohibition lost the support of moderate Americans as the dry forces became increasingly radical.

Efforts to End Prohibition

A growing number of Americans lost faith in the liquor ban, and the Association Against the Prohibition Amendment (AAPA) worked to politicize that disapproval in the late 1920s. The AAPA had been organized before adoption of the Eighteenth Amendment but was politically weak during the early years of Prohibition. Directed by wealthy Americans such as John J. Raskob, the Du Pont family, and Edward S. Harkness, some of whom were reacting to the increased tax burden placed on them by Prohibition, the AAPA and other Prohibition opponents in 1925 attempted to amend the ban to allow for local option and government liquor sales, to permit the manufacture of homemade beer, and to increase the permissible alcohol content from 0.5 percent to 2.25 percent. While unsuccessful, these efforts demonstrated the growing political might of Prohibition's detractors.

Like its opponent, the Anti-Saloon League, the AAPA enjoyed considerable financial backing, produced a massive advertising campaign, and applied political pressure on officeholders. It portrayed prohibitionists as puritans and old maids, and emphasized Prohibition's infringement on personal liberty. In the late 1920s, the Women's Organization for National Prohibition Reform joined the AAPA in calling for an end to Prohibition. Meanwhile, a series of bribery scandals tainted the Prohibition Bureau, and President Herbert Hoover brought it under the direction of the Civil Service Commission in an effort to end patronage in the department. The 1930 Prohibition Reorganization Act attempted to clean up the bureau's image, with mixed results.

As the new decade began, distaste for the liquor ban grew. The onset of the Great Depression in 1929 had discredited Anti-Saloon League claims that Prohibition would cure society's ills, including poverty. Opponents of the ban argued that repeal would provide jobs in a revived liquor industry. In 1931, the Wickersham Commission reported to Congress that Prohibition was not enforced adequately due to un-

The Legend of Izzy and Moe

Prohibition produced a colorful cast of characters—from the ruthless gang leader Al Capone to the straight-laced Treasury agent Eliot Ness. In New York, none captured the attention of the public more than the police duo of Isidor Einstein and Moe Smith, better known as Izzy and Moe. Working for the Prohibition Bureau of the New York City Police Department (NYPD), the two raided speakeasies throughout the city, confiscating more than 5 million bottles of liquor and making more than 4,900 arrests, with an astonishing conviction rate of 95 percent.

Their backgrounds could not have been more unlikely as preparation for police work. When the Eighteenth Amendment, making Prohibition possible, was ratified in 1919, Izzy was a postal clerk, and Moe owned a cigar store. But the two friends immediately applied for work with the NYPD.

They made a colorful team, and the roles they played seemed straight out of vaudeville. Izzy was the straight man. Modest and cerebral, he did much of the preliminary investigation that led up to their raids. Moe was the one who truly enchanted the public. A natural-born actor, he played every role imaginable—from banker to street sweeper—to gain entry into speakeasies in order to arrest their owners and patrons.

Some of the duo's raids became legend. They closed one speakeasy in the Bronx when Moe, dressed as a football player, demanded an end-of-season celebratory drink.

At a Coney Island establishment, Moe showed up shivering in a wet bathing suit, begging for a drink to warm him up. At a bar near a hospital, he arrived in the uniform of a hospital attendant. And in a particularly famous incident, he played *himself*, throwing his badge onto the bar of a Bowery tavern before asking for a drink. The bartender, thinking he was kidding, served him one and was promptly arrested. In one night alone, Izzy and Moe busted no fewer than forty-eight illegal liquor establishments. The press ate it up, though the publicity made the duo's job more difficult. So well known and feared had they become that speakeasies would close their doors on the mere rumor that Izzy and Moe were in the neighborhood.

Although their success led to many imitators around the country, more traditional agents in New York often resented them. Some regarded them as buffoons whose success made other officers look bad. Nor was the incorruptible duo appreciated by officers who made a side living by taking bribes. The NYPD released Izzy and Moe in 1925, claiming that the two had requested early retirement. Cynical reporters speculated that their retirement was the result of departmental resentments. Izzy and Moe remained silent on the subject.

James Ciment

derstaffing and a lack of funding. The report concluded that effective enforcement would necessitate a dramatic increase in tax revenues and an equally startling increase in police powers—measures unacceptable to most Americans. Industrialist John D. Rockefeller, Jr., who like his father had donated millions of dollars to the Anti-Saloon League in previous decades, announced in 1932 that he no longer supported the liquor ban. That same year, the AAPA, the Women's Organization for National Prohibition

Reform, and other anti-Prohibition groups merged to form the United Repeal Council. The American League and the American Federation of Labor supported repeal as well.

In early 1933, Congress increased the permissible level of alcohol in beverages to 3.2 percent, legalized beer, and adopted the Twenty-first Amendment to repeal Prohibition. In December of that year, the thirty-sixth state ratified the amendment, and national Prohibition officially came to an end.

James E. Klein

See also: Bureau of Investigation; Capone, Al; Crime, Organized; Drugs, Illicit and Illegal; Hoover, J. Edgar; Ness, Eliot; Speakeasies; Volstead Act (1919).

Further Reading

Asbury, Herbert. *The Great Illusion, An Informal History of Prohibition.* Garden City, NY: Doubleday, 1950.

Behr, Edward. *Prohibition: Thirteen Years That Changed America.* New York: Arcade, 1996.

Blocker, Jack S. *American Temperance Movements: Cycles of Reform.* Boston: Twayne, 1989.

Clark, Norman H. *Deliver Us from Evil: An Interpretation of American Prohibition.* New York: W.W. Norton, 1976.

Gusfield, Norman H. *Symbolic Crusade, Status Politics, and the American Temperance Movement.* 2nd ed. Urbana: University of Illinois Press, 1986.

Kerr, Norman H. *Organized for Prohibition: A New History of the Anti-Saloon League.* New Haven, CT: Yale University Press, 1985.

Kyvig, Norman H. *Repealing National Prohibition.* Chicago: University of Chicago Press, 1979.

Sinclair, Andrew. *Era of Excess: A Social History of the Prohibition Movement.* New York: Harper & Row, 1962.

Prostitution

Prostitution thrived in the United States in the early part of the twentieth century, but the profession was increasingly under attack. The sex trade had plagued American cities during the late 1800s and early 1900s, when Victorian standards of morality held that proper married women should be indifferent to sex. This assumption gave rise to a dramatic increase in prostitution, as well as the spread of sexually transmitted diseases, as married men went in search of sexual satisfaction.

The late 1800s and early 1900s were a time of urbanization and industrialization, which brought thousands of young women to America's growing cities. Many young women from rural areas or immigrant families entered into prostitution when their dreams of finding a good job or marriage in the city failed to materialize. Others joined the profession when a seduction or sexual encounter outside of marriage labeled them "fallen" women, no longer desirable as marriage partners. Madams and saloonkeepers often took in such women, leading or coercing them into the business.

Brothels and saloons were also often located in "red light" districts, a term originating from the practice of placing a red light in the window to indicate the nature of the business inside. Its first recorded use in the United States came in the 1890s, a time when madams used opulent decor and young women dancing to ragtime music to attract and entertain their customers. Part-time prostitutes and streetwalkers often plied their business outside the brothels and saloons.

Many American cities tolerated or legalized prostitution in red-light districts because of its profitability, as city governments benefited from the taxation of such establishments. Prostitution, like gambling, often benefited from police protection in exchange for profit sharing. City political machines helped stamp out periodic moral reform movements by helping those arrested and paying off judges.

Because it was such a lucrative business, many city guidebooks included advertisements for brothels. One of the most famous red-light districts was the Storyville area of New Orleans, where African American musicians sang and played jazz music in saloons and brothels. New Orleans established the area by ordinance in 1897. However, in response to a surge in such activity experienced during World War I, military authorities closed all brothels within a five-mile radius of a nearby naval base in 1917 to protect service members from sexually transmitted diseases. Most attempts to close such districts, however, met with failure.

During the 1920s and 1930s it became more common for prostitutes to work in hotels, apartments, and rooming houses and to communicate with customers by telephone. Prostitutes also adapted to the increasingly widespread ownership of the automobile by cruising the streets for clients, arranging with taxi drivers to supply customers, and working in roadhouses that sprang up just outside many city limits.

Challenges

More open sexual attitudes, a growing acceptance of female sexuality, and the birth control movement all hurt traditional brothels. And many reformers campaigned against prostitution, viewing it as immoral. Open prostitution fell out of favor, and the industry was driven underground. Prostitutes replaced blatant advertisements with a more secretive approach and moved from red-light districts to dance halls, massage parlors, automobiles, and other venues. Potential customers learned of a prostitute's whereabouts through whisperings and innuendo. And despite the laws prohibiting prostitution, many Americans continued to frequent prostitutes.

Prohibition brought prostitution closer to the illegal alcohol industry and organized crime. Many brothels and other establishments that housed prostitutes traditionally served as liquor outlets, and many continued to offer both alcohol and prostitutes to their clients during the Prohibition era. Successful bootleggers organized their criminal operations and extended their reach into other areas, such as prostitution and gambling. Gangsters such as Chicago's legendary Al Capone took control of much of the prostitution industry of the cities that they controlled.

Sex Slaves and Reform

At the beginning of the twentieth century, a "white slavery" scare caused some moral panic. The term referred to the abduction of white women into forced prostitution. Former abolitionists joined forces with "social purity" reformers to battle white slavery and the pimps, madams, and proprietors who were organizing the business.

Federal officials launched programs of protection and prevention. Prostitutes were treated more coercively with the creation of special courts and police vice squads. Social workers were brought into the prisons. Congressional legislation in the early 1900s outlawed the importation of prostitutes and permitted the deportation of immigrant prostitutes. The Mann Act of 1910 (also called the White Slave Traffic Act) made the transport of women across state lines for "immoral purposes" illegal. Local white slave acts, which were supposed to supplement the Mann Act, became effective tools for fighting commercialized vice.

In Minneapolis, the vice commission concluded that "nearly every city is infested with agents and everywhere these connect themselves with corrupt ward politicians and more secretly with men 'higher up' who give them police protection or immunity in exchange for votes." Even though there were not many documented cases of women being abducted and sold into prostitution, the white slavery scare changed the way Americans prosecuted urban vice. Laws were created or rewritten to address open prostitution and other vices associated with it. By the 1920s, almost every city in the United States had outlawed soliciting and had enacted laws to close down brothels. The era of the brothel and open prostitution had come to an end.

David Treviño

See also: Crime, Organized; Sex and Sexuality; Women and Gender.

Further Reading

Brandt, Allan M. *No Magic Bullet: A Social History of Venereal Disease in the United States Since 1880.* New York: Oxford University Press, 1987.

Decker, John F. *Prostitution: Regulation and Control.* Littleton, CO: Fred B. Rothman, 1979.

D'Emilio, John, and Estelle B. Freedman. *Intimate Matters: A History of Sexuality in America.* 2nd ed. New York: Harper & Row, 1997.

Hobson, Barbara Meil. *Uneasy Virtue: The Politics of Prostitution and the American Reform Tradition.* Chicago: University of Chicago Press, 1987.

Kaytal, Neal Kumar. "Men Who Own Women: A Thirteenth Amendment Critique of Forced Prostitution." *Yale Law Journal* 103:3 (1993): 791–826.

Protestantism, Mainstream

American Protestantism changed dramatically in the early years of the twentieth century, especially with regard to interfaith relationships. In 1905, representatives from thirty Protestant denominations gathered at Carnegie Hall in New York City to discuss possible plans for cooperation and unification. The meeting resulted in the creation of the Federal Council of Churches of Christ in America, with the stated purpose of working together to address matters of vital social and economic concern. Each fully independent denomination, represented by four delegates for every 50,000 communicants, agreed to surrender certain prerogatives with regard to general problems such as defense of the faith, spread of the gospel, and moral reform. Theological beliefs, however, were not even discussed.

All groups believed that their real priority was to apply the tenets and teachings of Christianity. It was time for action and not words. Waves of "pagan" immigrants, the Protestant theologians believed, were increasing the social problems of crime, poverty, and industrial strife. By 1908, the Federal Council was ready to take action and produced a Social Creed that would inform pulpit messages in the various churches. The creed emphasized such goals as complete justice for all people, abolition of child labor, and protection of the American worker from harsh working conditions. African American congregations were accepted by the group on an equal status with white congregations, and discrimination was declared a sin.

Many member denominations of the Federal Council, with the notable exception of the Lutherans and Episcopalians, believed that alcohol was a major social problem and advocated restricting or prohibiting the liquor industry. The council became a central figure in the battle over liquor. It also took a firm stand against war. Its Commission on Peace and Arbitration championed the teachings of Jesus as the model for settling national and international disputes.

When World War I erupted in 1914, most Americans' immediate reaction was to remain neutral. In April 1917, however, when Germany resumed its practice of unrestricted submarine warfare, influential pastors reacted to the situation by assisting in marshaling public opinion in favor of U.S. entry into the war. Council churches became recruitment centers and propaganda machines to invigorate a nation at war. The council's General War Time Commission coordinated this enterprise and helped to make congregations responsible for disbursing Liberty Loans. The rhetoric of Federal Council churches proclaimed that Americans were fighting to preserve Christian civilization from the Huns (a disparaging term for Germans).

In November 1918, peace finally returned. Churches proclaimed that democracy, Christianity, and civilization were once again safe. Playing off the rhetoric of the council, President Woodrow Wilson sought a just and honorable peace at the treaty conference in Versailles and the formation of a League of Nations to handle future disputes and prevent wars. The U.S. Senate, however, resisted participation in such an international body and refused to sign the treaty.

American Protestants felt betrayed, and clergy and laity alike felt deep remorse about the extremes to which they had gone in supporting and spreading prowar propaganda. This sentiment created a strong philosophy of pacifism within church ranks and an overwhelming rejoinder that the church would never again participate in advocating war. Liberal theology and Social Gospel emphasized that the teachings of Jesus should be the foundation of U.S. foreign policy.

The technological advancement and economic expansion of the postwar era led to a belief that a great period for Christian achievement was at hand, and the vision for congregational development changed. Lighted bulletin boards, printed Sunday bulletins, and advertising on billboards, in newspapers, and on radio turned the church into a business that needed to expand continually to be considered successful. The call to ministry was altered. Pastors had to have the instincts of a business executive and yet be as personable as salesmen. The hustle and bustle of ministry demands left little time for theological reflection, and theology was pushed aside.

People were urged to join churches on the premise that churches built strong communities. Moreover, it was simple to join a church, even more so than a service organization. The examination of personal faith or commitment to the church was no longer necessary as the focus now shifted to a church's numerical success.

Yet the growth and competition for communicants reminded Federal Council members of the need for unification. Many denominations were drawn together because of their concern for social well-being and public morality. International church federations began to take form among Lutherans, Baptists, Anglicans, Congregationalists, Methodists, and Presbyterians. As these groups formed, missionary-type activity and rhetoric made their way to the forefront of religious activities. The Union Theological Seminary, the Divinity School of the University of Chicago, and other institutions of religious instruction championed what came to be known as the Social Gospel. Greater emphasis and resources were devoted to the study of sociology, missions, social ethics, and graded religious education.

Still, the Social Gospel did not go unchallenged. Lutherans were concerned that it distorted Jesus' teachings into actions and a law of living rather than a tool of spiritual growth. Organized Fundamentalism, which grew rapidly in the 1920s, especially in the Baptist denominations, was concerned that too much interpretation was destroying the fundamental power and understanding of faith.

The devastating economic depression that followed the Wall Street crash of 1929 deeply affected the entire Protestant population. The social activism of Protestants seemed to be failing, as the government took up the slack in providing economic relief and reform. Large and expensive sanctuaries became too expensive for congregations to afford. Churches ran into debt and defaulted on loans. And at the beginning of World War II, Protestants were battling among themselves over whether the church should be neutral or active in the face of a growing world threat.

Matthew Drumheller

See also: Catholics and Catholicism; Evangelicals and Evangelical Christianity; Fosdick, Harry Emerson; Fundamentalism, Christian.

Further Reading

Brown, Stephen F. *Protestantism.* New York: Facts on File, 2002.

McGrath, Alister E., ed. *The Blackwell Companion to Protestantism.* Malden, MA: Blackwell, 2004.

Wolffe, John. *Global Religious Movements in Regional Context.* Burlington, VT: Ashgate, 2002.

Wuthnow, Robert, and John Evans, eds. *The Quiet Hand of God: Faith-Based Activism and the Public Role of Mainline Protestantism.* Berkeley: University of California Press, 2002.

Psychology

Psychology in America experienced a golden age during the 1920s. A number of existing theories were elaborated on and expanded in the research done by psychologists in the Jazz Age. And for the first time, psychological approaches to understanding personality development, behavior, mood, and mental disorders gained widespread popularity in the United States.

Background

Several developments before and during World War I contributed to the popular acceptance of psychology. Mental testing was first used on a widespread basis by the military in World War I to determine who was mentally fit to serve in uniform. While the focus of the testing was not necessarily psychological—it dealt mostly with intelligence—it did convey the idea to large segments of the public that science could offer a way of understanding the workings of the mind.

A second factor was the mental hygiene movement of the first two decades of the twentieth century. Progressives argued that social problems arose not because of moral defects in a person's character but because of the social environment in which he or she lived. The theory was given substantial support by the work done with World War I soldiers suffering from "shell shock," or what today is called post-traumatic stress disorder. The mental hygiene movement suggested that mental health education and guidance could help people overcome the problems they confronted in society—problems that led to criminal behavior and personality disorders. Proponents advocated improved care for those who were institutionalized for mental illness. The movement popularized the idea that trained professionals using applied scientific theories could alter or improve people's mental health.

A third factor behind the growing popularity of psychology was the visit to America in 1909 of pioneering Viennese psychoanalyst Sigmund Freud and the publication of his books under American imprints, which helped popularize his theories on the workings of the mind. Freud argued that unconscious desires are critical to an understanding of personality development. These desires, he contended, are shaped by the psychosexual experiences—both positive and traumatic—of early childhood. While many Americans rejected Freudian ideas during the World War I era—as they were associated with America's Austrian enemies—his theories quickly came back into vogue once the hostilities ended.

Competing with Freudian psychoanalytic theory in the early 1920s were the ideas of Carl Jung, a Swiss psychologist and a former disciple of Freud. Jung shared Freud's ideas on the importance of the unconscious to personality development and mental illness. Rather than locating the sources of unconscious desires in childhood experience, however, Jung saw them as the product of universal archetypes, or the psychological predispositions that all humans share. These predispositions shape how people interact with the world and with one another and can determine whether a person is psychologically well adjusted or not. Jung first began to put forth these theories in the early postwar period, and they quickly gained credence among some psychologists in the United States and with elements of the public.

The New Psychology

Freud and Jung agreed somewhat on methodology. Both subscribed to and helped develop the process of psychoanalysis: long-term, intensive discussions between psychoanalyst and patient that uncover the workings of the unconscious mind and thereby ease the power that unconscious desire or archetype has on mood and behavior. But it was the English psychologist A.G. Tansley who introduced psychoanalysis to most Americans in the 1920s. In accessible prose, Tansley turned psychological theory from a dry and academic discipline into an exciting, cutting-edge science that promised an understanding of the mind and new techniques for achieving mental health. Indeed, the title of his best-selling book *The New Psychology and Its Relation to Life* (1920) gave psychoanalysis its popular name—the "new psychology."

Even as psychoanalysis was winning a growing following in the early 1920s, another theory was catching on: the glandular theory of personality development, first popularized by a New York City internist named Louis Berman. Based on earlier research concerning the role of glands in regulating bodily functions, Berman argued that gland dysfunction could cause mental illness as well as physical disease. Scientists had already made the connection between glandular secretions and libido before World War I, but "glandular enthusiasts" now contended that such secretions played a role in everything from depression to megalomania. Clinics were set up in the early 1920s that specialized in glandular extracts and transplantation, with results that were much ballyhooed in the popular press. While not discounting the role of glands in regulating personality and behavior, later research concluded that the claim of a direct correlation between glandular secretions and behavior was overly simplistic.

Swiss physician Émile Coué argued that the subconscious could be influenced by suggestion, thereby altering its effect on behavior, mood, and personality. The means to achieve this was the repetition of what would later come to be called "affirmations." Coué popularized his theories in a well-publicized tour of the United States in 1923. While his ideas were somewhat more sophisticated than they were popularly portrayed, they were vulgarized in the press and among the public to suggest that all one had to do was stand in front of the mirror every day and repeat a phrase coined by Coué: "Day by day, in every way, I'm getting better and better."

While Coué's theories of suggestion were gaining acceptance among large segments of the public, psychologists in the middle and later years of the 1920s were advancing more elaborate theories connecting environmental stimuli to behavior and ultimately personality development. Building on the theories of Russian physiologist Ivan Pavlov, behaviorists, led by American psychologist John B. Watson, conducted a series of scientific experiments to put Pavlov's theories into practice with human subjects.

The Jazz Age offered a social environment in which all these theories could flourish. Above all, Americans of the 1920s—at least the trendsetting, urban, middle and upper classes that adopted psychology as a meaningful way to understand behavior and personality—were obsessed with the new and with themselves. Determined to reject old Victorian certainties about morality and character, many became preoccupied with self-improvement and self-understanding, not through old-fashioned ideas about moral regeneration and character, but by means of new findings and methodologies of science.

James Ciment

See also: Health and Medicine; Homosexuals and Homosexuality; Science; Sex and Sexuality.

Further Reading

Braeman, John, Robert Bremmer, and David Brody, eds. *Change and Continuity in Twentieth-Century America: The 1920s.* Columbus: Ohio State University Press, 1968.

Jansz, Jeroen, and Peter van Drunen, eds. *A Social History of Psychology.* Malden, MA: Blackwell, 2004.

Tansley, A.G. *New Psychology and Its Relation to Life.* New York: Dodd, Mead, 1921.

Watson, John B. *Behaviorism.* Chicago: University of Chicago Press, 1958.

Radio

The radio industry in America came of age during the 1920s. What had been a technology developed by the military for communicating with personnel in the field became a hobby for enthusiasts transmitting and receiving on homemade two-way radio sets. Then, quite rapidly, radio was transformed from a pastime for amateur "ham" operators to a multifaceted national industry—selling radio sets, setting up radio stations, marketing products, carrying information, and entertaining the American people.

Growth

Radio broadcasting, in which stations transmit programming by electromagnetic sound waves to receiving devices, began in 1920 with the first broadcast of station KDKA in Pittsburgh. By 1929, more than 600 radio stations, broadcasting from commercial studios, colleges, newspapers, and cities, were transmitting to an increasing number of receiver owners. Between 1923 and 1930, 60 percent of American families purchased a radio set. From the start of the industry, radio broadcasting was closely connected to the sale of radios; one could not exist without the other. As more radios were sold, more stations were set up to serve them, and more programming was produced and broadcast.

Thus, radio was several industries in one. As the producer of a household appliance, the industry went from $10 million in sales in 1921 to $843 million in 1929. Sets ranged from the inexpensive (around $50) to the very expensive (hundreds of dollars), which consumers bought on the installment plan. By the end of the decade, even though many Americans still did not own a radio, most had access to a set through friends, family, or community organizations.

Radio was also in the business of providing programming through a broadcast station. Initially, most radio stations in America were owned by individuals or businesses as a way to air their own views or, more important, as a way to sell more radios. News and entertainment were the staples of early radio. The fledgling medium was seen primarily as a means of giving people information faster than they could get it from newspapers, or to put them in the audience of a faraway or costly live performance.

As the demands and cost of radio programming increased, small stations became affiliated with larger ones to form networks, which shared programming. The Radio Corporation of America (RCA), one of the largest producers of radio sets, formed the first national network, the National Broadcasting Company (NBC) in 1926. The Columbia Broadcasting System (CBS) was formed in 1928, followed by the Mutual Broadcasting Company (MBC) in 1934. In addition to the major national networks, there were dozens of smaller regional networks, many owned by radio technology companies such as General Electric and Westinghouse.

Once they bought a radio, listeners could receive free programming in their own homes, but stations struggled with the cost of producing enough programming to meet demand and fill airtime. One solution became another business in itself—radio advertising. Tracing its origins to 1922, radio advertising originated when a local real estate corporation sponsored a program on WEAF in New York. Although the broadcast did not specifically promote products, the practice was established of selling airtime to businesses. By the end of the decade, the Ford Motor Company was paying up to $1,000 per minute of radio airtime.

Organization

As the number of radio stations grew, so did the need for order and regulation. Since the airwaves had not been regulated—except for limiting private radio transmissions to the AM band under the Federal Radio Act of 1912—the rapid growth of broadcasters resulted in competition for bandwidth. Stations broadcasting on nearby frequencies created signal interference. This led to passage of the Radio

David Sarnoff, general manager of the Radio Corporation of America, listens to one of his company's broadcasts in 1926. The founder of RCA's National Broadcasting Company, America's first network, Sarnoff pioneered the development of radio as a mass medium. *(G. Adams/ Stringer/Hulton Archive/Getty Images)*

Act of 1927 and the establishment of the Federal Radio Commission (FRC, later the Federal Communications Commission), which licensed broadcasters to use designated frequencies in the broadcasting spectrum.

Because the designated frequencies were limited in any broadcasting market, the FRC developed licensing criteria based on "public interest, convenience and/or necessity." Any station applying for a license had to show that its broadcasts would be in the public interest. While ensuring that free speech would not be abridged by the FRC, the Radio Act of 1927 stipulated that programming must be free of "obscene, indecent, or profane language." And if a station granted airtime to a candidate for public office, it "shall afford equal opportunities to all other such candidates." The law made no direct rules regarding the size of radio networks, and it stipulated that advertisers be announced as such in programming.

In these ways, the Radio Act of 1927 established federal oversight of the radio industry while preserving it as private enterprise—as opposed to the British model, in which the government ran the British Broadcasting Company (BBC, later the British Broadcasting Corporation). The legislation allowed the growing U.S. industry to consolidate into networks and take a pivotal role in keeping the public informed about events throughout the world.

Content

What Americans most desired from radio was what they could not get from other news and entertainment sources: immediacy. Live coverage of the 1920 presidential election returns (KDKA's first live broadcast), the 1920 World Series, the 1924 political conventions, and other events allowed listeners to experience history in the making. Radio supplanted newspapers as the preferred source of news. Sporting events such as baseball, boxing, and college football attracted larger audiences than most other programs, as announcers described the action in colorful language—sometimes enhanced by studio sound simulations. In some cases, the announcers were not at the games they were describing, but they gave a play-by-play account as reported to them via wire-service ticker.

The first live coast-to-coast radio broadcast in America was the Rose Bowl football game on January 1, 1927. Earlier "national" broadcasts were in fact chain broadcasts, in which one radio station relayed a broadcast to the next, as opposed to all of the stations getting a direct feed from one source, a true national broadcast.

Many of the earliest radio broadcasts were operatic and classical music performances, vaudeville, and entertainment from night clubs. Comedians, singers, and actors from vaudeville flocked to radio as live theater declined in the wake of movies. Performers such as the singer and bandleader Rudy Vallee made comedy and variety shows popular, featuring musical guests and skits. Stage melodramas were transformed into radio dramas. Minstrel show routines gave rise to one of the most popular radio shows, *Amos 'n' Andy,* which first aired in May 1928. Radio stations also broadcast concerts from symphony halls and ballrooms. New genres of entertainment arose, such as the quiz show and the soap opera, though it was not until the 1930s that these types of programs would dominate the airwaves.

Radio was instrumental in introducing the nation to jazz music. Radio stations in Chicago and New York broadcast live performances by such artists as Jelly Roll Morton, Joe "King" Oliver, and Louis Armstrong. People who had never been to a New Orleans club, Chicago speakeasy, or Harlem theater now discovered jazz, fueling the demand for jazz records and live performances. Radio allowed jazz to reach a much broader audience and helped to make jazz music, specifically in the form of Big Band swing, the most popular form of music in the 1930s and 1940s.

Charles J. Shindo

See also: Advertising; Appliances, Household; Country Music; Dance, Popular; Federal Radio Commission; General Electric; Jazz; Journalism; Leisure and Recreation; Radio Corporation of America; Sarnoff, David; Swope, Gerard; Vaudeville.

Further Reading

Barnouw, Erik. *A History of Broadcasting in America.* Vol. 1, *A Tower in Babel, to 1933.* New York: Oxford University Press, 1966.

Douglas, Susan J. *Inventing American Broadcasting, 1899–1922.* Baltimore: Johns Hopkins University Press, 1997.

Hilmes, Michele. *Radio Voices: American Broadcasting, 1922–1952.* Minneapolis: University of Minnesota Press, 1997.

Lewis, Tom. *Empire of the Air: The Men Who Made Radio.* New York: E. Burlingame, 1991.

Smulyan, Susan. *Selling Radio: The Commercialization of American Broadcasting, 1920–1934.* Washington, DC: Smithsonian Institution Press, 1994.

Radio Corporation of America

Founded in 1919, the Radio Corporation of America (RCA) was a pioneer in the development of commercial radio in the 1920s. RCA was involved in every facet of the early radio industry, developing new transmission technologies, marketing radio receivers, and in 1926, launching what would become the first national broadcasting network of radio stations, the National Broadcasting Company (NBC). As a technology innovator, RCA also became a favorite of Wall Street speculators, becoming the best-known exemplar of the high-flying securities market of the late 1920s.

Initially, radio, or wireless telegraphy, existed largely as a form of two-way communication where wired communication was impractical, such as on ships at sea. In 1899, radio inventor Guglielmo Marconi founded the Marconi Wireless Telegraph Company of America, better known as American Marconi. By the time America entered World War I, American Marconi was operating hundreds of marine radio stations across North America; it was also a major manufacturer of radio equipment at its factory in New Jersey.

During World War I, the U.S. Navy took control of American Marconi's transmission system. When the war ended, the government was reluctant to return control of such a vital operation to a company that was perceived as being foreign controlled (a controlling interest was owned by Marconi's Wireless Telegraph Company, Ltd, or British Marconi). The navy helped persuade General Electric (GE) to set up a company to buy out American Marconi. With funds from GE and American Telephone and Telegraph (AT&T), as well as investors on Wall Street, RCA was launched in 1919 as a publicly traded corporation.

RCA not only took over American Marconi's stations but also acquired its laboratories, equipment, and patents on radio equipment. These acquisitions, combined with patents from GE and Westinghouse, which took a large bloc of RCA stock in exchange, made RCA the leading manufacturer of radio equipment in the country. But perhaps the most important asset RCA acquired from American Marconi was David Sarnoff, head of that company's radio equipment manufacturing division.

Sarnoff had a different vision of radio. As early as 1915, he had proposed what he called a "radio music box," a device that would allow the growing number of amateur radio enthusiasts to listen to broadcast music. That would have put American Marconi in the business of broadcasting, as opposed to wireless telegraphy and telephony. But with World War I government contracts filling the company coffers, the leaders of American Marconi refused to support Sarnoff's idea.

Shortly after RCA took over American Marconi, Sarnoff became the new company's general manager. That same year, 1920, marked the launch of the first commercial broadcast station in the United States, KDKA in Pittsburgh. Sarnoff immediately recognized the potential of commercial broadcasting, not so much as a direct source of revenue but as a way of providing entertaining content that would spur sales of the company's radio receivers. In 1921, Sarnoff arranged to broadcast a boxing match featuring the popular heavyweight champion Jack Dempsey. Heard by more than 300,000 boxing fans in the Northeast, the broadcast sent sales of RCA equipment skyrocketing.

But the success had its downside. Equipment manufacturers sprang up, often stealing patented technologies used in the cutting-edge RCA receivers. At first, RCA engineers attempted to build equipment that would have to be destroyed in order to be examined. Efforts by RCA to shut down competitors ignited an antitrust investigation by the U.S. Justice

Department. By 1923, however, RCA had opted for a patent licensing system, whereby other manufacturers could use RCA technology and, in return, RCA would receive a percentage of their revenues.

Meanwhile, Sarnoff was developing plans for broadcasting. At first he opposed an idea pushed by AT&T of using advertisements to pay for radio, called "toll radio," seeing it as diminishing the quality of the broadcasts. He envisioned using increased sales of equipment to pay for on-air entertainment. But as programming became more sophisticated and costly, Sarnoff realized the necessity of advertising. He also recognized that, even with advertising, individually owned stations could not afford to create all their own content. By the middle of the decade, small regional networks of radio stations were forming, some of them owned by competing radio equipment manufacturers, in order to pool their resources to pay for higher-quality entertainment.

In 1926, RCA purchased the AT&T regional network in the Mid-Atlantic states and New England and combined it with its own growing network based in New York to form NBC. At first, NBC was a powerful regional rather than national network. Because some of its stations were in the same market, NBC divided into two entities: the Red Network, offering sponsored entertainment, and the Blue Network, which broadcast nonsponsored news and cultural shows.

As RCA and NBC grew during the late 1920s, the high-profile company attracted droves of small and large investors, who sent its share price soaring—from roughly $20 in 1927 to nearly $120 by the eve of the great crash in October 1929. Flush with revenues, RCA put money into researching the new technology of television and, in 1929, purchased the Victor Talking Machine Company, then the world's largest manufacturer of phonographs, changing its name to RCA-Victor.

As one of the highest-flying stocks of the great Wall Street boom of the 1920s, however, RCA also had some of the farthest distance to fall. By 1931, its share price had crashed to less than $10. Still, the company survived and even thrived during the Great Depression, moving its headquarters in 1932 to a new landmark, the RCA Building, in Manhattan's Rockefeller Center. RCA continued to operate as an independent, publicly traded company, with its subsidiary NBC, until purchased by GE in 1986.

James Ciment

See also: General Electric; Radio; Sarnoff, David; Swope, Gerard.

Further Reading

Albarran, Alan B., and Gregory G. Pitts. *The Radio Broadcasting Industry.* Boston: Allyn and Bacon, 2001.

Fisher, David E., and Marshall Jon Fisher. *Tube: The Invention of Television.* Washington, DC: Counterpoint, 1996.

Sobel, Robert. *RCA.* New York: Stein and Day, 1986.

Railroad Shopmen's Strike of 1922

The largest organized job action of the 1920s, the railroad shopmen's strike of 1922 represented both the promise and the precipitous decline of the post–World War I labor movement in the United States. Confident after several years of growth that wartime government labor policies had fostered, and angered by postwar wage cuts and railroad company attacks, the shopmen's unions called 400,000 members (about 90 percent) out on strike on July 1. For three months, the determined shopmen—workers who repaired railroad cars and equipment in thousands of shops on hundreds of different railroad lines across the country—battled equally staunch rail companies in a dramatic and often violent struggle that commanded the nation's attention.

Disorganized and weak at the turn of the century, the railway shopmen's unions grew considerably in numbers and strength in the years immediately before and during World War I. In 1909, the American Federation of Labor formed the Railway Employee's Department (RED). This body allowed the six craft unions representing railway shopmen to coordinate their efforts in an industry-wide organization. From 1914 to 1916, the RED, supported by mediators from the U.S. Department of Labor under President Woodrow Wilson, slowly organized unions on various rail lines, securing contracts that guaranteed union work rules, pay raises, nine-hour workdays, and overtime pay. However, the wartime need to ensure efficient rail transportation led the government to seize the nation's railroads in December 1917.

Facing a labor shortage and poor wages, the government was forced to concede some power to railroad labor. In 1918, the newly established Federal Railroad Administration standardized wages for all shopmen and granted them a wage increase, seniority rights, and an eight-hour workday. Government control of the industry provided protection for union organizing, and by the middle of that year, roughly 60 percent of all shopmen belonged to RED unions.

The RED's fortunes seemed promising until December 1918, when President Wilson announced that the railroads would be returned to private management after the war. This destroyed the hopes of rail unions and progressives who had rallied around the "Plumb Plan," then floating in Congress, to continue federal control. Although the RED wrested a national agreement covering all railroad shop workers in 1920, passage of the Federal Transportation Act later that year eroded federal protections for railroad unions. The legislation established the Railway Labor Board (RLB) to settle disputes between unions and owners but gave that body no binding legal authority over either party. While theoretically granting equal power to industry, labor, and the public, the RLB became increasingly antilabor with the addition of appointees selected by the new Republican administration of President Warren G. Harding. In 1921, the RLB, then under pressure from railway executives, an antilabor environment fostered by the Red Scare, and a national recession, delivered wage cuts and a series of decisions that threatened the wartime gains of the shopmen's unions. A final wage cut set for July 1 marked the beginning of the strike.

The RLB immediately condemned the action, authorized the use of replacement workers, and threatened to strip strikers of their seniority rights. Railroad companies quickly hired thousands of strikebreakers, along with armed guards to protect them and the rail facilities. In many cities and towns that were economically dependent on the railroad shops, the strikers initially enjoyed overwhelming and active support, sometimes even from local police. After one week of picketing, however, the strikers' determination to prevent work in the shops sparked heavy violence, which led to several deaths and the deployment of state National Guard troops and federal marshals. As the strike continued, some strikers formed "wrecking crews" to sabotage rail equipment and "auto-gangs" to harass and even kidnap strikebreakers along lengthy rail lines.

In late July and August, the Harding administration made two attempts to resolve the strike, but the majority of rail companies held firm against the RED. Determined to break the unions, the companies insisted on retaining strikebreakers and eliminating seniority, concessions too painful for the striking shopmen to accept.

Rail companies could not find enough skilled replacements, however, and as more rail equipment became unsafe, employees from other railroad unions refused to work on dangerous cars. An increasingly paralyzed rail system, combined with a massive strike of coal miners in the East, threatened the economy and compelled Harding to act decisively. On September 23, the government issued a sweeping federal injunction that outlawed picketing, fund-raising, and many other strike activities. Despite calls from rank-and-file shopmen to continue the strike, RED leaders capitulated and began to negotiate separate agreements with individual companies. This fatally fragmented the strike's original power, and throughout 1923 and 1924, strikes on most rail lines gradually melted away. The RED unions were eviscerated by the defeat; most strikers fortunate enough to return to work lost seniority and most other union protections.

To reverse government policy, rail unions in 1922 organized the Conference for Progressive Political Action, which helped to elect sympathetic politicians to Congress. However, they found little relief from Washington until passage of the Railway Labor Act of 1926, which established a more impartial board to mediate labor disputes and secured railway labor's rights to organize and to collectively bargain. The defeat of the shopmen's strike signaled the government's full retreat from the labor-friendly policies of the World War I period and secured the economic dominance of anti-union capitalism in the years before the Great Depression.

Justin F. Jackson

See also: American Federation of Labor; Labor Movement; Railroads and Railroad Industry; Railway Labor Act (1926).

Further Reading

Davis, Colin J. *Power at Odds: The 1922 National Railroad Shopmen's Strike.* Urbana: University of Illinois Press, 1997.

Zieger, Robert H. *Republicans and Labor, 1919–1929.* Lexington: University Press of Kentucky, 1969.

Railroads and Railroad Industry

The Jazz Age brought mixed blessings for America's railroads. The nation's rail system was returned to private ownership in March 1920, following more than two years of government control during and immediately after World War I. Free now to set their own agendas, railroad companies were eager to expand operations and attract new business. But radical changes in technology, competition, union work rules, and government regulation were in store for the decade, forever changing the nature of railroading in America.

In many ways American railroads hit their peak in the 1920s. Total track mileage reached an all-time high at the start of the decade, with 254,000 miles of line in service, and the industry employed slightly over 2 million Americans. Railroads were by far the largest movers of passengers and haulers of freight in the country, moving nearly 51 million tons of goods and 900 million people in 1920. During the course of the decade, however, the dominance of railroads in American transportation started to diminish. In particular, railroads began losing large numbers of passengers to motor vehicles, thanks largely to the affordability of the mass-produced Ford Model T. Motor vehicle registrations jumped from 9 million in 1921 to 23 million in 1929. In 1929 alone, U.S. automakers turned out 5 million new cars.

Intercity buses and trucks also started to compete with railroads for the movement of people and freight. By 1929, 15 percent of all intercity commercial passenger traffic moved by bus. While only 3 percent of commercial freight traffic moved by truck, the number was starting to grow as paved roads became more common and more reliable. The automobile, the bus, and the truck provided a flexibility that trains could never equal.

Railroads met the new competition in different ways. Increasing efficiency and speed became major goals for each individual operator. Railroads spent millions of dollars on new shop and freight-yard facilities, passenger stations, and lightweight freight cars. The nation's first continuously welded rail was laid, replacing the old-fashioned and much more dangerous bolted rail. The 1920s also saw the first use of diesel locomotives as yard switchers (engines that moved train cars within the rail yards) and an increased use of fuel-efficient gas and electric locomotive trolleys, or "doodlebugs," on many branch-line passenger routes.

In an attempt to keep passenger business away from buses and private automobiles, most American railroads also invested heavily in new dining and sleeping cars. Dining cars included large, modern kitchens and could seat up to forty passengers at a time. Meals became increasingly opulent, but competition forced the railroads to keep even the most ex-

pensive dish priced competitively low. During the decade, railroads lost roughly $9 million a year on dining services. For overnight accommodations, instead of the "open section" sleepers, in which passengers slept in curtained tiers of beds and shared communal bathrooms, passengers now had private sleeper compartments, each with its own toilet and washstand. But the cost of operating the private sleeper cars far outweighed the rates charged by the railroads. During the 1920s, passenger revenues dropped from 25 percent of freight revenue to 7 percent of freight revenue, with railroads losing almost $50 million a year on passenger service.

Railroads also increasingly found themselves under the thumb of federal regulation. Following a violent shopmen's strike in 1922, the government moved to legalize railroad unions in 1926 through the Railway Labor Act. In addition to its involvement in labor relations, the government also controlled many operational aspects of the railroad industry through the Interstate Commerce Commission (ICC). The ICC was created by Congress in 1887 to prevent various railroad abuses that were fixtures of the nineteenth century, when railroads held a virtual monopoly in American transportation. These abuses included shipping rate increases, biased shipping, and secret rebates to large shippers. The ICC was charged with establishing "reasonable and just" published rail rates by all carriers and with controlling mergers and maintenance of passenger service. Throughout the 1920s, the ICC continued to regulate railroads as if they still had a monopoly on transportation and did not compete with trucks, buses, and automobiles.

Following the imposition of federal control of the railroads during World War I, Congress charged the ICC to create a national plan for merging the nation's railroads into a limited number of systems. The idea was to eliminate redundant lines, equalize costs, and maintain fair competition. Published in 1929, the ICC plan called for the creation of a national system of nineteen lines, maintaining a rough balance of six lines for each major rail region of the country (East, South, Midwest, and West). No railroad line was pleased with the national system concept, and each believed that its competitors got better trackage rights. To complicate matters, by 1932 many of the lines included in the plan were either in or on their way to bankruptcy and receivership, and in 1940 Congress formally withdrew its request.

From that point forward, the ICC sought only to maintain a status quo among the railroads based on non-market-driven rates that often did not generate realistic economic opportunities. The result was an industry that wasted resources in maintaining nonproductive branch lines, was slow to embrace new technologies, and was forced to retain money-losing passenger service. Although no one knew it at the time, U.S. railroads had truly reached their peak by 1920. Changes in federal regulation, technology, work rules, and competition during the rest of the decade started a period of slow, painful decline for America's railroads that would ultimately hit bottom in the 1970s.

Matthew Hiner

See also: Railroad Shopmen's Strike of 1922; Railway Labor Act (1926).

Further Reading

Daniels, Rudolph. *Trains Across the Continent.* Bloomington: Indiana University Press, 2000.

Goddard, Stephen. *Getting There: The Epic Struggle Between Road and Rail in the American Century.* Chicago: University of Chicago Press, 1994.

Saunders, Richard. *Merging Lines: American Railroads, 1900–1970.* DeKalb: Northern Illinois University Press, 2001.

Stover, John. *American Railroads.* 2nd ed. Chicago: University of Chicago Press, 1997.

Railway Labor Act (1926)

The Railway Labor Act of 1926 was a groundbreaking federal law designed to govern labor relations in the railroad industry. The legislation grew out of series of contentious labor strikes dating back to 1877, and it was based on a number of earlier congressional measures intended to act as compromises between labor and management. The 1926 legislation sought to resolve labor disputes through collective bargaining, arbitration, and mediation rather than workers' strikes. The Railway Labor Act represented the first time the federal government guaranteed workers the right to organize unions without interference from employers. Although the law was amended many times after 1926, the fundamental principles of the Railway Labor Act later became the basis of other labor laws in the United States, and the legislation remains an important landmark in American labor and business history.

The origins of the Railway Labor Act date back to the bloody national railroad strike of 1877. A sour economy caused railroads across the country to radically cut wages throughout the 1870s, forcing workers in turn to participate in national work stoppages that culminated in a general strike in 1877. The walkout affected major lines throughout most of the country, and in many areas federal troops were called in to keep the railroads moving on schedule. The importance of railroads to the national economy during this period cannot be overstated. They were the essential means of transportation in the United States, moving people as well as raw materials and finished products, thereby facilitating the development of the Industrial Revolution. Conflicts between labor and railroad management thus affected not just each individual worker or company but the nation as a whole.

To prevent or curtail future strikes, Congress enacted the Arbitration Act of 1888. The legislation incorporated a voluntary arbitration board chosen by the union and the railroad involved in the dispute, along with a fact-finding board chosen by the president. Because neither board had any enforcement power, the law proved too weak to have any real impact on railroad labor–management strife. In 1898, Congress replaced the Arbitration Act with the Erdman Act, which abolished the fact-finding board and allowed for mediation as a precursor to arbitration. The measure also introduced a status quo provision, mandating that while disputes were in mediation, neither side could alter working conditions. The Erdman Act also made blacklisting of union organizers illegal, although the U.S. Supreme Court struck down that provision in 1908. The success of the mediation process helped to prevent major strikes for almost twenty-five years, and in 1913, the mediation board became permanent. However, neither the process of mediation nor the decisions rendered by the mediation board were compulsory.

In December 1917, American railroads were nationalized by the federal government for the duration of World War I. To prevent potential labor disputes during that period, the government granted workers the right to unionize and created local adjustment boards to help settle disputes. When the railroads were returned to private ownership after the war, Congress, as part of the Transportation Act of 1920, incorporated the adjustment boards into law by creating a Railroad Labor Board with the power to mediate disputes. That legislation increased the role of government in the rail industry and reduced emphasis on mediation and voluntary arbitration. As in earlier laws, however, the findings of the Railroad Labor Board were nonbinding.

Glaringly omitted from the Transportation Act was any guarantee that workers had the right to create and join unions. As a result, many railroads started to mandate that workers could only join "company unions," or those located at a single company, organized by that company, and not affiliated with another union group. The Railroad Labor Board never found a middle ground between workers seeking to maintain their right to collectively bargain and railroads seeking to erode that right. Two questionable decisions, one involving wage decreases and the other involving a shopmen's strike, which the board failed to prevent, doomed the Railroad Labor Board. As early as 1924, Congress started working on a new law to replace the Transportation Act.

The result was the Railway Labor Act (RLA) of 1926. The new law put almost complete assurance into collective bargaining for the settlement of labor–management disputes. When bargaining between unions and railroads broke down through local boards of adjustment, the act would provide for mandatory federal mediation; arbitration remained voluntary. The legislation was intended to avoid interruption of service, ensure the right of workers to create and join unions, provide organizational independence for workers and railroads, and assist in the prompt settlement of disputes over working conditions and existing contracts. Workers were free to join unions of any craft or class, provided that 35 percent of workers filed authorization cards.

To carry out these functions, the RLA created a five-person Board of Mediation (later renamed the National Mediation Board) appointed by the president and approved by the Senate. The board could act if invited by either party involved in the dispute, but it could also act on its own initiative. No time limit was placed on the mediation process, but if a "reasonable" attempt by all parties to reach a settlement failed, the board was required to persuade both parties to accept voluntary arbitration. The arbitration board, in turn, was given power to issue binding awards enforceable through the U.S. District Court.

If one or both parties rejected the process of arbitration, the Board of Mediation was required to notify the president, who in turn could create an Emergency Board to investigate the dispute. During this investigation, company management and the union were required to maintain the status quo in the workplace. Recommendations made by the Emergency Board were nonbinding, meaning that at the end of the status quo period, if no agreement was reached, either side became free to act in its own interests through a strike or implementation of proposals.

Should workers choose to strike, railroads were given the power to lawfully replace strikers, but the railroads could not legally discharge strikers or eliminate their jobs to retaliate for striking. In other words, once the strike was settled, workers were guaranteed to get their jobs back.

In many ways, the RLA was both a reflection of a more urban, industrial America of the 1920s and a logical outcome of labor–management disputes that had been brewing for almost forty years. The RLA strongly reflected concepts dating back to the 1888 Arbitration Act and incorporated the most workable features from forty years of railroad law into a compromise acceptable to both railroads and workers. Since its inception, the RLA has been remarkably proficient in preventing strikes in the railroad industry.

Matthew Hiner

See also: American Federation of Labor; Economic Policy; Labor Movement; Railroad Shopmen's Strike of 1922; Railroads and Railroad Industry.

Further Reading

American Bar Association. *The Railway Labor Act.* 2nd ed. Washington, DC: BNA Books, 2005.

Gohmann, John, ed. *Air and Rail Labor Relations: A Judicial History of the Railway Labor Act.* Dubuque, IA: Kendall/Hunt, 1979.

Rehmus, Charles, ed. *The Railway Labor Act at Fifty: Collective Bargaining in the Railroad and Airline Industries.* Washington, DC: U.S. Government Printing Office, 1976.

Wilner, Frank. *The Railway Labor Act and the Dilemma of Labor Relations.* Omaha, NE: Simmons-Boardman, 1988.

Reader's Digest

Most popular magazines of the late nineteenth and early twentieth centuries, such as *Harper's, Life,* and *The Saturday Evening Post,* were general-interest publications containing works of contemporary fiction, articles on current events, cartoons, and other material designed to attract a broad readership. Nevertheless, these magazines remained inaccessible or unappealing to a significant number of Americans because of their emphasis on urban life, contemporary culture, and mainstream progressive ideals. *Reader's Digest,* founded in Pleasantville, New York, in 1922 by salesman DeWitt Wallace and his wife, Lila Acheson Wallace, was also conceived as a general-interest magazine, but with a format, tone, and editorial policy that contrasted sharply with those of other popular periodicals.

Just as Henry Ford made the automobile accessible to mainstream America, the Wallaces sought to create a magazine that would be accessible to the average consumer. Emphasizing brevity and simplicity over detailed analysis, they selected articles from other popular publications and condensed them into shorter pieces designed to present the essential information in a manner quickly readable and easily processed by the largest possible segment of the public. The selection of articles tended to follow a set pattern: Each issue included thirty-one articles, one for each day of the month; topics varied but articles typically focused on noncontroversial issues and viewpoints, and emphasized self-help; stories were often inspirational and sometimes cautionary. Social and cultural diversity, while not overtly opposed or resisted, was de-emphasized. Short, light features, which appeared regularly, were sprinkled between the condensed articles. Among the more popular and enduring of these were a joke page titled "Laughter, the Best Medicine" and "Word Power," a vocabulary-building quiz. Other features included quotes, military anecdotes, and reader-submitted content.

The first issue of *Reader's Digest* was released on February 5, 1922, at ten cents per copy. Smaller in size than other popular magazines, it was designed for portability as well as conciseness. The magazine would include no advertising, generating revenue primarily through its subscription base, which grew sufficiently large during the 1920s that the Wallaces did not make copies available at newsstands until 1929. Its circulation grew steadily throughout the 1920s and remained strong even through the Great Depression, reaching the 1 million mark in 1935.

Like chain stores and mass-produced goods, *Reader's Digest* represented America's growing emphasis on convenience, simplicity, and standardization. Yet certain aspects of the magazine were strongly traditionalist. The Wallaces' insistence on shunning advertising (ads would not appear in the magazine until 1955) and relying exclusively on mail-order subscriptions in the magazine's early years stood in sharp contrast to the growing emphasis on advertising and street-level retailing during the 1920s. Nostalgia for a simpler, less uncertain age was also evident in the magazine's content. Optimistically patriotic, probusiness, and pro-Christian in its content, *Reader's Digest* reflected a postwar disillusionment and conservative reaction to the explosion of technology, mass media, consumerism, and progres-

sivism that prevailed in early twentieth-century America. Critics said the magazine promoted nativist and antilabor sentiments.

Reader's Digest embodied some of the contradictions of the Jazz Age, employing cutting-edge production and marketing techniques to promote a reactionary, traditionalist worldview. This formula, while controversial, proved successful and enduring. *Reader's Digest* continued to grow in popularity and profile in subsequent decades, introducing a British edition in 1938 and a Canadian edition in 1948. By the end of the twentieth century, it boasted forty-nine foreign editions. U.S. circulation declined steadily in the waning decades of the twentieth century, as magazines became more specialized in focus and graphic in presentation. Yet *Reader's Digest* continued to attract a loyal readership and remained a fixture in American and international popular culture.

Michael H. Burchett

See also: Journalism.

Further Reading

Canning, Peter. *American Dreamers: The Wallaces and Reader's Digest, an Insider's Story.* New York: Simon & Schuster, 1996.

Heidenry, John. *Theirs Was the Kingdom: Lila and DeWitt Wallace and the Story of the Reader's Digest.* New York: W.W. Norton, 1993.

Janello, Amy, and Brennon Jones. *The American Magazine.* New York: Abrams, 1991.

Schreiner, Samuel A., Jr. *The Condensed World of the Reader's Digest.* New York: Stein & Day, 1977.

Real Estate

During the 1920s, the value of urban land in America increased dramatically, while the value of rural land decreased just as dramatically, a dual trend that contributed to the growing economic and cultural divide between urban and rural America. The rise in value of urban real estate led to overdevelopment and speculation in city property. The sudden drop in rural land prices in 1926, revealing weaknesses in the critical agricultural sector of the economy, was an early indicator of the underlying weakness in the nation's economy as a whole.

Agricultural land values fell in the early 1920s when foreign demand for American farm products, especially wheat, dropped precipitously. The value of all farmland was $55 billion at the end of World War I. However, the reduced European demand for American foodstuffs resulted in an agricultural depression in 1921. By 1926, the value of all farmland had dropped roughly 33 percent to $37 billon.

While rural land values dropped precipitously, urban land values increased beginning in 1920. By 1926, the value of urban land in American cities with over 30,000 residents had risen from $25 billion at the end of World War I to more than $50 billion. The area of land within these cities was only one-fifth of 1 percent of all the land in the United States, and yet it was valued in 1926 at nearly one-third more than all the farmland in the United States, whose area was 200 times as great.

Urban land values increased in the 1920s because of an acute housing shortage. At the same time, 5 million soldiers and sailors were released from wartime service and seeking employment in large urban centers. From 1920 to 1930, American cities with more than 30,000 residents saw an overall population increase of nearly 9 million. Meanwhile, average construction costs in the United States dropped, and the cost of managing and operating buildings increased but slightly.

But the higher urban land prices had their downside as well, helping to fuel real estate speculation and urban sprawl. The number of lots platted in Florida during the boom reached 20 million. Portions of Los Angeles County experienced similar overdevelopment; 75 percent of the total platted area of Burbank, California, was vacant in the early 1930s. In 1929, 175,000 of Cleveland's 375,000 lots were empty. More than 65 percent of the total lot area in Duluth, Minnesota; 50 percent in Portland, Maine; and 30 percent in El Paso, Texas, was unused in the 1930s.

During the early 1920s, people flocked to Florida in ever-increasing numbers. Hundreds of promoters went to work selling lots and advertising new town sites, and large profits were sometimes realized in a quick series of property transactions. The area around Miami experienced a frenzy of speculative real estate investment. Miami grew from a population of 30,000 in 1920 to 75,000 by 1925. The Florida boom continued through 1925; early the next year, it began to fall off slightly as fewer people appeared for the winter. A severe hurricane struck the state on September 18, 1926, reducing many of the shoddily constructed developments to ruins, ending the boom, and wiping out virtually all of the ambitious speculators. As late as ten years afterward, the bulk of the lots were overgrown with weeds or underwater.

In the rest of the country, the disaster that ended the real estate boom of the 1920s was a man-made one. The collapse of the stock market in 1929 and the early 1930s led to the severest credit crunch in U.S. history, cutting off much of the financing for both real estate speculation and individual home mortgages. Not until the late 1940s, amidst renewed prosperity and a new federal commitment to mortgage financing, would the real estate market in the United States return to its pre–Great Depression levels.

Michael McGregor

See also: Credit and Debt, Consumer; Florida Land Boom; Housing.

Further Reading

Davies, Pearl Janet. *Real Estate in American History.* Washington, DC: Public Affairs Press, 1958.
Frazer, William Johnson, and John J. Guthrie, Jr. *The Florida Land Boom: Speculation, Money, and the Banks.* Westport, CT: Greenwood, 1995.
Hoyt, Homer. *One Hundred Years of Land Values in Chicago.* New York: Arno, 1970.
Miles, Mike E., Richard L. Haney, Jr., and Gayle Berens. *Real Estate Development: Principles and Process.* Washington, DC: Urban Land Institute, 1996.
Sakolski, A.M. *The Great American Land Bubble.* New York: Harper, 1932.

Recession of 1921–1922

The recession of 1921–1922 represented the worst economic downturn in the U.S. economy since the depression of the 1890s, and it stood in sharp contrast to the rest of the relatively prosperous Jazz Age. The years 1921 and 1922 were marked by a steep drop in retail and wholesale prices and the gross national product (GNP) as well as a sudden rise in unemployment. The economic decline was made more dramatic because it occurred after a long period of prosperity that began with the first years of World War I in Europe. A decline in exports, rapid demobilization, canceling of wartime contracts, a drop in wages, and excess inventory all contributed to the postwar recession. Government monetary policy played into the recession as well, as the Federal Reserve raised the rate it charged to member banks to 7 percent, thereby choking off borrowing and investment.

The economic numbers for the recession were certainly dramatic. Gross national product declined from $91.5 billion in 1920 to $69.5 billion in 1921, rising only to $74.1 billion by 1922. The GNP did not return to its 1920 level until 1925. Unemployment figures jumped from 5.2 percent in 1920 to 11.7 percent in 1921 before dropping back to

6.7 percent in 1922. Over 20,000 business failures occurred in 1921 alone.

The origins of the recession lay in the transition from a wartime to a peacetime economy. With the end of World War I, the demand for U.S. goods among European nations declined as their economies recovered from the war. U.S. agricultural exports dropped from $3.9 billion in 1920 to $2.6 billion in 1921 and to just $1.9 billion in 1922. Exports never fully recovered. During the course of the 1920s, annual exports rose above $2 billion only once, in 1925.

Nonagricultural unemployment in the early postwar years was caused in large part by the government's policy of rapid demobilization. Under pressure from voters, the government canceled wartime contracts and reduced the military at a hurried pace. From a high of 3.7 million troops at war's end in November 1918, the military reduced its ranks to 2.7 million the following June and to 1 million by year's end. The National Defense Act of 1920 called for a ceiling of approximately 300,000 troops, lowered to 136, 000 under 1922 legislation. Those released from the armed forces placed greater demands on the job market, driving up unemployment and pushing wages down. With wartime inflation, prices rose faster than wages, leading unions and workers to demand higher pay. About one in five workers went on strike at some point in 1919 and 1920.

Another cause for the economic troubles was overinvestment in inventories. During the war businesses had begun speculating on inventories. With prices rising because of wartime inflation, a business could make a profit between the time an item was purchased from the manufacturer and when it was sold by the retailer to a customer. As demand dropped due to low wages and increased unemployment, the inventory began eating into profits. To unload the excess inventory, companies lowered prices. Businesses then decreased payrolls to cut costs, which further hurt employment rates. The Woodrow Wilson administration provided little direction in the transition from a wartime to a peacetime economy. Government contracts were quickly and ruthlessly canceled as a cost-cutting measure.

Upon coming to office in March 1921, President Warren G. Harding took the unprecedented step of calling a conference to study the problems of the growing recession. Although recessions and depressions had happened in the past, this was the first time any president considered active measures to reverse the slump. The president's conference, chaired by newly appointed Secretary of Commerce Herbert Hoover, produced a report titled *Business Cycles and Unemployment,* which argued that such economic problems had human causes that could be addressed by the government.

The report suggested the government should focus on the high unemployment rate and advised major investment by the government in public works projects to help curb unemployment and increase spending power. As another course, Congress should pass a bonus bill granting veterans $50 for every month they served in uniform. Conservative Secretary of the Treasury Andrew Mellon argued against the measure, claiming it was special-interest legislation. Neither Mellon nor Harding liked either of these measures, as they would add to the already high national debt of $24 billion.

In the end, the government took no active measures to reverse the recession. Whether this was wise economic policy or not, market forces soon produced a sudden upturn in the economy at the end of 1922, largely the result of heightened demand for new consumer goods such as automobiles, radios, and appliances and increased worker productivity. The government's laissez-faire approach reinforced the idea that federal intervention in the economy in the face of recession was not necessary, an attitude that may have contributed to the sluggishness with which the Hoover administration responded to the Great Depression nearly a decade later.

Michael Faubion

See also: Agriculture; Credit and Debt, Consumer; Demobilization, Industrial; Economic Policy; Labor Movement; Stock Market; Wealth and Income.

Further Reading

Hicks, John. *Republican Ascendancy, 1921–1933.* New York: Harper, 1960.

National Bureau of Economic Research. *Business Cycles and Unemployment.* New York: McGraw-Hill, 1923.

Perrett, Geoffrey. *America in the Twenties.* New York: Simon & Schuster, 1982.

Wicker, Elmus R. "A Reconsideration of Federal Reserve Policy During the 1920–1921 Depression." *Journal of Economic History* 26:2 (1966): 223–38.

Red Scare of 1917–1920

In the wake of World War I, which ended in November 1918, the United States demobilized nearly 4 million soldiers, discontinued wartime economic controls, and ended much of the defense production that employed some 9 million workers. Wartime wage controls, along with inflation both during and immediately after the war, generated a pent-up demand for wage increases. The result was the greatest wave of strikes and lockouts in the United States to that time—some 3,600 incidents in 1919 alone. The government responded with an unprecedented crackdown on leftist and worker organizations believed to be fomenting industrial and political unrest. Historians refer to that crackdown as the Red Scare.

During the Great War, the U.S. federal government had passed a series of measures, including the 1917 Espionage Act, the 1918 Sedition Act, and a series of anti-alien laws, intended to prevent spying and squelch dissent against the war effort. Much of the opposition, according to the government and media, was fomented by immigrants and aliens. The Committee on Public Information had produced propaganda against Germans and foreigners, and some local jurisdictions went so far as to ban the teaching of German in public schools. Patriotic groups such as the American Defense Society, the National Security League, and the American Protective League attacked—usually verbally, but sometimes physically—radicals, German Americans, and others opposed to the war or seen as disloyal.

When the war was over, a reactionary, antiforeign mood settled over the country. Many Americans, who had been suspicious of Germans and other foreigners during the war, were eager to pass legislation strictly limiting immigration. There was also a fear of revolution, triggered by the 1917 Bolshevik takeover in Russia, a revolution that was praised initially by many American radicals. Postwar revolutionary movements in Germany and Hungary also set off fears in America.

Many Americans were in an isolationist mood, especially as the nation's wartime allies—particularly Great Britain and France—sought a vindictive peace that would compromise the democracy and self-determination for which President Woodrow Wilson had declared the war was being fought. The result was widespread bitterness about the war effort, skepticism about U.S. involvement in international affairs, and a sense that foreigners could not be trusted. All these factors produced a political climate in which dissent was treated as disloyalty.

Socialists and Radicals

One form of dissent in capitalist America was socialism. Although the Socialist Party routinely won hundreds of thousands of votes in national elections, its anticapitalist ideology was viewed suspiciously by the vast majority of Americans as a foreign import inimical to democracy, religion, and the American way of life. Moreover, during the war, the Socialists had been the only major party consistently opposed to U.S. involvement. Their active opposition helped provoke the various antidissent laws of the war years and resulted in the jailing of the party's presidential standard-bearer, Eugene V. Debs, on sedition charges in 1918. The following year, Congress refused to seat Socialist Party member Victor Berger, the elected representative from Milwaukee, because of his political views, his German ancestry, and his prior opposition to the war.

Even more radical than the Socialists were the Industrial Workers of the World (IWW), a union also known as the Wobblies. Departing from the moderate unionism of the American Federation of Labor (AFL), the IWW had an avowedly radical agenda of eventually overturning the capitalist system. And, unlike the AFL, the Wobblies went beyond skilled white male workers to organize African Americans, immigrants, the unskilled, and women. Their tactics seemed to threaten civil order, as far as management and the government were concerned. IWW methods included trying to shut down entire industries—and in one case, an entire city—to force its opponents to offer a better economic deal to workers. The IWW was one of the main organizers of the Seattle General Strike of 1919.

Also active around the country were anarchist agitators, such as Emma Goldman and Alexander Berkman. Some anarchists advocated violence in their crusade against capitalism. In fact, in the year or so following the end of World War I, more than thirty bombs were mailed to prominent industrialist and government targets.

Race also played a role in the fears that gripped the nation in the wake of the Great War. Riots, usually sparked by whites angry at the influx of blacks into industrial manufacturing and white neighborhoods, broke out in Boston, Chicago, Cleveland, New York City, and elsewhere. Efforts by the National Association for the Advancement of Colored People (NAACP) to end lynching and discrimination against black veterans were seen by some as Communist inspired.

Raids and Deportations

U.S. Attorney General A. Mitchell Palmer had already begun to investigate radicals during the war.

The first major postwar response to the fear of radical subversion emerged in New York State—New York City being home to many immigrants and radicals. In March 1919, the state legislature established the Joint Legislative Committee to Investigate Seditious Activities, better known as the Lusk Committee, after its chairman, Republican State Senator Clayton Lusk. The committee heard testimony and issued reports declaring that there were half a million active "Reds," or left-wing radicals, in America, and that revolution was imminent. But the committee went beyond words, raiding the offices of Socialists and the IWW, as well as the Socialist-sponsored Rand School of Social Science in New York City.

By the end of 1919, the federal government, under the leadership of Attorney General Palmer, was conducting its own raids. A Quaker and a progressive, Palmer had become increasingly hostile to radicals after his Washington home was bombed in June, presumably by anarchists. Between November 1919 and January 1920, the Justice Department conducted hundreds of raids on radical groups around the country. Within the Bureau of Investigation (later called the Federal Bureau of Investigation), Palmer established the General Intelligence Division, placing at its head the young and virulently anticommunist J. Edgar Hoover. Hoover used the division to create files on more than 200,000 radical organizations and radical publications.

With Congress and the public up in arms about foreign radicals threatening the country, demand grew for their deportation. The government organized "Red Specials," trains that would bring radicals detained in the raids to New York City to be prepared for deportation. Palmer and the bureau were convinced that 90 percent of radicalism was immigrant inspired. Good Americans, they believed, did not behave that way. The raids captured 450 people in eleven cities. Only thirty-nine were formally detained, but some were held without a hearing for weeks or months. After the federal agents took the lead, state and local governments also began raiding radical organizations. Although the raids turned up radical literature, there was little evidence of violent activities.

Civil libertarians complained that the raids violated due process, and Palmer's actions helped inspire the founding of the American Civil Liberties Union in 1920. Some in government questioned the legality of the raids. A few members of the House of Repre-

Fears of radicalism, anarchy, and revolution led to the Red Scare of 1917–1920. Here members of the Boston police force confiscate literature deemed subversive. *(Topical Press Agency/Stringer/Hulton Archive/Getty Images)*

sentatives investigated the detentions, and the commissioner of immigration resigned rather than agree to the mass deportations. He was replaced by a more amenable commissioner.

While the raids continued, the government prepared for the deportation of hundreds of foreign-born radicals by readying the U.S. Army transport *Buford*. Known as the "Soviet Ark," for the final destination of its passengers, the *Buford* sailed out of New York on December 21, 1919, with about 250 Socialists and anarchists—including Goldman and Berkman—guarded by more than 100 soldiers. Because the United States had no formal relations with the Soviet Union, the ship first landed in neighboring Finland. From there, the deportees—even those who were not from Russia—were to travel by train to the Soviet Union. Most of the deportees had no criminal records, though Berkman and Goldman were exceptions. Berkman had been convicted of attempted murder for trying to assassinate industrialist Henry Frick in 1892, and Goldman supposedly had mentored Leon Czolgosz, the 1901 assassin of President William McKinley, but authorities could never establish a relevant connection between the two and Goldman was released from custody.

In January 1920, Communists were the targets. The acting director of the Labor Department signed 3,000 warrants on December 27 and abandoned administrative protections, including the right to counsel. On January 2, some 4,000 people in twenty-three states were taken into custody. Most of the raids were conducted without a warrant, and detainees were held incommunicado and without counsel. Detention conditions were often deplorable.

Return to Calm

By the early months of 1920, the Red Scare was winding down, even though some states continued to pass laws banning anarchism, Communist flags, and some forms of radical speech. There were several reasons for the return to calm. In Europe, the threat of Communist revolution spreading from Russia to other countries never materialized. At home, many in the press and government began voicing increasing concern that the raids were a threat to democracy and the American way of justice. Government agencies began to reverse their loose deportation rules, and the judiciary began ruling for victims in a series of cases.

Congress held hearings on the deportations and came to the conclusion that much of the evidence for them was erroneous or absent. Of the 5,000 warrants issued between November 1919 and January 1920, fewer than 600 resulted in deportations. The media also joined in the criticism, and there was even talk of prosecuting the immigration commissioner who had approved the deportations.

By June 1920, Palmer was arguing against further raids, especially after the traditional prolabor May Day celebrations went off largely without incident across the country. Not even an anarchist bombing on Wall Street in September, which resulted in the deaths of thirty-three people and injuries to more than 200, set off a renewed panic.

John Barnhill and James Ciment

See also: Anarchism; Bureau of Investigation; Communist Party; German Americans; Hoover, J. Edgar; Immigration; Industrial Workers of the World; Labor Movement; Palmer, A. Mitchell; *Schenck v. United States* (1919); Socialism and the Socialist Party of America.

Further Reading

Bennett, David. *The Party of Fear: From Nativist Movements to the New Right in American History.* Chapel Hill: University of North Carolina Press, 1988.

Hoyt, Edwin P. *The Palmer Raids, 1919–1920: An Attempt to Suppress Dissent.* New York: Seabury, 1969.

Murray, Robert. *Red Scare: A Study in National Hysteria, 1919–1920.* New York: McGraw-Hill, 1964.

Preston, William, Jr. *Aliens and Dissenters: Federal Suppression of Radicals.* 2nd ed. Urbana: University of Illinois Press, 1995.

Reparations and War Debts

Europe suffered greatly from World War I. Millions died and many more suffered grievously. The war destroyed farms, homes, factories, and transportation and communication systems. Wanting revenge for these great losses, some of the Allied victors demanded that the vanquished nations, principally Germany, pay for the damage and thus provide funds for reconstruction. But Germany and the other Central powers had also suffered and could not make such payments easily.

The war had shattered economies, and the harsh peace broke apart old trading systems and relationships. Countries in the former Austro-Hungarian Empire and new nations carved out of western Russia were all cast adrift and had to develop new patterns of trade along with stable governments. Moreover, the U.S. government had lent its allies funds amounting to more than $10 billion to prosecute the war and to begin the reconstruction. Now Congress and most Americans expected full repayment.

International Credit System

Some reparations were handled through an international credit system whereby the U.S. government and American private agencies would lend Germany and Austria money to make reparation payments to the Allies, who in turn would repay their war debts to the United States. This system continued, with increasing modifications, until the onset of the Great Depression. The related issues of war debts and reparations, along with high tariffs limiting international trade, may well have helped make the Great Depression worse and more difficult to resolve.

The peace treaties ending World War I forced Germany to accept responsibility for the conflict and required the vanquished nations to pay extensive reparations to the victors. Such payments from the defeated to the victors, along with loss of territory, were accepted means of resolving wars involving the great powers, and France in particular wanted a measure of revenge for the human and physical losses it had suffered fighting Germany. Not only had France's infrastructure been heavily damaged by the war, but Paris held longtime fears of a powerful Germany, going back to France's devastating loss to German forces in the Franco-Prussian War of 1871–1872. Protected by the English Channel, Britain was less fearful of a strong Germany. Indeed, many British policy makers wanted to see Germany strong, so as to provide a bulwark against expansion from Communist Russia.

The Treaty of Versailles extracted a harsh peace. Subsequently, an international reparations commission determined in April 1921 that Germany owed $33 billion to repay its war guilt, an incredible sum for that era and an incredible burden for the war-ravaged German economy. Under the plan, Germany would pay $375 million per year until 1925 and $900 million a year thereafter. These terms were a compromise between hard-line France and the more moderate Britain.

The reparation plan fell apart when Germany, caught in an economic crisis at home, reneged on its payments in 1923. Britain preferred to reschedule payments, but France reacted by sending troops into the demilitarized Rhineland and seizing mines and factories. This led to American involvement.

During World War I, the United States moved from a debtor nation to the world's greatest creditor nation; the Allies borrowed from the U.S. government and from U.S. banks to finance wartime purchases of American manufactured and farm goods. The United States entered the war as an Associated rather than Allied nation and afterward made no territorial or reparations demands. But with the situation in Germany undermining the ability of the Allies to repay American war loans, successive U.S. presidents felt compelled to act.

The Dawes Plan

To deal with the reparations problem, a special commission led by Charles Dawes, who was President Warren G. Harding's director of the budget and later Calvin Coolidge's vice president, devised a plan through which the U.S. government cleared the way for private loans to Germany and Austria. This would enable the former Central powers to make their reparation payments to the victors, who could then repay their wartime loans to America. The Dawes Commission proposed a loan to Germany of $200 million and reduced debt payments until Germany's economy revived. The Dawes Plan became operational on September 1, 1924. As part of the agreement, French and Belgian troops soon withdrew from the Ruhr Valley.

From 1924 to 1929, Germany made its reparation payments, greatly helped by American loans. In February 1929, the Committee on German Reparations met in Paris to review the Dawes Plan and elected Owen D. Young to serve as chair. This committee proposed what became known as the Young Plan: The Allies would reduce total reparations to slightly more than $8 billion, and Germany could repay them over a period of fifty-five years.

As the world economy spiraled downward after the stock market crash of October 1929 and the disastrous impact of the Smoot-Hawley Tariff and reactive tariffs from other industrialized nations, Germany could not afford its payments, and the former wartime Allies ceased payments on war debts. In 1931, President Herbert Hoover proposed a twelve-month moratorium on Allied war debts and German reparation payments. But in 1933, Adolf Hitler, who had become chancellor of Germany in January, renounced all reparation payments. As the world began its march to World War II, these issues from the previous war faded into the background.

The experience of World War I reparations and war debts would figure prominently in American planning during World War II. The Bretton Woods monetary system and the International Monetary Fund, World Bank, and General Agreement on Trade and Tariffs (GATT) were all means to help restart the war-ravaged economies after World War II.

Charles M. Dobbs

See also: Dawes, Charles; Dawes Plan (1924); Europe, Relations with; Paris Peace Conference of 1919; Versailles, Treaty of (1919); Young Plan (1929–1930).

Further Reading

Hogan, Michael J. *Informal Entente: The Private Structure of Cooperation in Anglo-American Economic Diplomacy, 1918–1928.* Columbia: University of Missouri Press, 1977.

Kent, Bruce. *The Spoils of War: The Politics, Economics, and Diplomacy of Reparations, 1918–1932.* New York: Oxford University Press, 1989.

Marks, Sally. *The Illusion of Peace: International Relations in Europe, 1918–1933.* 2nd ed. New York: Palgrave Macmillan, 2003.

Schuker, Stephen A. *The End of French Predominance in Europe: The Financial Crisis of 1924 and the Adoption of the Dawes Plan.* Chapel Hill: University of North Carolina Press, 1976.

Trachtenberg, Marc. *Reparation in World Politics: France and European Economic Diplomacy, 1916–1923.* New York: Columbia University Press, 1980.

Republican Party

In the wake of the decisive presidential election of 1896—in which William McKinley swept to the first of his two terms—the Republican Party became the dominant political party in the United States and remained so through the onset of the Great Depression in the 1930s. The Republicans failed to retain control of the White House only between 1913 and 1921, when Democrat Woodrow Wilson occupied it. The House of Representatives was under Republican control except between 1911 and 1919, and the Senate except between 1913 and 1919. As the majority party from 1919 to 1929, the Republicans stood for probusiness economic policies, conservatism on social issues, a limited federal government, fiscal probity, and an isolationist foreign policy except in dealing with Latin America.

Ascendance

During the Progressive Era, from the late 1890s through World War I, the Republican Party was ideologically divided between conservatives and progressives, with the latter in ascendance until the war. The election of 1896 put the conservative McKinley in the White House, but party leaders—headed by political adviser Mark Hanna—agreed to add Spanish-American War hero Theodore Roosevelt to the ticket as a liberal counterbalance. When McKinley was assassinated eight months into his second term, in September 1901, the progressive Roosevelt became president.

Roosevelt immediately embarked on a progressive agenda at home and an aggressive foreign policy abroad, pushing for antitrust action against large corporations, a series of new laws and agencies designed to protect consumers and the environment, and bold international steps leading to the construction of the Panama Canal. In 1908, Roosevelt picked Vice President William Howard Taft to succeed him. But as president, Taft proved too conservative for Roosevelt's taste, and Roosevelt broke from the party to run for the presidency on the Bull Moose, or Progressive Party, ticket in 1912. With progressive and conservative Republicans divided between Taft and Roosevelt, the Democratic nominee, Woodrow Wilson, won the White House and Democrats took control of the Senate.

Four years later, the Republicans ran another moderate progressive, Charles Evans Hughes, for the presidency, but he also lost to Wilson. On the major issue of the day, both the Democrats and Republicans promised to keep the country out of World War I. Ongoing German belligerence, however, soon drew America into the fray. While conservative Republicans generally supported Wilson's increasingly hard line with Germany, the progressive wing of the party, led by Senators George Norris and Robert La Follette, of Nebraska and Wisconsin, respectively, continued to oppose U.S. entry. Once Wilson went to Congress and won a declaration of war, however, the vast majority of Republicans lined up with the president, in the tradition of bipartisan foreign policy during times of war. For the most part, Republicans supported the president's decision to expand government control of the economy during the war and his efforts to implement antidissent legislation, including the Espionage and Sedition acts.

But the Republicans and the country as a whole were becoming more conservative on domestic policy and more isolationist on foreign policy during the course of the war, and especially during the negotiations over the peace in 1919. Although Wilson engaged in an all-out push for U.S. membership in the League of Nations, an international conflict resolution organization, his efforts proved futile, dashed by the refusal of the Senate, led by isolationist Norris, to ratify the League treaty in 1919. In the elections of 1918, held just as World War I was ending, Republicans did well, taking control of the Senate by a margin of two seats, and the House by fifty seats.

By 1920, Republicans appeared poised to take control of the executive and legislative branches. While progressives remained a significant minority in the party, there was no question that conservatives were in ascendance with the nomination of Warren G. Harding for the presidency. A popular but relatively ineffective senator from Ohio, Harding was in fact a stalking horse for the old McKinley, probusiness wing of the party. Indeed, the two came from the same state. Well-financed, Harding spoke to rural and small-town America, where a majority of voters still lived. He coined the term "normalcy" to mean a turning away from reform crusades at home and interventionism abroad. After twenty years of progressive agitation, the public was more than open to the message, not only giving Harding a landslide victory—16 million votes to 9 million votes for opponent James M. Cox, a conservative Democrat who differed little from Harding on most major issues—but also

Republican President Warren G. Harding and Vice President Calvin Coolidge pose with their wives in early 1923. In August of that year, Harding died suddenly and Coolidge succeeded him. Republicans occupied the White House continuously from 1921 to 1933. *(Hirz/Hulton Archive/Getty Images)*

putting Republicans in a commanding position in Congress, with nearly 70 percent of House seats and more than 60 percent of Senate seats.

Harding and the Republicans in Congress immediately put into effect their probusiness platform. Led by Treasury Secretary Andrew Mellon, a wealthy financier, Congress passed a huge tax reduction as a means to reduce the federal surplus, with most of the cuts going to the nation's richest citizens. Mellon argued that this would spur investment, and to an extent, it did. Other than a sharp but brief recession in 1921–1922, the economy expanded dramatically during the decade, though many rural areas suffered from overproduction and low crop prices. Even more forceful was Secretary of Commerce Herbert Hoover, a former relief administrator, who established voluntary associations between industry and the federal government to promote big business.

The antiforeigner, antiradical hysteria of the immediate postwar era died down during Harding's administration, allowing relaxation in the enforcement of laws against sedition. Socialist leader Eugene V. Debs, jailed in 1918 for a speech criticizing the war, received a pardon.

Although Harding and Hoover, the two most prominent Republicans of the early 1920s, were

above reproach, this was not the case for other members of the administration. In 1923, a major scandal involving the nation's oil reserves at Teapot Dome, Wyoming, implicated a number of officials, but Harding died suddenly in August, before the full political impact could be felt. His successor, Vice President Calvin Coolidge, was a taciturn, law-and-order New Englander who had never even been close to scandal. While Coolidge helped repair the image of the party, he could not rescue it fully from setbacks in the 1922 and 1924 congressional elections, despite his own reelection in the latter year. He was also unable to block a defection of progressive Republicans, who broke from the party with La Follette as their presidential candidate in 1924. But the progressives were now a decided minority of Republicans and could not prevent Coolidge from scoring a landslide win.

Coolidge pursued the probusiness policies of his predecessor and even retained his two major domestic cabinet members, Mellon and Hoover. With still solid Republican majorities in Congress, the government remained committed to probusiness economic polices, social conservatism (especially in its continued support for Prohibition), and isolation from European affairs, despite a major intervention in Nicaragua in 1926 and continuing occupations of the Dominican Republic and Haiti.

Troubling Trends

Even as the Republicans continued their ascendance with increasing majorities in the Senate and House, and even as they continued to control the executive branch with the election of Hoover in 1928, their days as the majority party were numbered. Over the course of the 1920s, two forces came into play that doomed the Republicans to minority status. One was changing demographics. The base of Republican support was rural areas and small towns, with their populations of socially conservative, Protestant, native-born Americans. But the nation was becoming increasingly urban, immigrant, and Catholic. These voting blocs were more inclined to support government intervention in the economy and were generally hostile to the conservative social experiment of Prohibition.

The 1920 U.S. Census showed a majority of Americans living in urban areas for the first time, though it defined "urban" loosely, as any town with a population of 2,500 or more. Urban voters tended to be Democratic, and in 1928, they nominated as their presidential candidate the anti-Prohibition New

York Governor Al Smith, the first Catholic ever to run for the presidency on a major party ticket. Although Smith was swamped by Hoover in the November balloting, and Republicans made gains in both the House and Senate, the other great force favoring the Democrats was about to come into play.

Upon arriving in the White House in early 1929, Hoover promised continued prosperity and more of the probusiness policies he had pursued as commerce secretary. More progressive than Coolidge, Hoover nevertheless adhered to the idea that government involvement in the economy should remain limited. When Wall Street crashed in October 1929 and the economy began to tumble, accompanied by rising unemployment and bankruptcy rates, Hoover refused to reconsider his ideological positions. He argued that the economic downturn was temporary and that the government should not engage in public works to give jobs to the unemployed. This would lead only to federal debt, he contended, which would dry up capital needed by industry. He also believed that too much government relief would sap the initiative of the unemployed. Treasury Secretary Mellon, who remained on from earlier administrations, was even more committed to conservative economic policies. Even as the economy sank into a full-fledged depression in the early 1930s, Mellon argued that the downturn was good for America, weeding out less efficient businesses and industries.

Having been accorded credit for the economic prosperity of the 1920s, Republicans would now be punished by voters for the Depression, which began on the GOP's watch. In the 1930 midterm elections, the first following the crash, Democrats took control of the House and came within one vote of doing the same in the Senate. But it was the landslide victory of Democratic New York Governor Franklin D. Roosevelt in 1932 that spelled the undoing of Republican dominance. Roosevelt promised an activist federal government that would put America back to work. His New Deal coalition included not only urban, labor, and immigrant voters but also poor rural and small-town folk who were hurting from the Depression and blaming the Republicans for it.

Roosevelt also won over a majority of black voters. Until the 1920s, African Americans in the North had voted heavily for Republicans, the party of Abraham Lincoln and emancipation. (Those in the South had been largely disenfranchised since the late nineteenth century.) But blacks were especially hard hit by the Depression, and in 1932, the majority turned away from the Republicans to vote Democratic for the first time. So powerful was Roosevelt's New Deal coalition that Republicans would return to power in the 1950s only by promising not to tinker with its basic social and economic measures.

James Ciment

See also: Coolidge, Calvin; Democratic Party; DePriest, Oscar; Election of 1918; Election of 1920; Election of 1922; Election of 1924; Election of 1926; Election of 1928; Harding, Warren G.; Hoover, Herbert; Progressivism.

Further Reading

Goldberg, David J. *Discontented America: The United States in the 1920s.* Baltimore: Johns Hopkins University Press, 1999.

Leuchtenburg, William E. *The Perils of Prosperity, 1914–1932.* Chicago: University of Chicago Press, 1958.

Murray, Robert K. *The Politics of Normalcy.* New York: W.W. Norton, 1973.

Wilson, Joan Hoff. *Herbert Hoover: The Forgotten Progressive.* Boston: Little, Brown, 1975.

Retail and Chain Stores

The growing size and complexity of the American economy, combined with the introduction of new time-, cost-, and laborsaving technologies, inspired an increased emphasis on efficiency in American business during the early twentieth century. Innovations such as the assembly line allowed manufacturers to produce goods more quickly, easily, and cheaply, providing them with the capacity to expand operations and increase profits by making large volumes of goods available to American consumers at lower prices. An obsession with efficiency rippled through the nation's economy as a wide variety of businesses, following the successful example of the manufacturing sector, sought to streamline their operations.

The trend toward efficiency exerted a dramatic effect on the retailing sector. The territorial expansion and population growth of the nineteenth century had sparked an explosive demand for consumer goods, as vividly illustrated by the success of mail-order retail businesses in the late nineteenth century. The introduction of affordable mass-produced automobiles, beginning with the Ford Model T in 1908, led to a more mobile society, further increasing consumers' access to retail goods. In this environment, retail businesses with the capacity for purchasing larger volumes of goods and expanding into new markets enjoyed an advantage over other companies. Many of these concerns grew into chains: companies offering merchandise for sale to the public at two or more locations.

The first modern retail chain in the United States was the Great Atlantic and Pacific Tea Company (A&P), founded in 1858. Other retail firms, most notably the F.W. Woolworth Company, established chains in the late nineteenth century. The proliferation of chain stores increased dramatically during the early twentieth century, reaching a peak during the 1920s. In 1919, chain stores generated 5 percent of total U.S. retail sales; by 1929, chain store sales made up approximately 30 percent of the total retail market. Some retail concerns saw unprecedented growth during the 1920s. Sears, Roebuck and Company, which began as a mail-order company in the 1880s, opened its first retail store in 1925, operated twenty-seven stores by the end of 1927, and by 1930 had expanded its retail operations to more than 300 stores.

A number of factors created the ideal socioeconomic environment for the growth of chain retail businesses during the 1920s. The innovation in mass production, driven largely by the development of the assembly line, had revolutionized the means by which goods were made. Yet traditional methods of retailing had not kept pace with the increase in efficiency. Retail chains, however, applied the high-volume, standardized approach to manufacturing goods to the process of selling them in order to minimize costs and maximize efficiency. With the development of suburbs outside major cities, many Americans lost their usual familial and community ties, resulting in an increased sense of social alienation and a desire for the familiarity and predictability that chain stores provided. Economic growth in the 1920s contributed to an increase in Americans' disposable income, providing further impetus for the explosion of chain retailing.

The proliferation of chain retailing in the 1920s followed a period of progressive economic reform focused on the elimination of business practices such as monopolies, trusts, and price-fixing. Chain store competition eliminated a significant number of smaller retailers, forcing others to rely increasingly on cooperative purchasing and larger wholesalers to buy goods at lower prices. Lingering concerns over unfair business practices resulted in a backlash against retail chains, culminating in fair trade laws that regulated price setting and the ability of chains to obtain price advantages through mass purchasing. Additional taxes were imposed on chain retail activity.

The emergence of chain retailing in the 1920s, however, had transformed the American economy. Chain stores paved the way for the supermarkets and shopping centers of the postwar era—thus laying the foundation of the American consumer culture.

Michael H. Burchett

See also: Advertising; Beauty Industry and Culture; Credit and Debt, Consumer; Fashion, Men's; Fashion, Women's; Food and Diet; Suburbs.

Further Reading

Beckman, Theodore N., and H.C. Nolen. *The Chain Store Problem.* Chicago: Ayer, 1976.

Haas, Harold M. *Social and Economic Aspects of the Chain Store Movement.* Chicago: Ayer, 1979.

Lebhar, Godfrey M. *Chain Stores in America, 1859–1962.* New York: Chain Store Guide, 1963.

Rockne, Knute (1888–1931)

Knute Rockne, the charismatic football coach for the University of Notre Dame from 1918 to 1930, had more than a hundred victories and six national championships to his credit. He also achieved the highest winning percentage (.881) of any coach of a major college or professional football team in the history of the sport. Rockne helped to develop the modern style of football and to turn college football into a major spectator sport.

Born on March 4, 1888, in the small town of Voss, Norway, Rockne was five years old when his family immigrated to Chicago. He took up the sport of football as a boy, playing in pickup games in vacant lots and then in organized high school competition. After working for several years to raise money for tuition, he enrolled at Notre Dame in 1910. He participated in track and field, setting the school's pole-vaulting record, and football, but in the latter he was more a motivator than a star player. As team captain, he led the Notre Dame football team to one of the great upsets in the school's history, a win over the top-ranked U.S. Army cadet team in 1913.

An excellent student, Rockne was offered a position as a graduate assistant in chemistry when he graduated in 1914. He took the job only on the condition that he could help coach the school's football team as well. Three years later, upon the retirement of head coach Jesse Harper, Rockne was appointed to that position.

College football was just coming into its own as a national sport when Rockne took the helm at Notre Dame. Prior to World War I, the game's popularity was largely confined to the elite universities of the Northeast. Unlike baseball, which had emerged as a largely professional sport by the late nineteenth century, football was dedicated to the ideals of amateurism. Fans, particularly among school alumni, continued to view football as a gentleman's sport, a test of manhood for the nation's future leaders.

By World War I, the sport spread to major private and public universities across the country, gaining popularity and a new emphasis on winning. Recognizing that universities could make a name for themselves on the achievements of their football programs, administrators began to invest heavily in recruiting the best players and coaches and building facilities in which these athletes could display their prowess. No less than fifty-five large concrete stadiums—some seating 70,000 fans or more—were built in the 1920s, largely on or near college campuses. (Professional football was still in its infancy in the Jazz Age, its popularity eclipsed by the college game.)

An innovator on the field and in the head office, Rockne was a leading figure behind the sport's growing popularity. He helped pioneer the forward pass, a dramatic and crowd-pleasing play. He was instrumental in developing intersectional rivalries and a national playing schedule that assured wider popularity for the sport. One Jazz Age contest between Notre Dame and the University of Southern California—one of the great rivalries in college football history—was attended by 120,000 spectators at Chicago's Soldier Field. It is believed to be the largest crowd to ever attend a football game in American history.

Rockne was also noted for scouting and attracting some of the best talent in the history of the sport. He helped nurture the skills of quarterback George Gipp, one of the greatest players of his generation and a popular leader on the field. Rockne also coached the talented backfield of Jim Crowley, Elmer Layden, Don Miller, and Harry Stuhldreher, forever immortalized by sportswriter Grantland Rice as the "Four Horsemen of the Apocalypse." His contribution to picking up the speed of play—and hence making the game more popular with fans—was due to more than just his coaching from the sidelines. Rockne used his scientific training and understanding of the human body to design lighter equipment that did not sacrifice player safety. Rockne also introduced the school's dramatic gold-colored satin and silk uniforms.

But the intangibles were important, too. Rockne always had a colorful quote for the press, and he was the first coach of any sport to be featured on the cover of *Time* magazine, an honor he earned in 1927. Perhaps Rockne is best remembered for his rousing pregame pep talk as his team prepared to meet an undefeated Army team the following year. Recalling the premature demise of Gipp in 1920, Rockne quoted what was reportedly the deathbed speech of the late quarterback, exhorting the team to "win one for the Gipper." When underdog Notre Dame upset Army, 14–9, the Rockne legend was sealed.

Knute Rockne was killed in a plane crash outside Kansas City, Missouri, on March 31, 1931. He was on his way to Hollywood to act as an adviser to the film *The Spirit of Notre Dame*. Rockne, his Gipper speech, and George Gipp himself were immortalized in the film *Knute Rockne, All American* (1940), starring Pat O'Brien in the title role and Ronald Reagan as Gipp.

James Ciment

See also: Education, Higher; Football.

Further Reading

Brondfield, Jerry. *Rockne, the Coach, the Man, the Legend.* New York: Random House, 1976.

Robinson, Ray. *Rockne of Notre Dame: The Making of a Football Legend.* New York: Oxford University Press, 1999.

Rogers, Will (1879–1935)

Humorist, actor, and social commentator Will Rogers was perhaps the most popular, and most widely quoted, personality of the 1920s. With his homespun charm and cowboy background, Rogers embodied for many Americans a rural, frontier past that was rapidly vanishing in a modernizing and urbanizing country. Yet Rogers was a man of his time, a star of the new media of radio and film. And in his social commentary, delivered in his syndicated newspaper column, over the radio, and in public lectures, he applied a folksy wisdom—and a good dose of humor—to the pressing issues of the day.

A child of the frontier, William Penn Adair Rogers was born on November 4, 1879, on a ranch in Oklahoma Territory. Both of his parents were part Cherokee Indian, though his father was also part of the Anglo establishment of the territory, serving as a judge and helping to write the state's first constitution.

Humorist, actor, and newspaper columnist Will Rogers won a devoted following with his country charm and folksy wisdom before dying in a plane crash—with world-renowned aviator Wiley Post—in Alaska in August 1935. *(American Stock/Hulton Archive/Getty Images)*

Rogers famously said later, "My ancestors didn't come over on the Mayflower, but they met the boat." Although he attended military school through the tenth grade, a big part of his education came on his father's ranch, where he learned cowboy skills. After traveling in his early twenties to Argentina and South Africa, where he worked breaking horses and herding cattle, Rogers moved to New York, landing a job on the stage, performing roping and other cowboy tricks. In 1915, he secured a regular gig with Broadway impresario Florenz Ziegfeld at the New Amsterdam Theater, a leading venue for vaudeville acts.

An avid follower of the news, Rogers soon began mixing humorous social commentary with his roping tricks. The combination appealed to audiences, which included some of the country's most influential businesspeople, politicians, and cultural figures. Ziegfeld shifted Rogers to the immensely popular Ziegfeld Follies the following year, and by the beginning of the Jazz Age, Rogers was one of the top stars of the New York stage. He would perform with the Follies on and off through 1925.

Like many vaudeville performers, Rogers also worked in Hollywood, starring in numerous silent westerns and comedies from 1919 through 1923, though his efforts to produce his own films nearly bankrupted him. Rogers would not return to the screen until the era of talking film, in 1929. From then until his death in 1935, he was featured in pictures with some of the top stars of the day, including Dick Powell, Mickey Rooney, and Maureen O'Sullivan. He also starred in three films directed by the legendary John Ford.

But it was not so much his films that made Rogers a nationally recognized figure as his lectures and speeches, which gained him a national audience through their distribution on radio and phonograph records. When the Follies went on the road in the early 1920s, Rogers often took time off to give speeches to live audiences or on the radio. Victrola, a popular phonograph company, recorded several of these lectures, which became best-selling records.

In 1925, Rogers launched a national lecture tour that took him beyond major cities to small-town America. He did not pass up urban centers altogether: In 1926, he became the first humorist to ever perform at New York's Carnegie Hall. The tour lasted through 1928. His talks usually began with the disclaimer that "a humorist entertains, and a lecturer annoys." Rogers would then apply his trademark folk wisdom and down-home humor to some of the most controversial topics of the day—from Prohibition to the rise of the Ku Klux Klan, generally with a liberal slant. As Rogers once famously noted, "I don't belong to any organized party. I'm a Democrat." He also shared his personal stories of meeting celebrated and powerful figures, from Hollywood to Washington, D.C., with himself in the persona of a slightly naive but ultimately wise country cousin.

Rogers took time off to visit Europe in 1926. He was popular almost everywhere he went and became a goodwill ambassador for the United States, meeting with leaders in countries across the continent. He sent back a series of newspaper dispatches on everything from a general strike in Britain to Benito Mussolini's dictatorship in Italy to the goings-on in revolutionary Russia. In the tradition of Mark Twain, the commentary applied American common sense to the sophisticated world of European politics and culture. So popular were the dispatches that the McNaught Syndicate arranged to distribute what Rogers called his daily "telegram" to newspapers across the country. By the early 1930s, these dispatches were running in more than 400 papers on a regular basis.

While Rogers applied his trademark humor to almost every topic under the sun, there was one subject that he took especially seriously: aviation. He was a strong supporter of the new technology and loved to fly, if not as a pilot then as a passenger, at a time when commercial air travel was barely in its infancy. During his 1925 lecture tour, for instance, Rogers became the first civilian to fly coast to coast, hitching rides with airmail pilots. Two years later, he flew on a goodwill trip with famed aviator Charles Lindbergh to Mexico City.

In 1935, Rogers flew to and around Alaska on an experimental plane with renowned aviator Wiley Post. On August 15, the plane went down near Point Barrow and the two men were killed.

James Ciment and Michael McGregor

See also: Celebrity Culture; Film; Journalism; Radio.

Further Reading

Ketchum, Richard M. *Will Rogers: His Life and Times.* New York: American Heritage, 1973.

Rogers, Betty. *Will Rogers: His Wife's Story.* 2nd ed. Norman: University of Oklahoma Press, 1979.

Rogers, Will. *The Writings of Will Rogers.* Ed. Arthur Frank Wertheim and Barbara Bair. Norman: University of Oklahoma Press, 1996.

Rollins, Peter C. *Will Rogers: A Bio-Bibliography.* Westport, CT: Greenwood, 1984.

Rosewood Massacre (1923)

The massacre in Rosewood, Florida, in 1923 was one of the most notorious acts of white mob violence against African Americans in the twentieth century. The lynching and rioting that occurred over an eight-day period in January resulted in at least eight deaths and the destruction of the town. In the early 1920s, Rosewood was a small, predominantly African American village in Levy County, in the central part of the state, with a population of a little more than 300. Many of Rosewood's men worked at the sawmill in nearby Sumner; some of the women residents worked as domestics in Sumner.

The Rosewood massacre was one of a series of attacks on African American communities that occurred in Florida from 1912 through 1923, including the well-known 1920 Election Day race riot in nearby Ocoee. While lynchings of African Americans would decline in the 1920s, the early part of the decade was marked by heightened racism in many parts of the country, caused in part by white perceptions that blacks were refusing to play the subservient role assigned to them in the segregated South. Indeed, the Ku Klux Klan saw its membership rise to record levels in the South and across the country in the early 1920s.

The Rosewood attack began, as had many other instances of racial violence in the Jim Crow South, with rumors of a black sexual assault on a white woman. On New Year's Eve in 1922, Fannie Taylor, a white woman from Sumner, claimed that she had been attacked and raped by an African American man. But it may have been her white lover, John Bradley, who had assaulted her. Two black Rosewood residents who were washing clothes at the Taylor home—Sarah Carrier and her granddaughter, Philomena Goins—recalled that the couple had argued and believed that Bradley had caused Taylor's injuries. Angry Sumner residents, however, were convinced that an escaped African American convict named Jessie Hunter was the assailant. The men of the town organized a posse with dogs to track down Hunter and Rosewood residents they believed had aided his escape.

The group tortured and murdered Rosewood resident Sam Carter and his family, who had been hiding in the woods. Rosewood citizens began congregating at several barricaded homes and arming themselves. On January 4, the group of whites attacked Sylvester Carrier's home, where several Rosewood families had gathered, and killed several of its occupants. Some of the attackers were also killed. Many Rosewood residents then fled into nearby swamps, and the whites burned a church and several homes. The remaining structures in the town were burned over the next several days. Rosewood residents who survived the massacre credited two white train conductors, who snuck them aboard the train that ran through Rosewood, evacuating them to safety.

During the course of the Rosewood attacks, Levy County Sheriff Robert Walker refused Governor Cary A. Hardee's offer to send in the National Guard, claiming that the situation was under control. By the time the riot ended, there were at least eight dead, two of them white. Some scholars estimate that the death rate was actually much higher. Those Rosewood residents who survived the town's destruction fled and never returned. Governor Hardee ordered a special grand jury investigation into the Rosewood incident, and more than thirteen eyewitnesses testified. But the grand jury concluded that it did not have enough evidence on which to base indictments. Those involved rarely spoke of the incident, and the Rosewood massacre did not become widely known until many decades later.

In 1982, Arnett Doctor, son of Rosewood survivor Philomena Goins, shared his story with an investigative reporter from the *St. Petersburg Times*. Attorney Martha Barnett, a childhood friend of Doctor, convinced her firm, Holland and Knight, to represent the Rosewood survivors and their descendants free of charge in their battle to receive government redress. The Florida Conference of Black State Legislators joined the fight.

In 1994, the Florida legislature passed and the governor signed the Rosewood Compensation Bill, which appropriated state funds to survivors and their descendants who could demonstrate property loss from their displacement. The bill also established a state university scholarship fund for the descendants of Rosewood families. Including the scholarships, total compensation reached $1.85 million—an acknowledgment of past wrongs and a symbol of African American political strength. All that remains of the town of Rosewood, however, is a highway marker on State Road 24.

Marcella Bush Treviño

See also: African Americans; Chicago Race Riot of 1919; Lynching; Tulsa Race Riots of 1921.

Further Reading

D'Orso, Michael. *Like Judgment Day: The Ruin and Redemption of a Town Called Rosewood.* New York: G.P. Putnam's Sons, 1996.

Jenkins, Lizzie. *The Real Rosewood.* Gainesville, FL: BookEnds, 2003.

Jones, Maxine D., and Kevin McCarthy. *African Americans in Florida.* Sarasota, FL: Pineapple, 1993.

Ross, Harold (1892–1951)

Harold Ross rose to prominence in the mid-1920s as the editor of *The New Yorker* magazine, founded in 1925 by Ross and his wife, the journalist Jane Grant, with the financial support of investor Raoul Fleischmann, heir to a yeast fortune. By 1927, newsstand circulation was over 50,000, and the magazine had become a prominent voice in Jazz Age America.

Ross was born in Aspen, Colorado, on November 6, 1892. His mother was a schoolteacher, and his father was an Irish immigrant. When the mining economy of the town collapsed around 1900, the family moved to several other small towns before settling in Salt Lake City. There, Ross began his journalism career, working on his high school paper and as a contributor to the *Salt Lake Tribune*.

When he was thirteen, Ross dropped out of school, running off to his uncle's home in Denver, where he worked part-time for the Denver *Post*. He then took jobs at papers across the country, writing for no less than seven by the time he was twenty-five. When America entered World War I in 1917, Ross enlisted in an engineering regiment and was transferred to Paris to write for the army newspaper *Stars and Stripes,* where he soon became editor. There, he met *New York Times* journalist Jane Grant, as well as a number of other writers who would make names for themselves in New York literary circles in the 1920s, including critic Alexander Woollcott, columnist Franklin Pierce Adams, and illustrator Cyrus Baldridge.

In April 1919, Ross was in New York City, editing *Home Sector,* a magazine for veterans. When that publication folded in 1920, Ross took a job editing *Judge,* a humor magazine. He and Grant married in March 1920 (they would later divorce). Among their friends was a group of New York literary figures, including writers such as Woollcott, Dorothy Parker, and Heywood Braun, who would come to be known as the Algonquin Round Table, so named because they often met for lunch at the Algonquin Hotel. Encouraged by the Round Table, Ross and Grant began planning a new magazine. With financing from Fleischmann, they created *The New Yorker.* Round Table members were advisers and contributors to the publication from its inception.

On February 19, 1925, *The New Yorker* hit the newsstands with 15,000 copies and sold well. The novelty of the publication soon wore off, however, and sales began to decline by the spring. In response, Ross retooled some of the features, strengthening the "Talk of the Town" section at the beginning of each issue. "Talk of the Town" would become the magazine's signature article. He also hired a number of major editors and contributors throughout the first year. Two of his most important hires were E.B. White and James Thurber, whose playful styles helped define the magazine's sophisticated, witty tone. Ross's most trusted hire was probably Katharine Sergeant Angell, who helped steer the magazine's fiction selections. By 1927, *The New Yorker* was an unqualified success, with a circulation over 50,000.

In many ways, Ross was an odd fit for as literate a magazine as *The New Yorker*. He was described by staff members as having a temper, his private life was tumultuous, and his commitment to efficiency and organization often clashed with the more artistic temperaments of some *New Yorker* employees. Ross was never an aficionado of literature. Preferring nonfiction to fiction, he read reference books in his spare time. However, he was idealistic about journalism and editing, and he favored straightforward writing in the tradition of his hero, Mark Twain. These characteristics helped set *The New Yorker*'s style.

Ross planned on publishing a "funny little magazine." As such, in the words of E.B. White, he "allowed humor to infect everything." Ross led the magazine through 1,399 issues. He was still editing the magazine when he died from cancer on December 6, 1951.

Guy Patrick Cunningham

See also: Algonquin Round Table; Fiction; Journalism; *New Yorker, The.*

Further Reading

Grant, Jane C. *Ross, the* New Yorker, *and Me.* New York: Reynal, 1968.

Kunkel, Thomas. *Genius in Disguise: Harold Ross of the* New Yorker. New York: Carroll and Graf, 1996.

Kunkel, Thomas, ed. *Letters from the Editor: The* New Yorker's *Harold Ross.* New York: Modern Library, 2001.

Ruth, Babe (1895–1948)

George Herman "Babe" Ruth, who set home run records that remained unbroken for decades and who restored professional baseball to popularity in the wake of the 1919 Chicago Black Sox scandal, is still regarded by many as the greatest major league baseball player of all time. He was certainly was one of the great celebrities of the "golden age" of sports in America—the 1920s.

He was born on February 6, 1895, in Baltimore, Maryland, to Kate (née Schamberger) and George Herman Ruth, Sr. His parents managed and then owned a waterfront tavern, working long hours and allowing their son to roam the streets unsupervised. By age seven, Ruth was so unruly that his father signed over custody to the Catholic brothers who ran St. Mary's Industrial School for Boys, a reformatory

and orphanage. Ruth lived at St. Mary's for twelve years, seldom seeing his birth family. He struggled to adapt to the regimentation of institutional life but eventually fell under the wing of Brother Matthias, who coached baseball at the school and taught Ruth to field and hit. Ruth played the position of catcher before taking up pitching at age fifteen.

In 1914, when Ruth was nineteen, the owner of the Baltimore Orioles (then a minor league team), Jack Dunn, signed him to a contract. Because Ruth was still a ward of the reformatory, Dunn had to obtain legal custody of his new ballplayer, effectively adopting him. Referred to as Dunn's "new babe," Ruth earned the nickname by which he would be known for the rest of his life and beyond. Loyal Italian American fans called him the Bambino.

In October 1914, Ruth married seventeen-year-old Helen Woodford, a waitress. Not long after, the Orioles, who were part of the Boston Red Sox farm system, sold Ruth's contract to the major league team. He joined the starting rotation of pitchers in the spring of the following year and had a modest rookie season. In 1916, he compiled the lowest earned run average (ERA) in the American League (1.75), with the most shutouts (9). He also pitched thirteen scoreless innings during the fourth game of the World Series. In the first game of the 1918 World Series, Ruth pitched a 1–0 shutout. Then, in the fourth game, he held the Chicago Cubs scoreless until the eighth inning, setting up a 3–2 Sox win. Altogether, he pitched twenty-nine and two-thirds consecutive scoreless innings in the World Series, a record that stood for forty-three years.

It was his bat more than his arm, however, that began to attract attention. During the 1919 season, Ruth was switched from the mound to the outfield so that he could appear in every game. He responded by hitting twenty-nine home runs, a single-season record. But Red Sox owner Harry Frazee, who was strapped for cash because of investments he had made in Broadway shows, traded Ruth in the off-season to the New York Yankees for $125,000 plus a $300,000 loan. In the decades that followed, fans in Boston and New York came to regard Frazee's move as the "Curse of the Bambino." After 1918, the Red Sox did not win another World Series until 2004, while the Yankees won more championships than any other franchise in American professional sports.

In New York, as in Boston, tales of Ruth's appetite for life—in every sense of the word—

The home-run-hitting and larger-than-life personality of New York Yankees outfielder Babe Ruth revived fan interest in professional baseball after the taint of the 1919 Black Sox scandal. *(Library of Congress, LC-B2–5463–12)*

abounded. He was a charismatic man about town whose exploits off the field became an integral part of the Babe's legend. Even though he was suspended several times for fighting and curfew violations, companies paid top dollar to use his image in advertising. Fans, especially children, idolized him.

In 1920—the year the "dead ball" was replaced with a livelier one—Ruth hit fifty-four home runs, almost doubling his previous record and earning him another nickname: the "Sultan of Swat." He was suspended for the first thirty-nine days of the 1922 season for participating in a barnstorming tour, which was prohibited by his contract. Several times during the course of the season, he was suspended for fighting. But this did not quell the adoration of his fans. In 1923, so many people attended Yankees games that the franchise could afford to build its own stadium rather than continue to share the Polo Grounds with the New York Giants. The new Yankee Stadium became known as the "House That Ruth Built."

The year 1925 was a tumultuous one for the Babe. In April, he had emergency surgery for what was described as an intestinal abscess. Even after his return to the field, however, the team played badly. Late in the season, Ruth had a well-publicized fight with manager Miller Huggins. Also in 1925, Ruth and his wife decided to separate. They did not divorce because of religious beliefs. In April 1929, after Helen's death, Ruth married a widowed actress named Claire Hodgson.

On the field, the Bambino led the American League in home runs in every year from 1918 through 1931, except for 1922 and 1925. His total of sixty home runs in 1927 stood as a single-season record until 1961. One of the legendary moments of his career came in game three of the 1932 World Series, when he hit his memorable "called shot." Down in the count two balls and two strikes, Ruth lifted his bat and pointed to the center-field bleachers, apparently to indicate where his home run would land. Then the Bambino hit what may have been the longest home run in the history of Chicago's Wrigley Field.

Within two years, Ruth's age and lifestyle began to catch up with him. Turning down a managerial job for the minor league Newark Bears, he left the Yankees in 1935 to become a player-coach for the Boston Braves—for whom he hit the last of his record-breaking 714 career home runs that year.

In 1936, Babe Ruth was selected as one of the five initial inductees into the National Baseball Hall of Fame and Museum in Cooperstown, New York. In addition to 714 home runs, his career statistics include 2,211 runs batted in, 2,873 hits, a batting average of .342, and a slugging percentage of .690.

In 1946, Ruth was diagnosed with throat cancer and spent three months in the hospital, losing eighty pounds. On August 16, 1948, some two months after the Yankees honored him by retiring his uniform number (3), Babe Ruth died at the age of fifty-three. More than 200,000 people filed past his casket at Yankee Stadium.

Kelly Boyer Sagert

See also: Baseball; Celebrity Culture.

Further Reading

Creamer, Robert W. *Babe: The Legend Comes to Life.* New York: Simon & Schuster, 1974.

Ritter, Lawrence, and Mark Rucker. *The Babe: A Life in Pictures.* New York: Ticknor & Fields, 1988.

Sacco and Vanzetti Case (1920–1921)

Nicola Sacco and Bartolomeo Vanzetti were Italian immigrants living in the United States when they were accused of an April 1920 payroll robbery and murder in South Braintree, Massachusetts. The trial of the two anarchists was one of the most controversial legal cases in American history, receiving both national and international attention. The case unfolded at a time of great anxiety in American politics and culture. A fear of revolution led to wholesale arrests and deportations of radicals, and concerns about the rising tide of immigration led to restrictive laws that would keep broad categories of people from entering the country.

Sacco came to the United States in 1908 at the age of seventeen. Fleeing poverty, he hoped, like many Italian immigrants, to earn enough money to return to Italy. He found work as a shoemaker in several Massachusetts factories. Married and the father of one child, he became a union activist. Vanzetti also came to the United States in 1908. He held a variety of jobs and, like Sacco, was an avid student of politics. The two men became friends in 1917, when they joined a group of pacifists who fled to Mexico to avoid service in World War I. Both men were avowed political anarchists and friends of anarchist leader Luigi Galleani, whose associates had launched a series of bombings in 1919–1920 that prompted a federal crackdown on radicals.

The Crime

On April 15, 1920, Frederick Parmenter, paymaster of the Slater and Morrill Shoe Company in South Braintree, and guard Alessandro Berardelli were taking the company's payroll to the factory to be distributed. Two armed gunmen attacked them, robbing and mortally wounding them. The gunmen, along with two or three associates, drove off in a blue Buick, which they abandoned several miles outside of town. Area businesses were already uneasy because of a bungled armed robbery attempt on December 24, 1919, in the nearby town of Bridgewater.

Bridgewater Police Chief Michael Stewart thought the South Braintree robbery fit the pattern of the earlier attempt. Police suspected Mike Boda, a local Italian anarchist, and set a trap for him. Police watched a garage in which Boda had left a Buick for repairs, a vehicle similar to the one the robbers had abandoned. On May 5, 1920, Boda and three friends picked up the car. Sacco and Vanzetti, two of the friends, were arrested after boarding a nearby streetcar. Both men were carrying loaded guns. Sacco also had ammunition and a handbill for an anarchist meeting featuring Vanzetti as the main speaker. Both men lied during their initial questioning, claiming not to know Boda or to have been at the garage that night.

Police did not inform Sacco and Vanzetti of the charges against them during the first several days of questioning, which focused on their radical political beliefs. Although their belongings were searched thoroughly, the stolen money was never found. Nor did either of their fingerprints match those taken from the abandoned Buick used in the crime. Also, Sacco had a time card showing that he had been at work at the time of the robbery and slaying. During eyewitness identifications, Sacco and Vanzetti were made to stand alone in a room, and the eyewitnesses were told that the two were criminals. (Modern-day lineups, in which suspects are interspersed with non-suspects, were not yet the norm.)

Vanzetti was charged with assault and attempted robbery in the earlier Bridgewater crime. Judge Webster Thayer presided over the trial in June 1920. While Vanzetti had an alibi supported by eyewitnesses, most of them were Italian immigrants who had to rely on translators and may not have been trusted by the jurors. He did not take the stand in his own defense because he feared this would reveal his anarchist views. The jury convicted Vanzetti, and Judge Thayer imposed an unusually stiff sentence—twelve to fifteen years in prison—for a man with no criminal record and a crime in which no one had been hurt and nothing had been stolen.

Trial and Controversy

During the course of the summer, the police continued to gather evidence on the South Braintree robbery and murder, and in September, both Sacco and Vanzetti were indicted for those crimes. Five days later, a massive bomb exploded in New York City's financial district, targeting the Morgan Bank. The blast killed thirty workers on Wall Street and injured more than 200 others, three of whom later died. The incident, which officials denounced as the work of anarchists, possibly in revenge for the arrest of Sacco and Vanzetti, heightened antiradical feeling throughout the country and among the pool of people who would serve on the Sacco and Vanzetti jury.

As in the Bridgewater case, Judge Thayer presided over the trial, which commenced on May 31, 1921, in Dedham, Massachusetts. The Norfolk County district attorney in charge of prosecution was Frederick Katzmann. The chief defense counsel, Fred Moore, had taken part in numerous trials involving radical defendants and believed that, to ensure a fair trial, it was important to bring the national media spotlight on the case. His publicity campaign brought media attention from across the nation and around the world.

More than 160 witnesses testified during the six-week trial. Witnesses for the prosecution were native-born Americans, while the majority of the defense witnesses were Italian immigrants, many of whom required an interpreter. Much of the eyewitness testimony contained inconsistencies and contradictions. A ballistics expert testified for the prosecution that the bullets from Sacco's gun were consistent with those that killed Berardelli, although he did not claim that a definitive link had been established.

The final category of evidence consisted of Sacco and Vanzetti's evasive behavior before and after their arrests, which the prosecution characterized as "consciousness of guilt." The defense countered by introducing the defendants' political beliefs. The defense stated that the 1919 federal government crackdown on radicals was the real cause of Sacco and Vanzetti's suspicious behavior, because the two men feared possible persecution and deportation. The defense also claimed that Sacco and Vanzetti had been with Boda at the garage in order to use his car to remove radical literature from their homes. The fear of being caught with such literature caused them to lie about their whereabouts and their friendship with Boda.

The trial was marred by several procedural irregularities. Judge Thayer and other trial participants

Italian-born anarchists Nicola Sacco (right) and Bartolomeo Vanzetti (left) were found guilty of murdering two men during the robbery of a Massachusetts shoe factory in 1920. Before their execution in 1927, their case became a cause célèbre of civil libertarians. *(Stringer/Hulton Archive/Getty Images)*

discussed their views on the case outside the courtroom, revealing their prejudice against Sacco and Vanzetti's beliefs. Members of Thayer's social club told reporters that they had heard the judge denounce Sacco and Vanzetti as Bolsheviks and claim that he would do everything in his power to see they were convicted. Judge Thayer also appeared to harbor a bias against the defense attorney, calling him an anarchist in front of reporters. Thayer's bias was further reflected in his instructions to the jury, in which he falsely stated that the prosecution's ballistics expert had definitively linked Sacco's gun with the fatal bullets used in the crime.

The jury deliberated just five hours before returning its guilty verdict on July 14, 1921, and the defendants were sentenced to death the same day. The executions were postponed, however, as the irregularities in trial proceedings, Judge Thayer's apparent bias, and new evidence and eyewitnesses led to a series of legal appeals.

In the end, Sacco and Vanzetti went through six years of appeals on both the state and federal levels before the final appeal was denied on April 7, 1927. Defense counsel Fred Moore had withdrawn from the appeals process in 1924 in favor of William Thompson, a respected Massachusetts criminal lawyer. Any motion for a new trial had to be granted by the original trial judge; in other words, Judge Thayer had to hear and decide on evidence of his own prejudice before the case could go to an appeals court. The Massachusetts Supreme Judicial Court, the highest court of appeals in the state, denied hearings on three separate occasions because it could rule only on grounds of constitutional defects in Massachusetts law.

During the appeals process, Sacco received a note from fellow inmate Celestino F. Medeiros, connected to the notorious Morelli crime gang of Rhode Island, in which the latter confessed to the crime. Subsequent investigation revealed that one of the gang members closely resembled Sacco, that the gang carried similar guns, and that they drove a similar car. A number of the eyewitnesses from the original trial identified a picture of gang leader Joe Morelli. Thus, Judge Thayer's decision on October 1926 to reject the motion contributed to the public outcry over the case.

Sacco and Vanzetti were held at Charleston Prison in Boston throughout the appeals process. Various radical political groups, labor leaders, socialites, immigrant groups, liberals, artists, criminal lawyers, legal scholars, and civil libertarians supported their case. Harvard Law professor and future Supreme Court Justice Felix Frankfurter wrote a well-known article, "The Case of Sacco and Vanzetti," published in *The Atlantic Monthly* in 1927, that focused on what many felt was a miscarriage of justice. Protesters picketed, started petitions, and held vigils outside the prison as well as in major U.S. and European cities. Other groups, including political elites, nativists, and conservatives, remained convinced of the prisoners' guilt.

Sacco and Vanzetti continued to maintain their innocence. Sacco went on a hunger strike in February and March 1923 and had a nervous breakdown while in prison. Vanzetti wrote letters and speeches in his defense, including a clemency plea to Governor Alvan Fuller. After the Lowell Commission, an advisory panel summoned by Fuller, upheld the verdict and death sentence, Sacco and Vanzetti were executed on August 23, 1927. Some scholars have claimed that later ballistics tests confirmed Sacco's guilt, while others have argued that both men were innocent. Sacco and Vanzetti received a posthumous pardon from Governor Michael Dukakis in 1977.

Marcella Bush Treviño

See also: American Civil Liberties Union; Criminal Punishment; Immigration; Italian Americans; Law and the Courts.

Further Reading

D'Allesandro, Frank. *The Verdict of History on Sacco and Vanzetti.* New York: Jay Street, 1997.
Sacco, Nicola, and Bartolomeo Vanzetti. *The Letters of Sacco and Vanzetti.* Ed. Marion Denman Frankfurter and Gardner Jackson. Intro. Richard Polenberg. New York: Penguin, 1997.
Topp, Michael M. *The Sacco and Vanzetti Case: A Brief History with Documents.* New York: Bedford/St. Martin's, 2004.
Young, William, and David Kaiser. *Postmortem: New Evidence in the Case of Sacco and Vanzetti.* Amherst: University of Massachusetts Press, 1985.

Sanger, Margaret (1879–1966)

A pioneering advocate for birth control, Margaret Sanger was a heroine to millions of American women seeking family planning advice and aid during the first half of the twentieth century. At the same time, she was a target of government prosecutors for violating laws against obscenity and distributing birth control devices. Social conservatives denounced her as a promoter of sexual promiscuity. As founder and head of the American Birth Control League from 1916 to 1928, Sanger distributed information on birth control to hundreds of thousands of women across the country. In 1923, she opened the first legal birth control clinic in America.

Sanger was born Margaret Higgins in Corning, New York, on September 14, 1879. Her father, Michael, was a freethinking radical whom Sanger later credited for her own willingness to buck social convention. But it was her mother, Anne, who had perhaps the greatest impact on her choice of career. Eighteen pregnancies, including eleven live births, eventually crippled Anne emotionally and physically, Sanger later wrote. In 1897, Margaret attended Claverack College in Hudson, New York, before enrolling in a nursing program in White Plains. In 1902, she married an architect and artist named William Sanger, who, she later said, forced her to stop her training and become a full-time housewife and mother. Sanger gave birth to two boys and a girl over the next few years, though her daughter died in childhood.

Following a fire that destroyed their upstate New York home, the Sangers moved to Manhattan in 1912. Margaret had insisted on the move, hoping that her mother could watch the children so she could work to help support the family. Money problems continually beset the family and, in 1913, helped precipitate the marriage's breakup. Meanwhile, Sanger was doing social work in the immigrant slums of Manhattan, where she soon concluded that overly large families were both a source of poverty and a burden on poor and working-class women.

Sanger was also writing a column, "What Every Girl Should Know," for the social newspaper the

New York Call, in which, among other topics, she discussed birth control and sexually transmitted diseases. But it was her own monthly newspaper, the *Woman Rebel,* launched in 1914, in which Sanger coined the term "birth control," that led to her indictment on federal obscenity charges, as the newsletter was distributed through the U.S. mail. Rather than go to jail, Sanger fled to Europe. She returned to America a year later, long after the charges had been dropped.

In 1916, Sanger founded the first birth control clinic in America in Brooklyn. The facility opened on October 16; nine days later, it was shut down by police and Sanger was jailed for distributing obscene materials, which included birth control advice and contraceptive devices. She served thirty days in prison, but she appealed the decision, and in 1918, a state appellate court ruled that contraceptive devices and information were not in violation of New York's obscenity laws. Meanwhile, in 1916, Sanger founded the National Birth Control League (renamed the American Birth Control League, ABCL, from 1921 to 1942 and Planned Parenthood thereafter) to spread information about contraception. Branches quickly formed in cities across America and Canada, and by 1924 the organization had 27,500 members.

With her legal problems largely behind her by the end of World War I, Sanger spent most of the Jazz Age advocating birth control both in the United States and around the world. In 1923, the ABCL established the Clinical Research Bureau in New York, the first legal birth control clinic in America. The ABCL also answered hundreds of thousands of queries that poured in from women and men across the country, asking for birth control advice. That same year, Sanger launched the National Committee on Federal Legislation for Birth Control, serving as its president until it was dissolved in 1937. The organization pushed for liberalization of federal and state laws on birth control, which, at the time, meant making it legal for doctors to prescribe contraceptives to their patients. Sanger also toured the country giving lectures on birth control to any group that asked, regardless of its politics. A Socialist, Sanger described a 1926 talk in New Jersey to a woman's auxiliary of the Ku Klux Klan as "one of the weirdest experiences I had in lecturing." She also traveled to Japan frequently in these years to promote birth control in that country. In 1927, she helped organize the first World Population Conference on birth control, held in Geneva.

Despite growing acceptance of birth control in the Jazz Age, Sanger met with much criticism from social conservatives and religious leaders, for her advocacy not only of birth control but also of a healthy sex life for married persons. The 1920s was a critical time in the history of American sexuality, as psychologists and others began to promote the idea that sex was not just for procreation but also played a role in mental health. Some conservative social theorists argued that birth control would be used less by poor and working-class women than by middle- and upper-class women, thus increasing the percentage of supposedly inferior poor people in the country's population. Some on the Left denounced Sanger's efforts to advise the poor on birth control, arguing that she was diluting the strength of the working class in their struggle against capitalists.

Although she resigned as head of the ABCL in 1928, Sanger continued her advocacy of birth control through the Great Depression, World War II, the 1950s, and up through the development of the birth control pill in the early 1960s, which she promoted extensively. She also traveled the world, establishing birth control clinics in Europe, Africa, and Asia. Sanger died on September 6, 1966, less than one year after the landmark U.S. Supreme Court decision in *Griswold v. Connecticut* finally legalized birth control for married couples throughout the United States.

James Ciment

See also: Birth Control; Eugenics; Health and Medicine; Sex and Sexuality; Women and Gender; Women's Movement.

Further Reading

Chesler, Ellen. *Woman of Valor: Margaret Sanger and the Birth Control Movement in America.* New York: Simon & Schuster, 1992.

Douglas, Emily Taft. *Margaret Sanger: Pioneer of the Future.* New York: Holt, Rinehart and Winston, 1970.

Sarnoff, David (1891–1971)

As general manager of the Radio Corporation of America (RCA) from its founding in 1919 through his promotion to the company presidency in 1930, David Sarnoff helped usher in the age of commercial radio in America. Sarnoff pushed the company away from its original focus on radio as a means of two-way communication toward radio as a broadcasting medium. In the process, he made RCA one of the most profitable and prestigious corporations of the 1920s.

Sarnoff was born on February 27, 1891, to impoverished parents in the Russian village of Uzlian. To escape poverty and anti-Semitic persecution, Sarnoff's father, Abraham, immigrated to the United States in 1896. In 1900, Sarnoff and the rest of the family joined him, traveling by steerage to New York.

To help support the family, Sarnoff worked as a paperboy after school. From an early age, he showed an interest in communications, landing a job in his early teens as an office boy at the Marconi Wireless Telegraph Company of America, better known as American Marconi, a pioneer in radio communication. To advance himself, Sarnoff bought a telegraph key when he was fifteen so he could teach himself Morse code. At seventeen, he became a junior wireless telegraph operator. In 1912, Sarnoff was on duty when the first message came in from the *Titanic* that it had hit an iceberg and was sinking. He spent the next seventy-two hours at his post, relaying the names of survivors on rescue ships.

As important as radio was for marine communication, Sarnoff soon came to believe that it had even greater potential as a broadcast medium for news and entertainment. Shortly after radio's invention by the Italian Guglielmo Marconi at the end of the nineteenth century, amateur enthusiasts began using the technology to communicate with one another on their sets. By the 1910s, there were thousands of such operators throughout the country. In 1915, Sarnoff proposed in a memo to the management of American Marconi the idea for a "radio music box," which would turn the radio into a popular household entertainment device, like the piano or phonograph. With World War I under way, and lucrative government contracts filling company coffers, the idea went nowhere. Over the next several years, however, Sarnoff elaborated his vision of radio as a source of music, news, entertainment, and sports. He also developed a business model whereby radio equipment companies such as Marconi would create content that would further spur radio receiver sales.

During World War I, the U.S. Navy took over Marconi's network of radio communications stations. When the fighting was over, however, the federal government was reluctant to return such a strategic asset to a company essentially run by foreigners; controlling interest in American Marconi was held by Marconi's Wireless Telegraph Company, Ltd., also known as British Marconi. Instead, federal officials urged executives at General Electric (GE) and American Telephone and Telegraph (AT&T) to establish an independent company to take over Marconi's assets, both its manufacturing facilities and its radio trans-

mission stations. In 1919, the Radio Corporation of America (RCA) was founded as a publicly traded corporation, with Sarnoff as its second in command.

Sarnoff immediately began to put his idea for commercial radio into action. In 1921, he arranged to broadcast a heavyweight boxing championship featuring the popular Jack Dempsey. More than 300,000 listeners across the Northeast tuned in, spurring sales of RCA equipment. By 1924, the company had sold more than a million of its Radiola receivers at a price of $75 each, bringing the company revenues of more than $80 million. (The name Radiola was a play on the name of the popular Victrola phonograph.) By the end of the decade, more than 60 percent of American homes would own a radio.

RCA's very success bred problems, however, as its patented technologies were widely pirated by competitors. In using lawsuits to stop such theft, Sarnoff earned a reputation as an arrogant businessman set on eliminating all competition. This invited government antitrust investigations against RCA, which Sarnoff eventually avoided by developing a patent scheme in 1923 whereby other companies could use RCA technology by paying a percentage of their sales to the company.

Meanwhile, Sarnoff was coming to recognize another problem in radio broadcasting. In its first years, radio stations were content to merely put a microphone at a concert or sporting event. But soon radio listeners were expecting more sophisticated entertainment, in terms of both sound quality and content. This was expensive, beyond the means of many of the independent stations sprouting up across America. Moreover, few stations had the capacity to broadcast events from major cities. To overcome this problem, a few radio stations began to set up local networks. It was Sarnoff who came up with the idea of a national network. Using the revenues from RCA sales and from the company's patent scheme, Sarnoff purchased a string of stations along the Atlantic seaboard and, in 1926, launched the first nationwide broadcasting network, the National Broadcasting Company (NBC).

About this time Sarnoff also became intrigued by a new broadcasting technology, television. In 1923, he hired Russian inventor Vladimir Zworykin away from rival Westinghouse. Zworykin had developed what he called an iconoscope, a primitive form of television. Five years later, Sarnoff set up NBC's experimental television broadcasting station in New York.

Under Sarnoff's managerial leadership, RCA became one of the most successful companies in America and one of the highest-flying stocks on Wall Street, with share prices climbing from less than $20 a share in 1927 to nearly $120 on the eve of the stock market crash in October 1929. Flush with revenues, Sarnoff arranged to buy stations across the country and was the mastermind behind RCA's 1929 purchase of the Victor Talking Machine Company, the largest manufacturer of phonographs in the world. RCA subsequently changed its name to RCA-Victor.

Sarnoff was named president of RCA in 1930, moving the company to its new headquarters in the landmark RCA Building in New York's Rockefeller Center in 1932, and steering the company through the Great Depression. During World War II, Allied Commander Dwight D. Eisenhower hired him as his communications consultant, designating him a brigadier general. Sarnoff continued to run RCA through the first decades of television, retiring in 1970. He died on December 12, 1971.

James Ciment

See also: General Electric; Radio; Radio Corporation of America; Swope, Gerard.

Further Reading

Lyons, Eugene. *David Sarnoff*. New York: Harper & Row, 1966.
Sobel, Robert. *RCA*. New York: Stein & Day, 1986.
Stashower, Daniel. *The Boy Genius and the Mogul: The Untold Story of Television*. New York: Broadway, 2002.

Schenck v. United States (1919)

In the 1919 case of *Schenck v. United States,* the U.S. Supreme Court held unanimously that the conviction of Charles Schenck—a Socialist Party leader who called on men of draft age to resist conscription—under the World War I Espionage Act was not unconstitutional. The *Schenck* decision was a major ruling affecting freedom of speech.

In June 1917, two months after America's entry into World War I, the U.S. Congress passed and President Woodrow Wilson signed the Espionage Act. Among the most significant and widely invoked provisions of the legislation was one calling for prison sentences for anyone who intentionally interfered with the government's prosecution of the war in any of several ways. In May 1918, the Sedition Act—technically an amendment to the Espionage Act—removed the

"intentionality" clause of the earlier measure and added provisions against "disloyal, profane, scurrilous, or abusive" language aimed at the federal government. Although both laws were passed during the war, they remained in effect after the armistice of November 1918.

The language in both pieces of legislation was so broadly written, civil libertarians at the time argued, that the government could prosecute virtually anyone who said anything critical of the government or government officials with regard to the war effort. Indeed, most of the 2,000 or so indictments drawn up under the acts between mid-1917 and mid-1919, the period of heaviest enforcement, were for attempts to interfere with the government's war effort, rather than for actual interference. Altogether, some 900 people were convicted under the acts, the most well-known being Socialist Party presidential candidate Eugene V. Debs (found guilty of violating the Espionage Act in 1918). Most cases brought under the Espionage and Sedition acts were disposed of in federal district courts, while several made it to the U.S. Supreme Court on appeal. The first to do so—and the most important, according to constitutional scholars—was *Schenck v. United States.*

As general secretary of the Socialist Party of Philadelphia during World War I, Charles Schenck was responsible for the distribution of thousands of leaflets denouncing the draft as a form of "involuntary servitude" motivated by "capitalist" imperatives. The leaflets also called on citizens to resist the draft, albeit through peaceful and legal means, such as petitioning. Schenck was arrested, convicted, and sentenced to six months in a federal penitentiary under the Espionage Act. The case was appealed to the U.S. Supreme Court, which heard the arguments and issued its ruling in early 1919.

In speaking for the Court, Associate Justice Oliver Wendell Holmes, Jr., offered some of the most significant ideas concerning constitutional limits on freedom of speech in times of war: "Words which, ordinarily and in many places, would be within the freedom of speech protected by the First Amendment, may become subject to prohibition when of such a nature and used in such circumstances as to create a clear and present danger that they will bring about the substantive evils which Congress has a right to prevent. The character of every act depends upon the circumstances in which it is done." To clarify what he meant by the critical phrase "clear and present danger," Holmes offered a simple example:

"The most stringent protection of free speech would not protect a man in falsely shouting fire in a theatre and causing a panic."

By the summer of 1919, more than six months had passed since the end of World War I, and Holmes, after hearing the arguments in *Schenck,* began to reconsider the Espionage and Sedition acts. He discussed the case with a number of jurists, including the influential Learned Hand of the U.S. District Court for the Southern District of New York, an advocate of broad free speech rights. These conversations led Holmes to alter his ideas on what a person must do before he or she could be arrested on charges of posing a threat to the government.

In *Abrams v. United States* (1919), involving the convictions of five anarchists charged with opposing American intervention in the Russian Revolution, Holmes (joined by Justice Louis Brandeis) argued that "the ultimate good desired is better reached by free trade in ideas—that the best test of truth is the power of the thought to get itself accepted in the competition of the market." In other words, the government should, with limited exceptions, allow for the free exchange of ideas and let those ideas fall or fly on their own merit, not on the arbitrary decision of government prosecutors. Still, Holmes and Brandeis remained in the minority in *Abrams,* and the convictions were upheld by the Court, 7–2.

Similarly, in *Whitney v. California* (1927), the Court once again upheld the conviction of a radical dissenter. In this case, Anita Whitney had been convicted under California's 1919 Criminal Syndicalism Act for establishing a branch of the Communist Labor Party, which called for the violent overthrow of the U.S. government. Whitney claimed that she had not intended that the party become an instrument of violence. Holmes and Brandeis sided with the majority on technical reasons. But Brandeis, in his concurrence, offered one of the most powerful defenses of free speech, arguing that there was no "clear and present danger" if those who disagreed with the contents of the speech had time for rebuttal. In other words, mere fear of an idea did not constitute a "clear and present danger." Eventually, the Court would agree with Brandeis. During the Vietnam War era, the Supreme Court ruled in *Brandenburg v. Ohio* (1969) that free speech can be restricted only when it is intended to spark "imminent lawless action" and is likely to bring about that result.

As for the legislation that triggered *Schenck* and the other free speech cases of the Jazz Age, the Sedi-

tion Act was repealed in 1921, while the Espionage Act remains officially in force to the present day. It was barely used in World War II, and no one has been prosecuted under it since then; the United States must be formally at war for it to go into effect, and Congress has not passed an official declaration of war since 1941.

Scott Merriman and James Ciment

See also: American Civil Liberties Union; *Gitlow v. New York* (1925); Holmes, Oliver Wendell, Jr.; Law and the Courts; Socialism and the Socialist Party of America.

Further Reading

Kohn, Stephen M. *American Political Prisoners: Prosecutions Under the Espionage and Sedition Acts.* Westport, CT: Praeger, 1994.

Murphy, Paul L. *World War I and the Origin of Civil Liberties.* New York: W.W. Norton, 1979.

Peterson, H.C., and Gilbert C. Fite. *Opponents of War, 1917–1918.* Madison: University of Wisconsin Press, 1957.

Schultz, Dutch (1902–1935)

Arthur Simon Flegenheimer, better known by his nickname, "Dutch Schultz," was the ruthless head of a criminal syndicate that controlled much of the illegal liquor trade in New York and along much of the Atlantic seaboard during Prohibition. Schultz was born on August 6, 1902, on the Lower East Side of Manhattan. Soon after, his family moved to the Bronx. The son of German Jewish parents, he received a religious upbringing and attended public school until dropping out in the sixth grade. Abandoned by his father, he turned to crime and quickly moved from petty theft to burglary and armed robbery.

His first arrest at age seventeen was for burglary. Although this was the first of at least a dozen arrests in his life, it was the only incident for which he ever went to jail. He served about fifteen months, managing on one occasion to escape for a few hours. Upon his release, he told his Bergen Street Gang cohorts to refer to him as "Dutch Schultz," the name of a notorious member of the 1890s New York underworld. He later said that no one ever would have heard of him had he kept his real name.

Bronx Beer Baron

The coming of Prohibition in 1919 marked the rise of Dutch Schultz. He started as an enforcer, drove a beer truck, associated with gang leaders Lucky Luciano and

Legs Diamond, and was a partner in a speakeasy co-owned by childhood friend Joey Noe. Schultz soon gained a reputation for his ruthlessness and brutal temper. The partners expanded into the wholesale beer business, selling to rival speakeasy owners, who faced violence if they refused to do business with them. This strategy made Schultz and Noe the dominant beer bootleggers in the Bronx, and they began to assemble a gang of enforcers to intimidate rivals and perform executions.

By the mid-1920s, Schultz and Noe began to move into Manhattan, where they encroached on Legs Diamond's territory. In retaliation, Diamond's men ambushed and killed Noe in late 1928. Schultz may have ordered the killing of underworld financier Arnold Rothstein, who was friendly with Diamond. Several months later, Diamond was killed.

Schultz moved into slot machines, the Harlem numbers racket, and the restaurant protection racket. By the end of the 1920s, he had become such a powerful figure that he was invited to the 1929 conference called by Lucky Luciano in Atlantic City. The crime boss wanted to build a national organized crime network, with gangs divvying up territory across the country to avoid conflict. Partly as a result of this association, Schultz came to the attention of authorities, and he was indicted in January 1933 on tax evasion charges. After avoiding capture for nearly two years, Schultz was finally put on trial in April 1935. Threats by Schultz's associates silenced witnesses and led to a hung jury. A second trial was held in Malone, in upstate New York, but the verdict was not guilty.

During Schultz's second trial, Luciano moved in on his territory, causing Schultz to break with the national crime network he had helped create in 1929. Schultz then came under the suspicion of rival gang leaders, who believed that he was about to turn government witness against them. On October 23, 1935, he was shot by Luciano's hit men. Schultz died the following day.

Kevin Wozniak

See also: Crime, Organized; Prohibition (1920–1933).

Further Reading

Burroughs, William S. *The Last Words of Dutch Schultz.* New York: Grove, 1975.

Mappen, Marc. *Jerseyana: The Underside of New Jersey History.* New Brunswick, NJ: Rutgers University Press, 1994.

Sann, Paul. *Kill The Dutchman! The Story of Dutch Schultz.* New York: Da Capo, 1991.

Science

The United States was at the forefront of technological developments in communications, transportation, and materials during the 1920s. But in the dynamic field of theoretical physics, the United States took a backseat to Europe, and particularly Austria, Germany, and the United Kingdom. Still, some significant advances in physics were made in the United States during the Jazz Age, and the country was a leader in the field of astronomy. U.S. scientists pioneered what was probably the decade's most important advance in medicine—the discovery of vitamins and their role in human health. However, American scientists were also active in the now discredited field of eugenics.

Astronomy and Physics

No country made greater advances in astronomy during the 1920s than the United States. Working at the Mount Wilson Observatory in the mountains above Los Angeles—home to a 100-inch reflecting telescope, the largest in the world at the time—University of Chicago astronomer Edwin Hubble made a series of major discoveries, including what he became most famous for—the discovery in 1924 that matter in the universe is organized into many different galaxies. Three years later, Hubble made yet another elemental discovery in the structure of the universe—that it is expanding. In other words, galaxies are receding in their relationship to Earth, and the farther away they are, the faster they are moving away. In 1929, Hubble published his finding that the ratio of the speed of a galaxy to its distance from Earth never varies; the principle has since become known as Hubble's constant.

Other scientists were working on the structures of galaxies in the 1920s. American physicist Albert Michelson of the University of Chicago conducted a series of experiments to measure some of the basic phenomena of the universe. In 1920, using a stellar interferometer, an instrument that triangulates light waves from two separate sources, Michelson determined that the diameter of the star Betelgeuse was 300 times that of the sun; it was the first time the size of a star other than the sun had been measured. In 1923, Michelson made the most accurate measurement of the speed of light to date; with minor modifications, it still stands today. In 1925, U.S. astronomer Heber

Mount Wilson Observatory near Los Angeles—home to the world's largest reflecting telescope at the time—helped American scientists make great strides in astronomy during the 1920s, including Edwin Hubble's discovery of galaxies beyond the Milky Way. *(Hulton Archive/Getty UK)*

Curtis, along with Knut Landmark of Sweden, mapped the spiral structure of galaxies like the Milky Way.

In 1929, a team of U.S. and German scientists theorized that the thermonuclear process is the source of solar power. That same year, Princeton University's Henry Russell, considered the greatest theoretical astronomer of the first half of the twentieth century, published his ideas on stellar evolution, suggesting that stars have a life cycle.

Health Science, Eugenics, and Genetics

U.S. scientists of the 1920s made significant contributions to the study of vitamins and minerals. In 1922, University of California chemist Herbert McLean discovered vitamin E, and in 1926, Hungarian-born epidemiologist Joseph Goldberger became the first to isolate vitamins B and B2. Also in 1926, biochemist Elmer McCollum of the University of Wisconsin isolated vitamin D and successfully used it in the treatment of rickets, a bone disease suffered largely by children who lack adequate amounts of the vitamin

in their diets. A year earlier, University of Rochester pathologist George Whipple demonstrated the critical role of iron in the formation of red blood cells. These discoveries were quickly popularized by media and government reports emphasizing the importance of a balanced diet that included the necessary daily consumption of vitamins and minerals.

Less useful was the eugenics work of psychologist Carl Brigham. Having worked with the U.S. Army on its intelligence tests for recruits during World War I, Brigham, in 1923, published *A Study of American Intelligence,* in which he claimed that different races had different intelligence levels. Predictably, Brigham's theories reinforced prevailing racial stereotypes, as he contended that Northern Europeans were the most intelligent, Southern and Eastern Europeans had less capacity for theoretical thinking, and blacks were the least intelligent. Along with other eugenicists, Brigham argued that "racial degeneration"—the diluting of racial purity through intermarriage and interbreeding—was occurring in the United States at an increasing pace. Brigham also argued that the least intelligent races were breeding the fastest, an argument that led U.S. policy makers to oppose birth control, a practice mainly used by the middle and upper classes, and to advocate limiting immigration from Southern and Eastern Europe. Eugenics theories would eventually be questioned by much of the scientific community.

Some scientists in the field of genetics laid the groundwork for later breakthroughs on DNA, the basic molecular building block of life. Most notable was the mid-1920s work of U.S. geneticists Thomas Hunt Morgan, Alfred Sturtevant, and Calvin Blackman, which identified genes as the component parts of chromosomes, the macromolecules of DNA. In 1926, Morgan published his *Theory of the Gene,* in which he theorized that the gene would be the focus of all future work on the basic structures of life.

Institutional Changes

The 1920s witnessed the organization of hundreds of corporate research laboratories, most notably Bell Laboratories, founded jointly by American Telephone and Telegraph (AT&T) and Western Electric in 1925. While much of the work that went on in these laboratories was in the applied sciences and technology, pure research was also conducted at many of the larger facilities. Scientists at Bell Labs made significant discoveries in electrical wave amplitude, which would have

Edwin Hubble and the Discovery of Other Galaxies

Edwin Powell Hubble earned a bachelor of science degree from the University of Chicago in 1910 and studied law at Oxford University. In 1914, he returned to the University of Chicago's Yerkes Observatory as a graduate student in astronomy, where he used photographs from the 24-inch reflecting telescope to discover hundreds of nebulae, completing his doctoral thesis, "Photographic Investigations of Faint Nebulae," in 1917. In 1919, after serving in the U.S. Army during World War I, he joined George Ellery Hale at the Mount Wilson Observatory near Pasadena, California.

Mount Wilson's recently completed 100-inch reflecting telescope, then the largest in the world, would assist Hubble in ending centuries of debate over the nature of nebulae and the structure of the universe. Without powerful telescopes, nebulae appeared as cloudy, ill-defined patches of light. At the time, some astronomers believed nebulae were gaseous clouds; others contended that spiral-shaped nebulae were actually separate "island universes" similar to our galaxy, the Milky Way. Today, astronomers understand that some nebulae indeed are gaseous clouds, while others are clusters of stars that make up separate galaxies.

Beginning in 1923, Hubble used Mount Wilson's 100-inch Hooker telescope to systematically examine nebula M31 in the constellation Andromeda. By comparing his new photographs with old Mount Wilson photographic plates, Hubble noted an object of varying brightness in the Andromeda nebula. He had discovered a Cepheid, a pulsating star whose apparent brightness varies significantly. Early twentieth-century astronomers had studied similar stars in our own galaxy. In 1912, Henrietta Swan Leavitt of the Harvard College Observatory had discovered the period-luminosity relation: A longer pulsating period corresponds with greater luminosity or brightness. Using this information, astronomers could calculate a Cepheid's distance from Earth. Thus, over a period of thirty-one days, Hubble plotted the shape of the light curve of the Andromeda nebula's Cepheid. The long pulsating rhythm and faint appearance indicated that it was at a great distance.

By the end of 1924, Hubble had discovered many more Cepheid variables in the Andromeda nebula, nebula NCG 6822 (near the constellation Sagittarius), and nebula M33 (between the constellations Pisces and Triangulum). Based on the pulsation periods of these Cepheids, he calculated that the Andromeda nebula was a distance of nearly 1 million light-years from Earth. The maximum diameter of our galaxy was known to be 100,000 light-years, so the Andromeda nebula had to be outside the Milky Way. These calculations, presented at an American Astronomical Society meeting, proved the existence of island galaxies.

Hubble's discovery of other galaxies had a dramatic impact on cosmology and the popular conception of the universe. Scientists realized that the universe was much larger than the Milky Way. Hubble and other cosmologists soon began studying the structure of galaxies, their motion, and their distribution in space. The existence of other galaxies and their movements in relation to Earth helped scientists conclude that the universe is expanding, a discovery that Hubble helped to prove. All of this work contributed to research on the age and evolution of the universe.

Jodi Lacy

important applications in television broadcasting. In 1926, scientists at Bell Labs were the first to develop motion pictures that synchronized sound and image.

In addition, philanthropic money flowed into university research laboratories, particularly in the medical sciences. Most noteworthy were the contributions of philanthropic organizations set up by Standard Oil founder John D. Rockefeller. It is estimated that his philanthropies were responsible for roughly 90 percent of the foundation money that went into American medical research in the 1920s.

Meanwhile, policy makers and scientists began to recognize the importance of theoretical science to the nation's economy and strategic position in the world. Many began to urge a more systematic government, business, and university approach to the funding and conduct of theoretical research. As early as 1920, James Angell, chair of the private, nonprofit National Research Council, noted in an article in *Scientific Monthly* that "research work is capable of being organized in ways not dissimilar to the organization of our great industries." Angell further argued that scientific discovery should not be left to the whim of genius but should be pursued as a goal, in the same way that new technologies were developed by industrial laboratories such as Thomas Edison's in the late nineteenth century. While implemented to a limited degree in the Jazz Age, Angell's ideas would not be fully realized in America until World War II.

James Ciment

See also: Eugenics; Food and Diet; Health and Medicine; King Tut's Tomb; Mead, Margaret; Osborn, Henry Fairfield; Psychology; Scopes Trial (1925).

Further Reading

Christianson, Gale E. *Edwin Hubble: Mariner of the Nebulae.* New York: Farrar, Straus and Giroux, 1995.

Cravens, Hamilton, Alan I. Marcus, and David M. Katzman, eds. *Technical Knowledge in American Culture: Science, Technology, and Medicine Since the Early 1800s.* Tuscaloosa: University of Alabama Press, 1996.

Krige, John, and Dominique Pestre, eds. *Science in the Twentieth Century.* Amsterdam: Harwood Academic, 1997.

Scopes Trial (1925)

Labeled by the press of the times as the "trial of the century"—and still regarded by historians as a pivotal moment in twentieth-century American social and cultural history—the Scopes trial of 1925, also known as the "Monkey" trial, focused on a narrow legal question: whether John Thomas Scopes, a high school teacher in Dayton, Tennessee, had violated state law by teaching evolution in his classroom. But with former presidential candidate Williams Jennings Bryan as a prosecutor and nationally renowned attorney Clarence Darrow handling the defense, the trial became a media circus and a showdown between Evangelical Christianity and modern science.

Darwinism Versus Fundamentalism

When English naturalist Charles Darwin suggested in the mid-nineteenth century that human beings had evolved from lower forms of life, many Christians considered his ideas blasphemous, a refutation of the biblical story of creation. By the 1920s, however, large segments of the American public had come to accept Darwin's ideas. This included liberal Christians who believed that Darwin's message did not refute the basic principles of their religion.

At the same time, a significant segment of the American public continued to insist on a literal interpretation of the Bible. Darwin's theory ran counter to the opening passages of Genesis, in which God is said to have created the world and humanity in six days. Moreover, the idea that humans evolved from other primates called into question a central tenet of Christianity: that human beings were created in God's image.

The dispute between science and religion was not just an abstract one; it touched on a growing rift within American society in the early twentieth century. On the one hand were the forces of modernism, including urbanization, a growing belief in science and technology, and the easing of old moral strictures about sexuality. On the other hand were the inhabitants of America's small towns and the millions of rural migrants to urban areas. Many had embraced Fundamentalism, a form of Christianity that insisted, among other things, on the literal truth of every word in the Bible. Many Fundamentalists believed it was their Christian duty to fight godless modernism, which included Darwinism.

By the early 1920s, Bryan, the three-time Democratic presidential nominee and populist champion of workers and farmers, had taken a leading role in this crusade. Bryan's position in the evolution debate seemed a refutation of his earlier liberal politics, but he insisted his opposition to evolution was part of a seamless, philosophical fabric that embraced the sanctity of life. Among his most popular talks on the Chautauqua lecture circuit was one on the "Menace of Darwinism." In 1922, he turned the lecture into a

Bryan on the Stand

They were two of the most flamboyant personalities on the political and legal scene of Jazz Age America. And when they came to the small Tennessee town of Dayton in the summer of 1925 on opposing sides in the "Monkey" trial—to determine whether science teacher John Scopes had violated state law by introducing evolution to students at the local high school—a national newspaper and radio audience expected fireworks.

Representing the prosecution was three-time presidential candidate William Jennings Bryan, famous as the "Great Commoner" or "Boy Orator of the Platte," who had electrified the 1896 Democratic National Convention with his "Cross of Gold" speech. For the defense was Clarence Darrow, America's most celebrated trial lawyer of the early twentieth century.

With all the pretrial hype, nothing prepared those in attendance or the national audience for Darrow's dramatic decision to call Bryan to the witness stand to defend the Bible. Suddenly, a trial for a minor violation of Tennessee law became a confrontation between two great forces in Jazz Age America: the growing confidence in modern science versus the certainties of a resurgent Fundamentalism. On the trial's seventh day, the courtroom adversaries engaged in a two-hour exchange that included the following:

Darrow: You have given considerable study to the Bible, haven't you, Mr. Bryan?

Bryan: Yes, sir, I have tried to.

Darrow: Do you claim that everything in the Bible should be literally interpreted?

Bryan: I believe everything in the Bible should be accepted as it is given there. . . .

Darrow: The Bible says Joshua commanded the sun to stand still for the purpose of lengthening the day, doesn't it, and you believe it?

Bryan: I do.

Darrow: Do you believe at that time the entire sun went around the earth?

Bryan: No, I believe that the earth goes around the sun.

Darrow: Do you believe that the men who wrote it [the Bible] thought that the day could be lengthened or that the sun could be stopped?

Bryan: I don't know what they thought.

Darrow: You don't know?

Bryan: I believe that the Bible is inspired. . . .

Darrow: Do you think whoever inspired it believed that the sun went around the earth?

Bryan: I believe it was inspired by the Almighty, and He may have used language that could be understood at that time.

Darrow: So, it might have been subject to construction, might it not?

Bryan: Well, I think anybody can put his own construction upon it, but I do not mean necessarily that it is a correct construction.

Many saw Darrow's cross-examination as telling in its challenge to the underlying principles of Fundamentalist Christianity. But many others in small towns across America thought Darrow had simply displayed modern society's contempt for Christian beliefs.

Although the verdict went against Scopes, historians cite the cross-examination of William Jennings Bryan as a turning point in the culture wars of the 1920s. Although most Jazz Age Americans remained committed to their Christian faith, more and more came to embrace science and no longer saw the Bible as the final source on earthly questions. As for Bryan, the trial was his last hurrah. He died five days after it ended.

James Ciment

book, *In His Image,* in which he argued that accepting Darwin's principle of "survival of the fittest" and its application to human society—a popular late nineteenth-century doctrine known as Social Darwinism—led to the justification of brutality and indifference toward the weaker members of society.

Bryan was not alone in this kind of thinking. By the 1920s, a number of states had passed legislation banning the teaching of evolution in public schools. Tennessee passed just such a law, the Butler Act, in 1925. Meanwhile, other forces in American society were fighting to keep evolution in the classroom. Among them was the newly formed American Civil Liberties Union (ACLU), which saw such laws as a violation of constitutional free speech protections. To create a test case, the ACLU announced that it would provide financial assistance to anyone prosecuted for violating anti-evolution statutes.

Chicago defense attorney Clarence Darrow (left) and former presidential candidate William Jennings Bryan (right) faced off in the Scopes "Monkey" trial during the summer of 1925. *(Stringer/Hulton Archive/Getty Images)*

Business Interests and a Media Circus

That Dayton, Tennessee, was the place where these two forces would have their showdown had as much to do with commerce as it did religion. Although many people in the hill country of eastern Tennessee subscribed to Fundamentalist beliefs and did not want evolution taught in their public schools, it was largely a group of local businesspeople, led by mine owner George Rappelyea, who pushed for a legal showdown, believing that such a case would put Dayton on the map and boost the local economy. Just after the Butler Act was passed, Rappelyea and like-minded members of the school board recruited Scopes, a high school football coach and substitute science teacher, to test the statute. He was happy to oblige, leading a discussion of evolution in his classroom on May 5. Rappelyea and others expected the defense to be based more on a technicality than on constitutional principles. Tennessee mandated the use of a 1914 text called *Civil Biology,* which included a discussion of evolution. In effect, then, the state required its science teachers to break one of its own laws.

If attention was what the Dayton business leaders wanted, attention is what they got—especially when Bryan volunteered to help prosecute the case and Darrow, who proudly boasted of his atheism, was recruited by the ACLU to defend Scopes. Dayton quickly acquired a circus atmosphere as the trial approached in the summer of 1925. Stores put up cardboard cutouts of monkeys in their windows, drugstores served "simian sodas," and the town constable's

motorcycle sported a sign announcing that he was the "Monkeyville Police." A local church group hung a banner with the legend "Read Your Bible" across the walls of the courthouse.

The national media flocked to Dayton, including the famous Baltimore journalist H.L. Mencken, who used the trial to showcase his contempt for rural ignorance. The trial was also the first in history to be transmitted by radio; the judge delayed the proceedings by a day to allow microphones to be placed and adjusted. Eventually, as the trial wore on in the hot July weather, Judge John Raulston, concerned not only about the heat but the dangers of having so many people packed into an old building, moved the proceedings to a tent on the courthouse lawn.

From the first day of the trial, on July 13, Bryan and Darrow recognized that the narrow legal question at hand, Scopes's guilt, was a foregone conclusion. By admitting he had taught evolution, Scopes had already sealed his fate. Instead, the trial became a debate on the validity of evolution and, by implication, whether science or the Bible offered the true account of human origins. More broadly, both attorneys understood that the trial represented a showdown between two great forces in American society: liberalism and science versus conservatism and religion.

Darrow proved the more effective litigator. His expert witnesses not only showed the validity of the theory of evolution but also demonstrated how belief in evolution did not necessarily require a thinking Christian to abandon his or her faith. Bryan, meanwhile, got caught up in technical arguments about the use of such experts, which confused many of the jurors.

The highlight of the case came on the trial's seventh day, when Darrow unexpectedly called Bryan to the witness stand. In a series of pointed questions, Darrow put Bryan's ignorance of science and evolution on display and forced him to admit that the Bible was filled with contradictions and incidents that violated the basic laws of the universe. All Bryan could muster was the standby argument that God was all-powerful and so could dispense with natural law.

The jury reached the expected conclusion on July 21. After only nine minutes of deliberation, it pronounced Scopes guilty of violating the Butler Act. The judge fined him $100, which Bryan offered to pay. Scopes and his attorneys, however, appealed the case on a number of grounds, including the fact that the term "evolution" was so vague as to make the law unenforceable. In the end, they won the appeal, but on a legal technicality. Under Tennessee law, the jury was supposed to impose the fine, not the judge.

In a dramatic coda to the original trial, Bryan died in Dayton on July 26, just five days after the proceedings had drawn to a close. In his honor, a Bible institute called Bryan College was founded in Dayton in 1930.

James Ciment and Leigh Kimmel

See also: Fundamentalism, Christian; Osborn, Henry Fairfield; Science.

Further Reading

Ashby, LeRoy. *William Jennings Bryan: Champion of Democracy.* Boston: Twayne, 1987.

De Camp, L. Sprague. *The Great Monkey Trial.* Garden City, NY: Doubleday, 1968.

Ginger, Ray. *Six Days or Forever? Tennessee v. John Thomas Scopes.* Chicago: Quadrangle , 1958.

Hansen, Ellen, ed. *Evolution on Trial.* Lowell, MA: Discovery Enterprises, 1994.

Hanson, Freya Ottem. *The Scopes Monkey Trial: A Headline Court Case.* Berkeley Heights, NJ: Enslow, 2000.

Marsden, George M. *Understanding Fundamentalism and Evangelicalism.* Grand Rapids, MI: Eerdmans, 1991.

Scopes, John T., and James Presley. *Center of the Storm: Memoirs of John T. Scopes.* New York: Holt, Rinehart and Winston, 1967.

Seattle General Strike of 1919

On February 6, 1919, more than 65,000 American Federation of Labor (AFL) and other union workers in Seattle walked off their jobs in the first general strike in U.S. history. It began in the city's critical shipbuilding industry and then spread to other trades as workers struck in sympathy with the shipyard workers. In the wake of World War I, Seattle's laboring class and other workers across the country, in almost every industry, were dissatisfied. Wartime inflation had eaten away at their wages even as industry made record profits. While few workers were willing to strike for higher wages during the war—either seeing it as unpatriotic or fearing public backlash—the end of hostilities in Europe freed them to vent their frustration at management.

During World War I, Seattle's shipbuilding industry had benefited tremendously from wartime production, yet strict wage controls imposed by the federal government kept wages low. The Metal Trades Council, which represented the shipyard unions, and the larger Seattle Central Labor Council sought higher wages for union employees, nearly 100 percent of shipyard workers. The employers refused, but with the war on, the workers refrained from striking. With the war over in November 1918, the restraints fell away. Once again, union organizers approached the shipbuilders to request higher wages and were turned down.

On January 21, 1919, some 35,000 shipyard workers walked off their jobs. Seattle's powerful Central Labor Council then asked representatives of the city's 110 local unions to join in a sympathy walkout, and nearly all of them agreed. Before the sympathy walkout began, the General Strike Committee adopted the slogan "Together We Win" and set about making preparations for the strike. The committee handled hundreds of requests made by workers to keep the city's essential facilities operating; they set up cafeterias to feed workers who could not afford to eat at home; they got fuel and laundry to hospitals, mail delivered, government cargo unloaded, and milk stations set up; they also secured emergency transportation and fire protection.

At 10:00 A.M. on February 6, more than 60,000 of Seattle's organized AFL laborers walked off the job. They were joined by the segregated Japanese unions and more than 3,500 members of the Industrial Workers of the World (IWW). An additional 40,000 workers stayed home that fateful Thursday morning, fearing the strike might become violent. Other workers had no choice but to remain off the job, because their employers saw no reason to open their shops, restaurants, and theaters during the strike, and striking laborers had completely shut down Seattle's public transportation network. The Seattle General Strike of 1919 had begun.

The preparations paid off. The general strike proved orderly and peaceful. Not a single striker or antistrike protestor was arrested for a strike-related offense. Unfortunately for workers, however, no individual or group within the General Strike Committee existed to formulate a basic policy for establishing the goals and terms of the settlement of the strike. The committee's general lack of concern with the actions taken by government officials and owners to end the strike became apparent the second day of the walkout, when Seattle's mayor, Ole Hanson, with the support of the local press, issued a direct challenge to labor, threatening to intervene forcibly to end the strike. Three days later, on February 9, Hanson issued a statement to the national press claiming that revolutionaries and foreign agitators had organized the walkout, and demanding the "unconditional surrender" of strikers. The accusation was completely false but difficult for labor leaders to counter in the midst of the Red Scare.

Following Hanson's statements and facing a nearly total lack of support from local and national press, idle workers began to waver in their support for the walkout. When news of the strike became national, even the AFL urged workers to call it off. The fate of the strike was ultimately sealed when the powerful Citizens Committee, a group of 200 delegates from thirty-six local civic, cultural, fraternal, business, and humanitarian organizations, stated that they refused to negotiate with "revolutionists."

The Seattle General Strike ended without incident at noon on Tuesday, February 11, when most of Seattle's workers quietly returned to their jobs. The strike in the shipyards did not end, nor did the union busting and Red-baiting that characterized America's postwar Red Scare. But for a brief time in February 1919, workers had reigned supreme in Seattle.

Michael A. Rembis

See also: Labor Movement; Red Scare of 1917–1920.

Further Reading

Friedheim, Robert L. *The Seattle General Strike.* Seattle: University of Washington Press, 1964.

History Committee of the General Strike Committee. *The Seattle General Strike: An Account of What Happened in Seattle, and Especially in the Seattle Labor Movement, During the General Strike, February 6 to 11, 1919.* Seattle, WA: Seattle Union Record, ca. 1919.

Sex and Sexuality

The 1920s marked the emergence of a new morality in America, as many members of society, especially young people, began to accept new sexual attitudes and less restrictive sexual standards than had prevailed during the Victorian era of the late nineteenth and early twentieth centuries. The experience of World War I had eroded much of the idealism of the Progressive movement. Instead, many Americans exhibited the restlessness, boredom, and hedonism that came to characterize the decade known as the Roaring Twenties. The period was also marked by social and cultural conflict between those who espoused the newer attitudes and those—many of them older, rurally based, or religiously fundamentalist—who deplored the social and cultural changes. The new sexual attitudes were also linked to the increasing secularization of American life and the growing awareness of a generation gap between the old and the young.

A Sexual Revolution

The Jazz Age sexual revolution was coupled with the rise of the "New Woman." Women had won the right to vote with ratification of the Nineteenth Amendment to the U.S. Constitution in 1920, and many now sought to carry this new power into other areas of their lives. Seeking to overturn social taboos, they began smoking and drinking alcohol socially, activities that were shocking and almost unheard of during the Victorian era. This change in their cultural status was reflected in women's changing sexual status. Sexual independence became one of the most revolutionary aspects of the New Woman.

American women during the Jazz Age generally became more sexually assertive and viewed sex as less tied to marriage and motherhood than did their Victorian counterparts, who believed that respectable women had sex only for the purpose of conception within marriage. The New Woman reflected the growing belief that all women had a right to sexual pleasure and satisfaction. Young women began demanding equal opportunity for physical pleasure and the freedom to choose their mates. The decade saw increases in the rates of premarital sex, adultery, and divorce—the latter rising annually from five per 1,000 married women in 1920 to about seven per 1,000 in 1930. This increase can be attributed to a change in marital expectations. By the late 1800s, sensitivity and romantic love had begun to replace emotional control and practical matches as the marriage ideal. Divorce rates rose because couples were no longer as willing to remain in loveless or dysfunctional marriages.

The fashion and style of the 1920s embraced these independent attitudes. The New Woman was epitomized by the "flapper," who replaced the corseted Gibson Girl of the Victorian era as the feminine ideal. Gone were corsets and petticoats; flappers were characterized by their boyish appearance, which included short bobbed hairstyles and flattened breasts. These young women wore short skirts, rouged their faces, and used bright red lipstick. And the image of the flapper was everywhere—in magazine articles, drawings, photographs, books, and movies.

With their new look and new self-image, young women of the 1920s sought further independence in their living arrangements and social lives. Many single urban women lived outside their parents' homes for the first time. Flirting and dating became more common and acceptable. Young single women went on dates without chaperones. Words such as "petting" and "necking" became part of the American vocabulary.

Many people no longer considered sexual matters taboo, and sex became a popular topic for public discussion. Psychology in general, and the theories of Austrian psychoanalyst Sigmund Freud in particular, became highly popular in the 1920s. Freud's theories seemed to show that sexual repression was emotionally dangerous for both sexes, and many people viewed this as a license for letting down their inhibitions and indulging in sexual activity. Thus, the New Woman was, in part, a reflection of the decade's changing views of female sexuality. These views were perpetuated by psychologists and authors who advocated that women should enjoy sex and sought to educate women on sexuality and the female body. British birth control advocate Marie Stopes's book *Married Love,* for example, published in 1918, discussed a woman's orgasm. The book was banned by the U.S. Customs Service until 1931.

Family Planning and the Birth Control Movement

Methods of birth control in the 1920s included coitus interruptus, condoms, douches, sponges, diaphragms, cervical caps, and powders and potions of dubious effectiveness. There was also abortion, which was mostly illegal. Middle- and upper-class women were already practicing contraception and family planning. The trend toward contraception did not apply to the poor, however, many of whom sought information in vain, due to lack of education, published materials, and birth control clinics. Many working-class women had endured multiple pregnancies, miscarriages, and stillbirths, in addition to watching their children die young. Some desperately sought ways to limit the size of their families, who struggled with poverty.

Reformer Margaret Sanger launched a campaign in the early twentieth century to disseminate birth control information, which Congress had classified as obscene in 1873 under the Comstock Act. This federal legislation levied fines and imprisonment for providing information on contraception or abortion. The state of New York, where Sanger worked as a nurse, had a similar law. Sanger spoke out in favor of providing legal birth control information after witnessing a poor young slum mother die following an attempted abortion. Many people attacked Sanger as immoral, and she was arrested several times, once in 1916 after opening the first birth control clinic in the United States. In 1921, she organized the American Birth Control League, which later became Planned Parenthood. By 1930, there were more than 300 birth control clinics in the United States.

Arts, Literature, and the Entertainment Industry

Artists, writers, and filmmakers in the 1920s depicted women modeled on flappers, while journalists and others discussed the new gender roles and sexual openness. Some sought to defend the changes, some merely to explain them, and others to condemn their immorality. Some people blamed the country's loosening sexual mores on the media for displaying immoral content.

The general prosperity of the 1920s, the rise of mass-produced consumer products, and the advent of installment buying fueled the growth of the modern advertising industry. Advertising helped create and disseminate cultural ideals of the desirable man and desirable woman in an effort to sell a wide range of products. According to the advertisements, consumers would be criticized or ostracized by their peers if they did not use the advertised products. The smiling, sexy, confident people in the advertisements did not suffer from bad breath, dirty clothes, or other problems that might be keep the average person from

Sex and the Automobile

When Henry Ford set out to democratize the automobile in the early 1900s, he had a singular vision and purpose: to build a car that was cheap and reliable enough for farmers and workers to afford and maintain. For the farmer, it would offer the opportunity to go to town for shopping, socializing, and entertainment. For the worker, it would provide a means of escaping the crowd and soot of the city for the wholesome air of the countryside. But what the puritanical Ford never envisioned—and, indeed, came to rue—was the automobile as a vehicle for youthful escapade. As in the case of new technologies before and since, customers, or at least their children, soon discovered the potential of the automobile in the pursuit of sex.

Increasingly attractive to American youth, the automobile in the Jazz Age provided a new sense of freedom and a greater level of independence—not least in the realm of dating and sexual experimentation. Courtship during the nineteenth and early twentieth centuries had been conducted mainly in the home. Young men called on young women in their homes, under the watchful eyes of parents; attentive mothers and fathers could all but ensure that no inappropriate behavior took place. The motorcar, however, allowed a young couple to escape the gaze of their elders and, indeed, of society at large.

By the 1920s, the design of most motorcars included such comforts as an enclosed cab and a heating system. These innovations aided couples choosing to use their cars for all levels of physical intimacy. Those seeking a private spot to steal a kiss—or more—could park in a secluded lovers' lane, wooded park, or remote field. The new opportunity fostered public concern over illicit romance (especially premarital sex) in automobiles. Hoping to deter behavior that many viewed as immoral but was indeed widespread, a number of colleges forbade students to have cars on campus. In some locations, the outcry even led to passage of ordinances that barred couples from parking. The police often failed to enforce such measures, however, explaining that it was better to know where a community's teens were, even if they were engaging in sexual intimacy that society did not condone, than not to know at all. Arresting them, it was said, would only send them off later to who knew where to do who knew what.

While some young couples used the automobile as a venue for sexual experimentation, the motorcar also played host to less innocent meetings among adults and gave access to new sites of business for the world's oldest profession—prostitution. The motor hotels and drive-in restaurants that sprang up along America's roadways during the 1920s provided fertile ground for what was referred to as the "pillow trade," as well as extramarital affairs.

Although the fear of the automobile as a facilitator of sexual promiscuity has largely passed, the role of cars in the transformation of sexual mores among America's youth during the twentieth century remains unmistakable.

Margaret L. Freeman

achieving the same confidence. Sexual images proved highly effective and quickly became an advertising staple.

Motion picture exhibitors quickly realized the profits to be made from racy material. Many of the decade's most famous movie stars, such as Rudolph Valentino and Clara Bow, achieved their popularity through a combination of good looks and sex appeal.

Looser attitudes about sexuality marked the 1920s, as American youth experienced new freedom. The convenience of the automobile and the influence of motion pictures have been cited as causes of the new permissiveness. *(Fox Photos/Hulton Archive/Getty Images)*

But some Americans avoided movies because they did not want to be subjected to morally questionable content. Many reformers believed that movies corrupted children. These attitudes were not universal, however, and did little to stem the medium's soaring popularity.

Sexually charged female characters such as the "vamp," a woman who entices men only to destroy them, rose to popularity even before the 1920s. But more predominant in the Jazz Age was the flapper, personified by the "It Girl," Clara Bow. The flapper, typically silly and self-absorbed, used sexuality to appeal to men rather than to overpower them. Films also depicted career women who might defy social norms of behavior but were not openly promiscuous. Still, Hollywood tended to promote the ideal of marriage as glamorous and the ultimate life's goal of women.

The film industry came under attack as a number of sexual scandals emerged out of the Hollywood culture—most notoriously, the death of a young woman in the hotel room of comedic film star Fatty Arbuckle in 1921—that both titillated and shocked the public at large. In 1922, the industry created its first trade association, the Motion Pictures Producers and Distributors Association (later the Motion Picture Association of America), and appointed former post-master general and moral crusader Will Hays to help project a more wholesome image of Hollywood. Hays, increasingly frustrated by the explicit films of the era, invoked a strict code in 1930 to regulate the sexual content of movies. As a result of the Hays code, films became tamer in their depiction of sex and sexuality for a time.

The 1920s were also a time when African American music such as jazz and the blues flourished in the speakeasies and nightclubs of New Orleans, Chicago, New York, and other big cities. The blues especially was music steeped in themes of sexual passion and betrayal. Popular dances such as the Charleston and the black bottom emphasized sensual movement.

Taboos

Despite the sexual revolution and more open attitudes of the Jazz Age, several areas of sexuality remained taboo. One of these was miscegenation, or interracial dating and marriage. Many states had anti-miscegenation laws. Virginia passed the Racial Integrity Act in 1924 to create more stringent definitions of white and black racial categories; the law also required residents to file certificates testifying to their racial history and forbade residents from marrying anyone of another racial classification. Such laws appealed to Americans who desired racial purity, finding support among white supremacists and black separatists. White supremacist groups such as the Ku Klux Klan used sexually charged imagery, such as an African American man raping a white woman, in support of eugenics and other causes.

Many Americans did not welcome the sexual revolution, and its freedoms had limits. Most nonmarital sexual conduct was still considered criminal behavior and was attacked by moral reformers. Prostitution and red-light districts, which had flourished in the early part of the century, had largely been closed down or forced to go underground. Homosexuality, which flourished in more liberal urban areas, was illegal in most parts of the country.

Authors who were homosexual or bisexual had to hide that information from publishers and audiences to avoid rejection. When Charlie Chaplin and Lita Grey were divorcing in 1927, Chaplin faced charges that oral sex was part of his marriage; this alone was seen as sufficient grounds for divorce. Parents, progressive reformers, police, and juvenile courts all fought against the New Woman and her freedom. Many popular magazine articles expressed shock and dismay at the behavior of young women and called for a return to old-fashioned values. And though heavily critiqued, the ideal of the Victorian family continued among large sectors of the American population until well after World War II.

David Treviño

See also: Beauty Industry and Culture; Birth Control; Film; Homosexuals and Homosexuality; Marriage, Divorce, and Family; Psychology; Sanger, Margaret; Women and Gender; Youth.

Further Reading

Brandt, Allan M. *No Magic Bullet: A Social History of Venereal Disease in the United States Since 1880.* New York: Oxford University Press, 1985.

D'Emilio, John, and Estelle B. Freedman. *Intimate Matters: A History of Sexuality in America.* 2nd ed. New York: Harper & Row, 1997.

Gordon, Linda. *Woman's Body, Woman's Right: A Social History of Birth Control in America.* New York: Grossman, 1976.

Higashi, Sumiko. *Virgins, Vamps, and Flappers: The American Silent Movie Heroine.* St. Alban's, VT: Eden, 1978.

Hodes, Martha, ed. *Sex, Love, Race: Crossing Boundaries in North American History.* New York: New York University Press, 1999.

Thompson, Sharon. *Going All the Way.* New York: Hill and Wang, 1996.

Sheppard-Towner Act (1921)

The Sheppard-Towner Act (officially the Maternity and Infancy Care Act of 1921), which provided federal funding for maternity, child health, and welfare programs, was the first piece of federal social welfare legislation enacted in the United States. It was in many ways an extension of Progressive Era activism by women social reformers, a link between their work and the later New Deal. Sheppard-Towner programs were largely successful, but the law was repealed at the decade's end. The fate of Sheppard-Towner illuminates many of the decade's social and cultural trends.

The legislation was spearheaded by the federal Children's Bureau, established in 1912, whose statistics confirmed high infant mortality rates nationwide and the influence of social and economic causes. In response, Julia Lathrop, head of the bureau, and her predominantly female colleagues envisioned a program that would provide social welfare to all women and children as an entitlement from the government, regardless of financial need.

The federal legislation they conceived aimed to provide matching federal funds to state programs created to reduce infant and maternal mortality rates through education and preventive health care. Their proposed program would be comprehensive, national, run by women, and would rely in large part on local volunteer efforts. Originally introduced in 1918 by Jeannette Rankin, the first female member of Congress, the bill was changed and reintroduced several times before taking its final form in 1920.

Sponsored by Senator Morris Sheppard (D-TX) and Representative Horace Towner (R-IA), the bill faced fierce opposition. Right-wing organizations denounced the encroachment of the state into the realm of the private family, and the male medical establishment resented women taking control of health care. An enormous grassroots campaign by women's organizations countered these criticisms, and the bill was passed by a wide margin in Congress. But the opposition forced the Children's Bureau to compromise. Instead of a $4 million budget, Congress appropriated only $1.48 million for the first year and $1.42 million for the next five years. Moreover, the bureau would have only minimal control over the administration of funds, and the final bill had no provisions for medical care. The program would be purely educational.

By 1922, all but six states had put up funds for Sheppard-Towner programs, and programs eventually were running in every state except Connecticut, Massachusetts, and Illinois. Direction from Washington was minimal, but many volunteers and professionals worked at the state level distributing literature, corresponding with mothers, and holding conferences.

But attacks by the conservative American Medical Association, which saw almost any government involvement in health care as a step toward socialized medicine, grew louder and more intense. Conservative political groups decried Sheppard-Towner as Socialist legislation, and Lathrop and her colleagues were denounced as Bolsheviks. Supporters began falling away, and in 1927, although the House passed a bill to renew funding, the Senate blocked it. Ultimately, the Children's Bureau was forced to accept a bill that provided funding for two more years, until 1929, at which point Sheppard-Towner would be automatically repealed.

The Sheppard-Towner programs did succeed in lowering infant mortality rates, and maternal mortality rates as well, although infant mortality among babies of color did not significantly decrease. The extreme depths of poverty or illiteracy in some communities limited the effectiveness of the program. Many could not read the literature provided or were simply too poor to implement the dietary recommendations, and those without running water could not effectively implement the advice on infant and child hygiene. The success of Sheppard-Towner varied tremendously from region to region, depending on state funds, geography, and the degree of organization.

The legacy of the Sheppard-Towner Act is complex. Initiated and run by women, the program remains a testament to the power of women's reforms in the wake of the Nineteenth Amendment. Medical care for women and children was greatly improved, at least in some areas. Ultimately, however, the repeal of Sheppard-Towner signaled that responsibility for the welfare of children would rest in individual families and not in the hands of the state. Within six years of its repeal, however, the Franklin D. Roosevelt administration would revive the spirit of Sheppard-Towner with the Aid to Dependent Children program, a part of the landmark Social Security Act of 1935.

Erica J. Ryan

See also: Children and Child Rearing; Marriage, Divorce, and Family.

Further Reading

Ladd-Taylor, Molly. *Mother-Work: Women, Child Welfare, and the State, 1890–1930.* Urbana: University of Illinois Press, 1994.
Lemons, Stanley. *The Woman Citizen: Social Feminism in the 1920s.* Urbana: University of Illinois Press, 1973.
Muncy, Robyn. *Creating a Female Dominion in American Reform 1890–1935.* New York: Oxford University Press, 1991.
Skocpol, Theda. *Protecting Soldiers and Mothers: The Political Origins of Social Policy in the United States.* Cambridge, MA: Belknap Press, 1992.

Siberian Intervention

The Siberian intervention of 1918–1922 began as an action by the Allied powers of World War I, including the United States, to rescue some 50,000 Czechoslovakian soldiers in Siberia who were threatened by the Bolshevik government in Russia. Because of their long-standing demands for independence from their Austro-Hungarian rulers, the Czechs wanted to fight against the Central powers (Germany and Austria-Hungary primarily) in the war. The Allied powers, seeking more forces, were hoping to transport them to the Western Front. That, at least, was the official reason for the intervention. But many saw the intervention as a means to aid the antirevolutionary White Russian forces in their civil war against the Bolsheviks.

When the Bolsheviks came to power in Russia following the October 1917 revolution, they pulled Russia out of World War I, focusing instead on consolidating their revolution at home. Convinced that the war was really being fought over capitalist profits, the Bolsheviks had no interest in continuing Russia's participation, a move that angered the Western Allies, since it allowed the Central powers to shift forces to the Western Front.

The Czechs, as subjects of the Austro-Hungarian Empire, had been conscripted to fight against Russia, which had declared war against the Central powers in 1914. Thousands of the Czech soldiers had been captured by Russian forces during the war and placed in prisoner-of-war camps. But many of them wanted to fight for their independence against Austria-Hungary. The czarist government and then the noncommunist government that followed with the Russian Revolution in March had released these Czech soldiers and armed them. But before they could be sent to the front, the October Revolution overthrew the non-communist government in Moscow. The new Bolshevik government, under an agreement with Germany ending Russian participation in the war, agreed to reimprison the soldiers, whereupon the Czechs fled to Siberia aboard the Trans-Siberian Railroad. The Bolsheviks, however, occupied the central Siberian segment of the railroad and attempted to block their transit.

Meanwhile, the Allies were considering an occupation of Vladivostok, at the Pacific terminus of the railroad. The city held large stores of war materiel shipped to the prerevolutionary Russian government by the Allies. Now, in the summer of 1918, with the Czechs blockaded, the Allies decided to make their move. Because the United States and Japan had the easiest access to the Pacific coast of Russia, they formed the bulk of the expedition, though British, Canadian, French, and other European forces also took part. Under the command of Major General William Graves, some 7,500 U.S. troops of the Army Twenty-seventh and Thirty-first Infantry Regiments landed in Vladivostok in September, though a few had already arrived in August to prepare the way for the larger contingent. The Japanese officially sent about 30,000 troops.

The Allies issued assurances to Moscow that the expedition would respect Russian territorial integrity and that the troops would withdraw as soon as the mission was completed. They also insisted that they would not take sides in the Russian civil war. However, the Allies indeed ended up providing supplies to the White Russian forces.

Japan had bolder aims, and its troops penetrated deep into Siberia in several areas. Some of the Japanese forces moved north from Vladivostok. Others moved west through northern Manchuria to Irkutsk west of Lake Baikal. The Japanese aided virtually any anti-Bolshevik forces that sought their help. They also quickly established control of several areas. Ultimately, the Japanese effort was a failure. Not only did their forces fail to substantially help the White Russians, but also those who accepted foreign aid came to be viewed as unpatriotic and became the targets of a popular backlash.

Efforts by the Allies to aid the White Russian forces were failing by the end of 1919, as the Bolsheviks began to gain the upper hand in the civil war. In early 1920, the U.S. government announced its plans to pull out of Siberia, and on April 1, the Allied intervention ended with the evacuation of all non-Japanese forces from Vladivostok. For the American soldiers, the intervention had proved a disaster. Long supply lines left them with shortages of food, fuel, ammunition, and other materiel. The freezing weather did not help either. While some 150 died battling Bolshevik forces—the only time in history in which Soviet and American forces fought each other directly—more than 250 died of disease and frigid temperatures.

As the White Russian government collapsed in 1921, the Japanese found themselves isolated and unable to retain control of the areas they had occupied in Siberia. On October 25, 1922, the Japanese forces finally evacuated Vladivostok.

James Ciment and Andrew J. Waskey

See also: Europe, Relations with; Military Affairs.

Further Reading

Maddox, Robert James. *The Unknown War with Russia: Wilson's Siberian Intervention.* San Rafael, CA: Presidio, 1977.

Melton, Carol Willcox. *Between War and Peace: Woodrow Wilson and the American Expeditionary Force in Siberia, 1918–1921.* Macon, GA: Mercer University Press, 2001.

Unterberger, Betty Miller. *America's Siberian Expedition, 1918–1920: A Study of National Policy.* New York: Greenwood, 1969.

Sinclair, Harry (1876–1956)

Shrewd, confident, and willing to take risks, Harry Ford Sinclair worked his way up in the oil industry to become one of America's great oil barons. In less than fifteen years, he built the largest independent oil company in the nation. His drive to be a major player in the global petroleum market put him in competition with such giants as Standard Oil, the Anglo-Persian Oil Company (a predecessor to British Petroleum), and Royal Dutch Shell. For the most part, Sinclair's ambition served him well, but arrogance and greed led to some bad deals and a prison term in the 1920s.

Harry F. Sinclair was born to John and Phoebe Sinclair on July 6, 1876, near Wheeling, West Virginia. In 1882, the family moved to Independence, Kansas, where Sinclair's father, a pharmacist, ran a drugstore. With his father encouraging him to go into the family business, Sinclair enrolled in the pharmacy program at the University of Kansas in Lawrence. After graduation, he took over the family pharmacy but lost the business in 1901.

The pharmacy failure notwithstanding, Sinclair proved to be a formidable entrepreneur. While selling lumber in southeast Kansas, he sought out potential oil properties and brokered leases for investors. His venture was wildly successful, and colleagues claimed that Sinclair could "smell" oil. He also managed small oil companies for wealthy financial backers, buying and selling at his discretion and sharing in the profits. He eventually invested in companies himself. By 1913, Sinclair ran sixty-two companies, owned a number of drilling rigs, and sat on bank boards in Kansas and Oklahoma. In September 1919, Sinclair merged his companies under the umbrella of the Sinclair Consolidated Oil Corporation, a holding company for numerous subsidiaries.

As the automobile industry grew, so did Sinclair's business. In 1922, Sinclair Oil established the first full-service modern gas station in Chicago. The services offered—oil change, air, tire and mechanical repairs—were invaluable to the nation's many new automobile owners, who knew relatively little about how their vehicles worked. Sinclair educated his customers through a successful "Law of Lubrication" advertising campaign, which stressed the importance of Sinclair oils for smooth-running, reliable automobiles. He also tapped into the growing celebrity culture by sponsoring cross-country motorcyclists Floyd Clymer and Ernest G. "Cannonball" Baker, as well as racecar drivers Tommy Milton, Ralph De-Palma, and Gaston Chevrolet, who displayed the Sinclair logo on their vehicles and racing clothes. So successful was his advertising that many independent gas stations solicited Sinclair for the right to sell his products.

The American demand for oil soared in the 1920s. To conserve U.S. resources and prevent foreign interests from controlling global reserves, American companies explored overseas petroleum sources. During the course of the decade, Sinclair acquired leases throughout the United States, Mexico, Costa Rica, Venezuela, and West Africa. In 1923, he traveled to Russia with the dream of building Sinclair oil derricks, refineries, and pipeline systems throughout the country. Negotiations with officials in Moscow resulted in a contract granting a forty-nine-year partnership with the Soviet Union for oil in Baku and Grosni, as well as a monopoly on the Sakhalin oil field. In exchange, Sinclair agreed to arrange a $250 million loan for the Soviet Union with Wall Street and convince the U.S. government to formally recognize the Communist regime. But anticommunist sentiments ran strong at home, and neither the U.S. government nor Wall Street would support Sinclair's plan.

Sinclair also sought a foothold in Middle Eastern oil reserves. In December 1923, the government of Persia (modern-day Iran) granted Sinclair exploration rights in four northern provinces in exchange for his arranging a $10 million loan. Again, it was a contract he was unable to honor. In January 1924, a Tehran newspaper alleged that Sinclair had bribed the prime minister with $275,000 to coerce the deal. Further, the murder of U.S. diplomat Major Robert Imbrie in Tehran in July 1924 caused anti-Persian sentiment among American financiers. The deal fell apart.

Sinclair was also a key player in one of the biggest U.S. government scandals of the decade, Teapot Dome, which stemmed from the 1922 contract that granted a Sinclair subsidiary, Mammoth Oil Company, drilling rights on the Teapot Dome naval oil reserve in Wyoming. In 1924, Senate investigations revealed that Sinclair had bribed Secretary of the Interior Alfred B. Fall to obtain the exclusive twenty-year lease. A series of lawsuits followed that resulted in termination of the lease, a prison sentence for Fall, and a number of civil and criminal suits against Sinclair, who would have escaped further punitive actions had he kept his need for control in check.

In a brash move, Sinclair hired private detectives to follow the jurors and identify a weak link; one of them, Edward J. Kidwell, was offered a bribe of $25,000 to deadlock the verdict. Sinclair, on the advice of his attorney, refused to answer questions by the prosecution. In 1929, the Senate found him in contempt of court and sentenced him to six months in jail for jury tampering. During his brief stint in prison, Sinclair returned to his original profession—rolling quinine pills for the prison pharmacy.

In addition to oil, Sinclair enjoyed baseball and horseracing. He challenged the American and National League's monopoly on America's favorite pastime in 1914–1915 and founded the short-lived Federal League. In the 1920s, he invested heavily in the New Jersey Rancocas Stable, a thoroughbred horseracing training facility known for producing winners. Sinclair's horses went on to win the 1923 Kentucky Derby and three Belmont Stakes. Sinclair retired to Pasadena, California, in 1949 and died at his home on November 10, 1956.

Jennifer Aerts Terry

See also: Oil and Oil Industry; Teapot Dome Scandal.

Further Reading

Connelly, W.L. *The Oil Business as I Saw It: Half a Century with Sinclair.* Norman: University of Oklahoma Press, 1954.

Davis, Margaret Leslie. *Dark Side of Fortune: Triumph and Scandal in the Life of Oil Tycoon Edward L. Doheny.* Berkeley: University of California Press, 1998.

O'Connor, Richard. *The Oil Barons: Men of Greed and Grandeur.* Boston: Little, Brown, 1971.

Sinclair Oil Corporation. *A Great Name in Oil: Sinclair Through Fifty Years.* New York: F.W. Dodge, 1966.

Sloan, Alfred P. (1875–1966)

Next to Henry Ford, Alfred P. Sloan was America's most important automobile executive of the first half of the twentieth century. Under his leadership, General Motors (GM) became the leading car manufacturer in America, surpassing the Ford Motor Company. Sloan pioneered innovative techniques in marketing, management, and consumer credit, and he helped General Motors diversify and globalize, expanding into the defense industry, mass transit, and financing.

Alfred Pritchard Sloan, Jr., was born on May 23, 1875, in New Haven, Connecticut. A studious child, he later attended the Massachusetts Institute of Technology and graduated in 1895 with a degree in electrical engineering, completed in just three years. He then went to work for Hyatt Roller Bearing Company, where he used his organizational skills to turn a struggling company into a profitable operation. In 1916, Sloan convinced the owners of United Motor Company, which would later become part of General Motors, to buy the ball bearing company he was then president of; the deal also enabled him to join the auto manufacturer as a vice president. By 1923, thanks largely to his organizational acumen, he had risen to president of the company.

Instead of integrating the companies acquired by GM—Oldsmobile, Chevrolet, Pontiac, Cadillac—Sloan established them as divisions of the larger organization. Each division would continue producing cars for specific income levels, under its own brand name; all decisions for a division would be made by the division head, so long as they did not conflict with the policies of the GM corporation. Customers could upgrade to a different car within the GM family as their income level rose, a strategy that encouraged customer loyalty to the corporation. Each

While Henry Ford revolutionized the manufacture of automobiles, it was General Motors president Alfred P. Sloan who pioneered their marketing. Among his innovations were yearly model changes, vehicles in diverse price ranges, and optional features. *(Keystone/Stringer/Hulton Archive/Getty Images)*

division kept its own staff and had a high degree of autonomy in automotive design, so long as it did not compete with a model created by another GM division.

Sloan also introduced options, enabling consumers to modify cars to fit their own needs. Consumer surveys were used to find out what those needs were. The service policy, another marketing innovation, was offered by the Cadillac division in 1926. Engineering and design innovations offered in the 1920s included four-wheel brakes, chrome plating (standard by 1929), and safety glass. Each year's models were designed to look different from those of the previous year, and new options were offered to give them a distinctive look and feel. Some criticized the "planned obsolescence" strategy, but it succeeded in boosting sales as customers tried to keep up with the latest trends. Meanwhile, GM's biggest competitor in the 1920s, the Ford Motor Company, eschewed options and yearly changes.

Sloan also launched a financial service business to give credit to consumers. And he expanded GM's market by establishing assembly plants overseas. The first appeared in Copenhagen, Denmark, in 1924; by the beginning of World War II, GM had assembly and manufacturing plants in Argentina, Brazil, Uruguay, England, Belgium, France, Germany, Spain, Egypt, India, Japan, China, Australia, and New Zealand. By the end of the 1920s, GM was the largest corporation in the world.

In another expansion, Sloan and GM in 1926 purchased the Yellow Truck and Coach Manufacturing Company, a producer of trucks and buses. In the period that followed, GM became a strong proponent of buses as the preferred mass-transit system over rail. Critics later accused Sloan and GM of creating a monopoly for bus mass transit and then cutting back on routes to encourage the sale of its cars.

Under Sloan's leadership, research and development (R&D) were emphasized at GM. The company became the first auto manufacturer to have a dedicated R&D department, and Sloan made sure it had plenty of funding to keep GM ahead of its competition. Among the department's many important innovations in the 1920s was ethyl, or higher-grade, gasoline, which helped minimize wear on engine parts and allowed cars to run more smoothly.

Sloan's management style and consumer outreach became models for industrial organizations. He founded the Sloan School of Management at MIT in 1931 and another management program at Stanford University. He also became a strong advocate for industry and often clashed with government officials and unions. He resisted the New Deal programs of the 1930s and was an outspoken opponent of the auto safety movement. He retired from GM in 1956 and died on February 17, 1966.

Michael Faubion

See also: Automobile Industry; Automobiles and Automobile Culture; Credit and Debt, Consumer; General Motors.

Further Reading

Chandler, Alfred. *The Visible Hand: The Managerial Revolution in American Business.* Cambridge, MA: Harvard University Press, 1977.
Farber, David. *Sloan Rules: Alfred P. Sloan and the Triumph of General Motors.* Chicago: University of Chicago Press, 2002.
Freeland, Robert. *The Struggle for the Control of the Modern Corporation: Organizational Change at General Motors, 1924–1970.* Cambridge, UK: Cambridge University Press, 2000.
Freeman, Allyn. *The Leadership and Genius of Alfred P. Sloan: Invaluable Lessons on Business, Management, and Leadership for Today's Managers.* New York: McGraw-Hill, 2004.
Sloan, Alfred P., Jr. *My Years with General Motors.* New York: Doubleday, 1963.

Smith, Al (1873–1944)

Emerging out of the immigrant neighborhoods and Tammany Hall political machine of New York City, Al Smith served as a reform-minded Democratic governor of New York State from 1919 to 1921 and again from 1923 to 1929. But he is best remembered for his unsuccessful 1928 bid for the presidency, the first Catholic to ever run for president on a major party ticket.

Known as the "Happy Warrior," New York Governor Al Smith became the first Catholic candidate for president on a major party ticket in 1928. In an age of lingering religious bigotry and Republican hegemony, the Democrat was soundly defeated by Herbert Hoover. *(MPI/Stringer/Hulton Archive/Getty Images)*

Alfred Emanuel Smith was born on Manhattan's Lower East Side on December 30, 1873, the son of an Irish American mother and a father of Italian and German background. Smith always identified himself as an Irish American and remained a devout Catholic all his life. Equally important, Smith proudly called himself a son of New York's immigrant working classes throughout his political career.

When Smith was thirteen, his father died and Smith was forced to drop out of parochial school the following year to help support the family. He would never earn his high school diploma, but from an early age, Smith displayed the oratorical gifts that would serve him well in his political career. Most who knew him when he was in his teens and early twenties commented on his speaking ability. Smith also became an accomplished amateur stage actor in these years. In 1900, he married Catherine Dunn, with whom he would have five children.

Like most working-class politicians in New York City, Smith got his start with Tammany Hall, the political machine that had run the city on patronage—and some graft—for much of the late nineteenth and early twentieth centuries. Sponsored by Irish American political boss "Silent" Charlie McCarthy, Smith earned a patronage job as clerk in the Commissioner of Jurors office in 1895. Eight years later, he won his first elective office, as a New York assemblyman from the Lower East Side. Although Smith was a product of machine politics, he often bucked against it, supporting reform legislation and, in 1911, conducting investigations into the unsafe workshop conditions in the city that had led to the disastrous Triangle Shirtwaist Factory fire, which killed nearly 150 garment workers.

When Democrats won control of the assembly in the 1911 elections, Smith became chair of the powerful Ways and Means Committee, where he succeeded in pushing through laws to regulate unhealthy and unsafe factory conditions in the state. He rapidly rose up the ladder of power in Albany, becoming assembly majority leader in 1912 and speaker of the assembly, the state's second-most powerful position, a year later.

He held the job just two years, leaving to take what at first glance seemed a step down as sheriff of New York County. But the position offered Smith a chance to dole out patronage jobs on a major scale, winning him a large backing for his successful 1918 gubernatorial bid. In his terms as governor, Smith earned a reputation as a reformer and a builder. He put fellow reformer and close adviser Robert Moses in charge of creating the nation's first statewide park system. With the help of social worker and adviser Frances Perkins, a future U.S. secretary of labor, Smith also made New York State a leader in workmen's compensation laws, women's pensions, and laws protecting female and child laborers.

His enormous popularity in the state led him to seek the Democratic nomination for president in 1924. That meant winning delegate votes at the convention, held that year in New York City's Madison Square Garden. Smith campaigned as a liberal on economic and social issues, insisting on an anti-lynching law plank in the party's platform. He also spoke out against the nativist and racist Ku Klux Klan, which was experiencing an upsurge in popularity in the early part of the decade. These positions alienated critical Southern delegates, who were also wary of nominating a Northern urban Catholic. After more than a hundred ballots, Smith lost to conservative dark horse candidate John W. Davis. At the convention, however, Smith received his famous nickname when Franklin D. Roosevelt, putting Smith's name up for nomination, called him the "Happy Warrior" of American politics.

Four years later, as the Democratic Party's presidential candidate, Smith campaigned for an activist government after eight years of Republican laissez-faire rule. He promised public works programs and other economic reforms that later would be adopted by his protégé Roosevelt during the New Deal era of the 1930s. But in the prosperous times of the late 1920s, jobs programs were not as pressing with the voting public, many of whom were also turned off by Smith's Catholicism, his opposition to Prohibition, and his heavy New York accent, which played poorly with many rural and small-town Americans over the new medium of radio. Smith was swamped by Commerce Secretary Herbert Hoover in one of the largest landslides in presidential politics to that date.

Upon leaving the governor's office in 1929, Smith served as president of Empire State, Inc., the corporation then constructing the Empire State Building in Manhattan. In 1932, Smith again sought the Democratic nomination, this time against Roosevelt, his successor as governor of New York. But Smith's long-standing feud with newspaper magnate William Randolph Hearst, leader of the left wing of the New York Democrats, helped sink his chances with delegates, who were already reluctant to go with Smith again. Roosevelt gained the nomination, and the party sensed victory in the first presidential election of the Great Depression.

Feeling betrayed by the man he had considered his protégé, Smith became an outspoken conservative critic of President Roosevelt's New Deal, even though it incorporated many of the ideas and programs Smith had first developed for New York State. Smith died on October 4, 1944, in New York City.

James Ciment

See also: Anti-Catholicism; Catholics and Catholicism; Democratic Party; Election of 1928; Hoover, Herbert; Irish Americans.

Further Reading

Finan, Christopher M. *Alfred E. Smith: The Happy Warrior.* New York: Hill and Wang, 2002.

Slayton, Robert A. *Empire Statesman: The Rise and Redemption of Al Smith.* New York: Free Press, 2001.

Smith, Bessie (1894–1937)

The most successful blues singer of the early twentieth century and an influential vocalist in that musical genre, Bessie Smith—the "Empress of Blues"—cut numerous best-selling records during the 1920s and collaborated with some of the greatest blues and jazz performers of the era, including Louis Armstrong, Fletcher Henderson, and James P. Johnson.

Bessie Smith was born in Chattanooga, Tennessee. The date of her birth is open to some conjecture, but the most widely agreed upon one is April 15, 1894. Like many Southern African Americans of the day, Smith was born into poverty. Her father, William, was a day laborer who also worked as a Baptist preacher. Smith's father and her mother, Laura, died before Smith was ten years old, leaving her and five of her siblings to be brought up by their older sister Viola. To help raise money for the family, Smith formed a duet with her brother Andrew, and they performed on the streets of Chattanooga. In 1912, another brother, Clarence, helped get Smith a job as a dancer with the Moses Stokes Theater Company, where he performed. There, Smith received training from the legendary blues singer Gertrude "Ma" Rainey.

Soon, Smith gave up dancing for singing and was included in Ma Rainey's Rabbit Foot, a minstrel show that was part of the theater company's ensemble. Within a year, Smith was performing on her own in front of audiences across the Southeast and up and down the eastern seaboard. As she developed her singing style, she became a favorite with audiences and was soon the most popular performer in the troupe.

Known as the "Empress of the Blues," vocalist Bessie Smith sold more records in the 1920s than almost any other musician and became the nation's highest paid African American performer by the latter part of the decade. *(Frank Driggs Collection/Hulton Archive/Getty Images)*

Smith matured as a blues singer at a time when the genre was becoming increasingly popular with both black and white audiences. Unlike jazz, which emerged out of the theaters, brothels, and nightclubs of New Orleans, blues was originally a rural black musical form, fusing slave work songs, Negro spirituals, and old African rhythms. As African Americans began their Great Migration to urban centers throughout the country in the early part of the twentieth century, they brought with them this soulful music with simple chords. In the urban settings, the blues took on an edgier sound, borrowing from the syncopated rhythms of jazz. Smith helped establish the blues as a popular musical form.

In 1923, Smith made her first recording, "Down Hearted Blues," for Columbia Records. It was enormously successful, selling some 2 million copies, making it the most popular blues record to date. The record turned Smith into the most sought-after blues performer of her day. By the mid-1920s, she was the star performer of the Theater Owners' Booking Association, which produced shows for a national circuit of theaters and concert halls. Smith was now the highest paid African American performer of the time. In 1929, she began to star in her own show, the Midnight Steepers.

From her initial recording until 1933, Smith cut some 200 records, performing with some of the top jazz musicians of the day and earning the title "Empress of Blues" for the wide range and rich tone of her voice. Among her most famous recordings were "Reckless Blues" (1925), "Gin House Blues" (1926), "Black Water Blues" (1927), "Empty Bed Blues" (1928), and "Nobody Knows You When You're Down and Out" (1929). Smith's style, critics remarked, was more technically intricate than that of most other blues singers of the day, and she was noted for her great control of pitch, strong projection, equal emphasis on melody and lyrics, and clear diction.

Smith was also known for the tragic quality she leant to lyrics, and she frequently improvised and embellished her songs each time she performed them. One well-known feature of her music was a fall, or drop-off, at the ends of phrases. She might moan or break up a phrase to create tension or to emphasize certain words. The intensity she created during her performances produced a deep personal connection with her audiences, a major reason cited by musical historians for her fans' loyalty.

In an industry dominated by hard-living men, Smith developed a tough persona, relishing the nightlife, drinking heavily, and peppering her speech with foul language. Her 1923 marriage to a Philadelphia police officer named Jack Gee, with whom she had a son, was troubled, and the two soon separated. Her career began to decline in the early 1930s, a victim of the Great Depression and the impact of talking pictures on the vaudeville theater circuit, though she was featured singing in one 1929 film, *St. Louis Blues*. Smith was killed in an automobile accident in Mississippi on September 26, 1937.

James Ciment and Elizabeth Penn Whittenburg

See also: Blues; Jazz; Radio.

Further Reading

Albertson, Chris. *Bessie*. New Haven, CT: Yale University Press, 2003.

Schuller, Gunther. *Early Jazz: It's Roots and Musical Development*. Oxford, UK: Oxford University Press, 1968.

Snyder Act (1921)

The Snyder Act, passed by Congress on November 2, 1921, is the basic authoring law for all programs under the auspices of the Bureau of Indian Affairs (BIA). Enacted with the encouragement and support of former President William Howard Taft, the legislation reaffirmed that the BIA would remain under the control of the Department of the Interior (it had been part of the Department of War until 1849). It also outlined the specific responsibilities of the bureau and provided funding mechanisms to support Native American reservation life. Under Article I, Section 8, Clause 3, of the U.S. Constitution, the federal government served as the legal trustee of Native American lands, social services, and public programs. Years of neglect, harsh reservation conditions, broken-down infrastructures, health-care crises, and displacement of Native Americans finally spurred the U.S. government to attempt to restructure its stewardship.

As specified by the Snyder Act, the BIA became responsible for funding and providing the following services to the Native American reservation population: education; health care; administration of property; maintenance and improvement of irrigation systems and development of water resources; repair and expansion of reservation buildings and infrastructure; establishment of reservation bureaucracy, including police, judiciary, doctors, and inspectors; suppression of the influx of liquor and narcotic traffic; purchasing of vehicles for official, bureaucratic use on reservations; and providing general funds in connection with the management of Native American affairs.

In addition to reorganizing and funding federal stewardship, the Snyder Act expanded that stewardship significantly, specifying the precise services the government was responsible for providing Native American reservations. Tribal authority, long the support structure of Native American life, became legally subsumed by the authority of the federal government. American Indian tribes maintained traditional tribal structures, but the Snyder Act officially placed ultimate reservation authority, bureaucracy, and maintenance under the auspices of the BIA.

Specific funding was allocated for the establishment of school systems and the construction of school buildings on American Indian reservations. As explicitly outlined in the act, the U.S. government sought to bring "civilization" to Native American tribes through education. Thus, the schools attempted to assimilate Native Americans into American mass culture and social mores. A strong emphasis was placed on English-language training, while Native American languages, customs, and history were largely ignored. Organized efforts to teach Native American history and culture would not be enacted as public policy until the Indian Reorganization Act of 1934.

The need for improved health care among the Native American population was a major motivation for both Congress and President Taft to support the Snyder Act. Reservations had long suffered from high rates of infant mortality and low life expectancy, and from tuberculosis, trachoma, and other diseases. However, the government services provided under the Snyder Act generally ignored and even undermined traditional tribal medicine, homeopathic care, child rearing, and treatment of illness. In some cases, patients were removed from their communities and families and transported to off-reservation treatment facilities. Most tribes did not want the government to take control of their health-care services, the federal government had done so at least in part to promote their assimilation into mainstream American culture.

A second Snyder Act, the Indian Citizenship Act, passed in 1924, extended U.S. citizenship and the vote to all Native Americans, whether on reservations or not. But as most Native Americans had gained citizenship already through marriage, this legislation was more a symbolic gesture of inclusion.

Adam Shprintzen

See also: Native Americans.

Further Reading

Deloria, Vine, Jr., ed. *American Indian Policy in the Twentieth Century.* Norman: University of Oklahoma Press, 1985.

Kickingbird, Kirke, and Lynn Kickingbird. *Indians and the U.S. Government.* Washington, DC: Institute for the Development of Indian Law, 1977.

Kvansnicka, Robert M., and Herman J. Viola, eds. *The Commissioners of Indian Affairs, 1824–1977.* Lincoln: University of Nebraska Press, 1979.

Social Gospel

A liberal theological doctrine, the Social Gospel called upon Christians to live out their faith by improving society, particularly the living conditions of the urban poor. The Social Gospel arose in the last quarter of the nineteenth century, when immigration, industrialization, and urbanization created significant social problems in America. Middle-class Protestants believed that the nation's large influx of European immigrants, the abuse of poor workers by wealthy corporations, and the squalor of the nation's growing cities revealed the un-Christian elements existing in American society. The Social Gospel became a way to combat the problems the country faced, but even more importantly, the movement voiced an extreme optimism in the ability of ordinary people to make America into the kingdom of God on earth.

Organizations such as the Salvation Army (1880), Jane Addams's Hull House (1889), and the Religious Education Society (1903) attempted to achieve the practical objectives of the Social Gospel and transform America's inner cities. The phrase "What would Jesus do?" made famous by Topeka, Kansas, pastor Charles Sheldon in his novel *In His Steps* (1897), was at the heart of the Social Gospel movement. Sheldon's phrase aimed to inspire ordinary Christians to think about what they could do to reform American society one small act at a time.

The Jazz Age marked an important turning point in the Social Gospel movement. In 1918, as World War I came to an end, two leading proponents of the movement, Washington Gladden and Walter Rauschenbusch, died. In the postwar years, the movement, which never was institutionalized into a single organization, continued to operate as a coalition of pastors, churches, activists, and intellectuals trying to reform American society. However, the movement began a shift from a prewar vision focused on the Christianization of America, to a postwar vision that wanted to make the entire world Christian.

John Marshall Barker's *The Social Gospel and the New Era* (1919) enlarged the idea of what the Social Gospel could achieve in the aftermath of World War I. In the postwar years, most Americans embraced isolationism as the best solution to prevent the country from becoming involved in another costly war. The Social Gospel movement, however, resisted the turn to isolationism and embraced an internationalism aimed at Christianizing the world. The Social Gospel promoted America's involvement in the League of Nations as a means to ensure the spread of democracy and Christianity around the world. The ecumenical movement, which joined together Christians from a variety of denominational and theological backgrounds, became an essential part of the international vision of the Social Gospel during the 1920s. Meetings such as the Stockholm Conference of 1925 and books such as *The Christ of the Indian Road* (1925) by E. Stanley Jones attempted to create a Christian perspective for dealing with social problems beyond the United States.

The Social Gospel also directly influenced many other aspects of American life during the Jazz Age. The Eighteenth Amendment (ratified in 1919), prohibiting the manufacture and sale of alcoholic beverages, was widely embraced by supporters of the Social Gospel as a way to end the evils associated with alcohol abuse, particularly in urban areas. The Federal Council of Churches, one of the leading organizations of the Social Gospel movement, was active in the fight for the Child Labor Amendment in 1924. Throughout the 1920s, when the nation's newspapers rejected labor unions as Communist and anti-American, journals committed to the Social Gospel, such as the *Christian Advocate* and *Churchman,* encouraged readers to uphold the right of workers to form labor unions, fight for higher wages, and work fewer hours. The movement remained committed to the plight of the working classes throughout the 1920s by supporting labor strikes and helping resolve disputes between workers and business owners.

The most important development in the Social Gospel during the Jazz Age was an internal split in the movement that led some away from social evangelism (the belief that preaching proper behavior would change social attitudes) and social engineering (managing society through social services) to social reconstruction. Proponents of social reconstruction, such as Harry F. Ward and Francis J. McConnell, believed that institutions must be constantly evaluated according to their final impact on society. Capitalism, for example, initially contributes to human freedom, but, when combined with industrialization, creates a culture of economic pragmatism that threatens to undermine American society. Realist-minded radicalism soon became the hallmark of the social reconstruction perspective.

Social reconstructionists actively voiced their opposition to racial injustices, capitalism, and militarism. The radicalism of the social reconstructionists alienated others in the Social Gospel movement who believed that their goals could be achieved through preaching moral lessons and developing social institutions. These divisions in the Social Gospel movement reflected the broader realignments, along conservative, moderate, and liberal lines, taking place among American Protestants.

In 1929, Chester Charlton McCown published *The Genesis of the Social Gospel,* which argued that Jesus' earthly ministry was really a social gospel intended to confront the abuses of commercial Rome and end the exploitation of the poor in Palestine. McCown's book affirmed that Jesus Christ's life and teachings were central for understanding how America, and the world, could be saved through Christian-based social action. However, the optimism that had defined the Social Gospel at the beginning of the Jazz Age was shattered with the stock market crash of 1929 and the Great Depression that followed. The Social Gospel movement soon adopted a realist approach for dealing with both the difficult economic circumstances the country faced during the Depression and the change in world politics that defined the next decade.

Darin D. Lenz

See also: Immigration; Protestantism, Mainstream; Wealth and Income.

Further Reading

Ahlstrom, Sydney E. *A Religious History of the American People.* New Haven, CT: Yale University Press, 1975.

Carter, Paul A. *The Decline and Revival of the Social Gospel: Social and Political Liberalism in American Protestant Churches, 1920–1940.* Hamden, CT: Archon, 1971.

Gaustad, Edwin S., and Leigh E. Schmidt. *The Religious History of America: The Heart of the American Story from Colonial Times to Today.* Revised ed. San Francisco: Harper San Francisco, 2002.

King, William McGuire. "The Emergence of Social Gospel Radicalism: The Methodist Case." *Church History* 50:4 (1981): 436–49.

Socialism and the Socialist Party of America

Socialism, which called for the equitable division of wealth and the collective ownership of the means of production, distribution, and trade, originated in reaction to the negative effects of capitalism and industrialization on society. The theory gained increasing numbers of proponents throughout the nineteenth century, and the Socialist Party was organized in a number of countries.

By the time the Jazz Age began in 1919, the Socialist Party of America, founded in 1897, had spawned an urban-centered press that was varied, influential, and widely distributed in English and other languages. The party's goals had spread into rural areas, membership swelled, reaching about 118,000 between 1910 and 1912, and the party experienced a small boost in new members as a result of its antiwar stance in 1917. Ultimately, however, this position alienated it from the labor movement and heightened the distrust of many citizens. Government repression of the Socialist leadership during the war by means of the Espionage and Sedition acts, as well as the destruction of almost a third of its locals, all but collapsed the party.

However, socialism appealed to the progressive spirit and rebellious nature of the post–World War I generation. The Socialist Party's promise to improve job conditions and wages convinced workers to support its goals and objectives, and party membership covered nearly the full spectrum of class, race, and gender in America. Despite party leaders' espousal of traditional gender roles, women achieved leadership positions prior to passage of the Nineteenth Amendment in 1920. But the party failed to address issues of racism, as it lumped African Americans' concerns with general labor issues.

The strength of the party lay in its grassroots and regional organizations and the personal charisma of its chief standard-bearer, Eugene V. Debs. Audiences connected with his impassioned oratorical style and, for a short time, forged a unified front. In 1919, however, the party split when some members left to form the Communist Party and the Communist Labor Party.

Meanwhile, fear of a "Red threat" compelled U.S. Attorney General A. Mitchell Palmer to begin a campaign of arresting purportedly dangerous radicals. Under suspicion, a number of Socialists were held illegally without warrants, and Socialist Party assemblymen were ousted from their positions. Debs was convicted under the Espionage Act and sent to prison. Nevertheless, while still in prison, Debs received more than 900,000 votes in the 1920 presidential election, the highest total ever for a Socialist candidate in America.

Earlier that year, the party had applied for affiliation with the Comintern, the Moscow-run international organization of Communist parties, but the request was rejected. Debs was critical of some Comintern positions, and the Socialist Party ultimately abandoned its attempts to collaborate with the Communists. Instead, the party shifted to a more central ideology that would appeal to mainstream America.

The Socialist Party did not run a presidential candidate in the 1924 election. Along with the American Federation of Labor (AFL) and various railroad brotherhoods, the party backed the Progressive Party candidate, Senator Robert La Follette of Wisconsin, who received 17 percent of the total popular vote and thirteen electoral votes.

By 1928, the Socialist Party revived enough to run Norman Thomas as a candidate for president. With only 266,000 popular votes (0.7 percent), Thomas finished a distant third to the major party candidates, Republican Herbert Hoover and Democrat Al Smith. Thomas, who had opposed America's entry into World War I and later established the American Civil Liberties Union (ACLU), represented the Socialists on the presidential ballot five more times and, after Debs's death in 1926, took over leadership of the party.

With the failure of capitalism manifest in the stock market crash in October 1929, many people looked to the Left for solutions to the nation's woes. Both the Socialist and Communist parties experienced something of a revival in the 1930s, only to see their resurgence thwarted by the Cold War.

Rebecca Tolley-Stokes

See also: Communist Party; Labor Movement; Red Scare of 1917–1920; *Schenck v. United States* (1919).

Further Reading

Dick, William M. *Labor and Socialism in America: The Gompers Era.* Port Washington, NY: Kennikat, 1972.

Egbert, Donald Drew, and Stow Persons, eds. *Socialism and American Life.* Vol. 1. Princeton, NJ: Princeton University Press, 1952.

Lipset, Seymour Martin, and Gary Wolfe Marks. *It Didn't Happen Here: Why Socialism Failed in the United States.* New York: W.W. Norton, 2000.

Speakeasies

Speakeasies were illicit drinking establishments that first appeared during Prohibition (1920–1933). They were for many Americans a way to circumvent the Eighteenth Amendment to the U.S. Constitution, which outlawed the manufacture, sale, and transport of alcoholic beverages in the United States. Born in secrecy but flocked to in droves, thousands of speakeasies were established across the country to replace padlocked saloons. Their popularity peaked in the mid-1920s, by which time they had effectively displaced the existing network of saloons, taverns, and traditional clubs and offered in their place expensive liquor, nightclub acts, and jazz.

The speakeasy derived its name from the need to whisper, or "speak easy," as patrons slipped in and out of the illegal drinking establishment. Slang terms for speakeasies included "Blind Pig" and "Blind Tiger." At Prohibition's peak, Americans could find liquor and entertainment in as many as 500,000 speakeasies across the country. By 1925, it was estimated that 100,000 speakeasies were operating in New York City alone—about twice the number of saloons in business before 1919; the number dropped to just 9,000 speakeasies by 1933.

Speakeasies differed noticeably from saloons. They were usually hidden in back rooms, basements, or out-of-the-way places; entry was gained using a secret knock, password, or handshake. While some may have originated as havens for the working class, the cost of bootleg liquor became too expensive and the nightclub atmosphere too elaborate to allow the patronage of poorer customers. Speakeasies quickly became retreats for the middle and upper classes.

As the operators of illegal establishments, owners of speakeasies lived in fear of holdups, police raids, or loss of business due to closure. Speakeasies were also expensive to maintain, as it was not uncommon for law enforcement officials and their friends to drink for free, or to demand protection money to look the other way or in exchange for tip-offs about raids. Police raids were nevertheless commonplace, necessitating the creation of elaborate "security measures," including systems of drop-shelves, secret compartments, and false fronts that could be enacted at a moment's notice. Speakeasies also became the domain for organized crime. It was estimated that Al Capone's bootlegging cartel had a hand in every one of Chicago's 10,000 speakeasies. Mob-controlled liquor and gangster-owned speakeasies ruled major cities and fueled a plush nightlife culture.

Speakeasies proliferated in major cities where there were also endless supplies of musicians and entertainers looking for work. Competition among speakeasies contributed to a booming entertainment industry, and the establishments offered extravagant floor shows, cabaret singers, vaudeville acts, popular stars, and jazz. In New York, Fred and Adele Astaire entertained at the Trocadero, while Duke Ellington fronted the house band at the Cotton Club. The high-flying, musically charged speakeasy culture that quickly took root not only solidified the 1920s as the Jazz Age but contributed significantly to the development of jazz in general.

Studies of gender and Prohibition have addressed the role of speakeasies in a socially diverse drinking culture, as well as the importance of speakeasies in the creation of a new entertainment atmosphere that broke down racial, gender, and sexual barriers. Speakeasies generated a cultural ethos that was inclusive of African Americans and the white middle class, men and women, heterosexuals and homosexuals alike.

Although speakeasies came out of hiding after Prohibition's repeal, they could not survive the Great Depression. Many closed due to a lack of customers and the failure of speakeasies to take root as a middle-class custom. When alcohol became legal again, most people preferred to drink at neighborhood bars or more upscale cocktail lounges.

Matthew K. McKean

See also: Capone, Al; Crime, Organized; Ness, Eliot; Prohibition (1920–1933); Schultz, Dutch; Volstead Act (1919).

Further Reading

Powers, Madelon. *Faces Along the Bar: Lore and Order in the Workingman's Saloon, 1870–1920.* Chicago: University of Chicago Press, 1998.

Sinclair, Andrew. *Prohibition: The Era of Excess.* London: Faber and Faber, 1962.

Thornton, Mark. *The Economics of Prohibition.* Salt Lake City: University of Utah Press, 1991.

Walker, Stanley. *The Nightclub Era.* Baltimore: Johns Hopkins University Press, 1999.

Steel Strike of 1919–1920

When the national steel strike began in September 1919, several hundred thousand workers at U.S. Steel and other companies walked off their jobs over working conditions, hours, and wages. The strike continued through early January 1920 and ended in failure, as the workers won no concessions from the steel companies. For the leaders of the Amalgamated Association of Iron, Steel, and Tin Workers—usually referred to as the Amalgamated Association (AA)—who organized the strike, it was a major setback, as steel industry leaders refused to recognize the AA's right to collectively bargain for the workers. Most historians agree that the collapse of the strike set back the process of organizing the steel industry for nearly a generation.

The strike was foreshadowed by another major walkout in the industry, the Homestead Strike of 1892, named after the steel-making center in Pennsylvania where Carnegie Steel's main plant was located. That strike was also called in protest over wages, hours, working conditions, and union recognition. After much violence, the strike—also organized

A union leader speaks to striking steel workers in Gary, Indiana, in 1919. The national walkout in the steel industry was just one, albeit the largest, of thousands of labor actions in the period following World War I. *(Library of Congress, LC-USZ62–77539)*

by the AA—was broken by the company, backed by private security forces and the Pennsylvania state militia. Nine years later, the AA struck again, this time against the newly organized U.S. Steel, the nation's first billion-dollar corporation. While less violent, this strike also proved a failure, and the AA was left a shell of its former self through World War I.

Conditions remained appalling in many of the plants. The working environment was dangerous, and workers often put in twelve-hour days, six days a week. Many of them were recent immigrants desperate for work, and they were paid very low wages. An average steelworker earned about $2 a day in the early twentieth century, not enough to keep a family out of poverty. And conditions got worse during World War I. While there was plenty of work, and wages rose modestly, wartime inflation cut into earnings, leaving most workers with less money at the end of the war than at its beginning. Meanwhile, U.S. government and overseas contracts filled steel company coffers with record revenues and profits.

While abstaining from striking during the war, the American Federation of Labor (AFL), of which the AA was a member union, began to make plans for organizing the steel industry. Aside from industry resistance and workers fearing for their jobs, there was the problem of jurisdiction. The AFL was composed of craft unions, representing particularly trades, and no less than twenty-four member unions of the AFL

claimed jurisdiction over steel industry workers. To overcome this problem, fifteen of the unions met in Chicago in August 1918 to coordinate their organizing efforts by setting up the National Committee for Organizing Iron and Steel Workers.

The efforts to organize steel workers shortly after the armistice in November 1918 met with stiff resistance from both the steel industry and local officials, who cited health violations as an excuse to shut down meeting halls. Agents from the Pinkerton security firm, contracted by the steel industry, threatened organizers with violence. In May 1919, the AFL held another organizing conference, in Pittsburgh, but decided the time was not ripe for a strike. However, when the chair of U.S. Steel, Elbert H. Gary, refused to meet with union representatives in June to discuss wages and working conditions, the National Committee circulated a ballot among the workers in August on whether they should call a strike, set for September 22. No less than 98 percent of workers voted in favor.

With the threat of a strike as a bargaining tool, union leaders went back to Gary, who again refused to meet with them. The union leaders then turned to President Woodrow Wilson, asking him to organize a national conference between industry and union officials. But Wilson, caught up that summer in his efforts to win Senate ratification of the Treaty of Versailles and U.S. membership in the League of Nations, was distracted.

Much had changed since the National Committee was first formed in the summer of 1918. The country was now in the grip of the Red Scare, a fear of anarchist, Communist, or otherwise radical subversion of American institutions. In 1917, Communists had seized the government in Russia through revolution, and a series of revolutions rolled through postwar Europe. A wave of strikes had hit industries throughout America, including Pennsylvania's coal industry in April. A general strike in February had shut down the entire city of Seattle.

The steel industry, backed by Pinkerton agents, took advantage of the general fear. They exposed National Committee Chair William Foster's past association with anarchists and the radical Industrial Workers of the World. Reports circulated in the press about the influence of radical foreigners among the workers and union organizers, this at a time of rising nativist hostility to immigration.

Then, when several hundred thousand workers walked off their jobs on September 22—estimates range from 250,000 to 365,000—government officials responded with force. Mass meetings were usually prohibited in strike areas, which included not only the Pittsburgh area but also Youngstown, Ohio; Wheeling, West Virginia; Lackawanna, New York; and as far west as Pueblo, Colorado. When strikers clashed with police, martial law was sometimes declared, making even small meetings and picket lines illegal. Strikebreakers, many of them African Americans and Mexican Americans, were brought in to keep the mills running. Steel executives knew that racial prejudice and language differences would prevent alliances between strikers and strikebreakers. The steel industry, working with the local press, often spread rumors that the strike had collapsed in other cities.

Within a few weeks, the steel industry and government assault began to take its toll. Tens of thousands of workers began to cross picket lines in October and November. By the end of the year, even union leaders recognized the strike was failing and, on January 8, the AA told the National Committee to call off the strike. The committee refused, but few listened to it. By January 20, even the committee recognized the futility of going on and issued the end-of-strike order.

The impact of the strike on organizing in the industry could not have been worse. Although wages remained low and workweeks long, the AA faded into insignificance. By 1930, it had fewer than 10,000 members nationwide and would play virtually no role in the wave of successful organizing that swept the industry in the late 1930s.

James Ciment and Leigh Kimmel

See also: American Federation of Labor; Gary, Elbert H.; Labor Movement; Red Scare of 1917–1920.

Further Reading

Brody, David. *Steelworkers in America: The Nonunion Era.* Cambridge, MA: Harvard University Press, 1960.

Eggert, Gerald G. *Steelmasters and Labor Reform, 1886–1923.* Pittsburgh: University of Pittsburgh Press, 1981.

Warren, Kenneth. *Big Steel: The First Century of the United States Steel Corporation, 1901–2001.* Pittsburgh: University of Pittsburgh Press, 2001.

Stein, Gertrude (1874–1946)

A writer of complex and abstract prose during the 1920s, Gertrude Stein is perhaps best known for helping to nurture the "Lost Generation" of expatriate American writers, such as Ernest Hemingway, Ezra Pound, and F. Scott Fitzgerald, many of whom

A writer, art collector, and patron of the American expatriate artistic and literary community in Paris during the 1920s—which she dubbed the "Lost Generation"—Gertrude Stein hosted regular salons at her apartment on the rue de Fleurus. *(Keystone/Stringer/Hulton Archive/Getty Images)*

attended the weekly salons she hosted at her apartment at 27 rue de Fleurus in Paris. Stein was also well known for her long-term relationship with critic and editor Alice B. Toklas, from whose point of view Stein tells her own autobiography in her best-known work, *The Autobiography of Alice B. Toklas* (1933).

Stein was born on February 3, 1874, in Allegheny, Pennsylvania. Her parents were prosperous and well-educated German Jewish immigrants, and she grew up in Oakland, California, and in Europe, where her family spent long vacations. Stein attended Radcliffe College, studying under the philosopher and psychologist William James. After graduating in 1897, she studied marine biology and then attended the Johns Hopkins University medical school in 1900 and 1901, though she did not stay long enough to get her degree.

Increasingly interested in the arts, Stein moved to Paris in 1902, sharing an apartment with her art critic brother Leo from 1903 through 1912. The Steins lived comfortably on an inheritance left them by their father. Together, the two befriended early modernist artists, such as Henri Matisse and Pablo Picasso, who were making a name for themselves in Paris, then the center of the art world.

The Steins' Saturday night salons drew many of the city's best-known painters and writers, drawn not just by the siblings' hospitality but also by their perceptive critique of trends in the arts and literature of the day. When Stein met Toklas in 1907, the two quickly fell in love, and Toklas moved in with Stein and her brother in 1910. Stein and Toklas would remain lifelong partners.

Stein launched a prolific writing career during this period, beginning with *Three Lives* in 1913 and *Tender Buttons* in 1914. Captivated by cubist painting, in which images were represented from multiple perspectives simultaneously, Stein tried to convey stories from various angles. But multiple perspectives, critics noted, better suited the visual arts, and her work was largely dismissed as too abstract and even incomprehensible.

At the onset of World War I, Stein and Toklas moved to England and then the Spanish island of Majorca. With the threat of a German occupation of Paris receding, the couple moved back to the French capital in 1916, where they engaged in volunteer work, driving supplies to military hospitals.

Once the war ended, Paris again became the European destination of choice for many American artists and writers, lured by the rich culture and the inexpensive cost of living. Many of these Americans were in self-imposed exile from a culture they considered banal and frivolous. What united them, in Stein's mind, was their sense of alienation and disillusionment, having been witnesses to the pointless carnage of World War I. Stein dubbed them the "Lost Generation," a term that historians and critics continue to use to describe the talented cadre of American writers who came of age during World War I and worked in Europe when the war was over.

Stein continued to develop her literary theories, exploring how language can form landscapes of the mind. In what she called her "landscape plays," Stein said she was attempting to write theatrical pieces that had the stasis of a landscape painting, full of pastoral and animal imagery. In 1927, she teamed with composer Virgil Thompson to write her first opera libretto, *Four Saints in Three Acts,* a modernist effort that eschewed conventional narrative for an exploration of how language can convey complex reality through the sounds of words. The piece proved popular with critics

and audiences when it opened with an all-black cast on Broadway in 1934.

While Stein never won the following or literary renown of the writers she gathered at her salons, by the end of the 1920s, she had cemented her reputation as an innovative modernist, more appreciated by fellow writers for her experimentations in abstract prose than by a general public who could not make sense of what she was trying to say. That would change with the publication of *The Autobiography of Alice B. Toklas* (1933), a biography of Stein that Stein told from Toklas's perspective. Far more accessible than her other work, it became a best seller and propelled Stein to widespread fame. In 1934, she went on a well-attended lecture tour in the United States.

Stein continued to write and live in Paris during the late 1930s. And although both she and Toklas were Jews, the two remained in France during the German occupation of World War II, escaping persecution by living in the countryside. In 1945, Stein published *Wars I Have Seen,* her memoir of the war years. She died from cancer on July 27, 1946.

Beth Kattelman and James Ciment

See also: Art, Fine; Fiction; Hemingway, Ernest; Lost Generation; Poetry.

Further Reading

Souhami, Diana. *Gertrude and Alice.* London: Phoenix, 1991.
Stendahl, Renate, ed. *Gertrude Stein in Words and Pictures.* Chapel Hill, NC: Algonquin, 1994.

Stock Market

Perhaps nothing better symbolizes the economy of the United States during the Jazz Age than the click of the ticker tape printing out the dizzying rise of share prices for thousands of stock speculators across the country. Then suddenly, in late October 1929, the message became unrelentingly bleak. As share prices plummeted through a series of trading sessions, investors lost billions.

By twenty-first-century standards, the percentage of Americans investing in Wall Street in the 1920s was small, less than 1 percent of the population. Nevertheless, the hundreds of thousands who did invest in stocks represented a democratization of the securities industry that was unprecedented—and not repeated again until the 1960s.

Stocks did extraordinarily well through much of the 1920s. The Dow Jones Industrial Average—a measure of the securities industry based on the performance of selected "blue chip" stocks, representing established companies with stable earnings—had held steady around the 100 mark from the early 1900s through the end of World War I, but it rose to more than 200 in 1927 and nearly 450 by the summer of 1929. Whether these gains reflected genuine growth in the American economy is still a subject of debate among economic historians.

Solid Boom: 1924–1927

Most scholars agree that the gains made on Wall Street in the middle years of the 1920s were based on solid performance. The American economy was certainly buoyant in this period. After a few troubled years at the beginning of the decade, marked by an awkward transition from a wartime to a peacetime economy and a brief but sharp recession from late 1920 to early 1922, the American economy performed well. Unemployment remained low, and inflation was almost nonexistent. This happy combination of circumstances was the result of dramatic gains in productivity, made possible by new technology and more efficient management. As wages for the mass of unskilled laborers remaining stagnant, the productivity gains largely accrued to corporations, which saw their profits skyrocket. With share prices undervalued through the early 1920s, it was only natural that—with productivity and profits steadily rising—stocks would perform well.

But there were signs of trouble. While workers were buying many of the new consumer items made available through mass production, they were often going into debt to pay for them. Moreover, broad sectors of the American economy were performing quite poorly, including textiles, coal, and most notably agriculture, which never recovered from its post–World War I slump. As rural and working-class incomes remained stagnant, those of white-collar and skilled workers rose steadily. More dramatic was the vast increase in income and wealth among the economic elite. While the growing inequality in income would foster one of the long-term strains that contributed to the onset of the Great Depression in the early 1930s, the immediate effect was a mass investment in securities, as wealthy and many middle-income Americans sought a place to put their new earnings.

Speculative Boom: 1928–1929

Economic historians point to a subtle shift on Wall Street in late 1927 and early 1928, as investors began to put their money into companies that were not necessarily performing well in the real economy. Their earnings-to-assets ratios were not particularly favorable. Many of the companies had not paid dividends (a share of profits distributed to stockholders) in years, yet they remained popular among investors. As the price of their stocks rose, new investors were drawn in, regardless of the companies' profitability.

Adding to the buoyancy of stock prices was the newly popular practice of margin buying. Investors used their own money to purchase a percentage of a share's value, while the rest of the purchase price was borrowed, usually from the broker through which the stock was purchased, using the equity inherent in the stock shares as collateral. The brokers in turn borrowed the money for these loans from banks, both domestic and foreign, which were eager to cash in on the stock market boom.

Margin buying relies on several factors. One is steadily rising stock prices that create the equity the investor uses to borrow the money to buy the stock in the first place. The second factor is low interest rates, which make paying back loans affordable. Here the still new Federal Reserve Board obliged, keeping the discount rate (on money lent to bankers) very low. Economic historians cite the Federal Reserve Board's interest rate policies of the late 1920s as one of the main contributors to the spectacular gain in stock prices of the period. A final contributing factor was a lack of regulation. No laws prevented bankers from investing in securities, and there were virtually no controls on margin buying or broker's loans. Regulation or prohibition of these practices would only come after the great crash of 1929 and the advent of the Securities and Exchange Commission in 1934.

All of these factors contributed to a boom market of proportions never before seen on Wall Street. Following a dip of just over 10 percent in June 1928, the Dow Jones average began its spectacular rise. Brokers' loans increased about 50 percent between that month and June of the following year, to roughly $5 billion. At the end of June 1928, the Dow stood at about 200; on the last day of the year, it hit 300. Contributing to the gain was the election of Republican Herbert Hoover as president. Although he was wary of the stock speculation, Hoover was seen as the consummate businessman, and his elevation to the White House seemed to promise continuing economic prosperity.

Crowds of investors, brokers, and onlookers stand along Wall Street in Lower Manhattan, awaiting the latest news of the stock market crash of 1929. The dramatic plunge in the Dow Jones Industrial Average ended a near decade-long surge in share prices. *(Fox Photos/Stringer/Hulton Archive/Getty Images)*

Crash of 1929

The American economy had been weakening since 1927, as consumers began to cut back on purchases and merchants' inventories steadily rose, reducing orders to manufacturers, which drove up unemployment. Meanwhile, construction, one of the engines of the mid-1920s economy, was in decline. None of this seemed to matter to investors, however, who drove the Dow to 400 in June 1929 and 450 by August.

The press contributed to the euphoria, printing a stream of articles by supposed insiders and experts prophesizing an endless boom market and offering tips on how and where to invest. Regional stock markets sprang up around the country to cash in on the boom, and the number of new and existing companies making public offerings soared. Soaring stock prices drew in more and more investors, making even questionable companies' stocks perform well. By the summer of 1929, when the bull market was at its height, roughly 1 million Americans had money in stocks.

But with little regulation, vast amounts of money being borrowed for margin buying, and the underlying weaknesses in the real economy, the paper economy of Wall Street was a house of cards. In September 1929, it witnessed its first decline, followed by a ragged recovery through the middle of October. Then, on October 18, 1929, it began to fall again; the Dow dropped seven points that day. More worrisome was the sudden drop in share values for the highest-flying companies, in-cluding General Electric, Westinghouse, and Montgomery Ward. The following day, a Friday, was the heaviest trading day in the New York Stock Exchange's history, as stock prices fell steadily.

Over the weekend, *The New York Times* featured front-page stories on the new bear market. Still, stock prices held through Wednesday, October 23, when the Dow fell by 7.5 percent in one day, from 415 to 384. In a mere four hours, a share of Westinghouse fell by 25 points and a share of General Electric dropped 20 points, yielding a nearly $5 billion loss in paper assets. So heavy was trading that day—roughly 13 million shares—that the ticker fell behind by two hours in recording the losses.

The crash continued the following week. General Electric lost another 48 points and Westinghouse another 34 points on Monday alone. By the end of 1929, the Dow had lost all of the gains it had made since the beginning of the bull market in June 1928. In October, total U.S. stock values fell from $87 billion to $55 billion. The equity investors had used as collateral to borrow money in the first place quickly disappeared, and brokers called in their loans from investors. When the latter could not pay them, the brokerage houses found themselves unable to pay back the loans extended to them by the banks. By the time it hit bottom—just over 41 points in mid-1932—the Dow Jones Industrial Average had lost roughly 90 percent of its value. Not until 1954 would it reach its peak of October 1929.

Most economists agree that the stock market crash alone did not plunge the American economy into the Great Depression of the 1930s. Rather, the Depression stemmed from the same underlying weaknesses—inequality in wealth, stagnant wages, rising debt, and weak industrial and agricultural sectors of the economy—that caused the market to plunge in the first place. In other words, the great stock market crash of 1929 seems to have been more an omen of bad economic times than a cause of them.

James Ciment and Steven Koczak

See also: Credit and Debt, Consumer; General Electric; Kennedy, Joseph; Wealth and Income.

Further Reading

Galbraith, John Kenneth. *The Great Crash, 1929.* 1954 Boston: Houghton Mifflin, 1988.

Goldberg, David J. *Discontented America: The United States in the 1920s.* Baltimore: Johns Hopkins University Press, 1999.

Sobel, Robert. *The Great Bull Market: Wall Street in the 1920s.* New York: W.W. Norton, 1968.

Strong, Benjamin, Jr. (1872–1928)

The first governor of the Federal Reserve Bank of New York, from its formation in 1914 until his death in 1928, Benjamin Strong, Jr., exerted enormous influence on U.S. monetary policy during the Jazz Age. As head of the most powerful bank in the Federal Reserve System, he also helped establish the institution's independence from the Treasury Department and insulated it from White House pressure, traditions that would continue largely intact into the early twenty-first century.

Strong was born in Fishkill-on-Hudson, New York, in 1872 and began his banking career shortly after high school in 1891, rapidly rising up the ranks at several different companies. In 1907, as a financial analyst for Bankers Trust Company, one of Wall Street's largest trust firms, or investment banks, Strong was part of a team of investigators assembled by banker J.P. Morgan to look into the causes of the financial panic of 1907. Two years later, Strong was promoted to vice president of the company. Five years after that, he became its president, but not for long. In October of that year, he resigned the lucrative position to become the first governor of the newly created Federal Reserve Bank of New York.

The Federal Reserve Act, signed into law by President Woodrow Wilson in December 1913, established the Federal Reserve System to address the very problem that Strong had investigated in 1907. The national banking system was prone to panics because each bank set its own rules for the quantity of deposits to keep in reserve. Moreover, there was no central bank to provide loans to failing institutions. When a run on the deposits of one institution started, it often spread to other banks, setting off a financial panic that could plunge the economy into depression.

Many financial experts agreed that America needed a central bank, much like many European countries had, to set monetary policy as well as to be a lender of last resort. But there was much resistance to this idea. Some populists believed that a central bank would serve the interests of Wall Street, maintaining a tight monetary policy that kept interest rates up and the cost of loans high, thereby hurting farmers who were often in debt. If there was to be a central bank, they wanted it controlled by Congress, so that the people could have a voice in its decisions.

The financial community, which wielded great influence in the Republican Party and the conservative wing of the Democratic Party, feared that too much political interference would hurt their interests and that setting a loose monetary policy could lead to inflation and other economic problems.

The Federal Reserve System, then, was a compromise. It consisted of a seven-member Board of Governors, appointed by the president and confirmed by Congress for fourteen-year terms, as well as twelve regional Reserve Banks that were controlled largely by member banks, major private banks that owned stock in the Reserve Banks. (Another component of the Federal Reserve is the Federal Open Market Committee, responsible for buying and selling government securities.) Together, the Board of Governors and Reserve Banks regulate the flow of money in the economy by setting the interest rates with which they loan money to member banks.

Traditionally, as head of the Reserve Bank in the nation's financial capital, the governor of the Federal Reserve Bank of New York served as de facto head of the Reserve Bank component of the Federal Reserve System. Moreover, in the pre–New Deal era, the Reserve Banks had more influence over monetary policy than the Board of Governors. That would change in the wake of the Great Depression as there were calls for more government regulation of the economy.

When Strong took over as New York Reserve Bank governor, he was taking charge of a new quasi-governmental financial institution with potentially enormous power over monetary policy and hence the economy. Traditionally, central bankers had practiced passive monetary policy. With the national currency backed by gold, the central banks kept enough gold to cover currency deposits, thereby maintaining the currency's value. But in the financial maelstrom caused by World War I, countries went deeply into debt. As their currencies collapsed, people bought U.S. dollars, flooding the United States with gold by the end of World War I. Strong therefore had to adopt a more activist monetary policy, both at home and, as the United States was the world's largest creditor nation by 1918, abroad as well.

Strong set three major objectives for the Federal Reserve during his tenure: promoting price stability and stable business growth; curbing excessive use of credit for stock market speculation; and assisting in reconstruction of war-torn economies in Europe. To achieve these ends, he instituted a new and untried central bank policy of buying and selling government securities specifically for the purpose of regulating credit conditions. By selling government securities, or bonds, Strong could contract the money supply by soaking up excess funds in the economy; by buying back securities, he could pump more money into the economy. By regulating the money supply, he could determine interest rates, inflation, and the overall growth of the economy.

Despite this activist role, Strong believed that it would be better for the world's economies if they returned to the gold standard, which would establish monetary stability again. Britain, he felt, would have to move first, as that country remained the financial leader in Europe and so could influence other economies. To that end, he worked closely with Bank of England head Montague Norman after the war. During the early 1920s, Strong provided hundreds of millions of dollars in gold credits to Britain, which returned to the gold standard in 1925.

By the time of his death in October 1928, Strong had established the independence of the Federal Reserve through the principle of an active monetary policy, the terms of which were set by the Reserve Banks and the Board of Governors. With this active monetary policy, he laid the foundations for the decisive role of the Federal Reserve in the nation's economy.

James Ciment

See also: Credit and Debt, Consumer; Economic Policy.

Further Reading

Burgess, W. Randolph. *Interpretations of Federal Reserve Policy in the Speeches and Writings of Benjamin Strong.* New York: Harper & Brothers, 1930.

Chandler, Lester V. *Benjamin Strong, Central Banker.* Washington, DC: Brookings Institution, 1958.

Meltzer, Allan H. *A History of the Federal Reserve.* Vol. 1. Chicago: University of Chicago Press, 2003.

Wueschner, Sylvano A. *Changing Twentieth Century Monetary Policy: Herbert Hoover and Benjamin Strong, 1917–1927.* Westport, CT: Greenwood, 1999.

Suburbs

Suburbs are generally defined as communities surrounding urban cores where there is significant political, economic, social, and cultural interaction with city life. Suburbs in America arose with the expansion of the nation's cities in the middle and late decades of the nineteenth century, and they spread with the development of new transportation technologies. In the nineteenth and early twentieth centuries, that meant streetcars and suburban trains. In the Jazz Age, suburbs would become major population centers, largely the result of one new transportation technology—the automobile.

The demographics of suburban growth in the 1920s were nothing short of astonishing. In 1920, just over 46 million Americans lived in what the U.S. Census Bureau called standard metropolitan areas (SMAs), that is, central cities and a ring of suburbs around them. By 1930, that number had increased to 61 million, a roughly one-third increase; about 70 percent of that increase was accounted for by the suburbs. During the same period, America as a whole grew by about 15 percent, from roughly 106 million to 118 million.

The expansion of the suburbs was widespread, though it was particularly notable in the industrial areas of the Midwest. Garfield Heights and Shaker Heights around Cleveland grew by about 500 and 1,000 percent, respectively, between 1920 and 1930. Ferndale and Gross Pointe Park near Detroit grew by roughly 700 percent each. Park Ridge and Elmwood Park in the Chicago area expanded by some 200 and 700 percent, respectively.

One city that symbolized the rapid suburban growth of the 1920s was Los Angeles. Almost unique among big cities of the day, Los Angeles was largely a collection of suburbs. From 1920 to 1930, the Southern California metropolis saw its population climb from about 576,673 to 1,238,048—a roughly 115 percent increase—though this included numbers brought in through territorial acquisition. Individual suburbs in the Los Angeles area also saw rapid growth: Glendale at 363 percent, Inglewood at 493 percent, and Beverly Hills at an astonishing 2,485 percent, the ranks of that upscale city bolstered by members of the growing film community.

A number of factors—economic, political, and social—contributed to this rapid growth. Few members of the working class could afford a home in the suburbs in the 1920s. While banks were expanding the practice of mortgage lending, they still required large down payments of 50 percent or more, and the length of the mortgage was usually five or ten years, putting monthly payments beyond the reach of all but the highest-paid skilled workers. But the decade's prosperity allowed more middle-class Americans, especially those in the expanding ranks of corporate management, to afford a home in the suburbs. In addition, many in the largely native-born, white middle classes were eager to escape the overcrowded cities full of immigrants. The 1920s was a period in which the foreign-born population of American cities peaked, with New York, Chicago, Detroit, Cleveland, and Boston all recording roughly one-third of their residents as foreign born. This huge influx of immigrants produced a nativist backlash, evidenced not only in restrictive immigration laws but also in middle-class flight from U.S. cities.

Suburbanization in the 1920s did not involve just changes in residential patterns. The expansion of the electrical and communications grid allowed factories and businesses to move away from the commercial and industrial hubs within major cities. In 1919, roughly 85 percent of manufacturing output in America came out of just eleven major cities. By the early 1930s, that figure had dropped to just over 60 percent. Meanwhile, the number of workers in those cities fell from just over 2 million to under 1.9 million, while the number in those cities' outlying areas climbed from just above 365,000 to more than 1.2 million.

Although power sources were vital to that expansion, the key to the growth of suburbs in the 1920s was the spread of vehicles with internal combustion engines. Trucks allowed businesses and factories to move away from rail lines and city transportation hubs. Between 1919 and 1929, the number of registered trucks on American roads jumped from just under 800,000 to nearly 3.4 million. The growth in the number of cars on the road—from just over 6.5 million in 1919 to nearly 28 million in 1929—had a similar effect on the rise of residential suburbs, which could now expand beyond streetcar lines.

The government contributed to this growth by dramatically increasing the amount of money available for highway construction. The 1921 Federal Highway Act offered an unprecedented $75 million in matching funds to states for road construction. While much of the money was designated for intercity highway construction, the same roads could also be used by commuters. Meanwhile, the 1920s also witnessed the first construction of limited-access roads, providing for faster commuting times from the suburbs to urban cores. New York City pioneered this development with the Bronx River Parkway, opened in 1923, and the Saw Mill River Parkway, inaugurated six years later.

Suburban growth would slow in the 1930s and the early 1940s, as the Great Depression and World War II undermined the economics of building and buying homes. Fewer Americans could afford home ownership in the former period, and few resources were available for construction in the latter. It would not be until the late 1940s that the great postwar exodus of residents and businesses from cities to suburbs would commence. While suburban growth in the 1920s paled in comparison to growth in that later era, it nevertheless provided a prototype of what was to come.

James Ciment

See also: Appliances, Household; Automobiles and Automobile Culture; Housing; Marriage, Divorce, and Family; Population and Demographics.

Further Reading

Hayden, Dolores. *Building Suburbia: Green Fields and Urban Growth, 1820–2000.* New York: Pantheon, 2003.

Jackson, Kenneth T. *Crabgrass Frontier: The Suburbanization of the United States.* New York: Oxford University Press, 1985.

Lewis, Robert. "Running Rings Around the City: North American Industrial Suburbs, 1850–1950." In *Changing Suburbs: Foundation, Form, and Function,* ed. Richard Harris and Peter J. Markham. London: E & FN Spon, 1999.

Swanson, Gloria (1898–1983)

The film actress Gloria Swanson, the epitome of Hollywood glamour in the silent film era, will forever be linked with the character of Norma Desmond, the faded star she played in *Sunset Boulevard* (1950). Although the two women share biographical similarities—both were flamboyant, often-divorced, highly paid actresses of the silent screen era who became famous under the tutelage of director Cecil B. DeMille—Swanson did not suffer the grim decline played out by Desmond.

Gloria May Josephine Svensson was born in Chicago on March 27, 1898. Her father, a civilian, worked for the U.S. Army transport service. The family moved around during her childhood, living in Puerto Rico and Florida before settling back in Chicago. As a girl, Gloria loved to perform and wear beautiful clothes, and a visit to the Chicago branch of the Essanay movie studio when she was fifteen sparked a desire to break into show business. She made her film debut in 1914 as an extra at Essanay, where she met actor Wallace Beery, soon to become the first of her six husbands.

Beery persuaded her to move to Los Angeles, the new home of the movie industry. By then, she had adopted the name Swanson. In Hollywood, she won lead roles in Mack Sennett's slapstick comedies, such as *The Ambition of the Baron* (1915), *The Fable of Elvira and Farina and the Meal Ticket* (1915), and *Teddy at the Throttle* (1917), all shorts. Longing for dramatic, serious parts, she moved to Triangle Studios and made the melodramas *Her Decision* (1918), *The Secret Code* (1918), and *Shifting Sands* (1918), all full-length features.

Swanson's big break came in 1919, when she linked up with the Paramount Studios unit of the powerful director-producer Cecil B. DeMille, who made her a star by playing up her glamour and draping her in beautiful costumes. She was only in her early twenties, but she was convincing in roles as older and more sophisticated women. The films she made for DeMille, such as *Male and Female* (1919), *Don't Change Your Husband* (1919), and *The Affairs of Anatol* (1921), were Jazz Age sexual adventures in the guise of morality tales. Now a celebrity, Swanson became a favorite of the fan magazines, who followed her every move and recorded her purchases of furs, homes, and cars.

At Paramount, whose house style of sophistication Swanson helped to mold, she worked in prestige pictures opposite such stars as Rudolph Valentino and for such leading directors as Allan Dwan and Sam Wood. She was often cast as an upper-class woman contemplating adultery. During this period, she starred in *The Great Moment* (1921), *Under the Lash* (1921), *Don't Tell Everything* (1921), *Her Husband's Trademark* (1922), *Beyond the Rocks* (1922), *Her Gilded Cage* (1922), *My American Wife* (1922), and *Bluebeard's Eighth Wife* (1923). In 1924, Swanson went to Paris to make *Madame Sans-Gêne* and came home with a third husband, the Marquis de la Falaise. As the newlyweds traveled from Hollywood to New York, they were met by crowds of screaming fans and studio photographers at each train stop. Swanson had arranged for the photographers, but the fans had come on their own.

In 1927, Paramount offered her $17,500 a week to remain with the studio, but Swanson decided to produce her own star vehicles, releasing them through United Artists, as Mary Pickford, Douglas Fairbanks, and Charlie Chaplin were doing. She soon realized, however, that having complete control also meant having full responsibility. Her first release under the Swanson Producing Corporation banner, *The Love of Sunya* (1927), went well over budget—partly because of the generous salary Swanson gave herself—and failed at the box office. Her second film, *Sadie Thompson* (1928), adapted from a Somerset Maugham story and directed by Raoul Walsh, was more successful.

Although the risqué film ran into trouble with censors, it made a healthy profit and netted Swanson her first Academy Award nomination for best actress.

Her next project, however, nearly broke her. *Queen Kelly* (1928), which Swanson produced with her rumored lover Joseph P. Kennedy (father of the future president John F. Kennedy), fell victim to the perfectionism and lavish spending of its director, Erich von Stroheim. Swanson had to shut down production, and the film was never released (though footage would later be incorporated into *Sunset Boulevard*). Her next film, *The Trespasser* (1930), a sound film, earned her another best actress nomination. It was hardly the box office powerhouse of her earlier efforts, however, as tastes in movies had changed. Lavish, mannered, larger-than-life screen personas like Swanson's had begun to fall out of favor with Depression-era audiences, who preferred more naturalistic acting styles. In 1934 Swanson sang and danced her way through MGM's *Music in the Air*, then went into semiretirement.

After a half-hearted comeback in *Father Takes a Wife* (1941), she stayed out of the limelight for almost a decade. When Mae West and Mary Pickford turned down the lead role in *Sunset Boulevard*, Swanson saw an opportunity to get back on top. Her portrayal of a deluded, forgotten star was Swanson's last great role, but she hardly disappeared from public view and never fell victim to the nostalgia, self-pity, and despair of the character Norma Desmond. Indeed, Swanson went on to a highly visible career guest starring on television, often poking good-natured fun at her own silent films, ostentatious costumes, and dimmed celebrity.

Appearing on Broadway, promoting her own line of cosmetics, and consulting in the fashion industry, she was far from a recluse. Her final big-screen appearance was a cameo as herself in *Airport 1975* (1974), after which she married diet author William Duffy, her sixth and final husband. Her autobiography, *Swanson on Swanson* (1980), was well reviewed and a best seller. Swanson died in her sleep on April 4, 1983, in New York City.

Tom Cerasulo

See also: Celebrity Culture; DeMille, Cecil B.; Film.

Further Reading

Hudson, Richard, and Raymond Lee. *Gloria Swanson.* New York: A.S. Barnes, 1970.

Madsen, Axel. *Gloria and Joe: The Star Crossed Love Affair of Gloria Swanson and Joe Kennedy.* New York: Arbor House, 1988.

Quirk, Lawrence. *The Films of Gloria Swanson.* New York: Citadel, 1988.

Swanson, Gloria. *Swanson on Swanson.* New York: Random House, 1980.

Swope, Gerard (1872–1957)

With astute judgment and a keen eye for solutions, Gerard Swope managed to take General Electric (GE), an unwieldy company grown too large too quickly, and restructure it into an industry leader. He believed that employee welfare and company profits were intertwined, and he established innovative incentive programs in an era when big business and labor were commonly at odds.

Gerard Swope was born on December 1, 1872, in St. Louis, Missouri, to German immigrants Isaac and Ida Swope. Interested in science and engineering at an early age, he set up a basement workshop and experimented extensively. By the age of ten, he had invented an electric cloth-cutting machine. While an engineering student at the Massachusetts Institute of Technology (MIT), he traveled to Chicago to attend the World's Fair of 1893 and was offered a summer position by General Electric in its service shops, for a dollar a day.

Swope graduated from MIT with a degree in electrical engineering in 1895, after which he worked his way up, first at Western Electric and later at GE. During the 1890s, he volunteered at Jane Addams's Hull House, a Chicago settlement house (a community service organization), where he taught mathematics and principles of electricity to immigrant men. While there, he met and married Mary Hill, with Addams performing the wedding ceremony. Eventually, the Swopes moved to St. Louis, bought two houses in a working-class neighborhood, lived in one of them, and opened a settlement house in the other. Swope's settlement house experience greatly influenced his perspective on the working class; he believed opportunity made people more productive members of society.

Swope worked for Western Electric until GE executives took notice of him and offered him the vice presidency of their foreign department. Swope, a master negotiator, countered that he wanted the presidency and free reign to choose his own staff and board of directors; he also proposed the reorganization of the foreign department into an independent organization. His requests were granted, and he took over the presidency of the newly organized International General Electric Company in 1919. Swope excelled as the head of the company, and in 1921, he was offered the presidency of Goodyear Rubber. He declined the offer, however, stating that he "knew nothing about rubber" and enjoyed his job too much to change.

By 1921, General Electric had grown quite large but was deeply in debt. The company's aging president, E.W. Rice, Jr., and its chair, Charles A. Coffin, hand-picked their successors: Swope and up-and-coming businessman Owen D. Young. On May 16, 1922, the two men took the reins of the company. Young, as chairman, dealt with policy issues, while the new president, Swope, took a hands-on approach to running the company, under the motto "Analyze, Organize, Deputize, Supervise." In accordance with this maxim, Swope spent hours analyzing every aspect of the company, reorganized its departments, deputized through delegation, and supervised every operation. He toured the factories, laboratories, offices, and distribution centers. While on site, he interacted with the factory workers—unheard of with previous presidents—gaining insight into the company's workings. Swope found the company highly fragmented and inefficient. One of the problems was that GE subsidiaries were competing with one another for the incandescent lamp market. In a sweeping reorganization, Swope brought the subsidiaries under the General Electric umbrella.

Swope's philosophy on business and labor was contrary to most business practices of the day. Obsessed with profits, most chief executive officers pushed employees beyond their limits, with little or no concern for their well-being. Swope, on the other hand, believed that well-trained workers with adequate incentives were the key to production and profit. Where other executives disdained contact with workers, Swope opened the lines of communication between labor, foremen, managers, and executives. He established company camps for employee recreation and to provide a forum for open discussion of issues. Under his leadership, GE offered employees life and health insurance, profit sharing, savings plans, mortgage assistance, and, during the Great Depression, unemployment insurance. He was instrumental in establishing a national electrical workers union affiliated with the American Federation of Labor (AFL). He founded a fund to provide educational opportunities to employees and their families, and he created the Elfun Society in 1928 to promote employee investment and community service.

Together, Swope and Young worked to change General Electric's cold, corporate image. They hired advertising executive Bruce Barton to design a marketing campaign that would promote the virtues of modernization, thereby creating an increased demand for electrical products. Barton produced the "GE: A Symbol of Service, The Initials of a Friend" campaign, designed to increase public recognition of the trademark two-letter abbreviation and to help consumers equate the company with innovation and dependability.

General Electric experienced phenomenal growth under Swope's leadership. Until 1922, the company manufactured only incandescent lamps, fans, and heavy electricity generating and transmitting equipment. Recognizing the potential of the burgeoning home consumer market, Swope encouraged product diversification, resulting in a continuous stream of home appliance innovation. He revolutionized GE's marketing, distribution, manufacturing, and transportation systems, and he established the GE Credit Corporation to help consumers finance purchases.

Swope retired from General Electric in 1940 but returned temporarily when president Charles E. Wilson took a position with the War Production Board from 1942 to 1946. Swope then resumed his active retirement. On November 20, 1957, he died of pneumonia.

Jennifer Aerts Terry

See also: General Electric; Radio Corporation of America.

Further Reading

Gorowitz, Bernard, ed. *The General Electric Story: A Heritage of Innovation, 1876–1999.* Albany, NY: Fort Orange, 2000.

Loth, David. *Swope of G.E.: The Story of Gerard Swope and General Electric in American Business.* New York: Simon & Schuster, 1958.

Reich, Leonard S. "Lighting the Path to Profit: GE's Control of the Electric Lamp Industry, 1892–1941." *Business History Review* 66 (Summer 1992): 305–33.

Schatz, Ronald W. *The Electrical Workers: A History of Labor at General Electric and Westinghouse, 1923–1960.* Chicago: University of Illinois Press, 1983.

Taft, William Howard (1857–1930)

The only person in American history to head both the executive and judicial branches of the federal government, William Howard Taft served as the twenty-seventh president of the United States (1909–1913) and tenth chief justice of the Supreme Court (1921–1930). He presided over the Court during a period in which a conservative majority issued a number of probusiness decisions, from which he occasionally dissented.

Taft was born on September 15, 1857, in Cincinnati, Ohio, and raised there in a solidly Republican family and community. He graduated from Yale University in 1878 and earned his law degree from the Cincinnati Law School in 1880, passing the Ohio bar shortly thereafter. Active in Ohio Republican politics early on, he was appointed a superior court judge in 1887. While the appointment was to fill out a vacancy on the court, Taft won election to a full term in 1888.

Earning a reputation as both a party loyalist and a brilliant jurist, Taft soon won the attention of the national Republican Party and was appointed solicitor general of the United States in 1890. The following year, he was appointed judge on the U.S. court of Appeals for the Sixth Circuit. His many probusiness, antilabor decisions would come back to haunt him when he later sought progressives' support in his bids for the presidency in 1908 and 1912.

In 1900, President William McKinley appointed Taft head of the commission set up to decide how to govern the new U.S. colony of the Philippines. A year later, Taft was appointed governor of the islands. Taft turned down President Theodore Roosevelt's offer of a seat on the U.S. Supreme Court in 1904, saying his work in the Philippines, where the United States was then fighting a pro-independence insurgency, was not finished. He did, however, accept the position of secretary of war, believing that in this capacity he would aid in pacification efforts

there. Taft also sent troops to restore order in Cuba in 1906 and supervised early construction of the Panama Canal in 1907 and 1908.

When the popular Roosevelt stepped down from the presidency in 1908, he chose Taft as his successor, convincing progressives in the party to support Taft, although they thought he was too conservative on social and labor issues. Taft won that election but, indeed, proved too conservative and probusiness for Roosevelt over the next four years. In 1912, Roosevelt ran against Taft as a Progressive Party candidate, splitting the Republican vote and giving the presidency to Democrat Woodrow Wilson. Taft retired to Yale to teach constitutional law and served on the National War Labor Board during World War I.

In 1920, Republicans regained the White House, and with the death of Chief Justice Edward White, President Warren G. Harding appointed Taft to the Supreme Court. The Senate confirmed the appointment of the respected and experienced Taft without debate. It was the position Taft had always wanted.

An experienced administrator, Taft was disturbed to learn of the huge backlog of cases facing the Court, a problem exacerbated by the deep ideological divisions on the Court between liberals and conservatives. Arguing that justice delayed was justice denied, Taft moved to streamline the Court. His greatest legacy to the federal courts, say constitutional scholars, was modernizing how they functioned, rather than the decisions they reached during his tenure.

By 1922, he had planned the Conference of Senior Circuit Court Judges, a forum for jurists created by Congress to make policy concerning administration of the courts. Taft and the conference pushed Congress to adopt a law that permitted judges on one district court to help elsewhere if the caseload of one court was light and that of another was overburdened. It was the first step in developing coordination in the federal judiciary.

In his streamlining efforts, Taft broke the tradition of the Supreme Court that justices do not lobby for legislation; he actively lobbied Congress to pass the Judiciary Act of 1925. That law, also known as the Judges's Bill or Certiorari Act, gave the Supreme Court the discretionary power to issue a writ of certiorari to hear a case only if it so chose. The Court was now free to hear only suits raising major constitutional issues and federal problems. Limiting the right to appeal gave the Court control over its caseload.

Taft wrote nearly 250 opinions for the Court and several key dissents. While the Court as a whole proved conservative on the many business and labor cases it decided during this period, Taft's record was more balanced. In 1922, he wrote the majority opinion in *Bailey v. Drexel Furniture Company,* whereby the Court declared a state tax on child labor an unconstitutional penalty against private business. But in 1923, he dissented from the *Adkins v. Children's Hospital* decision, which declared state minimum wage laws a violation of liberty of contract.

Taft's most concrete legacy—quite literally—was his successful lobbying for a separate building for the Supreme Court. Until that time, the Court met in the old Senate chamber of the Capitol. While Taft was able to superintend the design for the building, he never saw it completed. Resigning from the Court in February 1930, he died on March 8.

James Ciment and Andrew J. Waskey

See also: *Adkins v. Children's Hospital* (1923); *Bailey v. Drexel Furniture Company* (1922); Law and the Courts; Republican Party.

Further Reading

Anderson, Judith I. *William Howard Taft: An Intimate History.* New York: W.W. Norton, 1981.
Burton, David H. *Taft, Holmes, and the 1920s Court: An Appraisal.* Cranbury, NJ: Associated University Presses, 1998.
Mason, Alpheus Thomas. *William Howard Taft: Chief Justice.* New York: Simon & Schuster, 1965.
Renstrom, Peter G. *The Taft Court: Justices, Rulings, and Legacy.* Santa Barbara, CA: ABC-CLIO, 2003.

Tariffs

See Economic Policy

Taxes and Taxation

See Economic Policy

Teapot Dome Scandal

The most notorious of a series of scandals of the early 1920s that tarnished the administration of President

Key figures in the Teapot Dome scandal stand outside a Washington, D.C., courtroom in October 1929. Former Secretary of the Interior Albert B. Fall (left) would be the only administration figure to spend time in jail for his involvement. Oil executive Edward Doheny (second from left) escaped prison time. The other two men in front are their attorneys. *(MPI/Stringer/Hulton Archive/Getty Images)*

Warren G. Harding, the Teapot Dome scandal involved a number of monetary gifts and unsecured loans made to Secretary of the Interior Albert B. Fall by several oil producers. In exchange, Fall granted them the right to pump oil from reserves in California and Wyoming previously set aside for use by the U.S. Navy. Teapot Dome, the name of the Wyoming reserve, came to symbolize the corruption that permeated the White House in the Harding years.

The origins of the scandal date back to the first decade of the twentieth century, when the U.S. Navy began to switch its fleet from coal-fired engines to more efficient and powerful diesel-fueled ones. While policy makers knew that America's coal supply was virtually unlimited, they were not so certain that its oil reserves were. This was before the major discoveries of oil in East Texas and Oklahoma. Thus, to ensure the navy a steady supply of oil, President William Howard Taft set aside two reserves in California in 1909. Six years later, with war in Europe, President Woodrow Wilson added a third reserve, at Teapot Dome. The name referred to a distinctive geological formation on the site.

Taft's and Wilson's decisions, while applauded by the military, met with resistance from private oil interests and their supporters in Congress. The reserves were said to be unnecessary, as U.S. oil companies could always be compelled to supply the navy in times of war. Moreover, there was ideological opposition to the idea of the federal government holding back resources that could be effectively exploited by private industry. Nevertheless, when Secretary of the Interior Robert Lane moved to lease the reserves to oil drillers at the end of World War I, the president fired him. As a progressive, Wilson was not always sure that private industry would serve the national interest, so he remained determined to keep the reserves under the navy's control.

In the election of 1920, however, the American people rejected progressivism by electing the probusiness Republican Harding to the White House and giving conservative Republicans an overwhelming majority in both the House and Senate. When Harding appointed Fall head of the Interior Department, it was a signal to developers that the nation's resources would be made more available to private interests. A Republican senator from New Mexico, Fall was also a rancher and a miner with a conservative, probusiness reputation. He persuaded Harding to shift control of the reserves from the Navy Department to the Department of the Interior. The navy, concerned about the growing power of the Japanese in the Pacific and believing it would have to expand its own fleet to meet that threat, was resistant. Fall, however, made a convincing argument. Because of the nature of the geological substrata, drillers on adjacent lands were siphoning oil from the reserves. If the government did nothing, which the navy recommended, the oil would be depleted. Better to lease the lands to private oil producers and take the 17 percent royalties from the oil companies to purchase oil and hold it in storage tanks at Pearl Harbor, Hawaii. The argument convinced Harding.

Fall wasted no time in leasing two of the reserves to oil producers. The reserve at Elk Hills, California, was leased to Californian Edward Doheny and his Pan-American Petroleum and Transport Company; the reserve at Teapot Dome was leased to Texan Harry Sinclair's Mammoth Oil Company. That's where things stood until Fall's resignation in March 1923 and Harding's death the following August. By that time, several scandals concerning administration officials were coming to light, including a bribery charge involving the sale of property seized by the government from enemy aliens in World War I and kickbacks from contracts with the Veterans' Bureau. Several of the scandals concerned members of the "Ohio Gang," a group of Harding's close advisers and friends.

As the Senate Committee on Public Lands launched investigations into the scandals, it began to cast an eye on other members of the Ohio Gang, including Fall. But committee head Robert La Follette (R-WI) did not believe that Fall was implicated in any of the scandals, and he appointed the committee's most junior minority member to look into corruption in the Interior Department. Senator Thomas Walsh (D-MT) soon learned, however, that Fall had made some elaborate improvements to his New Mexico ranch in the early 1920s, and he called on Fall to testify about them. In January 1924, Fall told the committee that the improvements were made by means of a $100,000 loan he had received from newspaper publisher Edward McLean. McLean, however, denied making the loan, even as Walsh began uncovering a paper trail that led to Sinclair and Doheny. The latter soon admitted that he had made an unsecured $100,000 loan to Fall in November 1921. Sinclair was also called to testify but refused to answer questions and was charged with contempt of the Senate.

Fearful that the scandal would taint his own administration and damage his chances for reelection in 1924, President Calvin Coolidge fired many holdovers from the Harding administration and appointed two special prosecutors to look into Teapot Dome. The effort worked and the Democrats were never able to pin the scandal on the new administration, perhaps because Doheny himself was a major contributor to Democrats.

The investigation dragged on through much of the decade. In 1928, it finally came to light that Sinclair had given Fall nearly $400,000 in cash and government bonds. Ultimately, Doheny escaped conviction; Sinclair was convicted, not for the original bribery but on the contempt charge. Appealing all the way to the U.S. Supreme Court and losing in 1929, Sinclair spent six months in jail. Fall suffered the worst. Convicted of taking bribes, he was sentenced to prison in 1931 and served a full year. He was the first cabinet officer in American history to be convicted of a felony committed in office.

James Ciment and Charles M. Dobbs

See also: Harding, Warren G.; Oil and Oil Industry; Republican Party; Sinclair, Harry.

Further Reading

Bates, J. Leonard. *The Origins of Teapot Dome: Progressives, Parties, and Petroleum, 1909–1921.* Westport, CT: Greenwood, 1963.

Davis, Margaret Leslie. *Dark Side of Fortune: Triumph and Scandal in the Life of Oil Tycoon Edward L. Doheny.* Berkeley: University of California Press, 1998.

Noggle, Burt. *Teapot Dome: Oil and Politics in the 1920s.* Baton Rouge: Louisiana State University Press, 1962.

Stratton, David H. *Tempest over Teapot Dome: The Story of Albert B. Fall.* Norman: University of Oklahoma Press, 1998.

Werner, M.R., and John Starr. *Teapot Dome.* New York: Viking, 1959.

Technology

During the Jazz Age, virtually every sector of American industry saw significant technological advances. Three fields especially stand out: communications, transportation, and the fabrication of materials. Some of the breakthroughs, notably in radio, were immediately put to commercial use. Others, like the transmission of images over radio waves, or television, would not reach their commercial potential for decades.

Perhaps more important than any single invention or technological breakthrough were the innovations in the administration of technology—how invention was financed and organized. Lone inventors had been giving way to commercial laboratories since Thomas Edison set up the world's first industrial research lab in the 1870s, but the 1920s witnessed an unprecedented expansion of corporate research facilities. By 1927, more than 1,000 U.S. corporations had set up research divisions, the most famous being the Bell Laboratories of American Telephone and Telegraph (AT&T), incorporated as a separate company in 1926. Many of the most important technological breakthroughs of the Jazz Age, including television and film sound, would occur in such laboratories.

Communications

Communications saw the most important technological advances of the Jazz Age, largely in the emerging field of radio. In 1920, the first commercial radio station, KDKA, began broadcasting in Pittsburgh; just four years later, there were over 600 licensed stations in the United States. In 1926, the Radio Corporation of America (RCA) launched the National Broadcasting Company (NBC), the nation's first radio network. By the end of the decade, fully 60 percent of all American households owned a radio.

While improved and expanded content, including music, news, and sports, fueled much of this growth, technological advances played a role as well. These advances fell into two basic categories: tuning and sound quality. The earliest radios of the pre–World War I era were largely crystal sets, which used crystalline minerals such as quartz to detect radio signals. Because crystal sets had no power to amplify sound, listening was done with headphones or through a horn-shaped device like a megaphone, but reception was poor and sound quality low. The 1918 development of superheterodyne receivers by electrical engineer Edwin Armstrong, later the inventor of FM radio, allowed sets to amplify and filter the signal. It took several more years for Armstrong's innovation to make an impact on commercial radio, as the technical requirements for tuning such devices were beyond the ability of most radio listeners. The development of the neutrodyne receiver in 1923 offered the advantage of receiving the same signal at a fixed position on the radio dial.

Advances in vacuum-tube technology in 1923 allowed radios to shift their power source from expensive low-power batteries to alternating current (AC) electricity. This extra power, combined with a shift from magnetic to electrical amplification, increased both the volume of radio play and the capacity to broadcast a stronger signal. Meanwhile, the introduction of the coil loudspeaker, invented in Britain in 1924 but quickly improved upon by RCA, made it possible for radios—and phonographs—to fill whole rooms with high-quality sound.

Other breakthroughs in radio technology were not immediately evident to the public but were significant nonetheless. The year 1921 saw the introduction of the radio compass and radio signals to guide

Radio technology underwent great advances in the 1920s. A high-power transmitter with banks of water-cooled amplifying tubes was used in the first transatlantic telephone transmissions in 1926. *(Topical Press Agency/Stringer/Hulton Archive/Getty Images)*

aviators, making it possible to fly longer distances in conditions in which visual landmarks were not available—at sea, at night, and in inclement weather. By 1928, a series of radio signal stations across the United States allowed pilots to find their coordinates through their radio sets. The technology used in these radio compasses would later be used to perfect radar detection in the 1930s and 1940s.

In retrospect, the most important breakthroughs in wireless technology were occurring in a field to which the general public had little access: television. Two basic forms of transmitting images over radio waves were being developed simultaneously in the 1920s. One was a mechanical scanning system of disks and drums, first developed by Scottish inventor John Logie Baird and improved upon through the prism system of American engineer C. Francis Jenkins. The other, an all-electronic system that would become the standard for television as it developed from the 1930s on, was invented simultaneously by Vladimir Zworykin of Westinghouse Laboratories and an independent technician named Philo Farnsworth. By 1927, both had perfected a system that included an image dissector vacuum-tube camera at the transmission end and a cathode-ray tube for the reception end.

Wired communication also saw advances in the Jazz Age, including the first dial telephones in 1919, the first transatlantic telephone cable in 1923, and the first transmission of photographs over telegraph wires in 1924. Film also underwent major advances, most notably the development of sound movies. Inventors, including Thomas Edison, had been experimenting with synchronized film and sound from the earliest days of film, but these were awkward contraptions that used mechanical devices to synchronize phonographs and projectors to run at the same speed. These devices often failed, producing disconnected images and sound. In 1926, the research laboratories of General Electric (GE) developed the first practical sound-on-film recording device. Later that year, Warner Brothers released *Don Juan,* the first motion picture incorporating the sound with the film, although the sound was background orchestration only. The first "talking picture" came out a year later with the release of *The Jazz Singer,* also by Warner Brothers.

Transportation and Materials

Transportation saw a host of important innovations in the 1920s, particularly in motor vehicles and

aviation, but these were largely improvements to existing technologies. The automobile was enhanced by hydraulic brakes, first developed by the Duesenberg Automobile Company of New Jersey in 1920. Ford introduced the solid cast-iron engine block that same year. In 1924, the Wills Sainte Clare line of automobiles introduced a fuel pump, allowing the gas tank to be placed a safe distance from the engine. In 1926, the upscale Pierce-Arrow Runabout offered power steering (this technology would not see widespread use until the 1950s).

The 1920s also saw the introduction of softer-riding pneumatic tires on buses and trucks. Previously, pneumatic tires had been available only on cars, while the heavy weight of commercial vehicles required solid rubber tires. But improvements in reinforcing tires with cords of stronger material made it possible to put pneumatics on heavier vehicles after 1925.

Motor transportation was also improved by the introduction in the early 1920s of the traffic light, more efficient road-building equipment (such as improved concrete-mixing and road-laying machines), and higher-performing fuels. Tetraethyl lead was introduced into gasoline for the first time in 1920, followed shortly thereafter by higher-octane gas, both of which reduced knocking and allowed for higher-performance engines. Catalytic cracking, a process that breaks up large hydrocarbons into smaller units, first invented in 1913 but not going into widespread use until the 1920s, made it possible to refine more higher-octane fuel. The same process also made it possible to produce higher-octane aviation fuels, allowing for faster airplanes that could travel longer distances without refueling.

The Jazz Age also witnessed the development or improvement of materials that would profoundly alter the way people lived. Improved refining technology made strong, light, flexible aluminum far cheaper to produce, making it suitable for use in airplanes, automobiles, and packaging. A number of synthetic materials underwent significant improvement, including rayon, cellophane, and plastic. These advances provided the public with a host of new products, including cellophane wrapping, artificial silk, and adhesive tape.

With the emergence of the corporate laboratory as the main engine of technological progress, Jazz Age America witnessed numerous improvements of existing technologies and their application to a wide variety of manufacturing processes and consumer products. Focusing on the bottom line and practicality over originality, the corporate managers of the new research laboratories put an emphasis on technologies that would increase profits as well as improve everyday life.

James Ciment

See also: Air-Conditioning; Architecture; Automobile Industry; Aviation; Birth Control; Coal Industry; Design, Industrial; Electricity Industry; Federal Highway Act of 1921; Federal Power Commission; Film Industry; Oil and Oil Industry; Railroads and Railroad Industry; Telephone and Telegraph.

Further Reading

Cravens, Hamilton, Alan I. Marcus, and David M. Katzman, eds. *Technical Knowledge in American Culture: Science, Technology, and Medicine Since the Early 1800s.* Tuscaloosa: University of Alabama Press, 1996.

Mowery, David C., and Nathan Rosenberg. *Paths of Innovation: Technological Change in 20th Century America.* New York: Cambridge University Press, 1998.

Oliver, John W. *History of American Technology.* New York: Ronald, 1956.

Telephone and Telegraph

The telegraph and the telephone were established technologies at the dawn of the Jazz Age, and both industries experienced significant changes in the period from the end of World War I to the beginning of the Great Depression. The telephone in particular saw a dramatic rise in use.

As electrical power lines were laid, so were telephones lines, doubling from about 25.4 million miles in 1920 to nearly 60 million by 1929. Lines were also extended internationally. Starting in 1921, direct telephone calls could be made from the United States to Cuba, and by 1927 across the Atlantic to London. However, the cost was prohibitively expensive: about $75 ($800 in 2007 dollars) for a three-minute connection, making international calling largely the preserve of businesses and the very rich.

Although international calling remained exclusive, telephones were becoming available to increasing numbers of ordinary citizens. From roughly 13.3 million, or one telephone for every eight persons, in 1920, the number increased to 20.2 million, or about one for every six persons, by 1929.

Much of the growth in the number of telephones was spurred by the big telephone manufacturing companies, including Westinghouse, General Electric (GE), and Western Electric, the equipment subsidiary of American Telephone and Telegraph (AT&T). The

companies offered different incentives to attract customers. For Westinghouse, it was a direct rotary telephone, which cut down on the need for switchboard operators. While invented back in 1888, direct dialing did not go into widespread use until the 1920s, and then only in certain urban areas. Until that innovation, telephone companies typically employed operators to connect parties wishing to talk. The telephone also became easier to use. In 1928, Westinghouse designed a telephone that incorporated the receiver and microphone in a single unit, requiring the use of only one hand. Previous models required the use two hands, one for the mouthpiece and the other for the receiver, or the user had to stand by a wall-based unit. A more ergonomic device, the one-piece handset extended the time of comfortable telephone conversation, which further increased profits for the telephone companies.

While the manufacture of telephone equipment was relatively competitive, telephone service was not. The AT&T family of companies, known as the Bell System, controlled the vast majority of lines—12.6 million of the nation's 13.3 million in 1920, and 20.1 million of its 20.2 million lines in 1929. The telephone seemed a natural monopoly—an industry in which it did not make economic sense to have competition—and AT&T remained largely immune from antitrust action in the Jazz Age, though rates were often carefully regulated by the state governments.

For all the growth in telephone usage, there remained social and cultural obstacles. When the telephone first came into widespread use in the late nineteenth and early twentieth centuries, many businesses and individuals thought it was antithetical to human interaction and commerce, and some feared that people would no longer talk face to face. As the telephone became a more familiar and accepted part of everyday family and business life, however, attitudes changed. People embraced the technology as a way of connecting families as well as doing business. The change was reflected in a rapidly increasing number of telephone calls. Whereas fewer than 19.4 million local calls were placed in 1917, the figure climbed to more than 28.1 million by 1927. The growth in domestic long-distance calls was even more dramatic. In 1917, Americans made fewer than 450,000 such calls; a decade later, the figure had climbed to more than 1.1 million.

But as telephones connected people in new ways, they also brought into question issues of privacy. While the increasing use of direct dialing made it less likely that an operator would listen in on a

Although technology for direct-dial telephoning was invented in the 1920s, switchboard operators were responsible for connecting the vast majority of calls. *(Lewis W. Hine/Hulton Archive/Getty Images)*

conversation, eavesdropping by law enforcement agencies was another matter. Was a telephone conversation private, given that it was conducted in the confines of a person's home or place of business? Was it covered by Fourth Amendment protections against unreasonable searches? Or was a telephone conversation more like a conversation conducted in the street, where there was no expectation of privacy? In 1928, the U.S. Supreme Court, in *Olmstead v. United States*, ruled that the government could listen in on telephone conversations without a warrant, as if they were conducted in public. Dissenting were the two liberal justices on the court, Oliver Wendell Holmes, Jr., and Louis Brandeis, the latter arguing that the courts had to take into account technological advances if constitutional protections were to have any meaning in the modern age. Subsequent legislation enacted by Congress would offer more protections.

Despite the spread of telephones in the Jazz Age, the telegraph remained vital, particularly for long-distance and overseas communication; sending a telegram was far cheaper than making a telephone call between cities and states, or overseas. Indeed, the growth in the number of telegrams sent between 1917 and 1927 significantly exceeded the growth in the number of telephone calls. While the latter increased by about 50 percent, the number of telegrams climbed more than 80 percent, from roughly 127 million in 1917 to about 230 million in 1927. There were nearly eight times as many telegrams as telephone calls. Nevertheless, telegraphy was an aging industry, reflected in the relatively anemic growth in miles of telegraph wires—from just under 1.9 million in 1917 to just over 2.1 million in 1927.

Technological changes in the communications industries were significant in the Jazz Age, with people becoming more comfortable using the telephone and making greater use of the telegraph. But as sociologists discovered, people often use new technologies to reinforce old social patterns. In 1926, the Knights of Columbus, a fraternal organization, conducted a survey to determine whether people would choose to communicate by telephone rather than visit in person. What they found was that people often used telephone calls to confirm face-to-face appointments rather than as a substitute for them.

Cord Scott and James Ciment

See also: General Electric; Radio; Radio Corporation of America; Technology.

Further Reading

Cowan, Ruth Schwartz. *A Social History of American Technology.* New York: Oxford University Press, 1997.
Fischer, Claude. *America Calling: A Social History of the Telephone to 1940.* Berkeley: University of California Press, 1992.

Tennis

Although similar games were played in ancient Greece and Egypt, the modern form of tennis was developed in Great Britain in the late nineteenth century but did not become popular in Europe or America until the 1920s. This development was true of a variety of other sports—including baseball, football, boxing, and golf—that first captured broad public attention during the Jazz Age.

The first lawn tennis club was formed in England in 1874, also the year of the first tennis match played in the United States. The four tennis championships, now referred to as the "Grand Slam," began during this era: Wimbledon (1877) in the United Kingdom, the U.S. Open (1881), the French Open (1891), and the Australian Open (1905). The Davis Cup, an annual competition for teams of men from different nations, began in 1900.

Tennis remained largely an amateur sport for members of the upper classes, primarily in Britain, the United States, Australia, and France, until the 1920s. As the sport became more popular and it became evident that a large audience was willing to pay to watch matches, the legendary promoter Charles C. "Cash and Carry" Pyle created the first professional tennis tour in 1926, starring Suzanne Lenglen of France and Vinnie Richards of the United States.

Pyle's professional tour had a formative influence on tennis worldwide because it created a two-tier system within the sport, with parallel tournaments and champions at the amateur and professional levels. Players had to decide in which tier they would participate: Once they played in a professional tournament, they were not allowed to compete again as an amateur. This system remained in place until 1968, when commercial pressures led to the abandonment of the two-tier system and the beginning of what is known as the open era, in which most tournaments make no distinction between professional and amateur players.

Emblematic of tennis in the 1920s was Bill Tilden, who in 1920 became the first American to win the singles title at Wimbledon. He won that championship twice more, in 1921 and 1930, and also won seven U.S. Open championships in the 1920s. When Tilden joined the professional tennis tour in 1930, he earned more than $500,000 in seven years. He became a well-known public figure, equal in fame to Babe Ruth, and the news media often remarked on his handsome appearance and his friendships with Hollywood celebrities such as Charlie Chaplin and Errol Flynn.

Suzanne Lenglen, the first international female tennis celebrity, won twenty-five Grand Slam titles in the years 1919–1926. She was also known for her revealing tennis costumes, which exposed her forearms and calves. American player Helen Wills Moody almost matched Lenglen's record. In the 1920s and 1930s, she won seven U.S. championships, eight Wimbledon titles, and four French championship titles.

Tennis was unique among major sports in the 1920s in that both men and women competed at the highest levels and achieved worldwide fame and popularity. Because tennis had begun as an amateur activity played by both men and women in private clubs, a large pool of female players existed, and it was socially acceptable for them to compete at this sport. However, African Americans, Jews, and other minorities were generally excluded from the private clubs where tennis developed. Consequently, mainstream tennis was largely restricted to white players in the 1920s. A separate system of leagues and tournaments was developed for African American players in the United States, but they did not participate in mainstream competitive tennis until much later in the history of the sport. In 1956, an African American—Althea Gibson—won the Grand Slam title.

Sarah Boslaugh

See also: Leisure and Recreation; Tilden, Bill.

Further Reading

Collins, Bud. *Total Tennis: The Ultimate Tennis Encyclopedia.* Toronto, Canada: Sport Media, 2003.

Grimsley, Will. *Tennis: Its History, People, and Events.* Englewood Cliffs, NJ: Prentice Hall, 1971.

Phillips, Caryl, ed. *The Right Set: A Tennis Anthology.* New York: Vintage Books, 1999.

Theater

The American theater was in transition during the Jazz Age. Since the early 1900s, theater had faced growing competition from movies. By the 1920s, movies had seriously undermined the popularity of vaudeville, or theatrical revues featuring comic sketches, dance and music performances, dramatic recitals, and other acts. In response, major theaters moved away from vaudeville-style revues while continuing to offer traditional comedies, melodramas, and musicals. At the same time, experimental developments on the European stage—including realism and expressionism—found new venues in smaller theaters in America and new voices in emerging American playwrights such as Eugene O'Neill.

Musical comedies were a specialty of Broadway in the 1920s. Most of the popular musical comedies of the Jazz Age featured large casts, elaborate staging, and numerous catchy tunes that became hits on radio and phonograph records. But they had largely forgettable books, or story lines. A minimal plot was designed to move the action from one musical number to the next. Popular works were Cole Porter's *Fifty Million Frenchmen* (1929), featuring the song "You Don't Know Paree," and Irving Berlin's *The Cocoanuts* (1929), featuring the Marx Brothers and the hit song "When My Dreams Come True." Perhaps the most successful of these lighthearted musical comedies were *Sally* (1920), with music by the up-and-coming songwriter Jerome Kern and lyrics by Clifford Grey, and *No, No, Nanette* (1925), an import from England.

Singer and actor Paul Robeson stars in the Ambassador Theater's 1925 production of Eugene O'Neill's hit drama *The Emperor Jones* (1920), the story of an American fugitive who sets himself up as the leader of a Caribbean island. *(Sasha/Stringer/Hulton Archive/Getty Images)*

The most successful Broadway musical writing team of the 1920s was Richard Rodgers and Lorenz Hart, who scored a string of hits, including *Garrick Gaieties* (1925), *Dearest Enemy* (1925), *The Girl Friend* (1926), *A Connecticut Yankee* (1927), and *Present Arms* (1928). Meanwhile, audiences made Eubie Blake and Noble Sissle's *Shuffle Along* (1921) Broadway's first hit musical written and performed entirely by African Americans.

Certainly there were exceptions to the trend toward musical comedies. One was Anne Nichol's *Abie's Irish Rose* (1922), a popular nonmusical romantic comedy that updated the Romeo and Juliet story to the immigrant neighborhoods of early twentieth-century New York. Breaking away from lighthearted, revue-style musical comedies was Jerome Kern and Oscar Hammerstein's *Show Boat* (1927), which many theater historians consider the first plot-driven, character-centered musical to play on Broadway. Soon, most Broadway musicals would move away from the revue tradition in the direction *Show Boat* had pioneered.

More serious drama was also emerging in theaters. The "Little Theater" movement emerged in the years immediately preceding World War I, determined to produce more experimental theater. Largely centered in Manhattan, the proponents included playwrights, actors, producers, and directors, most of whom held left-wing political views. They were determined to break free of the melodramatic conventions and capitalist business model of traditional Broadway theater. In 1915, they launched the Provincetown Players theater company, named after the Cape Cod town where many New York artists passed their summers. Within a year, the Players had relocated to New York City, where they began staging works by playwrights Susan Glaspell, Edna St. Vincent Millay, Theodore Dreiser, and Eugene O'Neill.

O'Neill introduced realism to the American stage in plays like *Beyond the Horizon* (1920), *Strange Interlude* (written in 1923 and first produced in 1928), and *Desire Under the Elms* (written in 1924 and produced in 1925). In these dramas, O'Neill took the elements of European-style realism—everyday language, alienated characters, and plots emphasizing disillusionment and despair—and placed them in an American setting. His plays were produced through the Provincetown Players and its successor organization, the Experimental Theatre, Inc., which O'Neill cofounded with set designer Robert Edmond Jones and drama critic Kenneth Macgowan in 1923.

In *The Hairy Ape* (1922), O'Neill experimented with expressionism, another European aesthetic, in which the artist distorts reality in order to heighten the emotional effect of the work. Perhaps the best-known example of expressionism in American theater is Elmer Rice's *The Adding Machine* (1923).

Other groups in the Little Theater movement were the Washington Square Players, founded in 1915, and the Theater Guild, begun in 1918. Like virtually all serious experimental theater groups in America, both were located in New York City. But even as New York was further consolidating its position in the 1920s as the center of American theater, many of its best talents were being lured away by Hollywood. Some of the leading theatrical talents of the 1920s—Buster Keaton, the Marx Brothers, Mae West, Ethel Merman, Fred Astaire—had largely decamped to Hollywood by the end of the decade.

James Ciment

See also: Anderson, Sherwood; Gershwin, George; O'Neill, Eugene; Vaudeville.

Further Reading

Chansky, Dorothy. *Composing Ourselves: The Little Theater Movement and the American Audience.* Carbondale: Southern Illinois University Press, 2004.

Jones, Robert Edmond. *The Dramatic Imagination: Reflections and Speculations on the Art of Theater.* New York: Theater Arts, 1969.

Wilmeth, Don, and Christopher Bigsby, eds. *The Cambridge History of American Theater.* Vol. 2, *1870–1945.* New York: Cambridge University Press, 1999.

Tilden, Bill (1893–1953)

The winner of ten Grand Slam singles tournaments in his career, all but one of them during the 1920s, Bill Tilden was America's first great tennis star. From 1920 to 1925, the temperamental and showy player was ranked number one in both America and the world. Although his abrasive personality made him less than adored by much of the public, his mastery of the game attracted millions of fans to a sport that was being transformed from a pastime of the elite to a recreational activity accessible to the middle class.

He was born William Tatem Tilden on February 10, 1893, to a wealthy family in Germantown, Pennsylvania. At seven years old, he was introduced to tennis at a country club in the Catskill Mountains, where his family summered. At the turn of the twentieth century, few courts were open to the general public, and most of those who played the game did so at exclusive clubs and resorts.

When his mother contracted the debilitating and ultimately fatal Bright's disease in 1908, Tilden went to live at the home of his aunt, where he continued to reside for the next thirty years. In the meantime, he attended Germantown Academy, where he rose to captain of the tennis team in his senior year. Tilden played at the University of Pennsylvania and began competing in national championships in 1913. Two years later, both his father and older brother, who had mentored him in tennis, died. At that point, Tilden dropped out of school and decided to make tennis his career.

He climbed the rankings of amateur tennis— there was virtually no professional circuit until the late 1920s—but enlisted in the U.S. Army in 1917 to fight in World War I. Tilden saw little fighting, however, participating in matches to entertain the troops and boost morale on the home front. He also continued to compete on the amateur circuit and won six tournaments before his discharge from the army in 1919.

Tall and slim, the right-hander was largely self-taught. In his first years out of the army, Tilden perfected an arsenal of shots, including a devastating "cannon ball" serve, as the press called it. Still, he remained ranked number two in the United States, after Bill Johnston. In 1920, the two anchored the U.S. team as it rolled over its European competitors in the Davis Cup tournament; Tilden and Johnston won every one of their matches. Upon his return to the United States, Tilden bested Johnston in the national championship, and he would remain ranked number one in the country through 1929. Tilden won the U.S. singles championship seven times during the 1920s and the U.S. doubles championship five times between 1918 and 1927. He also won the Wimbledon singles three times between 1920 and 1930.

While his dramatic style of play and oversized personality drew crowds to his matches, he was considered egotistical and short-tempered. He frequently argued with linesmen over disputed calls. He also angered the U.S. Lawn Tennis Association (predecessor of the U.S. Tennis Association) with his

One of the greatest American players in tennis history—and a major celebrity of the 1920s—Bill Tilden won six U.S. amateur championships during the course of the decade and led the U.S. team to a record seven straight Davis Cup titles. *(AFP/Getty Images)*

commentary on the state of the sport. A skilled writer, Tilden published a number of articles highly critical of tennis officials, prompting the association to pass a rule banning amateur athletes from writing about tennis for compensation.

Tilden lived expensively. An aspiring actor and playwright, he spent a fortune funding costly theatrical flops. More controversial were his sexual proclivities. Largely unknown to the general public, Tilden's homosexuality was familiar to those in the small world of 1920s amateur tennis, although he was never accused of sexual involvement with the many young tennis players he mentored.

By the mid-1920s, Tilden's reign as the world's greatest tennis player was threatened. While he remained number one in the United States through the end of the decade, he was toppled from the top seed in Europe by Frenchman René Lacoste at Wimbledon in 1926. With Lacoste and the French team rising to prominence, Tilden gained new popularity in the United States, as many came to see him as the representative of American tennis in the world.

In the latter years of the decade, professional tennis began to gain more attention as amateur players defected from the U.S. Lawn Tennis Association to play for money. Tilden held off until 1930, when he signed a movie contract with MGM to do films in which tennis was featured. Although he made no feature movies, under the strict rules of the day, his movie contract constituted a breach of his amateur status. (Tilden's only screen appearances came in non-MGM films about tennis technique and a 1941 documentary about himself entitled *Big Bill Tilden*.) In the early 1930s, Tilden formed a professional tennis tour, named after himself, which drew some of the biggest stars of the day.

Tilden moved from Germantown to Los Angeles in 1939, where he became a tennis pro to the stars and competed successfully in the burgeoning professional tour. He also wrote several best sellers about the game and played exhibition matches to raise money for the war effort during World War II. In 1945, he helped resurrect the professional tennis tour, which had been largely on hold during the conflict.

Many sports historians regard Tilden as the most influential figure in the history of American tennis—by promoting the amateur game in the 1920s and the professional circuit in the 1930s and 1940s. Tilden died on June 5, 1953, and was posthumously inducted into the International Tennis Hall of Fame in 1959. A decade later, an international panel of tennis journalists voted him the greatest male player in the history of the game.

James Ciment

See also: Celebrity Culture; Tennis.

Further Reading

Deford, Frank. *Big Bill Tilden: The Triumphs and the Tragedy.* New York: Simon & Schuster, 1976.

Tilden, Bill. *My Story: A Champion's Memoir.* New York: Hellman, Williams, 1948.

Voss, Arthur. *Tilden and Tennis in the Twenties.* Troy, NY: Whitston, 1985.

Time

Time was the brainchild of two twenty-five-year-old founding editors, Henry Luce and Briton Hadden, who had worked together at the *Yale Daily News* when both were undergraduates. The two began planning the magazine in 1921 and officially incorporated the venture in November 1922. Hadden served as the creative engine of the partnership while Luce focused more on business matters, though they took turns editing the magazine.

The pair had a lucky break when their mentor W.H. Eaton, editor of *World's Work* magazine, allowed them access to his subscriber lists so they could find potential subscribers for *Time*. Through direct marketing, *Time* recruited 6,000 early subscribers, double the goal. This success buoyed the editors as they searched for funding. Their efforts were further bolstered when famed financier Dwight Morrow purchased a small stake in the venture. Morrow's involvement gave the young editors credibility with other investors.

By March 1923, *Time* was ready to unveil its twenty-six-page inaugural issue. The black-and-white cover featured an illustration of "Uncle" Joe Cannon, the former Speaker of the House of Representatives, who was retiring from Congress after a record twenty-three terms. From the outset, the magazine committed itself to objective journalism, shunning editorials and muckraking in favor of a balanced approach that would present all sides of an issue and let readers draw their own conclusions.

Time made it a point to uncover interesting facts and statistics to spice up articles. In addition, Hadden encouraged *Time's* writers to use a light, sometimes playful style more akin to feature writing than hard reporting. This was all meant to make the magazine more entertaining, allowing *Time* to compete for the mass audience of general-interest publications like *The Saturday Evening Post.*

Articles ran 400 words at most and were written in a straightforward, accessible style. As Luce would later say, "The one great thing was simplification. Simplification by organization, simplification by condensation, and also simplification by just being damn simple." The magazine was divided into clear sections such as National Affairs, Foreign Affairs, the Arts, the Professions, and Sport. Each was further divided by subtopics—for example, the Professions section contained Business, Medicine, and Law subsections. Hadden and Luce also believed that many contemporary reporters failed to provide enough context for readers. Therefore, articles were to be written for a person who knew nothing about a particular topic.

Initially the magazine did not do its own reporting. Instead, editors at *Time* would sift through a week's worth of newspaper stories for important developments. The magazine was particularly dependent on *The New York Times.* However, *Time* did not simply republish the original reports. They used the previously published material as research for a broader article that not only summarized the week's events but offered historical or political background.

The first issue of *Time* attracted 9,000 readers. By the end of 1923, circulation was fewer than 20,000, reaching 70,000 subscribers by the end of 1924. The magazine's growth was bolstered in part by a rise in circulation in the Midwest. This prompted Luce to relocate *Time*'s offices to Cleveland in 1926, against Hadden's wishes. The move lasted less than one year, but it seriously damaged the relationship between *Time*'s founders.

By January 1926, *Time*'s subscriber base reached 100,000. However, advertisers wanted more newsstand sales. In an effort to attract these casual readers, *Time* added a distinctive red border around the cover of its January 3 issue. This splash of color helped boost sales enough that ad revenues rose to $415,000 by 1927.

The fall of 1927 saw another popular innovation when Hadden created *Time*'s first Man of the Year, an honor the magazine bestowed on Charles Lindbergh in January 1928. Hadden created the award at the last minute to attract more readers during a slow news week. It was so successful that it became an annual feature. The paper also drew attention for its extensive coverage of the 1928 presidential campaign.

Unfortunately, Hadden, a heavy drinker, died the following year. Luce then took on all editorial responsibilities himself, eventually becoming one of the most recognizable media figures in the country.

Guy Patrick Cunningham

See also: Journalism; Luce, Henry.

Further Reading

Baughman, James L. *Henry R. Luce and the Rise of the American News Media.* Boston: Twayne, 1987.
Elson, Robert T., ed. *Time Inc.: The Intimate History of a Publishing Enterprise.* 3 vols. New York: Atheneum, 1968–1986.

Tobacco

See Cigarettes and Tobacco

Travel and Tourism

American tourism increased dramatically from 1919 to 1929, a period in which a desire to cast off post–World War I cares and seek adventure seized the nation. Advances in transportation technology, increased automobile ownership, and more available leisure time for the expanding middle class stimulated new tourist markets and influenced Americans' quests for fun and adventure. People who had never traveled more than a few miles from home now ventured to the seaside or countryside, across the nation or around the world, by road, rail, air, and sea. Equipped with guidebooks, road maps, and travel brochures, Americans traipsed across the countries and continents, sending postcards by the millions to family and friends back home.

The affordability of mass-produced automobiles and the advent of consumer credit made automobile ownership a reality for approximately 23 million Americans by the end of the 1920s. Cars provided mobility, independence, and a sense of control and privacy not found in other modes of transportation. Sunday drives, picnics in the countryside, weekends at the beach, and cross-country treks gave Americans a better sense of their country. However, the dusty, sometimes muddy, rut-filled roads of the postwar era soon led to public demands for better thoroughfares. The automobile industry and towns that stood to benefit from tourist traffic sponsored many major highway projects. Additionally, the Federal Highway Act (1921) provided federal funds for interstate highway construction.

The automobile revolutionized travel in the 1920s, allowing tourists, including this group at New Mexico's Enchanted Mesa, to visit far-flung sights in relative comfort and ease. *(Paul Popper/Time & Life Pictures/Getty Images)*

Until the 1920s, most highway projects, such as the Lincoln Highway, the National Old Trails Highway, and the Dixie Highway, were local undertakings. The American Association of State Highway Officials simplified the system in 1926 by renaming regional highways with numbered U.S. highway designations. Route 66, an east–west highway running from Chicago to Los Angeles, is still the most famous numbered highway of the Jazz Era. It had become a piece of Americana and an attraction in itself by the 1950s.

Auto tourism created a new market for goods and services. Accommodations such as campgrounds, motels, and auto courts sprang up along major travel routes. Tourists purchased camping gear, picnic baskets, travel journals, travel wear, and even portable phonographs. Roadside attractions offered travel paraphernalia such as postcards, trinkets, and windshield stickers to commemorate the experience. Billboards lined the highways advertising attractions and lodging and miscellaneous goods. Small "snipe signs" nailed to fences and utility poles advertised that Coca-Cola or Wrigley's chewing gum was available in the next town. To meet increased fuel requirements, service stations opened along highways. Early stations

provided only fuel and perhaps minor mechanical repairs, but eventually the stations also offered snacks, cold drinks, and public restrooms.

Automobile travel offered new possibilities for women. Inspired by the 1909 cross-country drive of Alice Ramsey—the first women to accomplish the feat—many women embarked on road trips together. Some Americans condemned such trips, fearing the automobile would cause women to abandon their prescribed domestic responsibilities. Female travelers might encounter the disapproving remark, "A long way from home, ain't you?" But for the most part, women returned from these trips self-assured, invigorated, and confident in their newly discovered abilities to change tires and perform vehicle maintenance.

Nostalgia for the frontier made the American West a popular vacation destination. Some Native American tribes opened their villages to tourists and their money. Many tribes performed dances or other rituals for visiting tourists and sold handicrafts and jewelry. Restaurant and hotel entrepreneur Fred Harvey's "Indian Detours" were popular tourist activities. Passengers on the Atchison, Topeka, and Santa Fe Railway could disembark in various Southwestern towns, hire a luxury car and guide, and tour remote Indian reservations, villages, and ruins. For many travelers, California was the ultimate destination. A trip to the land of perpetual sunshine was a status symbol for Jazz Age travelers.

The National Park Service enhanced parks like Yellowstone, Yosemite, and the Grand Canyon in the 1920s to provide activities and opportunities for tourists to interact with the flora and fauna. Adventurers could ride mules down into the Grand Canyon, while tourists were encouraged to feed the bears at both Yellowstone and Yosemite. National park promoters correctly believed that the interaction with wildlife would draw more visitors. Unfortunately, increasing conflict between bears and humans nearly led to the bears' extinction in later years. And as the number of tourists increased, conservationists became concerned about the overall impact on the environment.

Rail and Air

Americans also explored the nation by railroad and increasingly by air. By 1920, Americans could travel coast to coast by rail in seventy-two hours. Pullman sleeper cars afforded a degree of comfort for long-distance overnight treks. The sleeping berths were cramped and afforded little privacy, but they were a welcome alternative to sitting up all night in coach. Wealthy travelers rented private sleeping compartments or even drawing rooms with all the comforts of a private hotel room. However, rail travel declined in the 1920s due to widespread mismanagement of the industry, increased passenger costs, and the growth of automobile travel.

World War I necessitated advances in aviation that resulted in faster, more reliable airplanes capable of transporting more weight for greater distances. Although commercial airlines were largely limited to airmail delivery in the 1920s, Ford Air Transport in 1925 combined airmail deliveries with passenger transport from Detroit to Chicago and Cleveland. Air travel was more novelty than practicality: Early passenger planes were loud, drafty, and lacked pressurization. Passengers wrapped themselves in blankets, stuffed cotton in their ears, and frequently got airsick or passed out at higher altitudes.

Charles Lindbergh's 1927 solo flight across the Atlantic encouraged greater public interest in air travel. Clement M. Keys, in association with Lindbergh; the

Pennsylvania Railroad; and the Atchison, Topeka, and Santa Fe Railway, devised a plan whereby passengers could travel coast to coast in just forty-eight hours by a combination of air and rail travel. Transcontinental Air Transport (TAT) launched its first trip on July 7, 1929, amid much publicity. Passengers took a train from New York's Penn Station to Columbus, Ohio, where they hopped on a Ford Trimotor airplane and flew to Waynoka, Oklahoma. There they caught the Santa Fe sleeper car to Clovis, New Mexico. After a hearty breakfast at the Clovis Harvey House restaurant, they boarded another plane for the last leg to Los Angeles. TAT offered speed and excitement, but delays due to weather and maintenance gave the company a bad reputation. It was popularly known as the "Take a Train" airline. Interest dropped off, and increasing expenses caused the airline to fold. Commercial air travel did not come into its own until after World War II.

International Travel

International travel, long a symbol of wealth and status, continued to attract upper-class American travelers. European ocean liners like the *Paris, Gripsholm,* and *Ile de France* provided luxurious accommodations for transatlantic crossings. Ocean liners were like small cities. Passengers had sumptuous staterooms, exercised in gymnasiums, swam in pools, and watched movies or live stage performances in theaters. They feasted on caviar, fillet of sole, petit fours, and ice cream in exquisite dining rooms. Especially appealing during the Prohibition era, bars opened once ships entered international waters, and alcohol flowed freely for the entire voyage.

By this time, however, international vacations were no longer limited to the upper class. At first, tourist-class accommodations differed little from the sparse offerings that immigrants encountered when crowded together in steerage. Competition for the middle-class dollar, however, led to upgraded dining facilities, lounges, and recreation areas. Some shipping lines converted entire ships to tourist class. In 1927, 40 percent of the 322,000 Americans who traveled to Europe went tourist third-class. Tourist agencies like American Express, Raymond-Whitcomb, and Thomas Cook and Son flourished. These companies offered Caribbean, Mediterranean, and around-the-world cruises, as well as packaged tours to Europe, Asia, Africa, and South America.

Motels and Autocamps

Between 1913 and the end of 1929, the number of registered automobiles in the United States skyrocketed from a little over 1 million to more than 27 million. With the soaring popularity of the automobile came a new kind of vacation, at first adventurous and difficult, then gradually more accessible to the average family: the automobile road trip. Key to making these trips so accessible—aside from improvements in the affordability and reliability of automobiles, as well as better roads—was the development of roadside accommodations. These stay-over sites began with the primitive (a tent at the side of the road) and progressed to the family-friendly forerunner of the modern motel: the cabin camp.

Although many of American's roads were still dirt tracks at the start of the Jazz Age, newspapers across the country began running articles that mapped out tours and gave travel tips to motorists, such as bringing along tire chains to help when mired in mud. The earliest long-distance car travelers slept in their vehicles or in tents. In fact, tent sales in the United States reached a record high in the early 1920s. Novelist Sinclair Lewis called this kind of travel "autobumming."

The next development in roadside accommodations was the free municipal campground, also known as an autocamp. Cities along the nation's developing road systems created free campgrounds, often in parks located near the center of town. The location of these camps helped to stimulate business, as traveling motorists would stock up on supplies at local establishments. The camps also deterred motorists from trespassing on or destroying private property. An early and especially elaborate example of the municipal autocamp was Denver's Overland Park, a $250,000 facility that included a clubhouse with a barbershop and a dance hall.

Between 1923 and 1926, many autocamps, especially in the West, began charging fees in order to maintain the facilities and keep out "undesirables." The charging of fees opened the market to entrepreneurs. It also raised consumer expectations, created competition, and soon led to new establishments—called cabin camps—that had many of the amenities of today's motels.

Some of the cabin camps were primitive, offering little more than four walls and a roof over the traveler's head. Others, like the one run by D.J. Flannigan near Macon, Georgia, featured iron beds, a dresser, a table and chairs, and a stove in each cabin—all for $1.00 or $1.50 per night. Also located on the property were a bathhouse, grocery, and laundry. According to one estimate, by 1926 some 2,000 cabin camps had been established across the United States. By the end of the Jazz Age, the great American road trip, while not quite the commonplace event it would become after World War II, was well on its way to becoming the modern experience of chain motels and swimming pools frequented by American travelers today.

William Toth

After World War I, France became a popular middle-class travel destination and a refuge for the "Lost Generation," the expatriate community that came of age during the war and questioned traditional American mores, capitalism, and imperialism. Many thought they could find happiness in the more liberal, Socialist French environment. Travel books and novels such as Ernest Hemingway's *The Sun Also*

Rises (1926) lured middle-class Americans to France and other destinations in search of romance, pleasure, and something they could not easily obtain in America: unlimited alcohol.

Jennifer Aerts Terry

See also: Automobiles and Automobile Culture; Aviation; Leisure and Recreation.

Further Reading

Biel, Alice Wondrak. *Do (Not) Feed the Bears: The Fitful History of Wildlife and Tourists in Yellowstone.* Lawrence: University Press of Kansas, 2006.

Darling, Harold. *Bon Voyage: Souvenirs from the Golden Age of Travel.* New York: Abbeville, 1990.

Gregory, Alexis. *The Golden Age of Travel: 1880–1939.* London: Cassel, 1998.

Heppenheimer, T.A. *Turbulent Skies: The History of Commercial Aviation.* New York: John Wiley and Sons, 1995.

Jakle, John A. *The Tourist: Travel in Twentieth Century North America.* Lincoln: University of Nebraska Press, 1985.

Patton, Phil. *Open Road: A Celebration of the American Highway.* New York: Simon & Schuster, 1986.

Scharff, Virginia. *Taking the Wheel: Women and the Coming of the Motor Age.* New York: Free Press, 1991.

Thompson, Gregory Lee. *The Passenger Train in the Motor Age: California's Rail and Bus Industries, 1910–1941.* Columbus: Ohio State University Press, 1993.

Tulsa Race Riots of 1921

In the late spring of 1921, the oil boomtown of Tulsa, Oklahoma, was convulsed by one of the worst race riots in American history, an outbreak of mob violence in which marauding whites attacked black neighborhoods, leaving dozens, perhaps hundreds, dead. Tulsa was one of several cities that experienced racial rioting, usually instigated by whites, in the World War I and postwar eras, a result of white resentment directed at blacks who moved into urban areas.

During the second decade of the twentieth century, Tulsa grew from a modest-sized agricultural town of 35,000 to a booming city of almost 110,000, largely because of the vast oil deposits discovered in its vicinity. People poured into the city from all regions of the country, looking to make a fortune drilling for oil. While few African Americans had the capital or business connections to engage in oil prospecting, they were drawn to Tulsa for the relatively high-paying jobs the oil industry offered. Thousands settled in the Greenwood section of the city, where entrepreneurs set up businesses from barbershops to banks. So prosperous was Greenwood's

commercial district that locals took to calling it the "black Wall Street." By 1920, Tulsa's black population numbered roughly 11,000.

Many whites resented Greenwood's well-to-do African Americans, and returning soldiers further contributed to Tulsa's racial volatility. Blacks who had served in the military often refused to give the deference whites expected of them. Adding to the rising tension was news of race riots in East St. Louis and Chicago in 1917 and 1919, respectively.

While Tulsa was prosperous, it was also prone to violence, an atmosphere of lawlessness, and weak law enforcement typical of boomtowns. Vigilantism that had nothing to do with race was common. In August 1920, for example, a white man named Roy Belton, accused of murdering another white man, was seized from police by a mob and lynched. In an environment where the law was unable to protect Tulsa's citizens from mob violence, rumors and a news report about a black man assaulting a white woman sparked one of the most deadly, destructive, and contested race riots of the twentieth century.

Although the details of the incident are unclear, on May 30, 1921, a young African American named Dick Rowland had a physical encounter with a young white woman, Sarah Page, on an elevator in the Drexel Building. Newspapers claimed that Rowland had attacked and attempted to rape Page, but all charges were dropped. Most historians now believe that either Rowland or Page accidentally stumbled into the other. In any event, the inflammatory reports of the day sparked the formation of a white lynch mob. In response, Greenwood blacks formed their own mob to protect Rowland. A confrontation at the courthouse

Smoke billows from the African American section of Tulsa, Oklahoma, during the race riots that rocked the city in 1921. Tulsa was home to one of the most prosperous African American communities in the United States, triggering white resentment. *(Library of Congress, LC-USZ62–33780)*

between the two groups led to an exchange of gunfire. The violence escalated, and rioting broke out.

Throughout the evening of May 31 and the early morning of June 1, mobs of whites carrying guns moved through Greenwood, looting, setting fires, destroying businesses and homes, and shooting black Tulsans, who tried to defend themselves but were outnumbered. More than eight hundred people were injured in the fighting, approximately ten thousand were left homeless, and more than one thousand homes and thirty-five city blocks in Greenwood were destroyed. Rioters and police marched blacks to makeshift prisons throughout the city; approximately half of Tulsa's black population was forcibly interned during the riot.

At a request from the mayor to the governor, the Oklahoma National Guard was dispatched to the city to restore order on June 1. By that time, however, the black commercial district had been decimated and Tulsans had suffered millions of dollars in property losses. The number of dead ranged anywhere from 27 to 250. Numbers have varied because funerals were banned, possible mass grave sites have never been examined, and newspaper accounts were notoriously unreliable.

Although the Tulsa Chamber of Commerce proclaimed that it would rebuild Greenwood, its actions indicated the opposite. The chamber decided to decline all outside donations to reconstruct the town, and much of the black population spent the winter of 1921–1922 living in tents. In the end, it was black Tulsans themselves who rebuilt their community.

In the aftermath of the riot, the governor ordered a grand jury to investigate the event and prosecute possible guilty parties. But like much of white Tulsa, the grand jury placed blame on black Tulsans and the presence of armed black men at the courthouse. Twenty-seven cases went through the grand jury, but no white Tulsans ever went to jail for looting or arson.

Accounts of the riot are contested. The exact sequence and nature of the events has remained unclear, and the memory of eyewitnesses has proven unreliable. In 1997, the Oklahoma legislature appointed a committee to reexamine the incident and explore the idea of reparations. Debate continues over liability for the injuries and damage sustained in the rioting.

Maria Reynolds

See also: African Americans; Chicago Race Riot of 1919; Lynching; Rosewood Massacre (1923).

Further Reading

Brophy, Alfred L. *Reconstructing the Dreamland: The Tulsa Riot of 1921, Race, Reparations, and Reconciliation.* New York: Oxford University Press, 2002.

Ellsworth, Scott. *Death in a Promised Land: The Tulsa Race Riot of 1921.* Baton Rouge: Louisiana State University Press, 1982.

Williams, Lee. *Anatomy of Four Race Riots: Racial Conflict in Knoxville, Elaine (Arkansas), Tulsa, and Chicago, 1919–1921.* Jackson: University and College Press of Mississippi, 1972.

Universal Negro Improvement Association

The brainchild of Jamaican-born black activist Marcus Garvey, the Universal Negro Improvement Association (UNIA) was organized in that British colony in 1914 as the Universal Negro Improvement and Conservation Association and African Communities League. The name was shortened after the organization moved its headquarters to New York City in 1917.

The UNIA promoted a pan-African identity for blacks dispersed throughout the world as a result of the slave trade. It advocated the creation of an independent black nation in Africa "of the Negroes, by the Negroes, and for the Negroes" and sought to instill a new racial self-pride among African Americans. In Harlem, the UNIA set up an international headquarters and quickly picked up approximately 1,500 members. The nightly meetings held at Liberty Hall usually culminated in a Garvey speech. From Harlem, the organization developed rapidly in the early 1920s, establishing chapters in various cities throughout the United States, Great Britain, and the West Indies.

Incorporated under New York State law, the UNIA served the needs of urban African Americans as a combination civil-religious body as well as a life insurance and health insurance company. Styling itself a confraternity, it patterned its organizational structure after that of traditional white fraternal orders, complete with elaborate rituals, secret practices, and exclusivity in membership. Members had to have a dark complexion and pay a fee of thirty-five cents per month: Twenty-five cents went to support the local chapter, with the other ten cents going to the Harlem headquarters. Members were expected to be practicing Christians. Infants and children would be baptized into the body of Christ and the UNIA jointly.

Literature

The UNIA developed an extensive array of literature during World War I and the 1920s, including its weekly newspaper, *The Negro World*. Other publications included Garvey speeches, hymns, poems, prayers, declarations, a motto, a catechism, an anthem, and a constitution, most of which were used either for advertising and recruiting or as part of the ritualized meetings. The organization's official motto was "One God, One Aim, One Destiny." Another favorite was "Europe for the Europeans; Asia for the Asiatics; Africa for the Africans." The official anthem of the UNIA was "Ethiopia, Thou Land of Our Fathers." The processional hymn of the Universal Negro Ritual, practiced at Sunday mass meetings, was "Shine on, Eternal Light." The most quoted Bible passage was Psalm 68:31: "Princes shall come out of Egypt; Ethiopia shall soon stretch out her hands unto God." (Ironically, the UNIA sought the new pan-African nation not in Egypt or Ethiopia but in Liberia, which officially repudiated the organization after 1924.)

Also recited at Sunday mass meetings was the "Universal Negro Catechism," by Chaplain General George Alexander McGuire. According to the catechism, God created man in his own image; if white Christians assert that God is white, then the UNIA would assert that he is black. The official statement of "General Objects" emphasized black pride, charity for destitute blacks, the civilization of the "backward tribes" of Africa, the establishment of black universities and colleges worldwide, and the development of international black business and industrial enterprises. The statement of "Beliefs" included a rebuke of racial miscegenation (said to produce "mongrels"), a call for racial purity for black and white alike, and an advocacy of physical separation of the races as the best solution to racial problems and the most sensible way to bring about racial peace and harmony.

Among the UNIA's principal writings was the "Declaration of the Rights of the Negro Peoples of the World," modeled after the U.S. Declaration of Independence; it had a preamble followed by a list of grievances against the white governments of the world. It also enumerated elements of the Jim Crow system of segregation, including inferior facilities for blacks and unequal treatment before the law. The declaration cited a list of economic grievances as well, such as underfunded black schools, wage discrimination, and the exclusion of blacks from civil service jobs.

In its literature and activities, the UNIA attacked racial discrimination in general, railing at the commonplace use of the term "nigger," the drafting of blacks to fight "white man's wars," and the taxation of blacks without adequate representation. It also issued denunciations of white imperialist control of Africa and the Caribbean islands and called on the European colonial powers to accept the UNIA's claim to rule Africa. It denounced the League of Nations as a racist organization and demanded that the white governments of the world recognize the UNIA as the official political body for the world's 400 million blacks and receive its diplomats and dignitaries accordingly.

On the cultural front, the UNIA attacked what it saw as the suppression of black freedom of the press, speech, and movement and denounced stereotypical depictions of blacks as savages and cannibals. It insisted that the press capitalize the word "Negro," that black children be taught "Negro history," and that August 31 be designated an official, annual, international holiday for all blacks.

Trade and Black Nationhood

To accomplish its goal of black nationhood in Africa (the "Motherland of all Negroes"), the UNIA began a fund-raising campaign in 1919. The immediate goal was to create a steamship company, called the Black Star Steamship Line, to transport American blacks to their new African homeland. The organization adopted a flag and declared red, black, and green the official colors of the black race and the soon-to-be-created "Empire of Africa" or "Interim-Provisional Government of Africa." The colors were symbolic: red, the color of blood, represented the sacrifice of the race in fulfilling its destiny; black symbolized the racial pride of black people; and green stood for the promise of a new and better life in Africa. Garvey and officers of the UNIA likewise developed official national regalia, which they wore during their parades, rallies, and ceremonies, complete with a plumed hat and gilded sword for President-General Garvey—who called himself the "Right Honorable Marcus Mosiah Garvey, the Universal African Redeemer."

For all its pomp, the UNIA failed to impress most black leaders in the United States. W.E.B. Du Bois of the National Association for the Advancement of Colored People (NAACP) became one of its harshest critics. It also drew the ire of the successors of Booker T. Washington at the Tuskegee Institute and the National Negro Business League. The sharpest criticism of the UNIA stemmed from Garvey's association with the Ku Klux Klan. In 1922, he essentially established a UNIA-KKK alliance based on the notion that both organizations professed the common goal of total racial separation, and on the fact that the Klan was at least "honest" in its assessment of the racial situation of America (which Garvey argued could not be said for the NAACP or the Bookerites).

Although most whites dismissed the opinions and declarations of the UNIA as nonsense, the U.S. government took the organization seriously. During World War I, the law enforcement officer in charge of monitoring subversives, J. Edgar Hoover, soon to head the Federal Bureau of Investigation (FBI), lumped the UNIA together with Communists, Socialists, and militant labor unions, despite the fact that Garvey consistently discouraged African Americans from joining such groups. The FBI kept tabs on UNIA activities, publications, and accounting records and Garvey's personal whereabouts. The Justice Department monitored the claims in UNIA advertisements for emigration via the Black Star Line and determined that Garvey was guilty of fraud, supposedly for soliciting funds from prospective emigrants and pocketing the money for personal use. Garvey was tried, convicted, and, after a failed appeal, incarcerated in 1925; more than two years later, President Calvin Coolidge ordered his release and deportation to Jamaica.

Garvey's ouster did not mark the official end of the UNIA, but the organization ceased to exist in any meaningful capacity after 1923. Thereafter, the remnants of the UNIA tried to salvage the emigration scheme by reconstituting the Black Star Line as the Black Cross Navigation and Trading Company, but to no avail. The international headquarters in Harlem shut down, unable to pay the rent. Garvey, meanwhile, continued to promote black nationalism out of Jamaica. In 1929, he started anew by founding the Parent Body of the UNIA-ACL, effectively dismissing the New York–based UNIA. The effort proved fruitless, but the organization has survived, if only in name, to the present day.

Thomas Adams Upchurch

See also: African Americans; Garvey, Marcus; Harlem Renaissance; Migration, Great.

Further Reading

Garvey, Amy Jacques. *Garvey and Garveyism.* New York: Collier, 1970.

————, ed. *Philosophy and Opinions of Marcus Garvey.* Vols. 1 and 2. Reprint ed. New York: Arno, 1968.

Hill, Robert A., ed. *The Marcus Garvey and Universal Negro Improvement Association Papers.* Vols. 1–7. Berkeley: University of California Press, 1984.

Martin, Tony. *Race First: The Ideological and Organizational Struggles of Marcus Garvey and the Universal Negro Improvement Association.* Westport, CT: Greenwood, 1976.

Vaudeville

Vaudeville shows, a form of theatrical entertainment, were made up of short acts ranging from singing, dancing, and comedy to magic, juggling, acrobatics, animal tricks, and dramatic recitation. The shows were America's most popular form of live entertainment at the turn of the twentieth century. At vaudeville's peak, almost every major city in the country had a vaudeville theater; the most famous and prestigious was the Palace Theater in New York City, which opened in 1913. Etymologists debate the word's derivation, though all agree it comes from the French. Possible origins include *voix de ville* (voice of the village), *vaux de vire* (songs from the Vire Valley region), or *vaux-de-vire* (to go and see).

The success of vaudeville is attributed to two businessmen, Benjamin F. Keith and Edward F. Albee (the grandfather of the modern playwright). The former was the first producer to use the term "vaudeville" to refer to variety shows that provided economically priced family entertainment. Keith and Albee joined forces and staged their first show in Boston in 1885. Performers referred to their theaters as "the Sunday school circuit" for the wholesomeness of the shows. After Keith's death, Albee merged Keith-Albee with Martin Beck's Orpheum Circuit, giving the new company control of vaudeville theaters in most major cities across the country. Orpheum managed the West Coast circuit; Albee kept control of the East Coast circuit.

During the golden years of vaudeville, from about 1900 to 1925, there were more than 1,000 theaters in the country. There were essentially two types of vaudeville theaters: small-time and big-time. Small-time vaudeville was cheaper and had fewer well-known acts; big-time vaudeville usually had two performances a day, eight acts per program, and at least one headliner to a show. Audiences paid anywhere from ten to seventy-five cents for a seat. To encourage patrons to stay for more than one live show, silent movies were often screened in between. Early motion pictures did not threaten vaudeville's form of live entertainment.

Vaudeville performers were skillful and well paid during the golden years, receiving from $1 to $10 per minute per show. Many early radio, movie, and television stars started their careers in vaudeville—among them Fred and Gracie Allen, Fred Astaire, Jack Benny, Edgar Bergen, Milton Berle, Fanny Brice, George Burns, James Cagney, W.C. Fields, Bob Hope, Al Jolson, Buster Keaton, the Marx Brothers, Will Rogers, Red Skelton, and Mae West.

Several factors contributed to the decline of vaudeville in the late 1920s. The most devastating blow was the advent of talking pictures. Warner Brothers released the first full-length talking feature film, *The Jazz Singer,* in 1927. An instant hit, the movie starred Al Jolson, who was already well known from the vaudeville stage. Other great vaudeville stars soon were flocking to Hollywood for a chance to star in the "talkies." Major film companies bought vaudeville theaters and converted them into movie theaters. Paramount purchased a large number of theaters and created its own type of live show, called a "unit show," to accompany its movies.

Another setback to vaudeville was the growing popularity of radio. The National Broadcasting Company (NBC), formed in 1926 by the Radio Corporation of America (RCA), and the Columbia Broadcasting System (CBS), founded in 1928, created radio shows that resembled the musicals, comedies, and one-act plays that had graced the vaudeville stage. As more Americans purchased radios, vaudeville stars flocked to the radio waves with hopes of reaching broader audiences.

By 1929, vaudeville was dying quickly. Albee clung to what was left of his empire, now including motion picture as well as vaudeville theaters. Financier Joseph P. Kennedy (the father of future president John F. Kennedy) purchased 200,000 shares of Keith-Orpheum stock and sold them to RCA—giving birth to Radio-Keith-Orpheum (RKO).

America loved vaudeville because it was simple, wholesome, inexpensive, and fun. No theatrical art equaled the popularity of American vaudeville during the first quarter of the twentieth century. Although there is no surviving film footage of an authentic vaudeville show, many of its greatest stars have preserved its spirit through radio, movies, and television.

Elizabeth Penn Whittenburg

See also: Film; Film Industry; Leisure and Recreation; Radio; Theater.

Further Reading

Slide, Anthony, ed. *Selected Vaudeville Criticism.* Metuchen, NJ: Scarecrow, 1988.

Stein, Charles W. *American Vaudeville as Seen by Its Contemporaries.* New York: Da Capo, 1984.

Wertheim, Frank. *Vaudeville Wars: How the Keith-Albee and Orpheum Circuits Controlled the Big-Time and Its Performers.* New York: Macmillan, 2006.

Versailles, Treaty of (1919)

The Treaty of Versailles, named for the seventeenth-century French palace in which it was signed, is perhaps one of the most intensely discussed diplomatic accords in history. The treaty, which ended World War I between Germany and the Allied powers, emerged from the Paris Peace Conference, held from January 18, 1919, to January 21, 1920. Seventy delegates representing twenty-seven countries were present at the conference. The great powers did not invite either Germany or Russia to attend the proceedings—the former because it had been the enemy of the Allies and the latter because it had pulled out of the war after the Bolshevik takeover of that country in 1917.

Differing Agendas

Each of the main powers at the conference—France, Great Britain, and the United States—had its own agenda. Most contemporary observers expected that President Woodrow Wilson would dominate the conference. The United States had emerged from World War I with the most powerful economy on earth, while Great Britain and France were deeply in debt to the U.S. government and financial institutions. Wilson also had a coherent vision for the postwar world.

Known as the Fourteen Points, Wilson's plan called for the spread of democracy and self-determination to the Eastern and Central European peoples once dominated by the Austro-Hungarian and Russian empires, which had collapsed as a result of the war. By implication, Wilson's ideas also could be applied to Britain and France's far-flung empires in Africa, Asia, and the Americas. Wilson also pushed for the creation of a League of Nations, an international body with a mandate to resolve international conflicts peacefully. Finally, the American president envisioned a lenient peace toward Germany, seeing an economically secure nation in Central Europe as a linchpin in the reconstruction of a peaceful, stable continent.

While France and Great Britain agreed about the need for the League of Nations—which they hoped to dominate—they were highly wary of the U.S. president's insistence on self-determination. Above all, they differed on how to deal with postwar Germany. France, which had suffered great destruction during the war, insisted on the harshest terms. President Georges Clemenceau, who represented France at the conference, wanted heavy reparation payments from Germany. And because the two countries shared a land border, the French also insisted on a buffer zone—a neutral, demilitarized corridor in the Rhineland. Finally, Clemenceau demanded control of all coal mines in the Saar region of Germany, to help provide the fuel France would need to rebuild its devastated countryside and cities.

Prime Minister David Lloyd George of Britain took a middle ground between France and the United States. Lloyd George wanted Germany to pay reparations to Britain and France, at least until the generation he claimed was responsible for the war had died. But the British leader was not sold on France's insistence on a separate Rhineland and control of the Saar coal mines. And whereas France wanted the Allies to administer the peace terms in Germany, the British thought that the Germans should do so themselves. The British also wanted to limit German rearmament and have it monitored by the League of Nations.

Terms

In the end, the Treaty of Versailles—like the accords ending the conflict between the other belligerents in the war—was a compromise intended to please all of the victorious parties but fully pleased no one. Most controversial was Article 231, the war-guilt clause, which displeased both the Americans and, to a lesser extent, the British. Both thought it too hostile and burdensome for Germany. The clause forced the

Germans to accept sole responsibility and blame for the conflict.

The Germans were required to pay more than 200 billion gold marks (an estimated 200 million pounds of gold) to the Allies. Even economists of the day considered the sum excessive for Germany's fragile postwar economy. The payments were to be made on a strict schedule, with the first installment of 20 billion marks due on May 1, 1921. The Allied nations would reconsider the final sum at that time, based on Germany's economic condition. The payments would then continue for thirty years or until the full war debt was paid. In addition, Germany would bear the burden of expenses for Allied occupation and construct 200,000 tons of shipping annually for the winning powers for a period of five years. Lastly, Kaiser Wilhelm II would stand trial, accused of war crimes, for his role in starting the war and for atrocities committed during the conflict.

Germany was also forced to accept severe limits on the amount of armaments it could possess and the size of the military it could field. The army would consist of no more than 96,000 troops and 4,000 officers, a fraction of its prewar size. The navy, which had contested with Britain for control of the world's sea lanes before the war, would be limited to just six warships and six support craft. The treaty also prohibited Germany from acquiring or possessing major artillery, military aircraft, or submarines. Even the number of small firearms would be restricted.

The treaty also called for territorial concessions, with Germany forced to relinquish its overseas colonies to the Allies and return some of its European territories to neighboring nations: Alsace-Lorraine to France; Moresnet, Eupen, and Malmédy to Belgium; and Posen and East Prussia to Poland. Danzig (now Gdańsk) would become an international city within the Polish customs union. The Rhineland would be demilitarized and occupied by the Allies for fifteen years.

Only one feature of the treaty pleased all of the signers—the establishment of the League of Nations—but even that accomplishment was soon undermined by developments in the United States. The country was in an increasingly isolationist mood after the war, a result, in part, of the Treaty of Versailles. President Wilson had sold the American people on the war with talk of spreading democracy and self-determination. It would be, he said, the "war to end all wars." But the results of Versailles seemed like a petty power play on the part of the other Allies, and

Americans wanted nothing to do with it. Despite his best efforts, the U.S. Senate, constitutionally mandated to approve all treaties, voted down U.S. participation in the League of Nations in November 1919.

Signing and Legacy

The Senate action was still some five months in the future when the Allied leaders sat down in Versailles's Hall of Mirrors to sign the treaty on June 28, 1919. Germany ratified the accord on July 7, followed by France on October 13, Great Britain and Italy on October 15, and Japan on October 30. The United States refused to ratify the treaty, choosing instead to conclude separate treaties with each of the defeated powers.

The legacy of the Treaty of Versailles was largely a negative one. As predicted by economists, Germany was unable to pay the reparations. Despite loans from the United States, Germany descended into economic chaos in the early 1920s. That crisis, which included massive inflation, created a sense of instability and resentment in the German people and later helped pave the way for the rise of the Nazis. While France tried to enforce the clauses on disarmament and a demilitarized Rhineland, Adolf Hitler ultimately violated the terms with impunity in the mid-1930s, leading to the even greater conflict of World War II.

As for the League of Nations, without U.S. participation and with the leading powers divided over how to deal with a resurgent and aggressive Germany, Italy, and Japan, it languished, unable to prevent the outbreak of the second global conflict of the twentieth century in the 1930s and 1940s. It was ultimately subsumed by the United Nations at the end of World War II.

James Ciment and April Smith Coffey

See also: League of Nations; Paris Peace Conference of 1919; Wilson, Woodrow.

Further Reading

House, Edward Mandell, and Charles Seymour, eds. *What Really Happened at Paris: The Story of the Peace Conference.* New York: Scribner's, 1921.

Sharp, Alan. *The Versailles Settlement: Peacemaking in Paris, 1919.* London: Macmillan Education, 1991.

Walworth, Arthur. *Wilson and His Peacemakers: American Diplomacy at the Paris Peace Conference, 1919.* New York: W.W. Norton 1986.

Veterans

When World War I ended on November 11, 1918, American "doughboys"—members of the American Expeditionary Force—were hailed as heroes and lauded with medals, parades, and memorials. Once the initial euphoria of victory wore off, however, former soldiers had to make the sometimes difficult transition to civilian life. As they adjusted to postwar life, veterans made a significant impact on the politics and culture of Jazz Age America.

Life After War

High unemployment levels in the years following World War I were exacerbated by the discharge of 600,000 soldiers shortly after the armistice was signed in November 1918. In all, more than 3.7 million service personnel were demobilized in the years immediately following the war. Given the contraction of the postwar economy, many returning veterans had difficulty finding work. Some also had to contend with acute housing shortages.

While many industrial workers had prospered from the wartime economy, the pay scale for veterans had not kept pace with that prosperity. Soldiers had been paid only $30 per month, from which the government deducted allotments for dependants and an additional $8 in war insurance premiums. To make matters worse, the returning soldiers' pay was frequently in arrears, and many veterans had unwittingly allowed their insurance to lapse. The $60 discharge bonus that service members received upon demobilization was deemed inadequate by many, particularly since prices had nearly tripled since 1915.

The glaring inefficiencies of the system responsible for dispensing veterans' benefits—coupled with First Lady Florence Harding's outspoken concern for veterans' welfare and pressure from the Disabled American Veterans of the World War (DAVWW, later shortened to DAV)—prompted President Warren G. Harding to launch an investigation of the government agencies charged with handling veterans' affairs. Acting on the recommendation of the Dawes Commission, the Harding administration combined the Federal Board for Vocational Education, the Bureau of War Risk Insurance, and those sections of the U.S. Public Health Service that handled veterans' affairs into a single agency known as the Veterans' Bureau. Harding placed Charles R. Forbes—former

director of the War Risk Insurance Bureau—in charge of the new government agency. However, Forbes was forced to resign when it was revealed that he had illegally sold government supplies and accepted kickbacks on bidding contracts for new veterans' hospitals. Frank T. Hines succeeded Forbes as director of the Veterans' Bureau in March 1923.

Pressure Groups and Legislation

Although President Harding was sympathetic to the plight of veterans and eager to improve the living conditions of disabled veterans in particular, he stopped short of supporting a federal cash bonus, as the Veterans of Foreign Wars (VFW) advocated. The VFW, which had been founded in 1899 following the Spanish-American War, came into its own as a major political force largely as a result of its campaign for veterans' benefits following World War I. The VFW increased both in number and lobbying power during the Jazz Age, so that by 1929, the organization included more than 76,000 veterans and constituted a powerful pressure group.

Another major veterans' organization, the American Legion, was initially divided on the issue of a cash bonus. While most members acknowledged the need for government relief in some form, the American Legion leadership under Theodore Roosevelt, Jr., initially opposed the notion of an "adjusted compensation" bonus for demobilized soldiers. Roosevelt and other critics opposed placing a cash value on patriotism, as the idea of a cash bonus seemed to imply. Before long, however, the dire socioeconomic position of so many of its members prompted the American Legion to join the VFW in lobbying for the cash bonus and other veterans' benefits. By the end of 1920, the American Legion had sponsored 473 different bills on Capitol Hill. Congress could not afford to ignore the highly organized network of American Legion posts, which averaged 8,000 veterans for every congressional district. Membership in the American Legion continued to grow throughout the Jazz Age, reaching more than 1.1 million prior to World War II.

In his inaugural address, President Harding had promised to cut taxes and reduce "abnormal" government expenditures. When the Senate Finance Committee approved a proposal in late June 1921 for additional payments to all ex-soldiers of $1.25 per day of overseas service, and $1 per day for service in the United States, Harding opposed the plan on the grounds that it would hinder economic recovery. The recession had worsened during the first year of the Harding administration; 100,000 bankruptcies were declared in 1921 and unemployment peaked at 12.5 percent. Secretary of the Treasury Andrew Mellon, one of the most powerful opponents of the proposed legislation, supported the president in his decision. Citing concerns about high taxes and fiscal irresponsibility, Mellon convinced first Harding and then his successor, Calvin Coolidge, to veto the veterans' bonus.

Congress overrode President Coolidge's veto, and in 1924, the World War Adjusted Compensation Act became law. The new law provided a bonus to each World War I veteran based on the duration and location of service. Rather than hand out cash payments, however, the government issued endowment certificates payable twenty years from the date of issue. The compromise was acceptable for a time, particularly since America was then entering an era of relative prosperity. Good will between veterans groups and the government was brought to a halt with the onset of the Great Depression, however, when veterans began clamoring for immediate payment of their bonuses.

Racial Tensions

The common experience of serving overseas did little to mitigate racial tensions between black and white soldiers, either during the war or in the decades that followed. The aggressive jingoism of the American Legion seemed to heighten animosity during the Jazz Age as the group asserted the supremacy of white and native-born Americans. Tensions were also exacerbated by the disillusionment that many black veterans felt upon returning to the United States, particularly after experiencing relative equality in French society.

When the United States entered World War I, African Americans had responded by enlisting in numbers disproportionate to their share of the general population. Despite the pervasive racism in the segregated American military, 350,000 African American soldiers and more than 600 African American officers joined the war effort. Many believed that their service and sacrifice on the battlefield would earn blacks acceptance and equal status with whites at the war's end. Black veterans were therefore disillusioned to return to a country in which they continued to be treated as second-class citizens. The resulting militancy is captured in Claude MacKay's poem "If We Must Die" (1919) and in W.E.B. Du Bois's editorial "Returning Soldiers" (*The Crisis*, May 1919). Both pieces called on African Americans to fight for the democratic ideals at home that so many had fought for overseas.

Increased militancy within some segments of the African American community was coupled with the mounting frustration experienced by many white veterans struggling to find housing and employment upon demobilization. America's entry into the war had accelerated the migration of Southern blacks to cities in the North to fill jobs in factories and mines. Racial tensions escalated in the industrial North as white veterans returned home expecting to reclaim their former jobs. Meanwhile, many white Southerners feared the return of black veterans who were trained in the use of arms and would now be demanding equal citizenship. The social dislocations experienced by both black and white veterans contributed significantly to the resurgence of the Ku Klux Klan and the unprecedented wave of racial violence in the immediate postwar years. In 1919, race riots broke out in more than twenty cities across the United States during the "Red Summer"—so called because of the amount of bloodshed, both as the result of racial violence and the government's crackdown on Communists, popularly referred to as "Reds." Veterans were not exempt from the violence; in the twelve months following the armistice, over seventy African American veterans were lynched, several of them while in uniform.

Culture

A number of Harlem Renaissance writers wrote about the war and the experiences of African American veterans. The plays *Mine Eyes Have Seen* (1918) by Alice Dunbar-Nelson and *Aftermath* (1919) by Mary Burrill, for example, call attention to the continued injustices faced by their race despite the honorable service of black soldiers. In the latter work, a young veteran returns home to South Carolina to find that his father has been lynched. Claude McKay's bestselling novel *Home to Harlem* (1928) traces the assimilation of a young veteran, albeit a deserter, into the life of interwar Harlem. One of the most influential scholars of the Harlem Renaissance, Charles Spurgeon Johnson, was a veteran, having served as regimental sergeant major with the 803rd Pioneer Infantry in France.

The American Legion

As the United States joined the Great War in Europe in the spring of 1917, thousands of farm boys, mill workers, and miners were quickly put into uniform. These members of the working class were joined by representatives of the middle and upper classes as well. Few had ever been out of the country; many had never traveled more than a few miles from home. After brief training at a military base, they were shipped to Europe across an Atlantic Ocean infested with German submarines. Most knew little of the countries they were fighting to protect, perhaps a little bit of their history barely remembered from school or a few tidbits picked up from an immigrant down the street or on the next farm.

They had been told they were fighting a "war to end all wars," to make the world "safe for democracy." But what they experienced was far less abstract and more horrifyingly real: artillery barrages raining destruction on mud-filled trenches; modern engines of war such as tanks and machine guns tearing up towns and the countryside; and most terrifying of all, mustard gas attacks that left them blind and gagging for oxygen. A few succumbed to "shell shock," a psychological paralysis induced by the horrors of warfare. Most would be changed forever, unable to explain to friends and family back home what they had gone through.

It was for them that a caucus of American Expeditionary Force (AEF) veterans met in Paris in March 1919, just five months after the armistice, to discuss the possibility of an organization to help veterans readjust to civilian life and to provide a kind of social club where they could meet, share their experiences, and alleviate the lingering effects of the battlefield. Two months later, in St. Louis, Missouri, they formed the veterans' organization known as the American Legion, which Congress officially chartered in September 1919.

The American Legion was an immediate success, as local chapters, called posts, were established across the country to provide support for the 2 million veterans who had served in the AEF. The Legion also worked for veterans' interests in Washington, D.C., proving instrumental in the formation of the U.S. Veterans' Bureau in 1921 (later the Veterans Administration and now the Department of Veterans Affairs).

The American Legion has never tried to hide its conservative ideology. The preamble to its constitution—drawn up in 1919 and still recited before every official Legion post meeting—states that one mission of the organization is to "foster and perpetuate a one hundred percent Americanism," a Jazz Age phrase that sums up the group's opposition to the wave of immigrants and the radical and Socialist politics of the period.

James Ciment

Other veterans of World War I also left their mark on the literary culture of the Jazz Age. Several prominent writers had served in the military and been profoundly affected by the experience of war. F. Scott Fitzgerald, considered by many the voice of the "Lost Generation," had enlisted in the U.S. Army but did not serve overseas. Ernest Hemingway, William March, Thomas Boyd, Hervey Allen, and John Dos Passos had experienced the war more directly and went on to offer scathing indictments of the brutality of modern warfare and what they perceived as the incompetence of the high command. Though the case should not be overstated, the ready audience that such works found suggests a level of disenchantment with the ideals that had drawn the United States into the war.

Kathleen Ruppert

See also: Military Affairs.

Further Reading

Palmer, Niall. *The Twenties in America: Politics and History.* Edinburgh, UK: Edinburgh University Press, 2006.

Parrish, Michael E. *Anxious Decades: America in Prosperity and Depression, 1920–1941.* New York: W.W. Norton, 1992.

Pearlman, Michael. *To Make Democracy Safe for America: Patricians and Preparedness in the Progressive Era.* Urbana: University of Illinois Press, 1984.

Perrett, Geoffrey. *America in the Twenties: A History.* New York: Simon & Schuster, 1982.

Severo, Richard, and Lewis Milford. *The Wages of War: When America's Soldiers Came Home, from Valley Forge to Vietnam.* New York: Simon & Schuster, 1989.

Slotkin, Richard. *Lost Battalions: The Great War and the Crisis of American Nationality.* New York: Henry Holt, 2005.

Ward, Stephen R., ed. *The War Generation: Veterans of the First World War.* Port Washington, NY: Kennikat, 1975.

Volstead Act (1919)

Before the Eighteenth Amendment to the U.S. Constitution took effect in 1920, banning the manufacture, sale, and transportation of alcoholic beverages, supporters of national prohibition believed that the federal government needed enabling legislation to enforce it. In order to ensure that the Eighteenth Amendment would be more than a "ceremonial enactment" defining the nation's values, it was, according to the Anti-Saloon League, "the obligation of Congress and the states to enact legislation necessary to put into effective operation the dry amendment." The legislative solution to enforcement of the Eighteenth Amendment was the National Prohibition Act of 1919, known as the Volstead Act for its author and congressional sponsor, Representative Andrew J. Volstead (R-MN).

Some have contended that the bill was in fact written by Wayne Wheeler, head of the Anti-Saloon League. At the very least, most contemporaries agreed that the measure was an Anti-Saloon League idea. Congress made several revisions to the original proposal, resulting in a final bill that was not only favorable to the legislature but also immune to executive veto. Indeed, Congress passed the Volstead Act on October 24, 1919, over the veto of President Woodrow Wilson. It was agreed that the legislation would take effect with the Eighteenth Amendment on January 16, 1920.

The act contained three major sections. One dealt with extending and enforcing the system of wartime prohibition in the early postwar era. Following World War I, supporters of Prohibition feared that the nation might become wet during the period of demobilization if the federal government did nothing to enforce wartime bans. Aware of alcohol's importance in medicine and industry, supporters of the Eighteenth Amendment recognized that there would be a need to manufacture certain amounts of the substance. Thus, another section of the law set up rules for the production and distribution of alcohol for industrial purposes. This section also attempted to keep alcohol out of the hands of most Americans by controlling the alcohol produced for medicine and making it unsafe for consumption.

The third section of the Volstead Act was the most important, as it set up a national code that banned the possession, sale, manufacture, and transportation of liquor. It created a permit system for distributing and manufacturing alcohol for medicinal purposes, and defined intoxicating liquors as one-half of 1 percent alcohol by volume, thereby making the consumption of beer illegal. Congress, however, made two exceptions to this section, allowing possession of alcohol in "one's private dwelling" and the home fermentation of fruit juices. These exemptions would eventually create major problems for law enforcement.

The national prohibition section divided authority over the enforcement of the Eighteenth Amendment between the Treasury Department and the Justice Department. William Anderson of the Anti-Saloon League and other proponents of the Volstead Act vested federal power with Treasury and revenue agents, believing "it would be foolish to construct a new department, when there was already in existence a bureau with the experience, personnel, and equipment that could be converted to new uses." Meanwhile, the Justice Department would handle prosecutions.

The Volstead Act, along with the Eighteenth Amendment, ultimately failed to curtail the illegal manufacturing and consumption of alcohol. The bill was rushed through Congress, making its language unclear and open to debate. It also presumed cooperation between the states and federal government in implementing and enforcing the ban. Many predicted that the Volstead Act would demonstrate to states how to enforce national prohibition, serving as a guide to local and state officials. Although it was successful in New York, states such as Maryland refused to accept any prohibition statute.

As lawlessness increased and criminal organizations expanded to fill the huge demand for illegal alcohol, a growing opposition constituency developed, known as "wets." With the Great Depression in the early 1930s, the wets began to argue that legalization would provide jobs, economic revival, and tax revenue. When the Democrats—who, outside the South, were usually less committed to Prohibition—took power in the 1932 election, both the Eighteenth Amendment and the Volstead Act appeared doomed.

Ratification of the Twenty-first Amendment in 1933, repealing the Eighteenth Amendment, also nullified the Volstead Act, and alcohol was no longer illegal.

Bruce E. Stewart

See also: Bureau of Investigation; Crime, Organized; Hoover, J. Edgar; Ness, Eliot; Prohibition (1920–1933).

Further Reading

Clark, Norman H. *Deliver Us from Evil: An Interpretation of American Prohibition.* New York: W.W. Norton, 1976.

Hamm, Richard F. *Shaping the Eighteenth Amendment: Temperance Reform, Legal Culture, and the Polity, 1880–1920.* Chapel Hill: University of North Carolina Press, 1995.

Timberlake, James H. *Prohibition and the Progressive Movement, 1900–1920.* Cambridge, MA: Harvard University Press, 1963.

Walker, Jimmy
(1881–1946)

Sometimes referred to as the "Mayor of the Jazz Age," Jimmy Walker was the debonair Democratic mayor of New York City from 1926 until he resigned the office in 1932, forced out by scandal. Much loved—if never completely respected—Walker embodied the carefree spirit that characterized America following World War I. He was a songwriter, would-be actor, lawyer, womanizer, partier (he was also known by the press as the "Night Mayor of New York"), fashion fiend, and affable official host to the dignitaries who visited New York during the 1920s.

James John Walker was born on June 19, 1881, in the city's Greenwich Village neighborhood. His father, William H. Walker, an Irish immigrant who had come to the United States as a teenager, was a carpenter, builder, and lumberyard owner who became part of New York's Tammany Hall political machine as a city alderman, state assemblyman, and superintendent of public buildings. Walker's mother, Ellen Ida Roon Walker, was the daughter of an Irish saloon owner.

Walker attended Saint Joseph's Parochial School, Xavier High School, and La Salle Business College in New York. He studied law—but not with great passion—and only passed the bar exam when he was in his early thirties. He spent his time acting in amateur theatricals and writing several one-act plays. He also had a passion for songwriting. In 1908, he wrote the lyrics to his only successful tune, "Will You Love Me in December as You Do in May." He is reported to have made $10,000 in royalties from the song, and to have spent most of it on clothes.

Walker began his career as a politician in 1909 when, with the backing of Tammany Hall, New York City's powerful and corrupt Democratic political machine, he was elected to the New York State Assembly. Like all would-be politicians and city job seekers, Walker learned that kickbacks, payoffs, and skimming off the treasury were common occurrences in New York City politics. He remained in the state assembly until 1914, when he was elected a state senator. Walker remained in that office until 1925, becoming the Democratic minority leader in 1921. Among his legislative accomplishments were a number of social welfare laws and the legalization of professional baseball on Sundays and professional boxing matches.

In 1925, with the help of Tammany Hall and Governor Al Smith, Walker defeated the incumbent John F. Hyland in the Democratic primary for mayor of New York City. He succeeded to the office the following year by defeating Frank D. Waterman in the citywide election. The popular composer Irving Berlin, a close friend, wrote Walker's campaign song. Another show business friend, actor George Jessel, often shared the podium when Walker gave speeches.

Jimmy Walker was more than just a playboy mayor. During his tenure, he worked to upgrade the city's public hospitals, created the Department of Sanitation, and launched major infrastructure projects to bring the city into the automobile age, including the construction of an elevated expressway in Manhattan, the Triborough Bridge, and the Queen's Midtown Tunnel. He also brought about the improvement of public parks and playgrounds.

But Walker often left much of the day-to-day business of running the city to his assistant, Charles F. Kerrigan—the "Day Mayor," as Walker nicknamed him. Walker frequently presided with enthusiasm over the city's glamour and glitz, always dressed impeccably in suits made by his private tailor. There were ticker tape parades for Charles Lindbergh, Queen Marie of Romania, Gertrude Ederle, and other celebrities. Walker attended Broadway plays, went to clubs and illegal speakeasies, and cheered the 1927 Yankees and Babe Ruth to the World Series. He also had a too-public affair with Broadway singer Betty Compton, whom he first saw in the musical *Oh, Kay!* in 1926. Six years later, he divorced his wife of twenty years, Janet Allen, to marry Compton.

Despite the affair, Walker won reelection in 1929 against Fiorello La Guardia, beating the reform candidate in a landslide. Even in triumph, however, the seeds of his downfall were being sown. Just prior to the election, the stock market had crashed and the mood of the city—and the country—began to change. For Jimmy Walker, a turning point had already come in the fall of 1928, with the shooting of the notorious gangster and gambler Arnold Rothstein. When the politically connected Rothstein eventually died, the New York City police proved either unable or unwilling to find his killer. Charges of Tammany Hall corruption began to circulate.

The public and press demanded an investigation, which began in 1931, led by Judge Samuel Seabury, who was known for his incorruptibility. At first, the investigation was limited to possible corruption in the Magistrates' Courts. By 1932, the investigation had reached city hall and Jimmy Walker. New York Governor Franklin D. Roosevelt subpoenaed Walker to appear before Judge Seabury; then the beleaguered mayor was to appear before Roosevelt himself. On September 1, 1932, just before Governor Roosevelt was to decide on the case, Walker resigned. Walker announced that he would run for mayor again, but instead he left for Europe on September 10.

Ultimately, no charges were brought against Walker, and he returned to New York in 1935. He was divorced from Compton in 1941, became the head of Majestic Records in 1945, and died on November 18, 1946.

William Toth

See also: Celebrity Culture; Democratic Party.

Further Reading

Mitang, Herbert. *Once Upon a Time in New York: Jimmy Walker, Franklin Roosevelt, and the Last Great Battle of the Jazz Age.* New York: Free Press, 2000.

Walsh, George. *Gentleman Jimmy Walker: Mayor of the Jazz Age.* New York: Praeger, 1974.

War Finance Corporation

The War Finance Corporation (WFC) was established in 1918 to ensure that federal money was available for loans to industries crucial to the war effort once the United States entered World War I. The WFC remained in operation after the war, making government-insured loans to industries and farmers to assist them through the recession of 1921–1922 and to encourage exports to other countries. Later in the 1920s and early 1930s, congressional investigations into the WFC's wartime operations revealed evidence of corruption and financial improprieties.

When the United States declared war on Germany on April 6, 1917, it was obvious to American leaders that financial mobilization was just as important as military mobilization. Great efforts were made to convert industry from peacetime production to war production. After a year of war, U.S. government officials found that many businesses were unable to finance expansions for war work because of a lack of capital from private sources; federal war bonds had absorbed most of that capital. As a result, Congress passed legislation on April 5, 1918, to create the War Finance Corporation.

The WFC was a federal corporation with capital of $500 million. The corporation was to issue bonds and extend credit to banks and other financial institutions so that they could make loans to businesses involved in war manufacturing. The WFC could also advance funds to any business important to the war effort that was unable to obtain funds through normal private channels. The managing director of the WFC was Eugene Meyer, Jr., a business partner of influential financier and government adviser Bernard Baruch. Under Meyer, the WFC issued nearly $1.9 billion in federal bonds.

Corruption in the WFC

While the WFC did indeed help private industries necessary to the war effort, later investigations by Congress revealed that Meyer and his business associates profited from some of the loans. Meyer set the amount of interest paid on the bonds after consultations with an assistant secretary of the treasury. These prices were apparently not based on market value but on arbitrary figures provided by Meyer. Meyer also used his old securities firm to buy and sell about $80 million in government bonds. He and his associates in private practice collected commissions on these sales, even though he had directed the sales in his capacity as managing director of the WFC. Meyer used the private accounting firm of Ernst & Ernst to audit the WFC's books. Witnesses later told congressional investigators that the books were altered nightly to cover up wrongdoing.

Congressional investigation also revealed that at least 7,000 duplicate bonds were issued. They ranged in value from $50 to $10,000 and were redeemed by private citizens by July 1, 1924. Additional securities were apparently destroyed to cover up a trail of fraud. Meyer and his associates in the WFC were accused of an attitude of "one for the government, one for me" toward the bonds the WFC issued. Despite questions of possible impropriety, Meyer was named to the Board of Governors of the Federal Reserve System in 1930.

Postwar Impact

After World War I, the federal government continued its unprecedented involvement in the nation's financial affairs. Peace brought a recession that threatened the economic stability of the United States. The WFC was authorized to continue to guarantee loans to railroads, since federal regulation of that industry was already a well-established practice. Agriculture was also suffering in the aftermath of World War I. Farmers had been encouraged to increase production during the war, and the surpluses continued in 1919 and 1920. In 1919, Congress authorized the WFC to make loans to American agricultural exporters. In turn, the exporters were allowed to extend credit to foreign buyers of agricultural products. The hope was that the WFC would encourage the sale of American agricultural products to foreign consumers, reducing the surpluses and keeping farm prices at a higher level. Agricultural cooperatives, such as the Staple Cotton Cooperative Association, benefited from multimillion-dollar federal loans.

By 1924, the WFC had lent $700 million in postwar loans. Its activities were largely replaced by those of the Commerce Department and by Federal Intermediate Credit Banks, established by the Agricultural Credits Acts of 1923. The WFC continued to exist on paper until formally abolished in 1939. During the Great Depression, however, it served as a model for the Reconstruction Finance Corporation (RFC), established in 1932 by President Herbert Hoover. The RFC followed the pattern of the WFC by extending public credit to private industries.

Tim J. Watts

See also: Demobilization, Industrial; Economic Policy; Military Affairs.

Further Reading

U.S. Department of the Treasury. *Liquidation of the War Finance Corporation.* Washington, DC: Government Printing Office, 1943.

War Finance Corporation Laws with Amendments. Washington, DC: Government Printing Office, 1936.

Willoughby, Woodbury. *The Capital Issues Committee and War Finance Corporation.* Baltimore: Johns Hopkins University Press, 1934.

Washington Naval Conference (1921–1922)

The Washington Naval Conference, held in the U.S. capital from November 1921 to February 1922, was a meeting of diplomats representing the world's major naval powers. The conference produced three major treaties—the Four-Power Treaty, the Five-Power Treaty, and the Nine-Power Treaty—each named after the respective number of signatories. Only one of the agreements—the Five-Power Treaty—dealt exclusively with limitations on naval armament; indeed, it became the first major arms limitation treaty in history. The two others concerned conflict resolution in the Pacific basin (Four-Power Treaty) and the sovereignty of China (Nine-Power Treaty). Although a host of countries were in attendance, the main powers in Washington that winter were France, Great Britain, Japan, Italy, and the United States. Notable by their absence were Germany and Russia, the former recently defeated in World War I and the latter internationally ostracized after Communists seized power in 1917.

Background

With the Meiji Restoration of 1868, Japan began to emerge on the world stage as a major industrial and military power. In 1905, it was powerful enough to become the first non-Western country to defeat a Western power, Russia, in a war. While America helped to resolve that conflict, policy makers in Washington were growing concerned that Japanese power in the western Pacific imperiled U.S. interests there, particularly its colony in the Philippines. In World War I, Japan extended its reach in the Pacific by seizing Germany's territories there, a move later ratified by the League of Nations.

Even as Japan's star was rising, China's was sinking. By the early twentieth century, several European powers, as well as Japan, had carved out what were known as "spheres of influence" along the populous coast of China, territories where the outside powers wielded exclusive trading rights and their citizens remained exempt from Chinese law. This was a humiliating development for the Chinese, but with their military backwardness and weak government, one they could do little to address, even after the founding of the Chinese republic in 1911. Of the world's great powers, the United States alone had abjured from claiming a sphere, arguing instead for an "open-door" policy in China, whereby all nations would have the right to trade freely throughout the country.

A more immediate factor behind the Washington Naval Conference was World War I and the vast expansion of the world's navies. Policy makers in Washington wanted to find a way to limit the size of national navies so as to decrease the possibility of another major war. At the time, the League of Nations was the most obvious place to conduct disarmament talks. However, as America had rejected membership in 1919, President Warren G. Harding and Secretary of State Charles Evans Hughes hoped to find a way to establish American leadership in world affairs outside the multilateral framework of that organization.

The U.S. Senate had rejected American membership in the League out of fear that it would entangle the nation in foreign alliances. But the Harding administration realized that the United States, as the greatest creditor nation in the world and still possessing one of the world's largest navies, had to play a role in world affairs. The Washington conference, then, offered America the chance to become engaged in international affairs without the permanent entanglement in foreign disputes implied in the League's charter.

Three Treaties

The Four-Power Treaty was the first to be signed, on December 13, 1921. The accord fixed a potentially dangerous anomaly in international affairs. London and Tokyo had signed the Anglo-Japanese Alliance of 1902, a mutual defense pact pledging that each country would come to the aid of the other in case of attack. But with tensions rising between America and Japan in the western Pacific, this presented the possibility of the United States having to go to war with Great Britain, its closest ally. With the alliance set to expire in 1922, a new framework for resolving conflict in the Pacific was needed. The Four-Power Treaty, signed by Great Britain, Japan, the United States, and France, pledged the signatories to respect one another's territories and League of Nations mandates in the Pacific. As Japan's possessions were the most recent, this part of the treaty was a concession to

Tokyo. In addition, the treaty set up a consultative process for resolving potential conflict.

The Five-Power Treaty and the Nine-Power Treaty both were signed about two months later, on February 6, 1922. The former, also known as the Washington Naval Treaty, sought to avoid conflict by reducing the size of the major navies of the world. This was done by a formula that dictated the relative sizes of the world's navies. Under the treaty, the United States and Great Britain would each be allowed five tons of gross ship tonnage to every three tons for Japan and 1.75 tons each for France and Italy. The United States and Britain claimed a rightful advantage because they already possessed the world's largest navies and operated them in all parts of the globe. While France was also a global power, it had never possessed a major navy. Japan and Italy were considered regional powers, so they did not need such large navies.

Japan was reticent to sign the treaty, demanding a higher ratio, but was mollified by a concession in the treaty whereby the United States would not establish major military bases west of the Hawaiian Islands, and Britain would not do so north of its equatorial possession of Singapore. Still, some feared an English-speaking alliance of the world's two largest navies, rendering the treaty suspect in many international capitals.

The Nine-Power Treaty was signed by all the conference attendees: Belgium, China, France, Great Britain, Italy, Japan, the Netherlands, Portugal, and the United States. The accord essentially established America's open-door policy as international law: The signatories agreed to respect China's independence, sovereignty, and territorial integrity and to end their rights to control trade and to exempt their citizens from Chinese law in their spheres of influence (effectively putting an end to those spheres). These changes would give China the chance to raise its own tariffs to protect local manufactures against imported goods, thereby allowing the country to industrialize. A well-intentioned effort to give China control over its own destiny, the Nine-Power Treaty was largely ceremonial, as it had no enforcement mechanisms.

The Washington Naval Conference represented America's first successful effort at global leadership. President Woodrow Wilson's efforts to shape the postwar world order at the Paris Peace Conference had largely failed. However, while initially successful, the treaties signed at the Washington Naval Conference failed in the long run, partly because the United States was not willing to make the financial and diplomatic sacrifices to see that they were enforced. Japan violated the Four-Power Treaty by seizing U.S. and British possessions in the Pacific in 1941. Despite two agreements signed in London in 1930 and 1936 to adjust the ratios, the Five-Power Treaty was undermined by Italy and nonsignatory Germany's rearmament in the 1930s and Japan's declaration in the mid-1930s that it would no longer abide by the treaty. The Nine-Power Treaty, never seriously enforced to begin with, was rendered null and void by Japan's invasion of Manchuria in 1931 and of China proper in 1937.

James Ciment and Charles M. Dobbs

See also: Europe, Relations with; Four-Power Treaty (1921); Geneva Arms Convention of 1925; Kellogg-Briand Pact (1928); League of Nations; Locarno Treaties (1925); Military Affairs.

Further Reading

Buckley, Thomas H. *The United States and the Washington Conference, 1921–1922.* Knoxville: University of Tennessee Press, 1970.

Cohen, Warren I. *Empire Without Tears: American Foreign Relations, 1921–1933.* Philadelphia: Temple University Press, 1987.

Ellis, L. Ethan. *Republican Foreign Policy, 1921–1933.* New Brunswick, NJ: Rutgers University Press, 1968.

Iriye, Akira. *After Imperialism: The Search for a New Order in the Far East, 1921–1931.* Cambridge, MA: Harvard University Press, 1965.

Wealth and Income

The Jazz Age is remembered in the popular imagination as a time of carefree, even hedonistic, pursuit of pleasure by the American people, made possible by an unprecedented prosperity. But the image of financial good times was partly a product of what followed. Compared to the historically high unemployment and hard times of the subsequent decade, the 1920s appeared like a shining moment of financial gain and freedom from economic want. Not surprisingly, the myth of the "Roaring Twenties" arose during the Great Depression and persists to the present day.

Still, there was some truth to the myth. While unemployment hovered around 20 percent through most of the 1930s, it averaged just 3.7 percent during the 1920s, at least after the end of the sharp but short recession of 1921–1922. Economists liken such an unemployment rate to a kind of full employment, as there is always a small percentage of people between jobs. Almost anyone who wanted a job in the Jazz Age could find one. There was also more money around. Per capita income increased by 37 percent between 1920 and 1929, while the overall price index barely rose, reflecting major productivity gains for the period.

But these glowing numbers masked some significant economic problems. The gains in per capita income largely reflected gains by the top quintile of the population. Large sectors of the economy, most notably agriculture, never recovered from the brief economic downturn of the early post–World War I period. And in the 1920s, agriculture did not represent the tiny sector of the workforce that it does in the twenty-first century; it still accounted for roughly one in four livelihoods in Jazz Age America. By the late 1920s, the woes besetting American farming began to spread to sectors of manufacturing, most notably the automobile industry. All of this was masked by a speculative fever—especially in the sales of corporate securities—that belied the underlying problems of the economy. The illusion was finally shattered by the collapse in stock prices in the last months of the decade, a crash that precipitated a depression in an economy that was never as sound as it appeared.

Poor and Rich

The inequalities in wealth and income during the 1920s were underlined by a number of exhaustive economic studies published at the time. Such studies showed that, amid the apparent boom times of the Jazz Age, a significant number of American families lived on income beneath what was considered minimal to meet bare necessities, and that an overwhelming majority had virtually no discretionary income beyond what it took to meet those basic needs, such as decent housing, adequate diet, and proper clothing.

In 1921, the newly created nonprofit research group the National Bureau of Economic Research (NBER) published the findings of its first study: "Whether the National Income Is Adequate to Provide a Decent Living for All Persons." The NBER chose an income of $2,000 as the minimum that permitted a married couple with three children to live in "modest comfort." Its findings for the period 1910–1919 were that 59 percent to 69 percent of American income earners received less than $2,000 a year. In 1929, the Brookings Institution, a private nonprofit think tank, reported that 71 percent of families earned less than $2,500, the minimum necessary for a decent family standard of living.

Among the Brookings study's other findings were that nearly 6 million families, or more than 21 percent of all families, had incomes of less than $1,000; about 12 million families, or more than 42 percent, had incomes of less than $1,500; and nearly 20 million families, or more than 71 percent, had incomes of less than $2,500. The researchers concluded that a family income of $2,000 was sufficient to supply only the most basic necessities, and that more than 16 million families, or nearly 60 percent of the total number, lived on a substandard income. The average working man with a wife and three children earned about $1,500 per year in the 1920s and spent 35 percent for food, 15 percent for clothing, 15 percent for rent, 5 percent for utilities, 5 percent for medical care, and about 20 percent for miscellaneous expenses; this left just 5 percent for savings, at a time when there was no social security program for retirement.

The upper rungs of the social ladder could not have been more different. While the vast majority of Americans saw their incomes stagnate in the 1920s, the wealthiest did quite well. Between 1919 and 1929, income for the top 1 percent of American households rose by 75 percent, and the share of income received by the wealthiest 1 percent of American households rose from 12 percent to 34 percent of all household income, the greatest leap in so short a period in American history. And at the very top, those with incomes of more than half a million dollars annually climbed from 156 in 1920 to 1,489 in 1929. The distribution of wealth was equally top-heavy. By 1929, the top 1 percent of American households owned 44.2 percent of all household wealth, while 87 percent of the population owned just 8 percent. Roughly one-third of all savings was held by the top 1 percent and fully two-thirds was held by the top 2.3 percent of households.

Much of the wealth came from corporate income. High productivity led to increased corporate profits, which rose 62 percent in the period 1923–1929; these profits in turn fed dividends, which climbed by 65 percent in the same period. The great bulk of the profit was earned by a small group of giant companies; the largest 2,300 firms in America, about one-quarter of 1 percent of all corporations, received roughly 60 percent of all corporate income

during the latter years of the 1920s. A smaller group, about 200 of the largest corporations (not including any banking corporations), controlled about one-half of all corporate wealth. Moreover, in the ten years from 1919 to 1929, these 200 corporations increased their holdings of the nation's corporate wealth to 85 percent while expanding at nearly twice the rate of smaller firms.

The rich received about three-quarters of their income from dividends and capital gains, and between 1920 and 1929, 82 percent of all dividends were paid to the top 5 percent of income earners. As a result, in 1929, some 36,000 high-income families received as much of the nation's income as the 11 million families with the lowest incomes.

For working Americans, from the end of the 1921–1922 recession to the stock market crash of 1929, wages and salaries rose just 5.1 percent; if inflation is taken into account, they rose just 2 percent. In other words, their wages and salaries were virtually stagnant. Indeed, in some industries, wages actually declined in the Jazz Age. Those in meatpacking, for example, fell between 10 percent and 20 percent, while those in coal mining fell by more than 25 percent, from 84.5 cents an hour in 1923 to 62.5 cents in 1929. Steel industry wages underwent a less dramatic but steady decline after the collapse of a nationwide strike in 1919. Skilled workers, such as railroad operators, auto and hosiery workers, printers, and those in the building trades, saw their wages go up at a faster clip than nonskilled workers during the period, but they only represented about 8.1 percent of workers.

Economic historians cite a number of factors for the growing disparities in wealth. The growth of corporate income was made possible largely by gains in productivity, which explains why the rich did so well in the period, since a significant portion of their income and wealth was derived from securities in the form of capital gains and dividends. Why workers did not share in the rising income and wealth created by those productivity gains is harder to ascertain. Many historians argue that the weakening of unions during the period—membership in trade unions fell by roughly 35 percent, from roughly 5 million in 1920 to less than 3.2 million in 1930—played a major role. Without the ability to bargain collectively, workers were unable to effectively demand a larger share of corporate profits, as evidenced by the fact that better organized skilled workers did see their wages go up faster.

Women, Minorities, and Farmers

At the very bottom of the social and economic ladder were three overlapping groups: women workers, minorities, and farmers. Some 25 percent of American women—and 10 percent of married women—were working at the end of the Jazz Age. Wages for women, who largely worked in the service sector and unskilled industries, generally stagnated, reflecting the overall picture of wages and salaries but at a lower level. Women were usually paid significantly less than men, even in the same line of work. Saleswomen, for example, earned between 40 percent and 60 percent of what salesmen earned. Even white-collar women lagged behind men, earning just $1,200 annually through the 1920s, about half of what their male counterparts earned. At the bottom of the income ladder were domestics, who represented about one-third of all employed women and about half of black and foreign-born women workers.

For African Americans, the picture was a bit more mixed. Black workers were far more likely to be unemployed during the decade, and they tended to find work in the lowest paying jobs in industrial America, often forced to work in custodial positions. Black workers tended to earn about 40 percent of what white workers earned in the 1920s. But the percentage of African Americans living in the rural South, where poverty was especially endemic, fell from 85 percent at the beginning of the decade to 79 percent at the end. No matter how poorly one was paid for a factory job in the North, it beat the income available to tenant farmers in the South.

Of the approximately 500,000 Mexican Americans who migrated to the United States in the 1920s, the vast majority lived in conditions of extreme poverty, many in homes that lacked toilets. In Los Angeles, the Mexican American infant mortality rate was roughly five times that for European Americans. According to one survey, many Mexican Americans had diets with virtually no meat or fresh vegetables, and 40 percent said they could not afford to give their children milk. But perhaps the poorest sector of the country's population was Native Americans. Still largely confined to reservations, roughly 70 percent of Native American households lived on less that $200 annually during the Jazz Age, or just 15 percent of what white families lived on.

The poverty endemic to African Americans and Native Americans was partly due to their living in rural areas and being engaged in agriculture. Even white farmers suffered during the 1920s. Indeed, some historians argue that the Great Depression of the 1930s actually began a full decade earlier for most farmers in America. While rural Americans earned about 40 percent of what urban Americans did in 1910, the figure fell to 30 percent by 1930, with most of the decline coming in the 1920s. Between 1919 and 1929, overall farming revenues in America plunged by nearly half, from $21.4 billion to $11.1 billion, and the percentage of national income accruing to farmers fell from 16 percent to 9 percent. For agricultural workers, the situation was especially dire, as they earned less than $300 annually during the 1920s. The poverty conditions of American farmers is reflected in their poor quality of life. As late as 1925, just 10 percent of farm households enjoyed indoor plumbing and 7 percent had electricity.

The depressed farming sector was caused by two related factors: declining crop prices and excessive debt. During World War I, American farmers enjoyed skyrocketing prices for their commodities. The European farm sector was badly hit by the war even as the food demands of the huge armies soared. American farmers expanded their operations in response to rising crop prices, often going deep into debt to buy equipment and land. But when the war ended and European farmers began to produce again, American crop exports declined and food prices dropped significantly. Farmers found themselves unable to pay off their wartime debts, forcing some into tenancy. Not surprisingly, a steady decline in tenant farming during the first two decades of the twentieth century reversed itself in the 1920s, as the percentage of tenants among all farmers rose from 38.1 percent in 1920 to 42.4 percent in 1930.

Economic Failures

When historians cite the reasons for the Great Depression of the 1930s, the stock market crash of 1929 is usually not high on the list. It was a symptom rather than a cause, they say, a reflection of underlying economic problems. More important, they say, were the gross income and wealth disparities between rich and poor in the 1920s. With productivity and profits going up, too few Americans shared in the bounty. They simply could not furnish enough buying power to sustain American industry. And when hard times and high unemployment came, they either had very little savings or were deeply in debt. Thus, any downward trend in income led to dramatically decreased consumption and further unemployment and poverty. Much of the social and economic legislation of the New Deal of the 1930s was created to address the basic failure of the 1920s economy to adequately distribute wealth and income to the majority of Americans.

Leslie Rabkin and James Ciment

See also: Credit and Debt, Consumer; Economic Policy; Housing; Progressivism; Real Estate; Social Gospel; Stock Market.

Further Reading

Bernstein, Irving L. *The Lean Years: A History of the American Worker, 1920–1933.* Boston: Houghton Mifflin, 1960.

Best, Gary Dean. *The Dollar Decade: Mammon and the Machine in 1920s America.* New York: Praeger, 2003.

Leuchtenburg. William E. *The Perils of Prosperity, 1914–1932.* Chicago: University of Chicago Press, 1958.

Weissmuller, Johnny (1904–1984)

As a world-champion swimmer and later a movie star, Johnny Weissmuller became one of the most popular Americans of the 1920s and one of the nation's first high-profile sports celebrities. Born Johann Weissmuller in Freidorf, Hungary, on June 2, 1904, he immigrated to the United States with his family as an infant, residing first in western Pennsylvania and later in Chicago.

At an early age, Weissmuller displayed an aptitude for swimming, winning numerous junior swim meets in the Chicago area and earning a spot on the local YMCA swim team. When his father died in 1920 of tuberculosis, Weissmuller was forced to quit school to help support the family. Yet he continued to swim competitively and to improve as he matured. In 1920, at the age of sixteen, he began training at the Illinois Athletic Club under the tutelage of renowned swimming coach Bill Bachrach, whom he later cited as a mentor and surrogate father. By his late teens, the six-foot, three-inch Weissmuller was one of the top amateur swimmers in the United States and an Olympic prospect.

Weissmuller entered Amateur Athletic Union (AAU) competition in 1921 with an innovative swimming style that he dubbed the "American Crawl," winning many of his early races by large margins. On July 9, 1922, he enhanced his reputation by winning a 100-meter freestyle race with a time of 58.6 seconds, becoming the first ever to swim that distance in less than one minute. Chosen to compete for the United States in the 1924 Olympic Games in Paris, Weissmuller won gold medals in the 100-meter freestyle, the 400-meter freestyle, and the 4x200-meter freestyle relay; he also won a bronze medal as a member of the U.S. water polo team.

Following his gold-medal performances in Paris, Weissmuller became known as the top competitive swimmer in the United States, continuing to amass victories and break national and world records. Numerous stories of his swimming prowess circulated, including reports that he routinely set new records in training with only his coach present. Other records were verifiable and long-standing: His 100-meter freestyle record of 57.4 seconds, set in 1924, would not be broken for ten years. At the 1928 Olympic Games in Amsterdam, Weissmuller was chosen to carry the U.S. flag in the opening ceremonies, and he won gold medals in the 100-meter freestyle and the 400-meter freestyle relay. Following the 1928 Olympics, Weissmuller retired undefeated from competitive swimming with fifty-two U.S. national championships, having set ninety-four American records and sixty-seven world records.

Despite his amateur status, Weissmuller was often compared to the most prominent sports celebrities of the decade, such as baseball player Babe Ruth, boxer Jack Dempsey, tennis player Bill Tilden, and golfer Bobby Jones (also an amateur). His innovative

After winning two gold medals at the 1924 Paris Olympics and another two at the 1928 Amsterdam Olympics, swimmer Johnny Weissmuller went on to a lucrative career as a Hollywood action star, including a dozen films in which he played Tarzan. *(FPG/Hulton Archive/Getty Images)*

style became a model for future competitive swimmers, and numerous contemporary swimmers and coaches studied details of his diet and training regimen. Newspapers of the era celebrated his swimming achievements, assigning him such colorful nicknames as the "Human Hydroplane" and "Aquatic Wonder." A burgeoning new medium, the cinematic newsreel, featured Weissmuller prominently, exposing him to a national audience of theatergoers, many of whom had never seen him in action. Weissmuller's good looks and affable personality enhanced his public appeal, and a 1927 boating accident in which he and his brother Peter rescued eleven people solidified his reputation as a hero.

Following his retirement from amateur competition, Weissmuller became an advertising spokesperson and model for the BVD swimwear company, traveling across the country for swimming exhibitions and personal appearances. In 1929, he made his motion picture debut in *Glorifying the American Girl,* in a nonspeaking role as Adonis. That year he also appeared in the first installment of *Crystal Champions,* a series of short films profiling American Olympic champions. Weissmuller remained popular with the American public and attracted the attention of Hollywood filmmakers.

In 1931, Weissmuller was invited to audition for the lead role in *Tarzan, the Ape Man,* a film based on the book by Edgar Rice Burroughs. Weissmuller later recalled that he did not expect to be chosen for the role and that, despite his reputation as a sports hero, the producer of the film was unaware of his athletic ability; the movie's numerous swimming scenes were added only after Weissmuller was selected. By the mid-1930s, Weissmuller had become a successful film star, as famous for his trademark Tarzan yell as for his legendary swimming exploits.

The initial film appearances marked the beginning of a long motion picture and television career for Weissmuller, highlighted by a recurring role as Tarzan in a series of films ending in 1948 and later the title role in the film and television adaptations of the *Jungle Jim* comic strip. He officially retired from acting in the mid-1950s but continued to make personal appearances and cameo film appearances until his health began to decline in the late 1970s. Weissmuller died at his home in Acapulco, Mexico, on January 20, 1984, after a series of strokes.

Michael H. Burchett

See also: Burroughs, Edgar Rice; Celebrity Culture; Film.

Further Reading

Dawson, Buck. *Weissmuller to Spitz: An Era to Remember, the First 21 Years.* Fort Lauderdale, FL: Hoffman, 1986.
Fury, David. *Johnny Weissmuller: Twice the Hero.* Minneapolis, MN: Artist's Press, 2000.
————. *Kings of the Jungle: An Illustrated Reference to Tarzan on Screen and Television.* Jefferson, NC: McFarland, 2001.
Onyx, Narda. *Water, World, and Weissmuller.* Los Angeles: Vion, 1964.
Weissmuller, Johnny, Jr. *Tarzan, My Father.* Toronto, Canada: ECW, 2000.

Welfare Capitalism

Welfare capitalism is an economic system in which employers voluntarily provide social services and economic benefits, beyond pay, to their employees that, in the absence of such a program, would be paid for by the employees themselves or provided by the state. These benefits can include subsidized housing, health care, skills training and education, pensions and stock-ownership plans, facilities and resources for sports and social clubs, and even company unions. Employers provide these services for a variety of reasons: to encourage employee productivity and loyalty; to prevent the passage of laws that might require employers to provide such services; to prevent the state from assuming such obligations and taxing businesses to pay for them; or out of benevolence toward their employees, often inspired by religious principles.

The Jazz Age was a high point for welfare capitalism in the United States for several reasons. One was the rise of the Social Gospel, a doctrine preaching the application of Christian principles to social problems; the movement was strongly supported in the mainline Protestant churches to which many business leaders belonged. Another reason was worker unrest and popular criticism of poor factory and living conditions among the working classes, along with the business community's fear of progressive government initiatives to regulate working conditions. Also, new theories of management emphasized the importance of worker satisfaction to productivity.

While many companies refused to recognize unions and used all their resources—often getting help from government—to crush strikes, there was also a growing recognition that cooperation, rather than confrontation, between workers and employers made for sounder business. By the early twentieth century, a school of management theory known as "scientific management" had emerged, spearheaded by engineer Frederick Taylor. While Taylor himself emphasized the close management of employees to increase output, other management theorists, those belonging to the school of "industrial relations," argued that easing workers' burdens and anxieties—by providing health care, pensions, and other programs—would increase their satisfaction and productivity and lower worker turnover.

Another economic trend behind welfare capitalism was business consolidation. The late nineteenth and early twentieth centuries saw a wave of corporate mergers, which gave the new big businesses the resources to offer their employees more services. Many corporate executives came to view mergers and welfare capitalism as part of a larger agenda of modernization and efficiency. Just as consolidation helped to eliminate ruinous competition, so welfare capitalism would help to avoid contentious and expensive strikes. Big business was also more conspicuous. Large businesses came under more public scrutiny, often the result of journalistic, or muckraking, exposés of harsh working conditions and unethical business practices in the early twentieth century. It was bad business to develop a reputation as a harsh employer.

The Progressive Era at the beginning of the twentieth century was a period of heightened antitrust action, culminating in the breakup of Standard Oil in 1911. While this action was usually taken in the name of business competition, not worker exploitation, the most high-profile advocate of trust-busting in the early twentieth century, President Theodore Roosevelt, had made it clear that he was not against bigness per se but against bigness that led to economic and social abuses. If major employers could show that bigness benefited employees, they could help ease antitrust sentiment on the part of the public and government officials.

And while the threat of antitrust action eased with the probusiness Republican ascendancy after 1918, public opinion continued to be suspicious of big business. Moreover, a new generation of businessmen, those who managed the big corporations rather than having built them from scratch, had taken over. These new managers saw themselves as trustees of institutions, responsible for satisfying not just stockholders but employees as well.

But perhaps the most important reason for the growth of welfare capitalism was profit. Aside from a brief recession early in the decade, the 1920s were marked by economic buoyancy, rising productivity, and relatively stagnant wages, all of which contributed to corporate coffers, allowing big business to offer various services to their employees.

It is hard to know how many companies, big and small, in the 1920s offered subsidized housing, training, or facilities for social clubs, because few statistics were kept. Nevertheless, data on several key welfare capital programs offer a glimpse into the extent of the practice. Group life insurance plans—offering cash payments to workers and their families if the former became injured, sick, or died—covered roughly 6 million workers by the end of the decade. More than 350 companies offered pension plans. And by 1929, nearly a million employees had invested more than $1 billion in stocks paid for by equity ownership plans (whereby employers aided their employees by helping them purchase shares in the company). Stock ownership plans were seen as the best way to achieve labor productivity, as workers could see a direct connection between the value of their stock and the quality of their work.

While businesses traditionally had been hostile to any kind of collective bargaining, a few began to recognize in the early twentieth century that, if labor unrest was to be avoided, employees needed some way to express their concerns and grievances to management. Company unions seemed to offer a solution, allowing for employees' input into their working conditions without turning over the process to independent trade union officials, who had their own agenda. The first to try this was John D. Rockefeller, Jr., who set up a company union at his Colorado Fuel and Iron Company after a violent strike there in 1913–1914. Its success in easing employer-worker relations led Rockefeller to promote his idea in a series of lectures across the country.

World War I contributed to the spread of company unions as well, as the National War Labor Board, which set rules for labor practices in the nation's defense plants, required the establishment of shop committees to settle labor grievances and ensure continuing production. In the decade that followed the war, then, hundreds of businesses—usually those with 500 or more employees—set up company unions. Their efforts were aided by the weakness of independent trade unionism in the period. After the great wave of postwar strikes ended—largely with the victory of management over labor—the number of workers in trade unions fell precipitously, from more than 5 million in 1920 to fewer than 3.4 million a decade later.

Reaching its peak in the Jazz Age, welfare capitalism virtually disappeared with the coming of the Great Depression. Disappearing profits forced many companies to abandon their programs. Rapidly falling share prices also took the sheen off company stock ownership plans. More generally, welfare capitalism was based on the idea that management and labor shared a common goal: If labor worked hard, they would be taken care of by employers; together, they would raise productivity, which would benefit both parties. But as employers cut wages, benefits, and jobs in response to the Great Depression, the compact broke down. Company unions were discredited as workers increasingly turned to independent industrial unions to fight for their interests. As for welfare capitalism's social services, they were supplanted by government programs such as Social Security.

James Ciment and Michael A. Rembis

See also: Ford Motor Company; Labor Movement.

Further Reading

Braeman, John, Robert H. Bremner, and David Brody, eds. *Change and Continuity in Twentieth-Century America: The 1920s.* Columbus: Ohio State University Press, 1968.

Brandes, Stuart D. *American Welfare Capitalism, 1880–1940.* Chicago: University of Chicago Press, 1984.

Cohen, Lizbeth. *Making a New Deal: Industrial Workers in Chicago, 1919–1939.* New York: Cambridge University Press, 1990.

Wheeler, Burton K. (1882–1975)

A reformist Democratic senator from Montana, Burton Kendall Wheeler was best known in the 1920s for his efforts to expose the Teapot Dome scandal in the Republican administration of President Warren G. Harding. He was also known for his support of progressive causes and his opposition to interventionist American foreign policy in Latin America. Born on February 27, 1882, in Hudson, Massachusetts, Wheeler attended public schools. After earning a law degree from the University of Michigan in 1905, he established a practice in Butte, Montana.

Wheeler was elected to the Montana state legislature in 1910 on a ticket supported by the region's powerful mining interests, but he quickly established his independence by supporting progressive Thomas J. Walsh for U.S. senator against their wishes. After serving as the U.S. district attorney for Montana, Wheeler unsuccessfully ran for governor in 1920, and in 1922, he was elected to the U.S. Senate. He was a fiercely independent voice of reform during the conservative 1920s, and his political career was marked by his stance against those who would bend the government to serve private interests.

Naval Oil Reserve Number Three, better known as Teapot Dome, was the spring that launched Wheeler onto the national stage. The Teapot Dome scandal involved the leasing of publicly owned oil reserves to private interests in exchange for bribes to several cabinet-level officials in the administrations of President Harding and his successor Calvin Coolidge. Senator Wheeler pursued an investigation of the actions of U.S. Attorney General Harry Daugherty relating to the oil scandals. On March 28, 1924, after several days of testimony supporting allegations that he had accepted bribes, Daugherty was forced to resign.

The administration took revenge on Wheeler when the Department of Justice brought federal corruption charges against him. An investigation by a Senate committee exonerated Wheeler on May 14, 1924, and it took less than ten minutes for a Montana jury to acquit him on April 24, 1925. Wheeler emerged with a national reputation as a tough crusader against the corrupt and powerful.

A Democrat throughout his political life, Wheeler was also a leading member of a bipartisan group of Western, independent, and reform-minded senators in their heyday during the 1920s. Often called the "insurgents" or "progressive bloc," senators such as Wheeler, William E. Borah (R-ID), and George W. Norris (R-NE) defied their own party leaders to fight against "the interests," which they generally defined as big business, Wall Street bankers, and other forms of concentrated power. When Senator Robert La Follette (R-WI) ran for president on the Progressive Party ticket in the election of 1924, Wheeler was his running mate, declaring that the major parties' candidates were beholden to Wall Street.

In 1928, Wheeler supported the Democratic presidential nominee, New York Governor Al Smith, whom he called a "true liberal." Key elements of Wheeler's domestic policy included support for the labor movement, the McNary-Haugen farm relief bill, railroad reform, and investigations into government abuse of Native Americans.

For Wheeler, U.S. interventionist foreign policy in Latin America symbolized the manner in which powerful interests forced American policy to serve their will. No incident better illustrated this than the American intervention in Nicaragua's civil war. After

1912, a small contingent of American troops had been maintained in Nicaragua to ensure stability, but the force was withdrawn in 1925. A coup promptly ensued against the democratically elected government, and President Calvin Coolidge dispatched troops to the region in 1926 to protect American lives and property. Wheeler played a particularly active role in challenging the administration's version of events in Nicaragua. He spoke out against what he regarded as the administration serving Wall Street's imperialistic designs in Latin America, and he called for the immediate withdrawal of American forces from Nicaragua.

Wheeler and other progressives were not powerful enough to force the administration to reverse course, but they were able to use their national prominence to focus attention on the issue. That pressure, combined with developments in Nicaragua, caused the administration to begin a shift from intervention to diplomacy and was a step on the path toward President Franklin D. Roosevelt's Good Neighbor Policy of the 1930s.

Wheeler was part of the progressive reform tradition that had thrived in previous decades. His was the voice of reform in a decade of conservatism. He supported Roosevelt's bid for the presidency in 1932, and he was an early supporter of the New Deal reforms. He maintained his fierce independence in the 1930s, never shying away from vocal opposition to many of Roosevelt's policies during the late 1930s and early 1940s. Wheeler left political life in 1946, and he died in Washington, D.C., on January 6, 1975.

Charles E. Delgadillo

See also: Democratic Party; Nicaragua, Intervention in; Teapot Dome Scandal.

Further Reading

Bates, J. Leonard. "The Teapot Dome Scandal and the Election of 1924." *American Historical Review* 60:2 (1955): 303–22.

Johnson, Robert D. *The Peace Progressives and American Foreign Relations.* Cambridge, MA: Harvard University Press, 1995.

Wheeler, Burton K., and Paul F. Healy. *Yankee from the West: The Candid, Turbulent Life Story of the Yankee-Born U.S. Senator from Montana.* New York: Octagon, 1977.

Wilson, Edith (1872–1961)

Among the most activist of first ladies, Edith Bolling Wilson virtually ran the White House from the time her husband, President Woodrow Wilson, suffered a major stroke in October 1919 to the end of Wilson's term in March 1921. Born in Wytheville, Virginia, on October 15, 1872, Edith Bolling was the seventh of nine children of William Bolling, a lawyer and judge, and Sallie White Bolling. For two years she attended Mary Washington College in Abington and the Powell School in Richmond, Virginia, and in 1896 she married her cousin-in-law Norman Galt, a prosperous Washington, D.C., jeweler. As a young matron, she traveled widely in Europe and became one of the first women in Washington to drive an automobile. Galt died in 1908, leaving no children, and Edith sold the business.

She met the widowed Woodrow Wilson during visits to the White House in the spring of 1915, winning the approval of Wilson's three adult daughters, who invited her to travel with them as part of the presidential entourage. Wilson faced enormous pressure from political advisers not to marry again less than a year after the death of his wife, Ellen Axton Wilson, but he proposed on October 5, 1915. Edith carefully weighed the pressure of an upcoming political campaign, as well as Wilson's affair with Mrs. Thomas Peck, which might be revealed during the campaign, but accepted his proposal. They were married on the evening of December 18, 1915, in a small ceremony at her Washington home.

Because she had never been part of Washington political circles, her status as first lady and center of the social scene ruffled established figures such as Alice Roosevelt Longworth (the daughter of former President Theodore Roosevelt). Edith Wilson accompanied her husband on the campaign trail for reelection in 1916, although she disapproved of his support for woman suffrage and the behavior of suffragists. After the U.S. declaration of war against Germany in 1917, she insisted on wheatless and meatless meals in the White House, and she served in Red Cross workshops and canteens in the Washington area. It is believed that she was behind the symbolic gesture of using sheep rather than hiring gardeners to crop the White House lawns, to free up manpower for the war.

Woodrow Wilson taught his wife his secret codes, which he had previously shared only with top adviser Colonel Edward House, and frequently included her in government decision making that excluded cabinet members. This enraged the president's political rivals, such as Senator Henry Cabot Lodge (R-MA), whom Edith Wilson considered a personal enemy.

First Lady Edith Wilson took over a number of executive duties after her husband, President Woodrow Wilson, suffered a massive stroke while campaigning for U.S. membership in the League of Nations in 1919. Some called her the "secret president." *(Stock Montage/Hulton Archive/Getty Images)*

The presidential couple traveled together to the Paris Peace Conference in 1919, with the first lady urging the president to ration his strength in his struggle to hold to the Fourteen Points despite suffering from influenza and exhaustion. Proudly refusing to curtsey before royal visitors, Edith Wilson demonstrated a sense of style and devotion to her husband that impressed European leaders and moved French Premier Georges Clemenceau to allow her to watch the reading of the treaty terms from a curtained room as the only nondelegate witness.

Back in the United States, she accompanied Wilson on his tour to promote the League of Nations and was a crucial support as his health began to fail. On October 2, 1919, Wilson suffered a stroke in the White House that left him paralyzed and gravely ill. From then until April 11, 1920, the first lady and family friend Dr. Cary Greyson isolated the president for medical reasons and made all decisions about his care. The first lady kept the president's condition largely hidden from the public and fought off attempts to allow Vice President Thomas Marshall to assume the presidency.

During this period, Edith Wilson handled all governmental papers and acted as a gatekeeper to the president's rooms, a move the press and political opponents disparagingly labeled "Mrs. Wilson's Regency." President Wilson returned to public view in April 1920, but his wife continued to act as his political agent, particularly after the final souring of their relationship with Colonel House.

With Wilson's term in office completed, the couple retired to a private residence on S Street in Washington, D.C., where the retired chief executive dictated to his wife *The Road Away from Revolution,* a pamphlet on how the West could avoid a Russian-style Communist revolution. Wilson died on February 3, 1924.

Edith Wilson voted for the first time in 1920—the Nineteenth Amendment to the U.S. Constitution had been ratified, enabling woman suffrage. She remained an ardent Democrat, addressing the Democratic National Convention in 1928 and traveling widely to promote the League of Nations. She served as a trustee of the Woodrow Wilson Foundation and helped to establish the Woodrow Wilson Birthplace in Staunton, Virginia. The former first lady published her autobiography, *My Memoirs,* in 1939 and campaigned enthusiastically for both Franklin D. Roosevelt and John F. Kennedy. She died in Washington, D.C., on December 28, 1961.

Margaret Sankey

See also: League of Nations; Wilson, Woodrow.

Further Reading

Hatch, Alden. *Edith Bolling Wilson.* New York: Dodd, Mead, 1961.

Levin, Phyllis. *Edith and Woodrow: The Wilson White House.* New York: Scribner, 2001.

Smith, Gene. *When the Cheering Stopped: The Last Years of Woodrow Wilson.* New York: Morrow, 1964.

Wilson, Woodrow (1856–1924)

Idealistic and progressive, but often stubborn and politically obtuse, Woodrow Wilson served as the twenty-eighth president of the United States, from 1913 through 1921. He led the nation during a time of domestic progressive reform, but also a period of increasing international tensions that culminated in the outbreak of World War I. He campaigned for reelection as a peace candidate in 1916, but he led the country into conflict the following year. His postwar efforts to create a just international order and establish the League of Nations were foiled by a growing isolationism in America, and he watched his internationalist ideas crash against the political and diplomatic realities at home and abroad.

Thomas Woodrow Wilson was born on December 28, 1856, in Staunton, Virginia. He graduated from Princeton University in 1879 and practiced law, becoming president of the university in 1902. In 1910, he served as the governor of New Jersey and was elected president of the United States in 1912 after a heated three-way campaign (his major opponents were William H. Taft and Theodore Roosevelt). As president, Wilson implemented such progressive policies as the eight-hour workday for federal workers, the establishment of the Federal Reserve, and various pieces of antitrust legislation. In 1916, he was reelected on the promise that he would keep the United States out of World War I. In 1917, after Germany's declaration of unrestricted submarine warfare, however, Wilson asked Congress to declare war and helped lead the Allies to victory.

Wilson was the only Ph.D. to serve as president, and he brought to the job a commitment to an activist government at home and a multilateral approach to world affairs. Much of his thinking on progressive government at home would be taken up and expanded during the New Deal, while his ideas about multilateralism abroad would form the basis of the post–World War II international order.

But Wilson could often be dogmatic, unwilling to participate in the normal give-and-take of the political arena. In 1919, he traveled to Paris for the peace conference ending World War I and was greeted as a hero by ordinary Europeans, but he soon fell out of favor with other Allied leaders, who were put off by his self-righteousness and unwillingness to accept their ideas and points of view. That same righteousness could make him appear hypocritical when reality required that he compromise on basic principles. After lecturing the Europeans on the dangers of secret diplomacy, he closeted himself with the leaders of Great Britain and France to work out critical issues such as reparation payments from Germany. Wilson's participation in these secret negotiations brought him much criticism at home, as many Americans had come to believe it was this kind of backroom diplomacy that had contributed to the outbreak of World War I in the first place. Indeed, the president was eventually forced to give up many of his cherished principles, including a just peace for Germany.

Wilson also compromised on self-determination for colonized people. In that regard, he shared many of the attitudes of European leaders. A son of the South, Wilson, many historians contend, was a racist; upon coming to office in 1913, one of the first acts of his administration was to impose segregation laws on the District of Columbia. And a delegation of African American leaders that came to the White House to protest these actions was told that segregation was "not a humiliation but a benefit" for black Americans. On only one principle was Wilson unwilling to compromise: the League of Nations. And for that, he was awarded the Nobel Peace Prize in 1919.

Before the war, Wilson was popular and enjoyed a string of legislative successes on domestic reform. After the war, he proved unable to push his internationalist agenda. Part of the problem was the changing political landscape. During his prewar tenure as president, he was fortunate to have fellow Democrats, along with some liberal Republicans, in control of both houses of Congress, allowing him to achieve much of his progressive agenda. But when voters gave Republicans control of both houses of Congress in 1918, partly in reaction to the war and to nearly two decades of progressivism, Wilson proved unable to adjust his strongly held beliefs or make the compromises necessary to gain such objectives as League ratification.

When resistance to the League of Nations arose in the increasingly isolationist Congress, Wilson tried to get around that body by appealing to the American people directly. In the course of a hectic national tour, he suffered a stroke that paralyzed him for several months. Rather than turn over some of the reins of government to cabinet officials and Vice President Thomas Marshall, Wilson allowed his wife, Edith, to act in his stead, running the daily affairs of the administration. In his last years in the White House, he cut himself off from longtime political adviser Colonel Edward House. The public, however, did not become aware of the full extent of his incapacity until after he left the White House. Wilson even contemplated running for an unprecedented third term, but Democratic leaders made it clear that he was more a liability than an asset to the party by 1920.

Wilson, and to a certain extent Wilsonianism, was massively repudiated in the 1920 election by voters, who voted the antiprogressive, isolationist Republican Warren G. Harding into the White House and gave overwhelming majorities to Republicans in Congress. In his retirement, Wilson turned to political science, which he had studied and taught as a younger man. In 1923, he published *The Road Away from Revolution,* a brief tract on the dangers of communism and what the West must do to avoid radical political upheaval of the kind that had turned Russia into a Bolshevik state in 1917. Wilson died in Washington, D.C., on February 3, 1924.

James Ciment and Dino E. Buenviaje

See also: Democratic Party; Election of 1918; Europe, Relations with; League of Nations; Paris Peace Conference of 1919; Progressivism; Versailles, Treaty of (1919).

Further Reading

Powaski, Ronald E. *Toward an Entangling Alliance: American Isolationism, Internationalism, and Europe, 1901–1950.* Westport, CT: Greenwood, 1991.

Rhodes, Benjamin D. *United States Foreign Policy in the Interwar Period, 1918–1941: The Golden Age of American Diplomatic and Military Complacency.* Westport, CT: Praeger, 2001.

Tilchin, William N., and Charles E. Neu, eds. *Artists of Power: Theodore Roosevelt, Woodrow Wilson, and Their Enduring Impact on U.S. Foreign Policy.* Westport, CT: Praeger, 2006.

Walworth, Arthur. *Wilson and His Peacemakers: American Diplomacy at the Paris Peace Conference, 1919.* New York: W.W. Norton, 1986.

Women and Gender

The lives of Jazz Age Americans varied greatly, depending on their race, class, region, ethnicity, and gender. Steady numbers of women entered the job market, but gender stereotyping placed women in subordinate positions, both in the workforce and in their own homes. The cause of women's rights, buoyed at first by the suffrage victory in 1920 with ratification of the Nineteenth Amendment, ultimately sputtered after a decade of setbacks. Women's traditional roles in marriage and the family were modernized by sweeping changes in American society, but popular perceptions of womanhood also limited the transformation of women's lives in this decade. Women generally benefited from an expansion of opportunity, and female autonomy was more recognized than ever before, yet the 1920s was not a decade of true economic, social, and political independence and equality for women.

Diversity of Work and Life

The carefree, sexually liberated flapper, an icon of the Jazz Age, represented a relatively small group of women who were urban, white, young, and middle class. Many young middle-class women, having graduated from high school in record numbers, chose higher education. Women attended both coeducational institutions and esteemed women's colleges, making up 43.7 percent of the total college population in 1920. After college, a few middle-class women chose a career and took advantage of the expansion of professional opportunities so often heralded in connection with the "New Woman." In reality, however, their options were limited to traditionally feminized occupations, such as social work, teaching, and nursing. Some women entered male-dominated fields such as medicine, law, and science, but they were often isolated and underpaid. By 1930, fewer than 15 percent of all women workers were employed in professional positions. And despite the hopes of feminists, most professional women in the 1920s had a difficult time combining a family and a career.

Most women married after college, and they used their analytic skills in a scientific approach to homemaking and child rearing, bringing to bear on the basic task of homemaking the latest scientific findings on health and hygiene, diet and nutrition, and developmental psychology. Efficiency in the home allowed for spare time, but most women stayed out of the job market and devoted those extra hours to religious and civic activities. Their daughters were more likely to follow in their footsteps than to agitate for sexual and social liberation.

Discrimination kept most African American women in poverty, but a few moved into the middle class in the 1920s. Often this transition was made possible by their attendance at one of the country's all-black or integrated colleges. Although they faced overwhelming discrimination, some found work in the fields of social work and teaching. These middle-class African American women continued to work through established, segregated institutions such as the National Association of Colored Women, and with groups like the YMCA and the Urban League, in their efforts to serve and uplift their own communities.

Ten million women worked for wages in the United States in the 1920s. A swift expansion of women in the workforce had taken place in the preceding two decades; 25 percent of all women worked outside the home in the 1910s, and the number held steady but did not increase during the 1920s. Most young women who were not in college were in the workforce, and the typical working woman was single and under twenty-five.

The types of jobs available to working-class women swelled as white-collar jobs increased, providing an alternative to manufacturing and domestic work. Women continued to work on assembly lines, in laundries, and in other people's homes, but many took positions as secretaries, stenographers, and sales clerks. By 1930, more women worked in offices than in manufacturing.

Most of these women were not unionized. A 1927 study showed that more than 3 million women were eligible for union membership, but only about 265,000 were actually members. In addition, heavily female fields like domestic work, clerical work, and teaching were not yet organized. Thus, female wage earners were more vulnerable than their male counterparts. By 1929, women made an average of fifty-seven cents per hour—compared to one dollar for men—in often unskilled, unstable, low-paying jobs. Protective labor laws for women were common in this decade; sixteen states banned female night work, thirteen fixed a woman's minimum wage, and all but four states limited a woman's workday. While the expansion of white-collar work and protective labor legislation improved working conditions, women were still relegated to traditional women's work, and employers still discriminated against women.

Many married women entered the workforce in the 1920s, despite the common preference for them to remain at home. The average minimum wage needed to support a family varied by state, from $1,500 to $2,000 annually. According to a 1927 study, unskilled male workers earned an average of $1,200 a year. A woman's paycheck was a necessity for many families.

One study of women in Philadelphia demonstrates the variety of their working lives. Italian immigrants usually took in piecework at home and often left the workforce completely after marriage. Irish women, once clustered in domestic work, increasingly moved into newly created white-collar positions. Polish women, often hindered by their lack of proficiency in English, cleaned the homes of other Polish immigrants or took boarders into their own homes. Jewish women tended to work in shops for relatives, keeping family traditions central. African American women, despite their native English and often higher levels of education, were forced into the lowest-paying positions available to women. They tended to work in agriculture, in laundries, in cigar factories, and most often as domestics. Mexican immigrants in the 1920s found even fewer options, working primarily in the agricultural sector. The vast majority of these working-class women entered the workforce in low-skill, low-paying jobs out of necessity, or struggled at home to raise children and care for their families, all the while holding fast to old cultural traditions.

Women's Rights

More than seventy years after women had begun the struggle for the right to vote, the Nineteenth Amendment was ratified in August 1920. The suffrage fight had held up a single pursuit to all women—an end to their collective disenfranchisement. Without such a focused goal, women's interests were bound to diverge. Recognizing this, suffragists transformed the National American Woman Suffrage Association into the League of Women Voters (LWV) in 1920. Carrie Chapman Catt and other leaders of the LWV saw enfranchised women as individuals with their own relationship to the state, and they set out to train these women in good citizenship.

Some women sought entry into the male-dominated world of partisan politics. Republicans and Democrats made a few token appointments of women to national committees, but never in real positions of power. Women interested in holding office were kept at the margins of party life, and by 1933, only thirteen women were serving in the U.S. House of Representatives and one in the Senate. In the 1920 election, fewer than half of all women turned out to vote; those who went to the polls tended to vote as their husbands did. Marriage, divorce, and property laws remained unfair to women. And by 1924, it was clear that the suffragists' great hope—that women voters would usher in social reform and greater economic equality—would not materialize.

Despite ratification of the Nineteenth Amendment, most African American women could not vote in the South, where Jim Crow laws kept most blacks from voting. Some prominent black women approached the LWV and the National Woman's Party (NWP) for assistance, but the white middle-class organizations hesitated to take on the issue of racial discrimination.

A further division within the women's movement was whether to claim equality with men or to seek solidarity in their difference from men. This split is most vividly illustrated by the battle over a proposed equal rights amendment in the 1920s. The

Flapper: Myth and Reality

To the present day, the image of the flapper remains one of the icons of the devil-may-care spirit of the Roaring Twenties, a symbol of how liberated young women after the Great War defied the old-fashioned Victorian moral code of their parents. Mythologized in the racy silent movies and magazines of the time, flappers had bobbed hair, rouged lips, and wore short dresses that revealed their ankles. They avoided church, marriage, and child rearing, popular opinion had it, preferring scandalously late-night dancing of the provocative Charleston, smoking, and drinking bootleg liquor in the illicit speakeasies that sprang up during Prohibition.

In contrast to the carefully chaperoned courting parlors in which prewar dating rituals primly unfolded, young women of the Jazz Age now took to riding around with men in Model Ts, unsupervised spaces of freedom condemned by church leaders as "houses of prostitution on wheels." In the culture wars of the 1920s, pitting traditionalists against modernists, those in the former camp saw the flapper as a sign that hedonistic "flaming youth"—and perhaps America itself—was headed straight to hell.

Like most stereotypes, however, the image of the flapper distorts the experience of millions of young women who indeed enjoyed new freedoms. In part, these freedoms were the fruit of women who had worked in factories and on farms during the war effort of 1917–1918. In part, they were an outgrowth of the long-deferred movement for woman suffrage, which finally achieved victory with ratification of the Nineteenth Amendment in 1920.

But the "New Woman" of the 1920s was largely a product of the economic opportunities and financial independence afforded by the industrial expansion of the times. Madge Krol and Helen Rydelek, sisters from a Polish American family, are good examples. As they later recalled, moving from the farm near the town of Goodells, Michigan, to take jobs in Detroit's booming auto industry exposed them to all the excitements of the big city and modern life, with the disposable income to ride streetcars (six cents a ride), see Mary Pickford movies (ten cents admission), and go roller-skating and dancing. Dressed up in fashionable new outfits and spit curls, they sometimes used fake identification to gain admission to "blind pigs" and "classy" places like the Greystone Ballroom. They learned to smoke, they sometimes drank alcohol, and they rode in cars with friends. But it was all "good, clean fun," and they retained the core values of their parents.

Madge and Helen shared living quarters with two other women in a one-room basement apartment. They worked hard and saved money from their small paychecks, sending some money to their family back on the farm. They went to church and visited home as often as they could. They deny being flappers like Daisy Buchanan in *The Great Gatsby*. In fact, their experience was closer to that of typical American women than that of the Hollywood vamp. But in exercising independence, they were pioneers, and represented a new ideal of womanhood unthinkable for their mothers and grandmothers.

Gregory D. Sumner

NWP, headed by Alice Paul, worked to secure an amendment to the U.S. Constitution that would protect against discrimination on the basis of sex. Waging a single-issue campaign, the NWP called for unity and worked with clarity of purpose. But a number of social reformers, such as Florence Kelly and the leaders of the Women's Trade Union League, criticized this equal rights legislation because it would invalidate protective labor laws for women workers. If women were guaranteed equality with men, they could not qualify for labor laws that distinguished them on the basis of their sex. They wanted equality, but they appreciated women's practical differences from men. Others argued that once gender equality was established under the law, social justice would follow.

Divisions between groups of women were bitter and deep. In an increasingly conservative decade, the equal rights amendment was attacked on many sides and obstructed in Congress. Social reform was largely unpopular, and women's activism went into a period of decline.

Marriage and Family

Changes in American society by the 1920s led to substantial changes in women's roles in marriage and the family. Women integrated with men in many ways as they lived through the disintegration of the Victorian era's separate spheres, or the belief that men and women should move in two different worlds. A new discourse on sex permeated American culture, and women who came of age during the late 1910s and 1920s encountered a changed social framework.

The break from Victorianism simmering among the working and upper classes broke into the middle class, marking the 1920s as a period of relative sexual liberalism. Popularized interpretations of Freudian psychology linked sexuality to notions of personal identity, the self, and individual liberation. Postwar youth were integrated with members of the opposite sex at an early age. Surveys of young women in college showed that 92 percent admitted to petting in the 1920s, and at least one-third of women who came of age in the 1920s had premarital sex.

Women's sexuality was acknowledged for the first time in the 1920s, and the sexual and emotional satisfaction of both partners became an integral part of marriage. Men said they wanted a woman they could talk to about the world. Women wanted to express their individuality, their sense of self, and their

sexuality—all afforded to them by a changing, modern culture.

The desire for partnership, along with social reformers' desire to rein in the sexual activities of the nation's youth, led to the idea of "companionate marriage" in the 1920s. In a period when the divorce rate rose from five per 1,000 in 1920 to about seven per 1,000 in 1930, here was a way to contain dangerous sexual disorder and promote the family. More people were marrying in the 1920s, and more were marrying younger, so physicians, social workers, social scientists, and psychologists incorporated new social patterns into traditional sexual values. The main tenets of companionate marriage, articulated in the popular press, prescriptive literature, and marriage manuals, were early marriage, birth control, easy divorce for the childless, and equality between the sexes.

But the ideal of companionate marriage did not translate into any real political or economic equality for women. Women's sexual expression was limited to the marital relationship, and the success of the marriage was largely placed on women's shoulders. A man's identity was tied to his work, but a woman's sense of identity and self-worth was tied to her ability to compete in the marriage market. Economic security and social status were tied to a successful marriage and the middle-class family. Women who rejected marriage were defined as deviant and possibly homosexual.

Perceptions of Women

Mass culture, modernity, and the rapidity of change shaped popular perceptions of women in the 1920s. Movie plots reflected but also influenced social behavior and societal expectations. Movie stars like "It Girl" Clara Bow were role models, urging women to embrace modern womanhood. The flapper—flirty, fun, and carefree—epitomized the liberation of American women from the inhibitions and restrictions of Victorian culture. The enthusiasm, freedom, and sexual adventurousness so highly prized by the flapper were conveyed throughout the country by mass culture.

The meteoric rise in advertising also played a significant role in constructing popular views of American womanhood in the 1920s. Women were recognized as the nation's top consumers, and sex was used to sell products. Womanliness was tied to cosmetics and cleansers. The independence of American women was channeled into consumer culture, as advertisements celebrated women's right to choose from a variety of detergents and vacuum cleaners. Ads created the perception that women were modern, empowered, and liberated, even as consumer culture prescribed female gender roles.

Despite modern colorful kitchens and access to cigarettes and dance halls, American women were regulated by many of their apparent advances. Electrical appliances saved time in the kitchen, but women were expected to devote that extra time to motherhood rather than to careers. Consumer culture channeled women into the act of shopping, and according to advertisements, a sparkling clean kitchen denoted a successful woman. Women may have relished their freedom from Victorian restrictions, but most faced a difficult choice between marriage and a career, as many found they could not successfully have both.

Yet the popular images of the middle-class wife and family were even less real for working-class women and farmwomen. Overall, the 1920s was a decade of modest gains, and despite perceptions, women did not achieve political, social, or economic equality.

Erica J. Ryan

See also: Adkins v. Children's Hospital (1923); Beauty Industry and Culture; Birth Control; Children and Child Rearing; Fashion, Women's; Homosexuals and Homosexuality; Marriage, Divorce, and Family; Office Work; Sex and Sexuality; Sheppard-Towner Act (1921); Women's Movement.

Further Reading

Brown, Dorothy M. *Setting a Course: American Women in the 1920s.* Boston: Twayne, 1987.

Coontz, Stephanie. *Marriage: A History.* New York: Viking, 2005.

Cott, Nancy F. *The Grounding of Modern Feminism.* New Haven, CT: Yale University Press, 1987.

Cowan, Ruth Schwartz. "Two Washes in the Morning and a Bridge Party at Night: The American Housewife Between the Wars." In *Decades of Discontent,* ed. Lois Scharf and Joan M. Jensen. Boston: Northeastern University Press, 1987.

D'Emilio, John, and Estelle B. Freedman. *Intimate Matters: A History of Sexuality in America.* Chicago: University of Chicago Press, 1997.

Evans, Sara M. *Born for Liberty.* New York: Simon & Schuster, 1997

Miller, Nathan. *New World Coming: The 1920s and the Making of Modern America.* New York: Scribner, 2003.

Mintz, Steven. *Domestic Revolutions: A Social History of American Family Life.* New York: Free Press, 1988.

Ryan, Mary P. "The Projection of a New Womanhood: The Movie Moderns in the 1920s." In *Decades of Discontent,* ed. Lois Scharf and Joan M. Jensen. Boston: Northeastern University Press, 1987.

Simmons, Christina. "Modern Sexuality and the Myth of Victorian Repression." In *Passion and Power: Sexuality in History,* ed. Kathy Peiss and Christina Simmons. Philadelphia: Temple University Press, 1989.

Women's Movement

After ratification of the Nineteenth Amendment to the U.S. Constitution in August 1920, guaranteeing woman suffrage, the women's movement in America lost momentum. By the time women went to the polls that November, only one original member of the 1848 Seneca Falls Convention, where the organized struggle for suffrage began, was alive to cast her vote. Many young women were seen as taking their hard-won, newfound freedoms for granted. Indeed, less than 50 percent of all eligible women turned out to vote in the presidential election of 1920.

Some former suffragists, however, saw passage of the Nineteenth Amendment as only the beginning of a movement that would expand the civil rights of women in America. Progressive feminists of the Jazz Age, for example, campaigned for women's ease of entry into the professions of their choice, better education for girls, greater governmental support for mothers, and easier access to birth control.

Organizations that had made suffrage their priority shifted their emphasis to encompass broader social goals. The National American Woman Suffrage Association (NAWSA), for example, became the League of Women Voters and tried to facilitate women's entry into politics. Nominal strides were made when in 1920 Congress created the Women's Bureau, a subdivision of the Department of Labor that was staffed entirely with women, to advance women's employment opportunities and improve women's working conditions.

Also, for the first time in its history, the U.S. Civil Service Commission in 1920 allowed women full admission into the civil service examinations required to secure a government job. However, because of the Veterans' Preference Act, which promised civil service positions to men who had served in the armed forces during World War I, most of the women who passed the exams were never actually hired for their positions of choice. In fact, many women who held jobs in government or industry during the war lost them to returning veterans.

Expanding women's professional options thus became a major goal and ongoing challenge for feminists.

After decades of struggle, women across America won the right to vote at the dawn of the Jazz Age. Here, suffragist Alice Paul unfurls a banner celebrating Tennessee's passage of the Nineteenth Amendment on August 13, 1920, ensuring final ratification. *(Stock Montage/Hulton Archive/Getty Images)*

But progress was slow during the course of the 1920s. At the start of the decade, there were a total of forty-one female licensed engineers in America; by 1930, there were 113. And although the decade also saw the number of woman lawyers double, they still represented only 2 percent of the total number of lawyers in the United States.

The women's movement during the Jazz Age was also attended by a significant backlash. Former suffragists were disheartened by the younger generation's apparent lack of interest in the overall advancement of women in America; many complained that once the Nineteenth Amendment was passed, feminists had little to rally around. Unity within the women's movement dissolved. Older feminists perceived younger women as placing a higher priority on their domestic lives than on their careers. And since many younger women in the workforce quit their jobs when they married or had children, many employers hesitated to hire marriageable women.

Institutional forces also hindered advances during the Jazz Age. In 1923, feminist leader Alice Paul proposed an equal rights amendment, but it failed to get through Congress even though it was put before that body every year during the 1920s. The proposed amendment met with great opposition from labor unions, who argued that protective restrictions on women's labor specified by the unions, such as capping the number of hours women were allowed to work in a day, sufficiently protected women from on-the-job exploitation. Members of the National Woman's Party (NWP) accused the unions of trying to secure jobs for male union members rather than protecting the interests of women in the workforce. This issue nearly divided the women's movement. Membership in the NWP, which peaked at 60,000 in 1920, declined to about 10,000 women over the course of the decade.

Another factor in the decline in NWP membership was that African American women were not entirely welcome as members. When voting officials, notably in the South, set up obstacles such as literacy tests to prevent African Americans from voting, many black women appealed to the NWP for help but were told that theirs was a race issue rather than a gender issue. Many perceived organizations such as the NWP as working for the interests of only white, upper-class women, and either marginalizing or ignoring the political needs and rights of poorer, nonwhite women.

The women's movement would not revive to its pre–World War I level of activism until well after World War II. In 1966, a group of more than two dozen feminists would found the National Organization for Women (NOW). As with the NWP, NOW would fight for gender equity in the workplace and a greater voice for women in politics. But the new movement spearheaded by NOW had a broader agenda than women's rights movements of the World War I era and the Jazz Age, emphasizing women's equality in the social and personal sphere as well.

Alison M. Perry

See also: Birth Control; League of Women Voters; Paul, Alice; Sanger, Margaret; Women and Gender.

Further Reading

Freeman, Jo. "From Suffrage to Women's Liberation: Feminism in Twentieth Century America." In *Women: A Feminist Perspective,* 5th ed., ed. Jo Freeman. Mountain View, CA: Mayfield, 1995.

Harvey, Anna. *Votes Without Leverage: Women in American Electoral Politics, 1920–1970.* New York: Cambridge University Press, 1998.

Matthews, Jean. *The Rise of the New Woman: The Women's Movement in America, 1875–1930.* Chicago: Ivan R. Dee, 2003.

Young Plan (1929–1930)

During the 1920s, one of the most vexing issues in international affairs was World War I debt and reparations. The matter was complicated not only by relations between Germany and its former war adversaries but also by America's relations with the other Allied powers. Among the efforts to resolve the divisions was the Young Plan, proposed by a committee headed by the American banker and industrialist Owen D. Young in 1929 and formally adopted in 1930.

The Great War had been enormously expensive. In the Treaty of Versailles (1919), the Allies tried to pass much of the financial responsibility onto Germany, presenting the vanquished nation with a bill for approximately $33 billion. Although historians have long debated whether the reparations burden exceeded Germany's ability to pay, the fact remains that the German regime did not meet its reparation obligations. In response, France and Belgium in 1923 occupied the Ruhr, a highly industrialized region in western Germany, which compounded Germany's economic problems by contributing to hyperinflation and soaring unemployment.

The Allied Reparations Commission asked American banker Charles G. Dawes to head a committee to investigate the reparations situation and prepare a report. As a result of its findings, the Dawes Committee in 1924 recommended the withdrawal of foreign troops from the Ruhr, a restructuring but not a reduction of reparation payments, reorganization of the German central bank, and massive loans to Germany. Although unpopular with some German politicians, including Adolf Hitler of the fledgling National Socialist German Workers' (Nazi) Party, implementation of the Dawes Plan helped to reduce hyperinflation and high unemployment and provided somewhat greater stability for the German economy. For the next five years, Germany was able to meet its reparation payments. By the late 1920s, however, it was becoming doubtful once again that the Germans could continue to do so.

In early 1929, the Allied Reparations Commission asked Owen D. Young—a former General Electric executive who had founded the Radio Corporation of America (RCA) and co-authored the Dawes Plan—to head an international committee to consider how best to deal with the reparations issue. Young's group submitted its initial report in June 1929 and, after considerable negotiations, submitted a final proposal that was accepted at the Second Hague Conference in January 1930.

The Young Plan called for a substantial reduction in the German reparations debt, to $26.3 billion to be paid over the next 58.5 years in annual payments of approximately $473 million. The payments consisted of two components: an unconditional one, representing about one-third of the annual total, and a postponable one, which could be delayed if conditions warranted. The funds for the reparations were to be raised by means of a German transportation tax and monies drawn directly from the country's budget. An international bank of settlement was to be created to oversee the payments. The plan was intended to facilitate the payment of reparations by reducing the total amount due and by dividing that amount into more manageable annual payments.

The Wall Street crash of October 1929 and the onset of the Great Depression spelled doom for implementation of the Young Plan. The availability of credit to Germany from the United States was an essential part of the plan, but as the Depression deepened, the United States could not provide the requisite credit. Furthermore, with the deterioration of international trade and the general economic turmoil resulting from the Depression compounding Germany's economic woes, it now lacked sufficient resources to meet its obligations under the plan. President Herbert Hoover, worried about the deteriorating economic situation across Europe, proposed a one-year moratorium on reparation payments, and with the agreement of fifteen nations, the moratorium went into effect for the 1931–1932 fiscal year. Once the moratorium expired, payments were to resume.

That prospect was dashed by Adolf Hitler's rise to power in 1933. Once he consolidated control, the German government defaulted on its debt under the plans. This marked the virtual collapse of the international reparations structure and contributed to considerable bitterness not only toward Germany but also among the former Allied nations. Europeans resented American demands that they repay their war debt, and the United States resented their failure to do so.

In 1953, an international conference agreed that Germany would not have to repay its World War I debt until the nation was eventually reunified—it had been divided into East and West Germany following World War II. Nevertheless, West Germany undertook responsibility for repayment and paid off the principal by 1980. In 1995, three-quarters of a century after the end of World War I, the reunified German government announced that it would begin repayment of the remaining interest due on the debt.

Robert F. Martin

See also: Dawes Plan (1924); Europe, Relations with; Reparations and War Debts.

Further Reading

Case, Josephine Young, and Everett Needham Case. *Owen D. Young and American Enterprise: A Biography.* Boston: David R. Godine, 1982.

Cohen, Warren I. *Empire Without Tears: America's Foreign Relations, 1921–1933.* New York: Alfred A. Knopf, 1987.

Youth

Americans during the Jazz Age were preoccupied with youth. Journalists, sociologists, and moralists chronicled and interpreted the antics, fads, and fashions of the young, particularly among the white middle class. Advertisers promoted their styles and interests to sell products ranging from clothing to popular music. Young Americans were the protagonists of many popular novels, plays, and films of the 1920s, and they continue to figure prominently in histories of the Jazz Age. In the somewhat extravagant parlance of the period, these young people were the "lost generation," the "beautiful and the damned," "flaming youth," and "prodigal daughters."

The public's fascination with youth was not unfounded, for it was the young who set the tone for many of the innovations attributed to the Jazz Age. They led the rebellion against Victorianism, particularly its emphasis on social and sexual restraint

(typically expressed as innocence). The young embraced a culture based on greater personal freedom and self-expression. They valued experience above innocence, and directness, immediacy, authenticity, and spontaneity above restraint and tradition. The new attitudes found expression in jazz, fast cars, less confining fashions, and dance fads such as the fox-trot that encouraged close contact between partners. The Charleston, a jazzier dance craze of the period, was an outlet for youthful high spirits and allowed young women to flaunt their legs and bare arms. The "jazz babies" were the first generation of Americans who were more likely to take their values from each other than from their parents. So pervasive was this cult of youth that even their elders sometimes emulated the young in an effort to be perceived as fashionable.

The convergence of a variety of factors and circumstances generated the youth culture of the Jazz Age. Young America's rejection of traditional values has been attributed to their disillusionment with the Great War. That disastrous episode, and the great influenza pandemic that followed it, may also explain why so many young people seemed determined to live for the moment and experience as much of life as possible in the possibly brief time allotted to them. The general prosperity of the period facilitated their zest for living. It enabled growing numbers of the young to complete high school and attend college. It afforded them leisure time, spending money, and access to popular entertainments and the latest fashions.

Even technology played its part. Movies promoted thrill-seeking behavior, romance, and sensuality. In keeping with the spirit of the times, Hollywood developed a new genre, the college movie, to appeal to young audiences. And many young people of the middle class had access to a family car, which enabled them and their companions to escape parental supervision, however briefly. It also freed them to indulge their appetites for speed, mobility, and sex.

Among the developments that set the stage for Jazz Age youth culture was the middle-class ideal of the affectionate, democratic, child-centered family. Unlike the hierarchical or paternalistic arrangements that had characterized family life through the turn of the century, middle-class families of the early twentieth century placed a premium on emotional satisfactions. They continued to be concerned about their children's educational opportunities and economic prospects, but more than ever before, they

Comic film star Harold Lloyd poses in a publicity still for *The Freshman* (1925), one of a number of Hollywood movies celebrating the supposedly carefree lives of America's college-age youth. *(Harold Lloyd Trust/Hulton Archive/Getty Images)*

were eager for their children to achieve happiness and personal fulfillment. Thus, young people led less structured lives, and parents interfered less in their development. Youth became a stage of life marked by greater independence and more experimentation. The results, however, were sometimes disconcerting. With only minimal discipline and structure in their lives, the young frequently fell into erratic and troublesome behaviors.

New Theories and Ideas

If the absence of traditional restraints and guidelines sometimes caused confusion on the part of the young and consternation among their elders, reassurance was readily available. The eminent social scientist G. Stanley Hall had only recently completed the first major study of adolescent psychology. In *Adolescence, Its Psychology and Its Relation to Physiology, Anthropology, Sociology, Sex, Crime, Religion, and Education* (1904), Hall held that the contradictions and excesses of youth were perfectly normal. Indeed, he maintained, they were essential for personal maturation. Most adolescent misbehaviors were the product of instinctive urges, said Hall, and any attempt by society to

repress its young would only impede their development and redirect their urges into more disruptive antisocial behaviors. Hall's work greatly influenced the public's perception of youth and led to greater permissiveness in parenting and schooling the young.

Many educators of the period also embraced John Dewey's philosophy of education. Dewey believed education should be student centered and socially progressive. Accordingly, American schools placed less emphasis on behavioral conformity and rote learning and more on each individual's potential. It was believed that the young should emerge from their secondary education with the knowledge essential for effective citizenship, and they should have either adequate preparation for college or the technical skills necessary to support themselves in a modern economy. The high schools of Muncie, Indiana, for instance, offered students twelve options. These included a general course and a college preparatory program, as well as specialized training in music and the arts. Other programs were purely vocational: shorthand, bookkeeping, applied electricity, mechanical drafting, printing, machine shop, manual arts, and home economics. Given their new functions, many school systems of the period provided significantly

The Image of Joe College and Betty Co-ed

Jazz Age illustrator John Held, Jr.—whose work appeared in *Life, College Humor, The New Yorker,* and other mass-circulation magazines—became famous for his depictions of college men and women of the time, whom he labeled "Joe College" and "Betty Co-ed." Conceived in a spirit of mockery, Held's drawings had the unanticipated effect of glamorizing and popularizing the demeanor and style of contemporary youth. Held depicted Joe College as a vacuous good-timer wearing a varsity sweater, blazer, and wide-bottom flannel trousers. Outdoors, in a raccoon coat, he carried a college pennant, a hip flask of illicit booze at the ready. Betty Co-ed is hardly distinguishable from Held's famous flappers. Her hair is bobbed, face rouged, arms and legs bare. Her dress is narrow and short enough to display a garter. Held frequently depicted Joe and Betty together in a party atmosphere, drinking, dancing, or cheering for their alma mater at the big football game. They seemed to have no purpose other than to enjoy their carefree lives.

College fiction of the Jazz Age—particularly F. Scott Fitzgerald's novel *This Side of Paradise* (1920) and several of the stories included in his *Flappers and Philosophers* (1920) and *Tales of the Jazz Age* (1922), Percy Marks's *The Plastic Age* (1924), and Dorothy Speare's *Dancing in the Dark* (1920)—depicted a generation making the most of its newfound freedoms, its rebellious spirit, and the nation's unprecedented prosperity. Like Held's graphics, these fictions were not always flattering, but they reinforced the public's fascination with "flaming youth" and campus high jinks, a fascination reinforced by Hollywood.

Certain themes and stereotypes were common to campus movies, such as *The Campus Flirt* (1926), *The College Hero* (1927), and *Hold 'Em Yale* (1928). The Big Man on Campus is always the sports hero, never the intellect, and he is popular with all the Betty Co-eds. Scholarly types are portrayed as timid and socially inept. Male friendships are just as important as romantic relationships. Young people in these films are lively, interesting, and attractive, while their elders are objects of pranks. Students justifiably scheme to outwit supercilious and stodgy professors, or contrive to enliven the campus by getting around antiquated rules backed by well-meaning but out-of-touch college officials.

In addition to its reliance on a few stock characters, the college genre employed a limited number of recurring plot issues that were often resolved during the climactic Big Game: Who will get the girl? Will State U. defeat its traditional rival? Will the hero prove himself on the field? Seldom does a hint of malice (or even seriousness) enter into the proceedings. If the genre conveyed any social concern at all, it was the fear that a young woman might fall in with a fast crowd and ruin her reputation. But pressing that moral message may simply have been the justification for including suggestive scenes of wild parties or hanky-panky at an off-campus roadhouse.

Hollywood continued to turn out campus capers movies, nearly all of them in the frivolous spirit of the Jazz Age, even after the stock market crash of 1929 and the Great Depression had radically altered the prospects and perspectives of Joe College and Betty Co-ed.

William Hughes

less in the way of traditional moral instruction, which was left to organizations such as the YMCA and YWCA, girls' and boys' clubs, and churches.

The new modes of parenting and schooling in the early twentieth century go a long way toward accounting for the gulf between Jazz Age youth and previous generations. As adult guidance of the young diminished, peer group influences increased. The schools and colleges facilitated that trend by bringing together ever-larger numbers of young people to engage in a broad range of activities—curricular and extracurricular, intellectual and athletic, social and recreational. In this way, the young soon established their own codes, behaviors, social networks, and fashions. They asserted greater personal autonomy than did prior generations, particularly in dating practices and sexuality. Among the young, however, autonomy was frequently accompanied by ambiguity, uncertainty, or sheer confusion.

In the absence of traditional dating guidelines, Jazz Age youth had to work out their own answers to such questions as: What is the meaning of a good-night kiss? Under what circumstances can petting be initiated? How far should it go? What can be done to avoid an unwanted pregnancy? And should social status supersede feelings in choosing a potential partner? For answers, young people frequently relied on hearsay or the sketchy information provided by acquaintances who claimed to have more experience in these matters. But if they managed, with the help of their peers, to negotiate the pitfalls of dating, courtship, and sex, Jazz Age youth were probably better prepared for marriage than prior generations had been.

Some social historians credit the adolescent subculture of the period with effectively socializing young people for adulthood generally. Peer pressures, for better or worse, defined gender roles and identities, established codes for courtship and sexuality, created and reinforced status systems, promulgated and maintained standards of style and taste, and devised environments in which the young could learn competitiveness and organizational skills. These developments were particularly pronounced among collegiate fraternities and sororities.

Class and Race

White working-class and minority youth were not full participants in the youth culture of the period. So long as they remained in school, white working-class youth were at least on the fringe of the youth movement—though few of them had the money for fashionable clothes, popular amusements, or the expense of dating. Many of them, however, necessarily dropped out of school as soon as the law allowed, because their families needed them to become self-supporting or at least contribute to the family income. Youthful rebellion was a luxury they could not afford. They were preoccupied with economic survival, which meant working on a family farm, getting a factory job, or, if they were both resourceful and fortunate, learning a craft or trade. Some working-class families, particularly among recent immigrant groups, placed a high value on education and made inordinate sacrifices so that their children could complete school and possibly even train to enter a profession. To such young people and their families, the youth culture must have seemed frivolous and irrelevant.

Class alone did not determine the experience of youth during the Jazz Age. Region and race also played their parts. The youth culture was largely an urban and suburban phenomenon; young people of the hinterlands were somewhat marginalized, while racism and segregation, not to mention poverty, assured that most African Americans, whether rural and urban, would be excluded from the youth culture of the period. True, there was a burgeoning black middle class that could provide for the educational advancement and material well-being of their young. Even so, black middle-class parents generally imposed stricter morality and exercised closer control over their children than did their white counterparts. And black middle-class youth often encountered the same patterns of discrimination experienced by poor blacks, which also impeded their participation in the youth culture of the period. For Native American youth, who faced abject poverty, discrimination, and cultural and geographic isolation the Jazz Age, including its youth culture, was a remote and meaningless concept.

William Hughes

See also: Automobiles and Automobile Culture; Child Labor; Children and Child Rearing; Education, Elementary and Secondary; Education, Higher; Leisure and Recreation; Marriage, Divorce, and Family; Population and Demographics; Sex and Sexuality.

Further Reading

Cremin, Lawrence A. *The Transformation of the School: Progressivism in American Education, 1867–1957.* New York: Vintage Books, 1964.

Erikson, Eric H. *Childhood and Society.* 2nd ed. New York: W.W. Norton, 1963.

——, ed. *Youth: Change and Challenge.* New York: Basic Books, 1963.

Fass, Paula S. *The Damned and the Beautiful: American Youth in the 1920s.* New York: Oxford University Press, 1977.

Handlin, Oscar, and Mary F. Handlin. *Facing Life: Youth and the Family in American History.* Boston: Little, Brown, 1971.

Kett, Joseph. *Rites of Passage: Adolescence in America, 1790 to the Present.* New York: Basic Books, 1977.

Lynd, Robert S., and Helen Merrill Lynd. *Middletown: A Study in Modern American Culture.* New York: Harcourt, Brace and Company, 1929.

Modell, John. *Into One's Own: From Youth to Adulthood in the United States, 1920–1975.* Berkeley: University of California Press, 1989.

Cultural Landmarks

Art and Architecture

American Radiator Building (New York City office building, 1924, designed by Raymond Hood)

Located on the west side of Midtown Manhattan, the 23-floor, 338-foot- (103-meter-) high American Radiator Building was commissioned as the corporate headquarters of the American Radiator and Standard Sanitary Company, a manufacturer of heaters and heating systems. Among the first New York skyscrapers to feature a stepped pyramidal shape, the building's Gothic-style pinnacles and distinctive black brick façade are meant to evoke the coal used in the company's products. The base, sheathed in black granite and bronze, features sculpted allegories of matter transforming into energy.

Raymond Hood, an industrial designer as well as an architect, was selected for the project by company executives impressed by his designs for radiator covers. This commission helped make Hood one of the 1920s' most sought-after American architects. Critics and historians regard the structure as one of the more significant skyscrapers of the era, citing its fusion of product and building design. The building currently houses the Bryant Park Hotel.

Black Iris II (painting, 1926, by Georgia O'Keeffe)

A notable early work of the avant-garde artist Georgia O'Keeffe, _Black Iris II_ (a follow-up to her _Black Iris_ of 1906) is an oil-on-canvas work created during the period in which she was emerging as one of the preeminent artists of her era. The piece is characteristic of O'Keefe's boldly magnified, brightly colored, sexually evocative representations of flowers.

Black Iris II and other contemporaneous works marked the start of a major transition in O'Keeffe's career, as she shifted her attention from paintings of modernist architecture—especially the buildings of New York City—to objects in nature such as flowers, animal bones, shells, and rock formations. She rendered these subjects as flat, clear forms evocative of abstract simplicity and mystical silence.

Chicago Tribune Tower (Chicago office building, 1925, designed by John Mead Howells and Raymond Hood)

The commission to design the Chicago Tribune Tower was awarded in an international competition. In 1922, chiefly as a publicity gimmick, the publishers of the _Chicago Tribune_ invited readers to submit designs for the "most beautiful and eye-catching building in the world," offering a prize of $50,000 for the best design. Of the more than 260 entries submitted, the prize was awarded to the young architects John Mead Howells and Raymond Hood for their neo-Gothic design. Although the two would become highly respected in their field—particularly Hood, who went on to design Rockefeller Center in New York—their plan for the Tribune Tower was widely criticized.

Chicago was, at the time, the heart of the modernist movement in architecture, and the design for the newspaper's building called for the very antithesis—an ornately decorated neo-Gothic tower. The _Tribune_'s publishers were undeterred by the criticism, however, and the 423-foot- (129-meter-) tall structure was completed on schedule in 1925. To further the publicity generated by the building, fragments from the Alamo, the Great Wall of China, and the Roman Colosseum were incorporated into the building during construction.

Chrysler Building (New York City skyscraper, 1930, designed by William Van Alen)

One of the foremost architectural landmarks in the world, the Chrysler Building—with its elegant lobby, high art deco design, and spires modeled after Chrysler automobiles of the 1920s—was constructed at a time when several New York architects were competing to build the world's tallest structure. Ground was broken on September 19, 1928, and as the 77-story building neared completion, it appeared that its final height would place it in a tie with H. Craig Severance's skyscraper being built at 40 Wall Street.

Then, on October 23, 1929, architect William Van Alen revealed that his crew had been working in secret on a 185-foot (56-meter) spire for the top of the building. Once installed, it pushed the Chrysler Building past the 1,000-foot (305-meter) mark, making it the first building in the world to reach that height.

Unfortunately, Van Alen's victory was rendered bittersweet when William Chrysler refused to pay the architect's fee. Although the Empire State Building and other structures eventually surpassed it in height, the Chrysler Building remains one of the most revered of all architectural achievements. As recently as 2005, a poll of New York architects indicated that the Chrysler Building is still the favorite building of professional designers.

City from Greenwich Village, The (painting, 1922, by John Sloan)

John Sloan began his career as an illustrator for *The Philadelphia Inquirer* before moving to New York's Greenwich Village to work as a fine artist. In 1908, shortly after his arrival in New York, Sloan joined with seven other artists to found the Ashcan School, which introduced realism into American painting and often took the gritty urban environment as its subject. By the 1920s, the work of Sloan and his colleagues had evolved into American Scene Painting, which extended the realistic perspective and focus on urban themes, but with a more naturalist style and an emphasis on everyday scenes.

Sloan was deeply enamored of his Greenwich Village stomping grounds. His 1922 oil painting, *The City from Greenwich Village,* recreates the artist's view from Washington Square one evening, looking down on the financial district and the Sixth Avenue elevated train. Although the city is dark, it is alive with activity, suggesting the energy and industry of modern America and of city life in particular.

City Night (painting, 1926, by Georgia O'Keeffe)

Like many of Georgia O'Keeffe's paintings of New York City in the 1920s, *City Night* takes the perspective of a person standing at ground level and looking up. Towering black structures crowd the view, thrusting skyward in converging vertical masses that are both ominous and abstract, conveying a sense of foreboding common in post–World War I modernism. A white skyscraper seen between the two buildings in the foreground—a sliver in the distance, all but hidden—serves as a counterbalance, suggesting hope and revealing the artist's basically romantic worldview.

O'Keefe's New York paintings were a product of her relationship with the pioneering photographer Alfred Stieglitz, who would eventually become her husband. In 1918, Stieglitz invited O'Keeffe to New York to work in his studio and introduced her to key members of the city's modernist art circles. By the end of the 1920s, O'Keeffe had largely abandoned New York building design as a subject, though later in life she returned to an architectural theme in a series of paintings of her adobe house in New Mexico.

Dempsey and Firpo (painting, 1924, by George Bellows)

The September 1923 boxing match between heavyweight champion Jack Dempsey and Luis Firpo of Argentina is notable in the annals of the sport as the first time a Latin American fighter challenged for the heavyweight crown. It was also an exceedingly dramatic match, as both fighters were knocked to the canvas several times in less than two rounds. At the end of the first round, Firpo sent Dempsey sprawling through the ropes.

This is the historic moment George Bellows captured in his painting. The work is an icon of American Scene Painting, characterized by its realistic style and emphasis on everyday American life. Bellows and other American Scene painters hoped to provide a counterpoint to the abstract modernist art emerging from Europe, which they rejected as trite and empty of meaning. *Dempsey and Firpo* would be one of Bellows's last contributions to this dialogue, however, as he died less than two years after completing the painting.

Dymaxion House (architectural design, 1928, by R. Buckminster Fuller)

In 1927, the daughter of designer and inventor R. Buckminster Fuller died of an infection contracted while the family weathered a harsh Chicago winter in substandard housing. Jobless and distraught, Fuller began work on an architectural concept intended to put an end to such tragedies and benefit all humanity—a lightweight, mass-produced residence that could be assembled from a kit at virtually any location.

The first sketches for Fuller's Dymaxion House were completed in 1928. The name Dymaxion—combining the words "dynamic," "maximum," and "tension"—was coined by a friend, and the house was unlike any ever seen. Round and slightly dome-shaped so as to retain heat, it was made of aluminum and designed to be autonomous—it did not need to be connected to municipal sewer systems, power lines, or communication services. The idea proved better in theory than in practice, however, as the design was too odd for the tastes of most Americans, required too much aluminum to be economical, and a number of the design concepts proved difficult to execute.

Only one Dymaxion House was actually built and occupied; it is now on display at the Henry Ford Museum in Dearborn, Michigan. Despite the high-profile failure—and that of such related projects as the Dymaxion car and Dymaxion world map—Fuller would achieve international fame for other design concepts, such as the geodesic dome.

Ennis House (Los Angeles residence, 1924, designed by Frank Lloyd Wright)

Designated as a national landmark, the Ennis House is located in the Los Feliz neighborhood of Los Angeles. Its interlocking concrete blocks were used at the request of the original owners, Charles and Mabel Ennis, who were deeply interested in Mayan culture and wanted a residence in the style of a Mayan temple.

The design of the Ennis House is considered one of the foremost examples of the genius of Frank Lloyd Wright, perhaps the preeminent American architect of the twentieth century. Wright later designed three other houses based on the same concept, but none was as impressive or well received. In disrepair due to poor upkeep, the 1994 Northridge earthquake, and heavy rains, today the Ennis House is closed to the public and classified as an endangered historic place.

Greta Garbo (photograph, 1928, by Edward Steichen)

When Edward Steichen first became interested in photography in the early 1900s, the vogue was pictorialism; photographers tried to make their photos appear as much like paintings as possible. Steichen toyed with this style for several years and then rejected it, believing that photography should be embraced as an art form in its own right.

In the early 1920s, Steichen became the chief photographer for *Vanity Fair* and *Vogue* magazines; in this capacity, he produced many of his best-known works. Among these were his photo portraits of Charlie Chaplin and Greta Garbo, two of the decade's great film stars. The Garbo photos show her dressed in black and hint at the air of mystery associated with the notoriously reclusive actress. The most famous shot, which became her defining image, features Garbo looking into the camera with her hair pulled back and her hands on the sides of her forehead as if covering her ears.

House by the Railroad (painting, 1925, by Edward Hopper)

Like several of the best-known American artists of the 1920s, Edward Hopper was trained as an illustrator. In the tradition of American Scene Painting, he focused on depictions of everyday life. Hopper was identified with the social realism wing of the movement, and his paintings typically dwell on themes of isolation and alienation.

House by the Railroad, among Hopper's best-known works, certainly embodies these themes. The painting's subject, a Victorian-style house, stands alone in a stark light and in a state of disrepair. The land around it is devoid of life—plant, animal, or human. The only other element is a railroad track in the foreground. The feelings of loneliness and uncertainty evoked by the painting are among the recurring themes of the post–World War I modernist movement.

I Saw the Figure 5 in Gold (painting, 1928, by Charles Demuth)

Inspired by a poem called "The Great Figure" by his friend William Carlos Williams, Charles Demuth's oil-on-board "portrait poster" is an emblematic composition in receding layers of geometric shapes and the number 5—all in shades of red, yellow, and gray. Demuth came to be identified with the precisionist style, a form of synthetic cubism with distinctively American themes.

I Saw the Figure 5 in Gold typifies Demuth's experimentation with geometric planes and his celebration of modernization, industrialization, and progress. Among the other artists and writers for whom Demuth executed portrait posters were Georgia O'Keeffe, Arthur Dove, John Marin, Gertrude Stein, Eugene O'Neill, and Wallace Stevens.

Lovell House (Los Angeles residence, 1929, designed by Richard Neutra)

The modernist Lovell House was the first steel-frame house in the United States. Designed by architect Richard Neutra for a Los Angeles physician, the home featured extensive terraced gardens, balconies supported by steel cables, and a swimming pool suspended in a U-shaped concrete cradle. The project took an uncommonly long time—two years—in part because the house was constructed on a hillside and in part because Neutra insisted on acting as his own contractor.

Perhaps the first example of modernist architecture with a distinctly Los Angeles flair, the Lovell House was certainly the first L.A. building to attract the attention of European architects, thereby marking a turning point in Neutra's career. He earned a reputation as one of the few modernists who was willing to prioritize function—in his view, the comfort of the interior—over form.

Lucky Strike (painting, 1921, by Stuart Davis)

On first examination, *Lucky Strike* appears to be a collage, a cutout composition popular among cubists of the 1920s. Executed in oils, however, the work is instead a suggestion of a collage. Composed of several fragments of a Lucky Strike cigarette package, the image approximates the appearance of such a wrapper after being flattened.

Like many artists of his time, Stuart Davis explored the themes and images of popular culture, and much of his work—including *Lucky Strike*—is critical of the emptiness of mass culture and the loss of individuality in the industrial age. His style has been characterized as "proto-pop," as his work had an obvious influence on Andy Warhol and other pop artists of the 1960s.

Monolith, The Face of Half Dome (photograph, 1927, by Ansel Adams)

Monolith, The Face of Half Dome is the most famous of a series of photographs by Ansel Adams taken at Yosemite National Park. Adams had joined the Sierra Club at age seventeen, and he remained a lifelong member, eventually serving as the group's director. It was on one of the Sierra Club's annual trips in the Sierra Nevada Mountains that he settled upon Yosemite as his first subject of photographic study.

Monolith, The Face of Half Dome depicts the massive granite outcropping in full shadow, rising upward from the snow-covered trees surrounding its base. Adams nearly failed to capture the shot, as nine of the twelve plates he carried with him that day had been used or damaged by the time he was in position to shoot. With his final plate and some help from a red filter, however, Adams got the image he wanted. He would characterize the resulting photograph as "majestic" and "wondrous." *Monolith, The Face of Half Dome,* along with Adams's other Yosemite photos,

which the photographer described as "an austere and blazing poetry of the real," propelled him to fame and became his signature works.

People of Chilmark (painting, 1920, by Thomas Hart Benton)

The Missouri-born muralist Thomas Hart Benton was a regionalist painter who primarily depicted everyday life on the farms and prairies of the American Midwest. *People of Chilmark (Figurative Composition),* a prominent example of early regionalism, depicts nine human figures—including Benton's wife, neighbors, and friends—in a complex and dynamic beach scene (in this case, on Martha's Vineyard, Massachusetts). A study in movement, balance, and sculptural human form, the painting elevates a scene of ordinary everyday life to monumental status and invests it with a sense of exuberance.

With its graceful curves and complete lack of abstraction, the painting also stands in stark counterpoint to the work of contemporary modernists, whom Benton abhorred. Calling himself an "enemy of modernism," Benton continued to produce rural-themed murals until his death in 1975 while serving as mentor to a new generation of students, most notably Jackson Pollock.

Portrait of Gertrude Stein (sculpture, 1923, by Jo Davidson)

Not to be confused with the 1906 Picasso painting of the same name, Jo Davidson's *Portrait of Gertrude Stein* is a bronze "portrait bust." The preeminent American sculptor of the 1920s, Davidson was known both for the realism of his work and for his unusual technique. Rather than have subjects sit for a formal portrait, he preferred to observe and interact with them and then sculpt from memory. His list of subjects reads like a "who's who" of the first half of the twentieth century: Mohandas Gandhi, Albert Einstein, Rudyard Kipling, Franklin D. Roosevelt, Charlie Chaplin, and dozens of other luminaries.

Portrait of Gertrude Stein, cast in bronze, is a nearly full-body portrait of the famous novelist and poet, seated and deep in concentration. "To do a head of Gertrude Stein was not enough," Davidson remarked. "She was so much more than that. So I did a seated figure of her—a sort of modern Buddha."

Shell (photograph, 1927, by Edward Weston)

Edward Weston, one of the master photographers of the twentieth century, was a cofounder of Group f/64, which included Ansel Adams and Imogen Cunningham among its members. The term "f/64" refers to the widest possible aperture on a standard camera, which creates a perfectly even photographic image from foreground to background. It was chosen as the group's name because of the members' belief in sharp, crisp photographs and the potential of the medium for perfect representations of the subject. These ideas stood in contrast to those of the pictorialists, who relied on soft lenses, darkroom manipulation, and a variety of other techniques to alter photographs and make the images look as much like paintings and etchings as possible.

Weston's *Shell,* a black-and-white photo of a nautilus seashell precariously balanced on its edge, is among the best-known examples of the work of Weston and Group f/64. In his journal, Weston commented on the difficulty of the shot: "The hour is late, the light is failing, I could not expose another film. So there stands my camera focused, trained like a gun, commanding the shell not to move a hair's breadth. And death to anyone who jars out of place what I know shall be a very important negative."

Although he earned an international reputation for his nature shots, in the 1930s Weston turned his attention to nudes, which would remain his focus for the rest of his career.

Terminal Tower (Cleveland skyscraper, 1928, designed by Graham, Anderson, Probst, and White)
The crown jewel of the Cleveland skyline, the 708-foot- (216-meter-) tall Terminal Tower was the tallest building in the world outside of New York City upon its completion in 1928 (and remained so until 1967). Designed as the downtown hub of Cleveland's public transportation system, it was built above three sets of railroad tracks. The construction of the tower and surrounding complex (completed in 1930) was thus a major feat of civil engineering, requiring the excavation of nearly as much earth as the digging of the Panama Canal.

The Terminal Tower is a prominent example of Beaux-Arts architecture, notable for its symmetry, extensive detailing, classical motifs, and grand entrances and staircases. While it is no longer the tallest building in Cleveland, the Terminal Tower remains the skyline landmark most identified with the city.

Wrigley Building (Chicago office building, 1925, designed by Graham, Anderson, Probst, and White)
Chewing gum magnate William Wrigley personally chose a triangle-shaped piece of land as the site of his new corporate headquarters. Situated on the north bank of the Chicago River and across the street from the Chicago Tribune Tower, the Wrigley Building marks the southern terminus of Chicago's "Magnificent Mile," earning it the designation "Jewel of the Mile."

With its two towers (the south rising thirty stories and the north standing twenty-one stories), the Wrigley Building is modeled after the Seville Cathedral in Spain, although French Renaissance features—columns, entablatures, round arches, detailed ornamentation—were incorporated into the design. The exterior is covered with 250,000 glazed terra-cotta tiles, which give the structure a gleaming white façade during the day and serve as backdrop for the nighttime illumination that is a Wrigley Building hallmark. It remains world headquarters of the Wrigley Corporation to this day, while also housing a number of other tenants.

Literature: Fiction, Nonfiction, and Poetry

Abraham Lincoln: The Prairie Years (nonfiction, 1925, by Carl Sandburg)

Abraham Lincoln: The Prairie Years chronicles the life of the sixteenth president of the United States up to the day he departed for the White House in February 1861. Earning praise for its elegant and readable prose, the two-volume work was the first great commercial success of poet, journalist, children's writer, and inveterate Lincoln admirer Carl Sandburg. This success afforded him the liberty of writing the much longer, four-volume *Abraham Lincoln: The War Years* (1939), for which he earned a Pulitzer Prize.

For many years, the two works were regarded as the definitive account of Lincoln's life. Today, however, they are not well regarded by historians because of their factual errors, romantic tone, and unabashed adoration for the subject.

Age of Innocence, The (novel, 1920, by Edith Wharton)

Critically acclaimed and popular among readers of the day, *The Age of Innocence,* which won the Pulitzer Prize for fiction in 1921, is a portrait of New York City high society during the 1870s. The protagonist, attorney Newland Archer, is betrothed to the beautiful but conventional May Welland and falls in love with her exotic and unhappily married cousin, Countess Ellen Olenska. In the end, Newland chooses to marry May and give up the great love of his life, who returns to Europe. In the novel's denouement, twenty-five years later and after May's death, Newland seeks out Ellen but she refuses to see him.

Contemporary readers were fascinated not just by the tragic love story but by Wharton's exquisite rendering of a lost age—a time predating the mass production of consumer goods—when the upper classes lived in a world of their own and it was not possible for the middle classes to mimic their way of life.

American Language, The (nonfiction, 1919, by H.L. Mencken)

Written by *Baltimore Sun* columnist H.L. Mencken, *The American Language* is a book-length tribute to the variety and versatility of American English. Mencken was inspired by Mark Twain—who incorporated various forms of American argot in his writing—as well as by the speech of ordinary Americans, particularly African Americans. A confessed Anglophobe, Mencken said that he had written the book to defend American English from its literary detractors in England and the halls of American academia.

A critical success and best seller, considering that it is a book on grammar and vocabulary, *The American Language* offered numerous examples of slang terms and their origins, and it explored regional and ethnic variations of American English. The book was published on the eve of what many scholars regard as the decade in which modern American literature came of age.

American Tragedy, An (novel, 1925, by Theodore Dreiser)

A satire on the American dream as well as a fictionalized account of a 1906 murder case, *An American Tragedy* is the story of Clyde Griffiths, a poor but ambitious young man from a small town who moves to the city in search of something better. However, in his new environs, his life spirals out of control, leading ultimately to the death of a young woman he impregnated. Although the death was inadvertent, he is convicted of murder and executed.

Dreiser clearly blames his protagonist's downfall on the society that both fostered his dreams and inevitably corrupted him. The idea that modern life in general, and urban living in particular, is damaging to human beings was a common theme in post–World War I literature. The book was criticized as obscene in some quarters for its amoral protagonist and sexual themes. Film versions appeared in 1931 and, under the title *A Place in the Sun,* in 1951.

Americanization of Edward Bok, The (nonfiction, 1921, by Edward Bok)

Winning a Pulitzer Prize in 1921, *The Americanization of Edward Bok* is both an inspirational rags-to-riches story and a case study in management style. An autobiography, it chronicles Bok's life from his immigration to the United States at the age of six through his rise to the upper echelons of the world of magazine publishing. The book was a progenitor of the professional self-help genre, whose other early examples include Bruce Barton's *The Man Nobody Knows* (1925) and Dale Carnegie's *How to Win Friends and Influence People* (1936).

Arrowsmith (novel, 1925, by Sinclair Lewis)

The third in his series of best-selling satirical novels of the 1920s about the narrowness of American life, *Arrowsmith* focuses specifically on an idealistic young doctor, Martin Arrowsmith, who becomes disillusioned with the complacency and commercialism of modern medicine. The novel begins with his days in medical school and continues through his marriage and career as a researcher before climaxing with the outbreak of a deadly plague on a Caribbean island.

The book is highly critical of the state of the medical profession in 1920s America—skewering incompetent public health workers, self-absorbed scientific researchers, and indifferent doctors—and holds up the dedicated and selfless Arrowsmith as an ideal to which all should aspire. The book earned a Pulitzer Prize in 1926, but Lewis declined the award.

Babbitt (novel, 1922, by Sinclair Lewis)

George F. Babbitt, the title character in Sinclair Lewis's satirical novel about small-town life, is a real estate salesman notable only for his willingness to conform. The self-centered Babbitt must always have the latest fashions, the newest gadgets, and much else he cannot afford. Although he becomes temporarily disenchanted with his shallow lifestyle, his inherent weakness eventually causes him to return to a life of conformity.

Babbitt is a scathing critique of the pretentiousness and emptiness of American consumerism, and "Babbittry" entered the lexicon as a term for blind adherence to middle-class values. Critics and the reading public embraced the book; the respected journalist and social commentator H.L. Mencken said, "I know of no American novel that more accurately presents the real America." When Sinclair Lewis was chosen as the winner of the Nobel Prize in Literature in 1930—the first American to be so honored—*Babbitt* was among the works specifically mentioned in the official citation.

Ballad of the Harp-Weaver, The (poem, 1922, by Edna St. Vincent Millay)

"The Ballad of the Harp-Weaver" is the best-known work of Edna St. Vincent Millay, one of America's most accomplished and popular poets of the early twentieth century. In the poem's thirty stanzas, the narrator describes his difficult childhood and his mother's attempts to put up a brave front in the face of suffering. Starving in the middle of a cold winter, mother and son sell all their possessions to pay for food, until they are left with only a harp. On Christmas Eve, the mother plays the harp for her son and uses it to weave warm clothes for him. It is their last moment together; in the morning, the son awakens to find his mother "frozen dead."

The poem's dark tone and complicated structure marked a departure from Millay's previous works, which were simpler and brighter. The title poem of her 1923 collection *The Harp-Weaver and Other Poems*, it earned its author a Pulitzer Prize.

Bridge of San Luis Rey, The (novel, 1927, by Thornton Wilder)

Set in the year 1714, *The Bridge of San Luis Rey* begins with the death of five people traveling across the "the finest bridge in all Peru" when it collapses. Brother Juniper, a Franciscan missionary who witnesses the tragedy, struggles to make sense of what happened and embarks on a quest to learn what he can about the five individuals. Juniper hopes to learn why God chose them to be the ones who fell victim to this fate. Never coming to a satisfactory answer, Juniper publishes his research notes as a book. Declared a heretic by church officials, Juniper is burned at the stake, along with his book.

The novel's central question—Why do bad things happen to innocent people?—was common in post–World War I literature, as people struggled to make sense of the horrors of that conflict. *The Bridge of San Luis Rey* was Thornton Wilder's first great success, winning him a Pulitzer Prize in 1928 and establishing him as one of America's foremost authors. With the exception of his ever-popular play *Our Town* (1938), Wilder's work waned in popularity after his death in 1975, but interest in *The Bridge of San Luis*

Rey revived in 2001 after British Prime Minister Tony Blair quoted the book during a memorial service for the victims of the September 11 terrorist attacks.

Cane (poetry and short-story collection, 1923, by Jean Toomer)

Cane is an innovative work of fiction comprising poems, short stories, and dramatic pieces by Jean Toomer, one of the leading lights of the Harlem Renaissance. It is a thin volume of less than 30,000 words and is divided into three parts, one set in Washington, D.C., and the other two in Georgia. The longest and best-known selection is a story titled "Kabnis," about an African American man who returns home to Georgia after graduating from college, only to find that he can no longer cope with the racism he finds there.

Cane was hailed by critics for its unflinching portrayal of race relations in the United States, but it would prove to be the author's last important work. Like other Harlem Renaissance writers, Toomer had difficulty getting published in the 1930s and 1940s, and he ultimately gave up writing altogether.

Color (poetry collection, 1925, by Countee Cullen)

Color is the first and best-known collection of poems published by Countee Cullen, regarded by many scholars as the finest poet of the Harlem Renaissance. Cullen was noted for his ability to blend European and African influences in his work. The poems in *Color*—including "Yet Do I Marvel" and "Incident," perhaps his most famous individual works—focus on themes such as the beauty of the black race, the progress of black culture, and the problem of racism in America.

Upon publication in 1925, *Color* was embraced by both white and black intellectuals, the latter including civil rights activist W.E.B. Du Bois. After *Color,* however, Cullen's star faded. Not wanting to be known as a "Negro poet," he chose to downplay the subject of race in subsequent volumes in favor of the themes of love and nature, and his readership largely abandoned him. Cullen's other collections of the 1920s are *Copper Sun* (1927), *The Ballad of the Brown Girl* (1927), and *The Black Christ* (1929).

Coming of Age in Samoa (nonfiction, 1928, by Margaret Mead)

Based on extensive fieldwork, *Coming of Age in Samoa* is an anthropological study of youth—mainly young women—on a South Pacific island. The book was based on Mead's firsthand observations of a Samoan village of 600 people and her in-depth interviews with selected females between the ages of nine and twenty.

The book attracted a great deal of attention for a pair of controversial theses: first, that Samoan children were happier than their American counterparts because Samoan parents emphasized cooperation whereas American children were taught to compete; and second, that Samoan teenagers were happier and more fulfilled because they engaged in sex with multiple partners before marriage.

Mead's provocative conclusions were embraced in some quarters and hotly denounced in others. Some academics criticized her research as sloppy or even fabricated, while social conservatives argued that she was projecting her personal beliefs about sex and sexuality onto her subjects. Mead defended her research for the rest of her life, and the work remains a classic in the field of anthropology.

Death Comes for the Archbishop (novel, 1927, by Willa Cather)

At a time when most authors were experimenting with new styles of writing or grappling with the great themes of existence, the former muckraker and schoolteacher Willa Cather was content to write more realistic stories—if subtle in character development and often unconventional in narrative structure—about the lives of everyday Americans, particularly the pioneers of the West. The central figure of *Death Comes for the Archbishop* is Bishop Jean Marie Latour, who is sent from Cincinnati to establish a diocese in New Mexico shortly after it has become a U.S. territory. After a long journey over water and land, he finally arrives in New Mexico and meets the entrenched Spanish priests he has been sent to replace. Some are simple, honest men who welcome Latour; others, greedy and fearing a loss of their power, resist him at every turn.

Beyond detailing this power struggle, the book is also notable for its vivid descriptions of the New Mexico landscape and its sympathetic portrayal of Native Americans. *Death Comes for the Archbishop* was a runaway critical and commercial success, going through thirty-four printings in its first seven years. It remains one of Cather's best-known and most widely read works.

Elmer Gantry (novel, 1927, by Sinclair Lewis)
A critique of Protestant revivalism in America, the satirical *Elmer Gantry* follows the career of a supremely hypocritical minister who conceals his greed and lust in the guise of religious zeal. At the start of the book, Gantry is in training for a career as a lawyer but soon switches to the ministry because of the power and prestige that come with the profession. Gantry continues his immoral behavior in his new line of work, and although he is nearly exposed as a fraud on several occasions, he always manages to squirm his way out of trouble. The novel ends with Gantry delivering a sermon on the importance of being a "moral nation"—while training his eyes on the object of his next sexual conquest.

The most controversial of Sinclair Lewis's novels, *Elmer Gantry* was banned in several cities, and the author was repeatedly threatened with bodily harm or imprisonment. Despite the controversy, Lewis won the Nobel Prize in Literature in 1930, and the book was made into a Broadway play in 1928 and an Academy Award–winning movie in 1960, with Burt Lancaster winning the Oscar for best actor in the title role and Shirley Jones winning for best supporting actress.

Enormous Room, The (memoir, 1922, by E.E. Cummings)
Although E.E. Cummings is known primarily for his poetry, the first published work of his career was *The Enormous Room,* a stylized memoir of his experiences as an ambulance driver during World War I. In August 1917, Cummings and fellow driver William Slater Brown (referred to in the book only as B.) were arrested by French authorities for writing letters that contained antiwar sentiments. They were interned in a French prison camp, La Ferté-Macé, for four months. The "enormous room" is the space in which Cummings, Brown, and thirty others were held prisoner.

With Cummings's sense of metaphor and knack for storytelling, his character sketches and descriptions of life in captivity evoke the chaos of the time and serve as an allegory for the "enormous room" of his own mind. *The Enormous Room* was one of the most powerful and popular books of the post–World War I era and a particular favorite of F. Scott Fitzgerald. "Of all the work by young men who have sprung up since 1920," he said, "one book survives—*The Enormous Room* by E. E. Cummings."

Etiquette in Society, in Business, in Politics, and at Home (nonfiction, 1922, by Emily Post)
The scion of one of Baltimore's elite families, Emily Post lived a life of privilege until financial reverses compelled her to take up writing to supplement her income. She began with light novels and travel books but soon turned to the subject that would make her famous. *Etiquette in Society, in Business, in Politics, and at Home* contains thousands of tips, most of them common sense, for proper conduct at weddings, funerals, parties, and other private and public settings.

At a hefty 627 pages, the book was a runaway best seller. Later known as *Etiquette: The Blue Book of Social Usage,* it went through ten editions and more than ninety printings during Post's lifetime. The book is credited with making the complexities of etiquette accessible to average Americans, and it established its author as the acknowledged arbiter of social conduct. In the 1930s, Post began a syndicated newspaper column that would run for nearly thirty years, and in 1946, she founded the Emily Post Institute, which continues to dispense advice on manners and etiquette.

Farewell to Arms, A (novel, 1929, by Ernest Hemingway)
A semi-autobiographical novel of World War I, Ernest Hemingway's *A Farewell to Arms* eschews flowery language and extended descriptions in favor of spare, straightforward narrative. The book's central character is Lieutenant Frederic Henry, who suffers leg wounds while driving an ambulance in the Italian Alps. Convalescing in a military hospital, Henry falls in love with his British nurse, Catherine Barkley; by the time he is sent back to the front, she has become pregnant. Henry ultimately deserts his post and is reunited briefly with Barkley, but she and the baby die in childbirth, leaving Henry, at the novel's end, with the realization that he is once again alone in the world.

A Farewell to Arms was adapted twice for the big screen: in 1932, starring Gary Cooper, and in 1957, starring Rock Hudson.

Flame and Shadow (poetry collection, 1920, by Sara Teasdale)
Sara Teasdale was one of the most respected American poets of the early twentieth century, and the lengthy volume *Flame and Shadow,* divided into twelve parts,

is one of her signature works. Like much of Teasdale's lyric verse, the poems in *Flame and Shadow* vary dramatically in tone. Some, like "Stars" and "Places," celebrate love and the beauty of nature. Others, like "Pain" and "The Broken Field," are much darker and dwell on death and suffering.

Writing poetry was a form of therapy for Teasdale, who suffered poor health, a difficult upbringing, and an unhappy marriage. The themes of darkness and pain become more pronounced in *Dark of the Moon* (1926) and *Strange Victory* (1933). She committed suicide in January 1933.

Frontier in American History, The (nonfiction, 1920, by Frederick Jackson Turner)

Frederick Jackson Turner became nationally famous in 1893 for an essay advancing his "frontier thesis." The unique American character, he contended, was forged in response to the challenges of conquering the Western frontier. Turner elaborated on this theory in his landmark work *The Frontier in American History*.

The book begins with his original essay on the significance of the frontier and expands on the concept in succeeding chapters. He identifies a series of geographic frontiers that Americans had to overcome, and he links these triumphs to specific elements of American political and social life. Although many of Turner's assumptions have been challenged, his frontier thesis revolutionized the writing of American history in general and the history of the American West in particular.

Gentlemen Prefer Blondes (novel, 1925, by Anita Loos)

Subtitled *The Illuminating Diary of a Professional Lady,* the hit novel *Gentlemen Prefer Blondes* tells the story of two young flappers named Dorothy Shaw and Lorelei Lee who leave their home state of Arkansas for careers as showgirls. Although the women at first seem vapid and interested only in pursuing wealthy husbands, they prove to be intelligent, resourceful, and adept at manipulating men.

Loos's story, while simple and entertaining on the surface, is now regarded by many scholars as an early feminist text, commenting on the place of women in society and the importance of challenging gender roles. *Gentlemen Prefer Blondes* won instant fame for its author and was translated into a dozen languages. It also spawned a successful sequel, *But Gentlemen Marry Brunettes* (1928), as well as two Broadway musicals (1926–1927 and 1949–1951), a silent film adaptation (1928), and a 1953 film musical directed by Howard Hawks and starring Jane Russell and Marilyn Monroe.

Great Gatsby, The (novel, 1925, by F. Scott Fitzgerald)

Among the most acclaimed works of modern American fiction—and perhaps the one most associated with the Jazz Age—*The Great Gatsby* is F. Scott Fitzgerald's evocative tale of the empty lives of the idle rich in the Roaring Twenties. The title character is Jay Gatsby, a larger-than-life romantic idealist and mysterious self-made multimillionaire who hosts opulent parties in his New York mansion. He is much admired by the narrator, neighbor Nick Carraway, a transplanted Midwesterner who aspires to follow in Gatsby's footsteps. As he grows closer to Gatsby, however, Carraway becomes disenchanted with the phoniness and hedonism of Gatsby's high-society friends and the inner emptiness of Gatsby's own existence.

Fitzgerald considered the novel his finest and was bitterly disappointed by its cool reception; it gained a wider audience after it was republished in 1945. Film versions exist from 1926, 1949, and 1974, the last starring Robert Redford as Gatsby.

Harmonium (poetry collection, 1923, by Wallace Stevens)

Harmonium was the little-noticed, first published collection of poems by Wallace Stevens, who would later be recognized as one of the masters of modernist American verse. The volume brought together a number of the writer's most original, most richly imaginative, and ultimately most famous poems. Many of them—including "Sunday Morning," "The Emperor of Ice Cream," and "Peter Quince at the Clavier"—had been previously published in magazines.

An insurance lawyer and corporate vice president in Hartford, Connecticut, Stevens quietly produced unconventional, philosophical, often elusive lyric verse that literary critics came to regard as some of the finest in twentieth-century American letters. It would be twelve years before Stevens published another collection, but the poems in *Harmonium* marked the debut of a unique and enduring voice.

Hugh Selwyn Mauberley (poem, 1920, by Ezra Pound)

Like his friend T.S. Eliot, Ezra Pound was among the founders of the modernist school of poetry. Influenced by his study of Chinese and Japanese verse, Pound was economical in his use of language and eschewed rhyme in favor of free verse. "Hugh Selwyn Mauberley," a long poem made up of eighteen parts in two sections, is one of the earliest examples of the modernist style. The poem's central figure is the semi-autobiographical Hugh Selwyn Mauberley, a struggling poet who works to make sense of the world. In telling Mauberley's story, Pound offers a damning critique of post–World War I society, which he describes as a "botched civilization."

The poem was a turning point in Pound's career. In addition to helping lay the groundwork for the modernist movement in poetry, "Hugh Selwyn Mauberley" was the last poem Pound completed before moving to Paris. He devoted much of the rest of his life—more than fifty years—to composing the encyclopedic and ultimately unfinished *Cantos*.

Kindergarten Chats on Architecture, Education, and Democracy (nonfiction, 1924, by Louis Sullivan)

A giant in the history of American architecture, Louis Sullivan is recognized as the creator of the modern skyscraper and a staunch advocate of the idea that a building's form should follow its function. Sullivan outlined his views on architecture and politics in a number of essays that were posthumously collected in *Kindergarten Chats on Architecture, Education, and Democracy*.

During his lifetime, Sullivan was responsible for some of the most important buildings constructed at the turn of the century, among them the Wainwright Building in St. Louis, the Guaranty Building in Buffalo, the Bayard-Condict Building in New York, and the Grand Opera House in Chicago. *Kindergarten Chats on Architecture, Education, and Democracy* introduced Sullivan's ideas to a new generation of architects and ensured his lasting influence.

Life and Labor in the Old South (nonfiction, 1929, by Ulrich Bonnell Phillips)

Life and Labor in the Old South is a comprehensive analysis of antebellum plantation culture and slavery by Ulrich Bonnell Phillips, the first prominent historian of the American South. Building on his 1918 work, *American Negro Slavery*, and influenced by his travels through Africa, Phillips argues that slavery in the American South emerged gradually in response to the region's geography and climate and was not the product of conscious design. He also asserts that slavery was generally not profitable but that the system was maintained because it produced social status and power for white slaveholders. In his most controversial assertion, Phillips insists that slaves generally were not the victims of brutal treatment and were well provided for materially.

As the first detailed analysis of the institution of slavery, Phillips's work was groundbreaking, and a few of his ideas—the influence of geography on the development of the Southern economy, for example—are still accepted today. However, his analysis of slavery and even his use of language are considered racist by modern historians and have led many to dismiss his work. Phillips hoped to produce an equally comprehensive analysis of the postbellum South, but his death from cancer in January 1934 prevented him from doing so.

Look Homeward, Angel (novel, 1929, by Thomas Wolfe)

The first novel by Thomas Wolfe, *Look Homeward, Angel* is an autobiographical coming-of-age story and a portrait of the South in the early twentieth century. The protagonist is the energetic and ambitious Eugene Gant, a perpetual outsider. The novel follows Gant from his childhood in the fictional town of Altamont—a thinly veiled evocation of Wolfe's hometown of Asheville, North Carolina—through his graduation from college.

One of the earliest works of the Southern Renaissance, *Look Homeward, Angel* was widely admired for its character portrayals and lyrical style—the contemporary novelist William Faulkner ranked Wolfe as the greatest writer of their generation. *Of Time and the River* (1935) picks up Gant's story as he leaves for graduate school at Harvard and follows him to New York City and Europe.

Main Street (novel, 1920, by Sinclair Lewis)

A satirical portrait of small-town life in the Midwest, *Main Street* was Sinclair Lewis's first popular success and thereby launched one of the most notable careers in the history of American literature. The novel is set in the fictional hamlet of Gopher Prairie, Minnesota, based on Lewis's hometown of Sauk Center, Minnesota. The protagonist is Carol Milford, a progressive young woman who moves to Gopher Prairie from Minneapolis after marrying Will Kennicott, a local doctor. She attempts to liven up the sleepy town—organizing women's clubs, holding fancy parties, introducing residents to great works of literature—but her efforts are met with indifference. After much unhappiness, she eventually accepts small-town life for what it is.

A biting and humorous critique of the vacuousness of conservative Midwestern life, *Main Street* was a surprise success, selling more than a quarter of a million copies in its first six months in print. Today, *Main Street* is widely recognized as Lewis's finest work and one of the first books by a male writer to embrace feminist themes.

Maltese Falcon, The (novel, 1930, by Dashiell Hammett)

California in the 1920s was full of outrageous characters, political corruption, and social turmoil. From this world and the pens of Dashiell Hammett, Raymond Chandler, and James M. Cain emerged the literature known as "hard-boiled" detective fiction—of which *The Maltese Falcon* is generally regarded as the first fully formed example. The novel's central character is detective Sam Spade, a drinker, cynic, and womanizer who is neither entirely good nor entirely bad. The novel opens as Spade's firm is hired to provide protection for an attractive but duplicitous woman named Brigid O'Shaughnessy. After Spade's partner is murdered, the detective becomes involved with O'Shaughnessy in a scheme to sell a golden statuette to a group of colorful villains.

Enormously popular and well received, *The Maltese Falcon* was adapted for the big screen in 1931 and 1941. The latter version, starring Humphrey Bogart in the role of Spade, is considered a film classic and has ensured the novel's continuing popularity.

Manhattan Transfer (novel, 1925, by John Dos Passos)

John Dos Passos rose to prominence in the early 1920s after publishing several books that explored the upheavals following World War I. *Manhattan Transfer,* which chronicles the struggles and triumphs of more than a dozen characters, was Dos Passos's third novel. Inspired by James Joyce and seeking to capture the chaos and social indifference of modern urban life, the author used the technique known as stream of consciousness—a series of thoughts presented in no particular order. Manhattan is portrayed as heartless and unforgiving, yet full of energy and life.

Dos Passos was pleased with the final product, which he described as "utterly fantastic and New Yorkish." The author would follow *Manhattan Transfer* with three books known as the *U.S.A.* trilogy, now considered his major accomplishment. All three books in *U.S.A.*—*The 42nd Parallel* (1930), *1919* (1932), and *The Big Money* (1936)—built on *Manhattan Transfer* thematically and stylistically.

Mental Growth of the Pre-School Child, The (nonfiction, 1925, by Arnold Gesell)

Psychologist and physician Arnold Gesell was an expert on child development who pioneered several new techniques for collecting data on child psychology and behavior. He was among the first researchers to use motion-picture cameras, and he invented the Gesell dome, a one-way mirror that allowed children to be observed without being disturbed. From his research, Gesell identified a number of milestones that could be used to assess a child's development, such as the refinement of motor skills, expressing emotions, and play. *The Mental Growth of the Pre-School Child,* which focuses on children under the age of six, is one of several books in which he identifies the hallmarks of a normally developing child.

Gesell's research revolutionized the fields of pediatrics and child psychology, providing tools for children's health professionals that continue to be used to this day.

Middletown: A Study in Modern American Culture (nonfiction, 1929, by Robert Staughton Lynd and Helen Merrel Lynd)

Based on a sociological case study of daily life in middle America, *Middletown* examines cultural norms and social change in an advanced industrial society. The object of the field study, conducted between 1890 and 1925, was later revealed to be Muncie, Indiana. Taking a rigorous anthropological approach, the Lynds (husband and wife) collected statistics, survey results, interviews, and documents to present a detailed analysis of changing behavioral patterns and social dynamics. The study proved influential as much for its methodology as for its substantive findings. A subsequent study conducted during the Great Depression was published as *Middletown in Transition: A Study in Cultural Conflicts* (1937).

New Hampshire (poetry collection, 1923, by Robert Frost)

Robert Frost is known especially for his pastoral poems about life in New England. *New Hampshire,* one of his earliest collections, showcases his characteristic style and subject matter. The forty-four selections in the volume—including "Fire and Ice," "Nothing Gold Can Stay," and "Stopping by Woods on a Snowy Evening"—address such sophisticated themes as the ambiguity of religion, the meaning of existence, and the future of the human race. Yet, because Frost preferred traditional rhyming verse and classical metrics, the poetry in *New Hampshire* is deceptively simple. The elegant "Stopping by Woods on a Snowy Evening" contains the oft-quoted closing refrain: "The woods are lovely, dark and deep. / But I have promises to keep, / And miles to go before I sleep, / And miles to go before I sleep." For *New Hampshire,* Robert Frost was awarded a Pulitzer Prize in 1923, the first of four in his career.

New Negro, The (nonfiction, 1925, edited by Alain Locke)

The New Negro is an anthology of works by Harlem Renaissance writers and poets edited by Howard University professor Alain Locke and heavily influenced by the ideas of W.E.B. Du Bois. The collection opens with an essay by Locke, in which the author expresses his disdain for the submissive, accommodationist "Old Negro" who was created by slavery and celebrates the rise of the confident, assertive "New Negro" at the start of the twentieth century. Locke's essay is followed by selections from Countee Cullen, Langston Hughes, Zora Neale Hurston, Claude McKay, and other prominent figures of the Harlem Renaissance.

Not all African American intellectuals embraced the book, however; Marcus Garvey and Eric Walrond dismissed Locke as a dark-skinned white and argued that the idea of a "New Negro" was a fad created by white society. Still, *The New Negro* was among the most significant books of the 1920s, spotlighting the cultural achievements of African Americans and the ideas and creative energy of the Harlem Renaissance.

One of Ours (novel, 1922, by Willa Cather)

Willa Cather's Pulitzer Prize–winning *One of Ours* is the story of Nebraska native Claude Wheeler, who finds little satisfaction in the life of a farmer, however successful. His search for a meaningful life leads to marriage, but his wife Enid is more interested in religion than her husband, and she leaves him to do missionary work in Asia. Shortly thereafter, the United States enters World War I and Claude joins the army. Despite the horrors of war, he finally finds the sense of purpose for which he has been searching.

One of Ours is characteristic of Willa Cather's style and subject matter—she preferred stories about average Americans and was particularly fascinated by pioneers and the challenges of life on the frontier. For the romantic and restless Claude Wheeler, however, the frontier has vanished and he is forced to look elsewhere for his fulfillment.

Psychology from the Standpoint of a Behaviorist (nonfiction, 1919, by John B. Watson)

One of the leading figures in the formative years of American psychology, John B. Watson was one of the founders and leading advocates for the behaviorist movement—the scientific study of human and animal behavior. Watson argued that such factors as emotion and mental state are scientifically unmeasurable, but that psychological problems can be understood as responses to external stimuli and treated accordingly. Thus, a behaviorist might treat a person's fear of snakes by forcing the patient to interact with snakes until the condition subsides, without making any effort to understand the underlying causes of the phobia.

Psychology from the Standpoint of a Behaviorist is Watson's magnum opus, laying out the ideas that would become his legacy. It was his last major contribution to the field; when it became known that he had had an affair with a student, the scandal forced him to leave academia. His book's influence was palpable, however, and shortly before his death in 1958, the work was recognized with a special citation from the American Psychological Association.

Public Opinion (nonfiction, 1922, by Walter Lippmann)

In addition to being a respected journalist, magazine publisher, and political commentator, Walter Lippmann served as a member of the committee charged with persuading the American people to support World War I. He drew on that experience when writing *Public Opinion,* a study of democracy and the power of the media to influence the masses. In it, Lippmann argues that the rise of mass media such as newspaper and radio allows political leaders to "manufacture consent" by controlling the flow of information to voters. He goes on to suggest how that power might properly be used, while also expressing concerns about the potential for abuse.

In many ways, the book laid the theoretical groundwork for the field of public relations, which was in its infancy during the 1920s. And though some of Lippmann's conclusions are no longer applicable, *Public Opinion* remains a classic in the fields of sociology and political science.

Reconstruction in Philosophy (nonfiction, 1920, by John Dewey)

Written as a series of lectures, John Dewey's *Reconstruction in Philosophy* helped introduce the world to pragmatism, a philosophical movement founded by Charles Sanders Peirce and William James and expanded upon by Dewey. Pragmatism constitutes a critique of traditional Western philosophy, particularly its reliance on logic and metaphysics. Dewey and his colleagues asserted that theory and speculation are essentially irrelevant, and that the meaning and truth of an idea or proposition are purely a function of its practical outcome. For example, if a person believes that God exists and that belief has a palpable impact on the person's life, then no further discussion of God's existence is needed. Dewey's work and the ideas of pragmatism influenced such fields as law, education, and linguistics.

Rise of American Civilization, The (nonfiction, 1927, by Charles Austin Beard and Mary Ritter Beard)

Charles and Mary Beard were among the most influential and controversial historians of their generation, and *The Rise of American Civilization* is their best-known work. Published in two volumes, it offers a comprehensive analysis of American history from an economic standpoint. The Beards, who had Socialist leanings, saw economic forces as the key to understanding nearly every significant event in America's past. Especially notable was their thesis that the Civil War was perpetrated on the South by Northern capitalists who hoped to extend their economic influence.

The Beards' ideas held sway for nearly thirty years after the publication of *The Rise of American Civilization* but fell out of favor in the 1950s and 1960s as mistakes were discovered in their research and historians became interested in issues other than economic forces. However, the Beards' influence continued in a generation of historians they trained, among them C. Vann Woodward and Howard Beale.

Sartoris (novel, 1929, by William Faulkner)

Far less experimental than *The Sound and the Fury* (1929) or *As I Lay Dying* (1930), *Sartoris* is among William Faulkner's most accessible novels. It is his first novel set in Yoknapatawpha County, Mississippi—a fictionalized version of the area in Mississippi where Faulkner was raised. The central character, Colonel John Sartoris, is based on Faulkner's great-grandfather, Colonel William Clark Falkner. Set in the years immediately after the Civil War, *Sartoris* chronicles the decline of Colonel Sartoris and the Mississippi aristocracy during the era of Reconstruction. The work raises several themes that would reappear in Faulkner's later works, among them racial tension, class struggle, and the romanticization of the past.

Though criticized by some reviewers as overwrought and melodramatic, *Sartoris* was popular enough to justify the publication of a follow-up, *The Unvanquished,* in 1938. In 1973, an unedited and much longer version of *Sartoris* was published under the book's original title, *Flags in the Dust.*

So Big (novel, 1924, by Edna Ferber)

With its strong female protagonist, *So Big* is characteristic of the work of Edna Ferber. Perhaps her most popular work, *So Big* chronicles the life of Selina Peake De Jong, the orphaned daughter of a gambler. She moves to a small farming town to be a teacher, and soon after arriving, marries a handsome but simple-minded cabbage farmer. They have a son named Dirk, nicknamed "So Big" because of his enormous size at birth. Although Selina must overcome challenges, including the death of her husband, she perseveres, all the while encouraging her son to pursue his dreams.

Despite the obvious appeal and uplifting message of the story, Ferber initially dismissed *So Big* as "a book about cabbages"—only to see it awarded a Pulitzer Prize in 1924. This elevated her to the first rank of American authors, and she would go on to produce such well-received works as *Show Boat* (1926), *Cimarron* (1930), and *Giant* (1952)—all successfully adapted for the stage or screen.

Sound and the Fury, The (novel, 1929, by William Faulkner)

Among the earliest novels of the Southern Renaissance, *The Sound and the Fury* is counted among the masterpieces of modern American literature. The work centers on the once prominent Compson family, whose fall from the Mississippi aristocracy has been caused by the racism, greed, and selfishness that William Faulkner believed was typical of white Southerners in the era of Reconstruction. At the center of the novel is Caddy Compson, whose story is told from the point of view of her three brothers and an anonymous narrator. The novel is divided into four sections, one for each of these perspectives, and is presented in stream of consciousness style.

Literary critics have offered a number of interpretations of *The Sound and the Fury*—a retelling of the story of Jesus, a modern Greek tragedy, or a loose adaptation of Shakespeare's *Macbeth,* the play from which the title of the novel is taken. *The Sound and the Fury* was almost universally praised upon publication and contributed to Faulkner's selection as the winner of the 1949 Nobel Prize in Literature.

Sun Also Rises, The (novel, 1926, by Ernest Hemingway)

The Sun Also Rises, a semi-autobiographical novel by Ernest Hemingway, was the first success of the author's distinguished career. The story recounts the experiences of a group of American expatriates who struggle to find meaning in their lives while living in post–World War I Europe. The novel tells the story of Jake Barnes, a journalist who has been rendered impotent by war wounds, and Robert Cohn, a romantic, who are rivals for the affection of the vivacious Lady Brett Ashley. The exploits and preoccupations of Jake and his friends from Paris, to Pamplona, to the festival of San Fermin, all chronicled in Hemingway's characteristically sparse narrative style, helped popularize the idea that World War I had created a "Lost Generation."

The Sun Also Rises would be followed by a string of other successes for Hemingway—among them *A Farewell to Arms* (1929), *For Whom the Bell Tolls* (1940), and *The Old Man and the Sea* (1952)—that would earn him the Nobel Prize in Literature in 1954.

This Side of Paradise (novel, 1920, by F. Scott Fitzgerald)

A novel of post–World War I American youth, *This Side of Paradise* was F. Scott Fitzgerald's debut work, published when he was only twenty-three. The book's central character is the handsome and wealthy Amory Blaine, who travels widely and receives the finest education money can buy before volunteering for service in World War I. Upon his return to civilian life, Amory is adrift, moving through a series of empty romantic encounters and failed relationships. Although he eventually finds solace in Socialist politics, his search for meaning continues.

This Side of Paradise was an overnight sensation, earning its author instant fame as one of the preeminent writers of his generation. The themes it introduced—the restlessness and alienation of the postwar generation—would play a central role in much of the literature of the 1920s.

Waste Land, The (poem, 1922, by T.S. Eliot)

T.S. Eliot's most famous work, a prototype of modernist poetics and one of the most written-about poems in the American canon, "The Waste Land" is a lengthy meditation on the decline of civilization and the emptiness of modern life. Beginning with the often-quoted words "April is the cruellest month," the 434-line work features a complex, elegiac flow of obscure cultural references, literary allusions, and original poetic images to evoke the spiritual void of modern Western civilization while suggesting the possibility of order and well-being.

Two years in the making, the poem is divided into five parts and reads like a lengthy dramatic monologue. The original version, nearly twice the published length, was edited by Ezra Pound, to whom the poem is dedicated. "The Waste Land" received a mixed reaction from critics of the day, but it has grown in stature over time and now ranks among the classics of American verse.

Weary Blues, The (poetry collection, 1926, by Langston Hughes)

Like other Harlem Renaissance writers and poets, Langston Hughes is known for his celebration of African American culture. *The Weary Blues,* his first book of poetry, fits squarely within that tradition. The title work and highlight of the volume is a poem that describes a Harlem blues performance in glowing terms. The anonymous narrator is dazzled by the musician's ability to make the "poor piano moan with melody," and the tone and meter of the poem are crafted to capture the feeling of a blues song.

The Weary Blues was published to much acclaim while Hughes was still a student at Lincoln University; after graduation he would produce a dozen more volumes of poetry, as well as numerous plays, books, and short stories in nearly four decades as a writer.

His 1925 essay "The Negro Artist and the Racial Movement" conveys his sense of excitement about the Harlem Renaissance and the idea of the New Negro.

Winesburg, Ohio (short-story collection, 1919, by Sherwood Anderson)

Winesburg, Ohio is a collection of loosely connected short stories about the inhabitants of a small Ohio town. The setting, Winesburg, is fictional but based on Sherwood Anderson's hometown of Clyde, Ohio. The central figure of the book is George Willard, a newspaper reporter whose presence is the only common thread in the stories. Among the "grotesques" introduced in the various vignettes—almost all leading lives of quiet desperation—are two young lovers who struggle to relate to one another, a man whose religious zeal leads him to attempt to sacrifice his grandson, and a married man who tries to convince his younger friend to avoid such commitments as marriage.

The book's general theme is the loneliness, frustration, and inhibiting quality of life in small-town, industrial America—a common leitmotif in the literature and art of the 1920s. Although *Winesburg, Ohio* was greeted with critical acclaim and is still popular with readers today, the original edition sold poorly.

Woman and the New Race (nonfiction, 1920, by Margaret Sanger)

Margaret Sanger was an early advocate of safe and effective birth control, and *Woman and the New Race,* a slender 128-page volume, outlines her views on that issue. Characteristic of its author, the book is straightforward and brutally honest, sometimes more so than 1920s audiences were prepared to accommodate. Chapter titles include "Woman's Struggle for Freedom," "The Wickedness of Large Families," and "Battalions of Unwanted Babies the Cause of War."

Although some of Sanger's ideas are out of step with modern feminism—for example, she characterizes abortion as "abhorrent," "abnormal," and a "disgrace"—the book is nonetheless considered one of the founding documents of the feminist movement, as well as an important step in the fight for safe and effective birth control.

Woman Suffrage and Politics: The Inner Story of the Suffrage Movement (nonfiction, 1923, by Carrie Chapman Catt and Nettie Rogers Shuler)

Carrie Chapman Catt was one of the foremost members of the woman suffrage movement, equaled in prominence only by Elizabeth Cady Stanton and Susan B. Anthony. Catt played an active role in the movement for more than forty years and was serving as president of the National American Woman Suffrage Association when women finally won the right to vote in 1920. She was therefore in an ideal position to tell the story of the fight for suffrage, which she did in *Woman Suffrage and Politics: The Inner Story of the Suffrage Movement.*

Although Anthony and Stanton wrote their own histories, both died well before the movement achieved victory. Because it chronicles both the struggle and the victory, *Woman Suffrage and Politics: The Inner Story of the Suffrage Movement* is perhaps the single most valuable inside history of the suffrage movement.

Women at Point Sur, The (poem, 1927, by Robinson Jeffers)

A lengthy and dramatic composition in the epic tradition, "The Women at Point Sur" is the work that elevated Robinson Jeffers to the first rank of American poets. The book-length poem tells the story of a renegade minister who searches for God and finally finds what he seeks in the beauty of nature. Like much of Jeffers's work, the poem is set in his native California, employs traditional styles of verse and meter, and calls on mankind to appreciate the majesty of the natural world.

Jeffers produced numerous collections of verse on nature-related themes. Not surprisingly, he was an early supporter of environmentalism and today is considered an icon of the movement.

Performing Arts: Film, Theater, and Music

Abie's Irish Rose (stage comedy, 1922, by Anne Nichols)

A twist on the age-old theme of star-crossed lovers, *Abie's Irish Rose* is a love story about a wealthy Jewish boy and a poor Irish girl. Unlike Shakespeare's *Romeo and Juliet,* however, this play is a comedy and the lovers end up happily married. In fact, they are married from the beginning, having deceived their prejudiced fathers about the ethnicity and faith of their partners. When the deception is discovered, the young couple are disowned and forced to live in poverty, but all are reconciled in the end.

Set in 1920s New York City, the play offers slapstick comedy and a host of platitudes about tolerance and the joys of diversity. Although it received almost uniformly poor reviews, *Abie's Irish Rose* was a huge hit on Broadway, running for more than 2,300 performances between 1922 and 1927. It was made into films in 1928 and 1946. *Abie's Irish Rose* was a product of its time, when many of the assimilated offspring of the turn of the century's great wave of immigration were coming of age and marrying outside their ethnic groups.

Adding Machine, The (stage drama, 1923, by Elmer Rice)

Elmer Rice's *The Adding Machine* is generally regarded as the first and most influential work of American expressionist theater, whose hallmarks include gross exaggerations of reality and exploration of the characters' angst. The play takes as its central theme the destruction of the human soul by modern society. Its main character, a white-collar worker named Mr. Zero, is fired in favor of an adding machine, then implicated in and executed for the murder of his boss.

Consistent with expressionist tradition, the play is an assault on the senses of the audience. The original production was performed on a rotating stage occupied almost entirely by an enormous adding machine. Screeching and jabbering sounds played incessantly in the background. Although the production was not a commercial success, a number of playwrights, notably Tennessee Williams, cited Rice's play as a major influence on their work.

Ain't Misbehavin' (musical recording, 1929, by Fats Waller)

Although the song "Ain't Misbehavin'" has become an American standard, inspiring hundreds of cover versions and a long-running Broadway musical (1978), Fats Waller's original recording remains the definitive performance. Trained as a classical musician before becoming interested in jazz as a young man, Waller helped create "stride style" piano playing, which blends classical and jazz formats while allowing room for improvisation. It is an exceedingly difficult style to play, and "Ain't Misbehavin'" showcases Waller's skill. Waller's music influenced a generation of jazz musicians, among them Duke Ellington and Thelonius Monk.

American in Paris, An (symphonic composition, 1928, George Gershwin)

An extended orchestral tone poem that premiered in New York City in 1928, *An American in Paris* was composer George Gershwin's homage to his life in the French capital during the 1920s. Along with many other artists, writers, and musicians, Gershwin was part of a large American expatriate community drawn to Paris for cultural, economic, and social reasons. A musical narrative combining standard orchestral instruments and everyday noises—including authentic taxi horns—*An American in Paris* evokes the sounds and atmosphere of typical Parisian life. The piece was the inspiration for a 1951 film musical of the same name starring Gene Kelly.

Anna Christie (stage drama, 1921, by Eugene O'Neill)

Eugene O'Neill's four-act drama *Anna Christie* is among the first American plays written in the realist style. Influenced by European playwrights Anton Chekhov, Henrik Ibsen, and August Strindberg, O'Neill strove to provide a frank and unflinching portrayal of his characters and the sordid aspects of human existence. The play's title character is a prostitute, driven to the life of a streetwalker after having been abandoned by her father, a sea captain. The action commences with a meeting between Anna and her father, Chris Christopherson, after an estrangement of many years. They leave together on a short voyage and begin repairing their relationship. In the midst of this domestic drama, they rescue four shipwrecked sailors, including an Irishman named Mat Burke with whom Anna gradually falls in love. Mat and Chris come to blows, and Chris and Anna go their separate ways, apparently never to see each other again. Their paths cross again by sheer chance, however, and the play ends with a reconciliation between Mat and Chris.

Happy endings of this sort are not typical of realist theater or the works of O'Neill, and some critics attacked *Anna Christie* for its sentimental ending. Most called it a masterpiece, however, and the play won O'Neill his second Pulitzer Prize.

Ben-Hur: A Tale of the Christ (film, 1925, directed by Fred Niblo)

Ben-Hur: A Tale of the Christ was the second silent film adaptation of Lew Wallace's 1880 novel about a Jewish prince who is betrayed into slavery by a boyhood friend, is eventually freed, and becomes a follower of Jesus of Nazareth. (The first film version was in 1907.) The Metro-Goldwyn-Mayer release starred Ramon Navarro and Francis X. Bushman, with many other well-known actors—Mary Pickford, Douglas Fairbanks, Lillian Gish, and Clark Gable among them—making cameo appearances.

Grossly overrunning its budget, *Ben-Hur* ultimately cost nearly $6 million to complete, making it the most expensive silent film ever made. It did exceedingly well at the box office, however, and helped establish fledgling MGM as a major studio. Today the film is known primarily for its legendary chariot race, which has been imitated in a number of other motion pictures, including the Academy Award–winning 1959 version of *Ben-Hur*. The chariot race was extraordinarily difficult to create, costing one stuntman his life and consuming over 200,000 feet (610 meters) of film. Only 750 feet (229 meters) of the footage were actually used, giving the movie an all-time record for the most edited scene in movie history.

Beyond the Horizon (stage drama, 1920, by Eugene O'Neill)

As playwright Eugene O'Neill's first success, *Beyond the Horizon* was responsible for launching the career of one of the most important figures in American drama. The play's complicated plot centers on two brothers, Robert and Andrew Mayo, who both fall in love with a woman named Kate. Kate chooses Robert, who abandons his plans for a career as a sailor and settles down to work as a farmer. The result is an unhappy life and a rocky marriage that leave Robert a bitter man. Andrew, meanwhile, seizes the opportunity that Robert declined and becomes successful, happy, and fulfilled.

Beyond the Horizon was written when O'Neill was still struggling to find his voice as a writer and to master the nuances of plot and tone. Although it does not measure up to some of his later works, it was well received in its day and earned O'Neill the first of his four Pulitzer Prizes.

Blackmail (film, 1929, directed by Alfred Hitchcock)

An early work by the master of film suspense Alfred Hitchcock, *Blackmail* tells the story of Alice White, who kills a man during an attempted rape and then is blackmailed about the incident. Groundbreaking in its use of camera angles and special effects, *Blackmail* is best remembered as the first British-made film to have a soundtrack.

The decision to produce it as a "talkie" was not reached until the film was more than halfway complete, creating a number of challenges for the director. The production company wanted to use as much of the silent footage as possible, and the star of the film, Anny Ondra, was a Polish immigrant with a poor command of English. Hitchcock resolved these problems by reshooting several scenes with sound and having an English actress read Ondra's lines off-camera. Because most theaters in 1929 were not equipped to show films with sound, *Blackmail* was released in both silent and sound versions. Their combined success helped cement Hitchcock's status as one of the world's foremost directors at a critical juncture in film history.

Broadway Melody, The (film, 1929, directed by Harry Beaumont)

Winner of the 1929 Academy Award for best picture, *The Broadway Melody* is generally regarded as the first motion-picture musical. The film, which paints a picture of backstage life at a Broadway musical, originally featured scenes in Technicolor and black and white, but all of the color footage has since been lost. It was an enormous financial and critical success, taking in over $4 million, which made it the top-grossing film of the year. "When talkies were new," observes film critic Pauline Kael, "this was the musical that everyone went to see." Beyond establishing the movie musical genre, *Broadway Melody* was also notable as one of the first American motion pictures to earn significant box-office revenues overseas and one of the first to spawn film sequels (three in all).

Charleston, The (musical recording, 1924, by Arthur Gibbs and Gang)

Although not a prolific group—with only two records to their name—Arthur Gibbs and Gang achieved a level of immortality as the first band to record the popular tune "The Charleston." Written by James P. Johnson for the moderately successful Broadway musical *Runnin' Wild,* the song was inspired by the city of Charleston, South Carolina, and the style of dancing favored by that city's African American community.

The Arthur Gibbs and Gang recording inspired a national and international dance craze, with various forms of the Charleston remaining popular into the 1940s. The fast and rhythmic Charleston was considered highly immoral in some quarters and was even banned in certain cities.

Cocoanuts, The (film, 1929, directed by Robert Florey and Joseph Santley)

Based on a George Kaufman play of the same name, *The Cocoanuts* was the first feature-length film to star the Marx Brothers. In addition to Groucho, Harpo, Chico, and Zeppo Marx, the film also featured Margaret Dumont, who would frequently costar with the brothers. A musical, with five songs contributed to the score by famed composer Irving Berlin, *The Cocoanuts* is set at a Florida hotel managed by Groucho and his assistant, Zeppo. The plot involves a number of schemes occurring under Groucho's nose: While Harpo and Chico hatch a plan to rob the hotel's guests, the Dumont character works to attract an upper-class husband for her daughter, unaware that the would-be husband is a con man. As in all Marx Brothers films, the plot is secondary to the slapstick antics of the stars, who had spent years on stage developing their act before making their foray into film.

The experience of making *The Cocoanuts* was not a good one for the brothers, and they disliked the final product so much, they offered to buy the negatives from Paramount Pictures in order to keep the film from being released. The studio refused, and the film became a hit, grossing $2 million and launching the Marx Brothers on the road to stardom.

Down Hearted Blues (musical recording, 1923, by Bessie Smith)

Known as the "Empress of the Blues," Bessie Smith was the most popular female blues singer of the 1920s. Born and raised in Tennessee, she spent more than a decade honing her craft on stage before signing a record contract with Columbia. Smith's debut on the label, "Down Hearted Blues," by jazz singer and songwriter Alberta Hunter, was an enormous commercial success, selling nearly a million copies (an extraordinary figure for that time).

Smith remained one of America's most popular recording and performing artists until her death in a 1937 car accident. But she continued to influence blues singers—among them Billie Holliday, Aretha Franklin, Sarah Vaughan, and Janis Joplin. As Joplin said of Smith, "She showed me the air and taught me how to fill it."

Emperor Jones, The (stage drama, 1920, by Eugene O'Neill)

Among his signature works, *The Emperor Jones* was one of Eugene O'Neill's first experiments with expressionist drama, which is characterized by an exaggerated realism, main characters elevated to symbolic or archetypal roles, and the tendency to turn common individuals into tragic figures. The protagonist of *The Emperor Jones* is an African American named Brutus Jones who is convicted of murder. Sent to prison, he escapes to a Caribbean island, where he proclaims himself emperor. After abusing his subjects and precipitating an uprising, Brutus flees into the jungle, only to be haunted by images from his past. Failing to separate fantasy from reality, Brutus is unable to defend himself and is killed by the rebels.

So positive were the initial audience response and critical reviews that a much larger theater had to be booked after the play's opening to accommodate the demand for tickets. A film version, with Paul Robeson in the title role, was released in 1933.

Four Horsemen of the Apocalypse, The (film, 1921, directed by Rex Ingram)

Based on the Vicente Blasco Ibáñez novel, *The Four Horsemen of the Apocalypse* was the highest-grossing film of the silent era, with a box-office take of nearly $10 million. It was also the movie that made actor Rudolph Valentino a household name. Valentino stars as Julio Desnoyers, a shiftless young Frenchman who carouses in bars and carries on an adulterous affair with a woman named Marguerite Laurier, played by Alice Terry. When World War I breaks out, Julio is initially unaffected but eventually enlists in the French army. He is killed in the trenches, and his spirit persuades Marguerite to return to her husband.

Because of its generally unfavorable portrayal of World War I—particularly the devastating impact of the war on the French countryside—historians regard *Four Horsemen* as the first antiwar film. It is also remembered for Valentino's passionate tango scene, which has been imitated or parodied in dozens of films in the decades since.

Freshman, The (film, 1925, directed by Sam Taylor)

If not as well known today as contemporaries Charlie Chaplin and Buster Keaton, Harold Lloyd was one of the giants of big-screen comedy in the 1920s, and *The Freshman* was one of his most successful films. Lloyd starred as Harold Lamb, a misfit college freshman who seeks desperately to capture the affection of a young lady named Peggy, played by Jobyna Ralston. After a series of embarrassing missteps, he joins the school's football team, comes off the bench to score the winning touchdown in the final game of the season, and thereby captures Peggy's heart.

A silent film classic, *The Freshman* inspired a wave of college-themed movies that lasted well into the sound era. Chosen in 1990 for preservation in the National Film Registry, it is one of the few Harold Lloyd films still widely available to audiences today.

Front Page, The (stage comedy, 1928, by Ben Hecht and Charles MacArthur)

Written by two former newspapermen, *The Front Page* is based loosely on actual events on the Chicago news beat. The play's protagonist is Hildy Johnson, a reporter whose last assignment before leaving the profession is to cover the execution of Earl Williams, a reputed Communist radical convicted of murdering a police officer. While awaiting execution, Williams escapes. Johnson discovers the condemned man's whereabouts and, realizing that Williams has been framed for the murder, helps him.

The play's blend of comedic elements and social commentary proved enormously appealing to audiences, making it one of the top grossing Broadway productions of the 1920s. It also grabbed Hollywood's attention, with screenwriters throughout the 1930s and 1940s emulating its rapid-fire, blue-collar dialogue in a number of projects, including at least four film versions of the play (under various titles) and several television adaptations.

General, The (film, 1927, directed by Buster Keaton and Clyde Bruckman)

Buster Keaton, affectionately dubbed the "Great Stone Face," was one of the best-known comic actors of the silent era, and *The General,* in which he starred, is his best-known work. The film, which Keaton codirected, is based loosely on actual Civil War events. When Union soldiers steal a train engine nicknamed the *General,* the Confederate train engineer, played by Keaton, gives chase, first on a hand-powered cart and then on a locomotive.

Making the film required Keaton to perform a number of dangerous stunts, among them running along the roof of the locomotive, jumping from the engine to a boxcar, and riding on the engine's cowcatcher. In the climactic scene—one of the most expensive produced to that time—a train is destroyed as it crosses a bridge sabotaged by Keaton's character. Although the film was Keaton's own favorite, it was panned by critics and was only moderately successful at the box office. Over time, however, it became one of the most loved comedies in the annals of film.

Gold Rush, The (film, 1925, directed by Charlie Chaplin)

Regarded by some as the peak of Charlie Chaplin's creative achievement, *The Gold Rush* certainly ranks as one of the best in which the comic actor plays his popular "Little Tramp" character. The film's plot has the Tramp heading to the Klondike in search of gold, only to suffer a series of misfortunes. In one famous scene, he is forced to boil and eat his boot to avoid starvation; in another, the Tramp spends a lonely New Year's Eve creating a dance for a pair of dinner rolls. The latter scene was said to be so popular with audiences that projectionists would sometimes stop the film and replay it. In the end, the Tramp survives his snowy ordeal to strike it rich—and win the love of a dance hall performer played by Georgia Hale.

The Gold Rush was Chaplin's personal favorite among all his movies and a smash hit at the box office. Indeed, with a gross in excess of $4 million, it earned more than any other silent comedy. Critics consistently rank it as one of the top ten films of all time.

Hairy Ape, The (stage drama, 1923, by Eugene O'Neill)

The Hairy Ape is among the foremost examples of expressionist drama, characterized by the exaggeration of reality for emotional effect. Characters in expressionist plays tend to be reduced to stereotypes, and Yank Smith, the main character in O'Neill's play, fits this model. A stoker on a transatlantic steamer, he is a classic bully—he treats everyone around him badly, inspiring both fear and resentment. He falls in love with a millionaire's daughter, but she is disgusted by his behavior and rejects him. The heartbroken sailor goes ashore but is ignored by high society types and rejected by both the poor and criminal alike, who think he is a Communist agitator. Smith then wanders into a zoo, where he sees a gorilla and recognizes him as a kindred spirit; he opens the cage and is killed.

A complex commentary on capitalism, the shallowness of the wealthy, and the alienation of the individual in modern America, *The Hairy Ape* was not as accessible as some of O'Neill's other plays and ran for a relatively modest 121 performances on Broadway. It is nonetheless viewed as one of the most important works of the greatest modern American playwright, helping earn him the Nobel Prize in Literature in 1936.

Homesteader, The (film, 1919, directed by Oscar Micheaux)

Oscar Micheaux's film *The Homesteader,* based on his 1917 novel, tells the story of a successful African American farmer in an otherwise all-white town in South Dakota. Both the novel and film drew heavily on Micheaux's own life. In addition to directing, Micheaux also wrote and produced the film, making it the first full-length release to have an African American director, screenwriter, and producer. *The Homesteader* was also the first film with a wholly African American cast and the first aimed specifically at an African American audience.

Although it earned only $5,000 in its initial release, the film cost so little to produce that it was considered a commercial success. More importantly, the experience persuaded Micheaux to devote himself to filmmaking; he went on to make forty more films dedicated to, in his words, "uplifting the race."

Iron Horse, The (film, 1924, directed by John Ford)

The first great success of director John Ford, *The Iron Horse* is a heavily fictionalized account of the genesis and construction of the transcontinental railroad, with a complicated storyline that squeezes the Civil War, Indian wars, the building of the railroad, the cattle boom, and a romance into a little more than two hours. The movie's protagonist is Davy Brandon, played by George O'Brien; his love interest, Miriam Marsh, is played by Madge Bellamy. Brandon helps build the railroad, with some help from close friend Abraham Lincoln, portrayed by Charles Edward Bull.

Although it was one of the most popular and successful westerns of the silent era, *The Iron Horse* is not well regarded by modern audiences because of its clumsy plot, stereotyped characterizations of women and minorities, and the message that progress should be pursued at any cost. Still, the film was the breakthrough work of a young John Ford, who would go on to become one of the icons of American film directing.

It (film, 1927, directed by Clarence Badger)

The definitive "flapper flick," *It* stars Clara Bow as a beautiful blue-collar worker named Betty Lou Spence. At the start of the film, Spence becomes interested in a wealthy playboy named Cyrus Waltham, Jr., played by Antonio Moreno, and decides to pursue him despite their obvious socioeconomic differences. Unexpected events, including the publication of a newspaper article that incorrectly identifies Spence as an unwed mother, conspire against her, but eventually all is resolved and the couple lives happily ever after.

One of the most culturally influential and commercially successful films of the silent era, *It* catapulted Bow to the top ranks of Hollywood stardom and identified her as the quintessential "It Girl"—a term that came to be used generically for a woman with strong sex appeal. Today the film is remembered primarily as one of the first romantic comedies.

Jazz Singer, The (film, 1927, directed by Alan Crosland)

The Jazz Singer ranks as one of the most important films ever made, as it was the first full-length feature with synchronized spoken dialogue. Although sound occurs in only a few minutes of the film, with the rest of the dialogue communicated through traditional title cards, the premiere of the *Jazz Singer* on October 6, 1927, marked the beginning of the end for silent films; they would all but disappear by 1931.

The Jazz Singer stars former vaudevillian Al Jolson as a young Jewish man named Jakie Rabinowitz whose father, played by Warner Oland, wants him to be become a cantor. Jakie defies his father's wishes in order to pursue a career as a stage performer. *The Jazz Singer* is rarely screened today because of its racist overtones—Jolson performs the climactic scene of the movie in blackface—but its place in history is secure. It has been remade three times, the most recent a 1980 production starring Neil Diamond and Laurence Olivier.

Kid, The (film, 1921, directed by Charlie Chaplin)

A silent classic, *The Kid* features Charlie Chaplin playing his popular "Little Tramp" character opposite six-year-old Jackie Coogan in the title role. The film begins with the Tramp finding an abandoned infant in an alley. As the child grows up, the two characters form a close bond and spend their time perpetrating scams against unsuspecting marks.

Described in the opening titles as "A picture with a smile, and perhaps a tear," *The Kid* has been recognized as the first film to effectively combine comedy and drama. Since its release in 1921, critics have praised the movie's tender and utterly believable portrayal of the relationship between the Tramp and the Kid—a circumstance that some Chaplin biographers attribute to the death of his infant son shortly before filming began. The film struck a chord with audiences as well, making it a smash hit and launching the career of Jackie Coogan as America's first child movie star.

King Porter Stomp (musical recording, 1923, by Jelly Roll Morton)

Ferdinand "Jelly Roll" Morton's "King Porter Stomp" is among the earliest recordings to showcase the Chicago style of jazz, which emerged as African American musicians migrated from New Orleans to the Windy City and absorbed the musical styles they found there. Chicago jazz is characterized by the prominence of the saxophone, use of instruments in nontraditional ways, and heavy improvisation.

Morton's star faded in the 1930s, and he and his work might have been forgotten were it not for a series of interviews he did late in life with folklorist Alan Lomax under the auspices of the Library of Congress. In them, Morton talks about the early days of jazz and plays a number of his songs, including "King Porter Stomp." The recordings provide invaluable insight into the world of 1920s jazz and remain vital documents for cultural historians today.

Makin' Whoopee (musical recording, 1929, by Eddie Cantor)

Known as "Banjo Eyes" and "the Apostle of Pep" to his fans, actor and singer Eddie Cantor was one of the most popular entertainers in America from the 1920s through the 1950s. Among his credits was a starring role in the successful 1928 Broadway musical *Whoopee,* and it was from that production that he borrowed the song "Makin' Whoopee," a tongue-in-cheek critique of the sexual excesses of the 1920s. It became one of Cantor's most popular songs and was among the last records he made before moving into radio and film during the 1930s.

Today, the song is remembered largely for its rendition in the extravagant 1930 film *Whoopee,* also featuring Cantor. "Makin' Whoopee" has been covered many times, most notably by Ray Charles, who had a hit with the song in 1965.

Nanook of the North (film, 1922, directed by Robert J. Flaherty)

Recognized as the first full-length film documentary, *Nanook of the North* follows an Inuit Eskimo and his family over the course of a year, recording their challenges and triumphs in the Canadian Arctic and documenting a culture that was disappearing in the face of encroachment by outsiders. Although many of the scenes were staged, movie critics have generally lauded the film and defended the filmmaker, observing that the documentary form was so new at that time that no clear production standards were in place. Moreover, it is pointed out, the motion-picture cameras of the time were essentially immobile, making it impossible to follow subjects while waiting for authentic action to occur.

Thanks to several breathtaking sequences, most notably a successful seal hunt, 1920s audiences loved the film. Made on a budget of only $50,000, *Nanook of the North* proved highly profitable and launched Flaherty's long career as a documentarian.

No, No, Nanette (stage musical, 1925, by Vincent Youmans, Irving Caesar, and Otto Harbach)

The romantic musical comedy *No, No, Nanette* was one of the biggest Broadway hits of the 1920s and the greatest success of producer Harry Frazee. The main characters are self-made millionaire Jimmy Smith and his frugal wife, Sue, who clash over how to spend their money and how to raise their daughter, Nanette, who is secretly involved in a romantic relationship. The show spawned several hit songs, including "Tea for Two" and "I Want to Be Happy," and captivated audiences with its tap dancing routines. Moreover, it was rumored that Frazee, then the owner of the Boston Red Sox, had sold the contract of baseball star Babe Ruth to the New York Yankees in 1920 to raise money for the production, leading generations of Red Sox fans to blame *No, No, Nanette* for the team's subsequent World Series losses.

Rhapsody in Blue (symphonic composition, 1924, by George Gershwin)

An innovative jazz composition, *Rhapsody in Blue* was commissioned from George Gershwin by bandleader Paul Whiteman, who was in search of a challenging piece for his orchestra to perform in concert. Gershwin, who finished the composition in only four weeks, took his inspiration from a train trip to Boston. He remarked that the sounds of the train, "with its steely rhythms, its rattle-ty bang," were "stimulating to a composer." Gershwin played piano for the New York City premiere of *American Rhapsody,* as the piece was originally titled, in February 1924. The clarinet glissando that opens the piece captured the attention of the audience, which remained rapt throughout the performance.

Some critics savaged the piece, with one going so far as to dismiss it as "negro music," but most enjoyed the melding of classical and jazz styles in an orchestral work. Renamed *Rhapsody in Blue* on the advice of Gershwin's brother, Ira, it established Gershwin as a serious symphonic composer and remains one of the most popular concert and recording selections in the modern American repertoire.

Robin Hood (film, 1922, directed by Allan Dwan)

Featuring Douglas Fairbanks in the title role and Wallace Beery as Richard the Lion-Hearted, Alan Dwan's 1922 version of *Robin Hood* was the first full-length film about the legendary English nobleman who takes to Sherwood Forest to defend the poor against the predations of the wealthy. With a budget of nearly $1.5 million—enormous for the time—the production was extravagant. The entire village of Nottingham was created from scratch, and the castle built for the film was the largest set ever constructed for a silent movie. *Robin Hood* was also the first film to premiere in Hollywood, at the lavish new Grauman's Egyptian Theater on October 18, 1922.

The pinnacle of silent film production in the 1920s, as well as a critical and popular success, *Robin Hood* remained lost for decades, until a single print was rediscovered in the late 1960s. Many film historians consider it the finest of the dozens of big-screen versions of the legendary tale.

Safety Last! (film, 1923, directed by Sam Taylor and Fred Newmeyer)

A classic silent comedy, *Safety Last!* is the story of a department-store clerk who suffers a series of misfortunes in his attempt to impress both his boss and his girlfriend. The clerk, identified in the film's credits simply as "The Boy," is played by the popular screen comedian Harold Lloyd; Mildred Davis and Bill Strother star as "The Girl" and "The Pal."

The success of the film was largely due to its impressive stunt work. The most famous stunt—creating one of the most enduring images of the silent film era—features Lloyd hanging from the hands of a clock on the side of a building, seemingly high above the ground and in grave danger. So skillful is the camerawork in this scene that some audience members reportedly fainted when it was shown in theaters. *Safety Last!* was Harold Lloyd's first smash hit and established him as one of the great film stars of the 1920s.

Sheik, The (film, 1921, directed by George Melford)

Based on the Edith Maude Hull novel of the same name, *The Sheik* stars the great "Latin lover" of the silent film era, Rudolph Valentino, as Sheik Ahmed Ben Hassan. Agnes Ayers costarred as Lady Diana Mayo. The plot is complex for a silent movie: The sheik kidnaps Mayo, then decides to free her, then loses her to a rival sheik, then recaptures her. In the course of these events, Mayo and the sheik fall in love and decide to remain together despite the initial kidnapping.

The film was poorly reviewed, but Valentino's presence made it a hit and secured his image as a romantic hero. "Sheik" became a popular slang term for a man who pursues women aggressively. A sequel, *Son of the Sheik* (1926), also starring Valentino, was another hit. While in New York City for the premiere of the sequel, Valentino was rushed to the hospital with a perforated ulcer and died a week later.

Show Boat (stage musical, 1927, by Jerome Kern and Oscar Hammerstein)

As the first Broadway play to blend songs and a dramatic plot in a cohesive production, *Show Boat* is regarded by many theater historians as the first modern musical. It was also Broadway's first racially integrated musical. Based on Edna Ferber's 1926 novel, *Show Boat* opens in 1890 on a Mississippi River showboat named the *Cotton Blossom*. Magnolia, the daughter of the ship's captain, dreams of being a star but abandons her plans after falling in love with, and marrying, Gaylord Ravenal, a gambler traveling on board. They have a daughter named Kim, but the marriage is rocky because of Gaylord's gambling. He eventually abandons the family, and Magnolia turns to her musical talents to support herself and her daughter, finally realizing her dream of becoming a great musical star. Kim also becomes a successful stage performer, and by the play's end she and Magnolia are reunited with Gaylord.

Aside from its engaging storyline, *Show Boat* featured a dazzling musical score highlighted by the song "Ol' Man River." One of the most loved American musicals, *Show Boat* ran for 575 performances in its initial incarnation and has had many new productions, including film versions in 1936 and 1951.

Shuffle Along (stage musical, 1921, by Eubie Blake and Noble Sissle)

Premiering in 1921 and running for 504 performances, *Shuffle Along* was the first Broadway hit to be written, produced, and performed entirely by African Americans. With only the vaguest semblance of a plot, the production was essentially a musical revue of songs by ragtime pianist Eubie Blake and songwriter Noble Sissle and featured the musical talents of up-and-coming stars Josephine Baker and Paul Robeson.

The production drew heavily on the conventions of minstrel shows, including the use of blackface makeup and racial stereotypes later considered offensive. Nevertheless, *Shuffle Along* proved popular with black audiences of the day, while also attracting a substantial number of white attendees. The show was revived in 1933 and 1952, and it served as a model for African American theater productions throughout the 1930s and 1940s.

St. Louis Blues (musical recording, 1922, by W.C. Handy)

One of the first blues songs to achieve success as a pop recording, "St. Louis Blues" was inspired by a woman whom composer W.C. Handy met on the streets of that city. Distraught over losing her husband to another woman, she complained, "Ma man's got a heart like a rock cast in de sea." Putting pen to paper, Handy created a song designed, he said, "to combine ragtime syncopation with a real melody in the spiritual tradition."

Published in 1914, "St. Louis Blues" was first recorded in 1915; Handy's own version, which remains among the best known, was not released until 1922. His recording was a hit and brought the foxtrot dance step, among the most popular dances of the Jazz Age, to a national audience. Cover versions of the song by Bessie Smith, Louis Armstrong, Glenn Miller, and others sold so well that Handy was still collecting tens of thousands of dollars a year in royalties at the time of his death in 1958.

Steamboat Willie (film, 1928, directed by Walt Disney and Ub Ilwerks)

An unassuming, eight-minute, black-and-white cartoon about a mouse and the boat captain he serves, *Steamboat Willie* is the film that made Mickey Mouse famous and launched the Disney empire. (The title is a parody of Buster Keaton's 1928 feature-length comedy *Steamboat Bill, Jr.*) *Steamboat Willie* was not the first appearance of the Mickey Mouse character—he had been featured in two previous cartoons—but it was the first to have music and dialogue synchronized with the action on screen. It was also the first sound cartoon to prove popular with audiences. Working with a budget of less than $5,000, codirector and cowriter Walt Disney did much of the animation and voice work himself.

An icon of American popular culture and a landmark in the history of animation, the film has also been the subject of much legal maneuvering. The Disney Corporation petitioned for and received several extensions of U.S. copyright protection; originally set to expire in 1998, the copyright will now remain in effect until 2023.

Strange Interlude (stage drama, 1928, by Eugene O'Neill)

One of the most ambitious works of modern American theater, Eugene O'Neill's *Strange Interlude* is a two-part drama in nine acts. The portrait of a woman from youth through sexual awakening to womanhood—in her roles as wife, daughter, lover, mother, and friend—*Strange Interlude* employs several dramatic techniques that were innovative at the time of its staging. Among these was the interior monologue, a soliloquy in which the actors tell their inner thoughts to the audience.

Strange Interlude was also unusual in its length—the audience would arrive at the theater in the afternoon and view the first two hours, then leave for dinner and return for the final two hours. Despite the time commitment, the play was a success with audiences, running for more than 400 performances on Broadway. It was revived twice and was adapted for the big screen in 1932. *Strange Interlude* also earned O'Neill his third Pulitzer Prize in a span of eight years.

Swanee (musical recording, 1920, by Al Jolson)
Written by George Gershwin and sung by Al Jolson, "Swanee"—not to be confused with the 1939 "Swanee River," also recorded by Jolson—was among the first and most popular musical hits of the 1920s. A nostalgic song about a man who longs to return to his home in the South, "Swanee" struck a chord with Americans still recovering from World War I. It was Gershwin's first commercial success as a songwriter, and it boosted Jolson's flagging career, securing the singer a recording contract. "Swanee" would serve as Jolson's signature tune for the rest of his life.

Ten Commandments, The (film, 1923, directed by Cecil B. DeMille)
Cecil B. DeMille's original, silent version of *The Ten Commandments* is essentially two films in one. The first half tells the story of Moses and the exodus of the Jews from Egypt; the second half is a modern morality tale about two brothers in which one follows the Ten Commandments but is poor and the other ignores them and is rich. Starring silent screen stars Theodore Roberts, Nita Naldi, and Agnes Ayers, *The Ten Commandments* is one of the first films to showcase what would become DeMille's signature epic style.

The movie was particularly notable for its clever use of special effects—the parting of the Red Sea, for example, was accomplished by placing blocks of blue gelatin side by side in front of a camera, heating them until they melted, and then running the resulting film in reverse. Still, DeMille was unhappy with the constraints of silent filmmaking and remade *The Ten Commandments* with sound in 1956; starring Charlton Heston, this version ran more than twice the length of the ninety-minute 1923 production.

Virginian, The (film, 1929, directed by Victor Fleming)
Based on Owen Wister's western novel, *The Virginian* stars Gary Cooper as a cattle ranch foreman. The story begins with the Virginian and his best friend, Steve (Richard Arlen), competing for the affections of the same woman. Steve becomes involved with a gang of cattle rustlers led by Trampas (Walter Huston). Choosing duty over friendship, the Virginian is compelled to track Steve down and order his death by hanging. He then avenges Steve's death by defeating Trampas in a climactic gun battle.

Among the first western "talkies," *The Virginian* helped propel both director Victor Fleming and actor Gary Cooper to stardom. It is considered a classic of the genre, perhaps best known for the Virginian telling Trampas: "If you wanna call me that, smile."

West End Blues (musical recording, 1928, by Louis Armstrong)
"West End Blues" is a jazz composition by Joe "King" Oliver about a summer resort in New Orleans. It was written and originally performed as an instrumental track, with lyrics later added by Clarence Williams. First recorded by King Oliver and his Dixie Syncopaters, the piece would be a favorite of jazz performers over the decades; the most famous recording being the 1928 version by Louis Armstrong and his Hot Five. Featuring a pair of dazzling trumpet solos by Armstrong, as well as some of the earliest examples of scat singing, the record quickly achieved legendary status and is now regarded as one of the classics of early jazz.

Bibliography

Abels, Jules. *In the Time of Silent Cal.* New York: Putnam, 1969.

Against the Odds: The Artists of the Harlem Renaissance. Videorecording. New Jersey Network. Alexandria, VA: PBS Video, 1995.

Aichele, Gary Jan. *Oliver Wendell Holmes, Jr.—Soldier, Scholar, Judge.* Boston: Twayne, 1989.

Aitken, Hugh G.J. *The Continuous Wave: Technology and American Radio, 1900–1932.* Princeton, NJ: Princeton University Press, 1985.

———. *Syntony and Spark: The Origins of Radio.* New York: Wiley, 1976.

Alchon, Guy. *The Invisible Hand of Planning: Capitalism, Social Science, and the State in the 1920s.* Princeton, NJ: Princeton University Press, 1985.

Alexander, Charles C. *Here the Country Lies: Nationalism and the Arts in Twentieth-Century America.* Bloomington: Indiana University Press, 1980.

———. *Ty Cobb.* New York: Oxford University Press, 1984.

Alexander, Michael. *Jazz Age Jews.* Princeton, NJ: Princeton University Press, 2001.

Allen, Frederick Lewis. *Only Yesterday: An Informal History of the 1920's.* New York: Wiley, 1997.

Alschuler, Albert W. *Law Without Values: The Life, Work, and Legacy of Justice Holmes.* Chicago: University of Chicago Press, 2000.

Alvarado, Rudolph, and Sonya Alvarado. *Drawing Conclusions on Henry Ford.* Ann Arbor: University of Michigan Press, 2001.

Ambrosius, Lloyd E. *Wilsonianism: Woodrow Wilson and His Legacy in American Foreign Relations.* New York: Palgrave Macmillan, 2002.

———. *Woodrow Wilson and the American Diplomatic Tradition: The Treaty Fight in Perspective.* Cambridge, UK: Cambridge University Press, 1987.

Andersen, Kristi. *After Suffrage: Women in Partisan and Electoral Politics Before the New Deal.* Chicago: University of Chicago, 1996.

———. *The Creation of a Democratic Majority, 1928–1936.* Chicago: University of Chicago Press, 1979.

Anderson, Paul Allen. *Deep River: Music and Memory in Harlem Renaissance Thought.* Durham, NC: Duke University Press, 2001.

Andreus, Alejandro. *Ben Shahn and the Passion of Sacco and Vanzetti.* Jersey City, NJ: Jersey City Museum, 2001.

Anthony, Carl Sferrazza. *Florence Harding: The First Lady, the Jazz Age, and the Death of America's Most Scandalous President.* New York: Morrow, 1998.

Arkes, Hadley. *The Return of George Sutherland: Restoring a Jurisprudence of Natural Rights.* Princeton, NJ: Princeton University Press, 1994.

Avrich, Paul. *Sacco and Vanzetti: The Anarchist Background.* Princeton, NJ: Princeton University Press, 1991.

Baiamonte, John V. *Spirit of Vengeance: Nativism and Louisiana Justice, 1921–1924.* Baton Rouge: Louisiana State University Press, 1986.

Bailey, Beth L. *From Front Porch to Back Seat: Courtship in Twentieth-Century America.* Baltimore: Johns Hopkins University Press, 1988.

Baker, Houston A. *Modernism and the Harlem Renaissance.* Chicago: University of Chicago Press, 1989.

Baker, Leonard. *Brandeis and Frankfurter: A Dual Biography.* New York: Harper & Row, 1984.

Baker, Liva. *The Justice from Beacon Hill: The Life and Times of Oliver Wendell Holmes.* New York: HarperCollins, 1991.

Baldwin, Neil. *Henry Ford and the Jews: The Mass Production of Hate.* New York: PublicAffairs, 2001.

Barber, William J. *From New Era to New Deal: Herbert Hoover, the Economists, and American Economic Policy, 1921–1933.* Cambridge, UK: Cambridge University Press, 1985.

Barkan, Elazar. *The Retreat of Scientific Racism: Changing Concepts of Race in Britain and the United States Between the World Wars.* Cambridge, UK: Cambridge University Press, 1992.

Barnouw, Erik. *Tube of Plenty: The Evolution of American Television.* New York: Oxford University Press, 1990.

Barry, John M. *Rising Tide: The Great Mississippi Flood of 1927 and How It Changed America.* New York: Simon & Schuster, 1997.

Baskerville, Stephen W. *Of Laws and Limitations: An Intellectual Portrait of Louis Dembitz Brandeis.* Rutherford, NJ: Fairleigh Dickinson University Press, 1994.

Batchelor, Ray. *Henry Ford, Mass Production, Modernism, and Design.* New York: Manchester University Press, 1994.

Bates, J. Leonard. *The Origins of Teapot Dome: Progressives, Parties, and Petroleum, 1909–1921.* Urbana: University of Illinois Press, 1963.

———. *Senator Thomas J. Walsh of Montana: Law and Public Affairs, from TR to FDR.* Urbana: University of Illinois Press, 1999.

Baughman, James L. *Henry R. Luce and the Rise of the American News Media.* Boston: Twayne, 1987.

Baughman, Judith, with Matthew J. Bruccoli. *F. Scott Fitzgerald.* Detroit, MI: Gale Group, 2000.

Beard, Mary Ritter. *A Woman Making History: Mary Ritter Beard Through Her Letters.* Ed. and Intro. Nancy F. Cott. New Haven, CT: Yale University Press, 1991.

Behr, Edward. *Prohibition: Thirteen Years That Changed America.* New York: Arcade, 1996.

Berg, A. Scott. *Lindbergh.* New York: G.P. Putnam's Sons, 1998.

Bergeen, Laurence. *Capone: The Man and the Era.* New York: Simon & Schuster, 1994.

Bernanke, Ben S. *Essays on the Great Depression.* Princeton, NJ: Princeton University Press, 2000.

Bernstein, Irving. *The Lean Years: A History of the American Worker, 1920–1933.* Boston: Houghton Mifflin, 1960.

Berry, Faith. *Langston Hughes, Before and Beyond Harlem.* Westport, CT: L. Hill, 1983.

Black, Edwin. *War Against the Weak: Eugenics and America's Campaign to Create a Master Race.* New York: Four Walls Eight Windows, 2003.

Blackwelder, Julia Kirk. *Now Hiring: The Feminization of Work in the United States, 1900–1995.* College Station: Texas A&M University Press, 1997.

———. *Women of the Depression: Caste and Culture in San Antonio, 1929–1939.* College Station: Texas A&M University Press, 1984.

Blanke, David. *The 1910s.* Westport, CT: Greenwood, 2002.

Blee, Kathleen M. *Women of the Klan: Racism and Gender in the 1920s.* Berkeley: University of California Press, 1991.

Blocker, Jack S. *American Temperance Movements: Cycles of Reform.* Boston: Twayne, 1989.

Blotner, Joseph Leo. *Faulkner: A Biography.* New York: Random House, 1984.

Blumhofer, Edith Waldvogel. *Aimee Semple McPherson: Everybody's Sister.* Grand Rapids, MI: W.B. Eerdmans, 1993.

Bolt, Christine. *The Women's Movements in the United States and Britain from the 1790s to the 1920s.* Amherst: University of Massachusetts Press, 1993.

Borus, Daniel H., ed. *These United States: Portraits of America from the 1920s.* Ithaca, NY: Cornell University Press, 1992.

Braeman, John, Robert H. Bremner, and David Brody, eds. *Change and Continuity in Twentieth-Century America: The 1920s.* Columbus: Ohio State University Press, 1968.

Brandt, Allan M. *No Magic Bullet: A Social History of Venereal Disease in the United States Since 1880.* New York: Oxford University Press, 1985.

Breen, W.J. *Labor Market Politics and the Great War: The Department of Labor, the States, and the First U.S. Employment Service, 1907–1933.* Kent, OH: Kent State University Press, 1997.

———. *Uncle Sam at Home: Civilian Mobilization, Wartime Federalism, and the Council of National Defense, 1917–1919.* Westport, CT: Greenwood, 1984.

Brian, Denis. *The True Gen: An Intimate Portrait of Ernest Hemingway by Those Who Knew Him.* New York: Grove, 1988.

Bristow, Nancy K. *Making Men Moral: Social Engineering During the Great War.* New York: New York University Press, 1996.

Brody, David. *Workers in Industrial America: Essays on the Twentieth Century Struggle.* New York: Oxford University Press, 1980.

Brown, Dorothy M. *Mabel Walker Willebrandt: A Study of Power, Loyalty, and Law.* Knoxville: University of Tennessee Press, 1984.

———. *Setting a Course: American Women in the 1920s.* Boston: Twayne, 1987.

Brown, JoAnne. *The Definition of a Profession: The Authority of Metaphor in the History of Intelligence Testing, 1890–1930.* Princeton, NJ: Princeton University Press, 1992.

Bruccoli, Matthew Joseph. *Some Sort of Epic Grandeur: The Life of F. Scott Fitzgerald.* San Diego, CA: Harcourt Brace Jovanovich, 1983.

Bruns, Roger. *Preacher: Billy Sunday and Big-Time American Evangelism.* Urbana: University of Illinois Press, 2002.

Buckley, Thomas H. *American Foreign and National Security Policies, 1914–1945.* Knoxville: University of Tennessee Press, 1987.

———. *The United States and the Washington Conference, 1921–1922.* Knoxville: University of Tennessee Press, 1970.

Bucklin, Steven J. *Realism and American Foreign Policy: Wilsonians and the Kennan-Morgenthau Thesis.* Westport, CT: Praeger, 2001.

Burk, Kathleen. *Britain, America and the Sinews of War, 1914–1918.* London: G. Allen & Unwin, 1984.

Burner, David. *Herbert Hoover: A Public Life.* New York: Alfred A. Knopf, 1979.

———. *The Politics of Provincialism: The Democratic Party in Transition, 1918–1932.* New York: Alfred A. Knopf, 1968.

Burns, James MacGregor. *The Workshop of Democracy.* New York: Alfred A. Knopf, 1985.

Burt, Robert. *Two Jewish Justices: Outcasts in the Promised Land.* Berkeley: University of California Press, 1988.

Burton, David H., ed. *Progressive Masks: Letters of Oliver Wendell Holmes, Jr., and Franklin Ford.* Newark: University of Delaware Press, 1982.

———. *Taft, Holmes, and the 1920s Court: An Appraisal.* Madison, NJ: Fairleigh Dickinson University Press, 1998.

Butler, Amy E. *Two Paths to Equality: Alice Paul and Ethel*

M. Smith in the ERA Debate, 1921–1929. Albany: State University of New York Press, 2002.

Calder, Lendol Glen. *Financing the American Dream: A Cultural History of Consumer Credit.* Princeton, NJ: Princeton University Press, 1999.

Calhoun, Frederick S. *Power and Principle: Armed Intervention in Wilsonian Foreign Policy.* Kent, OH: Kent State University Press, 1986.

Carter, Paul Allen. *The Twenties in America.* Arlington Heights, IL: Harlan Davidson, 1987.

Cash, Floris Loretta Barnett. *African American Women and Social Action: The Clubwomen and Volunteerism from Jim Crow to the New Deal, 1896–1936.* Westport, CT: Greenwood, 2001.

Cashman, Sean Dennis. *Prohibition, the Lie of the Land.* New York: Free Press, 1981.

Casper, Dale E. *Urban America Examined: A Bibliography.* New York: Garland, 1985.

Cebula, James E. *James M. Cox: Journalist and Politician.* New York: Garland, 1985.

Chafee, Zechariah. *Free Speech in the United States.* Cambridge, MA: Harvard University Press, 1967.

Chalmers, David Mark. *Hooded Americanism: The History of the Ku Klux Klan.* Durham, NC: Duke University Press, 1987.

Chambers, John Whiteclay. *To Raise an Army: The Draft Comes to Modern America.* New York: Free Press, 1987.

Chapman, Matthew. *Trials of the Monkey: An Accidental Memoir.* New York: Picador, 2001.

Chapman, Paul Davis. *Schools as Sorters: Lewis M. Terman, Applied Psychology, and the Intelligence Testing Movement, 1890–1930.* New York: New York University Press, 1988.

Chatfield, Charles. *For Peace and Justice: Pacifism in America, 1914–1941.* Knoxville: University of Tennessee Press, 1971.

Chauncey, George. *Gay New York: Gender, Urban Culture, and the Makings of the Gay Male World, 1890–1940.* New York: Basic Books, 1994.

Cherny, Robert W. *A Righteous Cause: The Life of William Jennings Bryan.* Norman: University of Oklahoma Press, 1994.

Chesler, Ellen. *Woman of Valor: Margaret Sanger and the Birth Control Movement in America.* New York: Simon & Schuster, 1992.

Chudacoff, Howard P. *How Old Are You? Age Consciousness in American Culture.* Princeton, NJ: Princeton University Press, 1989.

Clark, Norman H. *Deliver Us from Evil: An Interpretation of American Prohibition.* New York: W.W. Norton, 1976.

Clark, Paul F., Peter Gottlieb, and Donald Kennedy, eds. *Forging a Union of Steel: Philip Murray, SWOC, and the United Steelworkers.* Ithaca, NY: ILR Press, 1987.

Clayton, Douglas. *Floyd Dell: The Life and Times of an American Rebel.* Chicago: Ivan R. Dee, 1994.

Clements, Kendrick A. *Hoover, Conservation, and Consumerism: Engineering the Good Life.* Lawrence: University Press of Kansas, 2000.

———. *The Presidency of Woodrow Wilson.* Lawrence: University Press of Kansas, 1992.

———. *Woodrow Wilson, World Statesman.* Boston: Twayne, 1987.

Coben, Stanley. *A. Mitchell Palmer: Politician.* New York: Columbia University Press, 1963.

———. *Rebellion Against Victorianism: The Impetus for Cultural Change in 1920s America.* New York: Oxford University Press, 1991.

Cohen, Jeremy. *Congress Shall Make No Law: Oliver Wendell Holmes, the First Amendment, and Judicial Decision Making.* Ames: Iowa State University Press, 1989.

Cohen, Lizabeth. *Making a New Deal: Industrial Workers in Chicago, 1919–1939.* New York: Cambridge University Press, 1990.

Coleman, J. Winston. *Nathan B. Stubblefield: The Father of Radio.* Lexington, KY: Winburn, 1982.

Coleman, Leon. *Carl Van Vechten and the Harlem Renaissance: A Critical Assessment.* New York: Garland, 1998.

Conkin, Paul Keith. *The Southern Agrarians.* Nashville, TN: Vanderbilt University Press, 2001.

———. *When All the Gods Trembled: Darwinism, Scopes, and American Intellectuals.* Lanham, MD: Rowman & Littlefield, 1998.

Conn, Steven. *Museums and American Intellectual Life, 1876–1926.* Chicago: University of Chicago Press, 1998.

Conner, Valerie Jean. *The National War Labor Board: Stability, Social Justice, and the Voluntary State in World War I.* Chapel Hill: University of North Carolina Press, 1983.

Cooper, John Milton. *Breaking the Heart of the World: Woodrow Wilson and the Fight for the League of Nations.* New York: Cambridge University Press, 2001.

———. *The Warrior and the Priest: Woodrow Wilson and Theodore Roosevelt.* Cambridge, MA: Belknap Press, 1983.

Cooper, John Milton, Jr., and Charles E. Neu, eds. *The Wilson Era: Essays in Honor of Arthur S. Link.* Arlington Heights, IL: Harlan Davidson, 1991.

Cooper, Wayne F. *Claude McKay: Rebel Sojourner in the Harlem Renaissance: A Biography.* Baton Rouge: Louisiana State University Press, 1987.

Corn, Wanda M. *The Great American Thing: Modern Art and National Identity, 1915–1935.* Berkeley: University of California Press, 1999.

Costigliola, Frank. *Awkward Dominion: American Political, Economic, and Cultural Relations with Europe, 1919–1933.* Ithaca, NY: Cornell University Press, 1984.

Coté, Charlotte. *Olympia Brown: The Battle for Equality.* Racine, WI: Mother Courage Press, 1988.

Cott, Nancy F. *The Grounding of Modern Feminism.* New Haven, CT: Yale University Press, 1987.

Cottrell, Robert C. *Blackball, the Black Sox, and the Babe: Baseball's Crucial 1920 Season.* Jefferson, NC: McFarland, 2002.

Craig, Douglas B. *After Wilson: The Struggle for the Democratic Party, 1920–1934.* Chapel Hill: University of North Carolina Press, 1992.

———. *Fireside Politics: Radio and Political Culture in the United States, 1920–1940.* Baltimore: Johns Hopkins University Press, 2000.

Cray, Ed. *Chrome Colossus: General Motors and Its Times.* New York: McGraw-Hill, 1980.

Creamer, Robert W. *Babe: The Legend Comes to Life.* New York: Simon & Schuster, 1992.

Cremin, Lawrence Arthur. *The Transformation of the School: Progressivism in American Education, 1876–1957.* New York: Vintage Books, 1964.

Crunden, Robert Morse. *Body and Soul: The Making of American Modernism.* New York: Basic Books, 1999.

———. *From Self to Society, 1919–1941.* Englewood Cliffs, NJ: Prentice Hall, 1972.

———, ed. *The Superfluous Men: Conservative Critics of American Culture, 1900–1945.* Austin: University of Texas Press, 1977.

Curran, Thomas J. *Xenophobia and Immigration, 1820–1930.* Boston: Twayne, 1975.

Daniels, Roger. *Guarding the Golden Door: American Immigration Policy and Immigrants Since 1882.* New York: Hill and Wang, 2004.

———. *Not Like Us: Immigrants and Minorities in America, 1890–1924.* Chicago: Ivan R. Dee, 1997.

Daniels, Roger, and Otis L. Graham. *Debating American Immigration, 1882–Present.* Lanham, MD: Rowman & Littlefield, 2001.

Davis, John W. *The Ambassadorial Diary of John W. Davis: The Court of St. James's, 1918–1921.* Ed. Julia Davis and Dolores A. Fleming. Morgantown: West Virginia University Press, 1993.

Davis, Thadious M. *Nella Larsen, Novelist of the Harlem Renaissance: A Woman's Life Unveiled.* Baton Rouge: Louisiana State University Press, 1994.

Dawson, Nelson L., ed. *Brandeis and America.* Lexington: University Press of Kentucky, 1989.

———. *Louis D. Brandeis, Felix Frankfurter, and the New Deal.* Hamden, CT: Archon, 1980.

De Jongh, James. *Vicious Modernism: Black Harlem and the Literary Imagination.* Cambridge, UK: Cambridge University Press, 1990.

DeBenedetti, Charles. *Origins of the Modern American Peace Movement, 1915–1929.* Millwood, NY: KTO Press, 1978.

D'Emilio, John. *Intimate Matters: A History of Sexuality in America.* New York: Harper & Row, 1988.

Dennis, Michael. *Lessons in Progress: State Universities and Progressivism in the New South, 1880–1920.* Urbana: University of Illinois Press, 2001.

Deutsch, Sarah. *From Ballots to Breadlines: American Women, 1920–1940.* New York: Oxford University Press, 1998.

———. *No Separate Refuge: Culture, Class, and Gender on an Anglo-Hispanic Frontier in the American Southwest.* New York: Oxford University Press, 1989.

———. *Women and the City: Gender, Space, and Power in Boston, 1870–1940.* New York: Oxford University Press, 2000.

Dodge, Mark M., ed. *Herbert Hoover and the Historians.* West Branch, IA: Herbert Hoover Presidential Library Association, 1989.

Dorsett, Lyle W. *Billy Sunday and the Redemption of Urban America.* Grand Rapids, MI: W.B. Eerdmans, 1991.

Douglas, Ann. *Terrible Honesty: Mongrel Manhattan in the 1920s.* New York: Farrar, Straus and Giroux, 1995.

Douglas, Susan J. *Inventing American Broadcasting, 1899–1922.* Baltimore: Johns Hopkins University Press, 1987.

———. *Listening In: Radio and the American Imagination, from Amos 'n' Andy and Edward R. Murrow to Wolfman Jack and Howard Stern.* New York: Times Books, 1999.

———. *The Mommy Myth: The Idealization of Motherhood and How It Has Undermined Women.* New York: Free Press, 2004.

Drowne, Kathleen Morgan, and Patrick Huber. *The 1920s.* Westport, CT: Greenwood, 2004.

Dubofsky, Melvyn. *Industrialism and the American Worker, 1865–1920.* Wheeling, IL: H. Davidson, 1996.

———. *The State and Labor in Modern America.* Chapel Hill: University of North Carolina Press, 1994.

———. *We Shall Be All: A History of the Industrial Workers of the World.* Chicago: Quadrangle, 1969.

Dumenil, Lynn. *The Modern Temper: American Culture and Society in the 1920s.* New York: Hill and Wang, 1995.

Eastland, Terry, ed. *Freedom of Expression in the Supreme Court: The Defining Cases.* Lanham, MD: Rowman & Littlefield, 2000.

EAV History of Jazz, The. Videorecording. With Billy Taylor. Produced and directed by Ruth Leon; written by Gladys Carter and Billy Taylor. Chicago: Clearvue; Educational Audio Visual, 1986.

Eldot, Paula. *Governor Alfred E. Smith: The Politician as Reformer.* New York: Garland, 1983.

Elliott, Ward E.Y. *The Rise of Guardian Democracy: The Supreme Court's Role in Voting Rights Disputes, 1845–1969.* Cambridge, MA: Harvard University Press, 1974.

Ellis, Lewis Ethan. *Republican Foreign Policy, 1921–1933.* New Brunswick, NJ: Rutgers University Press, 1968.

Ely, Melvin Patrick. *The Adventures of Amos 'n' Andy: A Social History of an American Phenomenon.* New York: Free Press, 1991.

Epstein, Daniel Mark. *Sister Aimee: The Life of Aimee Semple McPherson.* New York: Harcourt Brace Jovanovich, 1993.

Esposito, David M. *The Legacy of Woodrow Wilson: American War Aims in World War I.* Westport, CT: Praeger, 1996.

Fabre, Geneviève, and Michel Feith, eds. *Jean Toomer and the Harlem Renaissance.* New Brunswick, NJ: Rutgers University Press, 2001.

Fabre, Michel. *From Harlem to Paris: Black American Writers in France, 1840–1980.* Urbana: University of Illinois Press, 1991.

Farber, David R. *Sloan Rules: Alfred P. Sloan and the Triumph of General Motors.* Chicago: University of Chicago Press, 2002.

Farwell, Byron. *Over There: The United States in the Great War, 1917–1918.* New York: W.W. Norton, 1999.

Fass, Paula S. *The Damned and the Beautiful: American Youth in the 1920's.* New York: Oxford University Press, 1977.

Faue, Elizabeth. *Community of Suffering and Struggle: Women, Men, and the Labor Movement in Minneapolis, 1915–1945.* Chapel Hill: University of North Carolina Press, 1991.

Fausold, Martin L. *The Presidency of Herbert C. Hoover.* Lawrence: University Press of Kansas, 1984.

Favor, J. Martin. *Authentic Blackness: The Folk in the New Negro Renaissance.* Durham, NC: Duke University Press, 1999.

Ferguson, Niall. *The Pity of War: Explaining World War I.* New York: Basic Books, 1999.

Ferrell, Robert H., ed. *America as a World Power, 1872–1945.* Columbia: University of South Carolina Press, 1971.

———. *Peace in Their Time: The Origins of the Kellogg-Briand Pact.* Hamden, CT: Archon, 1968.

———. *The Presidency of Calvin Coolidge.* Lawrence: University Press of Kansas, 1998.

———. *Woodrow Wilson and World War I, 1917–1921.* New York: Harper & Row, 1985.

Feuerlicht, Roberta Strauss. *Justice Crucified: The Story of Sacco and Vanzetti.* New York: McGraw-Hill, 1977.

Filene, Peter G., ed. *American Views of Soviet Russia, 1917–1965.* Homewood, IL: Dorsey, 1968.

Finan, Christopher M. *Alfred E. Smith: The Happy Warrior.* New York: Hill and Wang, 2002.

Finley, David E. *A Standard of Excellence: Andrew W. Mellon Founds the National Gallery of Art at Washington.* Washington, DC: Smithsonian Institution Press, 1973.

Fite, Gilbert Courtland. *American Farmers: The New Minority.* Bloomington: Indiana University Press, 1981.

———. *Cotton Fields No More: Southern Agriculture, 1865–1980.* Lexington: University Press of Kentucky, 1984.

Fleming, Robert E. *Sinclair Lewis: A Reference Guide.* With Esther Fleming. Boston: G.K. Hall, 1980.

Fleser, Arthur F. *A Rhetorical Study of the Speaking of Calvin Coolidge.* Lewiston, NY: E. Mellen Press, 1990.

Frank, Dana. *Purchasing Power: Consumer Organizing, Gender, and the Seattle Labor Movement, 1919–1929.* Cambridge, UK: Cambridge University Press, 1994.

Fuess, Claude Moore. *Calvin Coolidge: The Man from Vermont.* Hamden, CT: Archon, 1965

Galambos, Louis. *America at Middle Age: A New History of the United States in the Twentieth Century.* New York: New Press, 1983.

Galambos, Louis, and Joseph Pratt. *The Rise of the Corporate Commonwealth: U.S. Business and Public Policy in the Twentieth Century.* New York: Basic Books, 1988.

Gamm, Gerald H. *The Making of New Deal Democrats: Voting Behavior and Realignment in Boston, 1920–1940.* Chicago: University of Chicago Press, 1989.

García, Juan R. *Mexicans in the Midwest, 1900–1932.* Tucson: University of Arizona Press, 1996.

Gardner, Lloyd C. *The Case That Never Dies: The Lindbergh Kidnapping.* New Brunswick, NJ: Rutgers University Press, 2004.

———. *Safe for Democracy: Anglo-American Response to Revolution, 1913–1923.* New York: Oxford University Press, 1984.

Garraty, John Arthur. *Henry Cabot Lodge: A Biography.* New York: Alfred A. Knopf, 1953.

Gavin, Lettie. *American Women in World War I: They Also Served.* Niwot: University Press of Colorado, 1997.

Gerstle, Gary. *Working-Class Americanism: The Politics of Labor in a Textile City, 1914–1960.* New York: Cambridge University Press, 1989.

Gertz, Elmer. *A Handful of Clients.* Chicago: Follett, 1965.

Gilbert, Robert E. *The Tormented President: Calvin Coolidge, Death, and Clinical Depression.* Westport, CT: Praeger, 2003.

Gioia, Ted. *The History of Jazz.* New York: Oxford University Press, 1997.

Glad, Betty. *Charles Evans Hughes and the Illusions of Innocence: A Study in American Diplomacy.* Urbana: University of Illinois Press, 1966.

Goldberg, David Joseph. *Discontented America: The United States in the 1920s.* Baltimore: Johns Hopkins University Press, 1999.

———. *A Tale of Three Cities: Labor Organization and Protest in Paterson, Passaic, and Lawrence, 1916–1921.* New Brunswick, NJ: Rutgers University Press, 1989.

Goldberg, Ronald Allen. *America in the Twenties.* Syracuse, NY: Syracuse University Press, 2003.

Gordon, Colin. *New Deals: Business, Labor, and Politics in America, 1920–1935.* New York: Cambridge University Press, 1994.

Gordon, Robert W., ed. *The Legacy of Oliver Wendell Holmes, Jr.* Stanford, CA: Stanford University Press, 1992.

Gottlieb, Peter. *Making Their Own Way: Southern Blacks' Migration to Pittsburgh, 1916–30.* Urbana: University of Illinois Press, 1987.

Graham, Otis L. *The Great Campaigns: Reform and War in America, 1900–1928.* Englewood Cliffs, NJ: Prentice Hall, 1971.

Gray, Richard J. *The Life of William Faulkner: A Critical Biography.* Oxford, UK: Blackwell, 1994.

Gray, Susan M. *Charles A. Lindbergh and the American Dilemma: The Conflict of Technology and Human Values.* Bowling Green, OH: Bowling Green State University Popular Press, 1988.

Greenbaum, Fred. *Men Against Myths: The Progressive Response.* Westport, CT: Praeger, 2000.

Greenberg, Martin Alan. *Prohibition Enforcement: Charting a New Mission.* Springfield, IL: Charles C. Thomas, 1999.

Greenwald, Maurine Weiner. *Women, War, and Work: The Impact of World War I on Women Workers in the United States.* Westport, CT: Greenwood, 1980.

Gregory, Ross. *Modern America, 1914 to 1945.* New York: Facts on File, 1995.

Gross, David C. *A Justice for All the People: Louis D. Brandeis.* New York: Lodestar, 1987.

Guerin-Gonzales, Camille. *Mexican Workers and American Dreams: Immigration, Repatriation, and California Farm Labor, 1900–1939.* New Brunswick, NJ: Rutgers University Press, 1994.

Guinsburg, Thomas N. *The Pursuit of Isolationism in the United States Senate from Versailles to Pearl Harbor.* New York: Garland, 1982.

Gustafson, Melanie, Kristie Miller, and Elisabeth I. Perry, eds. *We Have Come to Stay: American Women and Political Parties, 1880–1960.* Albuquerque: University of New Mexico Press, 1999.

Gutiérrez, David. *Walls and Mirrors: Mexican Americans, Mexican Immigrants, and the Politics of Ethnicity.* Berkeley: University of California Press, 1995.

Hall, Jacquelyn Dowd, et al. *Like a Family: The Making of a Southern Cotton Mill World.* Chapel Hill: University of North Carolina Press, 1987.

Hall, Linda B. *Oil, Banks, and Politics: The United States and Postrevolutionary Mexico, 1917–1924.* Austin: University of Texas Press, 1995.

Halpern, Ben. *A Clash of Heroes: Brandeis, Weizmann, and American Zionism.* New York: Oxford University Press, 1987.

Halpern, Rick. *Down on the Killing Floor: Black and White Workers in Chicago's Packinghouses, 1904–54.* Urbana: University of Illinois Press, 1997.

Hamilton, David E. *From New Day to New Deal: American Farm Policy from Hoover to Roosevelt, 1928–1933.* Chapel Hill: University of North Carolina Press, 1991.

Hamm, Richard F. *Shaping the Eighteenth Amendment: Temperance Reform, Legal Culture, and the Polity, 1880–1920.* Chapel Hill: University of North Carolina Press, 1995.

Harbaugh, William Henry. *Lawyer's Lawyer: The Life of John W. Davis.* New York: Oxford University Press, 1973.

Harrison, Robert. *Congress, Progressive Reform, and the New American State.* New York: Cambridge University Press, 2004.

Harrison, S.L. *Mencken Revisited: Author, Editor, and Newspaperman.* Lanham, MD: University Press of America, 1999.

Hatch, James V., and Leo Hamalian, eds. *Lost Plays of the Harlem Renaissance, 1920–1940.* Detroit, MI: Wayne State University Press, 1996.

Hatchett, Louis. *Mencken's Americana.* Macon, GA: Mercer University Press, 2002.

Hawes, Joseph M. *Children Between the Wars: American Childhood, 1920–1940.* New York: Twayne, 1997.

Hawley, Ellis Wayne. *The Great War and the Search for Modern Order: A History of the American People and Their Institutions, 1917–1933.* New York: St. Martin's, 1979.

Haydu, Jeffrey. *Making American Industry Safe for Democracy: Comparative Perspectives on the State and Employee Representation in the Era of World War I.* Urbana: University of Illinois Press, 1997.

Haynes, John Earl, ed. *Calvin Coolidge and the Coolidge Era: Essays on the History of the 1920s.* Washington, DC: Library of Congress, 1998.

Heckscher, August. *Woodrow Wilson.* New York: Scribner's, 1991.

Helbling, Mark Irving. *The Harlem Renaissance: The One and the Many.* Westport, CT: Greenwood, 1999.

Hendel, Samuel. *Charles Evans Hughes and the Supreme Court.* New York: Russell & Russell, 1968.

Henri, Florette. *Black Migration: Movement North, 1900–1920.* Garden City, NY: Anchor, 1975.

Hersh, Burton. *The Mellon Family: A Fortune in History.* New York: Morrow, 1978.

Herzstein, Robert Edwin. *Henry R. Luce: A Political Portrait of the Man Who Created the American Century.* New York: Scribner's, 1994.

Higashi, Sumiko. *Cecil B. DeMille and American Culture: The Silent Era.* Berkeley: University of California Press, 1994.

———. *Virgins, Vamps, and Flappers: The American Silent Movie Heroine.* St. Alban's, VT: Eden, 1978.

Higham, John. *Strangers in the Land: Patterns of American Nativism, 1860–1925.* New Brunswick, NJ: Rutgers University Press, 1988.

Highsaw, Robert Baker. *Edward Douglass White, Defender of the Conservative Faith.* Baton Rouge: Louisiana State University Press, 1981.

Hijiya, James A. *Lee de Forest and the Fatherhood of Radio.* Bethlehem, PA: Lehigh University Press, 1992.

Hilliard, Robert L., and Michael C. Keith. *The Broadcast Century: A Biography of American Broadcasting.* Boston: Focal, 1997.

Hindman, Hugh D. *Child Labor: An American History.* Armonk, NY: M.E. Sharpe, 2002.

Hobbs, Sandy, Jim McKechnie, and Michael Lavalette. *Child Labor: A World History Companion.* Santa Barbara, CA: ABC-CLIO, 1999.

Hoff-Wilson, Joan. *American Business and Foreign Policy, 1920–1933.* Lexington: University Press of Kentucky, 1971.

————. *Herbert Hoover: Forgotten Progressive.* Ed. Oscar Handlin. Prospect Heights, IL: Waveland, 1992.

Hogan, Michael J. *Informal Entente: The Private Structure of Cooperation in Anglo-American Economic Diplomacy, 1918–1928.* Columbia: University of Missouri Press, 1977.

————, ed. *Paths to Power: The Historiography of American Foreign Relations to 1941.* New York: Cambridge University Press, 2000.

Hohner, Robert A. *Prohibition and Politics: The Life of Bishop James Cannon, Jr.* Columbia: University of South Carolina Press, 1999.

Hong, Sungook. *Wireless: From Marconi's Black-Box to the Audion.* Cambridge, MA: MIT Press, 2001.

Horowitz, Helen Lefkowitz. *Campus Life: Undergraduate Cultures from the End of the Eighteenth Century to the Present.* Chicago: University of Chicago Press, 1988.

Houck, Davis W. *Rhetoric as Currency: Hoover, Roosevelt, and the Great Depression.* College Station: Texas A&M University Press, 2001.

Hughes, Langston. *The Big Sea: An Autobiography.* New York: Thunder's Mouth Press, 1986.

————. *Remember Me to Harlem: The Letters of Langston Hughes and Carl Van Vechten, 1925–1964.* Ed. Emily Bernard. New York: Alfred A. Knopf, 2001.

Hull, Gloria T. *Color, Sex, and Poetry: Three Women Writers of the Harlem Renaissance.* Bloomington: Indiana University Press, 1987.

Hutchinson, George. *The Harlem Renaissance in Black and White.* Cambridge, MA: Belknap Press, 1995.

Iriye, Akira. *After Imperialism: The Search for a New Order in the Far East, 1921–1931.* Cambridge, MA: Harvard University Press, 1965.

Isaac, Paul E. *Prohibition and Politics: Turbulent Decades in Tennessee, 1885–1920.* Knoxville: University of Tennessee Press, 1965.

Isenberg, Michael T. *War on Film: The American Cinema and World War I, 1914–1941.* Rutherford, NJ: Fairleigh Dickinson University Press, 1981.

Jackson, Kenneth T. *The Ku Klux Klan in the City, 1915–1930.* Chicago: Ivan R. Dee, 1992. (First published 1967 by Oxford University Press)

James, Scott C. *Presidents, Parties, and the State: A Party System Perspective on Democratic Regulatory Choice, 1884–1936.* Cambridge, UK: Cambridge University Press, 2000.

Jeansonne, Glen. *Transformation and Reaction: America, 1921–1945.* New York: HarperCollins College, 1994.

Jensen, Joan M. *The Price of Vigilance.* Chicago: Rand McNally, 1969.

Jensen, Joan M., and Lois Scharf, eds. *Decades of Discontent: The Women's Movement, 1920–1940.* Westport, CT: Greenwood, 1983.

Johnson, Robert David. *The Peace Progressives and American Foreign Relations.* Cambridge, MA: Harvard University Press, 1995.

Johnston, Robert D. *The Radical Middle Class: Populist Democracy and the Question of Capitalism in Progressive Era Portland, Oregon.* Princeton, NJ: Princeton University Press, 2003.

Jones, Sharon L. *Rereading the Harlem Renaissance: Race, Class, and Gender in the Fiction of Jessie Fauset, Zora Neale Hurston, and Dorothy West.* Westport, CT: Greenwood, 2002.

Kamman, William. *A Search for Stability: United States Diplomacy Toward Nicaragua, 1925–1933.* Notre Dame, IN: University of Notre Dame Press, 1968.

Kammen, Michael G. *American Culture, American Tastes: Social Change and the 20th Century.* New York: Alfred A. Knopf, 1999.

Karl, Frederick Robert. *William Faulkner, American Writer: A Biography.* New York: Weidenfeld & Nicolson, 1988.

Keegan, John. *An Illustrated History of the First World War.* New York: Alfred A. Knopf, 2001.

Keith, Jeanette. *Country People in the New South: Tennessee's Upper Cumberland.* Chapel Hill: University of North Carolina Press, 1995.

Keller, Morton. *Regulating a New Society: Public Policy and Social Change in America, 1900–1933.* Cambridge, MA: Harvard University Press, 1994.

Kellner, Bruce, ed. *A Gertrude Stein Companion: Content with the Example.* New York: Greenwood, 1988.

Kellogg, Charles Flint. *NAACP: A History of the National Association for the Advancement of Colored People.* Baltimore: Johns Hopkins University Press, 1967.

Kellogg, Frederic Rogers. *The Formative Essays of Justice Holmes: The Making of an American Legal Philosophy.* Westport, CT: Greenwood, 1984.

Kennedy, David M. *Freedom from Fear: The American People in Depression and War, 1929–1945.* New York: Oxford University Press, 1999.

————. *Over Here: The First World War and American Society.* New York: Oxford University Press, 1980.

Kennedy, Kathleen. *Disloyal Mothers and Scurrilous Citizens: Women and Subversion During World War I.* Bloomington: Indiana University Press, 1999.

Kennedy, Sheila Suess, ed. *Free Expression in America: A Documentary History.* Westport, CT: Greenwood, 1999.

Kenney, William Howland. *Recorded Music in American Life: The Phonograph and Popular Memory, 1890–1945.* New York: Oxford University Press, 1999.

Kerr, K. Austin. *American Railroad Politics, 1914–1920: Rates, Wages, and Efficiency.* Pittsburgh, PA: University of Pittsburgh Press, 1968.

————. *Organized for Prohibition: A New History of the Anti-saloon League.* New Haven, CT: Yale University Press, 1985.

Kessler-Harris, Alice. *In Pursuit of Equity: Women, Men, and the Quest for Economic Citizenship in 20th-Century America.* Oxford, UK: Oxford University Press, 2001.

Keyssar, Alexander. *The Right to Vote: The Contested History of Democracy in the United States.* New York: Basic Books, 2000.

Kimeldorf, Howard. *Battling for American Labor: Wobblies, Craft Workers, and the Making of the Union Movement.* Berkeley: University of California Press, 1999.

King, Desmond S. *Making Americans: Immigration, Race, and the Origins of the Diverse Democracy.* Cambridge, MA: Harvard University Press, 2000.

Kirschke, Amy Helene. *Aaron Douglas: Art, Race, and the Harlem Renaissance.* Jackson: University Press of Mississippi, 1995.

Klan: A Legacy of Hate in America, The. Videorecording. Guggenheim Productions, Inc. Directed and edited by Werner Schumann; produced by Charles Guggenheim and Werner Schumann; written by Charles Guggenheim and Patsy Sims. Chicago: Films Incorporated Video, 1989.

Kline, Wendy. *Building a Better Race: Gender, Sexuality, and Eugenics from the Turn of the Century to the Baby Boom.* Berkeley: University of California Press, 2001.

Knapp, Bettina Liebowitz. *Gertrude Stein.* New York: Continuum, 1990.

Knickerbocker, Wendy. *Sunday at the Ballpark: Billy Sunday's Professional Baseball Career, 1883–1890.* Lanham, MD: Scarecrow, 2000.

Knock, Thomas J. *To End All Wars: Woodrow Wilson and the Quest for a New World Order.* New York: Oxford University Press, 1992.

Knopf, Marcy, ed. *The Sleeper Wakes: Harlem Renaissance Stories by Women.* New Brunswick, NJ: Rutgers University Press, 1993.

Kolata, Gina Bari. *Flu: The Story of the Great Influenza Pandemic of 1918 and the Search for the Virus That Caused It.* New York: Farrar, Straus and Giroux, 1999.

Kraut, Alan M. *The Huddled Masses: The Immigrant in American Society, 1880–1921.* Arlington Heights, IL: Harlan Davidson, 1982.

———. *Silent Travelers: Germs, Genes, and the "Immigrant Menace."* Baltimore: Johns Hopkins University Press, 1995.

Krog, Carl E., and William R. Tanner, eds. *Herbert Hoover and the Republican Era: A Reconsideration.* Lanham, MD: University Press of America, 1984.

Kühl, Stefan. *The Nazi Connection: Eugenics, American Racism, and German National Socialism.* New York: Oxford University Press, 1994.

Kurtz, Michael L. *The Challenging of America, 1920–1945.* Arlington Heights, IL: Forum, 1986.

Kwolek-Folland, Angel. *Engendering Business: Men and Women in the Corporate Office, 1870–1930.* Baltimore: Johns Hopkins University Press, 1994.

Kyvig, David E. *Daily Life in the United States, 1920–1939: Decades of Promise and Pain.* Westport, CT: Greenwood, 2002.

———. *Repealing National Prohibition.* Kent, OH: Kent State University Press, 2000.

Langley, Lester D. *The Banana Wars: United States Intervention in the Caribbean, 1898–1934.* Wilmington, DE: SR Books, 2002.

Larson, Edward J. *Summer for the Gods: The Scopes Trial and America's Continuing Debate over Science and Religion.* New York: Basic Books, 1997.

———. *Trial and Error: The American Controversy over Creation and Evolution.* Oxford, UK: Oxford University Press, 2003.

Latham, Angela J. *Posing a Threat: Flappers, Chorus Girls, and Other Transgressive Performers of the American 1920s.* Hanover, NH: University Press of New England, 2000.

Lay, Shawn. *Hooded Knights on the Niagara: The Ku Klux Klan in Buffalo, New York.* New York: New York University Press, 1995.

———, ed. *The Invisible Empire in the West: Toward a New Historical Appraisal of the Ku Klux Klan of the 1920s.* Urbana: University of Illinois Press, 1992.

———. *War, Revolution, and the Ku Klux Klan: A Study of Intolerance in a Border City.* El Paso: Texas Western Press, 1985.

Leach, William. *Land of Desire: Merchants, Power, and the Rise of a New American Culture.* New York: Pantheon, 1993.

Lears, T.J. Jackson. *Fables of Abundance: A Cultural History of Advertising in America.* New York: Basic Books, 1994.

Leffler, Melvyn P. *The Elusive Quest: America's Pursuit of European Stability and French Security, 1919–1933.* Chapel Hill: University of North Carolina Press, 1979.

———. *The Specter of Communism: The United States and the Origins of the Cold War, 1917–1953.* New York: Hill and Wang, 1994.

Lemons, J. Stanley. *The Woman Citizen: Social Feminism in the 1920's.* Urbana: University of Illinois Press, 1973.

Lentin, A. *Lloyd George, Woodrow Wilson, and the Guilt of Germany: An Essay in the Pre-History of Appeasement.* Baton Rouge: Louisiana State University Press, 1985.

Leuchtenburg, William Edward. *The Perils of Prosperity, 1914–1932.* Chicago: University of Chicago Press, 1993.

———, ed. *The Unfinished Century: America Since 1900.* Boston: Little, Brown, 1973.

Levin, Phyllis Lee. *Edith and Woodrow: The Wilson White House.* New York: Scribner's, 2001.

Lewis, David Lanier. *The Public Image of Henry Ford: An American Folk Hero and His Company.* Detroit, MI: Wayne State University Press, 1976.

Lewis, David Levering, ed. *The Portable Harlem Renaissance Reader.* New York: Penguin, 1995.

———. *When Harlem Was in Vogue.* New York: Penguin, 1997.

Lewis, Tom. *Empire of the Air: The Men Who Made Radio.* New York: E. Burlingame, 1991.

Lichtenstein, Nelson. *State of the Union: A Century of American Labor.* Princeton, NJ: Princeton University Press, 2002.

Liebovich, Louis. *Bylines in Despair: Herbert Hoover, the Great Depression, and the U.S. News Media.* Westport, CT: Praeger, 1994.

Link, William A. *The Paradox of Southern Progressivism, 1880–1930.* Chapel Hill: University of North Carolina Press, 1992.

Linkugel, Wil A., and Martha Solomon. *Anna Howard Shaw: Suffrage Orator and Social Reformer.* New York: Greenwood, 1991.

Livingston, John Charles. *Clarence Darrow: The Mind of a Sentimental Rebel.* New York: Garland, 1988.

Loeb, Carolyn S. *Entrepreneurial Vernacular: Developers' Subdivisions in the 1920s.* Baltimore: Johns Hopkins University Press, 2001.

Lovell, S.D. *The Presidential Election of 1916.* Carbondale: Southern Illinois University Press, 1980.

Ludmerer, Kenneth M. *Genetics and American Society: A Historical Appraisal.* Baltimore: Johns Hopkins University Press, 1972.

Lunardini, Christine A. *From Equal Suffrage to Equal Rights: Alice Paul and the National Woman's Party, 1910–1928.* New York: New York University Press, 1986.

Lunbeck, Elizabeth. *The Psychiatric Persuasion: Knowledge, Gender, and Power in Modern America.* Princeton, NJ: Princeton University Press, 1994.

Lundquist, James. *Sinclair Lewis.* New York: Ungar, 1972.

Lutholtz, M. William. *Grand Dragon: D.C. Stephenson and the Ku Klux Klan in Indiana.* West Lafayette, IN: Purdue University Press, 1993.

Lynd, Robert Staughton, and Helen Merrell Lynd. *Middletown: A Study in American Culture.* New York: Harcourt, Brace, 1956.

MacLean, Nancy. *Behind the Mask of Chivalry: The Making of the Second Ku Klux Klan.* New York: Oxford University Press, 1994.

MacMillan, Margaret Olwen. *Paris 1919: Six Months That Changed the World.* New York: Random House, 2002.

Madsen, Axel. *The Deal Maker: How William C. Durant Made General Motors.* New York: Wiley, 1999.

Maney, Patrick J. *"Young Bob" La Follette: A Biography of Robert M. La Follette, Jr., 1895–1953.* Columbia: University of Missouri Press, 1978.

Marchand, Roland. *Advertising the American Dream: Making Way for Modernity, 1920–1940.* Berkeley: University of California Press, 1996.

Marcus Garvey: Toward Black Nationhood. Videorecording. West German Television, Cologne. Produced by Orville Bennett et al. Princeton, NJ: Films for the Humanities & Sciences, 1993.

Margulies, Herbert F. *Senator Lenroot of Wisconsin: A Political Biography, 1900–1929.* Columbia: University of Missouri Press, 1977.

Marquis, Alice Goldfarb. *Hopes and Ashes: The Birth of Modern Times, 1929–1939.* New York: Free Press, 1986.

Marsden, George M. *Fundamentalism and American Culture: The Shaping of Twentieth Century Evangelicalism, 1870–1925.* New York: Oxford University Press, 1982.

Martin, Robert Francis. *Hero of the Heartland: Billy Sunday and the Transformation of American Society, 1862–1935.* Bloomington: Indiana University Press, 2002.

Marty, Martin E. *Modern American Religion.* Chicago: University of Chicago Press, 1986.

———. *Religious Crises in Modern America.* Waco, TX: Baylor University Press, 1981.

Maurer, Maurer. *Aviation in the U.S. Army, 1919–1939.* Washington, DC: Office of Air Force History, U.S. Air Force, 1987.

May, Lary. *The Big Tomorrow: Hollywood and the Politics of the American Way.* Chicago: University of Chicago Press, 2000.

———. *Screening Out the Past: The Birth of Mass Culture and the Motion Picture Industry.* New York: Oxford University Press, 1980.

McCann, Carole R. *Birth Control Politics in the United States, 1916–1945.* Ithaca, NY: Cornell University Press, 1994.

McCartin, Joseph A. *Labor's Great War: The Struggle for Industrial Democracy and the Origins of Modern American Labor Relations, 1912–1921.* Chapel Hill: University of North Carolina Press, 1997.

McChesney, Robert W. *Telecommunications, Mass Media, and Democracy: The Battle for the Control of U.S. Broadcasting, 1928–1935.* New York: Oxford University Press, 1993.

McClymer, John F. *War and Welfare: Social Engineering in America, 1890–1925.* Westport, CT: Greenwood, 1980.

McCormick, Richard L. *The Party Period and Public Policy: American Politics from the Age of Jackson to the Progressive Era.* New York: Oxford University Press, 1986.

McCoy, Donald R. *Calvin Coolidge: The Quiet President.* New York: Macmillan, 1967.

McCraw, Thomas K. *Prophets of Regulation: Charles Francis Adams, Louis D. Brandeis, James M. Landis, Alfred E. Kahn.* Cambridge, MA: Belknap Press, 1984.

McElvaine, Robert S. *The Great Depression: America, 1929–1941.* New York: Times Books, 1984.

McFadden, David W. *Alternative Paths: Soviets and Americans, 1917–1920.* New York: Oxford University Press, 1993.

McGerr, Michael E. *A Fierce Discontent: The Rise and Fall of the Progressive Movement in America, 1870–1920.* New York: Free Press, 2003.

McKernan, Maureen. *The Amazing Crime and Trial of Leopold and Loeb.* Holmes Beach, FL: Gaunt, 1996.

McShane, Clay. *The Automobile: A Chronology of Its Antecedents, Development, and Impact.* Westport, CT: Greenwood, 1997.

———. *Down the Asphalt Path: The Automobile and the American City.* New York: Columbia University Press, 1994.

Mee, Charles L. *The End of Order, Versailles, 1919.* New York: Dutton, 1980.

———. *The Ohio Gang: The World of Warren G. Harding.* New York: M. Evans, 1981.

Meikle, Jeffrey L. *Twentieth Century Limited: Industrial Design in America, 1925–1939.* Philadelphia: Temple University Press, 1979.

Mellow, James R. *Hemingway: A Life Without Consequences.* Boston: Houghton Mifflin, 1992.

———. *Invented Lives: F. Scott and Zelda Fitzgerald.* Boston: Houghton Mifflin, 1984.

Menand, Louis. *The Metaphysical Club.* New York: Farrar, Straus and Giroux, 2001.

Menchaca, Martha. *The Mexican Outsiders: A Community History of Marginalization and Discrimination in California.* Austin: University of Texas Press, 1995.

Mennel, Robert M., and Christine L. Compston, eds. *Holmes and Frankfurter: Their Correspondence, 1912–1934.* Hanover, NH: University Press of New England, 1996.

Meyers, Jeffrey. *Hemingway: A Biography.* New York: Harper & Row, 1985.

———. *Scott Fitzgerald: A Biography.* New York: HarperCollins, 1994.

Milkis, Sidney M., and Jerome M. Mileur, eds. *Progressivism and the New Democracy.* Amherst: University of Massachusetts Press, 1999.

Miller, Karen A.J. *Populist Nationalism: Republican Insurgency and American Foreign Policy Making, 1918–1925.* Westport, CT: Greenwood, 1999.

Miller, Zane L. *The Urbanization of Modern America: A Brief History.* New York: Harcourt Brace Jovanovich, 1973.

Milton, Joyce. *Loss of Eden: A Biography of Charles and Anne Morrow Lindbergh.* New York: HarperCollins, 1993.

Mink, Gwendolyn. *Old Labor and New Immigrants in American Political Development: Union, Party, and State, 1875–1920.* Ithaca, NY: Cornell University Press, 1986.

Mishkin, Tracy. *The Harlem and Irish Renaissances: Language, Identity, and Representation.* Gainesville: University Press of Florida, 1998.

Monagan, John S. *The Grand Panjandrum: Mellow Years of Justice Holmes.* Lanham, MD: University Press of America, 1988.

Montgomery, David. *The Fall of the House of Labor: The Workplace, the State, and American Labor Activism, 1865–1925.* Cambridge, UK: Cambridge University Press, 1987.

Moore, Leonard Joseph. *Citizen Klansmen: The Ku Klux Klan in Indiana, 1921–1928.* Chapel Hill: University of North Carolina Press, 1991.

Moran, Jeffrey P. *The Scopes Trial: A Brief History with Documents.* Boston: Bedford/St. Martin's, 2002.

Mowry, George Edwin. *The Progressive Era, 1900–20: The Reform Persuasion.* Washington, DC: American Historical Association, 1972.

Muncy, Robyn. *Creating a Female Dominion in American Reform, 1890–1935.* New York: Oxford University Press, 1994.

Munson, Gorham Bert. *The Awakening Twenties: A Memoir-History of a Literary Period.* Baton Rouge: Louisiana State University Press, 1985.

Murphy, Bruce Allen. *The Brandeis/Frankfurter Connection: The Secret Political Activities of Two Supreme Court Justices.* New York: Oxford University Press, 1982.

Murphy, Paul L. *World War I and the Origin of Civil Liberties in the United States.* New York: W.W. Norton, 1979.

Murray, Robert K. *The Politics of Normalcy: Governmental Theory and Practice in the Harding-Coolidge Era.* New York: W.W. Norton, 1973.

Nash, George H. *The Life of Herbert Hoover.* New York: W.W. Norton, 1983.

Nash, Gerald D. *The Crucial Era: The Great Depression and World War II, 1929–1945.* New York: St. Martin's, 1992.

———. *The Federal Landscape: An Economic History of the Twentieth-Century West.* Tucson: University of Arizona Press, 1999.

Nash, Lee, ed. *Understanding Herbert Hoover: Ten Perspectives.* Stanford, CA: Hoover Institution Press, 1987.

Nelson, Daniel. *American Rubber Workers and Organized Labor, 1900–1941.* Princeton, NJ: Princeton University Press, 1988.

———. *Shifting Fortunes: The Rise and Decline of American Labor, from the 1820s to the Present.* Chicago: Ivan R. Dee, 1997.

Neth, Mary. *Preserving the Family Farm: Women, Community, and the Foundations of Agribusiness in the Midwest, 1900–1940.* Baltimore: Johns Hopkins University Press, 1995.

Neuman, Shirley, and Ira B. Nadel, eds. *Gertrude Stein and the Making of Literature.* Boston: Northeastern University Press, 1988.

Nies, Betsy L. *Eugenic Fantasies: Racial Ideology in the Literature and Popular Culture of the 1920's.* New York: Routledge, 2002.

Ninkovich, Frank A. *The Wilsonian Century: U.S. Foreign Policy Since 1900.* Chicago: University of Chicago Press, 1999.

Novick, Sheldon M. *Honorable Justice: The Life of Oliver Wendell Holmes.* Boston: Little, Brown, 1989.

Oates, Stephen B. *William Faulkner, the Man and the Artist: A Biography.* New York: Harper & Row, 1987.

Ogren, Kathy J. *The Jazz Revolution: Twenties America and the Meaning of Jazz.* New York: Oxford University Press, 1989.

Oriard, Michael. *Reading Football: How the Popular Press Created an American Spectacle.* Chapel Hill: University of North Carolina Press, 1993.

Orleck, Annelise. *Common Sense and a Little Fire: Women and Working-Class Politics in the United States, 1900–1965.* Chapel Hill: University of North Carolina Press, 1995.

Palladino, Grace. *Teenagers: An American History.* New York: Basic Books, 1996.

Paper, Lewis J. *Brandeis.* Englewood Cliffs, NJ: Prentice Hall, 1983.

Parrish, Michael E. *Anxious Decades: America in Prosperity and Depression, 1920–1941.* New York: W.W. Norton, 1992.

———. *Felix Frankfurter and His Times.* New York: Free Press, 1982.

Patenaude, Bertrand M. "Herbert Hoover's Brush with Bolshevism" *Kennan Institute Occasional Papers.* Washington, DC: Woodrow Wilson International Center for Scholars, Kennan Institute, 1992.

Patterson, James T. *America's Struggle Against Poverty in the Twentieth Century.* Cambridge, MA: Harvard University Press, 2000.

Paulsson, Martin. *The Social Anxieties of Progressive Reform: Atlantic City, 1854–1920.* New York: New York University Press, 1994.

Payne, Elizabeth Anne. *Reform, Labor, and Feminism: Margaret Dreier Robins and the Women's Trade Union League.* Urbana: University of Illinois Press, 1988.

Pearlman, Michael. *To Make Democracy Safe for America: Patricians and Preparedness in the Progressive Era.* Urbana: University of Illinois Press, 1984.

Pegram, Thomas R. *Battling Demon Rum: The Struggle for a Dry America, 1800–1933.* Chicago: Ivan R. Dee, 1998.

———. *Partisans and Progressives: Private Interest and Public Policy in Illinois, 1870–1922.* Urbana: University of Illinois Press, 1992.

Peiss, Kathy. *Hope in a Jar: The Making of America's Beauty Culture.* New York: Metropolitan, 1998.

Peretti, Burton W. *The Creation of Jazz: Music, Race, and Culture in Urban America.* Urbana: University of Illinois Press, 1992.

———. *Jazz in American Culture.* Chicago: Ivan R. Dee, 1997.

Pernick, Martin S. *The Black Stork: Eugenics and the Death of "Defective" Babies in American Medicine and Motion Pictures Since 1915.* New York: Oxford University Press, 1996.

Perpener, John O. *African-American Concert Dance: The Harlem Renaissance and Beyond.* Urbana: University of Illinois Press, 2001.

Perret, Geoffrey. *America in the Twenties: A History.* New York: Simon & Schuster, 1982.

Perry, Elisabeth Israels. *Belle Moskowitz: Feminine Politics and the Exercise of Power in the Age of Alfred E. Smith.* New York: Oxford University Press, 1987.

Philp, Kenneth R. *John Collier's Crusade for Indian Reform, 1920–1954.* Tucson: University of Arizona Press, 1977.

Pohlman, H.L. *Justice Oliver Wendell Holmes: Free Speech and the Living Constitution.* New York: New York University Press, 1991.

Polenberg, Richard. *Fighting Faiths: The Abrams Case, the Supreme Court, and Free Speech.* New York: Penguin, 1989.

Pratt, Walter F. *The Supreme Court Under Edward Douglass White, 1910–1921.* Columbia: University of South Carolina Press, 1999.

Preston, William. *Aliens and Dissenters: Federal Suppression of Radicals, 1903–1933.* Urbana: University of Illinois Press, 1994.

Purcell, Edward A. *Brandeis and the Progressive Constitution: Erie, the Judicial Power, and the Politics of the Federal Courts in Twentieth-Century America.* New Haven, CT: Yale University Press, 2000.

Quarles, Chester L. *The Ku Klux Klan and Related American Racialist and Antisemitic Organizations: A History and Analysis.* Jefferson, NC: McFarland, 1999.

Radway, Janice A. *A Feeling for Books: The Book-of-the-Month Club, Literary Taste, and Middle-Class Desire.* Chapel Hill: University of North Carolina Press, 1997.

Rafter, Nicole Hahn. *Creating Born Criminals.* Urbana: University of Illinois Press, 1997.

Rampersad, Arnold. *The Life of Langston Hughes.* New York: Oxford University Press, 1986–1988.

Reagan, Patrick D. *Designing a New America: The Origins of New Deal Planning, 1890–1943.* Amherst: University of Massachusetts Press, 2000.

Reed, Miriam. *Margaret Sanger: Her Life in Her Words.* Fort Lee, NJ: Barricade, 2003.

Regal, Brian. *Henry Fairfield Osborn: Race, and the Search for the Origins of Man.* Burlington, VT: Ashgate, 2002.

Reilly, Philip. *The Surgical Solution: A History of Involuntary Sterilization in the United States.* Baltimore: Johns Hopkins University Press, 1991.

Renstrom, Peter G. *The Taft Court: Justices, Rulings, and Legacy.* Santa Barbara, CA: ABC-CLIO, 2003.

Ring, Frances. *Against the Current: As I Remember F. Scott Fitzgerald.* San Francisco, CA: D.S. Ellis, 1985.

Rochester, Stuart I. *American Liberal Disillusionment.* University Park: Pennsylvania State University Press, 1977.

Rollin, Lucy. *Twentieth-Century Teen Culture by the Decades: A Reference Guide.* Westport, CT: Greenwood, 1999.

Rosales, Francisco A. *Pobre Raza! Violence, Justice, and Mobilization Among México Lindo Immigrants, 1900–1936.* Austin: University of Texas Press, 1999.

Rose, Kenneth D. *American Women and the Repeal of Prohibition.* New York: New York University Press, 1996.

Rosen, Jerold A. *The Big Red Scare of 1919–1920.* Videorecording. Culver City, CA: Zenger Media, 1980.

Rosenberg, Emily S. *Financial Missionaries to the World: The Politics and Culture of Dollar Diplomacy, 1900–1930.* Cambridge, MA: Harvard University Press, 1999.

———. *Spreading the American Dream: American Economic and Cultural Expansion, 1890–1945.* New York: Hill and Wang, 1982.

Roses, Lorraine Elena, and Ruth Elizabeth Randolph, eds. *Harlem's Glory: Black Women Writing, 1900–1950.* Cambridge, MA: Harvard University Press, 1996.

590   Bibliography

Rubin, Joan Shelley. *The Making of Middlebrow Culture.* Chapel Hill: University of North Carolina Press, 1992.

Ruíz, Vicki. *From out of the Shadows: Mexican Women in Twentieth-Century America.* New York: Oxford University Press, 1998.

Rumbarger, John J. *Profits, Power, and Prohibition: Alcohol Reform and the Industrializing of America, 1800–1930.* Albany: State University of New York Press, 1989.

Russell, Francis. *Sacco and Vanzetti: The Case Resolved.* New York: Harper & Row, 1986.

Rutland, Robert Allen. *The Democrats: From Jefferson to Clinton.* Columbia: University of Missouri Press, 1995.

Sacco, Nicola, and Bartolomeo Vanzetti. *The Letters of Sacco and Vanzetti.* Ed. Marion Denman Frankfurter and Gardner Jackson. Intro. Richard Polenberg. New York: Penguin, 1997.

Salmond, John A. *Gastonia, 1929: The Story of the Loray Mill Strike.* Chapel Hill: University of North Carolina Press, 1995.

Salvatore, Nick. *Eugene V. Debs: Citizen and Socialist.* Urbana: University of Illinois Press, 1982.

Samuelson, Arnold. *With Hemingway: A Year in Key West and Cuba.* New York: Random House, 1984.

Sanchez, George J. *Becoming Mexican American: Ethnicity, Culture, and Identity in Chicano Los Angeles, 1900–1945.* New York: Oxford University Press, 1993.

Sarasohn, David. *The Party of Reform: Democrats in the Progressive Era.* Jackson: University Press of Mississippi, 1989.

Schaffer, Ronald. *America in the Great War: The Rise of the War Welfare State.* New York: Oxford University Press, 1991.

———. *The United States in World War I: A Selected Bibliography.* Santa Barbara, CA: Clio, 1978.

Scharf, Lois, and Joan M. Jensen, eds. *Decades of Discontent: The Women's Movement, 1920–1940.* Westport, CT: Greenwood, 1983.

Scharff, Virginia. *Taking the Wheel: Women and the Coming of the Motor Age.* New York: Free Press, 1991.

Schmitz, David F. *Thank God They're on Our Side: The United States and Right-Wing Dictatorships, 1921–1965.* Chapel Hill: University of North Carolina Press, 1999.

———. *The United States and Fascist Italy, 1922–1940.* Chapel Hill: University of North Carolina Press, 1988.

Schneider, Dorothy. *American Women in the Progressive Era, 1900–1920.* New York: Facts on File, 1993.

Schneider, Mark Robert. *"We Return Fighting": The Civil Rights Movement in the Jazz Age.* Boston: Northeastern University Press, 2002.

Schoenberg, Robert J. *Mr. Capone.* New York: Morrow, 1992.

Schrum, Kelly. *Some Wore Bobby Sox: The Emergence of Teenage Girls' Culture, 1920–1945.* New York: Palgrave Macmillan, 2004.

Schwabe, Klaus. *Woodrow Wilson, Revolutionary Germany, and Peacemaking, 1918–1919: Missionary Diplomacy and the Realities of Power.* Trans. Rita Kimber and Robert Kimber. Chapel Hill: University of North Carolina Press, 1985.

Schwarz, A.B. Christa. *Gay Voices of the Harlem Renaissance.* Bloomington: Indiana University Press, 2003.

Schwarz, Jordan A. *The Speculator: Bernard M. Baruch in Washington, 1917–1965.* Chapel Hill: University of North Carolina Press, 1981.

Scopes, John Thomas. *The World's Most Famous Court Trial: Tennessee Evolution Case.* Complete stenographic report. Union, NJ: Lawbook Exchange, 1997.

Sealander, Judith. *Grand Plans: Business Progressivism and Social Change in Ohio's Miami Valley, 1890–1929.* Lexington: University Press of Kentucky, 1988.

Selden, Steven. *Inheriting Shame: The Story of Eugenics and Racism in America.* New York: Teachers College Press, 1999.

Sellars, Nigel Anthony. *Oil, Wheat, and Wobblies: The Industrial Workers of the World in Oklahoma, 1905–1930.* Norman: University of Oklahoma Press, 1998.

Shack, William A. *Harlem in Montmartre: A Paris Jazz Story Between the Great Wars.* Berkeley: University of California Press, 2001.

Shaughnessy, Dan. *The Curse of the Bambino.* New York: Penguin, 2000.

Shaw, Arnold. *The Jazz Age: Popular Music in the 1920's.* New York: Oxford University Press, 1987.

Shoemaker, Rebecca S. *The White Court: Justices, Rulings, and Legacy.* Santa Barbara, CA: ABC-CLIO, 2004.

Sklar, Kathryn Kish, Anja Schüler, and Susan Strasser, eds. *Social Justice Feminists in the United States and Germany: A Dialogue in Documents, 1885–1933.* Ithaca, NY: Cornell University Press, 1998.

Slayton, Robert A. *Empire Statesman: The Rise and Redemption of Al Smith.* New York: Free Press, 2001.

Slotten, Hugh Richard. *Radio and Television Regulation: Broadcast Technology in the United States, 1920–1960.* Baltimore: Johns Hopkins University Press, 2000.

Smith, Page. *Redeeming the Time: A People's History of the 1920s and the New Deal.* New York: McGraw-Hill, 1986.

Smith, Richard Norton. *An Uncommon Man: The Triumph of Herbert Hoover.* New York: Simon & Schuster, 1984.

Smulyan, Susan. *Selling Radio: The Commercialization of American Broadcasting, 1920–1934.* Washington, DC: Smithsonian Institution Press, 1994.

Smythe, Donald. *Pershing, General of the Armies.* Bloomington: Indiana University Press, 1986.

Sobel, Robert. *Coolidge: An American Enigma.* Washington, DC: Regnery, 1998.

Spinelli, Lawrence. *Dry Diplomacy: The United States, Great Britain, and Prohibition.* Wilmington, DE: Scholarly Resources, 1989.

Springhall, John. *Youth, Popular Culture and Moral Panics: Penny Gaffs to Gangsta-Rap, 1830–1996.* New York: St. Martin's, 1998.

Stears, Marc. *Progressives, Pluralists, and the Problems of the State: Ideologies of Reform in the United States and Britain, 1909–1926.* Oxford, UK: Oxford University Press, 2002.

Steel, Ronald. *Walter Lippmann and the American Century.* Boston: Little, Brown, 1980.

Steigerwald, David. *Wilsonian Idealism in America.* Ithaca, NY: Cornell University Press, 1994.

Stein, Judith. *The World of Marcus Garvey: Race and Class in Modern Society.* Baton Rouge: Louisiana State University Press, 1986.

Steinson, Barbara J. *American Women's Activism in World War I.* New York: Garland, 1982.

Strasser, Susan. *Satisfaction Guaranteed: The Making of the American Mass Market.* New York: Pantheon, 1989.

Strom, Sharon Hartman. *Beyond the Typewriter: Gender, Class, and the Origins of Modern American Office Work, 1900–1930.* Urbana: University of Illinois Press, 1992.

Strum, Philippa. *Brandeis: Beyond Progressivism.* Lawrence: University Press of Kansas, 1993.

Szymanski, Ann-Marie E. *Pathways to Prohibition: Radicals, Moderates, and Social Movement Outcomes.* Durham, NC: Duke University Press, 2003.

Taylor, Ula Y. *The Veiled Garvey: The Life and Times of Amy Jacques Garvey.* Chapel Hill: University of North Carolina Press, 2002.

Teaford, Jon C. *The Twentieth-Century American City: Problem, Promise, and Reality.* Baltimore: Johns Hopkins University Press, 1986.

Tentler, Leslie Woodcock. *Wage-Earning Women: Industrial Work and Family Life in the United States, 1900–1930.* New York: Oxford University Press, 1979.

Thelen, David P. *Robert M. La Follette and the Insurgent Spirit.* Boston: Little, Brown, 1976.

Thompson, J.A. *Woodrow Wilson.* London: Longman, 2002.

Thompson, John A. *Reformers and War: American Progressive Publicists and the First World War.* Cambridge, UK: Cambridge University Press, 1987.

Tobin, Eugene M. *Organize or Perish: America's Independent Progressives, 1913–1933.* New York: Greenwood, 1986.

Trollinger, William Vance. *God's Empire: William Bell Riley and Midwestern Fundamentalism.* Madison: University of Wisconsin Press, 1990.

Tucker, Richard K. *The Dragon and the Cross: The Rise and Fall of the Ku Klux Klan in Middle America.* Hamden, CT: Archon, 1991.

Tucker, William H. *The Science and Politics of Racial Research.* Urbana: University of Illinois Press, 1994.

Tuttle, William M. *Race Riot: Chicago in the Red Summer of 1919.* New York: Atheneum, 1970.

Tygiel, Jules. *Past Time: Baseball as History.* New York: Oxford University Press, 2000.

Ulanov, Barry. *A History of Jazz in America.* New York: Da Capo, 1972.

Unger, Nancy C. *Fighting Bob La Follette: The Righteous Reformer.* Chapel Hill: University of North Carolina Press, 2000.

Urofsky, Melvin I. *Louis D. Brandeis and the Progressive Tradition.* Boston: Little, Brown, 1981.

Vaillant, Derek. *Sounds of Reform: Progressivism and Music in Chicago, 1873–1935.* Chapel Hill: University of North Carolina Press, 2003.

Vasey, Ruth. *The World According to Hollywood, 1918–1939.* Madison: University of Wisconsin Press, 1997.

Wade, Wyn Craig. *The Fiery Cross: The Ku Klux Klan in America.* New York: Oxford University Press, 1998.

Walch, Timothy, ed. *Uncommon Americans: The Lives and Legacies of Herbert and Lou Henry Hoover.* Westport, CT: Praeger, 2003.

Wall, Cheryl A. *Women of the Harlem Renaissance.* Bloomington: Indiana University Press, 1995.

Wallace, Max. *The American Axis: Henry Ford, Charles Lindbergh, and the Rise of the Third Reich.* New York: St. Martin's, 2003.

Walworth, Arthur. *Wilson and His Peacemakers: American Diplomacy at the Paris Peace Conference, 1919.* New York: W.W. Norton, 1986.

Warren, Donald I. *Radio Priest: Charles Coughlin, the Father of Hate Radio.* New York: Free Press, 1996.

Waterhouse, David L. *The Progressive Movement of 1924 and the Development of Interest Group Liberalism.* New York: Garland, 1991.

Waterhouse, John Almon. *Calvin Coolidge Meets Charles Edward Garman.* Rutland, VT: Academy, 1984.

Watson, Steven. *The Harlem Renaissance: Hub of African-American Culture, 1920–1930.* New York: Pantheon, 1995.

———. *Prepare for Saints: Gertrude Stein, Virgil Thomson, and the Mainstreaming of American Modernism.* New York: Random House, 1998.

Weisberger, Bernard A. *The La Follettes of Wisconsin: Love and Politics in Progressive America.* Madison: University of Wisconsin Press, 1994.

Wesser, Robert F. *Charles Evans Hughes: Politics and Reform in New York, 1905–1910.* Ithaca, NY: Cornell University Press, 1967.

White, G. Edward. *Creating the National Pastime: Baseball Transforms Itself, 1903–1953.* Princeton, NJ: Princeton University Press, 1996.

———. *Justice Oliver Wendell Holmes: Law and the Inner Self.* New York: Oxford University Press, 1993.

———. *Oliver Wendell Holmes: Sage of the Supreme Court.* New York: Oxford University Press, 2000.

Widenor, William C. *Henry Cabot Lodge and the Search for an American Foreign Policy.* Berkeley: University of California Press, 1980.

Wiebe, Robert H. *The Search for Order, 1877–1920.* New York: Hill and Wang, 1967.

Wiegand, Wayne A. *Patrician in the Progressive Era: A Biography of George Von Lengerke Meyer.* New York: Garland, 1988.

Williamson, Joel. *William Faulkner and Southern History.* New York: Oxford University Press, 1993.

Wintz, Cary D. *African American Political Thought, 1890–1930: Washington, Du Bois, Garvey, and Randolph.* Armonk, NY: M.E. Sharpe, 1996.

———. *Black Culture and the Harlem Renaissance.* Houston, TX: Rice University Press, 1988.

Woodson, Jon. *To Make a New Race: Gurdjieff, Toomer, and the Harlem Renaissance.* Jackson: University Press of Mississippi, 1999.

Wynn, Neil A. *From Progressivism to Prosperity: World War I and American Society.* New York: Holmes and Meier, 1986.

Yoo, David K. *Growing Up Nisei: Race, Generation, and Culture Among Japanese Americans of California, 1924–49.* Urbana: University of Illinois Press, 2000.

Young, James Van. *Landmark Constitutional Law Decisions: Briefs and Analyses.* Lanham, MD: University Press of America, 1993.

Young, Marguerite. *Harp Song for a Radical: The Life and Times of Eugene Victor Debs.* Ed. and Intro. Charles Ruas. New York: Alfred A. Knopf, 1999.

Young, William, and David E. Kaiser. *Postmortem: New Evidence in the Case of Sacco and Vanzetti.* Amherst: University of Massachusetts Press, 1985.

Young, William H., with Nancy K. Young. *The 1930s.* Westport, CT: Greenwood, 2002.

Zahniser, Marvin R. *Then Came Disaster: France and the United States, 1918–1940.* Westport, CT: Praeger, 2002.

Zenderland, Leila. *Measuring Minds: Henry Herbert Goddard and the Origins of American Intelligence Testing.* New York: Cambridge University Press, 1998.

Zieger, Robert H. *American Workers, American Unions, 1920–1985.* Baltimore: Johns Hopkins University Press, 1986.

———. *America's Great War: World War I and the American Experience.* Lanham, MD: Rowman & Littlefield, 2000.

Zimmermann, Warren. *First Great Triumph: How Five Americans Made Their Country a World Power.* New York: Farrar, Straus and Giroux, 2002.

Zinn, Howard, Dana Frank, and Robin D.G. Kelley. *Three Strikes: Miners, Musicians, Salesgirls, and the Fighting Spirit of Labor's Last Century.* Boston: Beacon, 2001.

Index